SIXTH EDITION

TEN STEPS
TO
BUILDING
COLLEGE
READING SKILLS

SIXTH EDITION

TEN STEPS
TO
BUILDING
COLLEGE
READING SKILLS

JOHN LANGAN

ATLANTIC CAPE COMMUNITY COLLEGE

Books in the Townsend Press Reading Series

Groundwork for College Reading with Phonics
Groundwork for College Reading
Ten Steps to Building College Reading Skills
Ten Steps to Improving College Reading Skills
Ten Steps to Advancing College Reading Skills
Ten Steps to Advanced Reading

Books in the Townsend Press Vocabulary Series

Vocabulary Basics
Groundwork for a Better Vocabulary
Building Vocabulary Skills
Building Vocabulary Skills, Short Version
Improving Vocabulary Skills
Improving Vocabulary Skills, Short Version
Advancing Vocabulary Skills
Advancing Vocabulary Skills, Short Version
Advanced Word Power

Supplements Available for Most Books

Instructor's Edition
Instructor's Manual and Test Bank
Online Exercises
PowerPoint Slides

Copyright © 2016 by Townsend Press, Inc.
Printed in the United States of America
9 8 7 6 5 4 3 2 1

ISBN (Student Edition): 978-1-59194-464-5
ISBN (Instructor's Edition): 978-1-59194-465-2

Send book orders and requests for desk copies or supplements to:

Townsend Press Book Center
439 Kelley Drive
West Berlin, New Jersey 08091

For even faster service, contact us in any of the following ways:

By telephone: 1-800-772-6410
By fax: 1-800-225-8894
By e-mail: cs@townsendpress.com
Through our website: www.townsendpress.com

Contents

Part Two

Part Three

Appendixes

Preface: To the Instructor

We all know that many students entering college today do not have the reading skills needed to do effective work in their courses. A related problem, apparent even in class discussions, is that students often lack the skills required to think in a clear and logical way.

The purpose of *Ten Steps to Building College Reading Skills,* Sixth Edition, is to develop effective reading and clear thinking. To do so, **Part One** presents a sequence of reading skills that are widely recognized as essential for sound comprehension:

- Knowing how to use the dictionary
- Understanding vocabulary in context
- Recognizing main ideas
- Identifying supporting details
- Locating main ideas in different parts of a passage
- Understanding relationships that involve addition and time
- Understanding relationships that involve examples, comparison and/or contrast, and cause and effect
- Making inferences
- Determining implied main ideas
- Evaluating arguments

In every chapter in Part One, the key aspects of a skill are explained and illustrated clearly and simply. Explanations are accompanied by a series of practices, and each chapter ends with four review tests. The last review test consists of a reading selection so that students can apply the skill just learned to real-world reading materials, including newspaper and magazine articles and textbook selections. Together, the ten chapters provide students with the skills needed for a solid understanding of reading materials.

Following each chapter in Part One are **at least six mastery tests for the skill in question.** The tests progress in difficulty, giving students the additional practice and challenge they may need to learn a skill. While designed for quick grading, the tests also require students to think carefully before answering each question.

Part Two is made up of ten additional readings that will improve both reading and thinking skills. Each reading is followed by *Vocabulary Questions* and *Reading Comprehension Questions* so that students can practice all of the skills presented in Part One. In addition, an *Outlining, Mapping,* or *Summarizing* activity after each reading helps students think carefully about the basic content and organization of a selection. *Discussion Questions* then afford instructors one more opportunity to engage students in a variety of reading and thinking skills and to deepen their understanding of a selection.

Part Three consists of an introduction to active reading, a set of eight relationships tests, and a series of twenty combined-skills tests that review skills in Part One and help students prepare for the standardized reading test that is often a requirement at the end of a semester.

Finally, the **Appendixes** contain chapters on separating fact from opinion and identifying an author's purpose and tone, writing assignments for all twenty readings in the text, and a limited answer key.

Important Features of the Book

- **Focus on the basics.** The book seeks to explain, in an extremely clear, step-by-step way, the essential elements of each skill. Many examples are provided to ensure that students understand each point. In general, the focus is on teaching the skills—not just on explaining or testing them.

- **Frequent practice and feedback.** Because abundant practice and careful feedback are essential to learning, this book includes numerous activities. Students can get immediate feedback on the practice exercises in Part One by turning to the limited answer key at the back of the book. The answers to the review and mastery tests in Part One, the reading questions in Part Two, and the relationships tests and combined-skills tests in Part Three are in the *Instructor's Manual.*

The limited answer key increases the active role that students take in their own learning. They are likely to use the answer key in an honest and positive way if they know they will be tested on the many activities and selections for which answers are not provided. (Answers not in the book can be easily copied from the *Instructor's Edition* or the *Instructor's Manual* and passed out at the teacher's discretion.)

- **High interest level.** Dull and unvaried readings and exercises work against learning. Students need to experience genuine interest and enjoyment in what they read. Teachers as well should be able to take pleasure in the selections, for their own good feeling about them can carry over favorably into class work. The readings in the book, then, have been chosen not only for the appropriateness of their reading level but also for their compelling content. They should engage teachers and students alike.

- **Ease of use.** The logical sequence in each chapter—from explanation to example to practice to review test to mastery test—helps make the skills easy to teach. The book's organization into distinct parts also makes for ease of use. Within a single class, for instance, teachers can work on a new skill in Part One, review other skills with one or more mastery tests, and provide variety by having students read one of the selections in Part Two. The limited answer key at the back of the text also makes for versatility: it means that the teacher can assign some chapters for self-teaching. Finally, the mastery tests—each on its own tear-out page—and the combined-skills tests make it a simple matter for teachers to test and evaluate student progress.

- **Integration of skills.** Students do more than learn the skills individually in Part One. They also learn to apply the skills together through the reading selections in Parts One and Two and the material on active reading in Part Three. They become effective readers and thinkers by means of a good deal of practice in applying a combination of skills.

- **Integrated online resources.** Through the use of TP's acclaimed Learning Center, *Ten Steps to Building College Reading Skills,* Sixth Edition, features powerful online components to enhance learning, including:

  1 **Online practice exercises and mastery tests.** Each chapter of the book features additional practice exercises *and* online versions of the book's mastery tests. These materials can be used to reinforce skills taught in the chapter *or* to assess students' learning.

  2 **Helpful PowerPoint files.** A comprehensive collection of PowerPoint files covering the book's ten skills chapters is available for immediate downloading.

3 **Downloadable supplements.** Electronic (PDF) versions of the instructor's manual and test bank can be downloaded directly from the Learning Center. These files give you the resources you need whenever and wherever you are—24 hours a day.

4 **Class management controls.** The Learning Center allows you to control which assignments and tests your students can access. It also allows you to create unique assignments for each class you teach, track students' progress, and simplify grading. To learn more, e-mail **cs@townsendpress.com** or visit the Learning Center at **www.townsendpress.net**.

● **Thinking activities.** Thinking activities—in the form of outlining, mapping, and summarizing—are a distinctive feature of the book. While educators agree that such organizational abilities are important, these skills are all too seldom taught. From a practical standpoint, it is almost impossible for a teacher to respond in detail to entire collections of class outlines or maps. This book, then, presents activities that truly involve students in outlining, mapping, and summarizing—in other words, that truly make students *think*—and yet enable a teacher to give quick feedback. Again, it is through continued practice *and* feedback on challenging material that a student becomes a more effective reader and thinker.

In addition, the final chapter in Part One, "The Basics of Argument," provides extensive explanation of and practice in the concepts of point and support that are central to critical thinking.

● **Supplementary materials.**

Print Supplement

An *Instructor's Edition* is available at no charge to instructors who have adopted the text. It can be obtained quickly by writing or calling Townsend Press (439 Kelley Drive, West Berlin, New Jersey 08091; 1-800-772-6410), by sending a fax to 1-800-225-8894, or by e-mailing Customer Service at cs@townsendpress.com. The IE is identical to the student book except that it also provides hints for teachers (starting on the inside front cover of the book), answers to all the practices and tests, and comments on most items. *No other book on the market has such detailed and helpful annotations.*

Online Supplements

Three online supplements are available through the TP website by going to the "Supplements" area for instructors at **www.townsendpress.net**.

1 A combined *Instructor's Manual and Test Bank* includes suggestions for teaching the course, a model syllabus, and readability levels for the text and the reading selections; as well as a complete answer key and a series of three short textbook selections that instructors can use to give students practice in taking notes. The test bank contains **four** additional mastery tests for each of the ten skills and **four** additional combined-skills tests—all on letter-sized sheets so they can be copied easily for use with students.

2 PowerPoint presentations.

3 Online exercises.

● **One of a sequence of books.** This text is the third in a series of six books.

Groundwork for College Reading with Phonics and *Groundwork for College Reading* are the basic texts in the series. They are suitable for ESL students and basic adult learners.

Ten Steps to Building College Reading Skills is often the choice for a first college reading course.

Ten Steps to Improving College Reading Skills is an intermediate text appropriate for the core developmental reading course offered at most colleges.

Ten Steps to Advancing College Reading Skills is a higher-level developmental text than the *Improving* book. It can be used as the core text for a more advanced class, as a sequel to the intermediate book, or as a second-semester alternative to it.

Finally, *Ten Steps to Advanced Reading* is the most advanced text in the series. It can also be used as a sequel (or a second-semester alternative) to either the *Improving* or the *Advancing* text.

A companion set of vocabulary books, listed on the copyright page, has been designed to go with the *Ten Steps* books. Recommended to accompany this book is *Building Vocabulary Skills* (300 words and word parts) or *Building Vocabulary Skills, Short Version* (200 words).

Together, the books and all their supplements form a sequence that should be ideal for any college reading program.

To summarize, *Ten Steps to Building College Reading Skills,* Sixth Edition, provides ten key reading skills to help developmental students become independent readers and thinkers. Through an appealing collection of readings and a carefully designed series of activities and tests, students receive extensive guided practice in the skills. The result is an integrated approach to learning that will, by the end of a course, produce better readers and stronger thinkers.

Changes in the Sixth Edition

Changes in this edition include six new readings (pages 288, 439, 455, 471, 493, and 512); a set of eight relationships tests (page 533) that will help strengthen students' reading and thinking skills; added combined-skills tests (page 549); an expanded offer for free books (pages 12–13); and a freshening of illustrations and practice materials throughout. In addition, the book will be available in electronic as well as print format, and online support for the book has been expanded.

Acknowledgments

I am grateful for the many helpful suggestions provided by the following reviewers: Barbara A. Cartwright, Bunker Hill Community College; Ronald Covil, Burlington County College; Nancy Deutsch, Cypress College; Mary Ellmann, Long Beach City College; Pam Franke, Blinn College; Nora R. Garza, Laredo Community College; Allan Hill, West Chester University; Iris Hill, Wake Technical Community College; Judith B. Isonhood, Hinds Community College; Karen Johnsen, Salt Lake Community College; Sherry Lindquist, Northland Community & Technical College; William McNeill, Robeson Community College; Barbara Nixon, Salem Community College; Spencer Olesen, Mountain View College; Therese Parr, Essex Community College; Betty Patton, Eastern New Mexico University; Betty Payne, Montgomery College; Florinda Rodriguez, South Texas College; Patricia L. Rottmund, Harrisburg Area Community College; Diane Schellack, Burlington County College; Carol G. Shier, Fullerton College; Julie Z. Uslan, Santa Monica College; Michael Vensel, Miami Dade College; Phyllis West, El Camino College; and, in particular, Joanne Nelson, Hillsborough Community College.

At Townsend Press, I thank Kathryn Bernstein, Bill Blauvelt, Denton Cairnes, Beth Johnson, Ruth A. Rouff, and Tanya Savory for the help they provided along the way. And I owe special thanks to two TP editors who brought their exceptional talents to this revision. Barbara Solot is responsible for a layout and full-color text design that are as clear as they are inviting. The result of her artistry is a strikingly attractive book that both students and teachers will appreciate. Janet Goldstein has provided design input along with her usual superb editorial skills. Her insights, coupled with her many years of classroom teaching, have strengthened the clarity and pedagogy of the book.

It is always a special pleasure to work with people who aspire toward excellence. With help from my colleagues in the teaching profession and at Townsend Press, I have been able to create a much better book than I could have managed on my own.

John Langan

Introduction

Hello, and welcome to this book. You're going to be using the book to learn reading skills that will help in your courses and on tests. But in addition to the reading skills, there are three other factors to your success: your attitude about learning, your use of study skills, and your involvement with reading. Each will be discussed in turn.

Your Attitude about Learning

Several years ago, my wife and I were vacationing in New Mexico. As we drove into one small town, we suddenly came upon a huge billboard. I was so struck by what it said that I stopped our car and wrote down the words.

If you never have a dream,

you'll never have a
dream come *true.*

I think your starting point must be a dream inside you—a belief and resolve in your heart that you will use this book as a step on your road to success. If you don't have the right attitude, you might as well throw this book in the trash.

I'm not kidding. Some students are just pretenders: they talk the talk, but they're not ready to walk the walk. This book will help you "walk the walk"; it will help you master the basic reading and thinking skills you need to succeed. But you must first have a dream and a resolve inside you.

Respecting Yourself

Consider this basic truth about human nature: **We all want to respect ourselves.** We all want to live our lives in such a way that we think well of our behavior and others think well of us. We do not want to be disrespected or seen as bad people. An equally basic truth is that the only way we can get respect is to earn it. At a certain point in growing up, we realize that life doesn't give us something for nothing. What is important and meaningful is what we earn through trying hard and working hard.

● Take a minute to think about the following question: Imagine two people. One person has drifted unhappily through life, putting in a minimal effort at a series of jobs and maybe even at times living off others. One morning the telephone rings and someone says to this person, "Congratulations. You have just won a million dollars in the state lottery." The other person works hard and eventually earns a million dollars; that person is well regarded by others and has a strong sense of accomplishment and self-worth. Which person would you rather be— the one who *won* a million dollars or the one who *earned* a million dollars?

_____

Chances are you would choose to be the person who worked hard, overcame obstacles, and achieved success. If you relate to that person, your attitude may be something like this: "I want to respect myself and have others respect me. To get this respect, I'm going to work hard to succeed. At this stage in my life, that means doing well in school because education is clearly a key to success." And if you've made mistakes in the past (and many of us have), your attitude should be: "I can change my behavior. I'm going to learn to work hard so I can get somewhere and be someone."

Doing the Work

You need to believe in the saying, "No pain, no gain." The only way to get self-respect and success is to work for them. When I was teaching full-time, I found that among the two hundred or so students I met each year, there was no way of telling at first which students had this attitude and which did not. Some time had to pass for people to reveal their attitude by what they did or did not do. What happened was that, as the semester unfolded and classes had to be attended and work had to be done, some people took on the work and persisted even if they hit all kinds of snags and problems. Others didn't take on the work or didn't persist when things got rough. It became clear which students had determined inside themselves, "I will do the work," and which had not.

The heart of the matter is not the *speed* at which a person learns; the heart of the matter is his or her determination—"I *will* learn." I have seen people who had this quality of determination or persistence do poorly in a course (often because of out-of-class problems or events), come back and repeat it, and finally succeed.

Through knowing such determined people, I've come to feel that the single most important factor for school survival and success is an inner commitment to doing the work. When the crunch comes—and the crunch is the plain hard work that school requires—the person with the commitment meets it head-on; the person without the commitment avoids it in a hundred different ways.

- If you have not yet taken charge of your life, the above paragraphs are the most important ones in the book for you. On the following scale of *Passive* to *Determined*, where would you rate yourself?

- Take several minutes to think about, or to discuss with others, why you rated yourself as you did. What are some of your strengths? What are some of the personal challenges you must overcome?

Key Study Skills

While it's not the purpose of this book to teach study skills, I do want to give you four important tips that can make you a better student. The tips are based on my thirty years of experience working with first-year college students and teaching both reading and study skills.

TIP 1:   Take Lots of Notes in Class

The most important steps you can take to succeed in school are to go to every class and take a lot of notes. If you don't go to class, or you go but just sit there without taking notes, chances are you're heading for a heap of trouble. The most important steps you can take to succeed in school are to go to every class and take a lot of notes. If you don't go to class, or you go but just sit there without taking notes, chances are you're heading for a heap of trouble.

Yes—I have deliberately repeated the above sentences. That's how essential the steps are. If I had only thirty seconds to speak to a student and offer advice, the above is the advice I would give.

I have interviewed hundreds of today's students who have said the same thing. Let me quote just two of them:

Ryan: "Attendance is as important as studying itself. So is taking notes. I take notes even in classes where they say you don't have to take notes. It's very easy to forget material otherwise."

Jhoselyn: "You definitely have to take a lot of notes. When the teacher is talking and you're just listening, everything is very clear. But you're just not going to remember it all. You have to get it down on paper."

● You may not realize just how quickly new information can be forgotten. For example, how much class material do you think most people forget in just two weeks? Check (✓) the answer you think is correct.

_____ 20 percent is forgotten within two weeks.

_____ 40 percent is forgotten within two weeks.

_____ 60 percent is forgotten within two weeks.

_____ 80 percent is forgotten within two weeks.

The truth is that within two weeks most people forget almost 80 percent of what they have heard! Given that fact, you need to get to class and take notes!

TIP **TIP 2:   Know Which Comes First—the Textbook or the Instructor**

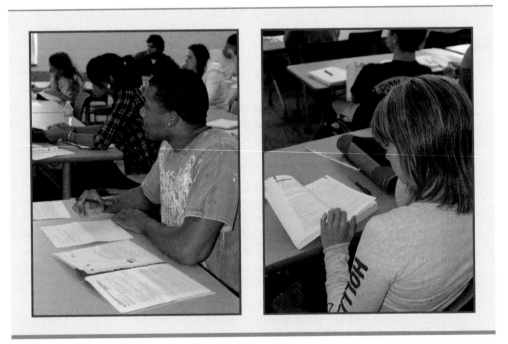

Let me ask you a question: Which is more important—learning how to read a textbook or learning how to read your instructor? Write your answer here:

You may be surprised at the answer: What is far more important is *learning how to read your instructor*—to understand what he or she expects you to learn in the course.

I remember becoming a good student in college only after I learned the truth of this statement. And I have interviewed hundreds of students over the years who have said the same thing. Let me quote just one of them:

> "You absolutely have to be in class. Then you learn how to read the teacher and to know what he or she is going to want on tests. You could read an entire textbook, but that wouldn't be as good as being in class and writing down a teacher's understanding of ideas."

TIP 3:   Have a Textbook Study Method

When I first began to teach study skills, I visited my students' classes to get a good sense of what skills they really needed. I was not too surprised to find out that very often students did not have to read their textbooks to do well on tests. I had had the same experience in school: If I took good notes in class, I seldom had to read or study the textbook. The bottom line is that teachers will test you on the ideas they feel are most important—and most of the time those are the ideas they cover in class.

For those times when you do have to read and learn a textbook chapter, do the following.

1   First, read the first and last few paragraphs of the chapter; they may give you a good overview of what the chapter is about.

2   Second, as you read the chapter, look for and mark off definitions of key terms and examples of those definitions. You'll learn about definition and examples in "Relationships II" (pages 261–294) of this book.

3   Third, as you read the chapter, number major lists of items. If there is a series of points and you number the points 1, 2, 3, and so on, it will be easier to understand and remember them. You'll learn about numbering lists of items in "Supporting Details" (pages 155–178) and "Relationships I" (pages 221–248) of this book.

4   Fourth, after you've read the chapter, take notes on the most important material, and test yourself on those notes until you can say them to yourself without looking at them.

TIP **TIP 4: Organize Your Time**

Are you an organized person? Answer these questions:

● Do you get out of bed on time, and do you get to places on time?

___ Yes   ___ No

● Do you have any trouble keeping up with schoolwork?

___ Yes   ___ No

● Do you allow enough time to study for tests and write papers?

___ Yes   ___ No

If you are not an organized person, you're going to have trouble in school. Here are three steps to take to control your time:

1   First, pay close attention to the course outline, or **syllabus**, that your instructors will probably pass out at the start of a semester. Chances are that the syllabus will give you the dates of exams and tell you when papers or reports are due.

2   Second, move all those dates onto a **large monthly calendar**—a calendar that has a good-sized block of space for each date. Hang the calendar in a place where you'll be sure to see it every day—perhaps above your desk or on a bedroom wall.

OCTOBER

Sun	Mon	Tues	Wed	Thurs	Fri	Sat
			1	2	3	4
5	6 English paper	7	8	9 Math test	10	11
12	13	14	15 History test	16	17	18
19	20	21 Math test	22	23	24	25
26	27	28	29	30 Speech report	31	

3   Third, buy a small notebook and write down every day a **"to do" list** of things that need to get done that day. Decide which items are most important and focus on them first. (If you have classes that day, going to those classes will be "A" priority items. Other items may be a "B" or a "C" in importance.) Carry your list with you during the day, referring to it every so often and checking off items as you complete them.

●   Look over the following "to do" list for one day. Label each of the items *A, B,* or *C* depending on what seems to be its level of importance.

> To Do – Monday
> 1. Go to History and English class.
> 2. Study for math test tomorrow.
> 3. Cash check at bank.
> 4. Meet Ben for lunch.
> 5. Recharge phone.
> 6. Pick up drinks and snacks for later.

●   Finally, answer these questions:

   1. Of the three steps for organizing time, which is the most important one for you, and why?

   _____

   _____

   2. Which step is the second most important for you, and why?

   _____

   _____

Your Involvement with Reading

I can make my point here by asking you two questions:

1. What is the best way to learn how to become a good driver?

   _____ A. Study the driver's manual.

   _____ B. Take a lecture class on how to drive a car.

   _____ C. Watch films of good drivers.

   _____ D. Sit in the passenger's seat with a good driver.

   _____ E. Drive the car.

You know the answer. The best way to learn how to be a good driver is to *drive the car.* In other words, the way to become good at a skill is to practice the skill.

2. What, then, is the best way to become a better reader?

    Based on question 1, you can probably guess. Write your answer here:

    _____

    The best way to become a better reader is to do a lot of reading. In this book, you will do a fair amount of reading at the same time you learn and practice key reading skills. All the reading and practice are sure to make you a better reader.

    At the same time, I strongly recommend that you not limit your reading to what is in this book. I know from my many years of working with students that you should **read even more**. It's like becoming a better driver: the more you drive, the better you become. The more you read, the better you become.

My Own Experience

In my experience, a lot of students come to college without having done much reading in their lives. I was lucky. Up until the end of my sophomore year in high school, I was not a reader. If I had to do a book report, I got a plot summary and slipped by. Then one idle summer day I saw a sign on a bus that said, "Open your mind. Read a book." I decided to read a book just to disprove the sign. I resented the suggestion that my mind was closed just because I did not read.

But here's what happened: When I read a book—*The Swiss Family Robinson,* about a family stranded on an island and having to survive until rescuers arrived—I knew in my bones that there was both pleasure and power in reading. I sensed that the more I read, the better off I would be, so I began to read a lot. I became an active reader, and it made all the difference. It is why I am now here writing to you.

A Question, and a Challenge

But enough about me. Let's get back to you.

● How many books would you guess you have read in your life? _____

I have had many students say they have never read a single book from cover to cover in their lives. At most they read a book or two in school, but their memories of such books are seldom pleasant ones. They often describe that reading as a kind of forced death march—a chapter at a time with lots of worksheets and quizzes. Such experiences are not true reading experiences.

A true reading experience would be to read an appealing story from cover to cover. To find a good story, you may want to do one of the following:

● Take advantage of the special offer on page 12 of this book.

● Or alternatively, you might ask for book suggestions from friends, family, or your instructor.

The important thing is that you give yourself a chance to develop a reading habit—for all the reasons shown below.

● Are you willing to take on this challenge: To read at least one outside book at the same time you are using this textbook?

___ Yes   ___ No   ___ Maybe

The Heart of the Matter: Regular Reading

Many people (and I am one of them) believe that regular reading is the very heart of education. Here is what they say:

1 Reading provides language power. Research has shown *beyond any question* that frequent reading improves vocabulary, spelling, and reading speed and comprehension, as well as grammar and writing style. If you become a regular reader, all of these language and thinking abilities develop almost automatically!

2 Reading increases job power. In today's world more than ever before, jobs involve the processing of information, with words being the tools of the trade. Studies have found that the better your command of words, the more success you are likely to have. *Nothing will give you a command of words like regular reading.*

3 Reading creates human power. Reading enlarges the mind and the heart. It frees us from the narrow confines of our own experience. Knowing how other people view important matters helps us decide what we ourselves think and feel. Reading also helps us connect with others and realize our shared humanity. Someone once wrote, "We read in order to know that we are not alone." We become less isolated as we share the common experiences, emotions, and thoughts that make us human. We grow more sympathetic and understanding because we realize that others are like us.

Regular reading can, in short, change your life. It can open the door to a lifetime of pleasure as well as learning. But you must be the one to decide whether to walk through that door.

A Special Offer

To promote your reading growth, Townsend Press will send you five books at no charge except for postage and handling. Here are the five books:

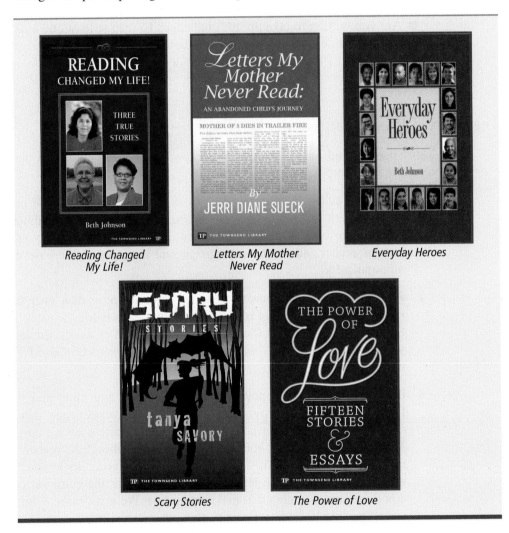

Reading Changed My Life!

Letters My Mother Never Read

Everyday Heroes

Scary Stories

The Power of Love

Use the order form on the next page, enclosing five dollars to cover the cost of shipping and handling. You'll then be sent these five very readable books.

ORDER FORM

YES! Please send me copies of *Reading Changed My Life!, Letters My Mother Never Read, Everyday Heroes, Scary Stories,* and *The Power of Love.* Enclosed is five dollars to help cover the shipping and handling of the books.

Please PRINT the following very clearly. It will be your shipping label.

Name _____

Address _____

City _____ *State* _____ *Zip* _____

MAIL TO: TP Book Center, 439 Kelley Drive, West Berlin, NJ 08091.

2 One Reader's Story

Preview

Ryan Klootwyk's childhood was torn apart by drugs, alcohol, and violence. He had no one to turn to for help. But as a little boy, he discovered a safe place he could always go when times were hard. That place was the world of books. Ryan's story shows how a love of reading can carry a person through painful experiences.

1   "Drink it. It will make a man out of you."

2   Ryan Klootwyk jerked his head away from the cup of beer that his stepfather Larry was shoving in his face. "But I don't like how it smells," he pleaded. For a moment, Larry just glared drunkenly at the eight-year-old boy, his bloodshot eyes like two cracked windows. Then he raised the cup high in the air and poured the contents on Ryan's head. As Larry stormed out of the room, Ryan sat quietly at the table, drenched in the stinking fluid. He was relieved. Larry could have done much worse; he usually did.

3   Nearly twenty years later, Ryan remembers that moment as if it were yesterday. He tells the story, sitting at another table—his own—with his wife, Ronda, and their two young sons. Watching his kids play, Ryan thinks how different their childhood is from his own. "My children will never have to go through what I went through," he says, shaking his head. "Never."

4   Ryan's childhood home was shattered by heroin. Both his parents were addicts. When Ryan was six years old, his father died, an apparent drug-related suicide. Alone and vulnerable, his mother soon brought a new man into their home. This was Larry.

5   When Larry first entered Ryan's life, he seemed friendly. He took Ryan and his brother Frank fishing. He bought new furniture for the house, and Ryan's mother told the kids to call him "Dad." The two lonely young boys started to accept Larry in his new role. But Larry was keeping a secret from the family. Underneath his pleasant exterior, Larry was a monster.

6   Ryan's first glimpse into Larry's true nature occurred a few months after he had moved in with the family. Ryan's dog—one that had belonged to Ryan's father—had an accident on the carpet. High and drunk, Larry announced he was going to kill the dog. Horrified, Frank shouted for him to stop. "That's

my dad's dog! That's my dad's dog!" he screamed.

7   Larry ignored Frank's screams, but when their mother heard the commotion and yelled, "Larry, what are you doing?" he snapped. Seven-year-old Ryan watched in helpless horror as Larry beat her, hitting her face with his fists. "My childhood ended that night," Ryan says today. "I hid behind the table and watched him. I had no idea why he acted that way. I only knew I was scared that he would kill one of us." Ryan, Frank and their mother fled into the boys' bedroom. Immediately, Larry cornered them there and issued a stern warning. "Don't you ever, *ever* mention your father to me again," he hissed. Terrified, the little boys could only stare.

8   As Larry wandered away, Ryan felt emptiness and terror threaten to overwhelm him. There was nowhere to go; there was no one to turn to. But a comforting thought broke through his despair. Reaching under his bed, he pulled out a battered copy of his favorite book, *The Five Chinese Brothers*. Crawling into bed, he quickly lost himself in the familiar pages. Thoughts of Larry's brutality, of fear, of pain, of humiliation faded as he read the story of the brave, clever little brother who saved everyone. Ryan was only seven, but he had already found the lifeline that would keep him afloat through the horrifying years ahead. He had discovered books.

9   Larry supported himself by robbing nearby households and businesses. With the police constantly trailing him, he had to keep moving. The moves

Ryan Klootwyk today.

would often occur without notice. "I would come home from school, and we'd be out the door," Ryan remembers. Traveling from motels to shelters, from friends' houses to apartments, Ryan lived in six different states and passed through fifteen separate schools, never staying in one place more than a year and a half. The constant moving took its toll. "I wanted to be a normal kid," he says, "but transferring from school to school made that impossible. The only people that were constant in my life were my mother and my brother. They were the only ones who knew how bad things were. My biggest fear as a child was that I would lose them, that I would be totally alone."

10   When Ryan was eight years old, that fear almost came true. This time, the family was in Texas. Even drunker and angrier than usual, Larry began kicking

and stomping on Ryan's mother. Frank, now nine years old, made a desperate effort to protect her. When he stepped between Larry and his mother, shouting "Don't hit her!" Larry turned on the boy. He kicked him in the face with his heavy black boots. Frank crumpled to the floor.

11   For the rest of that evening, little Ryan watched over his brother and tried to comfort him. "I could see that his eye was swollen shut, and pus and fluid were oozing out of it," he recalls. "Nothing Larry ever did hurt me inside more than when he hurt my brother like that," says Ryan, his voice wavering. Alone in the darkness with his silent, wounded brother, Ryan quietly sobbed through the night.

12   The next day Frank was a little better, and his mother took him to the hospital. Ryan went along. Larry instructed the boys to lie about what had happened. "Tell them you were playing baseball and Frank got hit in the head with the bat," Larry said. The boys and their mother obediently lied, but the injury still made people at the hospital suspicious. A police officer questioned the kids, but they stuck to Larry's story.

13   "I wanted to tell the truth, but we were so afraid of Larry," says Ryan. He still feels the frustration of those days. "We knew what would happen if we told the truth. They would take him away, he would be in jail for a short time, and then he would come out and get us, and he would kill Mom." Without the boys' cooperation, the police could do nothing. And a few weeks later, Larry,

aware of the watchful eye of the police, decided to move the family again. In yet another state and another school, the beatings continued.

14   Amazingly, amidst the constant abuse at home, Ryan did well in school. "School was the one safe place in my life. When I was in school, I was away from Larry. I was free from threats to my family. I could pretend to be a normal kid," recounts Ryan.

15   As a third-grader, Ryan won a school reading contest. The prize was a copy of *Charlotte's Web*. The book quickly became a new favorite. In it, a little runt pig, Wilbur, has his life saved twice: first by a kind little girl, and then by a clever and loving spider, Charlotte. Charlotte's first word to Wilbur is "Salutations!" Like Wilbur, Ryan had no idea what the word meant. He appreciated Charlotte's explanation to Wilbur: "Salutations are greetings," she said. "When I say 'salutations,' it's just my fancy way of saying hello." Ryan loved Charlotte for her friendship and kindness to lonely little Wilbur.

16   Charlotte and Wilbur joined the five Chinese brothers and Ryan's other favorite characters as pieces in a shield between him and the horrors of his home life. "Reading was a way I could forget about everything," he says. "It was the only thing that was completely in my control. I am not sure if I would have survived without it." He looked for things to read the way a hungry child might look for food that others had overlooked. "Once I even found some old history textbooks in the school trash

can. To someone, those old books were trash, but to me they were a treasure. I took them home and read them cover to cover."

17   Ryan's success at school had no effect on his troubled home. Each time he transferred to a new school, he concealed the painful truth of his home, of his mother's addiction, of the constant moves, and of Larry. Ryan's strong grades and good adjustment to school were all his teachers saw. Outwardly he seemed to be doing well. Inwardly, he was begging for help. "Sitting in all those classrooms, I remember thinking, 'Why doesn't anyone do something about what is happening?' I desperately wanted someone to ask about us, to investigate, to care. I was incapable of asking for help. I was ashamed about what was happening to us, ashamed at what Mom allowed to go on, ashamed that I couldn't do anything about it. And, on top of all that, I was afraid that if someone found out about our family, they might separate my mother and brother and me. I was so scared, I just kept it all inside," he explains. In silence, Ryan endured years of abuse, violence, and intimidation at the hands of Larry. "I just hoped that we would run away from Larry one day. That is what kept me going."

18   When Ryan was ten years old, his dream almost came true. His mother took the two boys and fled to Michigan, not letting Larry know where they were going. For three months, Ryan was free of the constant threat of violence. But the freedom did not last. Ryan returned from school one day to find Larry sitting on the couch with a smile on his face. "Hi," he said smugly.

19   Ryan could barely speak. "My soul dropped. I just wanted to cry. It was as if something inside me died." Again the cycle of terror began. This time, Ryan's mother sought legal help. A judge granted her a restraining order that barred Larry from being near her home. Larry's response was to stalk the family. Lying in bed one night soon after the order had been issued, Ryan heard a window break. When he went to investigate, he found Larry punching his mother. She managed to call the police, but Larry ran away before they arrived. For three more years the family ran from Larry, moving from town to town and from school to school.

20   As Ryan grew up, so did his tastes in reading. Instead of make-believe heroes like Charlotte and the clever Chinese brother, Ryan was drawn to real-life stories of brave men and women. He read biographies of Abraham Lincoln, once a poor boy who would walk miles to borrow a book. He read about Frederick Douglass, a former slave who became a fiery speaker for human rights. Larry's stalking continued until Ryan's mother became involved with a new boyfriend. The two men got into a fight in the street outside Larry's house, and Larry was almost killed. At last, he disappeared from Ryan's life.

21   At the age of 13, Ryan felt that life was starting at last. Ryan's mother

overcame her drug addiction and moved into a nicer apartment. For the first time in his life, Ryan was able to attend the same school for more than a year. He began to put down roots, make friends, feel at home. The future looked bright—briefly. Then Ryan's mother announced she could no longer afford the apartment they were living in. They were going to move again.

22   The news that he would have to uproot his life once again shocked Ryan. This time, he rebelled. "I was 13, and I had *had* it," he remembers. "I did not want to move any more. For the first time in my life, I had gotten a chance to have a normal, healthy life, and now someone was going to take it away again." Ryan begged and pleaded for his mother to stay, but she refused. "When we moved, something inside me snapped. It is sad to say, but in ninth grade I just stopped caring. I figured no one ever seemed to care about me, so why should I?"

23   Ryan's grades reflected his changing attitude. In just months he went from a B+ student to a student who got D's and F's. "I started skipping school, hanging out with the wrong crowd, and then using drugs. I just gave up. All the anger that had built up inside all those years was coming out, and nobody could do anything to stop me." A low point occurred when a cousin called, asking Ryan if he knew someone who would buy stolen jewelry. Ryan arranged the sale. After he and his cousin spent the eighty dollars they'd made on drugs and whiskey, Ryan asked who owned the jewelry. The cousin had stolen it from his own parents, Ryan's aunt and uncle.

24   Because of Ryan's poor performance in school, he was sent to a high school for troubled young people. There he was surrounded by students who spent much of their time trying to find a way to smoke marijuana in class. Fights were common. Far more attention was given to discipline than to learning. Once again, overwhelmed by the surrounding violence, Ryan retreated to the one safe place he knew—the world of books.

25   "I cut school to go to the public library and read," he remembers. "At school, it was clear that the teachers had given up on the students. They were more like babysitters than anything else. But at the library—away from the dangers of school—I could read and learn about anything I wanted." By this time, he was drawn to stories from the pages of military history books. He read about prisoners of war who survived long years of unspeakable torture. One book in particular, *The Forgotten Soldier,* moved him. It told the story of a man fighting his own personal war against himself as World War II rages around him. The author had been a prisoner. Ryan thought of himself as a kind of prisoner, too. But unlike Ryan, the author had pulled himself out of his prison and into a better life. Ryan was still locked inside his own private jail.

26   Somehow, despite poor grades and a complete lack of direction, Ryan managed to graduate from high

school. He went to work as an industrial painter. While working long hours at manual labor, Ryan had time to think about his life since Larry disappeared. "I realized that I had lost control of my life. I asked myself, 'Is this what I want? Is this all there is?'" In order to cope with his own dissatisfaction, Ryan continued reading. "I worked all day and read all night," says Ryan. "I read true stories about people who overcame incredible obstacles, about people who survived wars and concentration camps. I would get depressed because I'd read about people doing amazing things, and I wasn't doing anything except complaining."

27   Ryan's constant reading and the drudgery of his work forced him to rethink the choices he had made. "I said to myself, 'How did I get here? What am I doing? Where am I taking my life?'" His self-examination was painful. "I became aware of how I had hurt myself, how I had wasted time and made poor choices. But I could not see anything in my future except more of the same. It all seemed like a big nothing. I grew very depressed."

28   Then things got worse. On the job one day, Ryan slipped off a pedestal and shattered his wrist. He couldn't work. His wife was pregnant, and now she had to work more hours to support their household. Feeling scared and sorry for himself, Ryan went to see his brother Frank.

29   "I was looking for sympathy when I went over there," Ryan admits. "I told him I had no income, no food, no money to buy food, no way to support my wife." But Frank didn't want to listen to Ryan's complaints. Instead, Frank gave Ryan the best advice he could think of. With disgust in his voice, Frank said, "Why don't you go back to school and get an education so you can be somebody when you *do* grow up?"

Ryan works on a project in his home office.

30   "I wanted to punch his lights out," Ryan says. "I had come over to find a friendly, supportive brother, and instead I found someone telling me what to do." Angry and frustrated, Ryan barged out of his brother's home. Yet Frank's words lingered with him. "The more I thought about it, the more I realized that what Frank said was right. I needed to take charge of my life, and I needed to hear someone say it. Today I thank Frank for telling me the truth."

31   One of the next books to make an impression on Ryan was *Embattled Courage*. In that book, soldiers who fought the long-ago American Civil War spoke of what the war had done to them and their innocent dreams. "Once again, I realized that people who go through hell *can* learn to cope with life."

32   These long-dead soldiers were in Ryan's mind a year later when he enrolled in Muskegon Community College in Michigan. He was the first one in his family to go to college. The transition was not easy.

33   "The first day I set foot on campus, I was terrified," he says. "I looked around and saw that I was ten years older than most of my fellow students, and I thought, 'What am I doing here?' I was sure that everyone in the school was looking at me, thinking I was stupid for being so old. Sometimes I still feel that way," he admits.

34   "But worse than anything was my fear of failure. I was afraid that I wasn't prepared for the demands of college, since my high school years had been such a waste. I thought if I failed, then I would be a complete failure in life, that I wouldn't amount to anything, that everything that happened years earlier would have beaten me."

35   But over the course of his first semester, Ryan's fear faded. His constant reading over so many years had done more than help him to survive: it had helped prepare him for college. Ryan quickly became one of the strongest students in his classes. His love of learning had been buried under the years of abuse and poor choices, but it had not died. "I had given up on school for so long, but when I stepped into college, my mind woke up again," Ryan says. "It was like being reborn." After two years in community college, Ryan was a solid A student.

36   His college work inspired Ryan to decide on a direction for his life. "For years, I survived because I read books about people who kept on fighting, who kept on struggling in the face of horror. At college, I realized that I could teach these same stories to others. It became clear to me that what I wanted to do with my life was to be a history teacher."

37   Ryan has made his goal a reality. He went on to Grand Valley State University, where he earned a degree in secondary education. He is now teaching history at the same high school where he had once been a student.

38   "When I read books about extraordinary people, when Larry was hurting us or when I was depressed, I would say to myself, 'If they can survive, so can

I,'" says Ryan. "Today, there are people everywhere—kids and adults—who are fighting to survive, just as I was. Abuse, drugs, violence—the problems are still out there; they aren't going away. But if just one person can learn to make it, either by my story or the ones I teach, then all that I have been through is worthwhile," he says. "You have to learn from the past to build your future. That is the lesson of history."

39   "I have another mission too," he says, watching his two sons playing nearby. His older boy, Ryan Richard, is five years old; Reid, his second son, is three. "It is to be something for them that I never had. . . ." He pauses for a moment, picks up Ryan Richard, and gives him a warm hug. "A dad," he says, cradling his son. His eyes are moist when he puts Ryan Richard down. Reid doesn't notice his father coming over to hug him. He is engrossed in his favorite book—*Goodnight Moon*—one which has been read to him so many times that he can recite the words from memory. Ryan puts his big hand gently on Reid's small shoulder and embraces him. "They are what I live for most," Ryan says, drying his eyes. "When I look in their faces, when I see them looking back at me—safe, secure, and loved—I know why I am here. And despite all my anger and resentment for so many years, I feel thankful."

40   He sits on the floor with Reid. "Can we read, Daddy?" Reid asks hopefully.

41   "Yeah, but you have to start," Ryan replies.

Reid's childish voice carefully   42 recites the book's first line: *In the great green room there was a telephone and a red balloon . . .*

Ryan smiles. He is writing his own   43 kind of book, the book of his life. A painful chapter has ended, and a new one filled with promise and possibilities has begun.

An Update

"One Reader's Story" was written   44 in 1997, when Ryan Klootwyk was 31. Before reprinting the story, we caught up with Ryan to ask for an update on his life. This is what we learned.

Ryan, who is now 48, taught high   45 school for several years. But when budget cuts forced the school to reduce its staffing, Ryan was laid off. He was offered a teaching job in another Michigan city, but he and Ronda decided to stay in their home town of Muskegon. Ronda loved her job at the local hospital, and Ryan Richard and Reid were doing well in their schools. Ryan hated the thought of uprooting his sons—something he knew all too much about from his own childhood. Instead, he went to work for a company that provided online programs for long-term learning. He discovered, to his surprise, that he loved working in sales. "It makes all the difference if you're selling a product you truly believe in."

Sadly, Ryan's employer died   46 suddenly in 2010, and his widow sold the operation to a larger online learning company, which soon replaced all the sales force with new employees. Ryan found another job in sales, this time selling truck and trailer parts. His territory was the southeast United States, and he spent a week each month in cities such as Atlanta, Georgia, and Memphis, Tennessee, calling on clients. But then there was a change in management. Ryan's new boss wanted salespeople who lived in the areas they serviced. As of November 2014, Ryan was out of a job. "I'm doing OK, though," he said cheerfully. "I've got a few irons in the fire, and I'm confident I'll be back in sales soon."

47   Meanwhile, Ryan's family is thriving. Ronda has worked for more than 20 years at the hospital, where she is now in the purchasing department. "She loves the job, and everyone loves her," Ryan says proudly. "She's the kind who won't miss a day's work, no matter what." Looking back, Ryan gives his wife great credit for his stable life. "We dated for six years and have been married for 26, and through every day of it, she's kept me on the straight and narrow. When I was young and could have so easily gone wrong—more wrong than I did—she was the one who kept me focused on a different kind of life. I love her a lot and owe her everything."

48   Ryan Richard and Reid are now 22 and 20 years old. Both of them—as well as Ronda—attended Muskegon Community College, just as their dad did. Currently, Ryan Richard is a senior at Central Michigan University, where

he is majoring in business. Reid is a junior at the University of Michigan, where he is studying to be an actuarial scientist—a business professional that uses statistics to, for instance, help insurance companies figure out risks and benefits.

49   Ryan's mom and brother Frank are still close to Ryan and the family. After spending some years in Washington state, his mom moved back to Muskegon to be near her sons and grandchildren. And Frank works as a machinist with his own son and son-in-law. "They've got a real family affair going there!" says Ryan.

50   As time goes on and other things change, one thing in Ryan's life remains constant: his passion for reading. "Oh, I'll never stop that!" he chuckles. "I've got my library of books—mostly military history—and I'm running out of room for my new ones." Currently he's reading *A History of the End of the World*, a study of the biblical Book of Revelation and how it has figured into human history. "And I've got about three books waiting to start when I'm done with that," he adds.

51   It pleases Ryan that, years after it was first published, he still hears from readers of "One Reader's Story." "A young man who works with my wife asked her not long ago, 'Is this Ryan Klootwyk *your* Ryan Klootwyk?'" he reports with a chuckle. "He'd read the story in a college class, and wanted to meet me. It makes me so happy to think that my story might still be encouraging someone else."

*Ryan enjoys a late-summer day at home with his wife,
Ronda, and their sons, Ryan Richard and Reid.*

Questions for Discussion

1. As a child, Ryan used books as a "lifeline" to escape his troubled home life. When you are troubled or stressed, what do you like to do to make yourself feel better? Does your "lifeline" work as well for you as books worked for Ryan? Explain.

2. Ryan's favorite book was *The Five Chinese Brothers*. Later, he found a new favorite: *Charlotte's Web*. Judging from his story, why do you think these two books appealed so much to Ryan? If you also had a favorite book when you were younger, why did you like it so much? What did it teach you or make you think about?

3. Ryan tells about a "low point" in his life when he helped a cousin sell stolen jewelry and then spent the proceeds on drugs and liquor. Yet he managed to reject such behavior and eventually turned his life around. Have you or has anyone you've known come back from a similar low point in life? Describe the experience and its lessons.

4. "You have to learn from the past to build your future," Ryan says. What lessons has Ryan learned from his past? How, according to the update to Ryan's story, have these lessons helped build his future? What lessons from your past do you think can help you build *your* future?

3 How to Become a Better Reader and Thinker

The chances are that you are not as good a reader as you should be to do well in college. If so, it's not surprising. You live in a culture where people watch an average of *over seven hours of television every day!!!* All that passive viewing does not allow much time for reading. Reading is a skill that must be actively practiced. The simple fact is that people who do not read very often are not likely to be strong readers.

● How much TV do you guess you watch on an average day? _____

Another reason besides TV for not reading much is that you may have a lot of responsibilities. You may be going to school and working at the same time, and you may have a lot of family duties as well. Given a hectic schedule, you're not going to have much time to read. When you have free time, you're exhausted, and it's easier to turn on the TV than to open up a book.

● Do you do any regular reading (for example, a daily newspaper, weekly magazines, occasional novels)? _____

● When are you most likely to do your reading? _____

A third reason for not reading is that school may have caused you to associate reading with worksheets and drills and book reports and test scores. Experts agree that many schools have not done a good job of helping students discover the pleasures and rewards of reading. If reading was an unpleasant experience in school, you may have concluded that reading in general is not for you.

● Do you think that school made you dislike reading, rather than enjoy it?

_____

Here are three final questions to ask yourself:

● Do you feel that perhaps you don't need a reading course, since you "already know how to read"? _____

● If you had a choice, would you be taking a reading course? (It's okay to be honest.) _____

● Do you think that a bit of speed reading may be all you need? _____

Chances are that you don't need to read *faster* as much as you need to read *smarter*. And it's a safe bet that if you don't read much, you can benefit enormously from the reading course in which you are using this book.

One goal of the book is to help you become a better reader. You will learn and practice ten key reading comprehension skills. As a result, you'll be better able to read and understand the many materials in your other college courses. The skills in this book have direct and practical value: they can help you perform better and more quickly—giving you an edge for success—in all of your college work.

The book is also concerned with helping you become a stronger thinker, a person able not just to understand what is read but to analyze and evaluate it as well. In fact, reading and thinking are closely related skills, and practice in thoughtful reading will also strengthen your ability to think clearly and logically. To find out just how the book will help you achieve these goals, read the next several pages and do the brief activities as well. The activities are easily completed and will give you a quick, helpful overview of the book.

How the Book is Organized

The book is organized into four main parts:

Introduction (pages 1–31)

In addition to this chapter, which will give you a good sense of the book, there are two other parts to the introduction, "Getting Off to a Strong Start" and "One Reader's Story." "Getting Off to a Strong Start" describes several essential factors for success in school. In the space provided below, write the factor that is presented on pages 3–5.

_____

The next essential factor for success, "Key Study Skills," presents four tips that can make you a better student. If I had time to give just four tips to incoming college students, based on my thirty years of teaching experience, these are the things I would say. In the space below, write in the first and second of these tips, described on pages 5–7.

_____

_____

The last essential factor for school success is to increase your involvement with reading. Regular reading is seen as the very heart of education for three reasons. Turn to page 11 to complete the list of reasons:

1. Reading provides language power.

2. _____

3. Reading creates human power.

Part One: Ten Steps to Building College Reading Skills (pages 33–428)

To help you become a more effective reader and thinker, this book presents a series of ten key reading skills. They are listed in the table of contents on pages v and vi. Turn to those pages to fill in the skills missing below:

1 Dictionary Use

2 _____

3 Main Ideas

4 _____

5 Locations of Main Ideas

6 Relationships I

7 Relationships II

8 _____

9 Implied Main Ideas

10 The Basics of Argument

Each chapter is developed in the same way.

First of all, clear **explanations** and **examples** help you *understand* each skill. **Practices** then give you the "hands-on" experience needed to *learn* the skill.

● How many practices are there for the third chapter, "Main Ideas" (pages 113–142)? _____

Closing each chapter are **four review tests**. The first review test provides a check of the information presented in the chapter.

● On which page is the first review test for "Main Ideas"? _____

The second and third review tests consist of activities that help you practice the skill learned in the chapter.

● On which pages are Review Tests 2 and 3 for "Main Ideas"? _____

The fourth review test consists of a story, essay, or textbook selection that both gets you reading and gives you practice in the skill learned in the chapter as well as skills learned in previous chapters.

● What is the title of the reading selection in the "Main Ideas" chapter?

_____

Following each chapter are **six mastery tests** that gradually increase in difficulty.

● On what pages are the mastery tests for the "Main Ideas" chapter? _____

The tests are on tear-out pages and so can be easily removed and handed in to your instructor. So that you can track your progress, there is a score box at the top of each test. Your score can also be entered into the "Reading Performance Chart" on the inside back cover of the book.

Part Two: Ten Reading Selections (pages 429–522)

The ten reading selections that make up Part Two are followed by activities that give you practice in all of the skills studied in Part One. Each reading begins in the same way. Look, for example, at "Winners, Losers, or Just Kids?" which starts on page 431. What are the headings of the two sections that come before the reading itself?

● _____

Note that the vocabulary words in "Words to Watch" are followed by the numbers of the paragraphs in which the words appear. Look at the first page of "Winners, Losers, or Just Kids" and explain how each vocabulary word is marked in the reading itself.

● _____

Activities Following Each Reading Selection

After each selection, there are four kinds of activities to improve the reading and thinking skills you learned in Part One of the book.

1 The first activity consists of **vocabulary questions**—questions involving vocabulary words as they are used in the selection.

● Look at the vocabulary questions for "Winners, Losers, or Just Kids?" on pages 433–434. How many questions deal with understanding vocabulary in context? _____

2 The second activity consists of **reading comprehension questions**—questions involving main ideas (including the central point and implied main ideas), supporting details, transitions, patterns of organization, and inferences.

● Look at the questions for "Winners, Losers, or Just Kids?" on pages 435–436. Note that the questions are labeled so you know what skill you are practicing in each case. How many questions deal with the central point and main ideas? _____

3 The third activity involves **outlining, mapping,** or **summarizing**. Each of these activities will sharpen your ability to get to the heart of a piece and to think logically and clearly about what you read.

● What kind of activity is provided for "Winners, Losers, or Just Kids?" on page 437? _____

● What kind of activity is provided for the reading titled "The Right Words at the Right Time" on page 445? _____
Note that a **map**, or diagram, is a highly visual way of organizing material. Like an outline, it shows at a glance the main parts of a selection.

● What kind of activity is provided for the reading titled "How to Make It in College, Now that You're Here" on page 491? _____

4 The fourth activity consists of **discussion questions**. These questions provide a chance for you to deepen your understanding of each selection.

● How many discussion questions are there for "Winners, Losers, or Just Kids?" (page 438)—and indeed for every other reading? _____

Part Three: Active Reading, Relationships, and Combined Skills (pages 523–590)

This part of the book gives you tips on becoming an active reader and then provides a series of relationships tests and combined-skills tests that help you practice a number of the skills in the book.

● How many "Relationships" tests are there on pages 533–548? _____

● How many "Combined-Skills" tests are there on pages 549–590? _____
These tests are made up of short passages that closely resemble the ones typically found in standardized tests.

Appendixes (pages 591–622)

At the beginning of the "Appendixes" are two short chapters that your instructor may assign for additional skills practice.

- What is the topic of the first chapter (pages 593–596)?

_____

Another section, "Writing Assignments," presents writing assignments for all twenty of the reading selections in the book. Reading and writing are closely connected skills, and writing practice will improve your ability to read closely and to think carefully.

- How many assignments are offered for each reading? _____

Also included in the appendixes is a limited answer key.

Helpful Features of the Book

1 The book centers on *what you really need to know* to become a better reader and thinker. It presents key comprehension skills and explains the most important points about each one.

2 The book gives you *lots of practice*. We seldom learn a skill only by hearing or reading about it; we make it part of ourselves by repeated practice. There are, then, numerous activities in the text. They are not "busywork," but carefully designed materials that should help you truly learn each skill.

Notice that after you learn each skill in Part One, you progress to review tests and mastery tests that enable you to apply the skill. And as you move from one skill to the next, the reading selections help you practice and reinforce the skills already learned.

3 The selections throughout the book are *lively and appealing*. Dull and unvaried readings work against learning, so subjects have been carefully chosen for their high interest level. Almost all of the selections here are good examples of how what we read can capture our attention. For instance, begin "All the Good Things" on page 96 and try not to be moved by the conclusion. Or read Regina Ruiz's inspiring story on pages 373–375, which tells how she took charge of her life. Or look at the textbook selection on pages 503–507, which is full of helpful information about understanding and controlling one's feelings.

4   The readings include *selections from college textbooks*. Therefore, you will be practicing on materials very much like those in your other courses. Doing so will increase your chances of transferring what you learn in your reading class to your other college courses.

How to Use the Book

1   A good way to proceed is to read and review the explanations and examples in a given chapter in Part One until you feel you understand the ideas presented. Then carefully work through the practices. As you finish each one, check your answers with the "Limited Answer Key" that starts on page 617.

For your own sake, *don't just copy in the answers without trying to do the practices!* The only way to learn a skill is to practice it first and then use the answer key to give yourself feedback. Also, take whatever time is needed to figure out just why you got some answers wrong. By using the answer key to help teach yourself the skills, you will prepare yourself for the review and mastery tests at the end of each chapter as well as the other reading tests in the book. Your instructor can supply you with answers to those tests.

If you have trouble catching on to a particular skill, stick with it. In time, you will learn each of the ten skills.

2   Read the selections first with the intent of simply enjoying them. There will be time afterward for rereading each selection and using it to develop your comprehension skills.

3   Keep track of your progress. Fill in the charts at the end of each chapter in Part One and each reading in Part Two. And in the "Reading Performance Chart" on the inside back cover, enter your scores for all the review and mastery tests as well as the reading selections. These scores can give you a good view of your overall performance as you work through the book.

In summary, *Ten Steps to Building College Reading Skills,* Sixth Edition, has been designed to interest and benefit you as much as possible. Its format is straightforward, its explanations are clear, its readings are appealing, and its many practices will help you learn through doing. *It is a book that has been created to reward effort*, and if you provide that effort, you will make yourself a better reader and a stronger thinker. I wish you success.

John Langan

Part One

Ten Steps to Building College Reading Skills

1 Dictionary Use

This Chapter in a Nutshell

- You should own both a paperback and a hardbound dictionary.

- Your computer (if you have one) may have a built-in dictionary; also, you can easily visit an online dictionary.

- Use spelling hints to help you look up in the dictionary a word you cannot spell.

- A dictionary entry will tell you how a word is spelled and pronounced and give you the various meanings of the word. It will also provide other helpful information about the word.

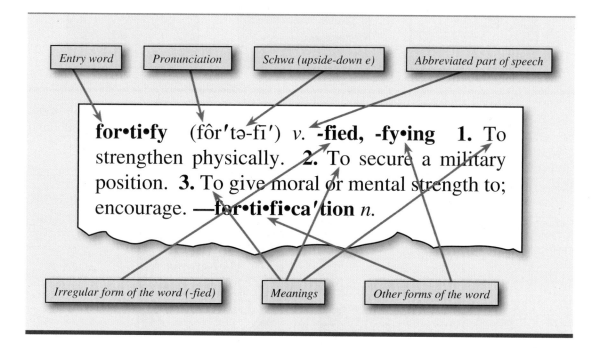

The dictionary is a valuable tool. To help you use it, this chapter explains in a clear and detailed way what you need to know about dictionaries and the information they provide.

Owning Your Own Dictionaries

You can benefit greatly by owning two dictionaries. The first dictionary you should own is a paperback edition you can carry with you. Any of the following would be a good choice:

The American Heritage Dictionary, Paperback Edition
The Merriam-Webster Dictionary, Paperback Edition
The New American Webster Handy College Dictionary

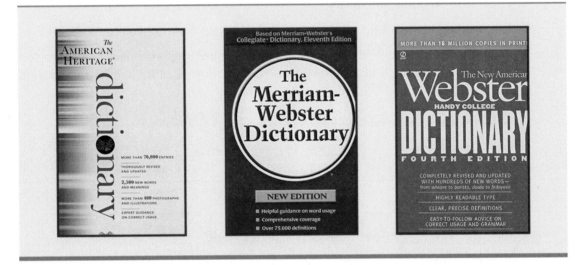

The second dictionary you should own is a desk-sized, hardcover edition, which should be kept in the room where you study. Here are two good hardbound dictionaries:

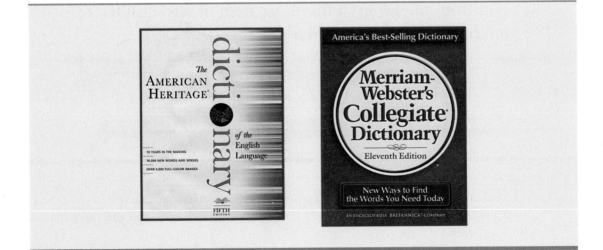

Hardbound dictionaries contain a good deal more information than the paperback editions. For instance, a hardbound dictionary defines far more words than a paperback dictionary. And there are more definitions per word, as well. Although they cost more, they are worth the investment, because they are valuable study aids.

Dictionaries are often updated to reflect changes that occur in the language. New words come into use, and old words take on new meanings. So you should not use a dictionary that has been lying around the house for a number of years. Instead, buy yourself a new dictionary. It is easily among the best investments you will ever make.

Online Dictionary

Copyright © by Randy Glasbergen.
www.glasbergen.com

GLASBERGEN

"How did you look up words before there were online dictionaries, Dad?"

If your computer is connected to the Internet, you may find it easy to check words online. Here is one dictionary site you can go to:

www.merriam-webster.com

For example, if you go online to **www.merriam-webster.com** and type in the word *fortify*, you will see something like this:

---

for·ti·fy ◀)) *verb*

for·ti·fied | for·ti·fy·ing

Definition of FORTIFY

transitive verb

: to make strong: as

a : to strengthen and secure (as a town) by forts or batteries

b : to give physical strength, courage, or endurance to <*fortified* by a hearty meal>

c : to add mental or moral strength to : ENCOURAGE <*fortified* by prayer>

d : to add material to for strengthening or enriching <*fortified* milk>

intransitive verb

: to erect fortifications
— **for·ti·fi·er** ◀)) *noun*
↗ See fortify defined for English-language learners »

Examples of FORTIFY

- *fortify* a city against attack

- a city *fortified* by high walls

- Support for his theories has been *fortified* by the results of these experiments.

(continued)

- He took a deep breath to *fortify* himself before stepping onto the stage.

- milk *fortified* with vitamin D

Origin of FORTIFY

Middle English *fortifien,* from Anglo-French *fortifier,* from Late Latin *fortificare,* from Latin *fortis* strong
First Known Use: 15th century

Synonyms: brace, forearm, nerve, poise, psych (up), ready, steel, strengthen

Antonyms: debilitate, enervate, enfeeble, weaken
[+]more

Rhymes with FORTIFY

abide by, Adonai, alibi, alkali, amplify, apple-pie, argufy, assegai, azo dye, basify, beautify, butterfly, by-and-by, caddis fly, calcify...
[+]more

Browse

- Next Word in the Dictionary: fortis
- Previous Word in the Dictionary: fortified wine
- All Words Near: fortify

By permission. From *Merriam-Webster's Collegiate Dictionary, 11th Edition* © 2011 by Merriam-Webster, Incorporated **(http://www.merriam-webster.com).**

Notice the speaker icon next to the word *fortify*. **If you click on this icon, the word will be pronounced for you.**

These sites also give you information on **synonyms** (words with similar meanings to the word you have looked up) and **antonyms** (words with opposite meanings to the word you have looked up). Synonyms and antonyms are explained further on pages 51, 80, and 83.

Note: Some computer programs come with a built-in dictionary. For example, if you use Microsoft Word on a Macintosh, click on "Tools" and then choose "Dictionary." If you are using Word for Windows, highlight a word in your document, scroll down to "Look Up," and then click on one of the dictionaries listed.

Finding Words in the Dictionary

Using Guidewords to Find a Word

One way to find a given word in a dictionary is to use **guidewords**—the pair of words at the very top of each dictionary page. Shown below are the top and bottom parts of a page in one paperback dictionary.

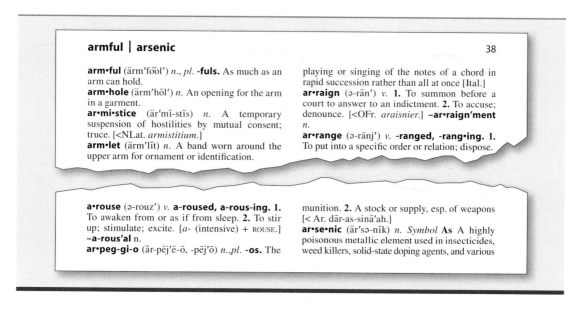

armful | arsenic   38

arm•ful (ärm′fŏŏl′) *n., pl.* **-fuls.** As much as an arm can hold.
arm•hole (ärm′hōl′) *n.* An opening for the arm in a garment.
ar•mi•stice (är′mĭ-stĭs) *n.* A temporary suspension of hostilities by mutual consent; truce. [<NLat. *armistitium.*]
arm•let (ärm′lĭt) *n.* A band worn around the upper arm for ornament or identification.

playing or singing of the notes of a chord in rapid succession rather than all at once [Ital.]
ar•raign (ə-rān′) *v.* **1.** To summon before a court to answer to an indictment. **2.** To accuse; denounce. [<OFr. *araisnier.*] **–ar•raign′ment** *n.*
ar•range (ə-rānj′) *v.* **-ranged, -rang•ing. 1.** To put into a specific order or relation; dispose.

a•rouse (ə-rouz′) *v.* **a-roused, a-rous-ing. 1.** To awaken from or as if from sleep. **2.** To stir up; stimulate; excite. [*a-* (intensive) + ROUSE.] **–a-rous′al** *n.*
ar•peg-gi-o (är-pĕj′ē-ō, -pĕj′ō) *n.,pl.* **-os.** The

munition. **2.** A stock or supply, esp. of weapons [< Ar. dār-as-sinā′ah.]
ar•se•nic (är′sə-nĭk) *n. Symbol* **As** A highly poisonous metallic element used in insecticides, weed killers, solid-state doping agents, and various

The first guideword tells what the first word is on that page; the second guideword tells what the last word is on the page. All the word entries on the page fall alphabetically between the two guidewords.

✓

Check Your Understanding

Now see if you understand how to use guidewords. Underline the three words below that would appear on the page with the guidewords *armful / arsenic*:

art   aroma   army   arrest   ax   allow

Explanation

The guidewords **armful / arsenic** tell us right away that every word on the page will begin with *ar*. That immediately eliminates *ax* and *allow*. The words that would fall on the page with those guidewords are *aroma, army*, and *arrest*. The word *art* also begins with *ar*, but alphabetically it comes after *arsenic*, the last word on the page.

PRACTICE 1

Below are five pairs of dictionary guidewords followed by other words. Underline the **three** words in each series that would be found on the page with the guidewords.

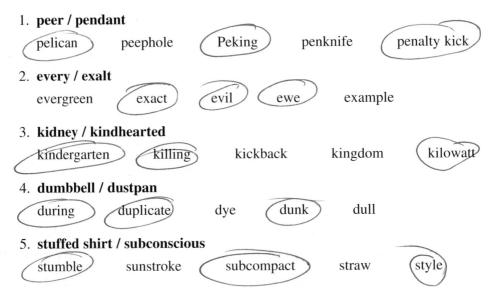

1. **peer / pendant**
   pelican   peephole   Peking   penknife   penalty kick

2. **every / exalt**
   evergreen   exact   evil   ewe   example

3. **kidney / kindhearted**
   kindergarten   killing   kickback   kingdom   kilowatt

4. **dumbbell / dustpan**
   during   duplicate   dye   dunk   dull

5. **stuffed shirt / subconscious**
   stumble   sunstroke   subcompact   straw   style

Finding a Word You Can't Spell

"If I can't spell a word," you might ask, "how can I find it in the dictionary?" The answer is that you have to guess what the letters might be.

Guessing is not too difficult with certain sounds, such as the sounds of *b* and *p*. But other sounds are more difficult to pin down because they can belong to more than one letter. And that's where the guessing comes in. Here are three hints to help in such cases:

Hints for Finding Words

Hint 1: If you're not sure about the vowels in a word, you will simply have to experiment. Vowels often sound the same. So try an *i* in place of an *a*, an *i* in place of an *e*, and so on. If, for example, you don't find a word that sounds as if it begins with *pa*, try looking under *pe*, *pi*, *po*, *pu* or *py*.

Hint 2: Below are groups of letters or letter combinations that often sound alike. If your word isn't spelled with one of the letters in a pair or group shown below, it might be spelled with another in the same pair or group. For example, if it isn't spelled with a *k*, it may be spelled with a *c*.

c / k	c / s	f / v / ph	g / j	qu / kw / k	s / c / z
sch / sc / sk	sh / ch	shun / tion / sion		w / wh	able / ible
ai / ay	al / el / le	ancy / ency	ate / ite	au / aw	ea / ee
er / or	ie / ei	ou / ow	oo / u	y / i / e	

Hint 3: Consonants are sometimes doubled in a word. If you can't find your word with a single consonant, try doubling it.

PRACTICE 2

For this practice you will need a dictionary. Try using your ear, the hints on this page, and guidewords to help you find the correct spelling of the following words. Write each correct spelling in the answer space.

1. occazion __occasion__
2. dooty __duty__
3. dicided __decided__
4. aksident __accident__
5. nieghbor __neighbor__

6. awtumn __autumn__
7. rimember __remember__
8. atenshun __attention__
9. experament __experiment__
10. fotocopy __photocopy__

Learning from a Dictionary Entry

Each entry word in a dictionary is in **boldface type**. Here is a sample entry:

Sample Dictionary Entry

dis•re•spect (dĭs′rĭ-spĕkt′) *n.* Lack of respect or regard; rudeness; discourtesy. —*tr .v.* **-spect•ed, -spect•ing, -spects.** To show a lack of respect for: *disrespect one's elders; disrespect the law.*

All of the following information may be provided in a dictionary entry:

1 Spelling and syllables

2 Pronunciation symbols and accent marks

3 Parts of speech

4 Irregular forms of words

5 Definitions

6 Synonyms

7 Usage labels

The rest of the chapter will look at each kind of information above.

1   Spelling and Syllables

The dictionary first gives the correct spelling and syllable breakdown of a word. Dots separate the words into syllables. Each syllable is a separate sound, and each sound includes a vowel. In the entry shown above, *disrespect* is divided into three syllables.

How many syllables are in each of the following words?

do•nate   com•pen•sate   o•be•di•ent

If you answered two for *donate*, three for *compensate*, and four for *obedient*, you were right.

PRACTICE 3

Use your dictionary to separate the following words into syllables. Put a large dot
(•) between the syllables. Then write down the number of syllables in each word.
The first one is done for you as an example.

1. b i r t h • p l a c e   _____2_____ syllables

2. d i s c l o s e   _____ syllables

3. h u r r i c a n e   _____ syllables

4. u n d e r t a k e r   _____ syllables

5. i n h u m a n i t y   _____ syllables

2   Pronunciation Symbols and Accent Marks

A dictionary entry word is followed by information in parentheses, as in the entry
for *disrespect*:

dis•re•spect (dĭs′rĭ-spĕkt′)

The information in parentheses shows you how to pronounce the word. It includes
two kinds of symbols: pronunciation symbols and accent marks. Following are
explanations of each.

Pronunciation Symbols

The **pronunciation symbols** tell the sounds of the consonants and the vowels in
a word. The sounds of the consonants are probably familiar to you, but you may
find it helpful to review the vowel sounds. Vowels are the letters *a, e, i, o,* and *u*.
(Sometimes *y* is also a vowel, as in *myself* and *copy*.) To know how to pronounce
the vowel sounds, use the pronunciation key in your dictionary. Here is a sample
pronunciation key:

Pronunciation Key

ă hat	ā pay	âr care	ä card	ĕ ten	ē she	ĭ sit
ī hi	îr here	ŏ lot	ō go	ô all	oi oil	ou out
o͝o look	yo͝o cure	o͞o cool	yo͞o use	ŭ up	ûr fur	th thick
th then	ə ago, item, easily, gallop, circus					

To use the pronunciation key, match the symbol (ă, ā, and so on) with the letter or letters in **bold print** in the short word that follows the symbol. For instance, ă (also called "short *a*") sounds like the *a* in *hat*.

You can pronounce the *i* and the first *e* in *disrespect* by first finding the matching symbol within the parentheses. Note that the matching symbol for both vowels is ĭ. Then look for that symbol in the Pronunciation Key. It shows you that ĭ has the sound of *i* in the short word *sit*. You can also use the Pronunciation Key to pronounce the second *e* in *disrespect* (ĕ). It shows you that ĕ is pronounced like the *e* in *ten*.

A long vowel (a vowel with a line over it) has the sound of its own name. Long *a* (ā) sounds like the *a* in *pay*; long *e* (ē) sounds like the *e* in *she*; etc.

Finally, note that the last pronunciation symbol in the key looks like an upside-down e: ə. This symbol is known as the **schwa**. As you can see by the words that follow it, the schwa has a very short sound that sounds much like "uh" (as in *ago, gallop,* and *circus*) or "ih" (as in *item* and *easily*).

PRACTICE 4

Refer to the pronunciation key to answer the questions about the following ten words. In the space provided, write the letter of each of your answers.

_____ 1. **kit•ten** (kĭt′n)
The *i* in *kitten* sounds like the *i* in
A. *sit.*   B. *hi.*

_____ 2. **blos•som** (blŏs′əm)
The first *o* in *blossom* sounds like the *o* in
A. *lot.*   B. *go.*

_____ 3. **live•ly** (līv′lē)
The *i* in *lively* sounds like the *i* in
A. *sit.*   B. *hi.*

_____ 4. **thun•der** (thŭn′dər)
The *u* in *thunder* sounds like the *u* in
A. *up.*   B. *fur.*

_____ 5. **gam•ble** (găm′bəl)
    The *a* in *gamble* sounds like the *a* in
    A. *hat.*   B. *pay.*

_____ 6. **bla•tant** (blāt′nt)
    The first *a* in *blatant* sounds like the *a* in
    A. *hat.*   B. *pay.*

_____ 7. **boast** (bōst)
    The *oa* in *boast* sounds like the *o* in
    A. *lot.*   B. *go.*

_____ 8. **fu•ture** (fyo͞o′chər)
    The first *u* in *future* sounds like the *u* in
    A. *up.*   B. *use.*

_____ 9. **ve•hi•cle** (vē′ĭ-kəl)
    The first *e* in *vehicle* sounds like the *e* in
    A. *ten.*   B. *she.*

_____ 10. **hyp•o•crite** (hĭp′ə-krĭt′)
    The *o* in *hypocrite* sounds like the
    A. *a* in *hat.*   B. schwa in the word *gallop.*

PRACTICE 5

A. Below are pronunciation symbols for five common words. Write in the word in each case and also the number of schwa sounds in each word. The first item has been done for you as an example.

Pronunciation symbols	*Word itself*	*Number of schwas*
1. (dĭs′ə-plĭn)	discipline	1
2. (mə-jôr′ĭ-tē)	_____	_____
3. (ī′sə-lāt′)	_____	_____
4. (är′tə-fĭsh′əl)	_____	_____
5. (năch′ər-əl)	_____	_____

B. Use your dictionary to find and write in the pronunciation symbols for the following words. Make sure you can pronounce each word. The first word has been done for you as an example.

6. cynic   ___sĭn′ĭk___

7. advocate   _____

8. optimist   _____

9. arrogant   _____

10. hypothesis   _____

Accent Marks

Notice the black marks in the pronunciation guide (the information shown in parentheses) for the noun form of *disrespect*. The marks look a little like apostrophes.

   dis•re•spect (dĭs′rĭ-spĕkt′)

The darker line (′) is a bold accent mark, and it shows which syllable has the strongest stress. That means the third syllable in *disrespect* is pronounced a little louder than the other two. Syllables without an accent mark are unstressed. Some syllables—like the first syllable in *disrespect*—are in between, and they are marked with a lighter accent mark (′).

The word *interview* is accented like this:

   in•ter•view (ĭn′tər-vyo͞o′)

Say *interview* to yourself. Can you hear that the strongest accent is on *in,* the first syllable? Can you hear that the last syllable, *view,* is also accented, but not as strongly? If not, say the word to yourself again until you hear the differences in accent sounds.

Here are some familiar words with syllable divisions and accent marks shown in parentheses. Use these guides to help you pronounce the words to yourself.

  ● ma•chine (mə-shēn′)
  ● de•ter•gent (dĭ-tûr′jənt)
  ● in•for•ma•tion (ĭn′fər-mā′shən)
  ● val•en•tine (văl′ən-tīn′)
  ● al•pha•bet•i•cal (ăl′fə-bĕt′ĭ-kəl)

Think for a moment of how each of these words would sound if you accented the wrong syllable.

PRACTICE 6

Answer the questions following each of the five words below.

1. **pro•cras•ti•nate** (prō-krăs′tə-nāt′)

    A. How many syllables are in *procrastinate?* _____

    B. Which syllable is most strongly accented? _____

2. **mag•nif•i•cent** (măg-nĭf′ĭ-sənt)

    A. How many syllables are in *magnificent?* _____

    B. Which syllable is most strongly accented? _____

3. **un•der•dog** (ŭn′dər-dôg′)

    A. How many syllables are in *underdog?* _____

    B. Which syllable is most strongly accented? _____

4. **so•phis•ti•ca•ted** (sə-fĭs′tĭ-kā′tĭd)

    A. How many syllables are in *sophisticated?* _____

    B. Which syllable is most strongly accented? _____

5. **ter•mi•nate** (tûr′mə-nāt′)

    A. How many syllables are in *terminate?* _____

    B. Which syllable is **least** strongly accented? _____

3   Parts of Speech

Every word in the dictionary is either a noun, a verb, an adjective, or another part of speech. In dictionary entries, the parts of speech are shown by letters in italics. In the entry for *disrespect*, for example, the abbreviations *v.* and *n.* tell us that *disrespect* is both a verb and a noun. The entry below for *insult* tells us that this word is both a verb and a noun.

in•sult (ĭn-sŭlt′) *v.* To speak to or treat with disrespect or contempt. —*n.* (ĭn′sŭlt′). An offensive or disrespectful action or remark.

When a word is more than one part of speech, the dictionary gives the definitions for each part of speech separately. In the above entry for *insult*, the abbreviation telling us that *insult* is a verb comes right after the pronunciation symbols; the verb definition follows. When the verb meaning ends, the abbreviation *n.* tells us that the noun definition will follow.

Parts of speech are abbreviated in order to save space. Following are the most common abbreviations for parts of speech:

n. — noun	*v.* — verb
pron. — pronoun	*conj.* — conjunction
adj. — adjective	*prep.* — preposition
adv. — adverb	*interj.* — interjection

Note: Many dictionaries use the abbreviations *tr.* and *intr.* (or *vt* and *vi*) to indicate two types of verbs, not other parts of speech. The abbreviations *tr.* and *vt* stand for a transitive verb (one that has a direct object); the abbreviations *intr.* and *vi* stand for an intransitive verb (one that does not have a direct object).

PRACTICE 7

Use your dictionary to list the parts of speech for each of the following words. Each word has more than one part of speech.

Parts of speech

1. praise   _____

2. bridge   _____

3. panic   _____

4. around   _____

5. level   _____

4   Irregular Forms of Words

Look at the following two words and the forms that follow them in most dictionaries.

know (nō) *v.* **knew** (no͞o, nyo͞o), **known, know•ing.**

fun•ny (fŭn′ē) *adj.* **-ni•er, -ni•est.**

When other forms of a word are spelled in an irregular way, these forms are shown. As you can see in the examples on the previous page, these forms are given after the part of speech in an entry. With irregular verbs, the dictionary gives the past tense (*knew*) and the past participle (*known*), as well as the present participle (*knowing*). With adjectives, the dictionary gives the comparative (*funnier*) and superlative (*funniest*) forms.

Plural forms with irregular spellings are also included in this spot in an entry. For example, the entry for *country* begins:

coun•try (kŭn′trē) *n., pl.* **-tries.**

After the part of speech of *country* (*n.* for noun), the entry gives the irregular form of the plural (*pl.*) of *country*.

Finally, comparative forms of adjectives and adverbs are also given at this point in the entry. Here are two examples:

good (gŏŏd) *adj.* **bet•ter** (bĕt′ər), **best** (bĕst)

wide (wīd) *adj.* **-er, -est**

PRACTICE 8

Below are the beginnings of three dictionary entries. In the blanks, write in the part of speech and irregular or other troublesome spellings in full (not abbreviated).

1. **write** (rīt) *v.* **wrote** (rōt), **writ•ten** (rĭt′n), **writ•ing**

    Part of speech: _____

    Spelling of past tense: _____

    Spelling of past participle: _____

    Spelling of present participle: _____

2. **cra•zy** (krā′zē) *adj.* **-zi•er, -zi•est**

    Part of speech: _____

    Spelling of form that means *most crazy* (with *-est* ending):

    _____

3. **qual•i•ty** (kwŏl′ĭ-tē) *n.* **-ties**

    Part of speech: _____

    Spelling of plural: _____

5   Definitions

Words often have more than one meaning. When they do, their definitions may be numbered in the dictionary. You can tell which definition of a word fits a given sentence by the meaning of the sentence. For example, the following are three of the definitions of the verb form of *revive* given in most dictionaries:

1. To bring back to life or consciousness.
2. To impart or regain health or vigor.
3. To restore to use.

Which of these definitions best fits the sentence below?

Modern technology can revive patients who have actually been considered medically dead.

The answer is definition 1: Modern technology can bring a patient back to life.

PRACTICE 9

Below are three words and their dictionary definitions. A sentence using each word is also given. Choose the dictionary meaning that best fits each sentence.

1. **idle: 1.** Not working; inactive. **2.** Avoiding work; lazy.

    Which definition best fits the sentence below? _____

    The streetcar tracks in our city have been *idle* since 1960, when the city switched from streetcars to buses.

2. **suspicion: 1.** The act of suspecting the existence of something, esp. of something wrong, with little evidence or proof. **2.** A faint trace; hint.

    Which definition fits the following sentence? _____

    There was a *suspicion* of rum in the chocolate cake.

3. **sterile: 1.** Incapable of reproducing sexually. **2.** Producing little or no vegetation. **3.** Free from microorganisms.

    Which definition fits the following sentence? _____

    The real estate agent had cheated young farmers by selling them *sterile* land.

6   Synonyms

© 2000 Randy Glasbergen.
www.glasbergen.com

GLASBERGEN

"This online dictionary is great! It gives me synonyms I can use to write a more impressive paper."

A **synonym** is a word whose meaning is similar to that of another word. For instance, two synonyms for the word *fast* are *quick* and *speedy.*

Dictionary entries sometimes end with synonyms. For example, the word *foreign* in some dictionaries ends with several synonyms: *alien, exotic, strange.* A hardbound dictionary in particular will provide synonyms for a word and explain the differences in meaning among the various synonyms.

More information on synonyms as well as **antonyms** (words with opposite meanings) can be found in a **thesaurus** (thĭ-sôr′əs), which is a collection of synonyms and antonyms. A thesaurus can improve your writing by helping you to find the precise word needed to express your thoughts. A thesaurus works much like a dictionary. You look up a word and, instead of definitions, you get a list of synonyms and perhaps an antonym of the word. To help you find the right word when writing, a thesaurus goes along well with your dictionary. If you have access to the Internet, you can find a free thesaurus online by going to

www.merriam-webster.com   or   www.thesaurus.com

Or see if your computer has a built-in thesaurus. For example, if you use Microsoft Word on a Macintosh computer, click on "Tools" and then choose "Thesaurus." (If you are using Word for Windows, click on "Review" and then choose "Thesaurus," or right-click a word in your document and then click "Synonyms.")

Or you may want to own a paperback thesaurus such as one of the following:

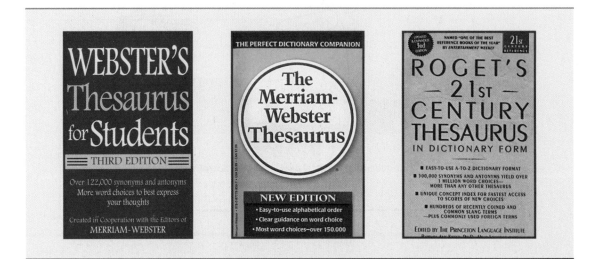

7   Usage Labels

Besides listing definitions, a dictionary often includes **usage labels**: terms that tell us if a meaning is considered something other than "Standard English." For example, the dictionary labels one meaning of the verb *crash*, "to go to sleep," as "*Slang*." Other common labels include "*Informal*" (the phrase *hang in,* meaning "to persist," is labeled as informal) and "*Nonstandard*" (the word *ain't* is labeled nonstandard). Such labels indicate language not considered appropriate in formal speech and writing.

In addition to usage labels, the dictionary provides **field labels**—special meanings of a word within a certain field. For instance, one dictionary definition of the word *mouse* is labeled "Computer Science" and is followed by a meaning that applies to the field of computers: "A hand-held input device used to move about a computer screen and operate programs."

CHAPTER REVIEW

In this chapter, you learned the following:

- It is helpful to own two dictionaries. One should be a small paperback edition you can carry with you. The other should be a large hardbound version for use at home.

- If you have a computer, you can easily use a dictionary site online. You may also have a dictionary that comes with the word-processing software on your computer.

- You can find a word in the dictionary with the help of guidewords, the two words at the top of each dictionary page.

- You can use the spelling hints on page 41 to help you find a word you cannot spell.

- A dictionary entry will tell you (1) how a word is spelled and broken into syllables; (2) how a word is pronounced; (3) a word's part (or parts) of speech; (4) irregular forms of the word; (5) definitions of the word; (6) in some cases, synonyms; (7) any usage or field labels for the word.

The next chapter—Chapter 2—will show you how you can use context, rather than a dictionary, to figure out the meaning of a word.

On the Web: If you are using this book in class, you can visit our website for additional practice in using the dictionary. Go to **www.townsendpress.com** and click on "Learning Center."

REVIEW TEST 1

To review what you've learned in this chapter, answer the following questions by writing the letter of the correct answer.

_____ 1. Guidewords can help you
    A. pronounce a word in a dictionary.
    B. find a word in a dictionary.
    C. define a word in a dictionary.

_____ 2. You can learn how to pronounce a word by using the pronunciation symbols and
   A. the part of speech.
   B. usage labels.
   C. the pronunciation key.

_____ 3. A dark accent mark shows
   A. which syllable has the strongest stress.
   B. which syllable has the weakest stress.
   C. that the word has only one syllable.

_____ 4. A schwa is an unaccented syllable that sounds like the *a* in the word
   A. *ago.*
   B. *cake.*
   C. *cat.*

_____ 5. Dictionary entries will show you all of the following *except*
   A. how to spell a word.
   B. how to pronounce a word.
   C. the meaning or meanings of a word.
   D. whether a word is a noun, verb, adjective or other part of speech.
   E. common spelling errors of a word.

REVIEW TEST 2

A. Where would you find the numbered words below—before, on, or following the page with the guidewords? Fill in each blank with a **B** (for *before*), an **O** (for *on*), or an **F** (for *following*).

Guidewords: **mace / magazine**

1. machine   _____

2. macaroni   _____

3. moody   _____

4. mailman   _____

5. Mafia   _____

B. Use your dictionary to find the correct spellings of the following words:

6. kabinit _____

7. sircus _____

8. dezign _____

9. jinjerbread _____

10. dinamite _____

C. Answer the questions about the five words below. The pronunciation key on page 43 will help you answer some of the questions.

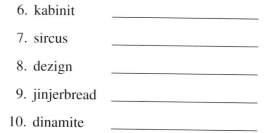

de•ter•mi•na•tion (dĭ-tûr′mə-nā′shən)   pro•file (prō′fīl′)

hu•man•ize (hyoo′mə-nīz′)   sa•vor (sā′vər)

lu•na•tic (loo′nə-tĭk)

11–12. Which two words have the sound of the long *a*, as in *pay*?

_____   _____

13–14. Which two words have the sound of the long *i*, as in *hi*?

_____   _____

15. Which word has the long *oo* sound, as in *cool*? _____

16. Which word has the long *yoo* sound, as in *use*? _____

17. In the word *savor,* a schwa sound appears in which syllable? _____

18. Which syllable is more strongly accented in the word *profile*? _____

19. Which syllable is most strongly accented in the word *determination?*

_____

20. How many syllables are in the word *determination*? _____

REVIEW TEST 3

Use your dictionary to do all of the following.

A. Place dots between the syllables in the following words. Then write the correct pronunciation symbols, including the accent marks.

1. s c a p e g o a t _____

2. e x h a u s t _____

3. d e c i s i o n _____

4. c e l e b r a t e _____

5. r e c i p r o c a t e _____

B. List the parts of speech for each of the following words.

6. before   *Parts of speech:* _____

7. desire   *Parts of speech:* _____

C. Write the irregular form or forms of the following words.

8. memory   *Irregular form:* _____

9. lively   *Irregular forms:* _____

D. What dictionary definition of *drown* fits the following sentence?

10. Elsie drowned her strawberry pancakes in strawberry syrup.

_____

REVIEW TEST 4

Here is a chance to apply your understanding of dictionary use to an excerpt from the longtime popular book *The Road Less Traveled*. The author, M. Scott Peck, a psychiatrist, explains a key first step in dealing with personal problems. He does so by offering examples of two people who fail to think clearly about their own problems.

Words to Watch

Below are some words in the reading that do not have strong context support. Each word is followed by the number of the paragraph in which it appears and its meaning there. These words are indicated in the selection by a small circle (°).

self-evident (1): not requiring any explanation
ludicrous (2): laughable because of being obviously ridiculous
clarified (19): made clear
amenable (23): agreeable
whining (29): childish complaining
glared (37): stared angrily

RESPONSIBILITY

M. Scott Peck

1   We cannot solve life's problems except by solving them. This statement may seem idiotically self-evident°, yet it is seemingly beyond the comprehension of much of the human race. This is because we must accept responsibility for a problem before we can solve it. We cannot solve a problem by saying, "It's not my problem." We cannot solve a problem by hoping that someone else will solve it for us. I can solve a problem only when I say, "This is my problem and it's up to me to solve it." But many, so many, seek to avoid the pain of their problems by saying to themselves: "This problem was caused by other people, or by social circumstances beyond my control, and therefore it is up to other people or society to solve this problem for me. It is not really my personal problem."

2   The extent to which people will go psychologically to avoid assuming responsibility for personal problems, while always sad, is sometimes almost ludicrous°. A career sergeant in the army, stationed in Okinawa and in serious trouble because of his excessive drinking, was referred for psychiatric evaluation and, if possible, assistance. He denied that he was an alcoholic, or even that his use of alcohol was a personal problem, saying, "There's nothing else to do in the evenings in Okinawa except drink."

3   "Do you like to read?" I asked.

4   "Oh yes, I like to read, sure."

5   "Then why don't you read in the evening instead of drinking?"

6   "It's too noisy to read in the barracks."

7   "Well, then, why don't you go to the library?"

8   "The library is too far away."

9   "Is the library farther away than the bar you go to?"

10   "Well, I'm not much of a reader. That's not where my interests lie."

11   "Do you like to fish?" I then inquired.

12   "Sure, I love to fish."

13   "Why not go fishing instead of drinking?"

14   "Because I have to work all day long."

15   "Can't you go fishing at night?"

16   "No, there isn't any night fishing in Okinawa."

17   "But there is," I said. "I know several organizations that fish at night here. Would you like me to put you in touch with them?"

18   "Well, I really don't like to fish."

19   "What I hear you saying," I clarified°, "is that there are other things to do in Okinawa except drink, but the thing you like to do most in Okinawa is drink."

20   "Yeah, I guess so."

21   "But your drinking is getting you in trouble, so you're faced with a real problem, aren't you?"

22   "This damn island would drive anyone to drink."

23   I kept trying for a while, but the sergeant was not the least bit interested in seeing his drinking as a personal problem which he could solve either with or without help, and I regretfully told his commander that he was not amenable° to assistance. His drinking continued, and he was separated from the service in mid-career.

24   A young wife, also in Okinawa, cut her wrist lightly with a razor blade and was brought to the emergency room, where I saw her. I asked her why she had done this to herself.

25   "To kill myself, of course."

26   "Why do you want to kill yourself?"

27   "Because I can't stand it on this

dumb island. You have to send me back to the States. I'm going to kill myself if I have to stay here any longer."

28   "What is it about living on Okinawa that's so painful for you?" I asked.

29   She began to cry in a whining° sort of way. "I don't have any friends here, and I'm alone all the time."

30   "That's too bad. How come you haven't been able to make any friends?"

31   "Because I have to live in a stupid Okinawan housing area, and none of my neighbors speak English."

32   "Why don't you drive over to the American housing area or to the wives' club during the day so you can make some friends?"

33   "Because my husband has to drive the car to work."

34   "Can't you drive him to work, since you're alone and bored all day?" I asked.

35   "No. It's a stick-shift car, and I don't know how to drive a stick-shift car, only an automatic."

36   "Why don't you learn how to drive a stick-shift car?"

37   She glared° at me. "On these roads? You must be crazy."

Dictionary Questions

Use your dictionary to answer the questions that follow. Each question is about a word taken from the selection.

1. What pronunciation does your dictionary give for *amenable?*

_____

2. Which syllable in *amenable* is accented?

_____

3. What part of speech is the word *amenable?*

_____

4. What pronunciation does your dictionary give for *ludicrous?*

_____

5. Which syllable in *circumstances* is most strongly accented?

_____

6. What part of speech is the word *clarified?*

_____

7. Use your dictionary to determine the number of syllables in the word *responsibility.* Write the word, with dots between the syllables, below:

_____

8. Use your dictionary to determine the number of syllables in the word *idiotically.* Write the word, with dots between the syllables, below:

_____

_____ 9. Below are dictionary definitions of *assume.* Choose the meaning that best fits *assuming* as used in the first sentence of paragraph 2 of the reading:
   A. To take upon oneself
   B. To put on
   C. To take for granted

   "The extent to which people will go psychologically to avoid assuming responsibility for personal problems, while always sad, is sometimes almost ludicrous."

_____ 10. Below are dictionary definitions of *glare*. Choose the meaning that best fits *glared* as used in paragraph 37 of the selection:
   A. To stare angrily
   B. To shine intensely
   C. To stand out in an obvious way

   "She glared at me. 'On these roads? You must be crazy.'"

Questions about the Reading

For each question, write the letter of your answer in the space provided.

_____ 1. In the excerpt below, the word *comprehension* probably means
   A. meaning.
   B. understanding.
   C. confusion.
   D. absence.

   "We cannot solve life's problems except by solving them. This statement . . . is seemingly beyond the comprehension of much of the human race." (Paragraph 1)

_____ 2. In the sentence below, the word *excessive* probably means
   A. good-natured.
   B. unwilling.
   C. moderate.
   D. more than normal.

   "A career sergeant . . . in serious trouble because of his excessive drinking, was referred for psychiatric evaluation and, if possible, assistance." (Paragraph 2)

_____ 3. Which sentence best expresses the central point of the entire selection?
   A. In Okinawa, Peck met two people who refused to take responsibility for their own problems.
   B. Some people find ways to come up with creative excuses for their irresponsibility.
   C. Many people, like the sergeant and the young wife, won't solve their problems because they refuse to take responsibility for them.
   D. The sergeant and the young wife would rather see their careers and lives ruined than take responsibility for their problems.

_____ 4. Which sentence best expresses the main idea of paragraphs 2–22?
   A. A career sergeant was in trouble because of his drinking.
   B. The sergeant denied that he had a problem with alcohol.
   C. Peck was expected to evaluate the sergeant and, if possible, help him.
   D. People will go to ridiculous lengths to avoid responsibility for their problems.

_____ 5. What seems to be the main idea of paragraph 23?
   A. Peck tried for some time to help the sergeant.
   B. Drinking has destroyed the lives of many people.
   C. Peck told the commander that he could not help the sergeant.
   D. The sergeant, whom Peck was unable to help, had to leave the service.

_____ 6. Peck states that the sergeant was not willing to be helped. What evidence does he give for that statement?
   A. The sergeant did not like to fish.
   B. The sergeant did not like to read.
   C. The sergeant refused every one of Peck's suggestions.
   D. All of the above

_____ 7. The young wife first saw Peck because she
   A. was drinking too much.
   B. had cut her wrist.
   C. had tried to return to the United States.
   D. wanted to learn to drive.

_____ 8. The young wife said she could not drive to the wives' club because
   A. she could not drive a stick-shift car.
   B. she had to be away at work all day.
   C. none of the other wives spoke English.
   D. she and her husband did not own a car.

_____ 9. Which statement would Peck be most likely to make to the young wife?
   A. "No one in your situation could be expected to be happy."
   B. "Since you're not willing to learn to drive a stick-shift car, you don't really want to help yourself."
   C. "Your neighbors really should learn English so that they can talk to you."
   D. "The military should make better arrangements for spouses who are living far away from home."

_____ 10. The sergeant and the young wife probably
  A. knew each other.
  B. wanted someone else to solve their problems.
  C. could have solved their problems if they were back in the United States.
  D. became happier and stronger after their meetings with Peck.

Discussion Questions

1. Peck says that some people will go to ridiculous lengths to avoid assuming responsibility for their personal problems. What is ridiculous about the sergeant's behavior? About the young wife's behavior?

2. What details might Peck have included in this selection if he had chosen students as examples? What responsibilities do students typically avoid? What excuses do they make?

3. Peck states that "we must accept responsibility for a problem before we can solve it." What does he mean by this statement? Do you agree? Use examples from your own life or someone else's to support your view.

4. Why do you think it's so difficult for people to take responsibility for their problems?

Note: Writing assignments for this selection appear on page 604.

Check Your Performance			DICTIONARY USE
Activity	Number Right	Points	Score
Review Test 1 (5 items)	_____	× 2 =	_____
Review Test 2 (20 items)	_____	× 1.5 =	_____
Review Test 3 (10 items)	_____	× 3 =	_____
Review Test 4 (10 items)	_____	× 3 =	_____
		TOTAL SCORE =	_____ %

Enter your total score into the **Reading Performance Chart: Review Tests** on the inside back cover.

DICTIONARY USE: Mastery Test 1

A. Answer the following questions about the dictionary entries for *avert* and *emerge*. Use the pronunciation key below for help as needed.

Pronunciation Key

ă hat	ā pay	âr care	ä card	ě ten	ē she	ĭ sit
ī hi	îr here	ŏ lot	ō go	ô all	oi oil	ou out
ŏŏ look	yŏŏ cure	ōō cool	yōō use	ŭ up	ûr fur	th thick
th then	ə ago, item, easily, gallop, circus					

a•vert (ə-vûrt′) *v.* **1.** To turn away: *avert one's eyes.* **2.** To ward off; prevent. —**a•vert′i•ble** or **a•vert′a•ble** *adj.*

_____ 1. Which syllable in *avert* is accented?
      A. The first   B. The second

_____ 2. The *e* in *avert* is pronounced like the
      A. *u* in *up.*   B. *u* in *fur.*

_____ 3. What part of speech is *avert*?
      A. Noun   B. Verb   C. Adjective

_____ 4. Which definition of *avert* best fits the sentence below—1 or 2?

Gene saw the other car swerve, but too late to avert a collision.

_____ 5. Which definition of *avert* best fits the sentence below—1 or 2?

The chef averted her face to avoid the heat from the oven.

(Continues on next page)

e•merge (ĭ-mûrj´) *v.* **e•merged, e•merg•ing. 1.** To rise up or come forth into view; appear. **2.** To become known or evident. **3.** To come into existence. —**e•mer´gence** *n.* —**e•mer´gent** *adj.*

_____ 6. The first *e* in *emerge* sounds like the
        A. *e* in *ten.*   B. *i* in *sit.*

_____ 7. How many syllables are in the word *emerged?*

_____ 8. What part of speech is *emergence?*
        A. Noun   B. Verb   C. Adjective

_____ 9. Which definition of *emerge* best fits the sentence below—1, 2, or 3?

        The sun emerged from behind the clouds.

_____ 10. Which definition of *emerge* best fits the sentence below—1, 2, or 3?

        The fact that the defendant was once a prison guard emerged in court last week.

B. Use your dictionary to find the correct spelling of the following words. (Feel free to use the spelling hints on page 41.)

    11. toona _____

    12. freaze _____

    13. tendancy _____

    14. paralel _____

    15. accelarate _____

C. Use your dictionary to put dots between the syllables in each word. Then write out the word with the correct pronunciation symbols, including the accent marks.

    16. i m p a i r_____

    17. s a d i s t i c _____

    18. i n e v i t a b l e _____

    19. a p p r e h e n s i v e _____

    20. s t e r e o t y p e _____

DICTIONARY USE: Mastery Test 2

A. Answer the following questions about the dictionary entries for *notable* and *undermine*. Use the pronunciation key below for help as needed.

Pronunciation Key

ă hat	ā pay	âr care	ä card	ĕ ten	ē she	ĭ sit
ī hi	îr here	ŏ lot	ō go	ô all	oi oil	ou out
ŏŏ look	yŏŏ cure	ōō cool	yōō use	ŭ up	ûr fur	th thick
th then	ə ago, item, easily, gallop, circus					

no•ta•ble (nō′tə-bəl) *adj.* **1.** Worthy of note or notice; remarkable. **2.** Widely known and celebrated. —**no′ta•ble•ness** *n.* —**no′ta•bly** *adv.*

_____ 1. *Notable* would be found on the dictionary page with which guidewords?
  A. **nostalgia / notation**   C. **notary / notify**
  B. **northwest / nostril**   D. **novice / noxious**

_____ 2. How many syllables are in the word *notable*?

_____ 3. Which syllable is accented?
  A. The first   B. The second   C. The third

_____ 4. The *o* in *notable* is pronounced like
  A. the *o* in *lot*.   B. the *o* in *go*.   C. the *a* in *hat*.

_____ 5. The *a* in *notable* is pronounced like
  A. the *a* in *hat*.   B. the *a* in *pay*.   C. the *a* in *ago*.

(Continues on next page)

un•der•mine (ŭn′dər-mīn′) *v.* **-mined, -min•ing, -mines. 1.** To weaken by wearing away a base or foundation. **2.** To ruin in an underhand way. **3.** To dig a mine or tunnel under.

_____ 6. *Undermine* would be found on the dictionary page with which guidewords?

    A. **underling / undershirt**   C. **understand / underworld**

    B. **under / undercover**   D. **underground / underhand**

_____ 7. How many syllables are in the word *undermine*?

_____ 8. The stronger accent is on the

    A. first syllable.   B. second syllable.   C. last syllable.

_____ 9. The *u* in *undermine* is pronounced like

    A. the *u* in *use*.   B. the *u* in *up*.   C. the *u* in *circus*.

_____ 10. What part of speech is *undermine*?

    A. Noun   B. Verb   C. Adjective

B. Use your dictionary to find the correct spelling of the following words. (Feel free to use the spelling hints on page 41.)

    11. consede _____

    12. retreave _____

    13. pessemist _____

    14. iluminate _____

    15. inevitible _____

C. Use your dictionary to put dots between the syllables in each word. Then write out the word with the correct pronunciation symbols, including the accent marks.

    16. a s p i r e _____

    17. r e p r i m a n d _____

    18. p r i n c i p a l _____

    19. t e r m i n a t e _____

    20. i m a g i n a t i o n _____

DICTIONARY USE: Mastery Test 3

A. Answer the following questions about the dictionary entries for *destiny* and *tentative*. Use the pronunciation key below for help as needed.

Pronunciation Key

ă hat	ā pay	âr care	ä card	ĕ ten	ē she	ĭ sit
ī hi	îr here	ŏ lot	ō go	ô all	oi oil	ou out
ŏŏ look	yŏŏ cure	ōō cool	yōō use	ŭ up	ûr fur	th thick
th then	ə ago, item, easily, gallop, circus					

des•ti•ny (dĕs′tə-nē) *n.* A fixed order of things that will inevitably happen in the future; fate.

_____ 1. *Destiny* would be found on the dictionary page with which guidewords?
    A. **designate / desperate**   C. **detach / determine**
    B. **despise / destructive**   D. **descent / design**

_____ 2. How many syllables are in the word *destiny*?

_____ 3. Which syllable is accented?
    A. The first   B. The second   C. The third

_____ 4. The *e* in *destiny* is pronounced like
    A. the *e* in *she*.   B. the *e* in *ten*.   C. the *a* in *hat*.

_____ 5. What part of speech is *destiny*?
    A. Noun   B. Verb   C. Adjective

(Continues on next page)

ten•ta•tive (tĕn′tə-tĭv) *adj.* **1.** Not definite; not final. **2.** Uncertain or unsure; hesitant. —**ten′ta•tive•ly** *adv.* —**ten′ta•tive•ness** *n.*

_____ 6. *Tentative* would be found on the dictionary page with which guidewords?
    A. **tennis / tentacle**   C. **tent / term**
    B. **tender / tension**   D. **tepid / terminate**

_____ 7. How many syllables are in the word *tentative*?

_____ 8. Which syllable is accented?
    A. The first   B. The second   C. The third

_____ 9. The *a* in *tentative* is pronounced like
    A. the *a* in *hat*.   B. the *a* in *pay*.   C. the *a* in *ago*.

_____ 10. What part of speech is *tentative*?
    A. Noun   B. Verb   C. Adjective

B. Use your dictionary to find the correct spelling of the following words. (Feel free to use the spelling hints on page 41.)

11. exersize _____

12. decieve _____

13. finaly _____

14. gullable _____

15. persistant _____

C. Use your dictionary to put dots between the syllables in each word. Then write out the word with the correct pronunciation symbols, including the accent marks.

16. e l a p s e _____

17. d u b i o u s _____

18. a n t i d o t e _____

19. i n g e n i o u s _____

20. p e r s e v e r a n c e _____

Name _____ Date _____

Section _____ SCORE: (Number correct) _____ x 5 = _____ %

DICTIONARY USE: Mastery Test 4

A. Answer the following questions about the dictionary entries for *suspend* and *universal*. Use the pronunciation key below for help as needed.

Pronunciation Key

ă hat	ā pay	âr care	ä card	ĕ ten	ē she	ĭ sit
ī hi	îr here	ŏ lot	ō go	ô all	oi oil	ou out
ŏŏ look	yŏŏ cure	ōō cool	yōō use	ŭ up	ûr fur	th thick
th then	ə ago, item, easily, gallop, circus					

sus•pend (sə-spĕnd′) *v.* **1.** To bar for a period from a privilege, office, or position. **2.** To cause to stop for a period; interrupt. **3.** To put off; defer: *suspend judgment.* **4.** To render ineffective temporarily: *suspend parking regulations.* **5.** To hang so as to allow free movement.

_____ 1. Which syllable in *suspend* is accented?
   A. The first   B. The second

_____ 2. The *u* in *suspend* sounds like
   A. the *u* in *up*.   B. the *u* in *circus*.

_____ 3. The *e* in *suspend* sounds like
   A. the *e* in *ten*.   B. the *e* in *she*.

_____ 4. Which definition of *suspend* best fits the sentence below—1, 2, 3, 4, or 5?

   The parade was suspended for a while on Broad Street while the police pushed back the crowds.

_____ 5. Which definition of *suspend* best fits the sentence below—1, 2, 3, 4, or 5?

   The bus driver was suspended until it could be determined if he had used marijuana.

(Continues on next page)

69

u•ni•ver•sal (yo͞o′nə-vûr′səl) *adj.* **1.** Extending to or affecting the entire world; worldwide. **2.** Including or affecting all members of a class or group. **3.** Of or pertaining to the universe; cosmic.

_____ 6. The stronger accent in *universal* is on the
        A. first syllable.   B. third syllable.

_____ 7. The *u* in *universal* is pronounced like
        A. the *u* in *use*.   B. the *u* in *up*.

_____ 8. The *a* in *universal* is pronounced like
        A. the *a* in *ago*.   B. the *a* in *hat*.

_____ 9. Which definition of *universal* best fits the sentence below—1, 2, or 3?
        Clean air and pure drinking water are a universal goal in our world today.

_____ 10. Which definition of *universal* best fits the sentence below—1, 2, or 3?
        The universal opinion of weekend moviegoers was disappointment in the new action film.

B. Use your dictionary to list the parts of speech given for the following words.

    11. muzzle _____

    12. moderate _____

    13. stray _____

    14. sedate _____

    15. compliment _____

C. Use your dictionary to write the irregular plural forms for the following words.

    16. strategy _____

    17. alumnus _____

    18. mother-in-law_____

    19. crisis _____

    20. passerby _____

DICTIONARY USE: Mastery Test 5

Using your dictionary, write the pronunciation and meaning of the boldfaced word in each sentence. Make sure that you choose the definition that best fits the sentence.

1. My sister, a kindergarten teacher, makes me laugh with every funny **anecdote** she tells about her young students.

   A. Pronunciation: _____

   B. Definition: _____

2. Suzanne is looking for a small used car—a Nissan Versa or something **comparable** in size and price.

   A. Pronunciation: _____

   B. Definition: _____

3. Ken is too **skeptical** to believe in UFOs visiting from other worlds. He would have to see the proof with his own eyes.

   A. Pronunciation: _____

   B. Definition: _____

4. My mother **imposes** on my brother's good nature by always asking him to run errands for her.

   A. Pronunciation: _____

   B. Definition: _____

5. I have asked my brother to **delete** an embarrassing photo of me that he posted on his Facebook page.

   A. Pronunciation: _____

   B. Definition: _____

6. A zoo is a place to see **exotic** animals, such as tigers from Asia and elephants from Africa.

   A. Pronunciation: _____

   B. Definition: _____

(Continues on next page)

7. Jesse is **susceptible** to headaches whenever her life becomes too stressful.

   A. Pronunciation: _____

   B. Definition: _____

8. I could not offer the teacher a **plausible** excuse for not handing in the paper.

   A. Pronunciation: _____

   B. Definition: _____

9. Some divorced parents who want to see more of their children use an illegal **strategy**: kidnapping.

   A. Pronunciation: _____

   B. Definition: _____

10. Many people are afraid of spiders and snakes, but some have a more unusual **phobia**, such as a fear of bridges or stoplights.

    A. Pronunciation: _____

    B. Definition: _____

DICTIONARY USE: Mastery Test 6

Using your dictionary, write the pronunciation and meaning of the boldfaced word in each sentence. Make sure that you choose the definition that best fits the sentence.

1. The staff at the drug store gave out the wrong medicine because they could not read the doctor's **illegible** handwriting.

   A. Pronunciation: _____

   B. Definition: _____

2. As the sprinkle turned into a downpour, the crowd at the baseball game began to **disperse**.

   A. Pronunciation: _____

   B. Definition: _____

3. In the court case, the decision of the jury was **unanimous**; everyone believed the defendant was innocent.

   A. Pronunciation: _____

   B. Definition: _____

4. The air escaping from the balloon **propelled** it across the table and into the fishbowl.

   A. Pronunciation: _____

   B. Definition: _____

5. It's important to keep household cleaners locked up safely away from children, as many of these products can be **lethal** if swallowed.

   A. Pronunciation: _____

   B. Definition: _____

6. A large part of war is **propaganda**: spreading information—which is often untrue—that makes the enemy look bad.

   A. Pronunciation: _____

   B. Definition: _____

(Continues on next page)

7. Although twins Jon and Ron look very much alike, there are a few **subtle** differences that help their friends tell them apart.

   A. Pronunciation: _____

   B. Definition: _____

8. Police officers used flashlights to **illuminate** the basement as they searched for the missing girl.

   A. Pronunciation: _____

   B. Definition: _____

9. The drug was pulled off the market when it was learned that researchers had **altered** test results to hide the fact that the drug was dangerous.

   A. Pronunciation: _____

   B. Definition: _____

10. Scholars believe the practice of drinking tea **originated** in China thousands of years ago when some leaves accidentally blew into a pot of boiling water.

   A. Pronunciation: _____

   B. Definition: _____

2 Vocabulary in Context

This Chapter in a Nutshell

- You don't always have to use a dictionary to learn the meanings of new words in your reading. You can often use *context* to figure out the meaning of a word:

    — *Examples* may provide clues to what a word means.

    — *Synonyms*—words that mean the same as an unknown word—may provide clues to a meaning.

    — *Antonyms*—words that mean the opposite of an unknown word—may help you figure out a meaning.

    — The *entire sentence* may provide clues to a meaning.

- Textbook authors often tell you a word's meaning; they *italicize* or **boldface** terms you may not know and give definitions and examples of those terms.

Do you know the meaning of the word *savor*? Look at the following cartoon and see if the sentences below it (spoken by the older brother) help you choose the correct answer.

_____ *Savor* (sā′vər) means
A. enjoy.
B. wonder about.
C. forget.

The older brother is advising his younger brother to take enough time to appreciate the taste of the candy. The **context**—the words surrounding the unfamiliar word—tells us that *savor* means "appreciate" or "enjoy." In this chapter, you will learn how to use the context to figure out the meanings of words.

Understanding Vocabulary in Context

Do you know the meaning of the word *vital*? How about the word *appropriate*? Or the word *passive*?

You may not know the meaning of one or more of these words. However, if you saw these words in sentences, chances are you could come up with fairly accurate definitions. For example, read each sentence below and see if you can understand the meaning of the word in *italics*. In the space provided, write the letter of the meaning you think is correct. Then read the explanation.

Do not use a dictionary for this work. Instead, in each sentence, try the word you think is the answer. For example, put *unimportant* or *necessary* or *surprising* into the sentence in place of *vital* to see which one makes the best sense.

_____ 1. All animals share the same *vital* needs, such as food, water, and shelter.

   Vital (vīt′l) means
   A. unimportant.   B. necessary.   c. surprising.

_____ 2. In the United States, shaking hands is the *appropriate* way to greet someone; in Japan, bowing is the right way.

   Appropriate (ə-prō′prē-ĭt) means
   A. proper.   B. artificial.   c. insulting.

_____ 3. Winners in life take an active role in making things happen, instead of being *passive* and waiting for good luck.

   Passive (păs′ĭv) means
   A. insincere.   B. inactive.   c. flexible.

In each sentence above, the context surrounding the unfamiliar word provides clues to the word's meaning. You may have guessed from the context that *vital* means "necessary," that *appropriate* means "proper," and that *passive* means "inactive."

Using context clues to understand the meaning of unfamiliar words will help you in three ways:

1 It will save you time when reading. You will not have to stop to look up words in the dictionary. (Of course, you won't always be able to understand a word from its context, so you should have a dictionary nearby as you read.)

2 It will improve your "working vocabulary"—words you recognize as you read and will eventually be able to use when you speak and write. You will therefore add to your vocabulary simply by reading thoughtfully.

3 It will give you a good sense of how a word is actually used, including any shades of meaning it might have.

Types of Context Clues

There are four common types of context clues:

1 Examples
2 Synonyms
3 Antonyms
4 General sense of the sentence or passage

In the following sections, you will read about and practice each type. The practices will sharpen your skills in recognizing and using context clues. They will also help you add new words to your vocabulary.

Remember *not* to use a dictionary for these practices. Their purpose is to help you develop the skill of figuring out what words mean *without* using a dictionary. Pronunciations are provided in parentheses for the words, and a guide to pronunciation is on page 43.

1 Examples

An unfamiliar word may appear with **examples** that reveal what the word means. For instance, note the examples in this sentence from the previous page: "All animals share the same vital needs, such as food, water, and shelter." The examples—food, water, and shelter—helped you figure out that the word *vital* means "necessary."

Look at the cartoon below and see if the example helps you choose the correct meaning of the word *vague*.

Copyright 2002 by Randy Glasbergen.
www.glasbergen.com

GLASBERGEN

"When my folks ask when I'm going to get a job, I always give some vague answer such as 'Oh, sooner or later.'"

_____ *Vague* (vāg) means

    A. angry.   B. humorous.   C. unclear.

Notice that the example of a vague answer—"Oh, sooner or later"—helps you understand that *vague* means "unclear."

✓ Check Your Understanding

Now read the items that follow. An *italicized* word in each sentence is followed by examples that serve as context clues for that word. These examples, which are **boldfaced**, will help you figure out the meaning of each word. On each line, write the letter of the answer you think is correct. Then read the explanation that follows.

    Note that examples are often introduced with signal words and phrases like *for example, for instance, including,* and *such as.*

_____ 1. In our house, clothes hangers have various odd *functions*. For instance, we use them to **scratch backs** and **hold up plants in the garden**.

    Functions (fŭngk'shənz) are
    A. shapes.   B. problems.   C. uses.

    Hint: Remember that in the exercises in this chapter, you can insert into each sentence the word you think is the answer. For example, substitute *shapes, problems,* or *uses* in sentence 1 in place of *functions* to see which one fits.

_____ 2. Our baseball team's pitcher has a few *eccentric* habits, such as **throwing exactly thirteen pitches when warming up** and **never wearing socks**.

    Eccentric (ĭk-sĕn'trĭk) means
    A. normal.   B. strange.   C. messy.

_____ 3. Throughout history, humans have built a wide variety of *dwellings*, including **simple mud huts, stone castles,** and **marble mansions**.

    Dwellings (dwĕl'ĭngs) are
    A. homes.   B. stores.   C. churches.

Explanation

In each sentence, the examples probably helped you to figure out the meanings of the words in italics:

1. The correct answer is C. In sentence 1, the examples of the odd functions of hangers—scratching backs and holding up plants—may have helped you to guess that *functions* are "uses."

2. The correct answer is B. In sentence 2, the examples of strange habits show that *eccentric* means "strange."

3. The correct answer is A. The examples in sentence 3 indicate that *dwellings* are homes.

Note that the examples in the sentences are introduced by the signal words *for instance*, *such as*, and *including*.

PRACTICE 1: Examples

Read each item below and then do two things:

1. Underline the examples that suggest the meaning of the word in italics.
2. Then write the letter of the word's meaning on the answer line.

Note that the last five sentences have been taken from college textbooks.

_____ 1. The *debris* in the stadium stands included numerous paper cups, ticket stubs, sandwich wrappings, and peanut shells.

   Debris (də-brē′) means
   A. products.   B. papers.   C. trash.

_____ 2. For his weak stomach, Mario ate a *bland* diet of white bread, rice, and mashed potatoes.

   Bland (blănd) means
   A. spicy.   B. varied.   C. mild.

_____ 3. New York, Boston, and Philadelphia are three of the oldest *urban* areas in the United States.

   Urban (ûr′bən) means
   A. empty.   B. city.   C. country.

_____ 4. Many people take dietary *supplements*—for example, extra calcium or large doses of vitamin C—in the belief that they will cure or prevent disease.

   Supplements (sŭp′lə-mənts) means
   A. additions.   B. losses.   C. suggestions.

_____ 5. My uncle often has embarrassing *mishaps*, such as backing his car into the side of his boss's BMW and trying to walk through a glass door.

   Mishaps (mĭs′hăps′) means
   A. clever moves.   B. accidents.   C. projects.

_____ 6. The death of a child and the death of a spouse are two of life's most
traumatic experiences.

Traumatic (trou-măt′ĭk) means
A. rare.   B. painful.   C. interesting.

_____ 7. A *transaction*, such as buying or selling a product, is the most basic part
of an economy.

Transaction (trăn-săk′shən) means
A. profit.   B. loss.   C. business deal.

_____ 8. Religious *rituals* like baptisms, church weddings, and funeral services
give many people a sense of peace and comfort.

Rituals (rĭch′ōō-əls) means
A. lessons.   B. ceremonies.   C. prayers.

_____ 9. Some wild dolphins are so *docile* that they will play with humans, eat
out of their hands, and even nuzzle them.

Docile (dŏs′əl) means
A. tame.   B. strange.   C. dangerous.

_____ 10. There are hundreds of different kinds of *retailers*, ranging from car
dealerships and department stores to frozen-yogurt stands and online
drugstores.

Retailers (rē′tāl′ərs) means
A. customers.   B. businesses that sell   C. businesses that
                          directly to users.   make products.

2 Synonyms

Context clues are often found in the form of **synonyms**: one or more words that
mean the same or almost the same as the unknown word. Look again at the sentence
on page 76: "In the United States, shaking hands is the *appropriate* way to greet
someone; in Japan, bowing is the right way." Here the synonym "right" tells you
the meaning of *appropriate*. A synonym may appear anywhere in a sentence as a
restatement of the meaning of the unknown word.

Now look at the cartoon on the following page.

"I try to refrain from overeating, but I can't stop myself!"

Notice that the synonym for *refrain*—expressed in the dog's words "stop myself"—helps you understand that *refrain* (rĭ-frān′) means "to hold oneself back."

✓ Check Your Understanding

Each item below includes a word or phrase that is a synonym of the *italicized* word. Underline that synonym in each sentence. Then read the explanation that follows.

1. The cat soon found it useless to smack her paws against the front of the fish tank; her effort to catch a fish was a *futile* (fyo͞ot′l) one.

2. My best friend *squandered* (skwŏn′dərd) all his money; his drinking and gambling wasted his earnings.

3. Because my boss runs the toy store like a *tyrant* (tī′rənt), all of the employees call her "the little dictator."

Explanation

In each sentence, the synonym given probably helped you understand the meaning of the word in italics:

1. In the first sentence, the synonym of *futile* is "useless."

2. In sentence 2, the synonym of *squandered* is "wasted."

3. In sentence 3, the synonym of *tyrant* is "dictator."

PRACTICE 2: Synonyms

Each item below includes a synonym of the *italicized* word. Write each synonym in the space provided.

Note that the last five items have been taken from college textbooks.

_____ 1. Everyone turned to look at the *arrogant* (ăr′ə-gənt) customer who spoke to the manager in a self-important voice.

   Hint: What does the voice reveal about the customer?

_____ 2. The medicine that Nina is taking is very *potent* (pōt′nt). It is so powerful that she must not take it for more than a week.

_____ 3. After the heavy rains, the stream became *murky* (mûr′kē); in fact, the water was so cloudy you couldn't see the bottom.

_____ 4. Some overweight people are called *furtive* (fûr′tĭv) eaters because they eat large quantities of food in secret.

_____ 5. A con artist was apparently very believable as he went door to door telling a *plausible* (plô′zə-bəl) story about having his wallet stolen and needing twenty dollars to get home.

_____ 6. The first step in reaching a peace agreement was to set up a *dialog* (dī′ə-lŏg′) between the two sides. Without discussion, peace was impossible.

_____ 7. You cannot *coerce* (kō-ûrs′) people into learning. If they are not interested, it is impossible to force them.

_____ 8. While Ved may not be *affluent* (ăf′lōō-ənt) by American standards, he is rich compared with most people in his homeland of India.

_____ 9. Several tests are necessary to *verify* (vĕr′ə-fī′) that a virus is present. One is never enough to prove a virus exists.

_____ 10. The *diversity* (dĭ-vûr′sĭ-tē) of the population of the United States is the result of accepting immigrants from a wide variety of cultures and nations.

3 Antonyms

Antonyms—words and phrases that mean the opposite of a word—are also useful as context clues. Antonyms are sometimes signaled by words and phrases such as *however, but, yet, on the other hand, instead of,* and *in contrast.*

Look again at the sentence on page 76: "Winners in life take an active role in making things happen, instead of being passive and waiting for good luck." Here the words *instead of* indicate that *passive* must be the opposite of *active.*

Now look at the cartoon below.

"What *do* you mean 'unreasonable,' Miss Jones? I think this is a perfectly rational way to keep myself organized."

Notice that the antonym "unreasonable" helps you figure out that *rational* (răsh′ə-nəl) must mean "reasonable."

✓ *Check Your Understanding*

In each of the following sentences, underline the word or phrase that means the opposite of the *italicized* word. Then, on the answer line, write the letter of the meaning of the italicized word. Finally, read the explanation that follows.

_____ 1. The coach takes every opportunity to *reprimand* his players, yet he ignores every chance to praise them.

   Reprimand (rĕp′rə-mănd) means
   A. approve of.　　B. criticize.　　C. choose.

_____ 2. "I am having *acute* pains in my chest now," said the patient, "but an hour ago, all I felt was a dull ache."

   Acute (ə-kyōōt′) means
   A. sharp.　　B. weak.　　C. no.

_____ 3. Some teachers are too *lenient*. I'd rather have strict teachers who take the class seriously.

Lenient (lē′nē-ənt) means

A. hard.   (B.) easygoing.   C. busy.

Explanation

In each sentence, the antonym given probably helped you understand the meaning of the word in italics:

1. The correct answer is B. *Reprimand* is the opposite of *praise*, so the answer to sentence 1 is *criticize*.

2. The correct answer is A. In sentence 2, the opposite of *acute* is *dull*, so *acute* must mean "sharp."

3. The correct answer is B. In sentence 3, "lenient" teachers are the opposite of "strict" teachers, so *lenient* means "easygoing."

Note that *reprimand* and *acute* are indicated by signal words: *yet* and *but*.

PRACTICE 3: Antonyms

Each item below includes a word or phrase that is an antonym of the *italicized* word. Underline each of those antonyms. Then, on the answer line, write the letter of the meaning of the italicized word.

Note that the last five items have been taken from college textbooks.

_____ 1. After his accident, Brad expected an in-depth examination at the hospital. Instead, a doctor gave him a quick, *superficial* checkup and said, "You're fine."

Hint: What would be the opposite of an in-depth examination?

Superficial (sōō′pər-fĭsh′əl) means

A. lacking depth.   B. complicated.   C. satisfactory.

_____ 2. A temporary cough is nothing to worry about, but a *chronic* one can be a sign of a serious illness.

Chronic (krŏn′ĭk) means

A. continuing.   B. brief.   C. mild.

_____ 3. When liquor sales were *prohibited* by the Eighteenth Amendment, alcohol became more popular with some people than it had been when it was allowed.

Prohibited (prō-hĭb′ĭt-ĭd) means

A. permitted.   B. defined.   C. forbidden.

_____ 4. "What we need is an *innovative* idea!" cried the chairman. "All I've heard so far are the same old ones."

   Innovative (ĭn′ə-vā′tĭv) means

   A. new.   B. traditional.   C. loud.

_____ 5. The class was in *turmoil* when only the substitute teacher was there, but it quickly came to order once the principal entered the room.

   Turmoil (tûr′moil′) means

   A. peace.   B. confusion.   C. attendance.

_____ 6. In ordinary life, people's facial expressions are *spontaneous*. However, actors must learn to use planned ways of showing emotion.

   Spontaneous (spŏn-tā′nē-əs) means

   A. varied.   B. unplanned.   C. hidden.

_____ 7. A computer *novice* is lucky if he or she knows someone who is an expert and is willing to offer advice.

   Novice (nŏv′ĭs) means

   A. a child.   B. a friend.   C. a beginner.

_____ 8. Some patients drop out of drug rehab programs before completing them. Instead of making progress, they may then *revert* to previous bad habits.

   Revert (rĭ-vûrt′) means

   A. say no.   B. improve.   C. go back.

_____ 9. Our Constitution would be in danger if all Americans were *indifferent to* it. However, history has shown that concerned citizens will always come forward to defend it.

   Indifferent to (ĭn-dĭf′ər-ənt tōō) means

   A. insulted by.   B. aware of.   C. uninterested in.

_____ 10. In warfare, as in chess, *impulsive* actions will fail. To win in either case, carefully thought-out moves are needed.

   Impulsive (ĭm-pŭl′sĭv) means

   A. fearful.   B. unplanned.   C. strong.

4   General Sense of the Sentence or Passage

Often, the context of a new word contains no examples, synonyms, or antonyms. In such cases, you must do a bit more detective work; you'll need to look at any clues provided in the information surrounding the word. Asking yourself questions about the passage may help you make a fairly accurate guess about the meaning of the unfamiliar word.

Look at the cartoon below about a job interview.

© 2005 by Randy Glasbergen.
www.glasbergen.com

"You're exactly what we need—
someone who will be ruthless about cutting costs."

There are no examples, synonyms, or antonyms in the woman's statement. However, the applicant's costume—that of an executioner—and the huge axe he carries suggest that *ruthless* (ro͞oth′lĭs) means "showing no mercy."

✓ Check Your Understanding

Each sentence below is followed by a question. Think about each question; then write the letter of the answer you feel is the meaning of the italicized word.

_____ 1. The newlyweds agreed to be very *frugal* in their shopping because they wanted to save enough money to buy a home.

(How would people shop if they wanted to save money?)

Frugal (fro͞o′gəl) means
A. thrifty.   B. wasteful.   C. interested.

_____ 2. So many customers have complained about the noise in the restaurant that the owners are trying to find ways to *mute* the noise.

(What would the restaurant owners probably want to do about noise?)

Mute (myo͞ot) means
A. increase.   B. quiet.   C. create.

_____ 3. Friends tried to *dissuade* ninety-year-old Mrs. Kellen from attending her son's trial, but she went anyway, to show her support.

(What would the elderly woman's friends have tried to do to her if they didn't want her to go to her son's trial?)

Dissuade (dĭ-swād′) means

A. question.   B. describe.   C. discourage.

Explanation

In each sentence, your answer to the question should have helped you figure out the meaning of the word in italics:

1. The correct answer is A. The first sentence provides enough evidence for you to guess that *frugal* means "thrifty." The newlyweds had to be thrifty if they wanted to save money.

2. The correct answer is B. *Mute* in the second sentence means "quiet"; a restaurant owner would probably want to reduce the noise.

3. The correct answer is C. *Dissuade* means "discourage"—Mrs. Kellen went to the trial despite her friends' attempts to discourage her.

   If you use context clues, you may not get the exact dictionary definition of a word, but you will often be accurate enough to make good sense of what you are reading.

PRACTICE 4: General Sense of the Sentence or Passage

Figure out the meaning of the word in *italics* by looking at clues in the rest of the sentence. First, try to answer the question in parentheses that follows each item below. Then, on the basis of your answer, write the letter of the meaning you think is correct.

Note that the last five items have been taken from college textbooks.

_____ 1. To reach a *sound* conclusion about an issue, you must carefully consider all the facts involved.

(What kind of conclusion would you reach by carefully considering all the facts?)

Sound (sound) means

A. early.   B. obvious.   C. reasonable.

_____ 2. My mother refuses to *divulge* the secret ingredients she uses in her fried chicken recipe.

(What would someone refuse to do with ingredients that are secret?)

Divulge (dĭ-vŭlj′) means

A. reveal.   B. hide.   C. invent.

_____ 3. Because the nicotine in cigarettes is harmful, many people favor *stringent* laws against their sale.

(What type of laws would be favored by people concerned about the harm of nicotine?)

Stringent (strĭn′jənt) means

A. strict.   B. weak.   C. confusing.

_____ 4. Taking the expression "raining cats and dogs" *literally*, the child looked for little animals on the ground after the storm.

(In what way did the child interpret the phrase "raining cats and dogs"?)

Literally (lĭt′ər-ə-lē) means

A. symbolically.   B. musically.   C. as the real facts.

_____ 5. It's too late to *alter* the plans for the party. The restaurant and band have been reserved, and all the invitations have been sent out.

(If the plans have all been made, what is it too late to do to the plans?)

Alter (ôl′tər) means

A. change.   B. surprise.   C. repeat.

_____ 6. Organ transplants will not succeed unless the *donor* has the same blood type as the person receiving the organ.

(Who would need to have the same kind of blood as the person receiving the transplant?)

Donor (dō′nər) means

A. one who receives.   B. one who gives.   C. one who doubts.

_____ 7. Few American officials in Iraq were *fluent* in Arabic, so all communication had to be in English.

(What would an American have to be in order to communicate in Arabic?)

Fluent (floo′ənt) means

A. able to remember.   B. able to teach.   C. able to speak well.

_____ 8. The placing of a huge cable on the floor of the Atlantic Ocean in 1866 made it possible to *transmit* telegraph signals from Europe to North America.

(What did the cable allow us to do with signals between Europe and North America?)

Transmit (trăns-mĭt′) means

A. check.   B. send.   C. lose.

_____ 9. Over years, the movement of water in a stream will *erode* the surrounding soil and rock. As a result, the stream will be wider and deeper.

(What does water do to soil and rock to enlarge a stream?)

Erode (ĭ-rōd′) means

A. wear away.   B. escape.   C. build up.

_____ 10. In the 1950s, Americans felt that the Soviet Union was a *menace* threatening their national security. As a result, Senator Joseph McCarthy was able to persuade millions of people that the Soviets had secret agents in the United States government.

(What would a country that threatened our national security be regarded as?)

Menace (mĕn′ĭs) means

A. puzzle.   B. friend.   C. danger.

An Important Point about Textbook Definitions

You don't always have to use context clues or the dictionary to find definitions. Very often, textbook authors provide definitions of important terms. They usually follow a definition with one or more examples to make sure that you understand the word being defined.

Here is a short textbook passage that includes a definition and an example. Note that the term to be defined is set off in **boldface** type, and the definition then follows.

[1]The changing work force has changed lifestyles and needs. [2]No wonder many workers have found **flextime** a desirable choice. [3]Instead of working the standard nine-to-five day, five days a week, they choose their own hours. [4]For instance, they may decide to work four days at ten hours a day rather than five days at eight hours.

Textbook authors, then, often do more than provide context clues: they set off the terms they are defining in *italic* or **boldface** type, as above. When they take the time to define and illustrate a word, you should assume that the material is important enough to learn.

More about textbook definitions and examples appears on pages 264–265 in the "Relationships II" chapter.

CHAPTER REVIEW

In this chapter, you learned the following:

- To save time when reading, you should try to figure out the meanings of unfamiliar words. You can do so by looking at their **context**—the words surrounding them.

- There are four kinds of context clues: **examples** (marked by words like *for example, for instance, including,* and *such as*); **synonyms** (words that mean the same as unknown words); **antonyms** (words that mean the opposite of unknown words); and **general sense of the sentence** (clues in the sentence or surrounding sentences about what words might mean).

- Textbook authors typically set off important words in *italic* or **boldface** and define those words for you, often providing examples as well.

The next chapter—Chapter 3—will introduce you to the most important of all comprehension skills, finding the main idea.

On the Web: If you are using this book in class, you can visit our website for additional practice in understanding vocabulary in context. Go to **www.townsendpress.com** and click on "Learning Center." To build your vocabulary, you may also want to consider the independent word study program called *VPi* that is available at the same web address.

 REVIEW TEST 1

To review what you've learned in this chapter, answer the following questions by writing the letter of each correct answer.

_____ 1. The context of a word is
  A. its meaning.   B. its opposite.   C. the words around it.

_____ 2. Which type of context clue often follows signal words like *including, such as,* and *for instance*?
  A. Example
  B. Synonym
  C. Antonym

_____ 3. In the sentence below, which type of context clue is provided for the italicized word?
   A. Example
   B. Synonym
   C. Antonym

   I'm looking for a *unique* (yōo-nēk′) gift for my boyfriend; he appreciates unusual things.

_____ 4. In the sentence below, which type of context clue is provided for the italicized word?
   A. Example
   B. Synonym
   C. Antonym

   Expecting that his license would be renewed, the pilot was surprised when it was *revoked* (rĭ-vōkt′) instead.

_____ 5. Often, when textbook authors introduce a new word, they provide a definition and help make the meaning of the word clear by including one or more
   A. examples.   B. synonyms.   C. antonyms.

REVIEW TEST 2

A. Look at the cartoon below about cavemen painting over drawings in their cave, and notice the caption, "First Graffiti Eradication Program." Then answer the question that follows.

FIRST GRAFFITI ERADICATION PROGRAM

_____ 1. Using the context clues in the cartoon, write the letter of the best meaning of *eradication* (ĭ-răd′ĭ-kā′shən) in the space provided.
   A. writing   B. removal   C. contest

B. Using context clues for help, write the letter of the best meaning for each italicized word. Use the space provided.

_____ 2. Though people who work nonstop can accomplish a great deal, they may also *forfeit* (fôr′fĭt) their health.
   A. strengthen   C. give up
   B. remember   D. talk about

_____ 3. The principal was known to *intimidate* (ĭn-tĭm′ĭ-dāt′) students by walking through the halls with a baseball bat and shouting through a bullhorn.
   A. encourage   C. frighten
   B. entertain   D. fail

_____ 4. My aunt has no *empathy* (ĕm′pə-thē) when it comes to other people's problems. She thinks only one person really has troubles, and that's herself.
   A. pleasure   C. pride
   B. fear   D. understanding

_____ 5. The crowd of protesters *dispersed* (dĭ-spûrst′) quickly when the police arrived with growling German shepherds.
   A. cheered   C. questioned
   B. scattered   D. paid

C. Using context clues for help, write the definition for each italicized word. Then write the letter of the definition in the space provided. Choose from the definitions in the box below. Each definition will be used once.

A. clear and brief	B. lazy	C. messy
D. violations	E. warning	

_____ 6. Paula was suspended from school because of several *infractions* of the rules, including smoking in the restroom and dressing inappropriately.

   Infractions (ĭn-frăk′shəns) means _____.

_____ 7. We began the picnic in spite of such *ominous* signs as dark clouds and a falling temperature.

   Ominous (ŏm′ə-nəs) means _____.

_____ B   8. While Luis is hardworking, his *indolent* brother spends most of his time texting or watching TV with friends.

   Indolent (ĭn′də-lənt) means _____.

_____ C   9. Although Alex usually looks *unkempt*, he had a very neat appearance at his job interview.

   Unkempt (ŭn-kĕmpt′) means _____.

_____ A   10. When you write a report, your statement of purpose should be *concise*. State your point clearly in as few words as possible.

   Concise (kən-sīs′) means _____.

 REVIEW TEST 3

A. Look at the cartoon below, and then answer the questions that follow.

© Randy Glasbergen.
www.glasbergen.com

GLASBERGEN

"My appearance is deceptive. I may look fierce, but that's untrue—I'm really a gentle, sensitive guy."

_____ C   1. Using the context clues in the cartoon, write the letter of the best meaning of *fierce* (fîrs) in the space provided.
   A. false   B. unhappy   (C.) scary

_____ C   2. Which kind of context clue helps you understand the meaning of the cartoon?
   A. Examples clue   B. Synonym clue   (C.) Antonym clue

B. Four words are **boldfaced** in the textbook passage below. Write the definition for each boldfaced word, choosing from the definitions in the box. Then write the letter of the definition in the space provided.

Be sure to read the entire passage before making your choices. Note that six definitions will be left over.

A. disliked	B. encourage	C. expensive	D. explanation
E. fearful	F. punishment	G. reward	H. small
I. warning	J. well-known		

¹Suppose someone asked you to sit on top of a flagpole for twelve hours and promised you a prize. ²After you returned to earth, you learned the prize was a stick of gum. ³Would you be likely to repeat the flagpole-sitting behavior? ⁴Chances are you would not unless there was a severe gum shortage and you were dying for gum. ⁵Although the gum was a prize, it was a **paltry** one. ⁶It would not serve as a **positive reinforcement** that would lead to more of the same behavior. ⁷What would it take to **induce** you to climb up and sit on top of the flagpole again? ⁸Perhaps a good positive reinforcement for you would be a more **lavish** prize, such as a new car, a screen test from a movie studio, or a free vacation in Hawaii. ⁹For such a reinforcement to be effective enough to shape behavior, it must be suitable.

_____ 3. *Paltry* (pôl′trē) means _____.

_____ 4. *Positive reinforcement* (pŏz′ĭ-tĭv rē′ĭn-fôrs′mənt) means _____

_____.

_____ 5. *Induce* (ĭn-do͞os′) means _____.

_____ 6. *Lavish* (lăv′ĭsh) means _____.

C. Four words are **boldfaced** in the textbook passage on the following page. Write the definition for each boldfaced word, choosing from the definitions in the box. Then write the letter of the definition in the space provided.

Be sure to read the entire passage before making your choices. Note that six definitions will be left over.

A. attracts	B. benefit	C. catch and eat	D. closes
E. danger	F. empties	G. explore	H. loosens
I. play with	J. rush away from		

¹While plants often provide food for animals, some plants turn the tables and **prey on** smaller members of the animal kingdom. ²One, the Venus flytrap, uses its leaves like a steel trap. ³It **lures** small insects with its sweet perfume and then **clamps** its "jaws" so it can digest the insects at its leisure. ⁴Another leafy hunter is the pitcher plant, whose sweet juices tempt insects to explore the plant. ⁵Once deep within the plant, the insect meets a watery death. ⁶Plants are essential for animal life, but for inhabitants of the insect community, they can also be a **hazard** that may end life.

_____   7. *Prey on* (prā ŏn) means _____.

_____   8. *Lures* (lŏŏrs) means _____.

_____   9. *Clamps* (klămps) means _____.

_____ 10. *Hazard* (hăz'ərd) means _____.

REVIEW TEST 4

Here is a chance to apply the skill of understanding vocabulary in context to a full-length selection. This story describes a moment in a teacher's life when she learned how important a single act of hers had been. Its author, Sister Helen Mrosla, was a Franciscan nun from Little Falls, Minnesota. Since 1991, when she wrote this account of a true incident in her life, the story has been reprinted many times and even circulated on the Internet. Read the selection, and then answer the questions on vocabulary that follow.

Words to Watch

Below are some words in the reading that do not have strong context support. Each word is followed by the number of the paragraph in which it appears and its meaning there. These words are indicated in the selection by a small circle (°).

> *mischievousness* (1): minor misbehavior
> *novice* (3): new
> *deliberately* (5): slowly and on purpose
> *concept* (8): idea
> *crankiness* (8): grouchy mood
> *lull* (13): brief silence
> *taps* (16): a bugle call sounded at night and at a military funeral
> *sheepishly* (20): with embarrassment
> *frazzled* (20): worn-out; ragged

ALL THE GOOD THINGS

Sister Helen P. Mrosla

1   He was in the first third-grade class I taught at Saint Mary's School in Morris, Minnesota. All thirty-four of my students were dear to me, but Mark Eklund was one in a million. He was very neat in appearance, but had that happy-to-be-alive attitude that made even his occasional mischievousness° delightful.

2   Mark talked incessantly. I had to remind him again and again that talking without permission was not acceptable. What impressed me so much, though, was his sincere response every time I had to correct him for misbehaving—"Thank you for correcting me, Sister!" I didn't know what to make of it at first, but before long I became accustomed to hearing it many times a day.

3   One morning my patience was growing thin when Mark talked once too often, and then I made a novice° teacher's mistake. I looked at him and said, "If you say one more word, I am going to tape your mouth shut!"

4   It wasn't ten seconds later when Chuck blurted out, "Mark is talking again." I hadn't asked any of the students to help me watch Mark, but since I had stated the punishment in front of the class, I had to act on it.

5   I remember the scene as if it had occurred this morning. I walked to my desk, very deliberately° opened my drawer, and took out a roll of masking tape. Without saying a word, I proceeded to Mark's desk, tore off two pieces of tape, and made a big X with them over his mouth. I then returned to the front of the room. As I glanced at Mark to see how he was doing, he winked at me.

6   That did it! I started laughing. The class cheered as I walked back to Mark's desk, removed the tape, and shrugged my shoulders. His first words were, "Thank you for correcting me, Sister."

7   At the end of the year I was asked to teach junior-high math. The years flew by, and before I knew it Mark was in my classroom again. He was more handsome than ever and just as polite. Since he had to listen carefully to my instruction in the "new math," he did not talk as much in ninth grade as he had talked in the third.

8   One Friday, things just didn't feel right. We had worked hard on a new concept° all week, and I sensed that the students were frowning, frustrated with themselves—and edgy with one another. I had to stop this crankiness° before it got out of hand. So I asked them to list the names of the other students in the room on two sheets of paper, leaving a space after each name. Then I told them to think of the nicest thing they could say about each of their classmates and write it down.

9   It took the remainder of the class period to finish the assignment, and as the students left the room, each one handed me the papers. Charlie smiled. Mark said, "Thank you for teaching me, Sister. Have a good weekend."

10   That Saturday, I wrote down the

name of each student on a separate sheet of paper, and I listed what everyone else had said about that individual.

11   On Monday I gave each student his or her list. Before long, the entire class was smiling. "Really?" I heard whispered. "I never knew that meant anything to anyone!" "I didn't know others liked me so much!"

12   No one ever mentioned those papers in class again. I never knew if the students discussed them after class or with their parents, but it didn't matter. The exercise had accomplished its purpose. The students were happy with themselves and one another again.

13   That group of students moved on. Several years later, after I returned from a vacation, my parents met me at the airport. As we were driving home, Mother asked me the usual questions about the trip—the weather, my experiences in general. There was a slight lull° in the conversation. Mother gave Dad a sideways glance and simply said, "Dad?" My father cleared his throat as he usually did before something important. "The Eklunds called last night," he began. "Really?" I said. "I haven't heard from them in years. I wonder how Mark is."

14   Dad responded quietly. "Mark was killed in the war," he said. "The funeral is tomorrow, and his parents would like it if you could attend." To this day I can still point to the exact spot on I-494 where Dad told me about Mark.

15   I had never seen a serviceman in a military coffin before. Mark looked so handsome, so mature. All I could think at that moment was, Mark, I would give all the masking tape in the world if only you would talk to me.

16   The church was packed with Mark's friends. Chuck's sister sang "The Battle Hymn of the Republic." Why did it have to rain on the day of the funeral? It was difficult enough at the graveside. The pastor said the usual prayers, and the bugler played taps°. One by one those who loved Mark took a last walk by the coffin and sprinkled it with holy water.

17   I was the last one to bless the coffin. As I stood there, one of the soldiers who had acted as pallbearer came up to me. "Were you Mark's math teacher?" he asked. I nodded as I continued to stare at the coffin. "Mark talked about you a lot," he said.

18   After the funeral, most of Mark's former classmates headed to Chuck's farmhouse for lunch. Mark's mother and father were there, obviously waiting for me. "We want to show you something," his father said, taking a wallet out of his pocket. "They found this on Mark when he was killed. We thought you might recognize it."

19   Opening the billfold, he carefully removed two worn pieces of notebook paper that had obviously been taped,

folded and refolded many times. I knew without looking that the papers were the ones on which I had listed all the good things each of Mark's classmates had said about him. "Thank you so much for doing that," Mark's mother said. "As you can see, Mark treasured it."

20   Mark's classmates started to gather around us. Charlie smiled rather sheepishly° and said, "I still have my list. It's in the top drawer of my desk at home." Chuck's wife said, "Chuck asked me to put his list in our wedding album." "I have mine too," Marilyn said. "It's in my diary." Then Vicki, another classmate, reached into her pocketbook, took out her wallet, and showed her worn and frazzled° list to the group. "I carry this with me at all times," Vicki said without batting an eyelash. "I think we all saved our lists."

21   That's when I finally sat down and cried. I cried for Mark and for all his friends who would never see him again.

Vocabulary Questions

Use context clues to help you decide on the best definition for each italicized word. Then, in the space provided, write the letter of each choice.

_____ 1. In the excerpt below, the word *incessantly* (ĭn-sĕs′ənt-lē) means
    A. slowly.
    B. constantly.
    C. quietly.
    D. pleasantly.

    "Mark talked incessantly. I had to remind him again and again that talking without permission was not acceptable." (Paragraph 2)

_____ 2. In the excerpt below, the words *accustomed to* (ə-kŭs′təmd tōō) mean
    A. afraid of.
    B. confused by.
    C. warned about.
    D. used to.

    "What impressed me so much, though, was [Mark's] sincere response every time I had to correct him for misbehaving—'Thank you for correcting me, Sister!' I didn't know what to make of it at first, but before long I became accustomed to hearing it many times a day." (Paragraph 2)

_____ 3. In the sentence below, the words *blurted out* (blûrt′ĭd out) mean
    A. said suddenly.
    B. watched for.
    C. ran away.
    D. looked at.

    "It wasn't ten seconds later when Chuck blurted out, 'Mark is talking again.'" (Paragraph 4)

_____ 4. In the excerpt below, the word *proceeded* (prō-sēd′ĭd) means

    A. stayed.   C. wrote.

    B. went.   D. threw.

"I walked to my desk, very deliberately opened my drawer, and took out a roll of masking tape. Without saying a word, I proceeded to Mark's desk, tore off two pieces of tape, and made a big X with them over his mouth." (Paragraph 5)

_____ 5. In the sentence below, the word *edgy* (ĕj′ē) means

    A. funny.   C. easily annoyed.

    B. calm.   D. happy.

"We had worked hard on a new concept all week, and I sensed that the students were frowning, frustrated with themselves—and edgy with one another." (Paragraph 8)

_____ 6. In the sentence below, the word *remainder* (rĭ-mān′dər) means

    A. what was left.   C. smallest part.

    B. beginning.   D. memo.

"It took the remainder of the class period to finish the assignment, and as the students left the room, each one handed me the papers." (Paragraph 9)

_____ 7. In the sentence below, the word *individual* (ĭn′də-vĭj′o͞o-əl) means

    A. day.   C. paper.

    B. person.   D. teacher.

"That Saturday, I wrote down the name of each student on a separate sheet of paper, and I listed what everyone else had said about that individual." (Paragraph 10)

_____ 8. In the excerpt below, the word *accomplished* (ə-kŏm′plĭsht) means

    A. forgotten.   C. been successful for.

    B. liked.   D. missed.

"The exercise had accomplished its purpose. The students were happy with themselves and one another again." (Paragraph 12)

_____ 9. In the excerpt below, the word *responded* (rĭ-spŏnd′ĭd) means

    A. answered.   C. asked.

    B. interrupted.   D. left.

"'The Eklunds called last night,' he began. 'Really?' I said. 'I haven't heard from them in years. I wonder how Mark is.'

"Dad responded quietly. 'Mark was killed in the war,' he said." (Paragraphs 13–14)

_____ 10. In the sentence below, the word *treasured* (trĕzh'ərd) means

    A. hid.
    B. valued.
    C. sold.
    D. lost.

> "I knew without looking that the papers were the ones on which I had listed all the good things each of Mark's classmates had said about him. 'Thank you so much for doing that,' Mark's mother said. 'As you can see, Mark treasured it.'" (Paragraph 19)

Discussion Questions

1. In this story, we read of two classroom incidents involving Sister Helen and her students. In one, she briefly taped a third-grader's mouth closed. In another, she encouraged junior-high students to think of things they liked about one another. In your opinion, what do these two incidents tell about Sister Helen? What kind of teacher was she? What kind of person?

2. Why do you think so many of Sister Helen's students kept their lists for so long? Why were the lists so important to them? What souvenir of the past have you kept for a long time? What does it mean to you?

3. At the end of the story, Sister Helen tells us that she "cried for Mark and for all his friends who would never see him again." Do you think she might have been crying for other reasons, too? Explain what they might be.

4. "All the Good Things" has literally traveled around the world. Not only has it been reprinted in numerous publications; many readers have sent it out over the Internet for others to enjoy. Why do you think so many people love this story? Why do they want to share it with others?

Note: Writing assignments for this selection appear on page 605.

Check Your Performance   **VOCABULARY IN CONTEXT**

Activity	Number Right	Points	Score
Review Test 1 (5 items)	_____	× 2 =	_____
Review Test 2 (10 items)	_____	× 3 =	_____
Review Test 3 (10 items)	_____	× 3 =	_____
Review Test 4 (10 items)	_____	× 3 =	_____
		TOTAL SCORE =	_____ %

Enter your total score into the **Reading Performance Chart: Review Tests** on the inside back cover.

VOCABULARY IN CONTEXT: Mastery Test 1

A. Look at the cartoon below, and then answer the questions that follow.

© 1998 Randy Glasbergen.

"I'm a little apprehensive about the new boss. His snoopiness makes me uneasy."

_C_ 1. Using the context clues in the cartoon, write the letter of the best meaning of *apprehensive* (ăp′rĭ-hěn′sĭv) in the space provided.
   A. pleased   B. forgetful   C. worried

_B_ 2. Which kind of context clue helps you understand the meaning of the cartoon?
   A. Examples clue   B. Synonym clue   C. Antonym clue

B. For each item below, underline the **examples** that suggest the meaning of the italicized word. Then, on the answer line, write the letter of the meaning of that word.

_A_ 3. Carol survived her freshman year despite various *adverse* (ăd-vûrs′) events. For instance, she missed two weeks of class because of a strep throat and had all her books stolen just before finals.
   A. unfavorable   C. fortunate
   B. evil   D. pleasant

_D_ 4. The new principal took *drastic* (drăs′tĭk) steps to deal with school funding cuts, including firing teachers and doing away with sports.
   A. funny   C. approving
   B. small   D. extreme

(Continues on next page)

C. Each item below includes a word or words that are a **synonym** of the italicized word. Write the synonym of the italicized word in the space provided.

show off   5. The old saying "If you've got it, *flaunt* (flônt) it" means that you should show off your good qualities.

signal   6. The company president made a brief *gesture* (jĕs'chər) with her hand. It was a clear signal that the interview was over.

D. Each item below includes a word or words that are an **antonym** of the italicized word. Underline the antonym of each italicized word. Then, on the answer line, write the letter of the meaning of the italicized word.

_D_   7. The chef hates a dirty kitchen. If the kitchen isn't *immaculate* (ĭ-măk'yə-lĭt) at the end of a day, he insists that somebody stay late to finish cleaning.
   A. large   C. crowded
   B. messy   D. spotless

_D_   8. If parents show *apathy* (ăp'ə-thē) toward their children's education, how can we expect the students to show interest?
   A. attention   C. teaching
   B. knowledge   D. lack of interest

E. Use the **general sense of each sentence** to figure out the meaning of each italicized word. Then, on the answer line, write the letter of the meaning of the italicized word.

_A_   9. My aunt is so *obstinate* (ŏb'stə-nĭt) that once she makes up her mind, nothing any member of her family says can change it.
   A. stubborn   C. easy-going
   B. clever   D. cooperative

_D_   10. Building the Brooklyn Bridge was a huge struggle involving men, materials, and nature. Numerous *obstacles* (ŏb'stə-kəls) had to be overcome in order to complete the structure in 1883.
   A. buildings   C. places
   B. causes   D. difficulties

VOCABULARY IN CONTEXT: Mastery Test 2

A. Look at the cartoon below, and then answer the question that follows.

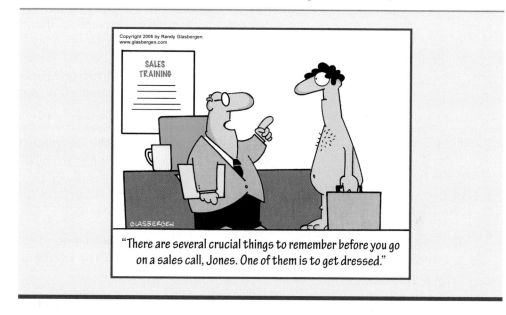

Copyright 2006 by Randy Glasbergen.
www.glasbergen.com

SALES
TRAINING

GLASBERGEN

"There are several crucial things to remember before you go
on a sales call, Jones. One of them is to get dressed."

_____ 1. Using the context clues in the cartoon, write the letter of the best
meaning of *crucial* (kro͞o′shəl) in the space provided.
   A. very important   B. expensive   C. unusual

B. For each item below, underline the **examples** that suggest the meaning of the
italicized term. Then, on the answer line, write the letter of the meaning of that
word.

_____ 2. The employees showed the *contempt* (kən-tĕmpt′) they felt for their boss
by ignoring his memos and making fun of him behind his back.
   A. admiration   C. fear
   B. envy   D. disrespect

_____ 3. The apples were on sale because many of them had *defects* (dē′fĕkts′),
such as brown spots, soft places, or small holes in the skin.
   A. imperfections   C. prizes
   B. peelings   D. leaves

(Continues on next page)

C. Each item below includes a word or words that are a **synonym** of the italicized word. Write the synonym of the italicized word in the space provided.

_____ 4. Textbook authors often *clarify* (klăr′ə-fī′) general statements with specific examples; the illustrations make clear what the general point is saying.

_____ 5. The event was *unprecedented* (ŭn-prĕs′ĭ-dĕn′tĭd)—the election of a pig to the student council is something that had never happened before.

_____ 6. The comedian waited for the laughter to *subside* (səb-sīd′) before going on with his next joke. The audience's reaction did not die down for two whole minutes.

D. Each item below includes a word or words that are an **antonym** of the italicized word. Underline the antonym of each italicized word. Then, on the answer line, write the letter of the meaning of the italicized word.

_____ 7. Before the game, the locker room had been cheerful; but now, after losing the game, the players were *morose* (mə-rōs′).
   A. sad and gloomy   C. pleased
   B. tired   D. happy and excited

_____ 8. "It is better to *retreat* (rĭ-trēt′) to safety," said the general, "than to go forward foolishly."
   A. attack   C. look
   B. investigate   D. move back

E. Use the **general sense of each sentence** to figure out the meaning of each italicized word. Then, on the answer line, write the letter of the meaning of the italicized word.

_____ 9. When I couldn't fall asleep last night, I realized I had been *imprudent* (ĭm-prood′nt) to drink so much coffee after dinner.
   A. pleased   C. unwise
   B. clever   D. fortunate

_____ 10. How you interpret the *ambiguous* (ăm-bĭg′yoo-əs) sentence "Visiting relatives can be boring" may depend on which you find annoying—relatives who visit or visits to relatives.
   A. long and boring   C. having a clear meaning
   B. difficult to say   D. having more than one meaning

VOCABULARY IN CONTEXT: Mastery Test 3

Using context clues for help, write the letter of the best meaning for each italicized word.

___A___ 1. Greg wanted to become *proficient* (prə-físh′ənt) on the saxophone, so he practiced every day for several hours.
   A. highly skilled   C. dependent
   B. very loud   D. tired

___C___ 2. Otis was faced with the *dilemma* (dĭ-lĕm′ə) of putting more money into his ancient Chevy or doing without a car.
   A. happy situation   C. unpleasant choice
   B. bad mood   D. victory

___D___ 3. Our children are so afraid of snakes that even a toy rubber snake *provokes* (prə-vōks′) panic in them.
   A. amuses   C. prevents
   B. closes   D. causes

___B___ 4. Janice often asks *impertinent* (ĭm-pûr′tn-ənt) questions such as "Where did you get that ugly shirt?" or "Did you cut your own hair?"
   A. clever   C. important
   B. rude   D. friendly

___C___ 5. At the family reunion, the older relatives sat together and *reminisced* (rĕm′ə-nĭst′) for hours about events of fifty years ago.
   A. forgot   C. discussed past events
   B. were irritated   D. argued

___B___ 6. The wolf was *wary* (wâr′ē), circling around the camp until he felt sure that all the hikers were asleep.
   A. hungry   C. brave
   B. cautious   D. tired

___C___ 7. Don't be *naïve* (nä-ēv′) enough to believe commercials and online ads that promise instant riches, effortless weight loss, and valuable free prizes.
   A. dishonest   C. unsuspecting
   B. absent-minded   D. critical

(Continues on next page)

105

___A___ 8. A fight between the two brothers seemed *inevitable* (ĭn-ĕv′ĭ-tə-bəl) that rainy Saturday; they had been teasing each other all morning.
A. unavoidable   C. impossible
B. welcome   D. unwanted

___C___ 9. The teacher decided that the test results were not *valid* (văl′ĭd) because some students had gotten hold of the questions before the test.
A. high   C. reliable
B. interesting   D. unusual

___D___ 10. Because Mac had left out a *vital* (vīt′l) ingredient, the apple cake came out looking like a pancake.
A. bad-tasting   C. small
B. unnecessary   D. very important

VOCABULARY IN CONTEXT: Mastery Test 4

Using context clues for help, write the letter of the best meaning for each italicized word. Note that all of the sentences have been taken from college textbooks.

_____ 1. After a baby is born, an older child may become jealous. Wanting the attention the newborn is receiving, the child may *regress* (rĭ-grĕs′) to such behavior as sucking a thumb or crying.
   A. look   C. talk
   B. go back   D. advance

_____ 2. Certain marine bacteria contain chemicals that produce light. Passengers sailing at night in the Indian Ocean often pass through "glowing seas" *illuminated* (ĭ-lōō′mə-nāt′ĭd) by countless bacteria.
   A. polluted   C. made dangerous
   B. cleaned   D. lit up

_____ 3. Nobody needs proof to know that conflict is part of life—it is *self-evident* (sĕlf′ ĕv′ĭ-dənt).
   A. obvious   C. unclear
   B. possible   D. unlikely

_____ 4. In historical novels, the main events that occur, such as the Civil War, are factual, but many of the characters are *fictitious* (fĭk-tĭsh′əs).
   A. old   C. unimportant
   B. not real   D. active

_____ 5. Teenagers are often *gregarious* (grĭ-gâr′ē-əs), finding status and a sense of identity by spending all their leisure time with a particular circle of friends.
   A. quiet and reserved   C. wanting their own way
   B. independent   D. seeking the company of others

_____ 6. It is a *fallacy* (făl′ə-sē) to assume that if one event happens before another, then the first event is the cause of the second one. Actually, the two events may be completely unrelated.
   A. promise   C. good idea
   B. mistake   D. truth

(Continues on next page)

_____ 7. Throughout history, governments have attempted to justify their actions through *propaganda* (prŏp′ə-găn′də), including political speeches, books and pamphlets, and media campaigns.
A. spending money
B. noise
C. information spread to support a cause
D. good behavior

_____ 8. Patients suffering from tuberculosis used to be placed in *seclusion* (sĭ-klōō′zhən), away from anyone who was in danger of catching the disease.
A. hospitals
B. bed
C. groups
D. away from others

_____ 9. Certain mental disorders can cause *delusions* (dĭ-lōō′zhəns), such as the false belief that one is being spied on by the police.
A. sudden actions
B. good feelings
C. mistaken ideas
D. strong objections

_____ 10. The popularity of social media has led to new legal and ethical problems, such as what should be done about people who use these sites to bully and *harass* (hə-răs′) one another.
A. support
B. ignore
C. agree with
D. attack

VOCABULARY IN CONTEXT: Mastery Test 5

A. Using context clues for help, write the letter of the best meaning for each italicized word.

_____ 1. The story the former drug addict told was so *engrossing* (ĕn-grō′sĭng) to the students that they didn't move even when the bell rang.
   A. pleasing   C. confusing
   B. boring   D. fascinating

_____ 2. Everyone *evacuating* (ĭ-văk′yoo-ā′tĭng) the burning hotel, including those as far up as the twentieth floor, had to use the stairs.
   A. staying in   C. paying for
   B. leaving   D. arriving at

_____ 3. Some members of organizations are good only at thinking up ideas. So although they are able to *initiate* (ĭ-nĭsh′ē-āt′) a project, they need others to complete it.
   A. start   C. try out
   B. name   D. work on

_____ 4. During high tide, waves advance, covering most or all of the beach; but during low tide, the water *recedes* (rĭ-sēds′), leaving behind seaweed and shells and occasionally leaving fish on the sand.
   A. appears   C. goes back
   B. comes forward   D. becomes dangerous

_____ 5. Colleges have several resources to aid students in determining which *vocations* (vō-kā′shəns) would be best for them. These include preference tests, a job placement center offering information about opportunities in various fields, and the services of career counselors.
   A. classes   C. study skills
   B. living arrangements   D. jobs

(Continues on next page)

109

B. Five words are **boldfaced** in the textbook passage below. Write the definition for each boldfaced word, choosing from the definitions in the box. Then write the letter of the definition in the space provided.

Be sure to read the entire passage before making your choices. Note that three definitions will be left over.

A. coating	B. drops off	C. enjoyable
D. enormous	E. increases	F. lie down
G. small	H. step forth	

¹One of the most unusual bodies of water in the world is the Dead Sea. ²Surrounded by desert, this "sea" is actually 26 percent dissolved minerals, 99 percent of which are salts. ³Over 45 miles long and 11 miles wide, the Dead Sea is so salty that its water actually feels oily and leaves a chalky **residue** on the skin. ⁴Bathers brave enough to **venture** just a few feet into the Dead Sea will discover that the human body floats in the salty mixture. ⁵Because of the **vast** amount of salt in the water, a person can actually **recline** on the surface of the Dead Sea as if it was a giant waterbed. ⁶While clear, the sea's water is so thick that ripples and waves are visible even beneath its surface. ⁷Unfortunately, this natural marvel is shrinking. ⁸Each year, the water level **diminishes** by three feet. ⁹At this rate, the Dead Sea will become a salty desert in a few centuries.

_____ 6. In sentence 3, *residue* (rĕz′ĭ-do͞o′) means _____.

_____ 7. In sentence 4, *venture* (vĕn′chər) means _____.

_____ 8. In sentence 5, *vast* (văst) means _____.

_____ 9. In sentence 5, *recline* (rĭ-klīn′) means _____.

_____ 10. In sentence 8, *diminishes* (dĭ-mĭn′ĭsh-ĭs) means _____.

VOCABULARY IN CONTEXT: Mastery Test 6

A. Using context clues for help, write the letter of the best meaning for each italicized word. Note that all of the sentences have been taken from college textbooks.

_____ 1. In deciding on a sentence, the judge often considers whether or not the criminal has shown *remorse* (rĭ-môrs'). If there is evidence that the convicted person is sorry for what he or she has done, the punishment tends to be less severe.

    A. regret and guilt   C. innocence

    B. evidence   D. pleasure and satisfaction

_____ 2. In the third stage of its life cycle, the caterpillar shuts itself into a cocoon. When it *emerges* (ĭ-mûrj'ĭs) months later, it will be a beautiful butterfly.

    A. folds up   C. comes out

    B. goes inside   D. cries out

_____ 3. The male woodpecker can be quite *persistent* (pər-sĭs'tənt) in his attempts to attract a female. He is usually not discouraged by her refusal and will continue to court her for several hours.

    A. late   C. afraid

    B. steady   D. uncaring

_____ 4. According to research, a majority of U.S. teenagers hold part-time jobs during the school year. Most teens consider their work *tedious* (tē'dē-əs), but some find their jobs to be an enjoyable social experience.

    A. exciting   C. helpful

    B. boring   D. educational

_____ 5. New employees should be reminded that it is *prudent* (prood'nt) to accept assignments and carry out orders without objecting. Workers who seem unwilling to go along with company policy will probably soon find themselves looking for new jobs.

    A. wise   C. risky

    B. friendly   D. unhelpful

(Continues on next page)

B. Five words are **boldfaced** in the textbook passage below. Write the definition for each boldfaced word, choosing from the definitions in the box. Then write the letter of the definition in the space provided.

Be sure to read the entire passage before making your choices. Note that three definitions will be left over.

A. dangerous	**B.** discouragement	**C.** done together
D. force	**E.** get involved	**F.** imitate
G. insincere	**H.** stand up to	

¹Studies of school violence suggest that as many as 80 percent of students who witness bullying do nothing to stop it. ²Why? ³According to sociologists, there are four main reasons students refuse to **intervene** and help their peers. ⁴First of all, most bystanders are simply afraid of getting hurt. ⁵Jumping into a fight is **treacherous**—it may lead to injury all too quickly. ⁶A second reason students don't stand up for their peers is that they are afraid bullies will turn on them. ⁷Fear of becoming a new target is such a powerful **deterrent** that most students choose to do nothing—even when their classmates are suffering. ⁸A third reason students don't **compel** bullies to stop is that most bystanders believe their actions can make a situation worse. ⁹In reality, however, doing nothing helps no one and can actually encourage bullies to attack. ¹⁰Last, bystanders do not **confront** bullies because they don't know what to do or how to do it. ¹¹Clearly schools need to teach students how to respond to bullying so that schools—and students—are safer.

_____ 6. In sentence 3, *intervene* (ĭn'tər-vēn') means _____.

_____ 7. In sentence 5, *treacherous* (trĕch'ər-əs) means _____.

_____ 8. In sentence 7, *deterrent* (dĭ-tûr'ənt) means _____.

_____ 9. In sentence 8, *compel* (kəm-pĕl') means _____.

_____ 10. In sentence 10, *confront* (kən-frŭnt') means _____.

3 Main Ideas

This Chapter in a Nutshell

- Recognizing an author's **main idea**, or point, is the most important reading skill.

- The main idea is a general idea supported by specific ideas and details.

- Learn to think as you read by asking yourself, "What is the author's point?"

What Is the Main Idea?

Copyright 2006 by Randy Glasbergen.
www.glasbergen.com

GLASBERGEN

"Things were good at work today. The boss was out sick. The computer network was working for a change. And the vending machine was giving everyone free cups of coffee."

"What's the point?" People ask this question when they want to know what main idea is being presented. Sometimes a main idea is clear right away, as in the cartoon above. What would you say is the speaker's point in the cartoon?

113

Explanation

The main idea is that the speaker had a good day at work. He then supports his point with three specific reasons: the boss was out, the computer network was working, and the vending machine was dispensing free coffee.

When you read, get in the habit of asking, "What is the main point the writer is trying to make?" Recognizing the **main idea**, or point, is the most important key to better reading.

✓ ## Check Your Understanding

For instance, read the following paragraph, asking yourself as you do, "What is the author's point?"

> ¹Poor grades in school can have various causes. ²For one thing, students may have financial problems. ³If they need to work long hours to make money, they will have little study time. ⁴Another cause of poor grades may be trouble with relationships. ⁵A student may be unhappy over family problems or a lack of friends. ⁶That unhappiness can harm schoolwork. ⁷A final cause of poor grades may be bad study habits. ⁸Some students have never learned how to take good notes in class, how to manage their time effectively, or how to study a textbook. ⁹Without such study skills, their grades are likely to suffer.

Here is a good two-step way to find an author's point, or main idea:

1   Look for a general statement.

2   Decide if that statement is supported by most of the other material in the paragraph. If it is, you have found the main idea.

Below are four statements from the passage about poor grades. Pick out the general statement that is supported by the other material in the passage. Write the letter of that statement in the space provided. Then read the explanation that follows.

Four statements from the passage

A.   Poor grades in school can have various causes.

B.   For one thing, students may have financial problems.

C.   A final cause of poor grades may be bad study habits.

D.   Some students have never learned how to take good notes in class, how to manage their time effectively, or how to study a textbook.

The general statement that expresses the main idea of the passage is: _____

Explanation

Sentence A: The phrase "various causes" in sentence A is a general one. It is broad enough to include all of the specific causes mentioned in the other sentences—financial problems, trouble with relationships, and bad study habits. Sentence A, then, is the sentence that expresses the main idea of the passage.

Sentence B: This sentence is about only one type of problem, financial problems. "Financial problems" is not general enough to include the other two listed causes of poor grades: trouble with relationships and bad study habits.

Sentence C: This sentence also mentions only one specific cause: bad study habits. "Bad study habits" is not general enough to include the other two causes presented in the paragraph.

Sentence D: This sentence lists three specific study problems. It does not cover the other material in the paragraph.

The Main Idea as an "Umbrella" Idea

Think of the main idea as an "umbrella" idea. The main idea is the author's general point. The other material in the paragraph fits under it. That other material is made up of **supporting details**—specific evidence such as examples, reasons, or facts. The diagram below shows the relationship:

The explanations and activities on the following pages will deepen your understanding of the main idea.

How Do You Recognize a Main Idea?

To recognize the main idea of a passage, you must **become an active reader**. Active readers *think* as they read. Instead of merely taking in words, an active reader constantly asks, "What's the point?" In addition, active readers use a variety of other strategies to determine an author's main idea. Below are three active reading strategies you can use to help find the main idea in a passage.

1 Look for general versus specific ideas.
2 Use the topic to lead you to the main idea.
3 Use key words to lead you to the main idea.

Each strategy is explained on the following pages.

1   Look for General versus Specific Ideas

You saw in the paragraph on the causes of poor grades that the main idea is a *general* idea that is supported by *specific* ideas. To improve your skill at finding main ideas, then, it will be helpful to practice separating general from specific ideas.

✓ Check Your Understanding

See if you can do the following brief exercises. Then read the explanations that follow.

1. You often use general and specific ideas without even realizing it. Consider the following:

● *Animal* is a general term. Write the names of three specific animals:

_____   _____   _____

● *Vegetable* is a general term. Write the names of three specific vegetables:

_____   _____   _____

● *Emotion* is a general term. Write the names of three specific emotions:

_____   _____   _____

Explanation

In answering the above items, you might have chosen such specific animals as a dog, raccoon, or bear; such specific vegetables as carrots, onions, or celery; such specific emotions as anger, sadness, or happiness.

2. Let's say that a new year is starting, and you decide to make some New Year's resolutions. Your general idea might be as follows:

General idea: Starting in January, I want to make some changes in my life.

● Now write three *specific* ideas—three resolutions that you might make:

_____

_____

_____

Explanation

Three examples of specific resolutions might be to get to bed earlier, to eat less junk food, and to spend at least a half hour reading each day.

3. In thinking about your teachers, you might decide that one of your high-school English teachers was your best teacher. Your general idea might be as follows:

General idea: _____ is the best teacher I ever had.

● Now write three *specific* reasons you thought so highly of this teacher:

_____

_____

_____

Explanation

You might, for instance, have liked a given teacher because he or she gave clear explanations of ideas, had a friendly manner, and spent individual time with each student.

4. Finally, suppose you have found a good part-time job. Your general idea might be as follows:

General idea: _____ has been a good part-time job for me.

● Now write three *specific* supporting reasons for liking the job:

_____

_____

_____

Explanation

Three particular reasons for liking a job might include pay of ten dollars an hour, convenient work hours after school each day, and a short travel time of only fifteen minutes to the job.

Now do the practices that follow, which will give you more experience in telling the difference between general and specific ideas.

PRACTICE 1

Each cluster of words below consists of one general idea and three specific ideas. The general idea includes all the specific ideas. Identify each general idea with a **G** and the specific ideas with an **S**. Look first at the example.

Example

_S_ frying
_S_ baking
_G_ cooking
_S_ steaming

(*Cooking* is the general idea. It includes three specific types of cooking: frying, baking, and steaming.)

1. ___ soup
   ___ water
   ___ liquid
   ___ coffee

2. ___ potato chips
   ___ pretzels
   ___ salted nuts
   ___ snacks

3. ___ cotton
   ___ fabric
   ___ silk
   ___ wool

4. ___ entertainment
   ___ movies
   ___ concerts
   ___ card games

5. ___ cans
   ___ boxes
   ___ bags
   ___ containers

6. ___ rock
   ___ classical
   ___ country
   ___ music

7. ___ necklace
___ jewelry
___ ring
___ bracelet

8. ___ fish
___ tuna
___ salmon
___ flounder

9. ___ coughing
___ sneezing
___ symptom
___ sore throat

10. ___ speaking
___ listening
___ writing
___ communicating

PRACTICE 2

In each item below, one idea is general and the others are specific. The general idea includes the specific ideas. In the spaces provided, write two more specific ideas that are covered by the general idea.

Example   *General:* school subjects
Specific: biology, Spanish,   _____history_____ ,   _____math_____

(*School subjects* is the general idea; *biology* and *Spanish* are specific subjects, as are *history* and *math.*)

1. *General:* beverages
Specific: iced tea, water,   _____ , _____

2. *General:* sport
Specific: baseball, soccer,   _____ , _____

3. *General:* relatives
Specific: cousin, mother,   _____ , _____

4. *General:* sandwich
Specific: ham, grilled cheese,   _____ , _____

5. *General:* reading material
Specific: textbook, comic book,   _____ , _____

6. *General:* seafood
Specific: clams, lobster,   _____ , _____

7. *General:* tone of voice
Specific: excited, surprised,   _____ , _____

8. *General:* negative personal quality
   Specific: greed, cowardice, _____ , _____

9. *General:* positive personal quality
   Specific: reliability, determination, _____ , _____

10. *General:* greeting
    Specific: "How are you," "Hello," _____ , _____

PRACTICE 3

In the following groups, one statement is the general point (and main idea), and the other statements are specific support for the point. Identify each point with a **P** and each statement of support with an **S.**

1. ___ A. A mosquito can find you in the dark.
   ___ B. A mosquito can keep you awake all night.
   ___ C. Though a mosquito is small, it has a lot of power.
   ___ D. A mosquito can make you scratch yourself until you bleed.

2. ___ A. The bread the waiter brought us is stale.
   ___ B. We've been waiting for our main course for over an hour.
   ___ C. The people at the next table are awfully loud.
   ___ D. It is time to speak to the restaurant manager.

3. ___ A. The apartment has no closets.
   ___ B. The kitchen is so small only one person can be there.
   ___ C. Each morning the apartment fills with exhaust fumes from a nearby bus station.
   ___ D. The apartment has some real drawbacks.

4. ___ A. That teacher is very demanding.
   ___ B. She calls on students who don't make eye contact with her.
   ___ C. Students must e-mail her if they intend to miss a class.
   ___ D. A paper handed in late is reduced a whole grade for each day it's late.

> ## PRACTICE 4

In the following groups—all based on textbook selections—one statement is the general point (and main idea), and the other statements are specific support for the point. Identify each point with a **P** and each statement of support with an **S**.

1. ____ A. Only one in three adults engages in regular physical activity.

   ____ B. The percentage of obese adults has more than doubled in the past 40 years.

   ____ C. About one in five adults still smokes cigarettes.

   ____ D. Americans are not as healthy as they should be.

2. ____ A. Couples committed to each other gain strength from their mutual support.

   ____ B. Committed couples are financially more successful than singles.

   ____ C. Committed relationships offer many benefits.

   ____ D. Happily married adults live longer and have fewer emotional problems.

3. ____ A. Finding safety in numbers, bats live in large colonies numbering from several thousand to a million or more.

   ____ B. Bats are creatures with a strong instinct to protect their own kind.

   ____ C. Mother bats, who usually have one offspring per year, leave their young only to get food.

   ____ D. When colonies containing mother bats are disturbed, the mothers will try to move their young to a safer location.

4. ____ A. In 17th-century Europe, people went through a lot of trouble to wear makeup.

   ____ B. To wear makeup at that time, men and women had to put an unpleasant mixture of lead, egg whites, and vinegar on their faces.

   ____ C. Once a person's makeup was applied, he or she had to be careful not to laugh, or the new "face" would crack.

   ____ D. The lead in the makeup caused scars and blemishes, which had to be covered with patches of cloth.

2   Use the Topic to Lead You to the Main Idea

You already know that to find the main idea of a selection, you look first for a general statement. You then check to see if that statement is supported by all or most of the other material in the paragraph. If it is, you've found the main idea. Another approach that can help you find the main idea of a selection is to look for its topic.

The **topic** is the general subject of a selection. It is not a complete sentence, but can be simply expressed in several words. Knowing the topic can help you find a writer's main point about that topic.

Textbook authors use the title of each chapter to state the overall topic of that chapter. They also provide many topics and subtopics in boldface headings within the chapter. For example, here is the title of a section in a psychology textbook:

Why We Communicate

And here are the subtopics:

Physical Needs
Identity Needs
Social Needs
Practical Goals

If you were studying the above chapter, you could use the topics to help find the main ideas. (Pages 5–9 explain just how to do so, as well as providing other textbook study tips.)

But there are many times when you are not given topics—with standardized reading tests, for example, or with individual paragraphs in articles or textbooks. To find the topic of a selection when the topic is not given, ask this simple question:

Who or what is the selection about?

For example, look again at the beginning of the paragraph that started this chapter:

Poor grades in school can have various causes.

What, in just a few words, is the above paragraph about? On the line below, write what you think is the topic.

Topic: _____

You probably answered that the topic is "poor grades in school." As you reread the paragraph, you saw that, in fact, every sentence in it is about poor grades.

The next step after finding the topic is to decide what main point the author is making about the topic. Authors often present their main idea in a single sentence. (This sentence is also known as the **main idea sentence** or the **topic sentence**.) As we have already seen, the main point about poor grades is "Poor grades in school can have various causes."

✓ ## *Check Your Understanding*

Let's look now at another paragraph. Read it and then see if you can answer the questions that follow.

> [1]Phobias are continuing fears of things that are not likely to be harmful. [2]For example, some people have a phobia about elevators. [3]They worry that if they enter an elevator, the cable will break and they will fall hundreds of feet to their death. [4]While such an accident can happen, it is extremely rare. [5]Another instance of a phobia is a fear of medical needles. [6]Some people will refuse to receive an injection, even if they are seriously ill. [7]They may faint if given a needle; so great is their fear that they are about to die. [8]Perhaps the most common phobia is fear of public speaking. [9]Some people will not go to school or take jobs if they have to speak before a group. [10]Their fear—that they will embarrass themselves and that people will pity or reject them—has little basis in reality. [11]These and other phobias can usually be overcome, often fairly quickly, with the right direction and treatment.

_____ 1. Write the letter of the *topic* of the paragraph. To find the topic, ask yourself what the paragraph is about. (It often helps as you read to look for and even circle a word, term, or idea that is repeated in the paragraph.)

    A. Dangers
    B. Phobias
    C. Worry about elevators

_____ 2. Write the number of the sentence that states the *main idea* of the paragraph. In other words, what point is the author making about the topic? (Remember that the main idea will be supported by the other material in the paragraph.)

Explanation

As the first sentence of the paragraph suggests, the topic is "phobias." Continuing to read the paragraph, you see that, in fact, everything in it is about phobias. And the main idea is clearly sentence 1: "Phobias are continuing fears of things that are not likely to be harmful." This idea is a general one that sums up what the entire paragraph is about. It is an "umbrella" statement under which all the other material in the paragraph fits. The parts of the paragraph could be shown as follows:

Topic: Phobias

Main idea: Phobias are continuing fears of things that are not likely to be harmful.

Supporting details:
1. Fear that an elevator ride will end in a fall to death.
2. Fear that an injection will cause death.
3. Fear that speaking in public will lead to pity or rejection.

The following practices will sharpen your sense of the difference between a topic, the point about the topic (the main idea), and the supporting details.

PRACTICE 5

Below are groups of four items. In each case, one item is the topic, one is the main idea, and two are details that support and develop the main idea. Label each item with one of the following:

T — for the **topic** of the paragraph
MI — for the **main idea**
SD — for the **supporting details**

Note that an explanation is provided for the first group; reading it will help you do this practice.

Group 1

_____ A. One pitcher smoothes the dirt on the pitcher's mound before he throws each pitch.

_____ B. One infielder sits in the same spot on the dugout bench during every game.

_____ C. Some baseball players think that certain superstitious habits help them win games.

___T___ D. Superstitious baseball players.

Explanation

All of the statements in Group 1 involve superstitious baseball players, so item D must be the topic. (A topic is expressed in a single word or short phrase and is not a complete sentence.) Statements A and B each describe specific superstitious habits of individual baseball players. Statement C, however, is more general—it states that some players think certain superstitious habits help them win games. Statement C thus gives the main idea, and statements A and B are supporting details that explain that main idea.

Group 2

_____ A. Houdini learned to pop his shoulder out of its socket in order to escape from straitjackets.

_____ B. Harry Houdini, the famous escape artist, worked hard at his career.

_____ C. Harry Houdini.

_____ D. Houdini trained to hold his breath for over five minutes in order to pull off underwater escapes.

Group 3

_____ A. At dinnertime, instead of cooking, many people simply go to a fast-food restaurant or order take-out.

_____ B. More and more families rely on prepared meals from the frozen-foods section or the deli counter.

_____ C. Home cooking is becoming a lost art.

_____ D. Home cooking.

Group 4

_____ A. Some cultures permit women to be denied an education or abused by men.

_____ B. Some male religious leaders teach that "women are inferior before God."

_____ C. The mistreatment of many women.

_____ D. Many women are mistreated in the world today.

PRACTICE 6

Following are four paragraphs. Read each paragraph and write the letter of the item you think is the topic of the paragraph. Then write the number of the sentence you think states the main idea of the paragraph.

Here is how to proceed:

1 Ask yourself, "What seems to be the topic of the paragraph?" (It often helps to look for and even circle a word or idea that is repeated in the paragraph.)

> *Hint*: When looking for the topic, make sure you do not pick one that is either **too broad** (covering a great deal more than is in the selection) or **too narrow** (covering only part of the selection). The topic and the main idea of a selection must include everything in that selection—no more and no less.

2   Next, ask yourself, "What point is the writer making about this topic?" This will be the main idea. In this practice, it is stated in one of the sentences in the paragraph.

3   Then test what you think is the main idea by asking, "Is this statement supported by all or most of the other material in the paragraph?"

Paragraph 1

[1]Some students use avoidance tactics when faced with college work. [2]They tell themselves, "I'm not bright enough," and so never make an honest effort to do the work. [3]Or they may say to themselves, "I'm too busy," and then they deliberately find an endless number of things to do other than study. [4]A third excuse that students use is to say, "I'm too tired." [5]As a result, they decide to take naps or to sleep late rather than try to study. [6]Finally, students may say, "I'll do it later." [7]In other words, they procrastinate and keep putting study off so they can spend more time watching TV or texting friends or playing games.

_B_ 1. The topic of the paragraph is
       A. college work.
       B. avoidance tactics.
       C. procrastination.

_1_ 2. Write the number of the sentence that states the main idea of the paragraph.

Paragraph 2

[1]The female black widow spider is not as terrible a killer as is generally believed. [2]While the creature is certainly poisonous, she is also very shy and will bite humans only when she feels cornered. [3]Also, the idea that the black widow always kills the male after mating is untrue. [4]The male is often spared—if he remembers to tap out a special signal as he ventures onto his mate's web. [5]The vibrations on the web let her know he is one of her own kind, not an insect to be rushed at and killed.

_A_ 3. The topic of the paragraph is
       A. the female black widow spider.
       B. poisonous spiders.
       C. the unlucky male black widow spider.

_1_ 4. Write the number of the sentence that states the main idea of the paragraph.

Paragraph 3

¹Potato chips got their start because of a hard-to-please restaurant customer in 1853. ²In that year, George Crum was working as a chef at an elegant resort in Saratoga Springs, New York. ³He prepared thick-cut French-fried potatoes for diners there. ⁴But one diner kept sending his potatoes back to the kitchen, complaining that they were too thick for his taste. ⁵Crum cut the potatoes thinner and thinner and finally, very annoyed, made a serving of potatoes too thin and crisp to eat with a fork. ⁶To his surprise, the guest loved them. ⁷Other guests demanded a taste. ⁸Soon "Saratoga Chips" were the most popular item on the menu.

_____ C 5. The topic of the paragraph is
  A. a hard-to-please customer.
  B. the origins of foods.
  C. potato chips.

_____ 1 6. Write the number of the sentence that states the main idea of the paragraph.

Paragraph 4

¹People have always loved bike riding. ²Biking, however, can be a dangerous activity. ³One danger is "getting doored"—having a car driver open his or her door directly into the path of an oncoming bike. ⁴Another risk is aggressive drivers who feel they have more right to the roads than bikes do. ⁵Such drivers will scream, honk, or gesture wildly. ⁶They may block off bikers without a signal or a look, giving the biker no time to avoid running off the road or into the car. ⁷An added source of danger for bikers is poor road design, which in many cases allows just enough room for a car on either side of the road, but no extra room for a biker to be on the same road. ⁸Recently, the U.S. Department of Transportation noted that bicycling is now more dangerous than flying in planes or riding in buses, boats, or trains.

_____ A 7. The topic of the paragraph is
  A. biking.
  B. transportation.
  C. getting "doored."

_____ 2 8. Write the number of the sentence that states the main idea of the paragraph.

3   Find and Use Key Words to Lead You to the Main Idea

Sometimes authors make it fairly easy to find their main idea. They announce it by using **key words**—words or phrases that are easy to recognize. These key words are clues to the main idea.

One type of key word is a **list word** or words, which tell you a list of items is to follow. For example, the main idea in the paragraph about poor grades was stated like this: *Poor grades in school can have various causes.* The expression *various causes* helps you zero in on the main idea. You realize that the paragraph will be about the causes of poor grades. As you read on and see the series of causes, you know your guess about the main idea was correct.

Below are some common words that often announce a main idea. Note that nearly all of them contain a word that ends in **s**—a plural that suggests the supporting details will be a list of items.

List Words

several kinds of	various causes	a few reasons
a number of	a series of	three factors
four steps	among the results	several advantages

When expressions like these appear in a sentence, look carefully to see if that sentence might be the main idea. Chances are a sentence with these words will be followed by a list of major supporting details.

✓   *Check Your Understanding: List Words*

Underline the list words in the following sentences.

> *Hint:* Remember that list words usually end in *s*.

Example   Being a middle child in a large family has <u>several drawbacks</u>.

1. The rising rate of obesity among young people seems to have <u>three causes</u>.

2. <u>Several symptoms</u> may indicate that a person is having a heart attack.

3. The Pilgrims faced a <u>number of challenges</u> during their first winter in America.

4. Community colleges have some real <u>advantages</u> over four-year colleges.

5. Students offer a <u>variety of excuses</u> for their homework being late.

Explanation

In the first sentence, you should have underlined the phrase *three causes*. Those words suggest that a list of the three causes of the rising rate of obesity among young people may follow. In sentences 2–5, you should have underlined these groups of words: *Several symptoms, a number of challenges, some real advantages,* and *a variety of excuses.* Each of those phrases also tells you that a list of supporting details may follow.

There is another type of key word that can alert you to the main idea. This type of key word, called an **addition word**, is generally used right before a supporting detail. Below is a box of words that often introduce major supporting details and help you discover the main idea.

Addition Words

one	to begin with	in addition	last
first	another	next	last of all
first of all	second	moreover	final
for one thing	also	furthermore	finally

Check Your Understanding: Addition Words

Reread the paragraph about causes of poor grades and underline the addition words that alert you to supporting details. Also, see if you can circle the list words that suggest the main idea.

¹Poor grades in school can have various causes. ²For one thing, students may have financial problems. ³If they need to work long hours to make money, they will have little study time. ⁴Another cause of poor grades may be trouble with relationships. ⁵A student may be unhappy over family problems or a lack of friends. ⁶That unhappiness can harm schoolwork. ⁷A final cause of poor grades may be bad study habits. ⁸Some students have never learned how to take good notes in class, how to manage their time effectively, or how to study a textbook. ⁹Without such study skills, their grades are likely to suffer.

Explanation

The words that introduce each new supporting detail for the main idea are *For one thing, Another*, and *final*. These addition words help you realize that all the details in the paragraph are supporting the idea that poor grades in school can have various causes. You should have underlined these three words.

Since *various causes* are list words, you should have circled them. Even before you saw the addition words, those list words could have suggested to you that the paragraph may list the different causes of poor grades. As you can see, in this paragraph (as in many others), list words and addition words work hand in hand.

PRACTICE 7

The chapters that follow will offer a good deal of practice in key words. For now, do the activity below.

A. Underline the list words in each of the following sentences.

1. Living alone has a number of advantages.

2. Physical punishment can be harmful to a child in several ways.

3. The Industrial Revolution came about quickly because of three major inventions.

4. A series of mistakes led to the arrest and imprisonment of the wrong person.

5. To memorize materials effectively, there are two important steps to follow.

6. The National Board of Medical Examiners has released some alarming facts about doctors.

B. (7–10.) Underline the four addition words or phrases in the following passage.

    [1]Women don't hold more political power in the United States for several reasons. [2]First of all, women are still a minority in law and business. [3]Those are the fields from which most politicians come. [4]In addition, political careers usually require a great deal of time spent away from home, and such hours don't tie in well with motherhood. [5]Also, women are less likely to have a supportive spouse at home, ready to help out with child care, housework, and the like. [6]Finally, men have not been eager to open up the "boys' club" of political power to women. [7]They tend to support and encourage upcoming male candidates, not female ones.

A Note on the Central Point

In selections made up of many paragraphs, the overall main idea is called the **central point**, also known as the **central idea** or **thesis**. You can find a central point in the same way that you find a main idea. First, identify the topic (which is often suggested by the title of the selection). Then look at the supporting material. The paragraphs within the longer reading will provide supporting details for the central point.

The following chapter, "Supporting Details," provides more information about (and practice in) the list and addition words that help signal main ideas and the details that support them.

CHAPTER REVIEW

In this chapter, you learned the following:

- Recognizing the main idea is the most important key to good comprehension. The main idea is a general "umbrella" idea. The specific supporting material of the paragraph fits under it.

- Three strategies that will help you find the main idea are to (1) look for general versus specific ideas; (2) use the topic (the general subject of a selection) to lead you to the main idea; (3) use key words to lead you to the main idea.

The next chapter—Chapter 4—will increase your understanding of the specific details that authors use to support and develop their main ideas.

On the Web: If you are using this book in class, you can visit our website for additional practice in recognizing main ideas. Go to **www.townsendpress.com** and click on "Learning Center."

REVIEW TEST 1

To review what you've learned in this chapter, answer each of the following questions by filling in the blank.

1. The umbrella statement that covers the material in a paragraph is the *(topic* or *main idea?)*_____.

2. The supporting details are always more *(general* or *specific?)* _____ than the main idea.

3. To help yourself find the *(topic* or *main idea?)* _____ of a paragraph, ask yourself, "Who or what is this paragraph about?"

4. To help you decide if a certain sentence is the main idea of a paragraph, ask yourself, "Is this sentence _____ by all or most of the other material in the paragraph?"

5. One way to help find the main idea is to look for **addition words** like *first, second, also,* and *finally.* Such words often introduce the supporting _____s for a main idea.

REVIEW TEST 2

A. Each cluster of words below consists of one general idea and three specific ideas. The general idea includes all the specific ideas. Underline the general idea in each group.

1. kneeling   position   standing   sitting

2. water   electricity   gas   utility

3. housing   condominium   palace   apartment

4. hearing   touch   sense   sight

5. nicotine   alcohol   drug   aspirin

6. flour   ingredient   yeast   eggs

7. tinsel   colored lights   decoration   wreath

8. car payment   credit-card bill   personal loan   debt

B. In each item below, one idea is general and the others are specific. The general idea includes the specific ideas. In the spaces provided, write two more specific ideas that are covered by the general idea.

9–10. *General:*   pet
      Specific: parakeet, hamster,   _____,   _____

11–12. *General:*   sharp object
      Specific: razor, broken glass,   _____,   _____

13–14. *General:*   footwear
      Specific: boots, slippers,   _____,   _____

15–16. *General:*   breakfast item
      Specific: orange juice, oatmeal,   _____,   _____

C. (17–20.) In the following group, one statement is the general point, and the other statements are specific support for the point. Identify the point with a **P** and each statement of support with an **S**.

_____ A. When you're speaking to Doug, he is often looking around the room.

_____ B. He never asks questions of the other person.

_____ C. Doug is not skilled at conversation.

_____ D. He interrupts when he thinks of something he wants to say.

REVIEW TEST 3

A. (1–12.) Each group of four items includes one topic, one main idea, and two supporting details. In the space provided, label each item with one of the following:

T — for the **topic** of the paragraph
MI — for the **main idea**
SD — for the **supporting details**

Group 1

_MI_ A. The human skeleton has certain important functions.

_SD_ B. The skeleton gives the body support and shape.

_SD_ C. The skeleton protects internal organs.

_T_ D. The human skeleton.

Group 2

_____T_____ A. Americans and exercise.

_____SD_____ B. Americans tend to ride everywhere instead of walking.

_____MI_____ C. Most Americans don't get enough exercise.

_____SD_____ D. Americans tend to watch sports instead of playing them.

Group 3

_____T_____ A. The Egyptian pyramids.

_____SD_____ B. More than 100,000 laborers worked to build Egypt's Great Pyramid.

_____MI_____ C. The Egyptian pyramids were built with manpower and skill, not secret engineering.

_____SD_____ D. Pyramid builders used ropes, wooden levers, and muscle power to move giant stones.

B. Read each paragraph below and write the letter of the item you think is the topic of the paragraph. Then write the number of the sentence that states the main idea of the paragraph.

Paragraph 1

[1]A dangerous mistake that students can make in life is not to take charge of their own lives. [2]If they do not sail their own ship but choose to drift with the tides and be part of the crowd, their ship may drift onto the rocks! [3]Their friends and peers may just be interested in smoking, drinking, socializing, playing games, and getting by. [4]They might not be interested in doing the hard work needed to succeed in life. [5]Studies have shown that countless students go through high school trying to be one of the gang. [6]Only later, sometime after high school, do some of them realize they must take responsibility for their lives. [7]Doing what other people in one's social group are doing may help make one popular, but it does not help one get a diploma that can lead to a job.

_____A_____ 13. The topic is

    A. a dangerous mistake students can make.

    B. being part of the crowd.

    C. getting a diploma.

_____1_____ 14. What is the number of the sentence that states the main idea?

Paragraph 2

[1]Almost every week you're likely to see a TV commercial or an ad for a new health product. [2]It might promise better sleep, more energy, clearer skin, firmer muscles, lower weight, brighter moods, longer life—or all of these combined. [3]The product is often endorsed by ordinary-looking people who have been carefully rehearsed. [4]However, if a health product sounds too good to be true, it probably is. [5]If, for example, a magic pill really *could* trim off excess pounds or remove wrinkles, the world would be filled with thin people with unlined skin. [6]Look around, and you'll realize that's not the case.

___B___ 15. The topic is
  A. TV commericals and ads.
  B. new health products.
  C. magic pills.

___4___ 16. What is the number of the sentence that states the main idea?

C. In the space provided, write the letter of the list words in each sentence.

___C___ 17. A teenager in serious emotional trouble is likely to display certain kinds of behavior.
  A. *serious emotional trouble*
  B. *likely to display*
  C. *certain kinds of behavior*

___c___ 18. The widespread pollution of the lakes in the region has a number of causes.
  A. *widespread pollution*
  B. *lakes in the region*
  C. *a number of causes*

D. In the space provided, write the letter of the addition word in each sentence.

___A___ 19. The best single way to become a better student is to attend every class; another important step is to take good notes in class.
  A. *another*
  B. *important*
  C. *better*

_____ 20. Extreme stress can lead some people to escape through drug abuse; stress may also lead to such severe depression that a person attempts suicide.
- A. *stress*
- B. *also*
- C. *depression*

REVIEW TEST 4

Here is a chance to apply your understanding of main ideas to a full-length reading. First read the following selection from the college textbook *Sociology, Third Edition*, by Rodney Stark—it will give you a fascinating view of the type of behavior we all witness every day. Then answer the questions that follow about topics, main ideas, and the central point. There are also vocabulary questions to help you continue practicing the skill of understanding vocabulary in context.

Words to Watch

Below are some words in the reading that do not have strong context support. Each word is followed by the number of the paragraph in which it appears and its meaning there. These words are indicated in the selection by a small circle (°).

conformity (2): behavior in accordance with group ideas and customs
confirming (2): proving true
perception (3): observation
at odds (8): in disagreement
stakes (10): something to be gained or lost

GROUP PRESSURE

Rodney Stark

1 It is self-evident that people tend to conform to the expectations and reactions of others around them. But what are the limits of group pressure? Can group pressure cause us to deny the obvious, even physical evidence?

2 Over thirty-five years ago, Solomon Asch performed the most famous experimental test of the power of group pressure to produce conformity°. Since then his study has been repeated many times, with many variations confirming° his original results. Perhaps the best way to understand what Asch discovered is to pretend that you are a subject in his experiment.

3   You have agreed to take part in an experiment on visual perception°. Upon arriving at the laboratory, you are given the seventh in a line of eight chairs. Other students taking part in the experiment sit in each of the other chairs. At the front of the room the experimenter stands by a covered easel. He explains that he wants you to judge the length of lines in a series of comparisons. He will place two decks of large cards upon the easel. One card will display a single vertical line. The other card will display three vertical lines, each of a different length. He wants each of you to decide which of the three lines on one card is the same length as the single line on the other card. To prepare you for the task, he displays a practice card. You see the correct line easily, for the other lines are noticeably different from the comparison line.

4   The experiment begins. The first comparison is just as easy as the practice comparison. One of the three lines is obviously the same length as the comparison line, while the other two are very different. Each of the eight persons answers in turn, with you answering seventh. Everyone answers correctly. On the second pair of cards, the right answer is just as easy to spot, and again all eight subjects are correct. You begin to suspect that the experiment is going to be a big bore.

5   Then comes the third pair. The judgment is just as easy as before. But the first person somehow picks a line that is obviously wrong. You smile. Then the second person also picks the same obviously wrong line. What's going on? Then the third, fourth, fifth, and sixth subjects answer the same way. It's your turn. You know without doubt that you are right, yet six people have confidently given the wrong answer. You are no longer bored. Instead, you are a bit confused, but you go ahead and choose the line you are sure is right. Then the last person picks the same wrong line everyone else has chosen.

6   A new pair is unveiled, and the same thing happens again. All the others pick an obviously wrong line. The experimenter remains matter-of-fact, not commenting on right or wrong answers but just marking down what people pick. Should you stick it out? Should you go along? Maybe something's wrong with the light or with your angle of vision. Your difficulty lasts for eighteen pairs of cards. On twelve of them, all the others picked a line you knew was incorrect.

7   When the experiment is over, the experimenter turns to you with a smile

and begins to explain. You were the only subject in the experiment. The other seven people were stooges paid by Professor Asch to answer exactly the way they did. The aim of the experiment was to see if social pressure could cause you to reject the evidence of your own eyes and conform.

8   In his first experiment, Asch tested fifty people in this situation. Almost a third of them went along with the group and gave the wrong answer at least half of the time. Another 40 percent yielded to the group some of the time, but less than half of the time. Only 25 percent refused to yield at all. Those who yielded to group pressure were more likely to do so as the experiment progressed. Nearly everyone withstood the group the first several times, but as they continued to find themselves at odds° with the group, most subjects began to weaken. Many shifted in their chairs, trying to get a different line of vision. Some blushed. Finally, 75 percent of them began to go along at least a few times.

9   The effects of group pressure were also revealed in the behavior of those who steadfastly refused to accept the group's misjudgments. Some of these people became increasingly uneasy and apologetic. One subject began to whisper to his neighbor, "Can't help it, that's the one," and later, "I always disagree—darn it!" Other subjects who refused to yield dealt with the stress of the situation by giving each nonconforming response in a progressively louder voice and by casting challenging looks at the others. In a recent replication of the Asch study, one subject loudly insulted the other seven students whenever they made a wrong choice. One retort was "What funny farm did you turkeys grow up on, huh?"

10   The Asch experiment shows that a high number of people will conform even in a weak group situation. They were required merely to disagree with strangers, not with their friends, and the costs of deviance were limited to about half an hour of disapproval from people they hardly knew. Furthermore, subjects were not faced with a difficult judgment—they could easily see the correct response. Little wonder, then, that we are inclined to go along with our friends when the stakes° are much higher and we cannot even be certain that we are right.

Reading Comprehension Questions

Vocabulary in Context

_____ 1. In the sentence below, the word *stooges* (st$\overline{oo}$j's) means
   A. comedians.
   B. people who played a role.
   C. true subjects in an experiment.
   D. educators.

   "The other seven people were stooges paid by Professor Asch to answer exactly the way they did." (Paragraph 7)

_____ 2. In the sentence below, the word *withstood* (wĭth-stŏod') means
   A. recognized.
   B. agreed with.
   C. resisted.
   D. understood.

   "Nearly everyone withstood the group the first several times, but as they continued to find themselves at odds with the group, most subjects began to weaken." (Paragraph 8)

_____ 3. In the excerpt below, the word *steadfastly* (stĕd'făst'lē) means
   A. constantly.
   B. wrongly.
   C. helpfully.
   D. comfortably.

   "The effects of group pressure were also revealed in the behavior of those who steadfastly refused to accept the group's misjudgments. Some of these people became increasingly uneasy and apologetic." (Paragraph 9)

_____ 4. In the excerpt below, the word *replication* (rĕp'lĭ-kā'shən) means
   A. memory.
   B. repeat.
   C. image.
   D. prediction.

   "In a recent replication of the Asch study, one subject loudly insulted the other seven students . . ." (Paragraph 9)

_____ 5. In the excerpt below, the word *retort* (rĭ-tôrt′) means
  A. genuine question.
  B. form of praise.
  C. choice.
  D. quick, sharp reply.

  "... one subject loudly insulted the other seven students whenever they made a wrong choice. One retort was 'What funny farm did you turkeys grow up on, huh?'" (Paragraph 9)

_____ 6. In the sentence below, the word *deviance* (dē′vē-əns) means
  A. going along with the crowd.
  B. an experimental test.
  C. differing from the normal group behavior.
  D. being a stranger.

  "They were required merely to disagree with strangers, not with their friends, and the costs of deviance were limited to about half an hour of disapproval from people they hardly knew." (Paragraph 10)

Central Point

_____ 7. Which of the following is the topic of the whole selection?
  A. Visual perception
  B. Solomon Asch
  C. Asch's experiment on group pressure
  D. Stooges in an experiment

_____ 8. Which sentence from the reading comes closest to expressing the central point of the whole selection?
  A. "Upon arriving at the laboratory, you are given the seventh in a line of eight chairs."
  B. "The experimenter remains matter-of-fact, not commenting on right or wrong answers but just marking down what people pick."
  C. "In his first experiment, Asch tested fifty people in this situation."
  D. "The Asch experiment shows that a high number of people will conform even in a weak group situation."

Main Ideas

_____ 9. The topic of paragraph 9 is
   A. the behavior of subjects who refused to accept the group's misjudgments.
   B. subjects who became uneasy and apologetic.
   C. a duplication of the Asch study.
   D. subjects who insulted others.

_____ 10. The main idea of paragraph 9 is expressed in its
   A. first sentence.
   B. second sentence.
   C. next-to-the-last sentence.
   D. last sentence.

Discussion Questions

1. Were you at all surprised by the results of Solomon Asch's experiment? If you had been one of the subjects, do you think you would have stuck to your answers, or would you have gone along with the group? Why?

2. What reasons might the subjects in the Asch experiment have had for eventually giving in and accepting the group's wrong answers?

3. Stark refers to the Asch experiment as a "weak group situation," one in which the group is made up of strangers and the stakes are not very high. What might a "strong group situation" be? Give examples.

4. Have you ever been in a situation when you wanted to resist group pressure? What was the situation, and why did you want to resist? What could you have done to resist?

Note: Writing assignments for this selection appear on pages 605–606.

Check Your Performance   MAIN IDEAS

Activity	Number Right	Points	Score
Review Test 1 (5 items)	_____	× 2 =	_____
Review Test 2 (20 items)	_____	× 1.5 =	_____
Review Test 3 (20 items)	_____	× 1.5 =	_____
Review Test 4 (10 items)	_____	× 3 =	_____
		TOTAL SCORE =	_____ %

Enter your total score into the **Reading Performance Chart: Review Tests** on the inside back cover.

MAIN IDEAS: Mastery Test 1

A. Each cluster of words below consists of one general idea and three specific ideas. The general idea includes all the specific ideas. Underline the general idea in each group.

1. oak	tree	maple	pine
2. iron	tin	metal	aluminum
3. insect	ant	roach	fly
4. basketball	hockey	tennis	sport

B. In each item below, one idea is general, and the other two are specific. The general idea includes the specific ideas. In the spaces provided, write **two** more specific ideas that are covered by the general idea.

5–6. *General:* fruit
   Specific: orange, pineapple, _____, _____

7–8. *General:* country
   Specific: Canada, Greece, _____, _____

9–10. *General:* holiday
   Specific: Independence Day,
   Labor Day, _____, _____

11–12. *General:* criminal
   Specific: kidnapper, arsonist, _____, _____

C. (13–20.) In each group below, one statement is the general point, and the other statements are specific support for the point. Identify the point with a **P** and each statement of support with an **S**.

Group 1

_____ A. Pet owners survive longer after a major illness than people who don't own pets.

_____ B. Daily time with pets aids relaxation and decreases stress.

_____ C. Pet ownership has positive effects on people's health.

_____ D. Petting an animal lowers blood pressure in humans.

(Continues on next page)

Group 2

_____ A. Certain harmless snakes eat poisonous ones.

_____ B. Snakes help control the rodent population by eating mice and rats.

_____ C. Medicines for humans have been developed from snake venom.

_____ D. Despite their poor public image, snakes have their good points.

MAIN IDEAS: Mastery Test 2

A. Each cluster of words below consists of one general idea and three specific ideas. The general idea includes all the specific ideas. Underline the general idea in each group.

1. rose	daisy	tulip	flower
2. sofa	furniture	table	chair
3. illness	flu	measles	pneumonia
4. socks	jacket	clothes	shirt

B. In each item below, one idea is general, and the other two are specific. The general idea includes the specific ideas. In the spaces provided, write **two** more specific ideas that are covered by the general idea.

5–6. *General:* beverages
     Specific: water, milk, _____, _____

7–8. *General:* bird
     Specific: parrot, turkey, _____, _____

9–10. *General:* natural disaster
      Specific: earthquake, hurricane, _____, _____

11–12. *General:* happy event
       Specific: birth of a child,
       getting an A, _____, _____

C. (13–20.) In each group below, one statement is the general point, and the other statements are specific support for the point. Identify the point with a **P** and each statement of support with an **S.**

Group 1

_____ A. Bringing homemade popcorn to the movies is cheaper than buying expensive theater popcorn.

_____ B. Buying candy at a grocery store, not a theater, cuts candy costs in half.

_____ C. Moviegoers can take several simple steps to save money at the movie theater.

_____ D. Going to movies early in the day can reduce ticket prices by several dollars.

(Continues on next page)

Group 2

___ A. Naps improve people's moods and alertness.

___ B. Taking a nap boosts energy and increases work productivity.

___ C. After a nap, it is easier to concentrate and make decisions.

___ D. People should take a nap every day.

MAIN IDEAS: Mastery Test 3

A. (1–12.) In each group below, one statement is the general point, and the other statements are specific support for the point. Identify each point with a **P** and each statement of support with an **S.**

Group 1

____ A. Tall buildings in the United States often have twelfth and fourteenth floors—but not a thirteenth floor.

____ B. Houses in France are never numbered thirteen.

____ C. Throughout the world, the number thirteen is viewed as unlucky.

____ D. Many global airlines have removed row number thirteen from airplane seating charts.

Group 2

____ A. Restaurant ratings are based on more than just food.

____ B. A restaurant's service can be almost as significant as the meal itself.

____ C. For many restaurant critics, the comfort of the surroundings will be a part of their evaluation.

____ D. Menu prices are always taken into consideration.

Group 3

____ A. The average American child is exposed to 12,000 violent acts—including rape and murder—on TV each year.

____ B. Adults who watch TV two hours a day increase their chances of obesity by 25 percent and Type 2 diabetes by 14 percent.

____ C. Toddlers who watch TV for an hour each day increase their risk of having attention problems by 10 percent.

____ D. TV watching can be an unhealthy activity.

(Continues on next page)

B. (13–20.) Each group of four items includes one topic, one main idea, and two supporting details. In the space provided, label each item with one of the following:

T — for the **topic** of the paragraph
MI — for the **main idea**
SD — for the **supporting details**

Group 1

_SD_ A. Researchers believe one quarter of "mysterious" fires in dwellings in the United States are caused by rats.

_T_ B. Problems caused by rats.

_SD_ C. Studies show that rats are to blame for 26 percent of electrical cable failures in houses and apartments.

_MI_ D. Rats cause serious problems to homeowners and apartment dwellers.

Group 2

_SD_ A. Young Americans are more likely to eat fast food, avoid exercise, be obese, or smoke cigarettes.

_SD_ B. Many do not have health insurance or get regular physical or dental exams and do not receive health care when they need it.

_MI_ C. Young Americans moving into adulthood face significant health risks.

_T_ D. Health risks for young Americans.

MAIN IDEAS: Mastery Test 4

A. (1–12.) In each group below, one statement is the general point, and the other statements are specific support for the point. Identify each point with a **P** and each statement of support with an **S**.

Group 1

P A. Some people find it difficult to live without technology.

S B. You never see them sitting quietly reading a book.

S C. When they are out during the day, they are constantly interacting with their phones.

S D. At home they watch TV, read e-mail, and spend time on Facebook and other social media.

Group 2

S A. Most teens who work do so to develop responsibility and gain independence from their parents.

S B. Almost all teens who work are motivated by a desire to earn spending money.

S C. For a majority of teens, work offers an opportunity to spend time with peers.

P D. Teenagers choose to work during the school year for a variety of reasons.

Group 3

S A. Panic disorder, a type of anxiety in which people experience feelings of panic, affects eight out of every thousand people.

P B. Anxiety is a widespread disorder that many people deal with each day.

S C. Five to 10 percent of Americans suffer from phobias, a type of anxiety in which people experience intense fear of things such as spiders, dogs, or bridges.

S D. About 12 million Americans experience strong fear in social situations— social anxiety—each year.

(Continues on next page)

B. (13–20.) Each group of four items includes one topic, one main idea, and two supporting details. In the space provided, label each item with one of the following:

       T — for the **topic** of the paragraph
     MI — for the **main idea**
    SD — for the **supporting details**

Group 1

  _SD_ A. Women have 15–20 percent more "gray matter" in their brains than men.

  _SD_ B. A man's brain is larger and has more "white matter" than a woman's.

  _MI_ C. When it comes to their brains, men and women are not equal.

  _T_ D. Men's and women's brains.

Group 2

  _MI_ A. Crocodiles have shown a remarkable ability to survive.

  _SD_ B. Crocodile-like creatures have existed for around 200 million years.

  _T_ C. The survival of crocodiles.

  _SD_ D. Crocodiles have been known to survive an entire year without food.

MAIN IDEAS: Mastery Test 5

A. (1–4.) In the group below, one statement is the general point, and the other statements are specific support for the point. Identify the point with a **P** and each statement of support with an **S**.

_____ A. On each square inch of your skin, there are millions of live bacteria.

_MI_ B. Your mouth is home to the "tooth amoeba," a tiny organism that feeds on food and dead cells.

_T_ C. Your body, like those of all humans, is home to many organisms.

_____ D. Tiny mites live in the roots of your eyelashes and feed on dead tissue.

B. (5–12.) Each group of four items includes one topic, one main idea, and two supporting details. In the space provided, label each item with one of the following:

T — for the **topic** of the paragraph
MI — for the **main idea**
SD — for the **supporting details**

Group 1

_____ A. One or two cups of coffee a day will relieve drowsiness and can increase concentration.

_____ B. Drinking a cup of coffee before a workout boosts strength and fights muscle fatigue.

_T_ C. The effects of drinking coffee.

_MI_ D. Coffee, when consumed in reasonable amounts, can produce positive effects on the body.

Group 2

_____ A. Sunglasses that block harmful ultraviolet light were first developed by the space program.

_MI_ B. Surprisingly, the U.S. space program has led to some useful items in everyday life.

_____ C. The material in football helmets and protective padding was first made to protect astronauts in space.

_T_ D. Some unexpected benefits of the U.S. space program.

(Continues on next page)

C. In the space provided, write the letter of the list words in each sentence. (List words are a clue to what supporting details to look for in a paragraph.)

___A___ 13. People who do not vote in national elections give a number of excuses.
    A. *a number of excuses*   C. *people who do not vote*
    B. *national elections*

___C___ 14. To decide whether or not to take a job, consider several key factors.
    A. *To decide*   B. *whether or not*   C. *several key factors*

___B___ 15. One study after another has found that cigarette smoking has long-term effects on the body.
    A. *One study after another*   C. *cigarette smoking*
    B. *long-term effects on the body*

___C___ 16. Advertising should not be permitted on children's television shows for a variety of reasons.
    A. *Advertising should not be permitted*   C. *a variety of reasons*
    B. *children's television shows*

D. Read the following passage. Then, in the space provided, write the letter of the addition words that introduce each supporting detail.

> ¹Illiterate people face great problems in our society. ²For one thing, people who cannot read or write are limited in a world full of print. ³They can't read stories in the newspaper or the menu in a restaurant. ⁴In a supermarket, they must depend on packages with familiar pictures and colors. ⁵In addition, illiterate people do not vote. ⁶As a result, they are "half-citizens" who cannot exercise their democratic rights. ⁷Another problem is in pursuing an education. ⁸Illiterate people find it difficult to take courses that might help them advance in their job or get a better job. ⁹Finally, they have trouble helping their children learn. ¹⁰They are not able to help with homework and often do not visit a school for fear of embarrassing their child or themselves.

___B___ 17. The addition words that signal the first problem of illiterate people are
    A. *limited in a world full of print.*
    B. *For one thing.*
    C. *familiar pictures and colors.*

___C___ 18. The addition words that signal the second problem of illiterate people are
    A. *"half-citizens."*   B. *democratic rights.*   C. *In addition.*

___A___ 19. The addition word that signals the third problem of illiterate people is
    A. *Another.*   B. *education.*   C. *courses.*

___C___ 20. The addition word that signals the fourth problem of illiterate people is
    A. *trouble.*   B. *embarrassing.*   C. *Finally.*

MAIN IDEAS: Mastery Test 6

A. (1–4.) In the group below, one statement is the general point, and the other statements are specific support for the point. Identify the point with a **P** and each statement of support with an **S**.

_____ A. In 1908, a meteor struck a remote region in Russia, destroying thousands of square miles of forest.

_____ B. In March 2004, an asteroid just missed the Earth, passing inside the moon's orbit.

_____ C. There is a real chance that an asteroid will collide with the Earth.

_____ D. In 2028, a mile-wide asteroid—big enough to destroy a continent—is expected to come dangerously close to Earth.

B. (5–12.) Each group of four items includes one topic, one main idea, and two supporting details. In the space provided, label each item with one of the following:

    T — for the **topic** of the paragraph
    MI — for the **main idea**
    SD — for the **supporting details**

Group 1

_____ A. Those exposed to secondhand smoke for 30 years or more are 23 percent more likely to get lung cancer.

_MI_ B. Exposure to secondhand smoke presents a number of serious health hazards to nonsmokers.

_T_ C. Exposure to secondhand smoke.

_____ D. Nonsmokers exposed to secondhand smoke at home have a 15 percent higher death rate than those exposed to clean air.

Group 2

_____ A. Advances in computer technology.

_____ B. E-mail is now used to steal people's identification and credit card information.

_____ C. High-speed Internet connections are used to send harmful viruses around the world.

_____ D. Advances in computer technology have created new tools for criminals.

(Continues on next page)

C. In the space provided, write the letter of the list words in each sentence.

_____C 13. Most mothers cradle their babies in their left arms for several reasons.
    A. *Most mothers*   C. *for several reasons*
    B. *cradle their babies*

_____ 14. Marriage has undergone a number of changes in recent years.
    A. *Marriage*   C. *in recent years*
    B. *a number of changes*

_____ 15. The original versions of famous fairy tales have some shocking outcomes.
    A. *original versions*   C. *some shocking outcomes*
    B. *famous fairy tales*

_____ 16. Although most celebrities would probably not choose different lives, they would agree that fame has some real drawbacks.
    A. *most celebrities*   C. *some real drawbacks*
    B. *different lives*

D. Read the following passage. Then, in the space provided, write the letter of the addition words that introduce each supporting detail.

> [1]There are several parenting styles. [2]The first is the authoritarian style. [3]Authoritarian parents give orders and punish their children if those orders are not quickly obeyed. [4]There is also the authoritative style. [5]Authoritative parents make it clear they are in charge, but they are open to seeing their children's point of view. [6]The next style is that of permissive parents, who avoid ever saying "no" and give the children a good deal of power. [7]The final parenting style is uninvolved. [8]An uninvolved parent does not ask much of children, and does not give much attention either. [9]Most child-raising experts feel that children's needs are best met by authoritative parents.

_____ 17. The addition word that signals the first parenting style is
    A. *several.*   B. *first.*   C. *punish.*

_____ 18. The addition word that signals the second parenting style is
    A. *also.*   B. *but.*   C. *point.*

_____ 19. The addition word that signals the third parenting style is
    A. *permissive.*   B. *avoid.*   C. *next.*

_____ 20. The addition word that signals the fourth parenting style is
    A. *uninvolved.*   B. *final.*   C. *best.*

4 Supporting Details

This Chapter in a Nutshell

- Supporting details are the evidence—such as reasons or examples—that backs up main ideas. Those details help you understand main ideas.

- Outlines and maps (diagrams) can show you a main idea and its supporting details at a glance.

- There are often two levels of supporting details—major and minor.

- List words and addition words can help you find major and minor supporting details.

Look at the following cartoon and see if you can answer the questions that follow.

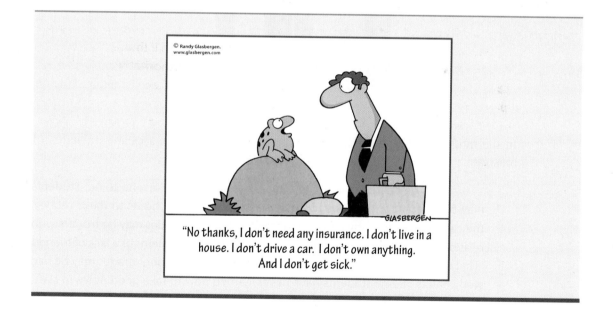

© Randy Glasbergen.
www.glasbergen.com

GLASBERGEN

"No thanks, I don't need any insurance. I don't live in a house. I don't drive a car. I don't own anything. And I don't get sick."

- What is the frog's *main idea*, or point?
- What is his *support* for his point?

Explanation

The frog's main idea, or point, is that he does not need any insurance. He supports his point by providing four reasons he doesn't need any insurance: no house, no car, no possessions, no health worries.

Chapter 3 introduced you to the most important reading skill—the ability to find the main idea. A closely related reading skill is the ability to locate supporting details. Supporting details provide the added information that is needed for you to make sense of a main idea.

What Are Supporting Details?

Supporting details are reasons, examples, steps, or other kinds of evidence that explain a main idea, or point.

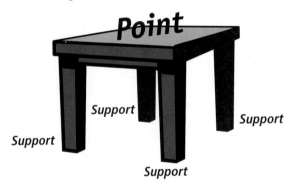

In the model paragraph in Chapter 3, the supporting details appear as a series of reasons:

> ¹Poor grades in school can have various causes. ²For one thing, students may have financial problems. ³If they need to work long hours to make money, they will have little study time. ⁴Another cause of poor grades may be trouble with relationships. ⁵A student may be unhappy over family problems or a lack of friends. ⁶That unhappiness can harm schoolwork. ⁷A final cause of poor grades may be bad study habits. ⁸Some students have never learned how to take good notes in class, how to manage their time effectively, or how to study a textbook. ⁹Without such study skills, their grades are likely to suffer.

✓ *Check Your Understanding*

See if you can complete the basic outline below that shows the three reasons that support the main idea. The first one has been added for you. Then read the explanation that follows.

> **Main idea: Poor grades in school can have various causes.**
>
> Supporting detail 1: Financial problems
>
> Supporting detail 2: _____
>
> Supporting detail 3: _____

Explanation

You should have added "Trouble with relationships" and "Bad study habits" as the two other supporting details. Notice that the supporting details provide the added information—the specific causes of poor grades—that is needed for you to fully understand the main idea. To read effectively, then, you must recognize both main ideas and the details that support those ideas.

In the paragraph on the previous page, about poor grades, the supporting details are *reasons*. Now look at the paragraph below, in which the main idea is explained by *examples*. In the outline provided, write in the main idea and the words that serve as examples.

> [1]Love them or hate them, smartphones have changed our lives in a number of ways. [2]To begin with, we can connect with friends and family instantly, no matter where we are. [3]In fact, we can show them pictures, even video, of what we're doing at any given moment. [4]We no longer have to wait until we can "get to a phone" or see someone in person to share our exciting lives. [5]Next, these small handheld gadgets take the place of many tools that we might otherwise have to drag around with us wherever we go. [6]Consider that a smartphone is a GPS, map, camera, computer, music player, video recorder, and even a flashlight—all in a handy little rectangular piece of metal or plastic. [7]Barely twenty years ago, a single road map would have taken up more space than a phone does today. [8]Finally, smartphones can be newsmakers! [9]Think about it. [10]How often is something that is captured on a phone noteworthy enough to make national news? [11]It happens multiple times a day. [12]Thieves have been caught, crimes solved, fires and floods captured, and inventions revealed thanks to these little electronic wonders. [13]They really *are* smart phones.

Main idea: _____

> Supporting detail 1: _____
>
> Supporting detail 2: _____
>
> Supporting detail 3: _____

Explanation

The main idea is the first sentence of the paragraph, and the supporting details are the three examples given: instant connection with friends and family, many tools in one, and newsmakers.

Outlining

Preparing an outline of a passage will help you clearly see the relationship between a main idea and its supporting details. Notice how the outlines on this page and the next page help you see and understand material at a glance.

Outlines are lists that show the important parts of a piece of writing. They begin with a main idea, with supporting details placed, in order, underneath the main idea. There may be two levels of supporting details—major and minor. The **major details** explain and develop the main idea. In turn, the **minor details** under them help fill out and make clear the major details.

Once you know how to outline, you can use the skill to prepare very useful study notes. Instead of studying fact after fact in sentence after sentence, you can organize the material into outlines. Good outlines clearly tie ideas together, making them easier to understand and remember.

Below is a more detailed outline of the paragraph on poor grades. This outline shows both major and minor details:

Main idea: Poor grades in school can have various causes.

Major detail: 1. Financial problems
   Minor details: a. Need to work long hours after school
                          b. No time left to study

Major detail: 2. Trouble with relationships
   Minor details: a. Unhappiness over family problems
                          b. Unhappiness over a lack of friends

Major detail: 3. Bad study habits
   Minor details: a. No skill in taking class notes
                          b. No skill in time management
                          c. No skill in studying a textbook

The main idea is supported and explained by the major details, and in turn the major details are supported and explained by the minor details. For example, the major detail of "bad study habits" is supported by three details: no skill in notetaking, time management, or textbook studying.

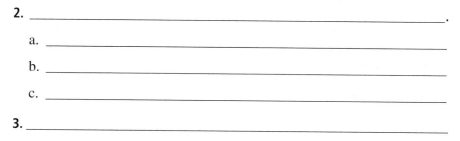

Check Your Understanding

See if you can fill in the missing major and minor supporting details in the outline of the following paragraph.

> ¹To motivate workers, managers should practice several methods of building self-esteem. ²One way to build self-esteem is to show a genuine interest in what workers have to say. ³Ask for their opinions, and really listen to their responses. ⁴A second method of improving self-esteem is to practice good conversational habits. ⁵Do so in three ways: by looking a worker in the eye, by smiling frequently, and by calling workers by their first name—the most important word in the language to every person. ⁶Last of all, managers can build esteem by admitting mistakes. ⁷Doing so, they show that it is simply human to do the wrong thing at times.

Main idea: **To motivate workers, managers should practice several methods of building self-esteem.**

1. Show genuine interest in what workers have to say.
  a. Ask for their opinions.
  b. Really listen to their responses.

2. _____.
  a. _____
  b. _____
  c. _____

3. _____

Explanation

You should have added two major details: (2) practice good conversational habits; (3) admit mistakes. And below the second major supporting detail, you should have added three minor details: (a) look a worker in the eye; (b) smile frequently; (c) call workers by first name.

Notice that just as the main idea is more general than its supporting details, major details are more general than minor ones. For instance, the major detail "to practice good conversational habits" is more general than the three minor supporting details: looking a worker in the eye, smiling, and using first names.

Outlining Tips

The following tips will help you prepare outlines:

 TIP 1   **Look for words that tell you a list of details is coming.** List words were introduced in Chapter 3 on page 128. Here are some common list words:

List Words

several kinds of	various causes	a few reasons
a number of	a series of	three factors
four steps	among the results	several advantages

For example, look again at the main ideas in two of the paragraphs already discussed, and circle the list words:

- Poor grades in school can have various causes.
- To motivate workers, managers should practice several methods of building self-esteem.

Explanation

In the main ideas above, the words *various causes* and *several methods* tell us that a list of major details is coming. You will not always be given such helpful signals that a list of details will follow. However, be ready to take advantage of them when they are present. Such list words can help you quickly understand the basic organization of a passage.

TIP 2   **Look for words that signal major details.** Such words are called **addition words**, and they were also introduced in Chapter 3 on pages 129–130. Here are some common addition words:

Addition Words

one	to begin with	in addition	last
first	another	next	last of all
first of all	second	moreover	final
for one thing	also	furthermore	finally

✓ *Check Your Understanding*

Now look again at the selection on poor grades, shown below, and answer the questions that follow.

> ¹Poor grades in school can have various causes. ²For one thing, students may have financial problems. ³If they need to work long hours to make money, they will have little study time. ⁴Another cause of poor grades may be trouble with relationships. ⁵A student may be unhappy over family problems or a lack of friends. ⁶That unhappiness can harm schoolwork. ⁷A final cause of poor grades may be bad study habits. ⁸Some students have never learned how to take good notes in class, how to manage their time effectively, or how to study a textbook. ⁹Without such study skills, their grades are likely to suffer.

- Which words signal the first major detail? _____
- Which word signals the second major detail? _____
- Which word signals the third major detail? _____

Look also at the selection on motivating workers, shown below, and answer the questions that follow.

> ¹To motivate workers, managers should practice several methods of building self-esteem. ²One way to build self-esteem is to show a genuine interest in what workers have to say. ³Ask for their opinions and really listen to their responses. ⁴A second method of improving self-esteem is to practice good conversational habits. ⁵Do so in three ways: by looking a worker in the eye, by smiling frequently, and by calling workers by their first name—the most important word in the language to every person. ⁶Last of all, managers can build esteem by admitting mistakes. ⁷Doing so, they show that it is simply human to do the wrong thing at times.

- Which word signals the first major detail? _____
- Which word signals the second major detail? _____
- Which words signal the third major detail? _____

Explanation

In the first selection, on poor grades, the addition word signals are *For one thing, Another,* and *final*. In the second selection, on motivating workers, the word signals are *One, second,* and *Last of all*.

TIP **TIP 3**   In your outline, put all supporting details of equal importance at the same distance from the margin. In the outline of the paragraph on poor grades (page 158), the three major supporting details all begin at the same distance from the left margin. Likewise, the minor supporting details are all indented at a slightly greater distance from the margin. You can therefore see at a glance the main idea, the major details, and the minor details.

✓ ## Check Your Understanding

Put appropriate numbers (*1, 2, 3*) and letters (*a, b, c*) in front of the major and minor details in the following outline.

> **Main idea**
> ____ **Major detail**
> > ____ Minor detail
> > ____ Minor detail
> ____ **Major detail**
> > ____ Minor detail
> > ____ Minor detail
> ____ **Major detail**

Explanation

You should have put a *1, 2,* and *3* in front of the major details and an *a* and *b* in front of the minor details. Note that an outline proceeds from the most general to the most specific, from main idea to major details to minor details.

The practice that follows will give you experience in finding major details, in separating major details from minor details, and in preparing outlines.

> *Hint:* As you read each passage in this practice and those that follow, circle the list words and underline the addition words. Another helpful technique is to number the major details in each passage *1, 2, 3,* etc.

PRACTICE 1

Read each passage. Then complete the outline that follows by filling in the missing major and minor details. (Some details have been added for you.) Finally, answer the questions that follow each outline.

Passage 1

[1]We all enjoy buying a new shirt or book or phone app. [2]According to experts, though, some people show signs of addiction to shopping. [3]One such sign is that a shopper develops serious money problems. [4]Checks are bounced, or credit card debt becomes so great that the minimum payment cannot be made each month. [5]A second sign of a shopping addict is a distinct mood pattern. [6]Before shopping, tension builds up in the addict as he or she looks forward to a "fix." [7]After shopping, there is a pleasant release from that tension, and for a time the shopper will feel happy and at rest. [8]Another sign of a shopping addict is shoplifting, especially if this has not been a behavior of the person in the past. [9]Last of all, a shopping addict often suffers from other addictive behaviors, such as overeating, overdrinking, or frequent gambling.

Main idea: Some people show signs of addiction to shopping.

1. _serious money problems_

   a. _checks bounce_

   b. _minimum monthly payments_

2. _____

   a. _____

   b. After shopping, a pleasant release from tension

3. _____

4. _____

Questions about the passage

● Which words in the main idea tell you that a list is coming?

_____

● Which word signals the first major detail?_____

● Which word signals the second major detail? _____

● Which word signals the third major detail? _____

● Which words signal the fourth major detail? _____

Passage 2

¹There are several advantages to watching a football game or other sports event on television instead of going to the game itself. ²One advantage is that it's cheaper to watch a game at home. ³Going to a sports event can cost at least $50 for parking and an admission ticket. ⁴Then it's all too easy to spend an added $30 for drinks and snacks. ⁵Moreover, it's more comfortable at home. ⁶There is no bumper-to-bumper traffic to and from a sports arena or stadium. ⁷There are no noisy, pushy crowds of people to deal with while trying to get to one's seat, which is made out of uncomfortably hard plastic or wood. ⁸Finally, watching a game on television is more informative. ⁹Camera coverage is so good that every play is seen close up, and many plays are shown on instant replay. ¹⁰At the same time, the game is explained in great detail by very informed commentators. ¹¹The fan at home always enjoys an insider's view about what is happening in the game at every minute.

Main idea: There are several advantages to watching a football game or other sports event on television instead of going to the game itself.

1. _____.

    a. $50 for parking and admission to event

    b. _____

2. _____.

    a. _____

    b. No noisy, pushy crowds or hard seats

3. _____.

    a. _____

    b. _____

Questions about the passage

● Which words in the main idea tell you that a list of details is coming?

_____

● Which word signals the first major detail? _____

● Which word signals the second major detail? _____

● Which word signals the third major detail? _____

Preparing Maps

Students sometimes find it helpful to use maps rather than outlines. **Maps**, or diagrams, are highly visual outlines in which circles, boxes, or other shapes show the relationship between main ideas and supporting details. Each major detail is connected to the main idea. If minor details are included, each is connected to the major detail it explains.

✔ *Check Your Understanding*

Read the following passage, and then see if you can complete the map and answer the questions that follow.

[1]People daydream for a variety of reasons. [2]One cause of daydreaming is boredom, at school or on the job. [3]To make life more interesting, people imagine being somewhere else. [4]For example, a student might dream of lying on the beach and flirting with an attractive person on a nearby blanket. [5]A production worker might dream about winning the lottery or becoming the big boss at the company. [6]Another cause of daydreaming is a lack of something. [7]For instance, a starving person might dream about food, or a poor person might dream about owning a house or a car. [8]A third cause of daydreaming is angry feelings. [9]An angry student might dream about getting a hated math instructor fired.

People daydream for a variety of reasons.

Example: Worker dreams about winning the lottery.

Example: Poor person dreams about owning a car.

Example: Angry student dreams about getting instructor fired.

Questions about the passage

● Which words in the main idea tell you that a list of details is coming?

_____

● Which word signals the first major detail? _____

● Which word signals the second major detail? _____

● Which word signals the third major detail? _____

Explanation

In the main idea above, the words *a variety of reasons* tell us that a list of major details is coming.

The word signals for the three major reasons are *One, Another,* and *third.* The map also includes minor details in the form of examples.

PRACTICE 2

Read each passage. Then complete the map that follows by filling in the missing major details. Finally, answer the questions that follow each map.

Passage 1

¹To complain to people and still keep them as friends, follow several sensible guidelines for criticism. ²First, be specific. ³Don't say, "Your behavior at the dinner was awful!" ⁴Instead, say, "You embarrassed me by getting drunk and loud and telling off-color jokes to my parents." ⁵Second, stick to the present. ⁶Hauling up old offenses from last month or last year just takes away attention from the problem at hand. ⁷In addition, don't use insults. ⁸Calling someone names like "idiot" or "animal" will only create anger and hurt any chance of getting the person to listen to you. ⁹The last guideline is to complain privately. ¹⁰Never criticize a person in front of friends, parents, children, or anyone else, for that matter. ¹¹Criticizing in front of others has the same effect as insults. ¹²It shames the person being criticized and makes it likely that he or she will want to put you down rather than listen to you.

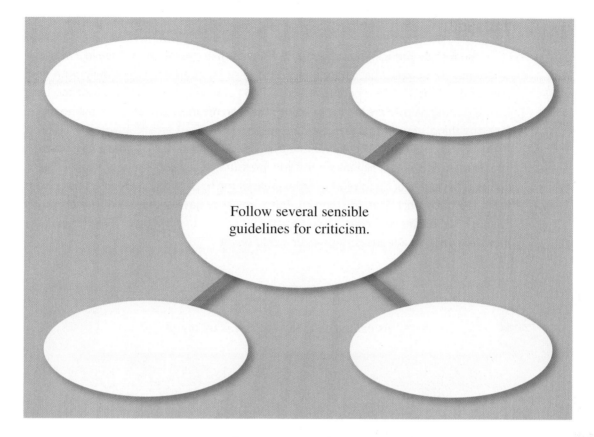

Follow several sensible guidelines for criticism.

Questions about the passage

● Which words in the main idea tell you that a list of details is coming?

_____

● Which word signals the first major detail? _____

● Which word signals the second major detail? _____

● Which words signal the third major detail? _____

● Which word signals the fourth major detail? _____

Passage 2

¹Some heart attacks are sudden and intense—like ones we might see in a movie—where no one doubts what's happening. ²But most heart attacks start slowly, with mild pain or discomfort. ³Often people affected aren't sure what's wrong and wait too long before getting help. ⁴Here are various signs that can mean a heart attack is taking place. ⁵For one thing, you may have chest discomfort. ⁶Most heart attacks involve discomfort in the center of the chest that lasts more than a few minutes, or that goes away but then comes back. ⁷It can feel like uncomfortable pressure, squeezing, fullness or pain. ⁸Next, you may have pain or discomfort in other areas of the upper body, including one or both arms, the back, neck, jaw, or stomach. ⁹Also, you may have shortness of breath. ¹⁰This feeling often comes with chest discomfort, but it can occur without it. ¹¹Finally, you may experience lightheadedness, nausea, or a cold sweat.

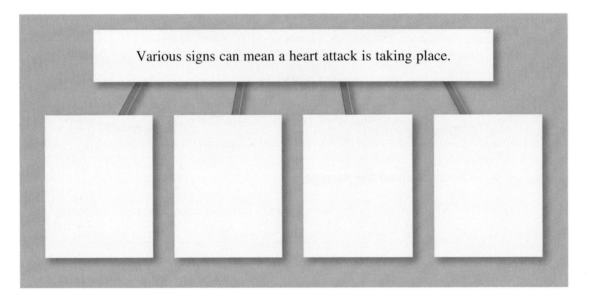

Various signs can mean a heart attack is taking place.

Questions about the passage

● Which words in the main idea tell you that a list of details is coming?

_____

● Which words signal the first major detail? _____

● Which word signals the second major detail? _____

● Which word signals the third major detail? _____

● Which word signals the final major details? _____

A Final Note

This chapter has centered on supporting details as they appear in well-organized paragraphs. But keep in mind that supporting details are part of readings of any length, including selections that may not have an easy-to-follow list of one major detail after another. Starting with the reading at the end of this chapter (page 173), you will be given practice in answering all kinds of questions about key supporting details. These questions will develop your ability to pay close, careful attention to what you are reading.

CHAPTER REVIEW

In this chapter, you learned the following:

- Supporting details go hand in hand with main ideas. They provide the added information you need to make sense of a main idea.
- There are often two levels of supporting details—major and minor.
- List words and addition words can help you to find major and minor supporting details.
- Outlining and mapping are useful note-taking strategies.
- Outlines and maps, or diagrams, show the relationship between the main idea, major details, and minor details of a passage.

The next chapter—Chapter 5—will deepen your understanding of the relationship between main ideas and supporting details.

 On the Web: If you are using this book in class, you can visit our website for additional practice in identifying supporting details. Go to **www.townsendpress. com** and click on "Learning Center."

REVIEW TEST 1

To review what you've learned in this chapter, fill in the blank or write the letter of your answer.

1. Two closely related skills are finding the main idea and identifying the

   major and minor ___Details___ that support the main idea.

2. Supporting details are reasons, examples, facts, steps, or other kinds of evidence that explain a ___main idea___ .

3. A ___map___ is a highly visual outline; it shows at a glance the relationship between a main idea and its supporting details.

___B___ 4. Words such as *several reasons, a number of factors,* and *three advantages* tell you that a series of details is coming. Such words are known as
   A. addition words.   B. list words.

___A___ 5. Words such as *first, also, another,* and *finally* often tell you that a new supporting detail is being introduced. Such words are known as
   A. addition words.   B. list words.

REVIEW TEST 2

A. Complete the outline below by filling in the missing major details. Then answer the questions that follow the outline.

[1]Researchers have learned that people lie for five main reasons. [2]The primary reason is to prevent discomfort. [3]For example, if a coworker asked, "Do you like my new haircut?" you might say yes even if you hate it, to avoid hurting his or her feelings. [4]Another common reason for lying is to avoid conflict. [5]If a friend angers you and asks, "Are you upset with me?" you might answer "No" to avoid a scene. [6]People also lie as a way of being socially acceptable. [7]For instance, they might say "That's interesting" when they actually find another person's conversation boring. [8]In addition, people lie to increase or decrease interaction with someone. [9]Many people rid themselves of undesired company with the lie "I have to go now." [10]Finally, people lie to have greater control over a situation. [11]For example, if someone asks you out at the last minute and you have nothing planned, you might still say "I have other plans" in order to be the one "in charge."

Main idea: People lie for five main reasons.

1. Prevent discomfort
2. Avoid conflict
3. to increase or decrease interaction
4. To have greater control
5. socially acceptable

B. Now answer the following questions about the passage you have outlined.

6. Which words tell you that a list of details is coming? _____

_____

7. Which word introduces the second major detail? _____

8. Which word introduces the third major detail? _____

9. Which words introduce the fourth major detail? _____

10. Which word introduces the last major detail? _____

 REVIEW TEST 3

A. (1–4.) Fill in the major details and one minor detail needed to complete the map below.

> [1]Colonial Americans experienced a number of dangerous medical treatments. [2]One of the most popular was bloodletting. [3]This involved cutting a patient's skin and allowing him or her to bleed enough to remove the cause of the disease. [4]Sometimes so much blood was lost that patients died. [5]Another harmful treatment used in colonial America was "sweating." [6]A patient would be kept in a small, hot room, covered in the heaviest clothing and blankets available. [7]The result was extreme weakness, heat exhaustion, and sometimes death. [8]A third harmful colonial treatment was purging. [9]Patients would be forced to swallow syrup that made them vomit in order to remove poison believed to be in the body. [10]With all these treatments, the "cure" was usually worse than the disease.

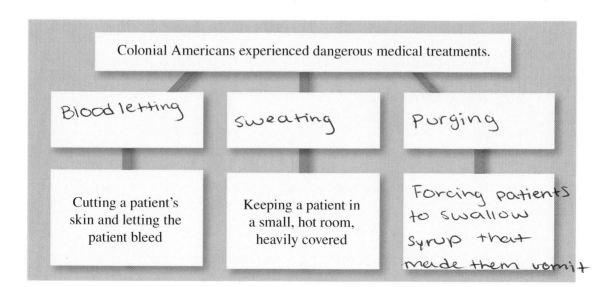

Colonial Americans experienced dangerous medical treatments.

Bloodletting

Sweating

Purging

Cutting a patient's skin and letting the patient bleed

Keeping a patient in a small, hot room, heavily covered

Forcing patients to swallow syrup that made them vomit

B. **(5.)**   What are the list words that tell you a series of details is coming?

_____

REVIEW TEST 4

Here is a chance to apply your understanding of supporting details to an excerpt from a recent autobiography. The author, Roxanne Black, describes her reactions when, as a teenager, she learned she had an incurable disease. Read the selection, and then answer the questions that follow about its supporting details.

To help you continue to strengthen your work on skills taught in previous chapters, there are also questions on vocabulary in context and main ideas.

Words to Watch

Below are some words in the reading that do not have strong context support. Each word is followed by the number of the paragraph in which it appears and its meaning there. These words are indicated in the selection by a small circle (°).

>   *foreboding* (15): a feeling that something bad is going to happen
>   *chronic* (18): lasting for a long time; continuing to occur
>   *remission* (21): lessening of the symptoms of a disease
>   *terse* (30): brief and to the point
>   *biopsy* (32): the removal of sample tissue for laboratory examination
>   *intoned* (37): said something in a slow and serious way
>   *muster* (39): gather

A DOOR SWINGS OPEN

Roxanne Black

1   I sat at my bedroom window in my wheelchair, watching my high-school rowing team pull away from the shore, eight friends smiling and waving as they moved into the choppy water. Not long ago, I'd been one of them.

2   I loved everything about rowing: the feeling of freedom, the teamwork, the sense of strength and accomplishment. When I rowed, I was at peace and forgot about my problems. Not that I'd had many then. In most ways, I was a typical New Jersey teenager, a shy high-school freshman who lived with her mother in a small row house that overlooked Lake's Bay. My mother and I didn't have two dimes to rub together, but with that view from our windows, we considered ourselves rich.

3   It was after rowing one afternoon that I had the first warning that something might be wrong with me—a sharp stab of back pain that took my breath away.

4   "What's the matter?" my mother asked when she saw me wincing.

5   "I don't know," I said, stretching. "I guess I strained a muscle."

6   By evening, the pain was almost too painful to bear. My mother filled a hot bath with Epsom salts, and later gave me a heating pad. I took a couple of Tylenol and decided I'd stay away from crew practice for a few days. In my young life, this had been the antidote for any ailment. Eventually everything passed, given time and a little rest.

7   But not this time. Instead of decreasing, the pain grew so intense that I could barely sit up in bed the next morning.

8   My mother took one look at me and said, "I'm taking you to the doctor."

9   But by the time we arrived at the office, the pain had subsided; and the doctor advised that we simply continue with the heating pad and baths.

10   Two days later, I developed chest pains that by evening were so acute I could barely breathe. Now I was beginning to worry.

11   This time the doctor prescribed antibiotics, thinking I might have an infection. The pains intensified over the next few days; then they too vanished.

12   This pattern of new symptoms that appeared, intensified, then vanished continued with an itchy red rash, which covered my body. After it mysteriously disappeared, my ankles swelled so severely that I was unable to fit into any of my shoes.

13   Although the doctor tracked my reports, took bloodwork, and examined me closely, he couldn't figure out what was wrong. My symptoms were elusive; it was hard to pin them down.

14   Finally he referred me to a specialist. By the day of my appointment, all my symptoms had subsided except for my swollen ankles. My mother and I arrived at his office, expecting this new doctor would prescribe another medication for what was probably an allergic reaction.

15   Although I'd never seen this

doctor's face before, his cool, sober expression as we walked in gave me a sense of foreboding°.

16   After a routine examination, he studied my bloodwork, then touched my ankles, which were so full of fluid they could be molded like lumps of clay.

17   Then he looked up and a strange word floated from his mouth. Lupus. I saw it, like in a cartoon caption, odd and ominous, hanging in the air.

18   The word meant nothing to me, but my mother's reaction did; she covered her face with her hands. In her work as a nurse, she'd spent years caring for patients with chronic° illness. As I watched her sniff and take out a Kleenex, it hit me that this must be serious, something that Tylenol and bed rest weren't going to solve.

19   My health had always been part of my identity, something I was as certain of as my strong legs and pumping heart. Now I was being told baffling facts about kidney function, inflammation, and antibodies.

20   But when the doctor said I was to be admitted to a children's hospital in Philadelphia the following day for testing, I realized a chapter of my life was suddenly ending and a new one was about to start.

21   When I returned home, I looked up lupus in our medical dictionary: a chronic autoimmune disease, potentially weakening and sometimes fatal, that was first discovered in the Middle Ages. The illness follows an unpredictable course, with episodes of activity, called flares, alternating with periods of remission°. During a flare, the immune system attacks the body's cells

and tissue, resulting in inflammation and tissue damage.

22   The words "sometimes fatal" stood out to me, as if they were written in blood. Just as alarming were the lists of possible signs: dermatological, musculoskeletal, hematological, renal, hepatic, pulmonary. What else was there?

23   How had this ancient disease—that only affected one in many hundreds in the United States—ended up in Atlantic City, residing in a teenager like me?

24   For that, there was no answer.

25   "There's always one moment in childhood when the door opens and lets the future in," Graham Greene wrote. I don't know if most people remember that moment, but I do.

26   At the children's hospital, I shared a room with a three-year-old girl with a charming face and shiny black hair cut in a bob. She was so energetic and lively, I assumed she was someone's daughter

or sister, until I glimpsed a tiny hospital ID bracelet on her wrist.

27 Her name was Michelle, and we bonded from the moment we met. She brought a herd of plastic ponies to my bedside, and we brushed their manes and made up stories.

28 "Why's she here?" I asked when her parents arrived, looking drawn and worried.

29 "She has a hole in her heart," her mother told me. "She's having open-heart surgery tomorrow."

30 A steady stream of doctors arrived to talk to Michelle's parents. I heard the terse° murmur of their voices behind the curtain that separated our room. Through it all, Michelle dashed between the beds, oblivious to the drama around her. She was so vital and energetic, it was hard to believe that anything serious was wrong with her.

31 I'd never known a sick child before, and now I was in a hospital full of them. It seemed unnatural seeing toddlers on IV's, babies on ventilators, adolescents with leg braces, struggling to walk. A parade of pediatric malfunction passed my door, children smashed in motor accidents, suffering from muscular dystrophy and leukemia. This alternate world had existed all along, behind my formerly sunny, innocent life.

32 The next day I was to find out the results of my kidney biopsy°, and Michelle was headed to surgery. Before she left, she walked over and hugged me so tightly that I could smell the baby shampoo in her hair. Then she solemnly handed me a drawing she'd made of a house, a girl, and a tree.

33 "This is you, isn't it?"

34 She nodded.

35 "Well it's beautiful, thanks. I'll see you later."

36 I waited all day for them to bring Michelle back, trying to distract myself by reading and crocheting, but it was no use. Breakfast came and went, then lunch, and still there was no sign of her.

37 Early in the evening, I was talking on the pay phone in the hallway when an alarm sounded, and doctors began running down the hall from all directions. A woman's voice intoned° a code over the loudspeakers, a foreign babble.

38 As I hung up, I saw two new figures running down the hallway. Their features grew terribly familiar as they approached. It was Michelle's parents, their faces smeared with tears, heading in the same direction as the doctors.

39 My mother came out and hurried me back into the room. When she shut the door, I stood there, looking at Michelle's bed, at the picture on the table she had drawn for me. I took out a little prayer book I'd brought along and began a prayer, filling it with all the love and intention I could muster°. A long, terrible female scream pierced the silence.

40 A young floor nurse walked in a short while later. Her sad face was statement enough, but then she told us. Michelle hadn't made it. She'd suffered a heart attack and died.

41 So there it was, and I had to face it: Life wasn't fair. Prayers weren't always answered. The young and innocent could be lost. The door had swung open, and I had been pushed through to the other side.

Reading Comprehension Questions

Vocabulary in Context

_B_ 1. In the excerpt below, the word *antidote* (ăn′tĭ-dōt′) means
   A. explanation.
   B. cure.
   C. cause.
   D. symptom.

> "I took a couple of Tylenol and decided I'd stay away from crew practice for a few days. In my young life, this had been the antidote for any ailment." (Paragraph 6)

_A_ 2. In the excerpt below, the word *subsided* (səb-sīd′-əd) means
   A. became less.
   B. gotten worse.
   C. returned.
   D. stayed the same.

> "My mother took one look at me and said, 'I'm taking you to the doctor.'
>
> "But by the time we arrived at the office, the pain had subsided; and the doctor advised that we simply continue with the heating pad and baths." (Paragraphs 8–9)

_B_ 3. In the sentence below, the word *acute* (ə-kyoōt′) means
   A. effortless.
   B. sharp.
   C. mild.
   D. predictable.

> "Two days later, I developed chest pains that by evening were so acute I could barely breathe." (Paragraph 10)

_D_ 4. In the excerpt below, the word *elusive* (ə-loo′sĭv) means
   A. difficult to treat.
   B. difficult to see.
   C. difficult to forget.
   D. difficult to identify.

> "Although the doctor tracked my reports, took bloodwork, and examined me closely, he couldn't figure out what was wrong. My symptoms were elusive; it was hard to pin them down." (Paragraph 13)

_A_ 5. In the excerpt below, the words *oblivious to* (ə-blĭv′ē-əs tōō) mean
  A. unaware of.
  B. saddened by.
  C. confused by.
  D. conscious of.

> "A steady stream of doctors arrived to talk to Michelle's parents. I heard the terse murmur of their voices behind the curtain that separated our room. Through it all, Michelle dashed between the beds, oblivious to the drama around her." (Paragraph 30)

Central Point

_D_ 6. The central idea of the selection is that
  A. Black was shocked to learn that she had a chronic disease.
  B. Black was saddened when a little girl she met in the hospital died.
  C. before becoming ill with lupus, Black had been in excellent health.
  D. as the result of her own chronic illness and the death of a child, Black realized that life isn't fair.

Main Ideas

_C_ 7. Which sentence best expresses the main idea of paragraph 2?
  A. When Black rowed, she forgot about her problems.
  B. Black lived with her mother in a small row house overlooking Lake's Bay.
  C. In most ways, Black, who loved rowing, was a typical teenager.
  D. Although Black and her mother didn't have much money, they considered themselves rich.

Supporting Details

_D_ 8. Black first thought the intense pain she was experiencing was
  A. an insect bite.
  B. an allergic reaction.
  C. an infection.
  D. a muscle strain.

_C_ 9. When the doctor tells Black she has lupus, her mother
  A. tells the doctor he's wrong.
  B. screams and then breaks out into loud sobs.
  C. covers her face with her hands and takes out a Kleenex.
  D. says she knew it all along.

_B_ 10. Michelle was in the hospital because she had
    A. leukemia.
    B. a hole in her heart.
    C. a brain tumor.
    D. been injured in an auto accident.

Discussion Questions

1. When Black enters the hospital, she becomes aware of an "alternate world" that "had existed all along, behind my formerly sunny, innocent life." What is this "alternate world"? What, in particular, does she find surprising about it?

2. Black quotes Graham Greene, who wrote, "There's always one moment in childhood when the door opens and lets the future in." What might this statement mean? According to Black's story, when did this experience happen to her? Why do you think she was so upset afterward?

3. Have you ever known anyone who, like Black, suffers from chronic illness? If so, how does it affect his or her life? What adjustments has the person made in order to live with this condition?

4. Do you remember a moment in _your_ life when "the door opened and let the future in"? Describe the event, and explain what it made you realize.

Note: Writing assignments for this selection appear on page 606.

Check Your Performance   **SUPPORTING DETAILS**

Activity	_Number Right_	_Points_	_Score_
Review Test 1 (5 items)	_____	× 2 =	_____
Review Test 2 (10 items)	_____	× 3 =	_____
Review Test 3 (5 items)	_____	× 6 =	_____
Review Test 4 (10 items)	_____	× 3 =	_____
		TOTAL SCORE =	_____%

Enter your total score into the **Reading Performance Chart: Review Tests** on the inside back cover.

SUPPORTING DETAILS: Mastery Test 1

A. (1–6.) Complete the outline below by filling in the missing major details. Then answer the questions that follow the outline.

> ¹If you are like most people, you feel that writing is not one of your talents and there's nothing you can do about it. ²The truth is that some common-sense tips can help you become a better writer. ³First of all, write often. ⁴Like other crafts, writing improves with practice. ⁵Also, organize your material with an outline. ⁶An outline will provide you with a good guideline without limiting you, as you can change it at any time. ⁷Next, write in a plain style. ⁸Don't try to use overly fancy language. ⁹Instead, just say what you mean simply and clearly. ¹⁰Finally, tighten your writing. ¹¹Nothing improves writing more than eliminating unnecessary words.

Main idea: Some common-sense tips can help you become a better writer.

1. _____

2. _____

3. _____

4. _____

Questions about the passage

5. Which addition words introduce the first major detail?

   _____

6. Which addition word introduces the second major detail?

   _____

(Continues on next page)

B. (7–10.) Fill in the major details needed to complete the map below.

[1]The 14th-century Italian poet Dante is probably best known for a work called *The Inferno.* [2]In it, he writes of visiting the nine circles of Hell. [3]As he goes down from each level to an even deeper one, he sees the worst of all evildoers. [4]Here are candidates for the people Dante might put in the lowest levels of Hell if he were writing today. [5]I think that child molesters would be suitable for the seventh circle of Hell. [6]Any person who would coldly rob a child of his or her innocence, trust, and physical and emotional well-being deserves no better. [7]Next, to the eighth circle, I would send selfish politicians who sit in comfortable offices and make decisions that send young men and women off to die in needless wars. [8]Politicians must be willing to fight those wars themselves—and send their own sons and daughters into battle—before they declare war. [9]Last, in the lowest circle of Hell, I would place terrorists of every nationality, faith, or cause. [10]There is no moral justification for spreading fear, death, and suffering as the bodies of the innocent are blown apart. [11]The lowest circle of Hell is the only place fit for terrorists.

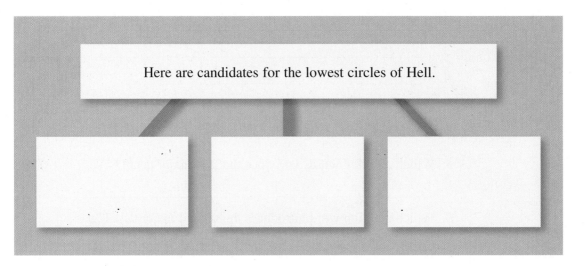

Here are candidates for the lowest circles of Hell.

10. Which two addition words introduce the people in the eighth and ninth circles?

_____   _____

SUPPORTING DETAILS: Mastery Test 2

A. (1–6.) Complete the outline below by filling in the missing major details.

¹There are a number of ways to tell if a person has a drug problem. ²First, a drug abuser cannot stop using or drinking. ³Secondly, the person turns into a "different" person when she or he is using the drug, acting in unusual ways. ⁴Another signal is that the user makes excuses for using drugs. ⁵He or she will say that it was an especially bad day at school or work, or that a relationship has become very stressful. ⁶Fourth, an abuser will try to cover up drug use, or will pretend that it "isn't that bad." ⁷Yet another signal is that the abuser will forget things that happen while he or she is high or drunk. ⁸Finally, the abuser will be the last to recognize that he or she has a problem.

Main idea: There are ways to tell if a person has a drug problem.

1. _cannot stop using or drinking_

2. _Turns into a "different" person_

3. _user makes excuses_

4. _abuser will try to cover up_

5. _Abuser will forget things_

6. _Abuser will be the last to recognize that they have a problem._

B. (7–10.) Fill in the major details needed to complete the map below. Then answer the question that follows the map.

[1]Experts have several theories to explain why people yawn. [2]One explanation is that yawns help boost oxygen levels in the blood. [3]By forcing the body to breathe deeply, yawns increase airflow to the lungs and rush oxygen to the bloodstream. [4]A second theory is that yawns help the body change its level of alertness. [5]It is for this reason yawns happen whether a person is waking up or getting sleepy. [6]Yet another explanation is that yawns, like stretches, give the body exercise. [7]When a person yawns, blood pressure and heart rate gently increase and muscles flex. [8]No matter what the cause for yawning, one thing is clear. [9]Fifty-five percent of the people who read this paragraph will yawn in less than five minutes.

Several theories explain why people yawn.

yawns help boost oxygen levels in the blood

yawns help the body change its level of alertness

yawns, like stretches, give the body exercise

10. What are **two** of the addition words used to set off the major details in the passage?

    One   *second*

SUPPORTING DETAILS: Mastery Test 3

A. (1–6.) Complete the outline below by filling in the missing major and minor details. Some details have been added for you.

> [1]There are several guidelines you can follow to avoid being bitten by a dog. [2]First of all, don't trust appearances. [3]A dog with a wagging tail isn't always friendly. [4]Even small dogs that look harmless can deliver a painful bite. [5]Secondly, be cautious. [6]Allow a dog to see and sniff you before you pet it. [7]Be especially careful around a dog when it's eating, sleeping, or caring for puppies. [8]Next, watch for warning signs. [9]Dogs that stare at you with their heads lowered are probably unfriendly. [10]Likewise, a dog that growls or shows its teeth should be avoided. [11]Fourth, learn defensive strategies to prevent a dog from biting you. [12]For example, stand still with arms at your sides if you find yourself facing an angry dog. [13]Also, avoid eye contact with the dangerous animal so that it knows you are not challenging it.

Main idea: **There are several guidelines you can follow to avoid being bitten by a dog.**

1. *Don't trust appearances*

   a. *A dog w/a wagging tail isn't always friendly*

   b. Small harmless-looking dogs can deliver a painful bite.

2. *Be cautious*

   a. *Allow a dog to see / sniff you*

   b. Be especially careful around a dog that's eating, sleeping, or caring for puppies.

3. *Warning signs*

   a. *Dogs that stare at you with their heads lowered are probably unfriendly*

   b. Dogs that growl or show their teeth should be avoided.

4. Learn defensive strategies.

   a. Stand still with arms at your sides if you face an angry dog.

   b. Avoid eye contact with a dangerous dog.

(Continues on next page)

B. (7–10.) Fill in the major details needed to complete the map below. Then answer the question that follows the map.

> ¹Practically everyone needs to complain at times about a product or service that has been unsatisfactory. ²It is helpful, then, to keep in mind some steps for effective written complaints. ³First, always address your complaint to a person in charge, such as a manager or the head of the company. ⁴You can get the person's name by calling the company directly. ⁵Next, write your complaint in a clear and matter-of-fact way. ⁶You will be taken less seriously if you sound emotional or threatening. ⁷Finally, explain exactly what action you want taken. ⁸If, for example, you want a company to replace a defective microwave, say, "Please give me the go-ahead to return this microwave. ⁹Then arrange for a new one to be sent to me." ¹⁰Don't leave it up to the company to figure out what you would consider a satisfactory response.

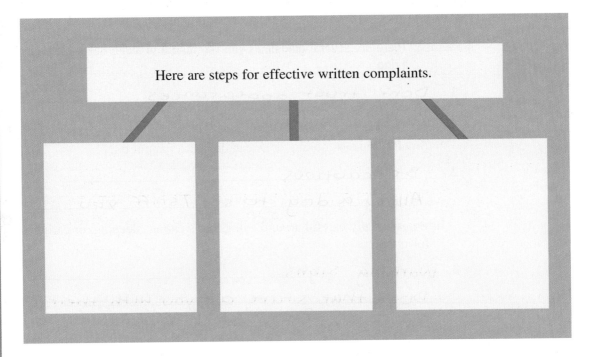

Here are steps for effective written complaints.

10. What are the **three** addition words used to set off the major details in the passage?

_____   _____   _____

SUPPORTING DETAILS: Mastery Test 4

A. (1–6.) Complete the outline below by filling in the missing major and minor details. Some details have been added for you.

[1]High schools should require all students to wear uniforms. [2]One reason for doing so is that uniforms would save money for parents and children. [3]Families could simply buy two or three inexpensive uniforms. [4]They would not have to constantly put out money for designer jeans, fancy sneakers, and other high-priced clothing. [5]A second advantage of uniforms is that students would not have to spend time worrying about clothes. [6]They could get up every day knowing what they were wearing to school. [7]Their attention, then, could be focused on schoolwork and learning and not on making a fashion statement. [8]Last, uniforms would help all students get along better. [9]Well-off students would not be able to act superior by wearing expensive clothes, and students from modest backgrounds would not have to feel inferior because of lower-cost wardrobes.

Main idea: High schools should require all students to wear uniforms.

1. _____

    a. Families could just buy two or three inexpensive uniforms.

    b. _____

    _____

2. _____

    a. Students would know what they were going to wear every day.

    b. _____

    _____

3. _____

    a. Well-off students would not be able to act superior.

    b. _____

    _____

(Continues on next page)

B. (7–10.) Fill in the major details and the one minor detail needed to complete the map below.

¹A number of factors influence the pace at which people age. ²First of all, genes—traits inherited from parents—play a major role in how people age. ³Genes play a role in how much hair loss we have or how much weight we gain. ⁴Genes also help explain why some people at 75 years old look 60, while others who are 60 appear to be 75. ⁵A second factor that influences aging is a person's lifestyle. ⁶Older-looking skin and wrinkles can be caused by too much sun exposure in youth—part of an outdoor, active lifestyle. ⁷On the other hand, a person who does not exercise is more likely to look and feel older than one who is physically active. ⁸Social forces are a third factor that influence aging. ⁹Older people who feel isolated or lonely often age faster than those who don't report having those feelings. ¹⁰But older people who are involved with others—their families, religious groups, or peer groups—age more slowly and live longer than those who don't.

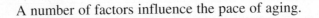

A number of factors influence the pace of aging.

Genes help explain hair loss or weight gain or how old we look.

A person with too much sun or too little exercise will look older.

SUPPORTING DETAILS: Mastery Test 5

A. (1–6.) Complete the outline below by filling in the missing major and minor details. Some details have been added for you.

[1]Certain physical conditions affect how well people perform their work. [2]Temperature is one factor that has been shown to greatly influence workers. [3]If a workspace is too warm, people become cranky and uncomfortable. [4]On the other hand, workers who are cold are more likely to pursue nonwork activities, such as chatting or making warm drinks. [5]Color is another factor that affects worker performance. [6]A workspace that has lots of red tends to stimulate and excite workers. [7]Blue, on the other hand, usually soothes workers, making them feel relaxed and comfortable. [8]Finally, lighting has a powerful effect on employees. [9]Bright, direct light encourages good listening, close concentration, and comfortable reading. [10]Low light, however, promotes relaxation and personal conversation—rather than getting work done.

Main idea: Physical conditions affect work performance.

1. _____

    a. _____

    _____

    b. Cold workers are more likely to pursue nonwork activities.

2. _____

    a. Reds tend to stimulate and excite workers.

    b. _____

    _____

3. _____

    a. _____

    _____

    b. Low light promotes relaxation and personal conversation.

(Continues on next page)

B. (7–10.) Fill in the major details and one minor detail needed to complete the map below.

¹Nearly every family has members who don't get along. ²But for some, these disagreements grow into painful feuds that can last for years. ³Fortunately, there are certain strategies that can help heal even the most difficult family feuds. ⁴The first step is to get people to share the blame for their disagreement. ⁵Family rifts are rarely caused by a single person. ⁶For healing to take place, then, everyone involved must accept responsibility for his or her part in the conflict. ⁷The second step is to increase the communication between family members. ⁸Writing a note, making a phone call, or attending a family event allows people to express their feelings to each other. ⁹Such actions show care and help rebuild damaged relationships. ¹⁰A third step is to set realistic goals. ¹¹A family feud that has lasted for thirty years will not be solved by a single talk. ¹²However, that talk may lead to a truce and help build a foundation for healing.

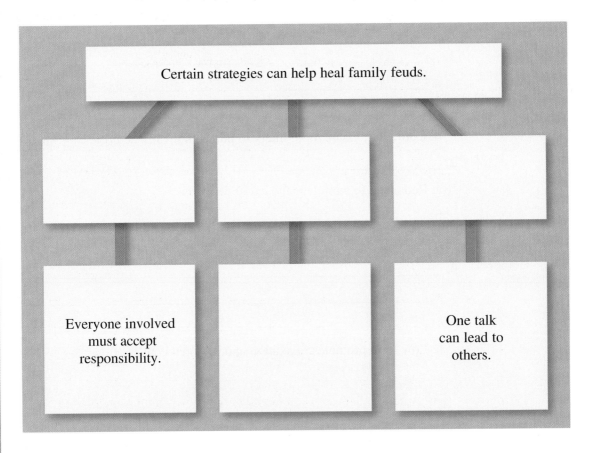

Certain strategies can help heal family feuds.

Everyone involved must accept responsibility.

One talk can lead to others.

SUPPORTING DETAILS: Mastery Test 6

A. (1–6.) Complete the outline below by filling in the missing major and minor details. Some details have been added for you.

> ¹People sometimes express their thoughts not by speaking, but by using their bodies in various ways. ²One way people use the body to communicate is through the eyes. ³By glaring, people can send the message that they are angry without saying a word. ⁴Likewise, people can show interest in what another person is saying by just looking at the person, using direct eye contact to send the message. ⁵Another way that people use their bodies to communicate is through facial expressions. ⁶Studies show that people all over the world use the same facial expressions to show emotions. ⁷Just by looking at a face, it is possible to tell if a person is sad, happy, afraid, or surprised. ⁸Body posture is a third way that people send messages to each other without speaking. ⁹For example, sitting upright or leaning forward shows great interest and attention. ¹⁰On the other hand, if a person has arms crossed at the chest, it is a sign that he or she dislikes or disagrees with the speaker.

Main idea: People can communicate by using their bodies.

1. _____

   a. _____

   _____

   b. People can show interest in a speaker through direct eye contact.

2. _____

   a. All over the world, people use the same facial expressions to show emotions.

   b. _____

   _____

3. _____

   a. _____

   _____

   b. A person with arms crossed dislikes or disagrees with the speaker.

(Continues on next page)

B. (7–10.) Fill in the major details and one minor detail needed to complete the map below.

¹Mysteries are questions in life without satisfying answers. ²One mystery is why there is so much hatred on the planet. ³We are all mortal and here on Earth for only a little while. ⁴Yet instead of being kind to one another, we continue to start wars—the main effect of which is to kill each other. ⁵A second mystery is how good and evil can exist together in the same person. ⁶For example, we have all heard of a person who is liked and even admired in the community. ⁷We then learn that the person has been abusing his wife or children. ⁸A third mystery is why some wealthy Christians do little to help the poor. ⁹They go to church on Sunday but act as if the lives of the poor are none of their concern. ¹⁰Yet the Bible says that it's easier for a camel to pass through the eye of a needle than for a rich man to enter the kingdom of Heaven.

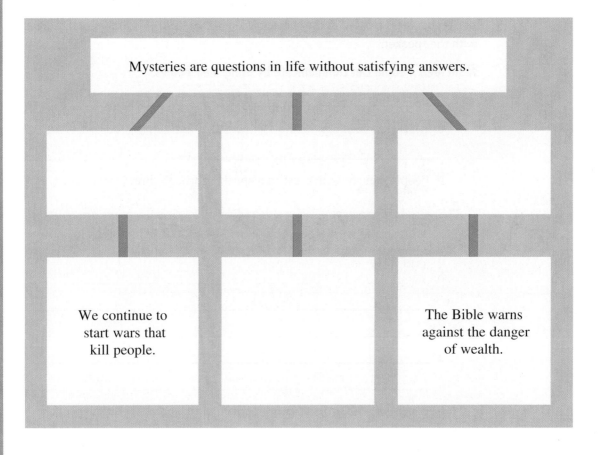

Mysteries are questions in life without satisfying answers.

We continue to start wars that kill people.

The Bible warns against the danger of wealth.

5 Locations of Main Ideas

This Chapter in a Nutshell

- The main idea most often appears in the first sentence of a paragraph.

- The main idea may include such list words as *various kinds* and *a number of.* Supporting details may be introduced with such addition words as *first of all, next,* and *finally.*

- Sometimes the first sentence or two of a paragraph act only as an introduction to the main idea. The main idea then appears in the second or third sentence. Often a word like *but* or *however* signals such a main idea.

- The main idea may also appear in the middle or at the end of a paragraph.

Like the freight train pictured above, a paragraph has a beginning, a middle, and an end. In the previous chapters, most of the main ideas were at the beginning: the first sentence of each paragraph. But the main idea "engine" may appear in the middle or at the end of the paragraph as well.

This chapter describes common locations of the main idea and gives you practice in finding the main idea in a series of paragraphs.

As you work through this chapter, remember what you have already learned about finding main ideas:

1   Look for a **general idea** and ask yourself, "Is this idea supported by all or most of the other material in the paragraph?"

2   See if you can decide on the **topic**—the general subject of the paragraph— and then ask, "What point is the paragraph making about the subject?"

3   Look for **list words** such as *several reasons* or *various factors* or *three steps*; such words often appear in the main idea sentence. (See page 128.) Also, look for **addition words** such as *first, another, also*, and *finally*; such words may introduce details that support the main idea. (See page 129.)

Main Idea at the Beginning

Authors often begin a paragraph with the main idea. The rest of the paragraph then supports the main idea with details.

 Check Your Understanding

See if you can underline the main idea in the following paragraph.

[1]Pain can cause aggression. [2]When two rats in the same cage were given foot shocks, they attacked each other immediately. [3]In addition, stronger shocks resulted in more violent aggression. [4]Pairs of various other animals reacted similarly. [5]A stubbed toe or a headache has been known to cause similar responses in humans. [6]A parent with a bad headache, for instance, is more likely to shout at or even slap children.

Explanation

The author's main idea is presented in the *first* sentence. The following sentences support the main idea with examples of pain that causes aggression.

But a main idea does not necessarily appear in the very first sentence of a passage. See if you can underline the main idea in this paragraph:

> [1]College is supposed to be a place of discovery. [2]But for some students, college can be a place of fear. [3]In the classroom, for example, many students are afraid of appearing stupid in front of their classmates or professors. [4]Such students often try to hide in class by sitting in the back of the room and avoiding eye contact with instructors. [5]Fear prevents them from raising their hands, answering questions, or being part of class discussions. [6]Fear also leads to problems outside the classroom. [7]Worried their peers won't like them, many college students smoke or drink heavily to blend in with the crowd. [8]They also try drugs, join in hurtful pranks, or practice unsafe sex—all out of fear. [9]And sadly, after getting in trouble, students are often too scared to seek the help they need to solve their problems.

Explanation

In the above paragraph, the main idea is stated in the *second* sentence. The first sentence introduces the topic (college), but it is the idea in the second sentence—college can be a place of fear—that is supported in the rest of the paragraph. So keep in mind that the first sentence may simply introduce or lead into the main idea of a paragraph.

> *Note:* In paragraphs beginning with one or more introductory sentences, very often a word like *but, however,* or *yet* then signals the main idea. In the above paragraph, the word *but* helps mark the main idea.

Main Idea in the Middle

At times, the main idea appears in the middle of a paragraph.

✓ Check Your Understanding

Here is an example of a paragraph in which the main idea is somewhere in the middle. Try to find and underline it. Then read the explanation that follows.

> [1]Exercise thickens the bones and can slow the loss of calcium that normally occurs with age. [2]Physical activity increases flexibility in the joints and improves digestion and elimination. [3]It builds lean body mass, so the body burns more calories and body fat decreases. [4]If exercise could be packed into a pill, it would be the single most widely used medicine in the world. [5]Exercise also lowers the risk of developing Type 2 diabetes. [6]It helps to prevent strokes and heart attacks, and it lowers the risk of certain cancers. [7]It can actually extend your lifespan and sharpen your memory and mind.

Explanation

If you thought the fourth sentence contains the main idea, you were correct. The first three sentences give some of the benefits of exercise. Then the writer presents the main idea, which is that if exercise were a pill, everyone would take it. The rest of the paragraph goes on to support this idea with even more benefits of exercise.

Main Idea at the End

Sometimes all the sentences in a paragraph will lead up to the main idea, which is stated at the end.

✓ Check Your Understanding

See if you can underline the main idea in the following paragraph.

> [1]A woman's son had just graduated from college. [2]So when a florist's truck pulled in front of her house, she was not surprised, thinking that a relative or friend was congratulating her son. [3]However, she was surprised when she saw that the dozen red

roses were addressed to her. ⁴The card read, "Thanks, Mom, for making this day possible. ⁵I could not have done it without your love and support." ⁶In an unusual switch, the graduate had given his mother a graduation gift.

Explanation

Here the supporting details appear first, and the point of the supporting details—that a son had surprised his mother with a gift—appears at the end.

> *Note:* At times, the main idea will appear at the beginning of a paragraph and also, in different words, at the end. Writers may repeat the main idea if they want to emphasize it.

PRACTICE 1

The main idea may appear at any place within each of the four paragraphs that follow. Write the number of each main idea sentence in the space provided.

Hints: Remember the three ways to find main ideas:

1 Look for a general idea and ask yourself, "Is this idea supported by all or most of the other material in the paragraph?"

2 See if you can decide on the topic—the general subject of the paragraph—and then ask, "What point is the paragraph making about the subject?"

3 Look for list words such as *several reasons* or *various factors* or *three steps*; such words often appear in the main idea sentence. Also, look for addition words such as *first, another, also*, and *finally*; such words may introduce details that support the main idea.

_____ 1. ¹One of the most important secrets of good communication is knowing how to ask return questions. ²For example, if someone asks, "Did you have a good weekend?" you should offer a reply and then ask a question in return. ³You might say something like "What did you do this weekend?" or "Is today going to be busy for you?" or "Do you think the weather is going to get better soon?" ⁴What you ask is not as important as the fact that you respond with a question of your own. ⁵Many adults are not good at conversation because they have not mastered this skill. ⁶All of us enjoy talking more with people who show interest in us.

_____ 2. [1]Americans tend to say directly what is on their minds. [2]However, people in Asian cultures are more likely to speak indirectly. [3]In Asia, if you visit a friend on a hot day and feel thirsty, you would not ask point-blank, "May I have a glass of water?" [4]Instead, you would state your request indirectly by saying, "Isn't it hot today?" [5]In Japan, at the end of a long business meeting, if you ask, "So will you do business with us?" the Japanese will always say "yes" even if they mean "no." [6]They will not say "no" directly because they do not want to embarrass you.

_____ 3. [1]The set of cooking knives is offered at an unbeatable price. [2]You hurry to the department store. [3]There, the sympathetic clerk tells you he is so sorry, but he's all sold out. [4]But, he adds, the quality of the knives wasn't that good, anyway. [5]If you want a real value, he suggests that you purchase another set. [6]True, it costs more, but the knives are certainly worth the extra money. [7]So you buy the more expensive knife set. [8]Later, you notice that the super-low-priced set of knives you had originally wanted is still being advertised. [9]The store ran an illegal operation called a "bait-and-switch": you were "baited" with an inexpensive item, then "switched" to something more expensive.

_____ 4. [1]Everyone has heard a few "Your mama is ugly" jokes. [2]"Your mama is so ugly that when she entered an ugly contest, the judge said, 'Sorry, no professionals.'" [3]"Your mama is so ugly that when she went to a haunted house, she came out with a paycheck." [4]"In the dictionary, your mother's picture is next to the word 'ugly.'" [5]There are several reasons why "your mama" jokes are popular. [6]First of all, humor usually contains something surprising or even shocking. [7]We aren't expected to make fun of someone's mom, so a "your mama" joke has the element of surprise. [8]Secondly, humor is a way we deal with taboos, or things that are forbidden. [9]Insulting anybody is bad enough, but insulting somebody's mother is really out of line. [10]Finally, "your mama" jokes are generally told between close friends as a way to express friendship and affection. [11]Mothers aren't really being insulted. [12]Instead of getting angry, the friend on the receiving end of the joke usually laughs.

PRACTICE 2

The main idea may appear at any place within each of the four paragraphs that follow. Write the number of each main idea sentence in the space provided.

_8_ 1. ¹One way poor spellers can improve their spelling is to keep a list of words they are constantly looking up in the dictionary. ²They can review and test themselves on a few of these words each day. ³Breaking up a word into its parts also makes spelling a less forbidding task. ⁴For example, the word *formidable* can be broken into three parts: *for*, *mid*, and *able*. ⁵Third, learning little verbal tricks is helpful. ⁶One such trick is "There's *a rat* in *separate*." ⁷Another is "*Iron* is found in the *environment*." ⁸Using these methods, poor spellers can become more reliable spellers.

_1_ 2. ¹When a company "downsizes"—that is, reduces its workforce—there are both positive and negative results. ²On the one hand, as labor costs are reduced, the company usually becomes more profitable. ³It makes more money for its shareholders, and the price of its stock is likely to rise. ⁴On the other hand, the remaining employees at a company must usually work harder and longer. ⁵Both managers and workers may have to deal with more stress and burnout. ⁶And morale often falls because employees feel that the company has no loyalty to them and cares only about the bottom line.

_2_ 3. ¹Today, we take many of the comforts of our everyday lives for granted. ²However, people living before 1900 had relatively few modern conveniences. ³Running water, bathtubs, and indoor toilets were luxuries of the rich. ⁴Most people washed with basins in their rooms and used outdoor privies. ⁵A metal bathtub might be hauled out once a week, but the water had to be carried from a well. ⁶The kitchen stove, which used coal or wood, did double duty for cooking and heating. ⁷Refrigerators were not yet made, but some people had iceboxes, which required regular supplies of ice. ⁸A few homes were lit by electricity, but most still used kerosene or gas.

_3_ 4. ¹Some people believe the superstition that cats have nine lives because they can fall from high places with few, if any, injuries. ²They may have minor injuries, such as a bloody nose or cracked teeth or ribs, but they recover. ³Cats are able to survive long falls because they possess several advantages. ⁴For one thing, their small size and low body weight soften the impact as they make contact with the ground. ⁵Also, their highly developed inner ears give them a keen sense of balance, so they can quickly adjust themselves in the air to ensure a landing on all fours. ⁶As a result, the impact is absorbed by all their legs. ⁷Additionally, cats bend their legs when they land, which cushions and spreads the impact, not only through bones that might break otherwise, but through the joints and muscles as well.

PRACTICE 3

The main idea may appear at any place within each of the four paragraphs that follow. Write the number of each main idea sentence in the space provided.

___2___   1. [1]Vocabulary is a major part of almost every standardized test, including college placement exams. [2]But there are reasons for building a strong vocabulary other than to prepare for standardized tests. [3]Common sense tells us that the more words we know, the better we will be able to understand what we read. [4]If our vocabulary is not large enough, our reading comprehension will suffer. [5]Another reason for building vocabulary is that words are the tools not just of better reading, but also of better writing, speaking, and thinking. [6]In addition, studies have shown that a good vocabulary, more than any other factor, is common to people enjoying successful careers.

___1___   2. [1]People with higher status are generally given more space and privacy. [2]For instance, we knock before entering our boss's office, but we walk into the office work area without hesitating. [3]In many schools, teachers have offices, dining rooms, and even toilets that are private, but students do not have such special places. [4]In the world of show business, stars receive their own dressing rooms or private trailers. [5]Among the military, greater space and privacy usually come with rank: privates sleep forty to a barrack, sergeants have their own rooms, and generals have government-provided houses.

___7___   3. [1]Have you ever seen a fast-food ad that shows the factories where French fries are made? [2]Or a fast-food ad that shows the slaughterhouse where cattle are turned into ground beef? [3]Or an ad that tells you what's really in your fast-food milkshake and why some strange-sounding chemicals make it taste so good? [4]Or an ad that shows overweight, unhealthy kids stuffing their faces with greasy fries at a fast-food restaurant? [5]You probably haven't. [6]But you've probably seen a lot of fast-food commercials that show thin, happy children having a lot of fun. [7]The fact is that companies that sell fast food don't want you to know where it comes from or how it's made or what eating too much of it might do to you.

___2___   4. [1]Many English people sailed to Jamestown, Virginia, in 1607 in order to get away from problems in England. [2]But a number of problems awaited the English settlers in the New World. [3]Of the first 10,000 who landed in Virginia, only 2,000 survived. [4]They died of disease, Indian attack, and hunger. [5]In a land of plenty, not all of them learned quickly enough how to hunt, or fish, or raise crops, or gather food. [6]Nor were they all ready to cope with the heat, which in August could reach 100 degrees. [7]Some of the English gentlemen felt they needed to wear sixty-pound suits of metal armor to be safe from

Indian arrows. ⁸Under the armor they wore wool clothing because that is what they would have done in England. ⁹It was impossible to hunt animals in such hot, heavy, noisy outfits. ¹⁰And the firearms that the settlers carried were not as accurate as rifles (which had not been invented yet) or even bows and arrows (which few settlers knew how to use).

CHAPTER REVIEW

In this chapter, you learned the following:

- The first place to check for the main idea is the first sentence. But the main idea can appear anywhere within a paragraph.

- At times the first sentence or two serve as an introduction to the main idea, which then appears in the second or third sentence. In such cases, a word like *but* or *however* often signals the main idea.

The next two chapters—Chapter 6 and Chapter 7—explain common connections between ideas and the ways authors organize supporting details.

 On the Web: If you are using this book in class, you can visit our website for additional practice in locating main ideas. Go to **www.townsendpress.com** and click on "Learning Center."

REVIEW TEST 1

To review what you've learned in this chapter, complete each of the following sentences.

1. The main idea appears most often in the (*first, second, final*) __First__ sentence of a paragraph.

2. Sometimes the first sentence or so of a paragraph may simply introduce or lead into the __main idea__, which may appear in the second or third sentence.

3. The main idea may occur at the beginning, in the middle, or at the __End__ of a paragraph.

4. _List words_ words such as *several reasons* or *various factors* or *three steps* often appear as part of the main idea sentence.

5. Addition words such as *first, another, also,* and *finally* often introduce _Details_ that support the main idea.

REVIEW TEST 2

The main idea may appear at any place within each of the four paragraphs that follow. Write the number of each main idea sentence in the space provided.

___1___ 1. ¹Soup has become more popular than ever, for good reasons. ²For one thing, it can help you lose and maintain weight. ³Since you can't eat soup on the run, you're forced to eat slowly. ⁴And slow eating usually means a lower calorie intake. ⁵Soup can also help you feel better when you've got a cold or bronchitis. ⁶Hot chicken soup, especially if it's spiced with pepper or garlic, helps to break up the congestion in your throat and chest. ⁷As a result, you can breathe more easily. ⁸In addition to being healthful, soup is available everywhere, it's inexpensive, and it's easy to prepare.

___11___ 2. ¹The man who washes cars may not own one. ²The clerk who files canceled checks at the bank may have less than $5 in her own account. ³The person who serves you a fast-food burger may have thousands of dollars in credit-card debt. ⁴The man or woman who helps you find merchandise at a dollar store may be worrying about having enough money to pay the next month's rent. ⁵These people might be climbing out of welfare, drug addiction, or homelessness. ⁶They may be trapped for life in a zone of low-wage work. ⁷Some of their children are malnourished. ⁸Some have been sexually abused. ⁹Some live in crumbling housing that contributes to their children's asthma, which means days absent from school. ¹⁰Some of their youngsters do not even have the eyeglasses they need to see the chalkboard clearly. ¹¹All around us, millions of people live on the hard edge of poverty.

___2___ 3. ¹Speaking before a group is more frightening to many people than almost anything else. ²But there are ways to overcome the fear of speaking and become an effective speaker. ³The first step to take is to think positively. ⁴Replace thoughts of failure with statements such as, "I am interested in my topic, and I will make my listeners interested, too." ⁵It also helps to plan a speech with only two or three major points and to develop each of those points with examples. ⁶Moreover, visualize yourself standing in front of your audience, feeling comfortable and relaxed. ⁷Finally, rehearse your speech a number of times, speaking naturally, almost the way you would in everyday conversation, rather than speaking in a formal way.

_1_ 4. ¹Roads of the nineteenth century were much different from roads of today. ²The average street in the 1800s was a dirt path between six and eight feet wide. ³In the fall and spring, these roads were often muddy and marked by holes and puddles caused by stagecoaches. ⁴In the summer, dry dirt roads would create huge clouds of dust whenever anyone traveled on them. ⁵Slightly better roads were made with wood. ⁶Workers would lay round logs on the ground next to each other. ⁷Often the logs rolled under the weight of coaches, causing horses to slip. ⁸Sometimes, ankles would get caught in the gaps between the logs, resulting in broken bones. ⁹Even the best roads of the time—those made with wooden planks—had problems. ¹⁰Plank roads were smoother, but their wooden surfaces would quickly rot away. ¹¹Only later in the century did workers use crushed stones, clay, and gravel to build roads.

REVIEW TEST 3

The main idea may appear at any place within each of the four paragraphs that follow. Write the number of each main idea sentence in the space provided.

_2_ 1. ¹Feeling chilly? ²To fight the cold, you should understand how to use clothing to stay warm. ³Because heat rises, one of the best ways to keep your whole body warm is to wear a hat or cap. ⁴Dressing in layers is another useful tip, since air trapped between layers stays warm. ⁵This principle also applies when choosing gloves. ⁶Loose-fitting gloves trap warm air near your skin. ⁷On the other hand, tight gloves are not as warm because they lack this layer of air.

_1_ 2. ¹A lack of social connections is dangerous to people's health. ²Individuals without strong bonds of friendship, family, or community get colds at four times the rate of people who have such bonds. ³According to research, a lack of relationships poses as great a health risk as smoking, obesity, high blood pressure, or lack of exercise. ⁴Divorced people are five times more likely to get cancer than married people of the same age. ⁵Loners are two to three times more likely to die prematurely than people with social ties.

_1_ 3. ¹Television ads urge you to buy products by scaring you, appealing to your desire for the comforts of home, or promising popularity. ²You can probably think of some mildly fearful ads: commercials for deodorants, soaps, mouthwash, denture adhesive, or diarrhea usually begin with someone suffering rejection or facing a problem. ³Other ads are more pleasant, with products associated with a warm, loving, old-fashioned atmosphere. ⁴For example, you may be told about cookies, breads, or spaghetti sauce such as Grandmother used to make. ⁵And some ads appeal to your desire for popularity. ⁶They imply, for instance, that if you wear the right brand of jeans or use the right perfume or drink the right kind of beer, you will have more friends.

___9___   4. ¹Near the end of the Civil War, the Confederate and Union forces met at Gettysburg, Pennsylvania. ²The Confederate general, Robert E. Lee, had his forces bombard the Union soldiers, who were camped on high ground at a site called Cemetery Hill. ³After two hours of nonstop cannon fire, Lee felt that most of the Union line had been destroyed. ⁴He did not realize that most of the poorly aimed cannons had done little damage to the Union soldiers. ⁵Lee then ordered his soldiers out of the protective woods and across a wide stretch of open field toward the Union forces. ⁶The sight was impressive: fifteen thousand men in gray uniforms, the bright sun reflecting off their silver bayonets and red flags. ⁷Elbow to elbow, as if in a parade, they marched forward in an orderly line almost a mile wide and half a mile deep. ⁸Protected by a low stone wall, the Union forces opened fire and mowed down row after row of the advancing Rebel soldiers. ⁹General Lee's ill-advised battle plan resulted in a shockingly bloody defeat for the Confederate Army.

REVIEW TEST 4

Here is a chance to apply your understanding of main ideas to a full-length selection. Read the following article, and then answer the questions that follow on the central point and main ideas. For review purposes, there are also questions on vocabulary in context and supporting details.

This selection tells what it might mean when your boss pats you on the back, when men and women run their hands through their hair, and more. The selection may convince you that no matter how quiet you are, your body has been speaking loudly and clearly.

Words to Watch

Below are some words in the reading that do not have strong context support. Each word is followed by the number of the paragraph in which it appears and its meaning there. These words are indicated in the selection by a small circle (°).

gestures (2): motions made that express thought or emphasize speech
context (2): overall situation
seductive (6): tempting, often in a sexual way
abrupt (10): rudely sudden
staging (11): performing
preening (14): grooming
meek (15): willing to yield to the power of another

BODY LANGUAGE
Beth Johnson

1   Imagine yourself in the following situation: You're a young woman interviewing for a new job. You have been talking for about half an hour with the interviewer, a pleasant man slightly older than yourself. You feel the interview has gone well, but you're not sure what he's thinking. Suddenly the mood in the room changes. Your interviewer sits back in his chair, crosses one ankle over his knee and begins tapping his pen against his shoe. Should you:

(a) Forget about the job?
(b) Congratulate yourself?
(c) Tell him you're not that kind of girl?

The answer is *b*—you're probably going to be hired, says Dr. Robert Rosenthal of Harvard University. Dr. Rosenthal, a clinical psychologist, is a pioneer in the study of how people send and receive nonverbal messages—in other words, "body language."

2   Researchers say that body language sends out messages far more powerful than we're generally aware of. At the same time, they warn that nonverbal communication—which involves gestures°, posture, tone of voice, and eye contact—is more complicated than the drugstore-type books on the subject suggest. Body language can be explained only within its context°, they say; you shouldn't expect to find a "dictionary" for reliable definitions of crossed arms, sideways glances, and tapping toes.

3   Still, those that study the field agree that a better awareness of nonverbal communication makes you a more sensitive observer of any situation. Such awareness can also help you understand how people perceive you.

4   Let's take an example: How would a student of body language explain the interview described above? What in the world does touching a shoe have to do with making a favorable hiring decision? Dr. Rosenthal admits he doesn't know for sure. But after watching many job interviews, he is certain that the foot-touching gesture means the interview subject has made a good impression. This is his theory: an interview is likely to make both persons involved feel uneasy. Both will probably sit stiffly in their chairs. But once the interviewer decides, "Yes, I'm going to hire this person," he relaxes. At that point, he's apt to shift into a more comfortable position, often bringing his foot within easy touching distance.

5   Status differences on the job offer other interesting examples, points out Allan Mazur, a professor of sociology at Syracuse University. When a respected executive talks with a lower-ranking employee, for example, the employee usually keeps his or her eyes glued to the boss's face. But when the employee is talking, the executive feels free to glance around the room. Another example is the manager who shows his or her superiority by patting a worker

on the back—something the employee would never do to the manager. In an office, the person with the most status even establishes how a conversation will take place: If the higher-status person stands, the lower-ranking person remains standing as well. If lower-status people violate any of these rules, they risk looking disrespectful.

6   Of course, the working world is not the only place where body language is used. Every would-be Romeo or Juliet knows that the language of courtship goes far beyond words. Much of our flirtatious behavior is instinctive, not consciously thought out. But if you can get them to admit it, many expert flirts are aware of their seductive° use of body language.

7   "I've got my tricks," admits Patti, 22, a college student who spends many evenings out dancing with a group of friends. Patti is not a beauty, but she always attracts men at the clubs she goes to.

8   "I don't know why some things work the way they do, but certain gestures make men feel more confident about coming up to me," she says. When asked to describe those gestures, she laughs nervously. "That's kind of embarrassing. . . . It's just little things like glancing sideways at a guy with a little smile. Then you look away as if you didn't do it. But a minute later you sort of let your eyes slide back to meet his while you're talking to someone else. After that, he'll usually get up and come over."

9   When you spend an hour observing Patti in action, you see other "tricks" she uses while talking to men she's attracted

to. She lightly draws her finger across her lip as she listens to a man. She plays with her hair. She tilts her head and gazes upward into his eyes. She lazily shrugs her shoulders. It's no wonder Patti gains all the attention she can handle, according to Dr. David Givens, an anthropologist at the University of Washington. Her "vocabulary" of body language sends out a strong signal: "I'm friendly. I'm approachable."

10   Taken a step further, the message becomes "I'm sexually available." Patti admits that the men she enjoys flirting and dancing with often read that message in her behavior. So she has become equally expert at "freezing" a too-insistent man with a nonverbal vocabulary of rejection: a stiff posture, expressionless face, and abrupt° gestures. Patti is a pro with body language, and as she says, "You can say about anything you want without words."

11   Where does nonverbal communication come from? Researchers trace various kinds of body language back to

our roots in the animal world. Courtship practices such as marking out one's territory, staging° battles before the object of one's affection, or grooming oneself in front of a would-be mate are all common animal behaviors that humans use as well.

12   An evening of observation at a singles bar demonstrates the links between animal and human body language. Si and Mark are a couple of factory workers in their early twenties out for an evening at Lights, their favorite hangout. As they settle at the bar, they automatically scatter their jackets, Si's car keys, and a cigarette lighter across the bar in front of them. They're marking out their territory—warning other men to stay away.

13   Before long they have spotted several women that they particularly like. As those women move into hearing range, Si and Mark's casual, low-volume conversation changes noticeably. Their voices rise and take on a challenging, though still good-humored, quality. They begin to argue: "You're crazy!" "You're outta your mind!" "I can't believe this guy." They are laughing, but their voices are loud and rough. They glance around, hoping to include the women in their conversation. But they are passed by, and Si and Mark's conversation quickly returns to a lower tone.

14   Later in the evening, however, Si has better luck with a second target. As she approaches, he and Mark go into their "arguing" routine. She pauses. Catching Si's eye, she leans against the wall and begins running her fingers through her already well-combed hair.

Si slowly makes his way across the room to speak to her. The message of her preening° in response to his masculine display is one he quickly recognizes—as would any animal scientist.

15   Animal behavior, however, is not the only source of nonverbal communication. As Dr. Givens points out, another rich source of nonverbal vocabulary is our childhood. When we want to seem meek° and friendly—which in the case of women often translates into "romantically available"—we may borrow gestures from as far back as babyhood. An infant scared by a loud noise will respond with the "startle reflex": a combination of lifting the shoulders, lowering the head and pulling in the chin. An older child will use the same gestures when being scolded, making the child seem cute and meek. But when used by Patti upon meeting new dance partners, the same moves seem less childish than seductive and feminine.

16   Dr. Givens further demonstrates this point by putting together photographs of children looking adorable and adult female fashion models looking sexy: the poses are identical.

17   Everyone uses body language. Because nonverbal communication, based in our animal roots and childhoods, is universal, it is useful to become more aware of it. What we and others "say" when we're not saying anything can enrich and entertain us as we spend each day in the human "laboratory."

Reading Comprehension Questions

Vocabulary in Context

__B__   1. In the excerpt below, the word *apt* (ăpt) means
   A. unlikely.   C. unable.
   B. likely.   D. not ready.

> "But once the interviewer decides, 'Yes, I'm going to hire this person,' he relaxes. At that point, he's apt to shift into a more comfortable position. . . ." (Paragraph 4)

__B__   2. In the sentence below, the word *instinctive* (ĭn-stĭngk′tĭv) means
   A. planned.
   B. natural.
   C. strange.
   D. poor.

> "Much of our flirtatious behavior is instinctive, not consciously thought out." (Paragraph 6)

__D__   3. In the excerpt below, the word *links* (lĭngks) means
   A. differences.
   B. questions.
   C. friendship.
   D. connections.

> "Researchers trace various kinds of body language back to our roots in the animal world. . . . An evening of observation at a singles bar demonstrates the links between animal and human body language." (Paragraphs 11–12)

Central Point

__D__   4. Which of the following sentences from the reading best expresses the central point of the selection?
   A. "Dr. Rosenthal, a clinical psychologist, is a pioneer in the study of how people send and receive nonverbal messages—in other words, 'body language.'"
   B. "Every would-be Romeo or Juliet knows that the language of courtship goes far beyond words."
   C. "Researchers trace various kinds of body language back to our roots in the animal world."
   D. "Because nonverbal communication, based in our animal roots and childhoods, is universal, it is useful to become more aware of it."

Main Ideas

_A_ 5. The main idea sentence of paragraph 5 is its
   A. first sentence.
   B. second sentence.
   C. third sentence.
   D. last sentence.

_A_ 6. The main idea of paragraph 9 is expressed in its
   A. first sentence.
   B. second sentence.
   C. third sentence.
   D. fourth sentence.

_D_ 7. A main idea sentence sometimes provides the main idea for more than one paragraph. The first sentence of paragraph 12 expresses the main idea for paragraphs
   A. 10–12.
   B. 11–13.
   C. 12–13.
   D. 12–14.

_B_ 8. The main idea of paragraph 15 is expressed in its
   A. first sentence.
   B. second sentence.
   C. next-to-last sentence.
   D. last sentence.

Supporting Details

_A_ 9. When people are having a talk with their boss, they
   A. usually look continuously at the boss.
   B. may glance around while the boss is talking.
   C. may sit while the boss is standing.
   D. may show approval by patting the boss on the back.

_D_ 10. Animal courtship practices that influence human body language include
   A. marking of territory.
   B. staging battles in front of a desirable female.
   C. grooming in front of a desired mate.
   D. all of the above.

Discussion Questions

1. How aware of body language were you before you read this article? After reading it, might you behave any differently in situations where you are meeting people for the first time? Explain.

2. What is some of the "vocabulary" of classroom body language? Consider both students' and teachers' nonverbal communication.

3. Johnson gives several examples of ritual and body language in courtship. What others could you add?

4. Johnson writes, "Body language can be explained only within its context . . . you shouldn't expect to find a 'dictionary' for reliable definitions of . . . tapping toes." Give some examples in which certain body language has different meanings in different situations. For example, what are some different meanings that tapping toes might have?

Note: Writing assignments for this selection appear on page 607.

Check Your Performance		LOCATIONS OF **MAIN IDEAS**		
Activity		*Number Right*	*Points*	*Score*
Review Test 1 (5 items)		_____	× 2 =	_____
Review Test 2 (4 items)		_____	× 7.5 =	_____
Review Test 3 (4 items)		_____	× 7.5 =	_____
Review Test 4 (10 items)		_____	× 3 =	_____
			TOTAL SCORE =	_____ %

Enter your total score into the **Reading Performance Chart: Review Tests** on the inside back cover.

LOCATIONS OF MAIN IDEAS: Mastery Test 1

The main idea may appear at any place within each of the five paragraphs that follow. Write the number of each main idea sentence in the space provided.

_____ 1. [1]"Ladies and gentlemen of the jury," said the prosecuting attorney, "two reliable witnesses—both respectable citizens—have testified that they saw the defendant commit the robbery at the jewelry store. [2]Three more witnesses have testified that they saw him fleeing the store just after the crime was committed. [3]In addition, his fingerprints were found in several places in the store. [4]What is more, he was caught just several blocks from the store, just minutes after the robbery, and arrested with the stolen jewelry still in his possession. [5]All the evidence proves that the defendant is guilty beyond a reasonable doubt, and you should convict him."

_____ 2. [1]Someone once said, "Seeing yourself as you want to be is the key to personal growth." [2]You can help yourself grow in self-knowledge through the following exercises. [3]First of all, take the tombstone test. [4]What would you like to have written on your tombstone? [5]In other words, how would you like to be remembered? [6]Your honest answer should reveal, in a few words, what you value most. [7]Next, see if you can describe yourself, as you are today, in a brief sentence. [8]You might want to ask friends or family members how they would describe you in a few words. [9]Then decide how you would have to change to become the person you want to be remembered as. [10]Finally, try the adjective test. [11]Choose three adjectives that you'd like to see connected with your name. [12]Then list what you've done or can do to earn such a reputation.

_____ 3. [1]The health-care field is now a stable middle-class career path for a number of Americans, especially women. [2]"We used to think about the men going out with their lunch bucket to their factory, and those were good jobs," said Jane Waldfogel, a professor at Columbia University who studies work and family issues. [3]"What's the corresponding job today? [4]It's in the health-care sector." [5]In 1980, 1.4 million jobs in health care paid a middle-class wage; today, the figure is 4.5 million. [6]The pay of registered nurses—now the third-largest middle-income occupation and one that continues to be overwhelmingly female—has risen strongly. [7]The median salary of $61,000 a year in 2012 was 55 percent greater, adjusted for inflation, than it was three decades earlier. [8]Back then, more than a quarter of middle-income jobs were in manufacturing, a sector long dominated by men. [9]Now, as of 2015, it is just 13 percent. [10]Tabitha Waugh is one success story; the daughter of a teacher's aide and a gas station manager, she now works as a registered nurse for $27 an hour.

(Continues on next page)

_____ 4. [1]Most people think the mind functions like a simple file cabinet—with all memories being stored in the same way. [2]Research, however, has proven that the human brain has three different types of memory. [3]Sensory memory records anything that comes in through the senses. [4]It can hold data from the eyes, ears, and so on, but just for a few seconds. [5]Short-term memory, the next type, holds memories longer—up to about twenty seconds. [6]It helps us in daily life, reminding us, for example, that we put sugar in our coffee or grabbed our books before heading to class. [7]Long-term memory, the most powerful memory type, can store information indefinitely, perhaps for life.

_____ 5. [1]Eating habits differ widely from one culture to another. [2]Many Japanese relish toasted grasshoppers, and members of some Brazilian tribes enjoy eating ants. [3]If you find such fare disgusting, keep in mind that many Europeans consider corn on the cob fit only for nonhuman animals, and many Asians and Africans reject cheese because they find it too smelly. [4]It's socially acceptable to eat dog flesh in Korea and horseflesh in France. [5]The thought of eating either dogs or horses offends most Westerners. [6]Orthodox Jews and Muslims avoid eating pork, which they consider sinful and unclean. [7]And orthodox Hindus—vegetarians who regard cows as sacred—find beef particularly offensive.

LOCATIONS OF MAIN IDEAS: Mastery Test 2

The main idea may appear at any place within each of the five paragraphs that follow. Write the number of each main idea sentence in the space provided.

_____ 1. ¹Storage facilities have become part of our culture. ²You see them everywhere—under overpasses, in industrial parks, and along busy highways. ³In the past, most people rented these climate-controlled, garage-like rooms only for brief periods. ⁴Perhaps they were moving from one state to another and needed to store their belongings while they looked for a new house. ⁵But today, people rent storage facilities year-round. ⁶Self-storage units are stuffed with unused clothes, bicycles, Grandma's old furniture, duplicate toasters and food processors, boxes of books, unwanted Christmas gifts, televisions, pool tables, model trains, cars, motorcycles, boats, sets of dishes, oriental rugs, pots and pans, and virtually anything else you can think of. ⁷Items that were once sold at yard sales, given to friends, or donated to charity now sit untouched for years at a time.

_____ 2. ¹They're moist, wiggly creatures, and many people don't like to touch them. ²Nevertheless, earthworms are very useful. ³People who like to fish, of course, know that worms make great bait. ⁴They also help improve the condition of the soil. ⁵As they dig under the ground, earthworms constantly take soil into their bodies. ⁶Their bodies use part of the soil and pass out the rest in the form of fine powder. ⁷That powder, called cast, makes the earth richer. ⁸In addition, the tunnels that worms create make the earth better able to absorb water and air.

_____ 3. ¹A dermatologist brought together sixty-five young people who were prone to acne. ²Every day for four weeks, he fed each of them either a super-chocolate bar, containing ten times the chocolate of an ordinary candy bar, or a look-alike candy bar that tasted like chocolate but contained none. ³None of the subjects knew whether or not they were eating real chocolate. ⁴Halfway through the experiment, the dermatologist switched bars on the subjects. ⁵The subjects' acne was not affected by including chocolate in their diets. ⁶The dermatologist's experiment suggests that chocolate is not to blame for complexion problems.

(Continues on next page)

_____ 4. [1]Congratulations: your tire is as flat as the road, you're supposed to be at an important meeting in an hour, and there's no help to be found anywhere. [2]What should you do? [3]You can change your own tire by following several safe, effective steps. [4]Park on level ground away from traffic, put the car in park, and put on the emergency brake. [5]Next, block the wheels at the opposite end from the flattened tire to prevent the car from rolling. [6]Take out the spare tire and the jack, and take off the hubcap. [7]Loosen the lug nuts; then jack the flat tire up at least two or three inches above the ground, remove the lug nuts, and put them inside the hubcap, where you won't lose them. [8]Then pull off the flat tire and put on the spare tire. [9]Replace the lug nuts, but don't tighten them all the way. [10]Jack down the car most of the way, and then finish tightening the lug nuts. [11]Finally, lower the car all the way, put away your tools, clean yourself up, and continue on your way.

_____ 5. [1]Preventing, not treating, social problems is the goal of an increasing number of programs. [2]By teaching teenagers to resist peer pressure, for example, one program helped them avoid serious problems with drinking and drugs. [3]In another program, nurses taught poor, young, pregnant women all the basics of good child care. [4]These young mothers then gave better care to their babies than mothers who did not receive such training. [5]A third program paired at-risk teenagers with adults from the community. [6]Each adult agreed to meet with the teenager on a regular basis through all four years of high school. [7]The result was that none of the teenagers dropped out of high schools in which the average dropout rate was close to 50 percent. [8]Instead, almost all of the teenagers went on to college.

LOCATIONS OF MAIN IDEAS: Mastery Test 3

The main idea may appear at any place within each of the five paragraphs that follow. Write the number of each main idea sentence in the space provided.

_____ 1. ¹According to Hollywood movies, the Middle Ages was a wonderful time of romantic castles and unbeatable knights. ²In reality, however, the Middle Ages was a difficult time to stay alive. ³Recent studies indicate that the average life span for English and Scottish kings between 1000 and 1600 A.D. was just 50 years. ⁴Nobles, including knights and other important people, had even shorter lives. ⁵In one study of a group of 23 noblemen, only one lived into his 70s. ⁶The rest died in their 20s, 30s and 40s. ⁷Common people had the shortest lives. ⁸For them, middle age began after adolescence, and death usually occurred in the mid- to late 30s.

__10__ 2. ¹Polar bears are excellent swimmers. ²They slip through the water at speeds up to six miles an hour, using their front legs to move them forward. ³With their nostrils closed and their eyes open, they can also dive underwater, staying there for as long as two minutes. ⁴When they emerge, they immediately shake the water off their fur before the water freezes. ⁵Polar bears are equally able to move well over the icy landscape. ⁶On very smooth, slippery slopes, a polar bear may move by sliding on its belly. ⁷With its legs stretched outward, it will descend in a spray of powdery snow. ⁸When walking over ice, the polar bear walks bow-legged with toes inward. ⁹This posture enables the huge animal to move along without slipping. ¹⁰Clearly, the polar bear is very skillful at moving around its watery and icy environment.

__2__ 3. ¹We believe one man because he has an "honest face," but we do not trust another person who, we notice, has "shifty eyes." ²In fact, a liar's body and voice do give clues that he or she is not telling the truth. ³When people are lying, they tend to speak in a higher voice than usual. ⁴They stumble over their words, saying "uh" and "er" a lot. ⁵People smile less when they are lying. ⁶When they do smile, the smile tends to look forced. ⁷Many people, when they lie, don't use their hands much. ⁸They keep them still or out of sight. ⁹And yes, "shifty" eyes can indicate that a person is lying. ¹⁰People telling a lie tend to look away from the person they are speaking to.

(Continues on next page)

_____ 4. ¹Studies have shown that people believed to have a high status tend to have more influence on others' actions. ²Researchers demonstrated the effect of status by first having a poorly dressed man violate the "wait" signal at street corners in Austin, Texas. ³His action triggered little jaywalking from other pedestrians. ⁴Then the same man dressed like a bank president. ⁵After his change in wardrobe, his going against the "wait" prompted many more pedestrians to jaywalk with him. ⁶A separate experiment in Sydney, Australia, had similar results. ⁷Pedestrians in Sydney were more cooperative when approached by a well-dressed survey taker than they were when approached by one who was poorly dressed.

_____ 5. ¹Sundays aren't what they used to be—a day for reading and rest. ²In the past, most stores and businesses were closed on Sunday. ³Liquor was unavailable by law. ⁴Worship and family time helped recharge people's energy for the week ahead. ⁵Today, religious services and family meals may still be on the agenda. ⁶Nevertheless, people use Sundays to catch up on errands, watch sports on TV, or work around the house or at their job. ⁷At present, more than thirty-eight states permit sales of alcohol on Sunday. ⁸Stores stay open because Sunday shopping offers additional profit. ⁹There's even a bank with an advertising campaign based on doing business on Sundays. ¹⁰And circulation of the Sunday newspaper has dropped dramatically, with people saying they no longer have time to read.

LOCATIONS OF MAIN IDEAS: Mastery Test 4

The main idea may appear at any place within each of the five paragraphs that follow. Write the number of each main idea sentence in the space provided.

___2___ 1. [1]Have you ever heard a kid in public pleading with a parent, saying over and over something like "Please? Please? Please?" or "Mom, Mom, Mom"? [2]Kids have a number of successful ways to nag their parents. [3]The riskiest type is the acting-out nag, in which kids throw an all-out tantrum in a public place—holding their breath, crying, and refusing to leave a store until they get what they want. [4]Sugar-coated nags promise love in return for a purchase and may rely on sweet, adorable comments like "You're the best dad in the world." [5]Pity nags claim that a kid will be heartbroken or humiliated or teased by friends if a parent refuses to buy something. [6]Threatening nags are the nastiest, with kids vowing to hate their parents forever or to run away from home if what they want isn't bought at once. [7]Kids may even use a number of nags at the same time.

___5___ 2. [1]The dandelion, widely known as an annoying weed, is also a nutritious vegetable that can be eaten raw or cooked. [2]Acorns, though bitter-tasting, are found everywhere and can be ground up into a paste that is safe to eat. [3]Grasshoppers, crickets, and beetles are also a widespread and healthy food source. [4]Even the common earthworms and some caterpillars can be eaten by humans. [5]As these examples suggest, there are many sources of food available in the outdoors—for those brave enough to eat them.

_____ 3. [1]"Take some chicken soup for your cold." [2]"Eating carrots will help you see better." [3]Just about everyone can cite old wives' tales like the ones above. [4]They've been around as long as mothers have, probably because they offer comforting advice about experiences we all share and worry about. [5]The amazing thing is that in our modern scientific world, some old wives' tales have actually been proven true. [6]For example, eating chicken soup really *does* help a cold. [7]Although it can't cure it, the soup opens the sinuses and helps fight head congestion. [8]In addition, chicken contains natural chemicals which thin the mucus in the lungs that causes coughing. [9]The carrots in the old wives' tale won't actually improve vision, but the beta carotene they contain helps fight against an eye disease that can eventually cause blindness. [10]Finally, Mom was also right about fish being brain food. [11]It contains zinc, which affects brain function, including memory, and it's healthy in other ways as well.

(Continues on next page)

___2___ 4. ¹No one likes a bully. ²So if your child has been terrorizing other children, you'll be glad to know you can redirect that antisocial behavior in several ways. ³Bullies need a physical outlet for their aggressive feelings. ⁴Encourage the child to join a sports team or get regular physical exercise. ⁵Also, reward the bully for cooperative social behavior, even if you have to arrange a situation where he or she can be pleasant to others. ⁶Point out the good qualities the bully does have, and say that those very qualities can get a person the attention he or she so much wants. ⁷Last, help the bully find a positive role model. ⁸Children often behave like their parents in social situations. ⁹Be prepared to change your behavior if you yourself use aggression to accomplish goals.

___1___ 5. ¹Aside from its enormous population—there are 4,000 different species of this insect worldwide—the lowly cockroach has some amazing characteristics. ²In the first place, the bug is fast. ³Even the smallest roach can run up to three miles an hour. ⁴What's more, cockroaches can change course as often as twenty-five times in a second, making them the most nimble animals known. ⁵Roaches are tough to catch. ⁶With sense organs located front and back, they can start to flee from predators within 0.054 seconds of detecting potential danger. ⁷Second, they are ideally adapted to living with people. ⁸They eat almost anything and are comfortable anywhere as long as the temperature is above freezing. ⁹Most species can fit through a crevice no wider than the thickness of a quarter, so any building gives them endless places to rest and breed. ¹⁰And they're perfect travelers, hitching a ride in pant cuffs or grocery bags. ¹¹Finally, the cockroach has an astonishing capacity for survival. ¹²It can hold its breath for nearly forty minutes under water. ¹³Because its brain is spread throughout its body, the roach can survive for several weeks if its head is removed carefully enough to prevent it from bleeding to death. ¹⁴And because roaches sample food before it enters their mouths, they have learned to avoid foul-tasting poisons. ¹⁵This makes them hard to kill with insecticides.

LOCATIONS OF MAIN IDEAS: Mastery Test 5

The main idea may appear at any place within each of the five paragraphs that follow. Write the number of each main idea sentence in the space provided.

6 1. [1]Studies of men's speech show that it is typically direct and positive. [2]Women's speech, on the other hand, tends to be less bold and more hesitant. [3]While a man is likely to state, "It's cold in here," a woman is more likely to ask, "Is it cold in here, or is it just me?" [4]Similar studies show that men interrupt women far more often than women interrupt men. [5]And in listening to couples' conversations, researchers have found that topics that succeed (those that are pursued in the conversation) are usually introduced by the man. [6]Apparently, men's greater social power influences how men and women speak.

3 2. [1]"Fatso!" "Goof-off!" "Jerk!" [2]Most people realize that such name-calling shows disrespect. [3]But verbal disrespect also comes in less obvious forms. [4]One such form is criticism that reduces a person to some undesirable behavior: [5]"All you ever do is sit around"; "You've always been a lousy cook." [6]Repeatedly interrupting someone also shows disrespect. [7]Such interruptions often indicate that what the person is about to say is unimportant to you. [8]Using someone's remark as a way of changing the subject to yourself also is disrespectful. [9]For instance, if someone says, "I can't find my car keys" and your only response is "I've been looking all day for my math book," you're suggesting that *your* concerns matter, but the other person's don't.

3 3. [1]Leadership style is the way a manager uses authority to lead others. [2]Every manager has a definite style. [3]Still, three broad categories of leadership have been identified. [4]First is the ruling style. [5]Rulers centralize leadership. [6]They do not involve others in decision-making. [7]Next is the democratic style. [8]Democratic leaders transfer authority. [9]They involve employees in decision-making and encourage open communication. [10]Yet they make it clear that the leader has the final say. [11]The third style of leadership is the hands-off approach. [12]Hands-off leaders take the role of consultants. [13]They provide encouragement for employees' ideas and offer opinions when asked. [14]Their goal is to assist but not to direct.

(Continues on next page)

_____ 1   4.   ¹Government agencies that collect information on crime divide illegal acts into three categories. ²The first type is crimes against people. ³These involve physical violence or the threat of it. ⁴Murder, assault, and rape fall into this category. ⁵So does robbery, which is theft by force, violence, or threat. ⁶The second group, crimes against property, involves taking something belonging to another. ⁷Burglary, which is unlawful entry for the purpose of theft, is an example. ⁸Stealing cars and setting fires are other types of property crimes. ⁹Unlike crimes against people, the victims of crimes against property generally do not fear for their lives or safety. ¹⁰Victimless crimes are the third group of unlawful acts. ¹¹They are harder to define than the other categories because there is no specific victim to make a complaint and no specific criminal to arrest and bring to trial. ¹²Instead, prostitution, gambling, and illegal drug use have an effect on society as a whole.

_____ 9   5.   ¹One man robs a gas station of $250 and is sent to prison for six months. ²Another man makes millions through illegal securities trading on Wall Street and is required only to pay a fine that he can easily afford. ³A man feuding with another man plants a bomb in his car. ⁴When caught, he is charged with conspiracy and murder. ⁵Ford Motor Company sold millions of a car called the Pinto, even though its own tests had shown that the rear-mounted gas tank might explode if the car was hit in the back. ⁶Over the next eight years, five hundred people were burned to death in accidents involving Pintos. ⁷Ford paid millions of dollars in damages, but was found not guilty of criminal charges. ⁸No one went to jail. ⁹As these cases suggest, the social response to corporate and white-collar crime is quite different from the treatment of "common criminals."

LOCATIONS OF MAIN IDEAS: Mastery Test 6

The main idea may appear at any place within each of the five paragraphs that follow. Write the number of each main idea sentence in the space provided.

_____ 1. ¹Thousands of children are sent home from school each year because tiny, blood-sucking lice have made their home on the children's little heads. ²Because of their behavior and size, children are much more likely to get head lice than adults. ³Children are very likely to spread lice to others through playing. ⁴They are often touching each other and roughhousing. ⁵Girls and boys commonly share hats and hooded sweatshirts at school. ⁶They also borrow each other's combs and brushes. ⁷Because children are short, their heads often rest against the tops of seats as they sit in classes, buses, airplanes, theaters, and restaurants. ⁸Lice can then transfer easily from one child to the next child who sits in that place. ⁹A single child may spread the condition to dozens of other children before receiving treatment.

_____ 2. ¹People's sense of what is morally right and wrong develops as they age. ²In childhood, people use rules to make moral choices. ³External factors such as punishments or rewards become the basis of a person's sense of right and wrong at this stage. ⁴Later, in adolescence, people begin to look to others in their social group to determine morality. ⁵At this stage, peer groups and social expectations are used to judge whether something is right or wrong. ⁶In adulthood, people develop their own standards of morality. ⁷At this stage, they may view "the rules" or "the crowd" as morally incorrect. ⁸While not everyone reaches this stage, those that do look to themselves—not others—to determine what is morally good and bad.

_____ 3. ¹Half of all the plant and animal species in the world live in rain forests. ²Many of the medicinal drugs used in the United States contain ingredients that originate in rain forests. ³For instance, 73 percent of the 3,000 plants identified as having cancer-fighting properties come from the world's rain forests. ⁴Rain forests also help regulate the flow of water on Earth. ⁵They soak up the water from heavy tropical rains like enormous sponges. ⁶They then release the water slowly, providing a supply for people living hundreds and even thousands of miles away. ⁷For all these reasons, it is essential that nations around the world work together to protect the rain forests.

(Continues on next page)

_____ 4. ¹As the weekend rolls to a conclusion, many people experience a downward mood swing around three o'clock on Sunday. ²No matter how much fun the weekend has been, they describe a sense of depression, sadness, or even loneliness late in the day. ³Scientists offer various explanations for the Sunday blues. ⁴The first three theories are physical. ⁵One says that feeling out of sorts is a result of too much eating and drinking the night before. ⁶A second explanation places the blame on caffeine withdrawal by students and workers who taper their coffee intake on the weekends. ⁷The third says that the internal body clock gets out of whack when people stay up later and sleep in. ⁸Other theories about Sunday's unhappy mood are much more psychological. ⁹After two days off, people with stressful jobs may actually desire the daily adrenaline rush by late Sunday. ¹⁰Then there are those folks who are so used to structure in their lives that they feel lost because of the free time they have later on Sunday. ¹¹And then there are those people who hate school, hate their job, or just plain hate Monday. ¹²From their perspective, the Sunday blues are a result of having nothing but a long, hard week to look forward to after the promise of the weekend.

_____ 5. ¹Scientists wondered why certain tiny, colorful frogs found in Central and South America are so poisonous. ²An American scientist then argued in convincing fashion that the poison results from the ants in the frogs' diet. ³Tests showed that the frogs were harmless when born. ⁴Only mature frogs produced a deadly coating of poisons. ⁵The poison is so deadly, in fact, that one single frog has enough poison on it to kill a hundred people. ⁶The American scientist then examined the stomach contents of various types of these frogs. ⁷("Imagine looking into a stomach the size of a speck," she said.) ⁸In those stomachs, she found 135 species of ants, with the ants containing 15 to 20 poisonous substances. ⁹The ants, she discovered, provide 70 percent of the diet of the most deadly of the frogs.

6 Relationships I

This Chapter in a Nutshell

- To help make their ideas clear, authors use **transitions**—signal words that carry the reader from one sentence or idea to the next.
  - Typical addition transitions are *for one thing, in addition, also,* and *finally.*
  - Typical time transitions are *first, next, then, after,* and *last.*
- In addition to transitions, authors also use **patterns of organization** to show relationships between ideas and to make their ideas clear.
  - The **list of items pattern** presents a series of reasons, examples, or other points.
  - The **time order pattern** presents steps or events in the order in which they happen.

Ideas in a reading selection are almost always connected to each other. Learning to recognize these connections, or **relationships**, will help you become a better reader.

As you will see, authors use two common methods to show relationships and make their ideas clear. These two methods—**transitions** and **patterns of organization**—are explained in turn in this chapter.

Transitions

Look at the following two items. Then check (✔) the one that is easier to read and understand:

____ Paperback books cost less than hardback books. They are easier to carry.

____ Paperback books cost less than hardback books. Also, they are easier to carry.

You probably found the second item a bit easier to read and follow. The word *also* makes it clear that the writer is discussing the advantages of paperback books. One advantage is that the books are less expensive. An *additional* advantage is that they are easier to carry.

Transitions are words or phrases (such as *also*) that show the relationship between ideas. They are "bridge" words, carrying the reader across from one idea to the next.

Paperback books cost less than hardback books. $\overset{\text{ALSO}}{\underline{\hspace{3cm}}}$, they are easier to carry.

Two major types of transitions are described in this chapter: words that show addition and words that show time.

Words That Show Addition

Once again, put a check (✔) beside the item that is easier to read and understand:

____ Climbing stairs is good exercise for your muscles. It burns a lot of calories.

____ Climbing stairs is good exercise for your muscles. In addition, it burns a lot of calories.

The words *In addition* in the second item helps make the relationship between the two sentences clear. The author is listing the benefits of climbing stairs. The first benefit is good exercise for the muscles. In addition, climbing stairs burns a lot of calories. *In addition* and words like it are known as addition words.

Addition words signal added ideas. These words tell you a writer is presenting one or more ideas that continue along the same line of thought as a previous idea. Like all transitions, addition words help writers organize their information and present it clearly to readers. In the cartoon on the next page, the words *To begin with* introduce a list, and the words *Second* and *Also* add to the list of reasons why the dog should be hired.

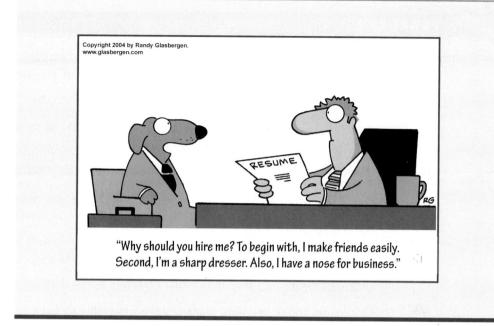

Copyright 2004 by Randy Glasbergen.
www.glasbergen.com

"Why should you hire me? To begin with, I make friends easily.
Second, I'm a sharp dresser. Also, I have a nose for business."

Below are some common words that show addition:

Addition Words

one	to begin with	in addition	last
first	another	next	last of all
first of all	second	moreover	final
for one thing	also	furthermore	finally

Examples

The following items contain addition words. Notice how these words introduce ideas that *add to* what has already been said.

- Hippos give birth under water. They *also* nurse their young there.

- One reason people have dogs is for companionship; *another* reason is for protection.

- The human body has six pounds of skin. *Furthermore*, it contains sixty thousand miles of blood vessels.

PRACTICE 1

Complete each sentence with a suitable addition word from the box. Try to use each transition once. Then, in the spaces provided, write the letter of the transition you have chosen.

A. also	B. another	C. for one thing
D. in addition	E. second	

Hint: Make sure that each addition word or phrase that you choose fits smoothly into the flow of the sentence. Test each choice by reading the sentence aloud.

___B___ 1. One good way to be friendly is to ask people questions about themselves. ___Another___ way is to listen carefully when they answer.

___A___ 2. Employers today say they want college graduates to have good writing and speaking skills. They ___also___ want them to be able to think critically and solve problems.

___D___ 3. Almost 80 percent of college students drink alcohol. ___In addition___, about 40 percent either binge drink or drink to get drunk.

___C___ 4. I find your attitude insulting. ___For one thing___, you pull out your phone and begin texting when I try to talk with you.

___E___ 5. There are different ways to solve problems. One way is simple trial and error. A ___second___ way to proceed is to break a problem into smaller, more manageable pieces. Each piece is easier to solve than the problem as a whole.

Words That Show Time

Check (✓) the item that is easier to read and understand:

____ I had blood work done. I went to the doctor.

____ I had blood work done. Then I went to the doctor.

The word *Then* in the second item clarifies the relationship between the sentences. After having blood work done, the speaker goes to the doctor. *Then* and words like it are time words.

Time words indicate a time relationship. These transitions tell us *when* something happened in relation to when something else happened. They help writers organize and make clear the order of events, stages, and steps in a process. In the cartoon below, the words *First, Then,* and *Finally* mark different stages in "growing up."

"Growing up isn't easy. First, in preschool, you have to learn to tie your shoes. Then in kindergarten, it's the alphabet. Finally, in first grade, they hit you with addition and subtraction."

Here are some common time words:

Time Words

before	next	while	later
previously	soon	during	after
first	often	until	eventually
second	as	now	finally
third	when	then	last

Note: Additional ways of showing time are dates ("In 1850 . . ."; "Throughout the 20th century . . ."; "By 2018 . . .") and other time references ("Within a week . . ."; "by the end of the month . . ."; "in two years . . .").

Examples

The following items contain time words. Notice how these words show us *when* something takes place.

● *After* our kids take their morning showers, there is usually no hot water left.

● It used to take me thirty-five minutes to get to school. *Now*, because of road construction, that time has nearly tripled.

● I begin my "Things To Do" list by writing down everything I need to do the next day. *Then* I label each item A (very important), B (important), or C (not important).

Helpful Tips about Transitions

Here are two points to keep in mind about transitions:

 TIP 1 Some transition words have the same meaning. For example, *also, moreover*, and *furthermore* all mean "in addition." Authors typically use a variety of transitions to avoid repetition.

 TIP 2 Certain words can serve as two different types of transitions, depending on how they are used. For example, the word *first* may be used as an addition word to show that the author is presenting a series of points, as in the following sentences:

● My mother has some strange kitchen habits. *First*, she loves to cook with the television on full blast. *Moreover*, she . . .

First may also be used to signal a time sequence, as in this sentence:

● The paramedics raced to the man who had collapsed on the sidewalk. *First*, they checked his pulse and breathing. *Then* . . .

PRACTICE 2

Complete each sentence with a suitable time word from the box. Try to use each transition once. Then, in the spaces provided, write the letter of the transition you have chosen.

| A. after | B. before | C. during |
| D. then | E. when | |

Hint: Make sure that each time word that you choose fits smoothly into the flow of the sentence. Test each choice by reading the sentence aloud.

A 1. __After_____ playing outside most of the day, the children fell asleep quickly that night.

E 2. ____When_____ I was in the shower, a hairy spider crept out of the drain.

D 3. First, my uncle studies the food ads to see which stores have the best specials. ____then_____ he clips all the cents-off coupons.

B 4. ____Before_____ the school lays off any teachers, it should reduce the size of its office staff.

C 5. Some people rudely talk with each other and use their phones ____during_____ a movie.

Patterns of Organization

You have learned that transitions show the relationships between ideas in sentences. In the same way, **patterns of organization** show the relationships between supporting details in paragraphs, essays, and chapters. It helps to recognize the patterns in which authors arrange information. You will then be better able to understand and remember what you read.

The rest of this chapter discusses two major patterns of organization:

● The **list of items pattern**
  (Addition words are often used in this pattern of organization.)

● The **time order pattern**
  (Time words are often used in this pattern of organization.)

Noticing the transitions in a passage often can help you become aware of its pattern of organization. Transitions can also help you find the major supporting details.

1   The List of Items Pattern

List of Items
Item 1
Item 2
Item 3

To understand the list of items pattern, try to arrange the following group of sentences in an order that makes sense. Put a *1* in front of the sentence that should come first, a *2* in front of the sentence that comes next, a *3* in front of the third sentence, and a *4* in front of the sentence that should come last. The result will be a short paragraph. Use the addition words as a guide.

____ Also, when you're on foot, you are more likely to meet neighbors and make new friends.

____ Finally, a brisk walk is an excellent and inexpensive form of exercise.

____ Walking can be a rewarding experience.

____ For one thing, walking lets you see firsthand what's going on in your neighborhood.

This paragraph should begin with the main idea: "Walking can be a rewarding experience." The next three sentences go on to list three reasons, resulting in the pattern of organization known as a list of items. The transitions *For one thing, Also,* and *Finally* introduce the points being listed and indicate their order. The sentences should read as follows:

> [1]Walking can be a rewarding experience. [2]For one thing, walking lets you see firsthand what's going on in your neighborhood. [3]Also, when you're on foot, you are more likely to meet neighbors and make new friends. [4]Finally, a brisk walk is an excellent and inexpensive form of exercise.

A **list of items** is a series of reasons, examples, or other points that support an idea. The items are listed in the order the author prefers. Addition words are often used in a list of items to tell us that another supporting point is being added to one or more points already mentioned. Textbook authors frequently organize material into lists of items, such as a list of the causes of climate change, the results of stress, or the reasons why some people never vote.

Addition Words Used in the List of Items Pattern

one	to begin with	in addition	last
first	another	next	last of all
first of all	second	moreover	final
for one thing	also	furthermore	finally

✔

Check Your Understanding

The paragraph below is organized as a list of items. Complete the outline of the paragraph by adding the three major details listed in the paragraph. Then read the explanation that follows.

To help you find the major details, do two things to the paragraph:

● Underline the addition words that introduce the major details in the list;

● Number (*1, 2, . . .*) each item in the list.

¹A number of different theories attempt to explain crime. ²One theory says that crime is caused by biology. ³This explanation says that people inherit the tendency to commit crime much as they inherit eye color. ⁴Another theory suggests that crime is caused by psychological factors. ⁵According to this view, anger caused in childhood—by such painful events as abuse and neglect—drives people to commit crimes. ⁶A third, more recent view is that crime is caused by social forces. ⁷According to this theory, economic, social, and political inequalities create an environment in which crime is likely to happen.

Main idea: A number of different theories attempt to explain crime.

1. _____

2. _____

3. _____

Explanation

The main idea is that a number of different theories attempt to explain crime. Note the list words: "a number of different theories." (At times you may also express the main idea in a short heading that describes what's being listed; the heading here could be "Theories to Explain Crime.") Following are the three theories you should have added to the outline:

1. Crime is caused by biology. (This item is signaled by the addition word *One.*)

2. Crime is caused by psychological factors. (This item is signaled by the addition word *Another.*)

3. Crime is caused by social forces. (This item is signaled by the addition word *third.*)

PRACTICE 3

A. The following passage uses a listing pattern. Outline the passage by filling in the major details.

> *Hint:* Underline the addition words that introduce the items in the list, and number the items.

> ¹Research has revealed three different types of kindness. ²First of all, there is natural kindness, based on our ability to identify with others and sense what they're feeling. ³This kindness shows up at a very early age. ⁴A grade-school child who says that a caged gorilla looks sad or who gets upset when another child is bullied has this natural kindness. ⁵The second type of kindness is rule-guided. ⁶Rule-guided people have learned "It's wrong to do that." ⁷For example, rule-guided children do not hit other children because they have been taught that hitting is wrong. ⁸The last type of kindness is imitative. ⁹We imitate the behavior of people we admire. ¹⁰For instance, imitative children who admire their parents will avoid behavior that their parents disapprove of—because they want to be like their parents.

Main idea: Research has revealed three different types of kindness.

1. *First of all, there is natural kindness, based on our ability*
2. *rule guided*
3. *imitative*

B. The following passage uses a listing pattern. Complete the map of the passage by filling in the missing major details.

> ¹Opossums use a few defense methods to cope with danger. ²The best-known defense is "playing dead." ³An opossum using this defense goes into a coma. ⁴In that state, it appears dead and can be dropped, kicked, or even cut without responding. ⁵This may seem to be a foolish method of defense, for it leaves the animal open to attack. ⁶But many predators will not eat what they haven't killed, and others won't attack something that doesn't run away from them. ⁷However, most opossums—over 90 percent—never use this method. ⁸Instead, their defense is simply to run away from danger immediately. ⁹Finally, others use the method of trying to scare off enemies—they hiss, salivate, bare their teeth, excrete wastes, or release a terrible odor.

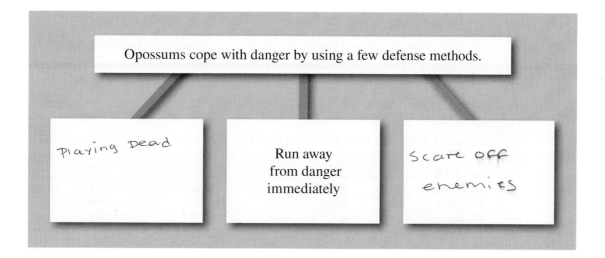

Opossums cope with danger by using a few defense methods.

Playing Dead

Run away
from danger
immediately

Scare off
enemies

2   The Time Order Pattern

To understand the time order pattern, try to arrange the following group of sentences in an order that makes sense. Put a *1* in front of the sentence that should come first, a *2* in front of the sentence that comes next, a *3* in front of the third sentence, and a *4* in front of the sentence that should come last. The result will be a short paragraph. Use the time words as a guide.

__3__   After the dish had been brought to Germany, a German cook decided to broil the meat, calling it Hamburg steak.

__4__   Finally, German immigrants took the dish to the United States, where it became known as "hamburger."

__1__   For centuries, a dish made of raw ground beef was eaten by the Tartars, a group living in central Asia.

__2__   Then a merchant from Germany discovered the Tartars' recipe for ground beef and took it to his hometown, Hamburg.

Authors usually present events in the order in which they happen, resulting in a pattern of organization known as **time order**. Clues to the pattern of the above sentences are time words (*Then, After, Finally*). The sentences should read as follows:

[1]For centuries, a dish made of raw ground beef was eaten by the Tartars, a group living in central Asia. [2]Then a merchant from Germany discovered the Tartars' recipe for ground beef and took it to his hometown, Hamburg. [3]After the dish had been brought to Germany, a German cook decided to broil the meat, calling it Hamburg steak. [4]Finally, German immigrants took the dish to the United States, where it became known as "hamburger."

Time Words Used in the Time Order Pattern

before	next	while	later
previously	soon	during	after
first	often	until	eventually
second	as	now	finally
third	when	then	last

As a student, you will see time order used frequently. Textbooks in all fields describe events and processes, such as the events leading to the uprisings in Egypt in 2011, the steps involved in writing a paper, the growth of Henry Ford's auto empire, or the stages in the development of a tadpole into a frog.

In addition to time transitions, signals for the time order pattern include dates, times, and such words as *stages, series, steps,* and *process.*

The two most common kinds of time order are (1) a series of events or stages and (2) a series of steps (directions for how to do something). Each is discussed below and on the pages that follow.

Series of Events or Stages

Authors sometimes describe a series of events—for example, the financial mistakes that led to the major recession that began in 2008 in the United States. Or authors may explain a series of stages, such as those that turn a caterpillar into a butterfly. In both cases, they use time order. They discuss the first event or stage, then the second, and so on until the final event or stage in the series is reached.

✓ *Check Your Understanding*

Here is a paragraph that is organized according to time order. Complete the outline of the paragraph by listing the missing stages in the order in which they happen.
   To help you find the stages, do two things to the paragraph:

   ● Underline the time words that introduce each stage in the process;

   ● Number (*1, 2, . . .*) each stage in the process.

   ¹Very young children in a hospital often go through three stages of separation anxiety. ²In the first stage, "protest," these children try actively to get the parent (especially the mother) back. ³For instance, they may shake their cribs and hurl themselves about. ⁴In the second stage, "despair," the babies and children become inactive and withdrawn. ⁵They may cry, but generally they are so quiet that they are mistakenly assumed to have accepted the hospital. ⁶In the final stage, "detachment," they respond to hospital workers—they eat, play with toys, and are friendly. ⁷But they fail to respond to a visiting parent.

Main idea: Very young children in a hospital often go through three stages of separation anxiety.

   1.   *protest*

   2.   *Despair*

   3.   *Detachment*

Explanation

You should have added the following stages to the outline:

1. Protest. (The author signals this stage with the time transition *first.*)

2. Despair. (The author signals this stage with the time word *second.*)

3. Detachment. (The author signals this stage with the time word *final.*)

As you can see by the transitions used, the relationship between the points is one of time: the second stage happens *after* the first, and the third stage *after* the second.

PRACTICE 4

The following passage describes a sequence of events. Outline the paragraph by filling in the major details. Note that the major details are signaled by time words.

Hint: Underline the time word or words that introduce each major detail, and number each major detail.

¹All of us have certain fears at different points in our lives. ²When we are young children, we worry that something bad will happen to our parents. ³We are afraid of being alone if our parents die or go away. ⁴Then, as teenagers, we fear that we will be socially rejected or seen as "uncool" nobodies. ⁵We often act against our better instincts in order to be accepted as one of the crowd. ⁶Later, if we become parents, our greatest fear is that someone or something will harm our children. ⁷Our sense of love and responsibility for our kids makes the thought of our children being hurt our greatest nightmare. ⁸Last, when elderly, we fear poor health and death. ⁹We worry about losing our independence, being a burden to other people, and, of course, the end of our lives.

Main idea: **All of us have certain fears at different points in our lives.**

1. *young children - something bad will happen to our par*
2. *teenagers - socially rejected*
3. *Parents - someone or something will harm our children*
4. *Elderly - poor health and death*

Series of Steps (Directions)

Time Order: Steps

Step 1
Step 2
Step 3

When authors give directions, they use time order. They explain step 1, then step 2, and so on through the entire series of steps that must be taken toward a specific goal.

✓ Check Your Understanding

Here is a paragraph that gives directions. Complete the outline of the paragraph that follows by adding the missing steps in the correct sequence. Then read the explanation that follows.

To help yourself identify each step, do two things to the paragraph:

● Underline the time words that introduce each item in the sequence;

● Number (*1, 2, . . .*) each step in the sequence.

[1]To improve your memory for names, follow this procedure. [2]First, when you are introduced to someone, make sure you hear the person's name clearly. [3]Next, repeat the name with your greeting: "Nice to meet you, Ms. Baron." [4]Then take a good look at the person and concentrate on matching the face with the name. [5]Last, repeat the name again when you are leaving the person: "Good meeting you, Ms. Baron."

Main idea: To improve your memory for names, follow this procedure.

1. Make sure you hear
2. _____
3. _____
4. _____

Explanation

You should have added these steps to the outline:

1. Make sure you hear the person's name clearly during an introduction. (The author signals this step with the time word *First*.)

2. Repeat the name as you greet the person. (The author signals this step with the time word *Next*.)

3. Concentrate on matching the name with the face. (The author's signal is the time word *Then*.)

4. When you leave the person, repeat his or her name. (The author signals this final step with the time word *Last*.)

PRACTICE 5

The following passage gives directions involving several steps that must be done in order. Complete the map below by filling in the three missing steps. To help yourself identify each step, do two things:

- Underline the time words that introduce each item in the sequence;
- Number (*1, 2, . . .*) each step in the sequence.

¹To study a textbook effectively, follow a few helpful steps. ²First, preview the reading. ³This means a quick reading of the first and last paragraphs and of the headings in the chapter. ⁴Previewing will help you understand the selection better once you do begin reading. ⁵After previewing, you are ready to read and mark the selection. ⁶Mark key definitions with "Def"; useful examples with "Ex"; important lists of items with "1, 2, 3"; and key points with underlines. ⁷Your next step is to write study notes for the selection. ⁸By selecting and writing down the important parts of the chapter, you will have already begun to learn them. ⁹The last step of this process is to study the ideas in your notes. ¹⁰Do so by repeating the material over and over to yourself. ¹¹When you can recite it without looking at your notes, you'll really know the material.

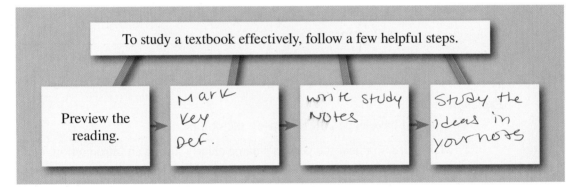

To study a textbook effectively, follow a few helpful steps.

Preview the reading. → Mark key Def. → write study Notes → Study the ideas in your notes

A Note on Main Ideas and Patterns of Organization

A paragraph's main idea may indicate its pattern of organization. For example, here's the main idea of the paragraph you just read: "To study a textbook effectively, follow a few helpful steps." The words *a few helpful steps* suggest that this paragraph will be organized according to time order. Another good example is the main idea of the earlier paragraph on the causes of crime: "A number of different theories attempt to explain crime." The words *different theories* suggest that this paragraph will be a list of items.

Paying close attention to the main idea, then, can give you a quick sense of a paragraph's pattern of organization. Try, for instance, to guess the pattern of the paragraph with this main idea:

While there are hundreds of opportunities for volunteering, most fall into four basic categories.

The statement that volunteer opportunities "fall into four basic categories" is a strong indication that the paragraph will list those categories. The main idea helps us guess that the paragraph will be a list of four items.

PRACTICE 6

Most of the main ideas below have been taken from college textbooks. In the space provided, write the letter of the pattern of organization that each main idea suggests.

_B_ 1. April 12, 1861, marked the beginning of the four years of bloodshed and bitterness called the Civil War.
  A. List of items   B. Time order

_A_ 2. America's highways would be safer if drivers followed three simple rules.
  A. List of items   B. Time order

_A_ 3. The widespread use of the Internet has changed American society in a number of ways.
  A. List of items   B. Time order

_B_ 4. A series of important world events led to the creation of the United Nations in 1945.
  A. List of items   B. Time order

_A_ 5. There are several guidelines that every person needs to follow for good health.
  A. List of items   B. Time order

_B_ 6. Children pass through various stages on their way to becoming adults.
  A. List of items   B. Time order

_A_ 7. The students who are most likely to drop out of school often share a few characteristics.
  A. List of items   B. Time order

_B_ 8. In order to create a mummy, ancient Egyptians followed a sequence of unusual steps.
  A. List of items   B. Time order

_A_ 9. Therapists use a broad variety of methods to help individuals cope with their lives.
  A. List of items   B. Time order

_____10. Income taxes have been part of society throughout history, from the time of the Bible to the present day.
      A. List of items   B. Time order

Two Final Points

1 While many passages have just one pattern of organization, often the patterns are mixed. You may find that part of a passage uses a list of items pattern, and another part of the same passage uses a time order pattern. (For example, in the paragraph on page 236 about studying a textbook, the steps are given in time order, but the second step contains a list of four kinds of items to mark.)

2 Remember that not all relationships between ideas are signaled by transitions. An author may present a list of items, for example, without using addition words. So as you read, watch for the relationships themselves, not just the transitions.

CHAPTER REVIEW

In this chapter, you learned how authors use transitions and patterns of organization to make their ideas clear. Just as transitions show relationships between ideas in sentences, patterns of organization show relationships between supporting details in paragraphs and longer pieces of writing.

You also learned two common kinds of relationships that authors use to make their ideas clear:

- **Addition relationships**
  - Authors often present a list or series of reasons, examples, or other details that support an idea. The items have no time order, but are listed in whatever order the author prefers.
  - Transition words that signal such addition relationships include *for one thing, in addition, also,* and *finally.*

- **Time relationships**
  - Authors usually discuss a series of events or steps in the order in which they happen, resulting in a time order.
  - Words that signal such time relationships include *first, next, then, after,* and *last.*

The next chapter—Chapter 7—will help you learn three other important kinds of relationships: definition-example, comparison and/or contrast, and cause-effect.

On the Web: If you are using this book in class, you can visit our website for additional practice in understanding relationships that involve addition and time. Go to **www.townsendpress.com** and click on "Learning Center."

REVIEW TEST 1

To review what you've learned in this chapter, complete each item by filling in the blank.

1. __Transitions__ are words or phrases (like *also* or *another* or *then* or *last of all*) that show the relationships between ideas. They are bridges that connect one idea with another.

2. Patterns of __Organization__ show the relationships between supporting details in a paragraph or longer passage.

3. Typical __Addition__ words are *for one thing, also, moreover,* and *another.* Such words tell us the writer is presenting one or more ideas that add to the same line of thought as a previous idea.

4. Typical __Time__ words are *then, next, later,* and *after.* They tell us when something happened in relation to when something else happened.

5. Sometimes the __main Idea__ of a paragraph may suggest the pattern of organization in the paragraph.

REVIEW TEST 2

A. (1–2.) Name the type of transition used in each of the following cartoons.

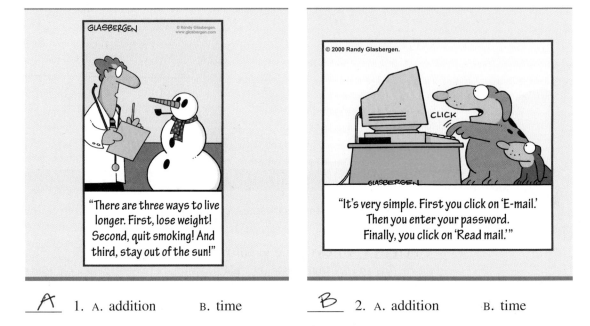

_A_ 1. A. addition B. time   _B_ 2. A. addition B. time

B. Fill in each blank with one of the transitions in the box. Use each word once. Then write the letter of the word in the space provided.

A. also	B. another	C. before	D. then

_C_ 3. ___Before___ the thunderstorm struck, the air was strangely quiet, and the sky was an odd yellow color.

_B_ 4. One good thing about my apartment's location is that it is close to school. ___Another___ benefit is that it's in a safe area.

_D_ 5. Break six eggs, separating the whites from the yolks. ___Then___ beat the whites at high speed until they are light and fluffy.

_A_ 6. I've found that a short nap before dinner relaxes me after the stresses of the day. The nap ___also___ gives me the energy I'll need to do homework in the evening.

C. Fill in each blank with an appropriate transition from the box. Use each transition once.

first	then	while

¹Few people are able to resist the following directions. ²They will keep trying over and over again to see if they can outsmart their foot, but they won't succeed. ³(7)_____First_____ sit down in a chair, preferably a straight chair. ⁴(8)_____Then_____ lift your right foot off the floor and make clockwise circles with it. ⁵(9)_____while_____ doing so, draw the number "6" in the air with your right hand. ⁶You will not be able to stop your foot from moving in the opposite direction. ⁷You and I both know how stupid this is, but before the day is done, you are going to try it again—if you've not already done so!

___B___ 10. The pattern of organization of the above selection is
      A. list of items.   B. time order.

REVIEW TEST 3

A. Fill in each blank with one of the transitions in the box. Use each transition once.

finally	first of all	second
then	when	

¹If I were the king (or queen) of America and had total power, there are certain things I would do in Washington. ²(1)_____First of all_____, I would see that every person in our country has the same high level of health care that our politicians do. ³Our elected officials should not get better medical treatment than ordinary American citizens. ⁴(2)_____Second_____, I would make Washington provide a maternal leave policy. ⁵A working mother should get at least ten weeks of time off, with pay, to be with her newborn baby. ⁶(3)_____Then_____ she will really have time to bond with her child and learn to be a caring parent. ⁷Most countries in North and South America provide a paid leave of at least ten weeks, and Canada provides up to fifty weeks. ⁸(4)_____finally_____, I would limit the power of lobbyists in Washington. ⁹Right now there are hundreds of thousands of well-paid lobbyists working full-time in Washington. ¹⁰They make sure that our politicians pass laws that are good for the companies they represent. ¹¹(5)_____when_____ companies benefit, the best interests of ordinary Americans often suffer. ¹²All Americans—not just the wealthy and powerful—should be the ones who matter most in Washington.

B. Below are the beginnings of five passages. Label each one with the letter of its pattern of organization. (You may find it helpful to underline the transition or transitions in each item.)

    A   List of items
    B   Time order

___B___ 6.   ¹Eskimos begin building an igloo by cutting blocks of ice from well-packed snow. ²The tops are cut at a slight angle, so when they are piled in a circle, they curve inward and form a dome. ³When the igloo is completed, a door is carved out. . . .

___A___ 7.   ¹Homeless people may resist being taken to city shelters, where they could get a hot meal and a bed for the night. ²For one thing, they may feel safer on their own than crowded together with others, some of whom may be mentally unstable. ³There is also the matter of simple pride. . . .

___B___ 8.   ¹The first printed ad appeared in about 1440. ²Hung on church doors, it advertised a prayerbook. ³The next big event for advertising came soon after the newspaper was born in the early 1600s. ⁴An ad in a London newspaper offered a reward for the return of some stolen horses. . . .

___B___ 9.   ¹In Edgar Allan Poe's story "The Tell-Tale Heart," the insane narrator describes his murder of an old man who had been a tenant in his house. ²First he tells how he treated the old man kindly during the week before the murder. ³Then he explains how, on the eighth night, he . . .

___A___ 10.   ¹Effective treatment of diabetes depends on early detection. ²Various symptoms suggest the presence of diabetes. ³Some are excessive thirst, hunger, weight loss, and blurry vision. ⁴Additional symptoms are frequent bouts of fatigue and frequent urination. . . .

REVIEW TEST 4

Here is a chance to apply your understanding of addition and time relationships to a full-length reading. The following selection from the college textbook *Sociology: An Introduction*, Third Edition, deals with a troubling aspect of family life.

To help you continue to strengthen your work on the skills taught in previous chapters, there are also questions on vocabulary in context, the central point and main ideas, and supporting details.

Words to Watch

Below are some words in the reading that do not have strong context support. Each word is followed by the number of the paragraph in which it appears and its meaning there. These words are indicated in the selection by a small circle (°).

unique (2): unusual
resolved (3): settled
virtually (3): almost entirely
brutalizes (5): treats cruelly
stakes (6): benefits that can be gained and lost
appalled (6): horrified
intensity (6): great strength of feeling
restraints (7): controls
intercede (7): become involved in order to bring about agreement
constitute (8): make up, form

BEHIND CLOSED DOORS: VIOLENCE IN THE FAMILY

Michael S. Bassis, Richard J. Gelles, Ann Levine

1   "And they lived happily ever after." Hundreds of stories about marriages and families end with this line. Typically, loved ones are reunited; obstacles to marriage overcome; problems with children resolved. Indeed, the very idea of living happily ever after is linked, in our minds, with the special warmth of the family. Yet if we look behind the closed doors of many American households, we discover that all is not peace and harmony.

Some Myths and Realities

2   With the exception of the police and the military, the family is the most violent social group in our society. The home is a more dangerous place than a dark alley. A person is more likely to be murdered in his or her home, by a member of the family, than by anyone else, anywhere else, in society. One in every four murders in the United States is committed by a member of the victim's family. Our country is not unique° in this respect.

3   In an earlier time, few Americans would have believed these statements. Then the sociologists Murray Straus, Richard Gelles, and Barbara Steinmetz conducted a national survey on family violence. Rather than relying on official statistics (incidents of physical abuse known to the police and other social agencies), the researchers asked a representative sample of Americans how they resolved° family conflicts, whether they had hit, spanked, punched, or otherwise assaulted a family member, and how often. The results of this survey exploded a number of myths about

violence in the home. The first myth was that incidents of family violence are rare. They are not. In a year-long study, nearly two million children had been punched, kicked, beaten up, or injured with a knife or gun by a member of their own family. Sixteen percent of couples reported at least one incident of violence in the year of the survey, and nearly a third had experienced violence at some point in their marriage. Two-thirds reported that they had hit a child at least once. In most cases, child abuse was not an isolated incident: if a child was assaulted once, he or she was usually assaulted several times. A second myth suggested that violence occurs only in poor, uneducated families. This, too, proved false. Economic stress does make family violence more likely. But someone had been slapped (or worse) in virtually° every household in the United States, regardless of family income. One reason for the belief that only poor families are violent is that the wealthy take their injuries to private doctors, who were more likely to treat the problem as a private matter than to report family violence to authorities.

4   As for educational level and family violence, 16 percent of college students in one survey knew of at least one physical fight between their parents during the preceding year. Nearly 50 percent of the students had been hit by their parents during their senior year of high school, and 8 percent had been injured severely enough to require first aid or medical attention.

5   Most of us assume that anyone who brutalizes° a loved one is "sick"—mentally ill. This is also a myth. The proportion of violent family members who are psychologically disturbed, in the clinical sense, is no higher than the proportion in the population as a whole.

Sociological Explanations

How do sociologists explain the high 6 levels of violence in the family? A number of factors seem to be at work. The first is *intimacy*. Family members are intensely involved with one another. They have deep emotional investments in one another. When quarrels break out or problems arise, the stakes° are higher than in other social groups. A man who is amused by the behavior of a female colleague who is drunk may become enraged if his wife has a little too much to drink. A politician who has been an active supporter of gay rights, at some risk to her career, may be appalled° to discover that her own child is homosexual. Why? Because the behavior of a member of our family is a direct reflection on ourselves. The intensity° of family relationships tends to magnify the most trivial things, such as a burned dinner or a whining child. When did you last hear of someone beating up the cook in a restaurant for preparing an unacceptable meal? But such minor offenses and small oversights often spark violent family fights.

A second factor contributing to 7 violence in the home is *privacy*: because family affairs are regarded as private, there are few outside restraints° on violence. When a family quarrel threatens to become a fight, there are no bystanders to break it up, as there might be on the street or in some other public place. Police are reluctant to intercede° in family quarrels—for good reason. More police are killed responding to calls about domestic disturbances than are killed chasing armed robbers. Neighbors may know that a parent is abusing a child but resist "getting involved." The family, after all, has a right to privacy. Victims may be too ashamed to report family violence to the police. Indeed, a small child may not know something is wrong or unusual when Mother holds his or her hand in a flame as punishment.

8   Third, and perhaps most disturbing, there is a good deal of *social and cultural support* for the use of physical force in the family. Parents are allowed—indeed, encouraged—to spank their children. "Spare the rod and spoil the child," the old saying goes. Most people do not think of spanking a child as violence. But suppose a total stranger in the supermarket smacked your daughter because he disapproved of something she said? Suppose a teacher hit her across the face? Either would constitute° assault and battery in a court of law. What makes parents different? In effect, parenthood confers a "license for hitting" in our society. So, according to some, does marriage. In one survey, one out of four people agreed that it is sometimes justifiable for a husband to hit his wife. Battered wives often say (and believe), "I asked for it" or "I had it coming." (Imagine if the attacker had been her boss, another "authority" figure, but one whose authority is limited. Because it was her husband who beat her, the situation is viewed quite differently.)

Finally, in the process of *sociali-*   9
zation, we learn to associate violence with the family. Our first experience of force nearly always takes place at home. Most of our parents use physical punishment on occasion—for our own good, of course, and because they love us. (The child is told, "This hurts me more than it hurts you.") From here it is only a small step to the conclusion that the use of violence is legitimate whenever something is really important. And the things that are most important to us are often family matters. In addition, we learn how to be violent from our families. (It takes observation and practice, perhaps with siblings, to learn how to beat up another person.) Study after study has shown that the more violence an individual experiences as a child, the more violent he or she will be as a parent. Brutality breeds brutality.

Reading Comprehension Questions

Vocabulary in Context

_____ 1. In the sentence below, the word *trivial* (trĭv′ē-əl) means
  A. rare.
  B. colorful.
  C. pleasant.
  D. unimportant.

> "The intensity of family relationships tends to magnify the most trivial things, such as a burned dinner or a whining child." (Paragraph 6)

_____ 2. In the excerpt below, the word *confers* (kən-fûrs′) means
  A. denies.
  B. gives.
  C. repeats.
  D. destroys.

> "Parents are allowed—indeed, encouraged—to spank their children. . . . In effect, parenthood confers a 'license for hitting' in our society." (Paragraph 8)

Central Point and Main Ideas

_____ 3. Which sentence best expresses the central point of the selection?
  A. Numerous murders take place at home.
  B. The American family is more violent than previously thought, a situation for which several causes have been identified.
  C. According to sociologists, there are a number of factors that explain family violence.
  D. Because family affairs are considered private, there are few outside controls on violence in the home.

_____ 4. The main idea of paragraph 7 is best expressed in its
  A. first sentence.
  B. second sentence.
  C. third sentence.
  D. last sentence.

Supporting Details

_____ 5. The major details of paragraphs 6–9 are
   A. myths about family violence.
   B. steps to take to counteract family violence.
   C. factors that explain the high levels of violence in the family.
   D. the effects of family intimacy.

_____ 6. TRUE OR FALSE? People who experience violence as children are more likely to avoid using violence with their own children.

Transitions

_____ 7. The sentences below express a relationship of
   A. addition.
   B. time.

   "In an earlier time, few Americans would have believed these statements. Then the sociologists Murray Straus, Richard Gelles, and Barbara Steinmetz conducted a national survey on family violence." (Paragraph 3)

8. Find the addition transition in the sentences below and write it here:

   _____

   "Most of us assume that anyone who brutalizes a loved one is 'sick'— mentally ill. This is also a myth." (Paragraph 5)

Patterns of Organization

_____ 9. Just as paragraphs are organized according to patterns, so are groups of paragraphs. What is the main pattern of organization of paragraphs 3–5?
   A. List of items
   B. Time order

_____ 10. Which words signal the pattern of organization of paragraphs 6–9?
   A. *Intimacy, privacy, social and cultural support, socialization*
   B. *Number, factor, force, process*
   C. *First, second, third, finally*
   D. *Family, home, parents, legitimate*

Discussion Questions

1. Why do you think the researchers "asked a representative sample of Americans how they resolved family conflicts" instead of using official statistics such as police reports? What did their method accomplish that relying on official statistics would not have accomplished?

2. What myths about family violence did the survey disprove? Why might these myths have existed in the first place?

3. Were you or was someone you know ever punished with physical force as a child? If so, what do you think have been the effects of this use of force?

4. What can society—for instance, schools, religious institutions, government, the media—do to prevent further violence in families?

Note: Writing assignments for this selection appear on pages 607–608.

Check Your Performance   **RELATIONSHIPS I**

Activity	Number Right	Points	Score
Review Test 1 (5 items)	_____	× 2 =	_____
Review Test 2 (10 items)	_____	× 3 =	_____
Review Test 3 (10 items)	_____	× 3 =	_____
Review Test 4 (10 items)	_____	× 3 =	_____
		TOTAL SCORE =	_____%

Enter your total score into the **Reading Performance Chart: Review Tests** on the inside back cover.

RELATIONSHIPS I: Mastery Test 1

A. Fill in each blank with an appropriate transition from the box. Use each transition once. Then, in the space provided, write the letter of the transition you have chosen.

A. after	**B.** another	**C.** before
D. second	**E.** then	

Hint: Make sure that each word or phrase that you choose fits smoothly into the flow of the sentence. Test your choices by reading each sentence to yourself.

_A_ 1. ¹____After____ a bad nightmare awakened me in the middle of the night, I decided to turn on the bedroom lights for a while.

_E_ 2. ¹Blinking helps to keep your eyes healthy. ²When you close your eyes, your eyelids sweep away dirt and other harmful particles. ³Fluids ____Then____ moisten and bathe the surface of your eyes.

_D_ 3. ¹Many parents today are busier than ever. First of all, they must raise their own children. ²And often their ____Second____ responsibility is to care for aging parents, even to the point of having the parents live with them.

_B_ 4. ¹A major trend in education has been the return of adults to the classroom. ²One type of nontraditional student is the adult worker seeking to advance in a job or retrain for a new career. ³____Another____ type is the homemaker preparing to enter the job market in middle age. ⁴A third type is the retired person now pursuing interests there was no time for in earlier years.

_C_ 5. ¹The American custom of dating has changed. ²____Before____ the 1970s, dating was more formal. ³Males usually had to ask for a date at least several days in advance. ⁴These days, dating has become more casual. ⁵In fact, the word "date" now sounds a bit old-fashioned to many young people. ⁶"Getting together" and "hanging out" are more likely ways of referring to dating today.

(Continues on next page)

B. Fill in each blank with an appropriate transition from the box. Use each transition once.

after	before	then	when

¹(6)___when___ President Theodore "Teddy" Roosevelt visited the South in 1902, he was invited to a hunting party. ²The organizers staked a bear cub to the ground so that the President could not miss. ³(7)___After___ he realized that the bear was pinned down, Roosevelt refused to fire. ⁴A political cartoon based on the incident appeared in a number of newspapers. ⁵The cartoon, with a drawing of the small bear, was seen by a shop owner in Brooklyn. ⁶The shop owner (8)___Then___ made up a window display version of the little bear in a soft, plush material. ⁷(9)___Before___ offering the bear to customers, the shop owner asked Roosevelt for permission to sell the new toy as "Teddy's Bear." ⁸The President gave his approval but wrote, "I don't think my name is worth much to the toy bear cub business." ⁹He was clearly wrong, for a bear-buying frenzy swept the country, and the teddy bear has been popular ever since.

___B___ 10. The pattern of organization of the above selection is
    A. list of items.
    B. time order.

RELATIONSHIPS I: Mastery Test 2

A. Fill in each blank with an appropriate transition from the box. Use each transition once. Then, in the spaces provided, write the letter of the transition you have chosen.

A. also	**B.** another	**C.** before
D. during	**E.** second	

_A_ 1. [1]Ice is the safest and most effective immediate treatment for athletic injuries. [2]It can be used, for example, on torn ligaments, strained muscles, and bruises. [3]Ice relieves pain while slowing the blood flow. [4]Ice ___Also___ helps reduce internal bleeding and promotes faster healing.

_E_ 2. [1]There are excellent reasons for taking a night class. [2]One is that it is a good way to develop a new interest or hobby. [3]A ___second___ reason is that it's a great way to meet people with similar interests.

_D_ 3. [1]Only a little over a century ago, guns were considered a necessity for American pioneers. [2]People hunted with guns to provide food for their families. [3]Guns were used for protection against threats from the wilderness. [4]___during___ the 1800s and into the early 1900s, a gun was as common as a coffeepot in most American homes.

_C_ 4. [1]Some simple methods can improve your ability to relax. [2]One method, called progressive relaxation, involves tensing a muscle group and then slowly relaxing the muscles in that group. [3]Your whole body feels relaxed after you repeat this process for all the major muscles. [4]Another simple relaxation method is to stop what you are doing and take a few deep breaths. [5]Next time you watch a basketball game, notice how a player will use this technique just ___before___ shooting a free throw.

_B_ 5. [1]Hispanic Americans, also called Latinos, are the largest minority group in the United States. [2]The group includes Mexican Americans, Puerto Ricans, and immigrants from Cuba and other Central and South American countries. [3]The Spanish language is the unifying force among Hispanic Americans. [4]___Another___ source of common identification is religion: at least 85 percent are Roman Catholic.

(Continues on next page)

251

B. Fill in each blank with an appropriate transition from the box. Use each transition once.

finally	first of all	moreover	secondly

[1]United States schools are not entirely to blame for the lower achievements of their students compared with the achievements of Japanese students. [2](6) _First of all_, our schools deal not just with learning (the only concern of Japanese schools) but also with such social problems as alcohol and drug abuse and teenage pregnancy. [3](7) _Secondly_, American parents are often too stressed, tired, or self-absorbed to do what Japanese mothers do— help with their children's homework and make sure they study three or four hours a night. [4](8) _Moreover_, many American teenagers hold part-time jobs, reducing their ability to hit the books after school. [5]Working after school is almost unheard of in Japan. [6](9) _Finally_, American teenagers are under great pressure from their peers to look good, drink, date, or even have sex. [7]With Japanese teenagers, the pressure instead is to study hard.

_A_

____ 10. The pattern of organization of the above selection is
  A. list of items.
  B. time order.

RELATIONSHIPS I: Mastery Test 3

A. (1–4.) Arrange the scrambled sentences below into a logical paragraph by numbering them *1, 2, 3,* and *4* in an order that makes sense. Then, in the space provided, write the letter of the main pattern of organization used.

Note that transitions will help you by making clear the relationships between sentences.

__3__ Another method is acupuncture, in which a tiny needle is placed in a smoker's earlobe to remove the craving for a cigarette.

__4__ Finally, many feel that being strongly motivated and quitting "cold turkey" is the best way to conquer the habit.

__2__ One method involves chewing a special nicotine gum whose nicotine content decreases at regular intervals.

__1__ Several ways have been suggested to help long-time smokers stop smoking.

__A__ 5. The pattern of organization of the above selection is
    A. list of items.
    B. time order.

B. Read the passage and answer the question that follows. You may find it helpful to underline transitions as you read.

[1]There is a false idea that lemmings, small mouselike creatures that live in northern regions, often commit suicide. [2]The truth is, however, that lemmings end their lives by accident. [3]Normally they live quietly in underground nests, feeding on roots and moss. [4]But every few years, the lemming population grows so large that the food supply becomes too small to feed them all. [5]Then all the lemmings leave their nests and go in search of food. [6]As they travel, the lemmings eat everything in their path. [7]After traveling for weeks, they reach the shore—but they don't stop there. [8]Still searching for food, the tiny rodents plunge into the ocean and begin swimming. [9]In a short time, the little creatures become exhausted and drown.

__B__ 6. The pattern of organization of the above selection is
    A. list of items.
    B. time order.

(Continues on next page)

C. Fill in each blank with an appropriate transition from the box. Use each transition once.

after	then	when

¹Gary began stealing liquor from his parents at the age of fourteen, and within two years, he regularly came to school drunk. ²(7)____When____ he was in his early twenties, he realized that he was completely dependent on alcohol, but he continued to drink. ³Gary's moment of truth came at age twenty-five. ⁴He narrowly escaped death in a drunk-driving accident, and he was responsible for injuring someone else. ⁵He soon committed himself to the local alcohol-recovery center. ⁶(8)____After____ an intensive four-week treatment and a ninety-day follow-up program, Gary was free of alcohol for the first time in over ten years. ⁷He (9)____Then____ returned to college and received a degree. ⁸Today Gary works as a counselor in the same treatment center that gave him his second chance. ⁹Gary's story should inspire many of his own clients at the alcohol-recovery center.

__B__ 10. The pattern of organization of the above selection is
   A. list of items.
   B. time order.

RELATIONSHIPS I: Mastery Test 4

A. (1–4.) Arrange the scrambled sentences below into a logical paragraph by numbering them *1, 2, 3,* and *4* in an order that makes sense. Then, in the space provided, write the letter of the main pattern of organization used.

Note that transitions will help you by making clear the relationships between sentences.

___4___ Then, often quite suddenly, a chimp would grab the stick, poke it through the bars of the cage, and drag the banana within reach.

___1___ A series of experiments showed how chimps solved the problem of reaching a banana placed on the ground outside their cage.

___3___ After a while, the chimps would start looking at what was lying around the cage, including a stick left there by the experimenters.

___2___ The chimps almost always tried first to reach the food with their hands.

___B___ 5. The pattern of organization of the above selection is
   A. list of items.
   B. time order.

B. Read the passage and answer the question that follows. You may find it helpful to underline transitions as you read.

[1]Every year, about 35,000 Americans commit suicide. [2]Sadly, research shows that many of these deaths can be avoided. [3]In order to prevent this needless loss of life, people must learn to recognize the warning signs of a potential suicide. [4]Such signs include, first of all, severe depression and withdrawal, often combined with the inability to sleep or eat. [5]Extreme mood swings, from joy to deep depression, are also danger signs. [6]In addition, suicidal people may begin giving away valued belongings. [7]Last, any life crisis, such as the death of a loved one or the loss of a job, may make a potentially suicidal person feel that he or she can't go on.

 6. The pattern of organization of the above selection is
   A. list of items.
   B. time order.

(Continues on next page)

C. Fill in each blank with an appropriate transition from the box. Use each transition once.

later	now	then	when

¹Popcorn has long been a favorite food. ²An early Spanish explorer in the Americas wrote of toasted corn that burst and looked very much like white flowers. ³In 1621, Indians brought corn to the first Thanksgiving. ⁴They taught the colonists to hold oiled ears on sticks over the fire and chew the popped kernels off. ⁵Two centuries (7)___*later*___, in 1846, the first cookbook to mention popcorn was published. ⁶The recipe directed the cook to pour corn kernels into a kettle of hot fat. ⁷When the corn popped, it was skimmed off the top. ⁸Popcorn appeared, too, in recipes for soup and beer. ⁹Popcorn balls became a holiday treat, and candied popcorn was flavored with lemon, rose, peppermint, honey, vanilla, or molasses. ¹⁰(8)___*when*___ the first corn poppers were invented in the 1890s, boys in large cities and small towns sold popcorn on street corners. ¹¹It was a good way to make a profit since vendors could buy twenty-five pounds of popping corn for a nickel and sell multiple individual bags for the same price. ¹²Movie theaters (9)___*then*___ brought the taste treat indoors. ¹³During World War II, when sugar was rationed, Americans ate three times as much popcorn as they had before. ¹⁴(10)___*now*___ we nibble approximately seventy quarts of the snack food per person a year.

RELATIONSHIPS I: Mastery Test 5

Read each textbook passage, and then answer the questions or follow the directions provided.

A. [1]People have differing feelings about their work. [2]First of all, for some it can be just a job, something done only for the paycheck, with a limited emotional reward. [3]For a second type of worker, work is a career and a part of the person's self-image. [4]A career person is challenged by the work and cares about the power and prestige that the job offers, not just the money. [5]Last, work can be a calling. [6]A person with a calling is passionately committed to the work itself, apart from the money or status that it may bring. [7]In general, people with callings are happier than those with mere jobs or careers.

_A_ 1. The pattern of organization of the above selection is
   A. list of items.
   B. time order.

2–3. Two of the transitions that signal major details of the paragraph are

   __First of All__   __Last__

B. [1]In 1814, a military victory was won—not with soldiers or guns, but with animals! [2]The battle took place in Chile when a Chilean leader named O'Higgins was fighting to win his country's independence from Spain. [3]The Chilean patriots were surrounded by a larger, well-armed Spanish army. [4]Wounded and seemingly without any options, O'Higgins came up with an idea. [5]He ordered his soldiers to gather together as many cows, mules, sheep, and dogs as possible. [6]Then, using gunshots to frighten the herd, O'Higgins got the animals to stampede toward the Spanish camp. [7]In a short time, the Spanish forces were being attacked by a frightened crowd of charging beasts. [8]While the Spanish were busy trying to protect themselves from the animals, O'Higgins and his men escaped into the nearby mountains. [9]Three years later, O'Higgins and an army of four thousand men returned from the mountains and defeated the Spanish once and for all.

_B_ 4. The pattern of organization of the above selection is
   A. list of items.
   B. time order.

5–6. Two of the transitions that signal major details of the paragraph are

   __Then__   __In a short time__

(Continues on next page)

257

C. ¹A good conclusion should tie a speech together and give the audience the feeling that the speech is complete. ²It should not introduce any new ideas. ³There are several kinds of conclusions to speeches that have proved their value time and time again. ⁴One is a summary of the main ideas of your speech. ⁵This type of conclusion is especially useful if you want your audience to remember your main points. ⁶Another common and useful type of conclusion is a quotation. ⁷If you can find a quotation that fits your subject, the conclusion is one good place to use it. ⁸For example, if your speech was about the importance of reading aloud to little children, you could end with this quotation by Dr. Ruth Love: ⁹"If we could get our parents to read to their preschool children fifteen minutes a day, we could revolutionize the schools." ¹⁰A quotation such as this gives added authority to what you have said. ¹¹A third useful conclusion is one that inspires the audience to action. ¹²When you give a speech, especially a persuasive speech, your goal is often to inspire the audience to some course of action. ¹³If this has been your goal, conclude by telling audience members precisely what they should do.

_____A__ 7. The pattern of organization of the above selection is
   A. list of items.
   B. time order.

8–10. The paragraph is about three kinds of conclusions to speeches.

   ● Which transition word signals the first kind of conclusion?

   _____One_____

   ● Which transition word signals the second kind of conclusion?

   _____Another_____

   ● Which transition word signals the last kind of conclusion?

   _____third_____

RELATIONSHIPS I: Mastery Test 6

Read each textbook passage, and then answer the questions or follow the directions provided.

A. [1]The history of books is marked by many important milestones. [2]Among the earliest of these would have to be the establishment of the first public library. [3]This event took place in Athens, Greece, in 540 B.C. [4]Books then had to be copied by hand until 1456, when another important milestone was reached. [5]The German inventor Johann Gutenberg built a printing press capable of producing multiple copies of one book. [6]After printing presses were established, books spread everywhere. [7]By the 1800s, American publishing houses were pumping out works to satisfy a reading-hungry public. [8]An example of a best-selling book was *Uncle Tom's Cabin*, which was published in 1852 and sold seven million copies. [9]The next chapter in the history of books began in the 1980s, with the publishing of books on audiotape. [10]Today, we even have electronic books that can be downloaded from the Internet.

_B_ 1. The pattern of organization of the above selection is
    A. list of items.   B. time order.

2–3. Two of the transitions that signal major details of the paragraph are
    _____Dates_____   _____Next_____

B. [1]There's no foolproof way to keep a burglar out, but there are precautions you can take. [2]First of all, the best defense against a break-in is lights. [3]Keep an inside and an outside light on at night. [4]Second, if you are going to be home late or away, use timers to turn the lights, radio, and television on and off to give the appearance that someone is home. [5]Also, think of your house as a fort. [6]In many burglaries, thieves simply breeze in through unlocked doors or windows. [7]Keep doors locked even when you are home. [8]A final step is to deprive burglars of what they need. [9]Keep bushes and trees trimmed, if they are near windows and doors, to eliminate places for burglars to lurk. [10]Put away ladders, rakes, brooms, and other equipment that thieves might use to help them break in. [11]These steps won't guarantee that your house will be safe, but they will help minimize the risk.

_A_ 4. The pattern of organization of the above selection is
    A. list of items.   B. time order.

5–6. Two of the transitions that signal major details of the paragraph are
    _____First of all_____   _____Second_____

(Continues on next page)

C. ¹For several reasons, some people find it hard to show appreciation or give praise to others. ²One reason is that they may have received little praise or appreciation themselves. ³Not having received it, they don't know how to give it. ⁴Another reason for not making positive remarks about others is insecurity. ⁵Insecure people often have a need to put others down. ⁶If they can make someone else feel bad, they feel better by comparison. ⁷A final reason for not complimenting others is fear. ⁸Showing affection or appreciation is a way of opening oneself up to someone else, of offering friendship. ⁹But people are afraid they may be rejected, so they decide it is safer not to try.

A 7. The pattern of organization of the above selection is
    A. list of items.
    B. time order.

8–10. Complete the map of the selection.

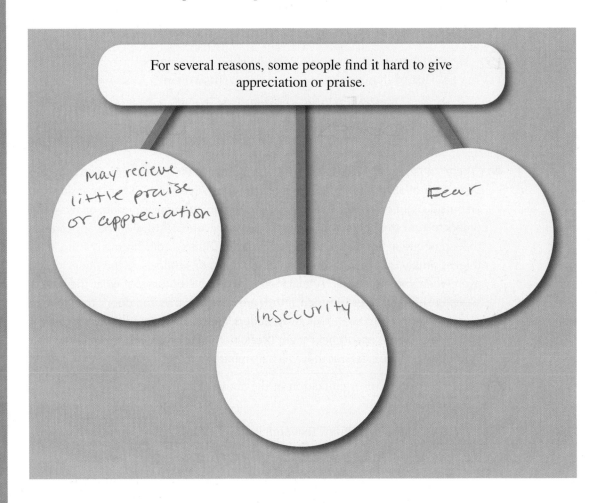

For several reasons, some people find it hard to give appreciation or praise.

May recieve little praise or appreciation

Fear

Insecurity

7 Relationships II

This Chapter in a Nutshell

This chapter explains three other types of relationships:

- Relationships that involve **illustration**
  - — Typical illustration transitions are *for example* and *for instance*.
- Relationships that involve **comparison and/or contrast**
  - — Typical comparison transitions are *alike* and *similar*.
  - — Typical contrast transitions are *but* and *however*.
- Relationships that involve **cause and effect**
  - — Typical cause-effect transitions are *reasons, because,* and *therefore*.

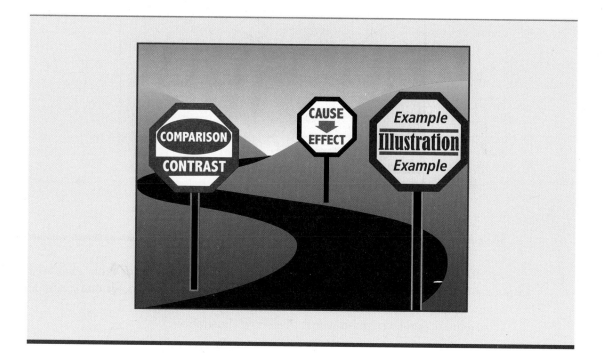

In Chapter 6, you learned about two common types of relationships: ones that involve addition and ones that involve time. In this chapter, you will learn about relationships involving **illustration**, **comparison**, **contrast**, and **cause and effect**.

1 Illustration

Words That Show Illustration

Check (✔) the item that is easier to understand:

___ Anyone can become a safer driver. Do not talk or text on your phone while driving.

___ Anyone can become a safer driver. For instance, do not talk or text on your phone while driving.

The second item is easier to understand. The words *For instance* make it clear that not talking or sending text messages on a phone while driving is one way to be a safer driver. *For instance* and other words and phrases like it are illustration words.

Illustration words tell us that an author will provide one or more *examples* to clarify a given idea. In the cartoon above, the man gives his doctor one example of how he tries to limit what he eats—having only one dessert!

Here are some common words that show illustration:

Illustration Words

(for) example	(for) instance	to illustrate
including	such as	once

Examples

The following items contain illustration words. Notice how these words signal that one or more *examples* are coming.

- Some birds, *such as* the penguin and the ostrich, cannot fly.

- People came to America for many reasons. The Puritans, *for example*, arrived in 1620 seeking religious freedom.

- My mother's love of chocolate has led to some pretty weird combinations. *Once* she put Hershey's syrup on a cheese sandwich.

PRACTICE 1

Complete each item with a suitable illustration word or phrase from the box on the previous page. Try to use a variety of transitions.

> *Hint:* Make sure that each word or phrase that you choose fits smoothly into the flow of the sentence. Test each choice by reading the sentence aloud.

1. A large part of what seems to be taste is really smell. _For example_, try eating some bread while holding a banana or piece of onion near your nose.

2. When we were young, my older brother liked to tease me. _Once_ he put raisins in my cereal and told me they were roaches.

3. The Italian restaurant offers pizza with unusual toppings, _such as_ sweet corn, sunflower seeds, and carrots.

4. Some children are very caring. _for instance_, they will want to share their toys with others, or they will reach out to comfort a crying friend.

5. Power is the ability to control the behavior of others, even against their will. If a robber forces us to hand over our wallets, that is an _example_ of power.

Illustration words are common in all types of writing. One way they are used in textbooks is in the definition and example pattern of organization.

The Definition and Example Pattern

To understand the definition and example pattern, try to arrange the following sentences in an order that makes sense. Put a *1* in front of the sentence that should come first, a *2* in front of the sentence that comes next, and a *3* in front of the sentence that should be last. The result will be a short paragraph. Then read the explanation that follows.

_2_ When acupuncture is used to kill pain, needles are inserted far from the area of pain.

_1_ Acupuncture is a Chinese medical technique that involves inserting special needles in certain places in the body.

_3_ In one stomach operation, for instance, four needles in the patient's outer ears eliminated pain.

This paragraph begins with a definition: "Acupuncture is a Chinese medical technique that involves inserting special needles in certain places in the body." The second sentence further explains acupuncture by discussing a special use: "When acupuncture is used to kill pain, needles are inserted far from the area of pain." Finally, an example of the use of acupuncture for pain is given: "In one stomach operation, for instance, four needles in the patient's outer ears eliminated pain." The third sentence includes the illustration words *for instance*. As you can see, the **definition and example pattern of organization** includes just what its name suggests: a definition and one or more examples.

> ***An Important Study Hint:*** Good textbook authors want to help readers understand the important ideas and terms in a subject—whether it is psychology, sociology, business, biology, or any other field. Such authors often take time, then, to include key definitions. These ideas and terms are usually set off in *italic* or **boldface** type, and the definitions are signaled by such words as *is, are, is called, termed,* and *refers to.* Here are some definitions from a variety of textbooks:
>
> - A **placebo** is a "sugar pill" without any significant medical properties.
> - **Hypotheses** are predictions stated in a way that allows them to be tested.
> - A low sense of personal worth is what psychologists call **negative self-esteem.**

- The chemical change in which a solid turns into a liquid is termed **melting.**

- **Narcolepsy** refers to an uncontrollable need to sleep for short periods during the day.

- Many critics argue that tests like the SAT are **culturally biased—** favoring one ethnic or racial group over others.

(*Note:* Sometimes a dash is used to signal a definition.)

If an author defines a term, you can assume that it is important enough to learn. So when reading and taking notes on a textbook, always do two things:

1) Write down key definitions.

2) Write down a helpful example for each definition. When a definition is general and abstract, authors often provide examples to help make a meaning clear.

✓ Check Your Understanding: List Words

The paragraph below defines a term, explains it a bit, and then gives an example of it. After reading the paragraph, see if you can answer the questions below. Then read the explanation that follows.

[1]Self-fulfilling prophecies are predictions that come true because we predict them. [2]For example, Tyrone may tell himself, "I bet I can get a good grade in this history class." [3]This thought makes Tyrone likely to work hard, making his prediction come true. [4]Children get their self-fulfilling prophecies from others. [5]For instance, if someone tells a child that he or she will "never amount to much," there is a good chance that is what will happen. [6]But if someone keeps saying to a child, "You can be one of the stars of your class," that child is likely to do well.

1. What term is being defined? _____

2. Which sentence contains the definition? _____

3. In which sentence does the first example begin? _____

4. How many examples are given in all? _____

Explanation

The term *self-fulfilling prophecies* is defined in sentence 1: "predictions that come true because we predict them." (Note that the definition is signaled by the word *are*.) The first example, about Tyrone's self-fulfilling prophecy, begins in sentence 2. A second example, about a child, appears in sentence 5, and a third example begins in sentence 6. Note that the author introduces two of the examples with the transition words *for example* and *for instance*. By providing clear examples, the author helps the reader understand the new term.

PRACTICE 2

Each of the following passages includes a definition and one or more examples. Underline the term being defined. Then, in the spaces provided, write the number of the definition sentence and the number of the sentence where each example begins.

A. ¹Have you ever been up at one o'clock in the morning, trying to finish the last chapter of the text on which you are being tested in the morning? ²If so, you may have turned to a stimulant to keep you awake. ³A stimulant is a substance that temporarily increases one's activity or alertness. ⁴One common stimulant is caffeine, which is found in coffee, tea, soft drinks, and chocolate. ⁵Another example of a common stimulant is nicotine, which is found in cigarettes. ⁶Both caffeine and nicotine cause a rise in your heart rate and blood pressure, making you feel more wide-awake.

Definition ___**3**___   Example 1 ___**4**___   Example 2 ___**5**___

B. ¹Frequently, members of a group will develop a jargon, or specialized language, which distinguishes the group from the wider society. ²The police are well known for their use of distinctive jargons. ³For instance, members of New York City's police department refer to a suspect as a "perp" (short for "perpetrator"), to a gun as a "piece," and to the police shield as the "tin." ⁴Chicago police also have their own terms, such as calling a suspect an "offender"; they call a gun a "biscuit" and the police shield the "button."

Definition ___**1**___   Example 1 ___**3**___   Example 2 ___**4**___

2 Comparison and Contrast

Words That Show Comparison

Check (✓) the item that is easier to understand:

____ Human infants suck their thumbs; baby elephants suck their trunks.

____ Just as human infants suck their thumbs, baby elephants suck their trunks.

The first item makes us wonder what the author is focusing on—how human infants and baby elephants are alike or how they are different. The words *just as* in the second version show the author is focusing on the similarity. *Just as* and words like them are comparison words.

"Do you realize how much we resemble each other? We'll both eat anything. We both like to sleep on the furniture. And we're both overweight."

Comparison words signal similarities. Authors use a comparison transition to show that a second idea is *like* the first one in some way. In the above cartoon, the words *resemble* and *both* show the dog is making a comparison between himself and the man. The dog names three ways he and the man are similar: both of them eat anything, sleep on the furniture, and are overweight.

Here are some common words that show comparison:

Comparison Words

(just) as	in like (similar) manner	same
(just) like	similar(ly)	in the same way
alike	similarity	resemble
likewise	both	equally

Examples

The sentences below contain comparison words. Notice how these words show that things are *alike* in some way.

● The carpet was so old and faded it looked *like* a gray shadow.

● Parents today often dislike the music their children listen to, *just as* their own parents disliked the Beatles or the Rolling Stones.

● Tattoos, which used to be seen as lower class, are part of our culture today. *Likewise*, many middle-class people now have body piercings.

PRACTICE 3

Complete each sentence with a suitable comparison word or phrase from the box on the previous page. Try to use a variety of transitions.

1. Bats and frogs hibernate during the winter, _Just like_ bears do.

2. Many Hispanic girls have a special party for their fifteenth birthday. _similarly_, Anglo girls often celebrate their sixteenth birthday in a special way.

3. Good teachers are _as_ _____ skilled in praising what students have accomplished as they are in challenging them to do more.

4. We are often attracted to people who have a social and religious background _similar_ _____ to our own.

5. As we turned onto the country road, the view in front of us—a bright rainbow rising over a gentle hill—looked _just like_ _____ a scene in a fairy tale.

Words That Show Contrast

Check (✓) the item that is easier to understand:

____ The weather in Florida is usually wonderful, but the summers are hot and humid.

____ The weather in Florida is usually wonderful. The summers are hot and humid.

In the second item, we're not sure if the author feels that the weather in Florida is wonderful *because of* or *in spite of* the hot and humid summers. The transition *but* in the first item makes the relationship clear: the weather in Florida is wonderful in spite of the summer heat and humidity. *But* and words like it are known as contrast words.

"That's the difference between us.
You like to read at meals, and I like to talk."

Contrast words signal differences. A contrast word shows that two things *differ* in one or more ways. Contrast words also inform us that something is going to *differ from* what we might expect. In the cartoon above, the woman uses the word *difference* to contrast what her husband likes to do at meals (read) with what she likes to do (talk).

Here are some common words that show contrast:

Contrast Words

but	instead	still	difference
yet	in contrast	as opposed to	different(ly)
however	on the other hand	in spite of	differs from
although	on the contrary	despite	unlike
nevertheless	even though	rather than	while

Examples

The sentences below contain contrast words. Notice how these words signal that one idea is *different from* another idea.

- *Although* the movie had an exciting plot, the actors in the lead roles were not very convincing.

- A laptop computer is convenient and portable; *on the other hand*, a desktop computer is usually less expensive.

- Only 10 percent of the population is left-handed. *In contrast*, of babies that are born more than two months prematurely, 54 percent are left-handed.

PRACTICE 4

Complete each sentence with a suitable contrast word or phrase from the box on the previous page. Try to use a variety of transitions.

1. Our Toyota is ten years old, ___ *But* ___ it still runs perfectly.

2. ___ *Although* ___ many people own running shoes, most of these people are not runners.

3. American women have been dyeing their hair for years. American men, ___ *However* ___, only recently started coloring theirs.

4. ___ *Despite* ___ the fact that the sign in the corner market window said "Open," the door was locked and no one was in sight.

5. Fast-food chains sell French fries for prices much higher than what they paid for them. The farmer who planted and grew the potatoes, ___ *however* ___, doesn't get such a good deal. Out of every $1.50 that you spend on a large order of French fries, maybe 2¢ goes to the farmer.

Comparison and contrast transitions often signal the pattern of organization known as the comparison-contrast pattern.

The Comparison-Contrast Pattern

To understand the comparison-contrast pattern, arrange the following group of sentences in an order that makes sense. Put a *1* in front of the sentence that should come first, a *2* in front of the sentence that comes next, and a *3* in front of the sentence that should be last. The result will be a short paragraph. Then read the explanation that follows.

_____ The snakes have similar markings: red, yellow, and black bands.

_____ The coral snake and the milk snake may look alike, but there's an important difference between them.

_____ However, the milk snake is harmless, while the coral snake is very poisonous.

The first sentence of this paragraph is the general one, the one with the main idea: "The coral snake and the milk snake may look alike, but there's an important difference between them." The words *alike, but*, and *difference* suggest a comparison-contrast pattern. As the comparison word *similar* and the contrast words *however* and *while* suggest, the other two sentences do in fact compare and contrast two things: "The snakes have similar markings: red, yellow, and black bands. However, the milk snake is harmless, while the coral snake is very poisonous."

The **comparison-contrast pattern** shows how two things are alike or how they are different, or both. When things are compared, their similarities are pointed out. When things are contrasted, their differences are discussed.

Authors often find it useful to compare and/or contrast. Here are two examples.

Comparison

[1]House cats and their larger relatives, jungle cats, have traits in common. [2]Both have eyes suited for night vision, and both prefer to sleep by day and move about at night. [3]Also, just as pet cats use their tails to keep their balance and show emotions, so do lions and other large cats. [4]In addition, both kinds of cats can leap great distances. [5]Finally, cats at home are not the only ones that purr: cats in the wild also purr when content.

Contrast

[1]Times have changed, and I know this because I have children, two of them, one born in the old days and one in modern times. [2]One was born back before seat belts, when a child might ride standing up in the front seat next to Daddy as he drove 75 mph across North Dakota, and nobody said a word, though nowadays Daddy would do jail time for that. [3]In contrast, my younger child rides in a podlike car seat, belted in like a little test pilot. [4]She likes it. [5]Another difference is that the older child grew up inhaling clouds of secondary smoke, while the younger one lives in a house in which nobody even thinks about smoking.

✔ Check Your Understanding

In the following paragraph, the main idea is stated in the first sentence. As is often the case, the main idea suggests a paragraph's pattern of organization. Here the transition *differ* is a hint that the paragraph may be organized in a comparison-contrast pattern. Read the paragraph, and answer the questions below. Then read the explanation that follows.

¹Humans differ from other primates, but not as much as one might think. ²It's true that there are important differences in size and shape between humans and other primates. ³And, of course, humans are by far the more intelligent. ⁴It is also true that there are striking similarities between the two. ⁵To use chimpanzees as an example, both they and humans have the same muscles and bones, located in almost the same places and working in nearly the same ways. ⁶The internal organs of both animals are also very much alike, as are their blood and other body fluids. ⁷Seen under a microscope, even their genes are strikingly similar.

1. Is this paragraph comparing, contrasting, or both? _____

2. What two things are being compared and/or contrasted? _____

   _____

3. Write out four of the comparison and/or contrast words that are used in the

   paragraph. _____

   _____

Explanation

The paragraph both compares and contrasts—it discusses both similarities and differences. First, it contrasts humans and other primates in terms of size, shape, and intelligence. The words used to indicate that contrast are *differ, but*, and *differences*. The paragraph also discusses similarities between humans and other primates—in their muscles, bones, internal organs, body fluids, and genes. The words used to indicate comparison are *similarities, both, same, alike*, and *similar*.

PRACTICE 5

The following passages use the pattern of comparison or contrast. Read each passage and answer the questions which follow.

A. ¹The lives and deaths of two assassinated Presidents, Abraham Lincoln and John F. Kennedy, contain a number of odd similarities. ²Lincoln was elected to Congress in 1846; Kennedy was elected to Congress in 1946. ³Lincoln was elected President in 1860, and Kennedy in 1960. ⁴Both presidents were shot on a Friday, and both were shot in the head. ⁵After their deaths, they were succeeded by men with the same name: Johnson. ⁶Lincoln's assassin, John Wilkes Booth, was born in 1839, while Kennedy's killer, Lee Harvey Oswald, was born in 1939. ⁷Both presidents' assassins were themselves murdered before they could stand trial.

Check (✔) the pattern used in this paragraph:

__✔__ Comparison   _____ Contrast

What two things are being compared or contrasted?

1. _Abraham Lincoln_ 2. _John F. Kennedy_

B. ¹High school and college offer very different educational experiences for students. ²In high school, teachers often treat students like children. ³For instance, teachers may call parents if a student skips class or fails to hand in an assignment. ⁴On the other hand, college teachers treat students like adults. ⁵Students are expected to take full responsibility for their attendance and their work. ⁶Also, in high school, students typically live at home and depend on their parents. ⁷In college, however, students live in apartments (or dorms) and have no one to depend on but themselves.

Check (✔) the pattern used in this paragraph:

_____ Comparison   __✔__ Contrast

What two things are being compared or contrasted?

1. _____ 2. _____

3 Cause and Effect

Words That Show Cause and Effect

Check (✓) the item that is easier to understand:

___ Nina cares for her elderly parents. She has very little free time.

___ Because Nina cares for her elderly parents, she has very little free time.

In the first item, we are not sure of the relationship between the two sentences. Does Nina have little free time *with which* to care for her parents? Or does she have little free time *because* she cares for her parents? The word *because* in the second item shows the connection between the two ideas. *Because* and words like it are known as cause and effect words.

"The reason I got the promotion is that I always dress for success."

Cause and effect words signal that the author is explaining *the reason why* something happened or *the result* of something happening. In the cartoon above, the dog explains that dressing for success (the *cause*) has led to his promotion (the *effect*).

Here are some common cause and effect words:

Cause and Effect Words

therefore	so	because (of)	thus
(as a) result	effect	as a consequence	results in
cause	explanation	consequently	led to
affect	due to	since	reason

Examples

The following items contain cause and effect words. Notice how these words introduce a *reason* for something or a *result* of something.

- People eat fewer hamburgers today than they did in the past. *Therefore*, fast-food restaurants have developed new items for their menus.

- *Because* roses are considered the flowers of romance, many people give them for Valentine's Day.

- Digital cameras do not require the use of film; *as a result*, they have become more popular than conventional cameras.

PRACTICE 6

Complete each sentence with a suitable cause and effect word or phrase from the box on the previous page. Try to use a variety of transitions.

1. __Because__ there's no room in your mouth for your wisdom teeth, they will have to be removed.

2. Gail wanted a large wedding reception. __Therefore__, her parents had to rent a hall.

3. The construction of a Home Depot and a Wal-Mart right outside of the town __resulted in__ the closing of a number of small businesses in the area.

4. Elephants were killed for many years for the valuable ivory in their tusks. __Therefore__, the elephant population declined significantly.

5. The __reason__ our skin wrinkles when we're in the water a long time is that the top layer of skin absorbs much more water than the lower ones.

Cause and effect transitions often signal the cause and effect pattern of organization.

The Cause and Effect Pattern

Arrange the following group of sentences in an order that makes sense. Put a *1* in front of the sentence that should come first, a *2* in front of the sentence that comes next, and a *3* in front of the sentence that should be last. The result will be a short paragraph. Then read the explanation that follows.

____ Accidents are also caused by speeding, as drivers try to get home as quickly as possible.

____ Traffic accidents are more likely to result during evening rush hour.

____ Because drivers are tired at the end of the day, they are not able to respond quickly enough to changes in traffic.

As the words *result*, *Because*, and *caused* suggest, this paragraph is organized in a cause and effect pattern. In paragraph form, the sentences would read as follows:

> [1]Traffic accidents are more likely to result during evening rush hour. [2]Because drivers are tired at the end of the day, they are not able to respond quickly enough to changes in traffic. [3]Accidents are also caused by speeding, as drivers try to get home as quickly as possible.

The paragraph begins with an effect—that more accidents occur during rush hour—and then follows with two causes.

Information in a **cause and effect pattern** addresses the questions "Why does a behavior or event happen?" and/or "What are the results of a behavior or event?" An author may then discuss causes, or effects, or both causes and effects.

Authors usually don't just tell *what* happened. They both describe what has happened and try to explain *why*. For example, a sociology textbook would not just say that the test scores of American students have declined for most of the last thirty years. The book would also explain the likely *causes* of this decline. Or a health textbook would not just describe the ways that medical care has changed in the last few years. It would also examine the *reasons* for such changes.

☑ *Check Your Understanding*

Read the paragraph below and see if you can answer the questions about cause and effect. Then read the explanation to see how you did.

> [1]Experts point out four reasons why the divorce rate has increased in the United States. [2]One explanation is a lack of time for many couples to work at their marriage. [3]With husband and wife often holding down jobs outside the home, there may be little energy for everything else that goes into a partnership. [4]Another cause is the "me-first" attitude in today's society. [5]Some people put their own personal happiness ahead of the well-being of a spouse and family. [6]In addition, women now have more freedom of choice. [7]Their ability to support themselves means that they can more easily leave an unhappy marriage. [8]Finally, because divorce is so much more common, it has also become more socially acceptable. [9]People are no longer embarrassed to say they are divorced.

1. What are the four *causes* described in this paragraph?

   a. _____

   b. _____

   c. _____

   d. _____

2. What is the *effect* of these causes?

   _____

3. What three cause-effect transitions are used?

   a. _____

   b. _____

   c. _____

Explanation

The paragraph presents four causes: lack of time to work at the marriage, the "me-first" attitude in today's society, more freedom of choice for women, and divorce becoming more socially acceptable. The four causes lead to one effect: the increased divorce rate. The cause-effect transitions used are *explanation, cause,* and *because.*

PRACTICE 7

A. Read the paragraph below, looking for the **one** effect and the **two** causes. Then complete the map that follows. (The effect has been added for you.)

¹For centuries, Japan had one of the lowest rates of obesity in the world. ²But that is changing. ³About a quarter of adult Japanese are now considered significantly overweight. ⁴Two reasons in particular explain this weight gain among the Japanese. ⁵For one thing, lifestyles have become less active as more and more rural Japanese move into cities. ⁶More importantly, many Japanese are turning away from their traditional low-fat diet emphasizing rice, fish, and vegetables. ⁷They are instead adopting a more Western diet that features lots of processed food that is high in fat.

Two reasons explain weight gain among the Japanese.

Less active lifestyle

higher fat Diet

B. Read the paragraph below, looking for the **one** cause and the **three** effects. Then complete the outline that follows.

¹Increases in the numbers of elderly people will have a major impact in Europe, Canada, and the United States. ²One effect of the aging of these populations is that the number of working-age people will go sharply down, leaving fewer people available to fill jobs. ³Also, as the number of retired people increases, there will be a bigger demand on the countries' pension systems. ⁴A third effect will be an immense strain on national medical services. ⁵Elderly people draw upon far more of a society's health-care services than do young people.

Main idea (*the cause*):_____

_____

    Major supporting details (*the effects*):

       1. _____.

       2. _____.

       3. _____.

A Note on Main Ideas and Patterns of Organization

As mentioned on page 236, a paragraph's main idea often indicates its pattern of organization. Try, for instance, to guess the pattern of the paragraph with this main idea:

> For various reasons, as many as half of all battered women do not leave their abusive husbands.

The word *reasons* suggests that the author is using a cause-effect pattern. The paragraph will go on to explain the reasons why many abused women stay with their husbands.

    Recognizing a main idea, and the pattern of organization that may be implied in a main idea, are both helpful steps in understanding the material in a paragraph.

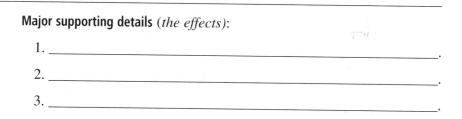

PRACTICE 8

Most of the main ideas below have been taken from college textbooks. In the space provided, write the letter of the pattern of organization that each suggests.

___B___ 1. One of the major differences between men and women is their degree of aggression.

    A. Definition and   B. Comparison-   C. Cause and effect
       example   contrast

___A___ 2. A stereotype is an oversimplified, inaccurate mental picture of others, such as the idea that the poor are lazy.

    A. Definition and   B. Comparison-   C. Cause and effect
       example   contrast

_C_ 3. People often form strong first impressions of others for unusual reasons.
   A. Definition and   B. Comparison-   C. Cause and effect
      example   contrast

_B_ 4. The eyes of newborns are both similar to and different from those of adults.
   A. Definition and   B. Comparison-   C. Cause and effect
      example   contrast

_C_ 5. Strong emotions tend to affect the flow of digestive juices and upset digestion.
   A. Definition and   B. Comparison-   C. Cause and effect
      example   contrast

_A_ 6. Self-esteem refers to how one feels about oneself; people with low self-esteem, for instance, do not like themselves.
   A. Definition and   B. Comparison-   C. Cause and effect
      example   contrast

_C_ 7. Viruses that cause colds and flu are often spread through sneezing, coughing, and unsanitary habits.
   A. Definition and   B. Comparison-   C. Cause and effect
      example   contrast

_B_ 8. Irish-Americans were once harshly discriminated against in the United States, just as Italian immigrants were.
   A. Definition and   B. Comparison-   C. Cause and effect
      example   contrast

_A_ 9. A closed shop is a business with an employment agreement that requires the company to hire only union workers.
   A. Definition and   B. Comparison-   C. Cause and effect
      example   contrast

_C_ 10. Childhood dental problems in the United States have decreased significantly because of the widespread use of fluoride in drinking water and toothpaste.
   A. Definition and   B. Comparison-   C. Cause and effect
      example   contrast

A Final Point

Keep in mind that a paragraph or a longer passage sometimes contains more than one pattern of organization. For instance, the paragraph in this chapter about the reasons for the increased divorce rate in the United States uses a cause-effect pattern. But the reasons themselves—lack of time to work at the marriage, a "me-first" attitude, more freedom of choice for women, and the greater social acceptability of divorce—are presented as a list of items. In other words, the paragraph combines two patterns.

Or consider the following passage:

[1]People with more wealth tend to have more power. [2]This fact is apparent in the domination of top government positions by the wealthy. [3]Higher-income persons are also more likely to feel a strong sense of power. [4]As a result, they are more likely to be politically active, working to keep or increase their power. [5]In contrast, lower-income people are more likely to feel powerless to influence major political decisions. [6]Therefore, they are more indifferent to politics and less likely to be involved in political activity.

The paragraph partly uses a contrast pattern, noting the *difference* between higher-income people and lower-income people with regard to political activity. But it also uses a cause-effect pattern: it describes the *effect* of feeling a sense of power or feeling no sense of power.

CHAPTER REVIEW

In this chapter, you learned about three kinds of relationships that authors use to make their ideas clear:

● **Definitions and examples**

— To help readers understand the important ideas and terms in a subject, textbook authors often take time to include key definitions (often setting them off in *italic* or **boldface**) and examples of those definitions. When reading a textbook, it is usually a good idea to mark off both definitions and examples.

— Transition words that signal the definition and example pattern include *for example* and *for instance*.

(Continues on next page)

● **Comparison and/or contrast**

— Authors often discuss how two things are alike or how they are different, or both.

— Transition words that signal comparisons include *alike* and *similar*.

— Transition words that signal contrasts include *but* and *however*.

● **Cause and effect**

— Authors often discuss the reasons why something happens or the effects of something that has happened.

— Transition words that signal causes and effects include *reason*, *because*, and *therefore*.

Note that pages 307–312 list and offer practice in all the transitions and patterns of organization you have studied in "Relationships I" and "Relationships II."

The next chapter—Chapter 8—will develop your skill in making inferences about what you read.

On the Web: If you are using this book in class, you can visit our website for additional practice in understanding relationships that involve examples, comparison or contrast, and cause and effect. Go to **www.townsendpress.com** and click on "Learning Center."

 REVIEW TEST 1

To review what you've learned in this chapter, write the letter of each correct answer in the space provided.

_____ 1. Words such as *but, although,* and *however* are known as
   A. cause and effect words.
   B. illustration words.
   C. contrast words.

_____ 2. Words such as *for example, for instance,* and *including* are known as
   A. definition words.
   B. illustration words.
   C. cause and effect words.

_____ 3. Words such as *reason, because,* and *therefore* are known as
   A. comparison words.
   B. definition words.
   C. cause and effect words.

_____ 4. Words such as *likewise, in the same way,* and *just as* are known as
   A. comparison words.
   B. definition words.
   C. cause and effect words.

_____ 5. When textbook authors provide a definition of a term, they often help make that definition clear by providing one or more
   A. comparisons.
   B. causes.
   C. examples.

REVIEW TEST 2

A. (1–2.) Name the type of transition used in each of the following cartoons.

"The reason you should hire me is that I can really bring home the bacon."

PSYCHOLOGY

"The trouble is my wife and I are exactly the same. We both like to spend more money than we earn."

_____ 1. A. Example
           B. Comparison
           C. Cause and effect

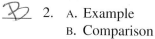

_____ 2. A. Example
           B. Comparison
           C. Cause and effect

B. Complete each sentence by filling in the blank with one of the transitions in the box. Use each word once. Then write the letter of the word in the space provided.

A. for example	B. however	C. like	D. therefore

_C_ 3. Transitions are __like__ bridges—they carry the reader across from one thought to another.

_D_ 4. Sports injuries can keep even a champion on the sidelines. __therefore__, experts urge every athlete to do warm-up exercises, which help prevent injuries.

_A_ 5. Clothes reflect society's values. __for example__, in Victorian times, when women were expected to be inactive, they wore clothing that limited their movements.

_B_ 6. Research shows that married people are healthier than people who have never been married. Marriage does pose one health hazard, __however__: weight gain. Married men are more likely to be overweight.

C. Below are the beginnings of four passages. Label each one with the letter of its pattern of organization. (You may find it helpful to underline the transition or transitions in each item.)

    A Definition and example
    B Comparison-contrast
    C Cause and effect

_C_ 7. ¹Because there are so few parking spaces downtown, people have had to change their shopping habits. ²One effect of the lack of parking is that shoppers are going to suburban malls instead of downtown stores. ³Another consequence has been significant growth in online shopping. . . .

_B_ 8. ¹There have always been homeless people in the United States. ²But the homeless today differ in some ways from their counterparts of thirty years ago. . . .

_A_ 9. ¹Snap judgments are opinions formed on the spot, often on little evidence. ²One instance of such a judgment is deciding that someone is a no-good after meeting him or her briefly at a party. . . .

_e__ 10. ¹There are several reasons why travelers so often become ill. ²The unfamiliar foods and water in foreign countries cause digestive upsets. ³Fatigue—from jet lag and the strain and exertion of traveling—lowers travelers' resistance. ⁴Finally, travelers may be exposed to infectious diseases to which their bodies have never developed any natural immunity. . . .

REVIEW TEST 3

Read each paragraph and answer the questions that follow.

A. ¹Recent studies indicate that male and female babies act very differently after only a few months of life. ²Baby girls seem to be more interested in people. ³They can recognize individual faces and voices at four months, well before baby boys can. ⁴In addition, they begin to smile and speak earlier than boys, and their vocabularies are larger. ⁵In contrast, baby boys react to objects with as much interest as they react to human beings. ⁶They will try to talk to the brightly colored toys that hang over their cribs just as often as they will try to talk to a parent. ⁷And before long, they will attempt to take these objects apart.

_____ 1. The main pattern of organization of the selection is
    A. definition-example.
    B. cause-effect.
    C. comparison-contrast.

    2. One transition that signals the paragraph's pattern of organization is

_____.

B. ¹Events leading to alcohol abuse in the United States took place in the eighteenth century. ²At that time, developments in agriculture had caused a surplus of grain. ³Farmers in the Midwest wanted to sell their surplus grain on the East Coast, which was more heavily populated. ⁴The most profitable way to do this was to convert the extra grain into something Easterners would buy: whiskey. ⁵As a result, whiskey production rose. ⁶And the increase in whiskey led to an increase in its use. ⁷Before long, alcohol consumption in the country rose to alarming proportions.

_____ 3. The main pattern of organization of the selection is
    A. definition-example.
    B. cause-effect.
    C. comparison-contrast.

    4. One transition that signals the paragraph's pattern of organization is

_____.

C. ¹An altruistic person is someone who will help others even when he or she expects no benefits in return. ²Consider the example of one of the passengers on a plane that crashed into the Potomac River one cold January day in 1982. ³Most of the passengers died under the ice, but six passengers escaped into the icy waters. ⁴Every time a life preserver was lowered by a helicopter, one man passed it on to one of the other five. ⁵When the helicopter had lifted out all five, it returned to pick up that last survivor. ⁶But he had disappeared under the ice.

_____ 5. The main pattern of organization of the paragraph is
       A. definition and example.
       B. contrast.
       C. cause and effect.

      6. One transition that signals the paragraph's pattern of organization is

_____.

D. ¹As news sources, websites have several advantages over newspapers. ²Online news sources can publish a story within minutes of an event happening, or continually update an existing story. ³On the other hand, a daily newspaper is published just once a day. ⁴Websites are more friendly to the environment; they require no raw material, while newspapers mean the destruction of many trees. ⁵And the search feature on most news websites lets readers find the story they want quickly, as opposed to wading through many pages looking for it.

_____ 7. The main pattern of organization of the paragraph is
       A. definition and example.
       B. comparison-contrast.
       C. cause and effect.

      8. One transition that signals the paragraph's pattern of organization is

_____.

E. ¹Although caffeine is the world's most widely consumed drug, few of its users realize how powerful it is. ²Caffeine is a drug that acts fast. ³In less than five minutes after you've drunk a cup of coffee, caffeine is racing to every part of your body. ⁴Its effects are many, including increasing the flow of urine and stomach acid, relaxing involuntary muscles, and stepping up the intake of oxygen. ⁵Caffeine also boosts the pumping strength of the heart, and too much caffeine can cause an irregular heartbeat. ⁶A small dose of caffeine can improve your performance as you type or drive, but the effect of too much caffeine is that you'll feel shaky and unsteady.

_____ 9. The main pattern of organization of the paragraph is
        A. definition and example.
        B. contrast.
        C. cause and effect.

10. One transition that signals the paragraph's pattern of organization is

_____.

REVIEW TEST 4

Here is a chance to apply your understanding of transitions and patterns of organization to a selection about the art of conversation. While all of us crave connection to other human beings, we are often at a loss as to how to connect through conversation. The following selection offers tips—and encouragement.

Words to Watch

Below are some words in the reading that do not have strong context support. Each word is followed by the number of the paragraph in which it appears and its meaning there. These words are indicated in the selection by a small circle (°).

> _scenarios_ (1): situations
> _impersonal_ (25): unfriendly
> _cliché_ (32): an overused idea or saying
> _baffled_ (36): confused
> _inclinations_ (36): leanings toward doing certain things
> _en route_ (36): on the way

CONVERSING IN REAL LIFE

Sarah Rice

1   Talking to other people is not something that we necessarily think that much about. After all, conversation is typically a daily activity that we take for granted. However, we may occasionally find ourselves in a conversation failure. Consider the following three scenarios°:

2   **#1.** Brad could hardly believe his good luck. He had finally gotten up the nerve to ask Maggie out to dinner, and she had actually said yes. Nervous about making a good impression, Brad spent most of Saturday thinking about all the things he would talk about that evening when he and Maggie went out. And when Brad was finally face-to-face with Maggie, he definitely had plenty to say. He talked about his love of sports, his travels to other countries, his old car, his friends, and his new job.

3   By the end of the evening, Brad was sure that dinner had been a big success. Maggie had smiled and laughed at everything he had said. So Brad couldn't understand why Maggie turned him down the next two times he tried to ask her out. When he ran into her a few weeks later, she was polite but definitely uninterested.

4   "I don't get it," Brad complained to his best friend. "I chatted her up all evening. I thought we got along great."

5   "Did you ask her about her interests?" Brad's friend asked. "Did you let her talk at all?"

6   "What do you mean?" Brad asked.

7   Brad's friend just shook his head. "Man, she probably couldn't wait for that evening to end!"

8   **#2.** Gail had just sat down to eat lunch at the small restaurant near her office when her boss sat down at the table right next to her. Immediately, Gail began to panic. She rarely talked to her boss, and she had no idea what to say to her. Should she talk about work? What if her boss thought she was stupid? What if she said the wrong thing?

9   "Hi there, Gail," her boss said in a friendly voice. "What's new?"

10 Gail looked away, embarrassed, and mumbled, "Not much."

11 "How's your holiday shopping going?" her boss asked as she glanced at the menu. "Do you shop early, or do you put everything off like I always do?"

12 Gail wondered what she should say. Would it be better to appear organized and say that her shopping was done? Or would her boss be offended by that? Should she just agree and say that she hadn't done any shopping yet? Confused, Gail just said, "It's going okay."

13 Now there was a long pause that made Gail extra nervous. She knew she should be saying something,

but she couldn't think of what to say to her boss that wouldn't sound boring. Finally, in desperation, Gail picked up her phone and pretended to be sending a text. After all, her boss was looking at the menu. They didn't have to talk, right?

14   After another few minutes of awkward silence, Gail's boss just smiled and said, "You know, I think I'll take lunch to go. See you back at the office."

15   Gail just nodded and said, "Okay." After her boss left, Gail worried that her boss would now think Gail didn't like her. In reality, Gail admired her boss a lot. So why was it so hard to have a simple conversation with her?

16   **#3.** Michael met his friend Jake at the coffee shop. Michael had been stressed out over his rocky relationship with his girlfriend, and he needed someone to listen to him and maybe offer advice.

17   "I just don't know what to do," Michael concluded after explaining what was going wrong in his relationship. Jake had been sitting across from him, nodding now and then. But, mostly, Jake kept glancing around the room. He yawned and stretched a few times.

18   "Yeah, that's rough," Jake finally said as he checked his phone. "Hey, did you hear about the new club down on Fifth Street? That'd be a great place to meet a girl."

19   "What? But I don't want to meet . . . ," Michael began.

20   "There's supposed to be live music every night," Jake interrupted. "Sounds awesome. You want to go there on Friday?"

21   "No," Michael said irritably. "I don't care about some stupid new club."

22   "What's wrong with you?" Jake asked in a surprised voice.

23   Michael sighed and said, "Nothing. Never mind."

24   Michael had just poured his heart out for twenty minutes, and now he wondered if his so-called friend had heard anything he'd said at all.

25   Have you ever experienced any of these "conversation failure" situations? When we make blunders in conversations with others, we often feel as if we're the only ones who ever experience these mistakes. In reality, however, the art of skilled conversation is becoming more and more rare. In an age in which much of our communication is electronic and impersonal°, face-to-face interaction often makes us seem flustered or, worse yet, rude.

26   Luckily, learning how to be a good conversationalist is not particularly complicated. All it takes is some practice, thoughtfulness, and a bit of self-confidence.

27   To begin with, keep in mind that we all love to feel as though we are interesting to others. In conversation, the way to make people feel interesting is by asking them questions about their interests, work, hobbies, and so on. Consider the first scenario. By the end of the evening, Maggie probably knew way more than she really wanted to know about Brad. She most likely left their dinner together thinking Brad was a self-centered jerk who was not at all interested in anything about her. In Brad's jittery preparation for "conversation," he made a common mistake. He planned to talk only about himself.

28   Of course, no one wants to be put under a microscope, so avoid bombarding someone with a series of rapid-fire questions. Instead, ask about something that you're genuinely curious about (without getting too personal!), and this will often lead into a natural and rewarding conversation. For example, asking someone about where he or she grew up can lead to interesting stories and childhood experiences that both of you may have had. A good conversation that "flows" is usually a matter of both parties asking questions and finding common ground that creates a friendly bond. More often than not, once this common ground is discovered, conversation becomes natural and enjoyable. It is no longer something either party has to worry about "creating."

29   Next, remember that nearly everyone feels a little awkward when attempting to make conversation with someone for the first time. When Gail ended up being seated next to her boss, she felt so awkward that she couldn't talk at all! So what do you talk about when you don't really know someone? The answer is simple: almost anything. And almost no topic of conversation is too insignificant. That is why this kind of conversation is sometimes referred to as "small talk."

30   Some people feel that engaging in small talk makes them appear boring or not very bright. However, the truth is that no one ever really remembers the topics of a small-talk conversation. What people *do* remember is an uncomfortable interaction. It is likely, for example, that Gail's boss will remember Gail's awkwardness far more than she would a brief conversation about holiday shopping, the weather, or even the food at the restaurant. Making small talk is a polite way of putting both parties at ease.

31   Again, asking questions is often the best way to deal in small talk. Was Gail's boss really that interested in how Gail's shopping was going? Probably not, but she knew it was a simple, non-personal question that might lead to further, and less "small," conversation. Unfortunately, Gail was so worried about what she was supposed to say that the conversation died before it even started. Yes, it takes some practice and confidence to make small talk with people you don't know or might be intimidated by, but it's a lot less nerve-wracking than sitting in

dead silence. It would have been easy enough (and not too frightening!) for Gail to make a comment or two about holiday shopping and then ask her boss something simple such as, "Do you have a big family to shop for?" or "Are you traveling over the holidays?" or even, "Do you think it will snow this year?"

32   Sure, talking about the weather is a small-talk cliché°, but it works.

33   Finally, remember that when it comes to the art of conversation, listening is as important as, and sometimes more important than, talking. Consider poor Michael and his self-absorbed friend, Jake. As much as we want to feel interesting to others, we also want to feel that our words are being heard.

34   And when someone is speaking, there are certain things we can do to let that person know that he or she *is* being heard. Make occasional eye contact, and don't look around at other people or things. Avoid mannerisms that indicate boredom, like stretching or yawning. It isn't necessary to comment on everything the person is saying, but nodding and making brief remarks ("I see," "Wow," "Really?") lets the other person know you're engaged.

35   But beyond just *appearing* to be listening, it is obviously most important of all to truly *be* listening. Instead of thinking about what you are going to say next or, in Jake's case, about something that has nothing to do with what is being said, listen to what you are being told. There is no greater conversational blunder than making a comment that reveals that you haven't really heard a word the other person has said. You can be assured that it will be the last time that other person will waste his or her time attempting to have an important conversation with you!

36   The old Mexican proverb, "Conversation is food for the soul," is certainly true. Human beings are naturally social creatures who crave interacting and communicating with others. Even so, we are sometimes baffled° by the art of conversation. Luckily, it is an art that can be learned simply by being interested in others and by being willing to set our self-absorbed inclinations° aside for a while. And, happily, it can be learned en route° to making friends.

Reading Comprehension Questions

Vocabulary in Context

 1. In the sentence below, the word *blunders* (blŭn′dərz) means
   A. lies.
   B. errors.
   C. attempts.
   D. progress.

   "When we make blunders in conversations with others, we often feel as if we're the only ones who ever experience these mistakes." (Paragraph 25)

_D_   2. In the excerpt below, the word *mannerisms* (măn′ə-rĭz′əmz) means
   A. conversations.
   B. relationships.
   C. comments.
   D. gestures.

> "And when someone is speaking, there are certain things we can do to let that person know that he or she *is* being heard.... Avoid mannerisms that indicate boredom, like stretching or yawning." (Paragraph 34)

Central Point and Main Ideas

_C_   3. Which sentence best expresses the central point of the selection?
   A. Today, young people, in particular, have a difficult time making conversation.
   B. A friend who won't listen to you is not really a friend at all.
   C. The art of conversation isn't always easy, but it's important to learn.
   D. Nearly everyone feels awkward at some point when it comes to making conversation.

_C_   4. Which sentence best expresses the main idea of paragraphs 33–35?
   A. If you don't listen to your friends, soon you'll have no friends.
   B. While someone is telling you something, you should respond to everything he or she says with a nod and brief remark.
   C. When someone is talking to you, it is important to appear to be listening and to actually *be* listening.
   D. It is not always easy to listen to another person discuss his or her problems, but it is polite to make an effort to appear to be listening.

Supporting Details

_B_   5. Maggie would not go out with Brad again because
   A. she had another boyfriend.
   B. all he did was talk about himself.
   C. she did not find him to be attractive.
   D. her parents didn't approve of him.

_C_   6. Small talk
   A. makes the speaker seem boring and not very bright.
   B. is fine in formal settings but should be avoided on dates or between friends.
   C. is good for putting two people who don't know each other well at ease.
   D. often leads to more awkward silences in a conversation.

Transitions

 7. The relationship of the second sentence below to the first is one of
   A. contrast.
   B. comparison.
   C. addition.
   D. illustration.

> "When we make blunders in conversations with others, we often feel as if we're the only ones who ever experience these mistakes. In reality, however, the art of skilled conversation is becoming more and more rare." (Paragraph 25)

_C_ 8. The relationship of the second sentence below to the first one is one of
   A. cause and effect.
   B. addition.
   C. illustration.
   D. comparison.

> "Instead, ask about something that you're genuinely curious about (without getting too personal!), and this will often lead into a natural and rewarding conversation. For example, asking someone about where he or she grew up can lead to interesting stories and childhood experiences that both of you may have had." (Paragraph 28)

Patterns of Organization

_D_ 9. On the whole, paragraphs 29–31
   A. compare and contrast small talk with more meaningful conversation.
   B. present a list of ways to talk to someone you are intimidated by.
   C. narrate a series of events that happened during a conversation.
   D. define *small talk* and present examples and tips for using it in conversation.

_B_ 10. What is the main pattern of organization of this essay?
   A. Time order: the author describes one conversation from start to finish.
   B. Contrast: the author contrasts failed and successful conversations.
   C. Comparison: the author shows the similarity between small talk and meaningful conversation.
   D. List of items: the author lists ways to turn small talk into a meaningful conversation.

Discussion Questions

1. Of the three "conversation failures" presented at the beginning of this selection, which one can you relate to the most? Explain.

2. Nearly all of us have felt "tongue-tied" when in the presence of someone who intimidates us, as Gail did with her boss. Who have you felt unable to talk to because of nervousness? Why do you think you felt that way? On the other hand, has someone been too afraid to make conversation with you? What happened?

3. Do you think Brad's date, Maggie, should have told him why she wouldn't go out with him again? If you were with someone who spent all of his or her time talking about himself/herself, would you say something about it? Or, like Maggie, would you just avoid that person in the future? Why?

4. The author writes: "In reality, however, the art of skilled conversation is becoming more and more rare. In an age in which much of our communication is electronic and impersonal, face-to-face interaction often makes us seem flustered or, worse yet, rude." In your opinion, is electronic communication replacing human interaction—or making face-to-face conversation more difficult? Why or why not?

Note: Writing assignments for this selection appear on page 608.

Check Your Performance   **RELATIONSHIPS II**

Activity	Number Right	Points		Score
Review Test 1 (5 items)	_____	× 2	=	_____
Review Test 2 (10 items)	_____	× 3	=	_____
Review Test 3 (10 items)	_____	× 3	=	_____
Review Test 4 (10 items)	_____	× 3	=	_____
		TOTAL SCORE	=	_____%

Enter your total score into the **Reading Performance Chart: Review Tests** on the inside back cover.

RELATIONSHIPS II: Mastery Test 1

A. Fill in each blank with an appropriate transition from the box. Use each transition once. Then, in the space provided, write the letter of the transition you have chosen.

A. as a result	B. because	C. for example
D. however	E. just as	

Hint: Make sure that each word or phrase that you choose fits smoothly into the flow of the sentence. Test your choices by reading each sentence to yourself.

_____ 1. ¹If you go to a website for medical information, go to one recommended by doctors. ²_____, the famous Mayo Clinic offers a one-stop health center: **http://mayoclinic.com**.

_____ 2. ¹Small feet were admired in ancient China. ²_____, some parents had their female infants' feet tightly bound. ³The feet then grew into a tiny deformed shape. ⁴Some of the women could barely walk.

_____ 3. ¹One way to own a book is to take possession by paying for it, _____ you pay for clothes or furniture. ²But full ownership comes only when you have made the book a part of yourself by reading it closely.

_____ 4. ¹In many European countries, a kiss on the cheek is used as a greeting by men and women, regardless of the sex of the other person, or of how well they know each other. ²In Britain and Germany, _____, the cheek-kiss is used only between women, or between men and women who know each other well.

_____ 5. ¹In the search for food, wood mice explore fields that don't contain many landmarks such as large rocks and tall trees. ²When they find new food sources, they build their own signposts out of piles of leaves, twigs, and seed casings. ³This method is safer than leaving scents that could be traced by enemies such as weasels. ⁴_____ of these signposts, wood mice are known as the only mammals other than humans that mark their trail.

(Continues on next page)

B. Below are the beginnings of five passages. Label each one with the letter of its pattern of organization. (You may find it helpful to underline the transition or transitions in each item.)

>   **A** Definition and example
>   **B** Comparison-contrast
>   **C** Cause and effect

_____ 6. ¹The first railroad cars were very similar to horse-drawn carriages. ²Both were called "coaches" and held the same number of passengers—just six people. ³Likewise, train cars and horse carriages also featured the same shape, windows, and decorations. ⁴Even though trains could carry many more people than horse-drawn carriages, builders simply followed old plans when they built the first cars for the "iron horse." . . .

_____ 7. ¹The depression of the 1930s had powerful effects on families. ²It forced many couples to delay marriage. ³Another effect was a sharp drop in the divorce rate because many couples could not afford to keep up separate households. . . .

_____ 8. ¹Good listeners can paraphrase well. ²To paraphrase is to state in your own words what someone else has said. ³For instance, after a person has given you directions for getting to a certain place, you might paraphrase, saying, "In other words, what I should do is . . . " ⁴Or if someone tells you a story and you then tell that story to someone else in your own words, you would be paraphrasing the story. . . .

_____ 9. ¹Various experiments reveal there are several reasons why people will or will not help others. ²One reason is how deserving the victim is thought to be. ³This was shown in an experiment in which people pretended to be in need of help. ⁴If they carried a cane, they were helped more promptly than if they carried a liquor bottle. . . .

_____10. ¹In contrast to schools in other countries, the educational system in the United States can be seen as placing limits on teachers. ²Our teachers often cannot choose their own textbooks but must use whatever books are chosen by a local school board or district office. ³On the other hand, teachers in France are free to do their job in almost any way they want. ⁴Teachers are permitted to pick the books for their classes or even not to use any books. . . .

RELATIONSHIPS II: Mastery Test 2

A. Read the textbook excerpts that follow, and fill in each blank with an appropriate transition from the box. Use each transition once. Then, in the spaces provided, write the letter of the transition you have chosen.

A. explanation	**B.** for instance	**C.** however
D. same	**E.** therefore	

_____ 1. [1]Why is it that about half of America's eligible voters do not take part in national elections? [2]One _____ may be that many of our political leaders do not appeal to voters.

_____ 2. [1]Importing is purchasing products in other nations and bringing them into one's own country. [2]_____, buyers for Target might purchase shirts in India or sneakers in Indonesia or raincoats in England and have them shipped to the United States for sale there.

_____ 3. [1]Before the 1900s it was widely believed that schoolwork "would make women sick" and would take blood away "from their wombs to their brains," so that they would be less suited to have children. [2]_____, women were often denied opportunities for higher education and were kept from entering many colleges and universities.

_____ 4. [1]For twenty years, Asian Americans were the fastest-growing minority in the United States. [2]They are now about 4 percent of the U.S. population. [3]_____, they are a much smaller minority than African Americans, who are more than 13 percent, and Latino Americans, who are now nearly 16 percent of the population.

_____ 5. [1]*For example* and *for instance* mean the _____ thing, just as *therefore* and *as a result* do. [2]Words and phrases with the same meaning allow authors to include more variety in their writing.

(Continues on next page)

B. Below are parts of five passages. Label each one with the letter of its pattern of organization. (You may find it helpful to underline the transition or transitions in each item.)

> **A** Definition and example
> **B** Comparison-contrast
> **C** Cause and effect

_____ 6. ¹There are notable differences between people with high self-esteem and those with low self-esteem. ²People with good self-concepts tend to be more accepting of others and also more accepting of their own failures. ³In contrast, people with low self-esteem tend to be very critical of others. . . .

_____ 7. ¹Schools all too often teach students to be passive, viewing instructors as experts who serve up "truth." ²Students are expected to quietly listen and take notes. ³As a result, researchers estimate, just 10 percent of college class time is used for discussion. . . .

_____ 8. ¹Stepfamilies and "natural" families have similarities and differences. ²Both types of families have a similar range of everyday values, and both types have backgrounds that tend to be alike as well. ³However, the stepfamily includes more people—ex-husbands, ex-wives, ex-in-laws, and various other relatives on both sides. ⁴Another difference is that the stepfamily has anger, guilt, and conflicts stemming from issues that "natural" families do not face. . . .

_____ 9. ¹"Let's go shopping!" ²These familiar words echo across America like a battle cry. ³Every day, Americans get another fix of their favorite drug: shopping. ⁴There are probably several causes of this shopping madness. ⁵One reason is that we are competitive. ⁶If our neighbors have something, we want it as well, or we feel like losers or feel that we're losing out. . . .

_____ 10. ¹Great actors have more than talent. ²They also have a quality known as charisma—a mysterious "x" factor that can't be learned. ³Charisma is that extra something you can't describe but can feel flowing out of them, whether they are on stage or on the screen. ⁴For example, an acting teacher talked about seeing Marlon Brando in a play at the start of his career, before his name was known. ⁵"Suddenly a man came on the stage whom I had never seen or heard of. ⁶Before he even spoke, it was as if a leopard had entered the room." . . .

RELATIONSHIPS II: Mastery Test 3

A. (1–4.) Arrange the scrambled sentences below into a logical paragraph by numbering them *1, 2, 3,* and *4* in an order that makes sense. Then, in the space provided, write the letter of the main pattern of organization used.

Note that transitions will help you by making clear the relationships between sentences.

____ Another result is a higher proportion of male children than normal.

____ First of all, it has led to a greater number of divorces.

____ The Chinese policy of allowing only one child per family has had some disturbing effects.

____ The major reason for this imbalance in the sexes seems to be abortions of female fetuses, because male children are preferred.

_____ 5. The primary pattern of organization in the selection is
    A. comparison.
    B. contrast.
    C. cause and effect.
    D. definition and example.

B. Read the paragraph and answer the questions that follow.

> [1]Have you ever heard the term "sandwich generation"? [2]Some people might guess that it refers to a generation that spends more time eating sandwiches than sitting down to meals. [3]In fact, the term refers to adults who are "caught in the middle," so that they have to care for both their own children and their aging parents at the same time. [4]As people live longer, more and more adults end up taking care of their elderly parents. [5]For instance, a single mother named Rose has to care for her two children, one just six years old, and the other a troubled thirteen-year-old. [6]She must also care for her sixty-six-year-old mother, who has not been able to live independently since suffering a stroke.

_____ 6. The main pattern of organization in the selection is
    A. definition-example.
    B. cause-effect.
    C. comparison-contrast.

7. A transition that signals the pattern of organization is _____.

(Continues on next page)

C. Read the paragraph and answer the questions that follow.

> [1]In recent years, health-care costs in the United States have skyrocketed. [2]The result is that a large number of people—particularly the poor and those in the lower middle class—have not been able to afford health care. [3]There are many reasons for the increase in health-care costs. [4]One cause is the aging of the U.S. population. [5]Greater numbers of older Americans have created added demand for medical care, leading to higher prices. [6]Another reason that health-care costs are so high is that medical care is better. [7]As a result, patients who once died quickly from conditions such as comas and strokes can now live much longer—but need expensive medical care that often goes on for years. [8]Soaring costs have been caused as well by the way in which health care is used in the United States. [9]American medicine tends to focus on treating a disease, not preventing it. [10]Therefore, simple steps that could prevent illness and save money—such things as prenatal care and free exams for the elderly—are often ignored. [11]When people finally get to a doctor, they are more likely to have advanced problems that cost more money to treat.

_____ 8. The main pattern of organization in the selection is
   A. definition-example.
   B. cause-effect.
   C. comparison-contrast.

9–10. Two transitions that mark the paragraph's pattern of organization are

_____   _____

RELATIONSHIPS II: Mastery Test 4

A. (1–4.) Arrange the scrambled sentences below into a logical paragraph by numbering them *1, 2, 3,* and *4* in an order that makes sense. Then, in the space provided, write the letter of the main pattern of organization used.

      Note that transitions will help you by making clear the relationships between sentences.

_____ For example, the tailbone is what remains of a tail, something our ancestors once needed to survive.

_____ Body hairs, too thin to keep us warm or protect our skin, are another example.

_____ Vestigial organs are those parts of our body that serve little or no purpose to us today but were useful to our pre-human ancestors.

_____ A final example, the appendix, is believed to have once helped our ancestors digest rough vegetable matter.

_____ 5. The primary pattern of organization in the selection is
    A. comparison.
    B. contrast.
    C. cause and effect.
    D. definition and example.

B. Read the paragraph and answer the questions that follow.

    [1]Streetcars had dramatic effects on the character of city life. [2]Before their introduction, cities were limited in size by the distances people could conveniently walk to work. [3]The "walking city" could not easily extend more than two and a half miles from its center. [4]Streetcars increased this radius to six miles or more. [5]As a result, the area of a city expanded enormously. [6]A later effect was a shift in population as those who were better off moved away from the center of the city. [7]In search of air and space, they left the jam-packed older neighborhoods to the poor. [8]This flight of middle-class people from urban centers led to the growth of inner-city ghettos.

_____ 6. The main pattern of organization of the selection is
    A. definition-example.
    B. cause-effect.
    C. comparison.

    7. One transition that signals the paragraph's pattern of organization is

_____.

(Continues on next page)

C. Read the paragraph and answer the questions that follow.

> ¹When life brings setbacks and tragedies to optimists, they weather those storms better than pessimists do. ²Optimists look on the bright side. ³They bounce back from defeat, and, with their lives perhaps somewhat poorer, they pick up and start again. ⁴In contrast, pessimists give up and fall into depression. ⁵Optimists take more risks to get what they want, while pessimists are so sure of failure they don't even try. ⁶Optimists also have better health and may even live longer. ⁷However, even when things go well for pessimists, they are haunted by fears of catastrophe.

_____ 8. The main pattern of organization in the selection is
         A. cause-effect.
         B. comparison.
         C. contrast.

    9. One transition that signals this pattern of organization is

    _____.

  10. Another transition that signals the pattern of organization in the selection

    is _____.

RELATIONSHIPS II: Mastery Test 5

A. (1–4.) Arrange the scrambled sentences below into a logical paragraph by numbering them *1, 2, 3,* and *4* in an order that makes sense. Note that transitions will help you by making clear the relationships between sentences.

____ Or if you believe that a certain group has a particular talent, you may be disappointed when a member of that group cannot do what you expect.

____ For instance, if you believe that a particular group is pushy, you will automatically judge someone belonging to that group as pushy—without waiting to see what that person is really like.

____ Stereotyping is holding a set of beliefs about the general nature of a group of people.

____ It can greatly interfere with making accurate judgments about others.

_____ 5. The primary pattern of organization in the selection is
    A. comparison.
    B. contrast.
    C. cause and effect.
    D. definition and example.

B. Read the paragraph and answer the questions that follow.

> [1]The Industrial Revolution led to dramatic changes in American society. [2]At the beginning of the nineteenth century, it could take weeks to produce a single shirt. [3]Wool had to be turned into yarn, then dyed, made into fabric, and sewn into patterns—all by hand. [4]When machines were introduced, this whole process could be done in a fraction of the time. [5]Many workers' lives were affected by the industrial changes. [6]Instead of working in their homes or on farms, men, women, and children were soon working twelve- and fourteen-hour days in factories. [7]Workers such as tailors or carpenters, who previously had their own trade, found themselves employed in the very places that drove them out of business. [8]Another result was that whole villages started being built around factories, providing families with jobs, houses, schools, churches, and stores—all in one place.

_____ 6. The main pattern of organization of the selection is
    A. definition-example.
    B. cause-effect.
    C. comparison-contrast.

    7. One transition that signals this pattern of organization is

    _____.

(Continues on next page)

C. Read the paragraph and answer the questions that follow.

¹In a book titled *The Art of Loving*, a psychologist describes the difference between "mother love" and "father love." ²Mother love says, "I will always love you no matter what. ³Nothing you ever do or fail to do will make me stop loving you." ⁴On the other hand, father love says, "I will love you if you *earn* my love and respect. ⁵You must do things like obey me, get good grades, make the team, choose the right friends, get into a good college, and earn a good salary." ⁶In contrast to mother love, father love may seem harsh. ⁷But sometimes we want to hear that we are loved because we deserve it, not only because the other person cares for us without conditions.

_____ 8. The main pattern of organization in the selection is
    A. cause-effect.
    B. comparison.
    C. contrast.

9–10. Two word signals that mark the paragraph's pattern of organization are

_____   _____

RELATIONSHIPS II: Mastery Test 6

A. Read the textbook paragraph below. Then answer the question and complete the outline that follows.

> [1]There are some common reasons that small businesses fail. [2]One is managers who don't have enough knowledge or experience. [3]Some people think that managing a business is just "common sense." [4]But if managers do not know how to make basic business decisions, they are unlikely to succeed in the long run. [5]Another reason for failure is neglect. [6]After the excitement of the grand opening, some business owners fail to focus on business as much as they should. [7]Small-business owners who are unwilling to work long hours and perform many jobs are likely to fail. [8]A third common reason small businesses fail is poor record-keeping. [9]By keeping careful track of sales and costs, a manager can spot serious troubles and make changes before it is too late to do so. [10]Finally, many small businesses fail because of lack of money. [11]Here is a well-known rule of thumb: A new business should have enough money to operate at least six months without earning a profit. [12]Owners of new businesses are almost certain to fail if they expect to pay the second month's rent from the first month's profits.

_____ 1. The patterns of organization of the paragraph are list of items and
   A. definition-example.
   B. cause-effect.
   C. comparison.
   D. contrast.

2–5. Complete the outline of the paragraph by writing in the four major supporting details.

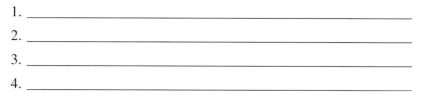

Main idea: There are common reasons that small businesses fail.

   1. _____

   2. _____

   3. _____

   4. _____

B. Read the textbook paragraph below. Then answer the question and complete the map that follows.

¹When people get sick during the flu season, they are not always sure whether what they have caught is the flu or a cold. ²It's true that the symptoms of the two overlap. ³However, there are some distinct differences between cold and flu symptoms. ⁴First of all, people rarely get a fever when they have a cold. ⁵In contrast, people with the flu typically get a fever of about 100 to 104 degrees Fahrenheit, which lasts three to four days. ⁶Also, although a cold is at times accompanied by a headache, headaches are much more likely with the flu. ⁷Third, cold victims experience at most a few slight aches and pains. ⁸But aches and pains are a usual feature of the flu and can often be quite severe. ⁹Finally, even though a cold never exhausts its victims, someone with the flu may suffer extreme fatigue.

_____ 6. The paragraph lists a series of
   A. definitions.
   B. examples.
   C. comparisons.
   D. contrasts.

7–10. Complete the map of the paragraph by writing in the missing supporting details.

A cold and the flu often have different symptoms.

Cold

1. Fever is rare.

2. _____

   _____

3. Aches and pains, if any, are slight.

4. Victims never suffer exhaustion.

Flu

1. _____

   _____

2. _____

   _____

3. Aches and pains are usual and can be severe.

4. _____

   _____

TO THE STUDENT

The pages that follow contain two mastery tests that offer additional practice in the skills covered in Chapters 6 and 7.

- Relationships that involve **addition**
- Relationships that involve **time**
- Relationships that involve **illustration**
- Relationships that involve **comparison and/or contrast**
- Relationships that involve **cause and effect**

For ease in reference, the lists of words that show these relationships have been reprinted on the next page.

Addition Words

one	to begin with	in addition	last
first	another	next	last of all
first of all	second	moreover	final
for one thing	also	furthermore	finally

Time Words

before	next	while	later
previously	soon	during	after
first	often	until	eventually
second	as	now	finally
third	when	then	last

Illustration Words

(for) example	(for) instance	to illustrate
including	such as	once

Comparison Words

(just) as	in like (similar) manner	same
(just) like	similar(ly)	in the same way
alike	similarity	resemble
likewise	both	equally

Contrast Words

but	instead	still	difference
yet	in contrast	as opposed to	different(ly)
however	on the other hand	in spite of	differs from
although	on the contrary	despite	unlike
nevertheless	even though	rather than	while

Cause and Effect Words

therefore	so	because (of)	thus
(as a) result	effect	as a consequence	results in
cause	explanation	consequently	led to
affect	due to	since	reason

RELATIONSHIPS I & II: Mastery Test 1

A. Fill in each blank with an appropriate transition from the box. Use each transition once. Then, in the spaces provided, write the letter of the transition you have chosen.

> **A.** because   **B.** for example   **C.** in addition
> **D.** just like   **E.** on the other hand

_____ 1. [1]If you have ever eaten spicy food, you may have noticed that drinking water will not calm the fire on your tongue. [2]_____ spices are usually oily, water will simply roll right over them. [3]To get some relief, you should eat a piece of bread to absorb the oily spices.

_____ 2. [1]Many prescription drugs are now available in the form of patches, which offer significant advantages over oral drugs. [2]Patches generally allow the use of lower doses of a drug, so that there is less risk of side effects. [3]_____, patches can deliver a steady dose of medication for several hours or even several days.

_____ 3. [1]Making people feel old is a poor way to sell products. [2]_____, the Heinz company once produced a diet food for seniors that it called Senior Foods. [3]The product flopped. [4]As someone explained, "People didn't want to be seen eating the stuff. [5]It was labeling them as old—and in our society, that is an embarrassment."

_____ 4. [1]People who favor dogs over cats make the following argument. [2]If you are the owner of a dog and you are suddenly shrunken to the size of a mouse, the dog will still know that you are its owner. [3]_____, if you are the owner of a cat and you are suddenly reduced to the size of a mouse, the cat will probably eat you.

_____ 5. [1]According to one eye expert, there is no harm in reading in dim light. [2]Reading in dim light is _____ sniffing hard to smell a faint odor. [3]You will not injure your eyes any more than you will injure your nose. [4]The worst thing that will happen is that your eyes will get tired because you're struggling to see instead of reading comfortably.

(Continues on next page)

B. Fill in each blank with an appropriate transition from the box. Use each transition once. Then, in the spaces provided, write the letter of the transition you have chosen.

A. another	**B.** before	**C.** however
D. such as	**E.** then	

_____ 6. [1]To recognize whether someone has just had a stroke, ask the person three simple questions. [2]First, ask the person to smile. [3]_____ ask him or her to raise both arms. [4]Finally, ask the person to speak a simple sentence. [5]The person might say, "It's sunny out today" or "I'm wearing brown pants." [6]If he or she has trouble with any of these tasks, call 9-1-1 immediately.

_____ 7. [1]All of us are subject to social control—attempts by society to regulate people's thoughts and behavior. [2]Often, these attempts are informal, _____ when parents praise or scold in order to control their children. [3]Another instance is friends who make fun of someone in their group who studies too much or wears the wrong clothes or is otherwise seen as a threat to their own behavior.

_____ 8. [1]Valentine's Day had a romantic, if tragic, beginning. [2]When Rome was about to go into battle in the third century, the emperor canceled all marriages so that men would be more willing to join the army. [3]However, a priest named Valentine secretly continued to marry couples. [4]On February 14, he was caught and jailed. [5]_____ his execution, Valentine fell in love with the jailer's daughter. [6]He signed his final note to her, "From your Valentine."

_____ 9. [1]Diamonds are the hardest natural substance on earth. [2]_____, they are easier to destroy than you might think. [3]If a diamond is baked at a temperature of 1405 degrees Fahrenheit, it will vanish, without leaving any ash.

_____ 10. [1]When you cut an onion, the chemicals in the onion's cells mix together. [2]This mixing creates a substance which makes your eyes water. [3]If you want to avoid crying when you cut an onion, you should cut it under running water. [4]The onion's chemicals will dissolve and run into the drain. [5]_____ way to avoid tears is to put an onion in the freezer for a few minutes before cutting it. [6]Cold temperatures will slow down the onion's chemical reactions.

RELATIONSHIPS I & II: Mastery Test 2

Read each selection and answer the questions that follow.

A. [1]During World War II, a cat named Oscar lived on the *Bismarck*, a German battleship. [2]When the *Bismarck* was torpedoed by a British ship, a sailor rescued Oscar. [3]Five months later, the British ship sank, but another British ship saved Oscar from drowning. [4]Just three weeks after that, Oscar was rescued yet again when a German U-boat destroyed the British ship. [5]Oscar was then returned to land, where he died peacefully in 1955, ten years after the war ended.

_____ 1. The main pattern of organization of the selection is
A. list of items.
B. cause and effect.
C. time order.

2. One transition that signals the pattern of organization of this paragraph

is _____.

B. [1]In 1996, three-fourths of Americans approved of capital punishment; in 2000, only two-thirds did. [2]Public support for the death penalty continues to decline. [3]There are at least three reasons why. [4]Crime itself has declined over the past decade; when people feel less threatened by crime, they're less likely to favor harsh punishment. [5]Another reason for the loss of support for the death penalty is that the public has become more aware of cases in which people were sentenced to death and later found to be innocent, often as a result of new DNA evidence. [6]A third cause of declining support for the death penalty is a greater mistrust of the entire judicial system, partly due to reports of incompetent or corrupt lawyers, judges, and police officers.

_____ 3. The main pattern of organization of the selection is
A. time order.
B. cause and effect.
C. definition and example.

4. One transition that signals the pattern of organization of this paragraph

is _____.

(Continues on next page)

C. ¹The effects of climate change are visible all over the world. ²In Antarctica, temperatures are rising five times faster than in the rest of the world, and penguins are finding it more and more difficult to survive. ³In Montana, glaciers in Glacier National Park are shrinking at an alarming rate and may be gone by 2020. ⁴Rising temperatures have also led to an 85 percent decline in the ice cap on Africa's tallest mountain. ⁵This ice is expected to disappear completely in less than 20 years.

_____ 5. The main pattern of organization of the selection is
      A. cause-effect.
      B. comparison and/or contrast.
      C. definition and example.

      6. One transition that signals the pattern of organization of this paragraph

      is _____.

D. ¹Television advertising is what pays for much of television programming. ²But many people have a number of objections to TV advertising for children. ³First, critics dislike the whole idea of ads for kids. ⁴Young children, they point out, do not understand the self-serving nature of advertising. ⁵They tend to simply accept ads as true. ⁶Another concern is the promotion of war-related toys in a country where kids are already exposed to too much violence. ⁷A third concern is the many ads that promote sugar-coated cereals and other unhealthful "kiddie" foods.

_____ 7. The main pattern of organization of the selection is
      A. list of items.   B. time order.   C. definition and example.

      8. One transition that signals the pattern of organization of this paragraph

      is _____.

E. ¹A stroke is very much like a heart attack. ²In a heart attack, the supply of blood to muscles of the heart is reduced or cut off, so that some of the heart's cells die. ³Similarly, in one common type of stroke, the supply of blood to the brain is hindered, so that some brain cells die. ⁴Just as in a heart attack, how many cells are killed and where they are located—which indicates what their functions were—will determine how severe the stroke is. ⁵In fact, the two events are so alike that a stroke has been called a "brain attack."

_____ 9. The main pattern of organization of the selection is
      A. time order.
      B. comparison and/or contrast.
      C. definition and example.

      10. One transition that signals the pattern of organization of this paragraph

      is _____.

This Chapter in a Nutshell

- Ideas are often suggested rather than being stated directly. We must **infer**, or figure out, those ideas.

- Discovering ideas that are not stated directly is called **making inferences**.

- We make inferences all the time—in life and in visual and reading materials of all types.

- To make logical inferences, we must look closely at the information available and use our own experience and common sense.

An Introduction to Inferences

Inferences are ideas that are not stated directly. They are conclusions we draw from what we see, hear, and read.

Look at the cartoon below. What conclusions can you draw about it? Check (✓) the **two** inferences that are most logically based on the information suggested by the cartoon. Then read the explanation on the next page.

"It's Junior's report card. The good news is that he's passing his gym class."

_____ 1. The parents have several children in school.

_____ 2. Junior is not doing well in most subjects.

_____ 3. The parents are angry about Junior's grades.

_____ 4. The wife is trying to be positive about a bad situation.

_____ 5. The parents were both good students when they were in school.

Explanation

1. Nothing in the cartoon indicates that the husband and wife have other children. The only child they are talking about is Junior.

2. If "the good news" is that Junior is passing gym, we can infer that there is also bad news: he is not passing some, or even all, of his other classes. You should have checked this item.

3. Nothing suggests that the husband or the wife is angry. They might, for example, be used to Junior's poor performance in academic subjects.

4. By presenting "the good news" about gym class first, the wife is trying to be as positive as possible. You should also have checked this item.

5. There is no evidence that the husband and wife were good students. In fact, they might have had the same kind of academic difficulties as their son, but there's no way to tell.

We make inferences all the time. We hear a sound in the night and infer it is just a squirrel on the roof. We walk into a friend's house for dinner, and the smells coming from the kitchen help us infer that we are about to have a delicious meal. We greet someone and infer from that person's body language or tone of voice that something is troubling him or her. We sense the air suddenly getting cooler and the light changing in the sky and infer that a storm is approaching.

With visual material such as cartoons, book covers, and photographs, we can infer a great deal from all the clues provided. With written material, we can "read between the lines" and pick up ideas the author only suggests, or implies. This chapter will give you practice in making inferences from both visual and reading materials.

Inferences about Visual Materials

Cartoons

How well a cartoon works often depends on the reader's inference skills. Take a moment to look at the *New Yorker* cartoon on the next page. What can you infer about this cartoon? Put a check (✓) by the **two** inferences that are most logically based on the information given in the cartoon.

"He didn't do anything, Gregory. This is a zoo."

© David Sipress/The New Yorker Collection/**www.cartoonbank.com**.

___ 1. The boy doesn't like monkeys.

___ 2. The boy has probably never seen animals in a zoo.

___ 3. The father is angry with the boy.

___ 4. The boy thinks the monkey is being punished.

___ 5. The boy and his father go to the zoo often.

Explanation

1. Nothing the boy says or does suggests he dislikes monkeys. His expression may even suggest that he is concerned about the monkey.

2. The boy would not be so apparently puzzled or upset if he were accustomed to seeing animals behind bars. And the father has to explain to the boy that "This is a zoo." You should have checked this item.

3. Nothing indicates that the father is angry.

4. From what the father is saying, we know that the boy thinks the monkey is in jail. You should have checked this item.

5. The cartoon suggests the boy has not seen an animal in a cage before, so this is not likely.

✓ *Check Your Understanding*

Now look at the following *Peanuts* cartoon:

Put a check (✓) by the **two** inferences that are most logically based on the information given in the cartoon. Then read the explanation that follows.

_____ 1. The light-haired girl read *Silas Marner* for a school assignment.

_____ 2. Marcie doesn't like to read.

_____ 3. The light-haired girl very much enjoyed reading *Silas Marner.*

_____ 4. The cartoonist suggests that reading for true understanding requires real attention.

_____ 5. Marcie and the other girl are sisters.

Explanation

1. Since Marcie says that the light-haired girl should write a report on *Silas Marner*, we can assume that reading the book was a school assignment. This inference is a matter of common sense: Children usually don't write reports on books they read on their own. You should have checked this item.

2. Nothing in the pictures or words suggests that Marcie does not like to read.

3. The light-haired girl says that she "didn't pay any attention" as she read the book. To say the least, this is not the sort of comment one makes about a book one has very much enjoyed.

4. The comment "I didn't pay any attention" suggests that it's possible to read with too little attention. You should have checked this item.

5. The light-haired girl is standing at the door as if she had come to visit Marcie. We must therefore assume that the two girls don't live together and aren't sisters.

Book Covers

Look at the following cover for a book titled *Reading Changed My Life!* by Beth Johnson. Put a check (✓) by the **two** inferences that are most logically based on the information given on the cover.

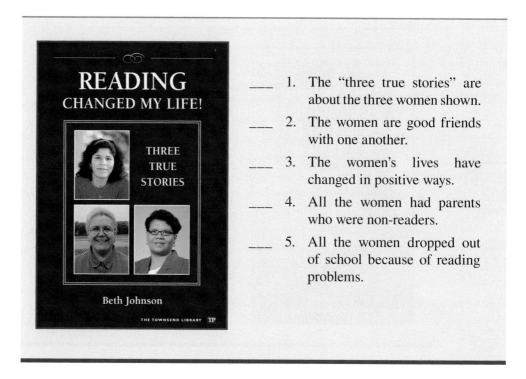

___ 1. The "three true stories" are about the three women shown.

___ 2. The women are good friends with one another.

___ 3. The women's lives have changed in positive ways.

___ 4. All the women had parents who were non-readers.

___ 5. All the women dropped out of school because of reading problems.

Explanation

1. It is logical to assume that people shown on the cover would be the book's subjects. (What other reason would there be for their pictures to be on the cover?) You should have checked this item.

2. There is no evidence given that the women know each other. Also, they are in separate photos, rather than together in one photo.

3. The title of the book and the smiling faces of the women suggest that the changes in their lives have been positive. You should have checked this item.

4. We are not given any information about the women's parents.

5. We are not told that the women dropped out of school.

✓ *Check Your Understanding*

Now look at the following book cover for the classic story *Gulliver's Travels*, by Jonathan Swift. Put a check (✓) by the **two** inferences that are most logically based on the information given on the cover.

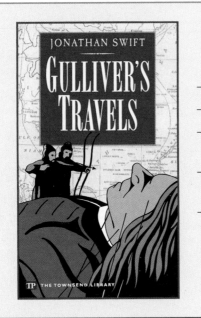

_____ 1. *Gulliver's Travels* is a true story.

_____ 2. The man on the ground is dead.

_____ 3. The book has something to do with a journey.

_____ 4. The man on the ground is probably Gulliver.

_____ 5. The story in the book takes place in modern times.

Explanation

1. The illustration shows either an impossibly huge man or two impossibly tiny men, so the story must be fiction.

2. The fact that the man is being threatened suggests he is alive. If he were dead, he would pose no threat.

3. The word *Travels* in the title and the map in the background suggest that the story indeed is about a journey. You should have checked this item.

4. The title states that the story is about the travels of one man, Gulliver. Therefore, the man shown alone, on the ground, is probably the main character. You should have checked this item.

5. The type of weapons and the clothing shown suggest that the story takes place in another time period.

Poster and Ad

Look at the following poster. Put a check (✓) by the **two** inferences that are most logically based on the information shown.

© GettyImages

____ 1. The woman has been handcuffed by the police.

____ 2. The woman is a former addict.

____ 3. The woman is addicted to food, cigarettes, and alcohol.

____ 4. Alcohol is more addictive than cigarettes or food.

____ 5. People who are addicted are not free.

Explanation

1. The picture shows nothing to support the idea that the woman has broken any law or been in contact with the police.

2. The fact that the woman is chained suggests she is still addicted.

3. All three substances are shown with her, so this is a logical inference.

4. Nothing in the poster suggests that one substance is more addictive than the others.

5. Addicts like this woman are "chained" by their addiction. This inference is also logical.

Check Your Understanding

Now look at the following advertisement. Put a check (✓) by the **two** inferences that are most logically based on the information given in the ad. Then read the explanation that follows.

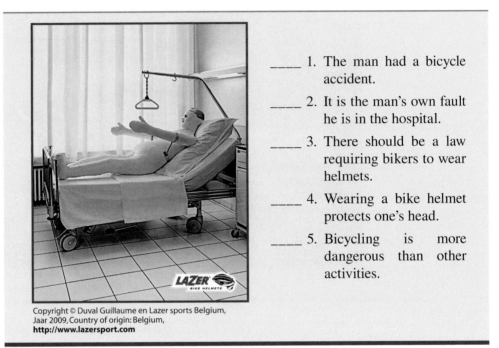

_____ 1. The man had a bicycle accident.

_____ 2. It is the man's own fault he is in the hospital.

_____ 3. There should be a law requiring bikers to wear helmets.

_____ 4. Wearing a bike helmet protects one's head.

_____ 5. Bicycling is more dangerous than other activities.

Explanation

1. The ad is for Lazer bike helmets. It is clear that the man in the picture has been in some sort of accident. His entire body is in a cast except for the top of his head; this is the part that would be protected by a bicycle helmet. Taken together, these details suggest the man has had a bicycle accident. You should have checked this item.

2. None of the information in the ad indicates who is at fault for the man's accident.

3. The ad suggests that it makes sense to wear a bike helmet. However, nothing indicates that there should be a law requiring bikers to wear helmets.

4. The one part of the man that is not in a cast is a helmet-shaped area at the top of his head. This suggests that wearing a bike helmet protects one's head. You should have checked this item.

5. The ad does not compare the dangers of biking with the dangers of other activities. This is not a logical inference.

A Final Comment about Visual Materials

As the preceding examples—the cartoons, the book covers, the poster and ad—make clear, we live in a world full of images, and we make inferences about such visual materials all the time. In other words, making inferences is a skill all of us already possess.

This chapter will now go on to strengthen your ability to make good inferences when reading.

Inferences about Reading Materials

You have already practiced making inferences while reading an earlier chapter of this book. Do you remember, for example, the following sentence from "Vocabulary in Context"?

In the United States, shaking hands is the *appropriate* way to greet someone; in Japan, bowing is the right way.

The sentence does not give us a definition of *appropriate*, but it does suggest that *appropriate* is close in meaning to "right." Thus we can infer in this sentence that *appropriate* means "right" or "proper." As you looked at all the sentences in Chapter 2, you inferred the meanings of words by looking closely at the surrounding context.

In all of our everyday reading, we make logical leaps from the information given directly on the page to ideas that are not stated directly. To draw such inferences, we use the clues provided by the writer, and we also apply our own experience, logic, and common sense.

Inferences in Passages

Read the following passage and then check (✔) the **two** inferences that are most firmly based on the given information.

> [1]I once hired a roofer to put a new roof on my home. [2]He checked the roof and then quoted me a price of $1,000. [3]I agreed. [4]He tore the old roof off, then came back down. [5]I noticed a barely hidden smile on his face.
>
> [6]"Sorry," he said, "it's gonna cost you $1,800. [7]I didn't know it needed so much work."
>
> [8]"No way," I said, folding my arms.
>
> [9]"Whatever you say," the roofer said. [10]He looked up at the sky and commented, "You know, it looks like rain."
>
> [11]I sighed, shook my head, and said, "With my luck, it will rain for three days. [12]Finish the job."

____ 1. At first, the author did not want to spend the extra $800.

____ 2. The author's old roof would have held up for another year or two.

____ 3. The roofer may have planned all along to raise the price after the old roof was torn off.

____ 4. The author believes that all roofers are con men.

____ 5. The roofer had been recommended to the author.

Explanation

1. When the roofer first tells the author that the job would cost $1,800, the author says, "No way." Using our common sense, we can conclude that the author of the selection refuses because he doesn't want to spend the extra $800. So you should have checked this item.

2. Nothing in the passage discusses the actual quality of the roof. You should not have checked this item.

3. The roofer says, "I didn't know [the roof] needed so much work." However, in telling us that the roofer had a smile on his face, the author implies that the roofer may have known all along that he planned on charging an extra $800. So you should have checked this item.

4. The passage makes no mention of the author's view of all roofers. We see only his reaction to this roofer. You should not have checked this item.

5. There is no mention in the passage of how the author came to hire the roofer. You should not have checked this item.

✓ *Check Your Understanding*

Now read the following textbook passage. Then answer the questions about it by writing the letters of the inferences that are most firmly based on the given information. Hints are provided to help you think through the choices for each question.

> [1]A twenty-eight-year-old woman named Catherine Genovese was returning home from work one day. [2]Kitty, as she was called by almost everyone in her Queens neighborhood, had just parked her car. [3]Then a man with a knife grabbed her. [4]She screamed, "Oh my God, he stabbed me! [5]Please help me! [6]Please help me!"
>
> [7]For more than half an hour, thirty-eight neighbors listened to Kitty's screams as the attack continued. [8]The last time he stabbed her, she was slumped on the foot of the stairs to her apartment. [9]According to newspaper reports, not one person telephoned the police during the fatal attack. [10]Later, the police gathered statements from the witnesses. [11]Among their comments were, "I didn't want to get involved," "We thought it was a lovers' quarrel," and "I was tired. [12]I went back to bed."

_____ 1. We can infer that Kitty was attacked
   A. while she was on vacation.
   B. in her own neighborhood.
   C. on her way from work to her car.

   Hint: The passage tells us that Genovese "was returning home from work" and that she "had just parked her car."

_____ 2. We can conclude that the man who stabbed Genovese
   A. was someone she knew.
   B. intended to kill her.
   C. was a convicted criminal.

   Hint: Is there evidence that Genovese knew her killer or that he was a convicted criminal? Also, Genovese's killer stabbed her even after he was sure she was wounded and weak.

_____ 3. We can infer that the witnesses
   A. might have stopped the attack if they had called the police.
   B. wanted the man to kill Genovese.
   C. would not want someone else to get involved if they themselves were being attacked.

   Hint: The attack continued for at least half an hour.

Explanation

Here is an explanation of each item:

   1. The answer to the first question is B. We have solid evidence to conclude that Genovese was attacked in her neighborhood: she was returning home from work and had parked her car. Since she was returning home from

work, she was not on vacation. Also, we know she had just parked her car after coming home from work. So the attack could not have taken place before she got into the car to go home.

2. The answer to the second question is B. We can conclude that Genovese's attacker wanted to kill her. If his goal was to rob or rape her, he could have done so long before the last time he stabbed her. And no evidence in the passage indicates that Genovese knew her attacker. Finally, although we cannot be sure the attacker was never convicted of a crime, there is absolutely no evidence in the passage to support the conclusion that he was—his past is not referred to at all.

3. The answer to the third question is A. The crime took at least a half hour; thus we can conclude that if the police had been called, there is a chance they would have arrived in time to save Genovese. However, we have no reason to believe the witnesses actually wanted the man to kill Genovese. Most people, in fact, would be horrified to see someone stabbed to death. And on the basis of our knowledge of human nature, we can be pretty sure the witnesses would have wanted others to get involved if they were victims.

Guidelines for Making Inferences

The exercises in this chapter provide practice in making careful inferences when you read. Here are three guidelines to that process:

1. **Never lose sight of the available information.** As much as possible, base your inferences on the facts. For instance, in the paragraph about Kitty Genovese's attack, we are told that she "was returning home from work." On the basis of that fact, we can readily conclude that she was not on vacation.

   It's also important to note when a conclusion lacks support. For instance, the idea that the attacker was a convicted criminal has no support in the selection. We are told of only one instance of his criminal behavior, the attack on Genovese.

2. **Use your background knowledge, experience, and common sense to help you in making inferences.** Our experience with people, for instance, tells us that witnesses would themselves have wanted help if they had been in Genovese's place.

   The more you know about a subject, the better your inferences are likely to be. So keep in mind that if your background in an area is weak, your inferences may be shaky. If you are having study problems, for example, the inferences of a tutor about what you need to do are likely to be more helpful than those of another student.

3. **Consider the alternatives.** Don't simply accept the first inference that comes to mind. Instead, consider all of the facts of a case and all the possible explanations. For example, the tutor may be aware of many helpful study habits that would work for you.

PRACTICE 1

Read each of the following passages. Then write the letter of the most logical answer to each question, based on the information given in the passage.

A. ¹When Oprah Winfrey was a child, she lived with her mother and two younger half-siblings in a Milwaukee apartment without electricity or running water. ²One Christmas Eve, her mother told her there would be no celebration that year. ³There was no money to buy presents. ⁴"But what about Santa Claus?" Oprah asked. ⁵Her mother answered that there wasn't enough money to pay Santa to come. ⁶As she went to bed that night, Oprah dreaded the following day. ⁷She knew the neighbor children would be outside playing with their toys and comparing presents. ⁸She tried to think of a story she could tell the other kids to explain why she had nothing. ⁹Then she heard the doorbell ring. ¹⁰Three nuns had come to the apartment. ¹¹They brought a turkey, a fruit basket, and toys for the children. ¹²"I've never had a stronger feeling of someone lifting me up," she says today. ¹³"Their kindness made me feel so much better about myself." ¹⁴Oprah remembers that Christmas as the best she ever had.

_____ 1. We can infer that before the nuns came, Oprah dreaded the next day because she
  A. would not have any new toys to play with at home.
  B. now knew Santa Claus was not real.
  C. would be shamed in front of her friends.

  Hint: The paragraph tells us Oprah "knew the neighbor children would be outside . . . comparing presents" and that she felt she'd have to "think of a story she could tell the other kids to explain why she had nothing."

_____ 2. We can conclude this was Oprah's best Christmas because
  A. she was so relieved and grateful for what the nuns had done.
  B. the toys she received were exactly what she had wanted.
  C. she had never received Christmas presents before.

  Hint: The paragraph says that after the nuns arrived, Oprah had the "feeling of someone lifting" her up and felt "so much better" about herself.

_____ 3. What can we infer Oprah would most likely have done the next day if the nuns had not come?
  A. She would have been angry and hostile toward her mother.
  B. She would have made up a lie about the presents somehow being delayed.
  C. She would have gone out and stolen some toys.

  Hint: The passage states that Oprah knew the next day "the neighbor children would be outside playing with their toys and comparing presents" and that she "tried to think of a story she could tell the other kids to explain why she had nothing."

B. [1]The British prime minister Winston Churchill was a master of the elegant put-down. [2]At one fancy dinner party, he was seated next to a favorite target—a woman whose political views were opposed to his own. [3]The two argued more or less continually throughout the meal. [4]Totally annoyed, the lady said, "Sir Winston, if you were my husband, I'd put poison in your coffee!" [5]"Madam," replied Churchill, "if you were my wife, I'd drink it."

_____ 4. We can conclude that Churchill
   A. constantly put people down.
   B. liked to put down his political opponents.
   C. was rarely invited to fancy dinner parties.

_____ 5. When Churchill said, "If you were my wife, I'd drink it," he meant to imply that
   A. he admired the woman so much he would do whatever she said.
   B. he would never insult the woman by refusing her coffee.
   C. if she were his wife, he would prefer to die.

_____ 6. We can conclude that the author of the passage admires
   A. Churchill's politics.
   B. the woman's politics.
   C. Churchill's wit.

PRACTICE 2

Read the following article, which originally appeared in the newspaper *USA Today*. Then check (✓) the **five** inferences that are most logically based on the information in the article.

In Fall, a Young Man's Fancy Turns to His Teacher

Craig Wilson

[1]Her name was Miss Meinke. [2]Or maybe it was Menke.

[3]What did I know? [4]I was in first grade and she was my teacher. [5]I couldn't even spell my own name at the time, let alone hers.

[6]It didn't matter. [7]I was going to marry her and change her name to mine, and that would take care of that problem once and for all.

[8]I loved her. [9]And I know she loved me. [10]It was obvious, just by the way she winked at me when I came in the room.

[11]She was kind and good and noble—all the things a first-time love should be. [12]She never shouted, never scolded. [13]She praised my every move.

[14]For hours we'd push mahogany-colored chestnuts back and forth across the table. [15]She called it a counting exercise, but I knew it was more than that.

[16]I remember she was tall and willowy. [17]Maybe she was short and dumpy, but in 1954, when I was three feet high, she was tall and willowy. [18]And she had a long and beautiful neck, like a ballerina.

[19]She smelled good too. [20]Nothing racy. [21]Not Miss Meinke. [22]She wasn't that kind of girl.

[23]I was by no means the first student to fall in love with his teacher, and I certainly wasn't going to be the last.

[24]This fall millions of kids will have crushes on their own Miss Meinkes, staying late for special help they don't need, asking questions they already know the answers to. [25]Some will even offer up the proverbial shiny apple to the newest woman in their lives. [26]Could her first name be Eve?

[27]I didn't know Miss Meinke's first name. [28]First-grade teachers didn't have first names back then. [29]Nor did they have personal lives.

[30]I remember seeing her at the supermarket once and thinking how odd that was. [31]She buys food? [32]She cooks? [33]She eats at places other than the teachers' table in the cafeteria?

[34]To me she lived only in that crowded and cluttered pastel-colored classroom. [35]Maybe she slept under her desk. [36]I never asked. [37]But I would be the one to take her away from all that. [38]Who cared if there was a thirty-year age difference? [39]Not me. [40]Why wouldn't she want a younger man? [41]Someone to look after her later on.

⁴²It was a perfect match. . . .

⁴³We've all heard about lovers writing passionate letters to their beloved. ⁴⁴Miss Meinke never wrote me such a letter. ⁴⁵I understand now that she really couldn't, seeing that everything I took home I immediately showed to my mother. ⁴⁶So she did the only thing she could. ⁴⁷She sent messages on my report card.

⁴⁸The first came in October. ⁴⁹On it she wrote that basically I was the ideal young man. ⁵⁰"A delight to have in my classroom," were her exact words. ⁵¹I still have the card. ⁵²Now, if that wasn't a thinly veiled "I'm in love with Craig," I don't know what was.

⁵³But it wasn't meant to be.

⁵⁴She left me. ⁵⁵For another man, I found out later. ⁵⁶Out in California. ⁵⁷She left upstate New York the next fall and never looked back. ⁵⁸Never wrote. ⁵⁹Never called.

⁶⁰In retrospect, I understand it was her way of coping. ⁶¹What else could she do? ⁶²I had already moved on to an older, more mature woman. ⁶³Mrs. Baine, who lived down the hall in a place called second grade.

_____ 1. Miss Meinke was a kind, caring teacher.

_____ 2. Wilson's mother and Miss Meinke were close friends.

_____ 3. Wilson still feels bitterness toward Miss Meinke for leaving his school.

_____ 4. Wilson probably also "fell in love" with his second-grade teacher.

_____ 5. Miss Meinke was annoyed by young Wilson's feelings for her.

_____ 6. Young students often adore their teachers.

_____ 7. First-graders may find it hard to imagine their teacher anywhere but at school.

_____ 8. Now, Wilson realizes that Miss Meinke was not a very good teacher.

_____ 9. Miss Meinke must have been an extraordinarily beautiful woman.

_____ 10. Wilson is making lighthearted fun of his childhood crush.

PRACTICE 3

The ability to make inferences will help you in all kinds of reading, including textbook material. Read the following textbook passages. Then, for each passage, check (✓) the **two** inferences that are most logically based on the given facts.

A. ¹A question that interests many is why a woman will remain with a husband who abuses her. ²Interviews with violent families revealed that the decision is related to three major factors. ³First, the more severe and more frequent the violence, the more a woman is likely to end her marriage or to seek help from social agencies or the police. ⁴The second factor has to do with how much violence she experienced as a child. ⁵The more she was struck by her own parents, the more inclined she is to stay with an abusive husband. ⁶Third, wives who have not completed high school and those who are unemployed are less likely to leave their husbands. ⁷It appears that the fewer resources a woman has, the fewer alternatives she sees and the more trapped in her marriage she becomes.

_____ 1. Abusive husbands tend to be rich.

_____ 2. People who were beaten as children learn to tolerate being abused.

_____ 3. Women who are dependent on their husbands economically are more likely to stay in an abusive marriage.

_____ 4. Employed women who are well educated are never abused by their husbands.

_____ 5. The more abused a woman is, the less likely she is to leave her husband.

B. ¹It may be important to have a job, but does work make people happy? ²In many studies during the last two decades, workers have been asked whether they would continue to work if they inherited enough money to live comfortably without working. ³More than 70 percent replied that they would. ⁴Asked how satisfied they were with their jobs, even more—from 80 to 90 percent—replied that they were very or moderately satisfied. ⁵But asked whether they would choose the same line of work if they could begin all over again, most said no. ⁶Only 43 percent of white-collar and 24 percent of blue-collar workers said yes. ⁷And when asked, "Do you enjoy your work so much that you have a hard time putting it aside?" only 34 percent of men and 32 percent of women answered positively.

_____ 1. The only reason people work is to earn money.

_____ 2. Work provides people with rewards other than money.

_____ 3. For most people, work is as enjoyable as a hobby.

_____ 4. Most people like their jobs but are not thrilled by them.

_____ 5. For most people, work is the most important thing in their lives.

CHAPTER REVIEW

In this chapter, you learned the following:

● Making inferences is a skill we practice all the time: for example, with cartoons, book covers, ads, other visual images, and everything that we read.

● Many important ideas in reading are not stated directly, but must be inferred.

● To make good inferences, we must look closely at all the information presented and also draw upon our own experience and common sense.

The next chapter—Chapter 9—will also involve making inferences, with the focus on finding main ideas that are implied, rather than stated directly.

On the Web: If you are using this book in class, you can visit our website for additional practice in making inferences. Go to **www.townsendpress.com** and click on "Learning Center."

REVIEW TEST 1

To review what you've learned in this chapter, complete each of the following sentences about inferences.

1. To fully understand a cartoon, book cover, ad, or other visual image, we often must make _____.

2. Inferences were part of an earlier chapter in this book when the meaning of vocabulary words was figured out by looking at the _____ in which they appeared.

3. When we read, we often "read between the lines" and pick up ideas that are implied rather than directly _____.

4. When making inferences, it is (*a mistake, useful*) _____ to draw upon our own experience as well as clues provided.

5. When making inferences, it is (*a mistake, useful*) _____ to draw upon our own common sense as well as clues provided.

REVIEW TEST 2

A. (1–2.) Put a check (✓) by the **two** inferences that are most logically based on the information given in the following cartoon.

That's Life used with the permission of Mike Twohy and the Cartoonist Group. All rights reserved.

____ 1. The dog is afraid of the man.

____ 2. The dog wants to go for a walk.

____ 3. The man doesn't mind leaving his television set.

____ 4. The man has been ignoring the dog.

____ 5. The television set is brand new.

B. Read the following passage. Then, in the space provided, write the letter of the most logical answer to each question, based on the information given in the passage.

> ¹The real heroes of the fight against drugs are the teenagers who resist the ghetto's fast track—those who live at home, stay in school, and juggle their studies and a low-paying job. ²The wonder is that there are so many of them. ³"Most of our youngsters are not involved in crack," says the chief judge of one juvenile court in Michigan. ⁴"Most are not running around with guns. ⁵Most aren't killing people. ⁶Most are doing very well—against great odds." ⁷They are the youngsters who fit these words of Jesse Jackson: "You were born in the slum, but the slum wasn't born in you."

_____ 3. We can conclude that the author's attitude toward ghetto teenagers who live at home, stay in school, and work is
   A. disapproving.
   B. admiring.
   C. neutral.

_____ 4. We can infer that the author believes resisting crime in the ghetto
   A. is a challenge.
   B. requires no effort at all.
   C. is impossible.

_____ 5. When Jackson says, ". . . but the slum wasn't born in you," he implies that
   A. being born in the slums is good.
   B. people can rise above their slum environment.
   C. people can never overcome the problems of the slums.

REVIEW TEST 3

A. (1.) Read the following passage and check (✓) the **one** inference that is most firmly based on the given information.

> ¹At a White House dinner during the Civil War, an elderly guest waved his hat and cried out, "Mr. President, I'm from New York State, where we believe that God Almighty and Abraham Lincoln will save this country."
> ²Lincoln—a modest man whose political thought was guided and shaped by his religious faith—smiled and nodded. ³"My friend," he said, "you're half right."

_____ 1. Lincoln believed the guest was right in saying God would save the country.

_____ 2. Lincoln believed the guest was right in saying that he, Lincoln, would save the country.

_____ 3. Lincoln believed that the man was supporting the wrong political party.

B. (2–3.) Put a check (✓) by the **two** inferences that are most logically based on the information given in the following passage:

> ¹When I look back at myself in high school, I am amazed by two things: how smart I thought I was, and how much I didn't know. ²It seems to me now that I learned few, if any, important lessons in high school. ³For example, I learned a good deal about "romance." ⁴That is, I learned about fighting, jealousy, spreading rumors, breaking up, gossip, and using other people. ⁵I don't think I learned anything about genuine love and concern for a partner. ⁶I learned about "fun." ⁷That meant partying, drinking, smoking, putting off work, and lying to my parents. ⁸I learned very little about the satisfaction of doing a job well or the rewards of discipline. ⁹Finally, I learned all about fitting in and going along with the crowd and being one of the cool people. ¹⁰I didn't learn anything about standing up for what I believed, or even figuring out what that was. ¹¹I learned almost nothing about being me.

_____ 1. The author had low self-esteem in high school.

_____ 2. The author was not popular in high school.

_____ 3. Schoolwork was not a priority for the author during high school.

_____ 4. The author is proud of his or her behavior in high school.

_____ 5. If the author could go to high school again, he or she would do things differently.

C. (4–5.) Read the following textbook passage and check (✓) the **two** inferences that are most firmly based on the given information.

> ¹In America during the 1700s, the typical woman gave birth to her children at home. ²Female relatives and neighbors would gather at her bedside to offer support and encouragement. ³Records show that the daughter of a Puritan official gave birth to her first child on the last day of January 1701. ⁴At least eight other women were present at her bedside, including her mother and four or more other neighbors. ⁵Most women were assisted in childbirth not by a doctor, but by a midwife. ⁶Skilled midwives were highly valued. ⁷Communities tried to attract experienced midwives by offering a salary or a house rent-free. ⁸In addition to assisting in childbirth, midwives helped farm animals give birth and attended the baptisms and burials of infants. ⁹During labor, midwives gave no painkillers except alcohol. ¹⁰Pain in childbirth was considered God's punishment for Eve's sin of eating the forbidden fruit in the Garden of Eden. ¹¹After delivery, new mothers were often treated to a banquet. ¹²Women from well-to-do families were then expected to spend three to four weeks in bed recovering. ¹³Women from poorer families were generally back at work in one or two days.

_____ 1. In colonial America, there were no doctors.

_____ 2. Giving birth in colonial America was typically a lonely experience.

_____ 3. In colonial America, midwives filled several community roles.

_____ 4. Society's view of pain in childbirth has changed since the 1700s.

_____ 5. Poor women recovered more slowly from childbirth than rich women.

REVIEW TEST 4

Here is a chance to apply your understanding of inferences to a longer reading selection. Jean Sutton grew up in West Oak Lane, a mostly African American community in northwest Philadelphia, and attended Franklin & Marshall College in rural Lancaster, Pennsylvania. There, she met her future husband. Jean's essay offers valuable suggestions about preparing for adult life, choosing a mate, and building a strong marriage.

Following the reading are questions on inferences. There are also questions on the skills taught in previous chapters.

Words to Watch

Below are some words in the reading that do not have strong context support. Each word is followed by the number of the paragraph in which it appears and its meaning there. These words are indicated in the selection by a small circle (°).

vulnerable (5): not protected
mentor (9): someone older and more experienced who provides advice and
       support
savvy (10): well-informed
potential (11): the possibility of becoming something in the future
acknowledged (12): accepted
monks (14): priests
advocate (22): supporter
despair (27): a feeling of hopelessness

A PATH TO MARRIAGE

Jean Sutton

1 "If I died, you'd have nothing. I have nothing to leave you."

2 Those are harsh words to hear when you're only 11, but I knew my mother was only telling me the truth.

3 "Don't make the same mistake I did," she said. "Educate yourself. Don't grow up expecting that a man will always provide for you. Anything can happen."

4 She knew what she was talking about. She had learned that lesson the hard way. With only an eighth-grade education, she had few job opportunities available to her. She provided childcare out of our home, a row house in a working-class neighborhood of Philadelphia. My father was a high-school graduate who had joined the military, and had then gone to work in a steel plant.

5 Then my father died suddenly. My mother and I were forced onto the emotional roller coaster that follows the death of a loved one. Our sorrow was compounded by the financial impact of my father's loss. My mother struggled to make ends meet. We had to give up our car, and we very nearly lost our house. At a very early age, I realized how vulnerable° an uneducated woman is.

6 I think that was my first lesson in selecting a mate and in preparing myself for adulthood. I learned that I wanted to be a financial equal in a marriage. I didn't want to have to marry in order to survive. I didn't want to be unable to support myself if my man was no longer around. I set about the task of becoming self-sufficient. I completed my formal education and am now an assistant vice president at an insurance company. I am

happily married, but I have also prepared myself for life's unexpected events.

7   From my elementary years on, I was a good student. I enjoyed school, but beyond that, I never forgot that education would provide me with the opportunities my mother hadn't had. When it was time for college, Franklin & Marshall College in Lancaster, Pennsylvania, offered me a scholarship. F&M is a very good school with a small minority enrollment. When I attended, there were 1,500 students, of whom about 50 were African American. I had gone to a Catholic high school with white students, so being with white people was not that big a deal. For me, the adjustment was more about class than about race. In high school, we'd all worn uniforms, so it wasn't so obvious who had money and who didn't.

8   But at F&M I really saw the difference. Now that I was living around people who had always had money, I felt poor in a way I never had before. My classmates were surprised that I took my work-study job in the cafeteria so seriously. If they had jobs, it was just to earn pocket money. But I needed my job so that I could buy a winter coat. In the summers I worked full-time in order to buy textbooks for the next year. Although I tried hard to find affordable used books, one year I ran out of money before the second semester began. That term I developed a new schedule. I would sleep in the evening while my dorm mates studied. Then I would borrow the books I needed and study through the night. I took special satisfaction in making the dean's list that term!

Because F&M didn't have a large   9
enrollment of Black students, the Black Student Union made special efforts to help us get to know each other. The BSU assigned each of us incoming students a mentor°, and early in my freshman year they hosted a dance. My mentor noticed me sitting on the sidelines and asked one of the older students to invite me to dance. That student was Rod Sutton, the man I would later marry. I told Rod that I didn't feel like dancing. He said, "Okay, but then I'm going to sit and talk with you."

What I first noticed about Rod was   10
the same thing most people notice— that he's *big*: a big, tall man with a big voice. And being from inner-city Newark, New Jersey, he's very street savvy°. As we sat and talked, however, I sensed that this big, loud guy was also kind and gentle. I felt a bond with him, as we had both grown up in the city without much money.

For a full year after that first meeting,   11
Rod and I were just friends. Yes, for real, *friends*. And since I was just his friend, he wasn't trying to impress me. He was

just being himself. During that year, we had long talks about how we wanted our lives to turn out. He talked about his plan to teach and to attend graduate school. He told me that he wanted to complete his education before he got married. He talked about the girls he'd known in his old neighborhood who had become teenage mothers, and how sad he was that those smart, talented girls would be unlikely to ever realize their full potential°. He said he didn't want to bring a child into this world before he was ready to be a devoted, responsible parent.

12   Wow, I thought. Even as he was criticizing teenage pregnancy, he did it in a way that didn't trash the girls involved. He acknowledged° that they were smart and talented. He respected them. That impressed me.

13   Other things impressed me as well. During our friendship, I had the chance to hang out with Rod and his friends. Many of those friends were good-looking guys, attractive and smart. But some were disrespectful of their own girlfriends or were involved in relationships built on guilt or control. Once I heard one of these guys call his girlfriend the "b" word right to her face. She shrugged it off as if it were nothing. Can you believe that the next day she was walking across the campus with him, arm in arm? When Rod heard such things, he always spoke up to the guy. He would criticize the disrespectful attitude toward "the young lady," as he always carefully referred to the girl.

14   As Rod and I exchanged our life stories, I came to respect him even more.

I learned that this gentle, kind man had been an angry, troubled kid who had been repeatedly kicked out of school for fighting. He'd finally been sent to a kind of last-chance school, one run by monks°. There, gradually, he had turned around. As I heard him talk about how his attitude had changed and as I watched him in his daily life, I could see he was for real. He was consistent in his actions as well as his words. He wasn't saying things because he thought they were what I wanted to hear. He didn't just talk the talk—he walked the walk.

15   We began to date, and my good opinion of Rod kept growing. After we graduated from F&M, he got a job teaching elementary school. He lived in Philly but commuted to Camden, New Jersey, every day. That first winter, the temperature fell to zero after a storm that dropped seven inches of snow. The schools in Philly and Camden were closed, but Rod left for work so early in the morning that he missed the announcement and drove all the way to Camden anyway. Here was a single guy, no wife or children to support, and yet he had such a strong work ethic he always showed up at work, often earlier than anyone else.

16   Watching him, I thought, *He's hard-working, considerate, respectful, and a communicator. What more could a girl ask for?*

17   Then I saw him interact with an elderly woman. When we were in a department store, Rod noticed her carrying a heavy shopping bag and struggling to open the door. "Let me help you with that, ma'am," he said. He

took her bag and opened the door for her. "Thank you!" she said with a smile. He stood and watched her go until he was sure she was okay.

18   That sealed the deal for me. On top of everything else, he cared about our elderly! To this day, he respects the senior women in our church. He visits the sick and shut-ins. He goes beyond simply opening the door or helping with a bag. He engages them in a way that makes each one feel like the most important person in the world. I tease him about how he flatters the seniors, but I admire the care and respect that he shows. Given all the wonderful things I'd observed in Rod over the years, there was no question in my mind about what to say when he asked me to marry him.

19   My appreciation for his good qualities has only continued to grow since our wedding many years ago. Before my mother passed away, she was seriously ill for many months, and I was her sole caregiver. When I came down with the flu, Rod stepped in without hesitation. He visited her every single day, making sure she had a good meal and fresh water by her bedside. Some days he sat with her for hours, just to keep her company.

20   In parenthood, as well as elsewhere in our lives, Rod and I are true partners. We agreed that we wanted to wait to start our family until we felt really ready. I know that during the years before we had a child, Rod took some criticism from men he knew. They'd pressure him, saying things like "Don't you know how to make a baby?" They'd say it in a joking way, but you know a lot of guys would have been bothered by that. They were implying he wasn't a "real man" until he had fathered a child. But Rod never let such things get to him. He made it clear that *we* were going to make that decision; that we were a team, and that no outside pressure was going to influence us. I am so grateful that Rod felt the same way I did—that bringing a new human being into the world is a very serious decision, and not something to be done lightly.

21   We did make that decision in our own time, and our family now includes Paige, who is 13; Justin, 11; and Abu, an 8-year-old we're in the process of adopting. Abu has gone through a lot in his short life, and we are all excited about his move from the foster-care system to his forever home. In Rod's career as a teacher and now as an assistant principal, he has seen so many angry, scared, neglected children. He's worked very hard to help them, but as a teacher you can do only so much. We feel we've been very blessed in our own lives, and we've always wanted to share our good fortune with another child.

22   So by now you know that I'm a big fan of my husband and an advocate° of marriage. But rest assured that marriage is not easy. It takes a lot of negotiating and hard work. That's why it is so important to have patience in selecting and getting to know your mate. You cannot get to know someone in a day, a week, or even a month. It takes time. A good rule of thumb is to know your mate through at least four seasons before you get married. Don't rush!

23   And don't just listen to what a

guy *says*. Words are easy. Observe his *actions*. Observe how he treats his family and close friends. That will be a good indication of how he'll treat you.

24   I see so many of the girls I grew up with settle for, in my opinion, far less than they deserve. We African American women face some special challenges. To begin with, we simply outnumber our marriageable men. So many of our men are in prison. And there is a widespread belief that high-achieving Black men don't marry Black women, that they go outside the race. I don't know how true that is, but many women believe it.

25   So I think a lot of women end up saying, "Well, this guy is halfway decent and not in prison," and they settle. And the result is so much divorce and so many children growing up without fathers. I understand why it happens. When your friends are getting married and having babies, it's easy to get swept up in the excitement of that. You don't want to be left behind. But marriage and parenthood are too important to go into for less than the right reasons.

26   I am convinced that good men, loving men, dependable men who hold themselves to high standards, are out there. Hold out! Give it time. Look in the right places—places like school, church, and work. I'll tell you where *not* to look—in bars and clubs. Sure, a good guy could be at a club. But in general, guys hanging out in clubs are looking for someone for a while, not for a lifetime.

27   Ladies, love yourself enough to, first, be the best person that you can be. Then love yourself enough to demand of your partner all that is rightfully yours. Take the time to be certain that the love you have is a love that will always be there. I'm not talking about the sexy love of your youth. I'm talking about a love that will be there at the end of your life, holding your hand when you take your last breath—a love that lasts not only through joy and fun, but also through sickness and despair° and whatever life may bring. Do not settle for less. Love yourself enough to hold out for all that you deserve.

Reading Comprehension Questions

Vocabulary in Context

_____ 1. In the excerpt below, the word *compounded* (kŏm-pound′əd) means
   A. hidden.
   B. weakened.
   C. increased.
   D. explained.

   "Then my father died suddenly. My mother and I were forced onto the emotional roller coaster that follows the death of a loved one. Our sorrow was compounded by the financial impact of my father's loss." (Paragraph 5)

_____ 2. In the excerpt below, the words *self-sufficient* (sĕlf′sə-fĭsh′ənt) mean
   A. attractive.
   B. important.
   C. interesting.
   D. independent.

> "I didn't want to have to marry in order to survive. I didn't want to be unable to support myself if my man was no longer around. I set about the task of becoming self-sufficient." (Paragraph 6)

Central Point and Main Ideas

_____ 3. Which of the following sentences best expresses the central point of the selection?
   A. Sutton's father died when she was still a girl, leaving herself and her mother without much money.
   B. Sutton met her future husband when both were students at Franklin & Marshall College.
   C. Sutton believes that young Black women should not rush into marriage, but should first become self-sufficient and wait for a respectful, considerate partner, as she did.
   D. Sutton noticed that Rod Sutton was a hard worker, respectful of women, and kind to elderly people.

_____ 4. Which sentence best expresses the main idea of paragraph 8?
   A. Despite not having as much money as her classmates at F&M, Sutton succeeded academically.
   B. Sutton needed her work-study job so that she could buy a winter coat.
   C. One year, Sutton ran out of money before the second semester began.
   D. Sutton took special satisfaction in making the dean's list at F&M.

Supporting Details

_____ 5. What "sealed the deal" for Jean about marrying Rod Sutton was that he
   A. spoke up to guys who called their girlfriends the "b" word.
   B. traveled through a snowstorm to get to his teaching job in Camden, New Jersey.
   C. helped an elderly woman carrying a shopping bag.
   D. helped to care for Jean's elderly mother when she became seriously ill.

Transitions

_____ 6. The sentence below begins with a word that signals
   A. time order.
   B. cause and effect.
   C. a contrast.
   D. a comparison.

   "Because F&M didn't have a large enrollment of Black students, the Black Student Union made special efforts to help us get to know each other." (Paragraph 9)

Patterns of Organization

_____ 7. In paragraph 24, Sutton mainly
   A. lists some special challenges African American women face.
   B. gives reasons why so many African American men are in prison.
   C. contrasts the attitudes of Black men with the attitudes of Black women.
   D. compares attitudes toward marriage within the African American community.

Inferences

_____ 8. From paragraph 13, we can infer that
   A. Jean liked some of Rod's friends more than she liked him.
   B. Rod sometimes called Jean the "b" word.
   C. Jean would never tolerate a boyfriend calling her the "b" word.
   D. Jean forced Rod to speak to his friends about the way they treated women.

_____ 9. Paragraph 15 suggests that
   A. Jean Sutton thought Rod was crazy for going to work in seven inches of snow.
   B. Jean Sutton admires people who have a strong work ethic.
   C. Jean Sutton had never met a hard-working man before she met Rod.
   D. Rod Sutton nearly had an accident on his way to work.

_____ 10. On the basis of "A Path to Marriage," we can infer that
   A. Rod Sutton's respectful attitude toward women earned Jean's love and admiration.
   B. Rod Sutton hadn't always had a respectful attitude toward women.
   C. finding a good, dependable man to love is impossible for most African American women.
   D. physical attraction is the most important factor in selecting a mate.

Discussion Questions

1. After reading what Jean Sutton has to say about relationships, do you think she believes in "love at first sight?" Why or why not?

2. Sutton says several times that it's more important to pay attention to what a romantic partner *does* than what he *says*. Do you think her advice is worthwhile? Why or why not?

3. Sutton mentions that her husband, Rod, was teased by some male friends for not having a child sooner. Why do you think men would put pressure on each other that way? What did you think of Rod's response?

4. Jean Sutton describes her husband Rod as a true partner. Based on her description, what qualities must a mate have to be considered a true partner? Are those qualities ones that are important to you? Are there others you would add?

Note: Writing assignments for this selection appear on pages 608–609.

Check Your Performance   **INFERENCES**

Activity	Number Right	Points	Score
Review Test 1 (5 items)	_____	× 2 =	_____
Review Test 2 (5 items)	_____	× 6 =	_____
Review Test 3 (5 items)	_____	× 6 =	_____
Review Test 4 (10 items)	_____	× 3 =	_____
		TOTAL SCORE =	_____%

Enter your total score into the **Reading Performance Chart: Review Tests** on the inside back cover.

INFERENCES: Mastery Test 1

A. (1–4.) Shown below is a note that was actually found on a car windshield in Chicago. Put a check (✓) by the **four** inferences that are most logically based on the information given in the note.

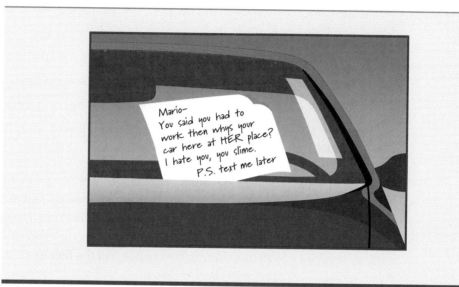

_____ 1. The note was written by Mario's girlfriend.

_____ 2. The car was not really Mario's.

_____ 3. Mario had gotten out of work early.

_____ 4. Mario's car was parked at another woman's house.

_____ 5. Mario had lied to his girlfriend.

_____ 6. The author of the note will never speak to Mario again.

_____ 7. The author of the note thinks Mario is cheating on her.

_____ 8. Mario and the author of the note are married.

(Continues on next page)

B. After reading each short passage, check (✓) the **two** inferences that are most logically based on the given information.

5–6. [1]There's an old story about a certain state legislator who had spent some time in a mental institution. [2]For years after, when debate in the legislature got heated, he would wave his release papers and declare, "I've got papers that prove I'm sane! [3]What about the rest of you?"

_____ A. The legislator was ashamed of having been in a mental institution.

_____ B. When he left the institution, the legislator was considered sane.

_____ C. The legislator had been reelected despite his mental problems.

_____ D. The legislator should never have been released from the mental institution.

7–8. [1]"Most people don't believe me when I tell them that reading aloud is the single most important factor in reading success," author Jim Trelease says as he prepares to speak to an audience of parents and teachers. [2]"They don't believe me for three reasons: One, it's simple. [3]Two, it's free. [4]And three, the child enjoys it. [5]But if reading required a $149 machine, we'd have it in half the homes of America. [6]And if kids hated it, we'd have it in every classroom."

_____ A. The use of a machine is the best way to teach a child to read.

_____ B. If something is simple, free, and enjoyable, people believe it's too good to be true.

_____ C. Jim Trelease has probably written a book about children and reading.

_____ D. Learning to read is a complex and difficult challenge for any child.

9–10. [1]A well-known prayer goes as follows: "God, grant me the courage to change what I must change, the patience to bear what I must bear, and the wisdom to know the difference."

_____ A. It sometimes takes courage to change one's life.

_____ B. Courage is more important than patience.

_____ C. Courage and patience are much the same.

_____ D. We sometimes aren't wise enough to know when we must simply accept a situation.

INFERENCES: Mastery Test 2

A. (1–4.) Put a check (✓) by the **four** inferences that are most logically based on the information given in the following cartoon.

_____ 1. The figure on the left does not work out at all.

_____ 2. The figure on the left probably spends lots of time working out.

_____ 3. The two figures do very different things when they work out.

_____ 4. The two figures do not like each other.

_____ 5. Spending time at the library has had no effect on the figure on the right.

_____ 6. Spending time at the library has made the figure on the right mentally strong.

_____ 7. Working out at the library has the same effect as working out at the gym.

_____ 8. Working out at the library involves mental—not physical—effort.

(Continues on next page)

B. After reading each short passage, check (✓) the **two** inferences that are most logically based on the given information.

5–6. ¹A doctor calls a patient into his office to reveal the results of some recent tests. ²"I have some bad news and some worse news," says the doctor. ³"The bad news is that you only have 24 hours to live."

⁴"Oh no," says the patient. ⁵"What could be worse than that?"

⁶The doctor answers, "I've been trying to reach you since yesterday."

_____ A. The patient learns he has cancer.

_____ B. The patient learns he will die that very day.

_____ C. The patient learns he will die a painless death.

_____ D. The patient at first cannot believe anything is worse than having only one day to live.

7–8. ¹Americans tend to see old age negatively, as a time of physical and mental decline. ²In Japan, the situation is very different. ³For instance, elderly guests arriving at a hotel in Japan are asked their age—a tradition meant to ensure that they will receive the proper respect. ⁴Japanese grandmothers wear red to show their high status. ⁵And to celebrate reaching age 60, a Japanese man wears a red vest. ⁶This, too, is a sign of great honor.

_____ A. The Japanese tend to view old age more positively than Americans do.

_____ B. Old people in Japan do not experience as much physical or mental decline as old people in the United States.

_____ C. Guests at a Japanese hotel would probably be embarrassed to state their age.

_____ D. The color red apparently has a special meaning in Japan.

9–10. ¹"I hate war," said U.S. General Dwight Eisenhower, "as only a soldier who has lived it can, as one who has seen its brutality, its futility, its stupidity. ²Every gun that is made, every warship launched, every rocket fired, signifies in the final sense a theft from those who hunger and are not fed, those who are cold and not clothed."

_____ A. Eisenhower did not like the military.

_____ B. Eisenhower's involvement in war made him hate war.

_____ C. Eisenhower believed that the money spent on war could be put to better use.

_____ D. Eisenhower believed the military was directly responsible for poverty and hunger.

INFERENCES: Mastery Test 3

A. (1–4.) After reading each short passage, check (✓) the **two** inferences that arc most firmly based on the given information.

1–2. [1]For centuries, coca leaves have been chewed by South American Indians to combat fatigue, hunger, and thirst. [2]When processed into cocaine, coca becomes much more powerful. [3]Cocaine was once believed to be a safe painkiller and was prescribed by doctors. [4]In fact, Coca-Cola originally contained a small amount of cocaine. [5]In recent times, cocaine has been recognized as a dangerous addictive drug.

_____ A. Cocaine is not an effective painkiller.

_____ B. Coca grows naturally in South America.

_____ C. Coca leaves are more dangerous than processed cocaine.

_____ D. Cocaine was once legal in the United States.

3–4. [1]A small private plane developed engine trouble while still many miles from a suitable landing strip. [2]The pilot, realizing there was nothing he could do to keep the plane in the air, rushed back to where his three passengers sat and explained the situation. [3]He added, "I am a married man with two small children. [4]I regret to tell you there are only three parachutes aboard." [5]And with that, he grabbed one of the parachutes and bailed out.

[6]One of the passengers reacted quickly to the pilot's exit. [7]"I am a brilliant scientist!" he announced. [8]"I am the world's smartest man! [9]The world cannot do without me!" [10]And with that, he too bailed out.

[11]The other two passengers, an elderly priest and a Boy Scout, were quiet for a moment. [12]"Son," the priest said finally, "I am old and have lived a full life. [13]I am ready to meet my Maker."

[14]"You'll have to cancel the meeting, Father," the Boy Scout answered, smiling. [15]"The world's smartest man just bailed out with my backpack!"

_____ A. Scientists tend to think highly of themselves.

_____ B. The "world's smartest man" wasn't as smart as he thought.

_____ C. Scientists are more important to the world than priests and Boy Scouts.

_____ D. No matter how smart someone is, he or she needs to examine the facts closely before acting.

(Continues on next page)

B. After reading each short passage, check (✓) the **three** inferences that are most firmly based on the given information.

5–7. ¹A radio announcer in Dallas asked his listeners to send him money, and they did. ²One day, Ron Chapman of station KVIL simply told his listeners, "Go to your checkbooks. ³Write a check payable to KVIL Fun and Games. ⁴Make it in the amount of $20 and mail it to this address." ⁵He never stated why listeners should send the money, only that they should. ⁶Chapman expected that about three or four hundred listeners would respond. ⁷He intended to return their checks and send them a bag of goodies from his sponsors. ⁸However, instead of four hundred checks, over twelve thousand were received, amounting to $244,240. ⁹The station donated the money to charity.

_____ A. People will sometimes do what they're told without knowing exactly why.

_____ B. The station gave the money to the homeless.

_____ C. Chapman made his announcement to play a trick on his listeners.

_____ D. Chapman's sponsors were furious about the stunt.

_____ E. Chapman assumed that a small percentage of his listeners would send money without knowing why.

8–10. ¹At Wellness Community meetings, cancer patients give each other various types of support, including the opportunity to laugh. ²They laugh with each other about things that would make outsiders uneasy. ³One joke told by patients is about a man with cancer who has just learned that he has only one more night to live. ⁴He asks his wife to come to the bedroom with him for one last sexual encounter. ⁵His wife says, "Gosh, Hugo, I'd love to, but I'm too tired." ⁶Hugo says, "Oh, come on." ⁷And his wife says, "That's easy for you to say. ⁸You don't have to get up in the morning."

_____ A. In real life, cancer patients cannot participate in sex.

_____ B. Cancer patients can laugh about their problems.

_____ C. The author feels that healthy people may be uncomfortable over jokes about death.

_____ D. The wife in the joke is aware that Hugo will die the next morning.

_____ E. All cancer patients in the Wellness Community meeting will die from their illness.

INFERENCES: Mastery Test 4

A. Read each passage and check (✓) the **two** inferences that are most firmly based on the given information.

1–2. ¹"You're just like an ostrich, burying your head in the sand!" ²We say this about a person who foolishly pretends not to notice danger approaching. ³Actually, the ostrich does not do anything quite so silly. ⁴When threatened, an ostrich may sit down and stretch its long neck against the ground. ⁵In that position, the bird resembles a grassy mound of earth. ⁶This is also the ostrich's position while guarding its nest. ⁷During the day, the dull-brown-colored female stretches out across the nest. ⁸At night, the black male takes over.

____ A. During the day, the natural environment of the ostrich probably is a dull brown color.

____ B. Ostriches are among the most intelligent of animals.

____ C. If they mistake the ostrich for a mound of earth, unfriendly animals will ignore it.

____ D. People should feel complimented when they are compared to ostriches.

3–4. ¹Trial lawyers point out that eyewitness accounts of crimes—often used to build a case against a suspect—are not always reliable. ²Experiments back up their claim. ³In one experiment, for example, a group of students was shown a film of a car accident. ⁴Then the students were questioned about the film. ⁵Some were asked, "How fast was the white sports car going when it passed the barn?" ⁶A week later, all the students were asked whether there had been a barn in the film. ⁷Nearly 20 percent of the students who had been asked the initial question "remembered" the barn. ⁸In fact, there was no barn in the film.

____ A. Experiments support trial lawyers' claim that eyewitness testimony is not always reliable.

____ B. Students are obviously less reliable than many firsthand witnesses in trials.

____ C. Eyewitnesses are the least reliable sources of evidence.

____ D. Eyewitnesses can be influenced into giving untrue testimony without realizing it.

(Continues on next page)

B. Read each passage and check (✓) the **three** inferences that are most firmly based on the given information.

5–7. ¹In Brazil, life moves slowly, and personal relationships are more important than financial success. ²Social life revolves around friends, relatives, and special occasions, like weddings or communions. ³People greet each other with a peck on each cheek or a hearty embrace, and being too much on one's own is seen as abnormal. ⁴Businesspeople in the cities go home to nearby apartments for lunch. ⁵Shops close from noon to 2:00 p.m. so the family can be together. ⁶No one feels a need to always be "on time," and people get there when they get there. ⁷The important thing is to enjoy life.

_____ A. Life in Brazil is more difficult than life in the United States.

_____ B. Brazilians are less concerned with financial success than Americans.

_____ C. Brazilians are a warm, social people.

_____ D. Brazilians place a high value on promptness.

_____ E. Brazilians place a high value on family life.

8–10. ¹There are two strong influences on the content of dreams. ²One influence is the time of your dream. ³When you are closest to waking, your dreams are apt to be about recent events. ⁴Those are the dreams you are most likely to remember because you tend to remember dreams you have had just before waking up. ⁵In the middle of the night, however, your dreams are more likely to involve childhood or past events. ⁶The other influence on the content of dreams is presleep conditions. ⁷In one study, subjects who had six hours of active exercise before sleep tended to have dreams with little physical activity. ⁸The researcher concluded that dream content may offset waking experiences to some extent. ⁹Other research supports that conclusion. ¹⁰For instance, subjects who had experienced a day of social isolation had dreams with a great amount of social interaction. ¹¹Also, subjects who had been water-deprived dreamed of drinking.

_____ A. Some people rarely dream.

_____ B. The researchers sometimes woke people up to ask what they were dreaming about.

_____ C. If you dream about your tenth birthday, the dream is likely to occur in the middle of the night.

_____ D. A student studying for finals will probably dream about studying.

_____ E. People who go to bed hungry probably tend to dream of eating.

INFERENCES: Mastery Test 5

A. Read the passage and then write, in each space provided, the letter of the inference most logically supported by the information given.

> [1]Beware! [2]Right now, a movie filled with blood, gore, and severed body parts is on its way to a theater near you. [3]The movie's title doesn't matter. [4]It will follow the same plot as the countless other "slash and gore" movies that have come before it. [5]These movies are easy to spot. [6]All involve young, attractive teens having sex and then getting sliced and diced. [7]The chopping is usually done by an evil villain with bad teeth and a deep, threatening laugh. [8]And if one of these movies does well at the box office, a sequel will be made—usually with an even larger dose of gore and butchery. [9]Such movies manage to draw large audiences because they offer date-night appeal. [10]People tend to hold, squeeze, and grab each other when they're scared. [11]These movies also offer some privacy to teens intent on making out. [12]Any sensible adult wouldn't be caught dead at one of these movies.

_____ 1. We can conclude that the movies to which the author refers
   A. attract only adults.
   B. are uninteresting to teens.
   C. attract teens.

_____ 2. We can infer that the author of the passage feels that the audience of horror movies
   A. likes to be scared at the movies.
   B. does not like to be scared at those movies.
   C. is never scared at the movies.

_____ 3. We can infer that the author of the paragraph feels the "slash and gore" plots are generally
   A. harmful to audiences.
   B. surprising.
   C. not very creative.

B. (4–8.) Read the following passage from *Homecoming*, an autobiography by Floyd Dell (1887–1969). Then check (✔) the **five** statements that are most logically supported by the information given.

> [1]That fall, before it was discovered that the soles of both my shoes were worn clear through, I still went to Sunday school. [2]And one time the Sunday school superintendent made a speech to all the classes. [3]He said that these were hard times, and that many poor children weren't getting enough to eat. [4]It was the first

(Continues on next page)

that I had heard about it. [5]He asked everybody to bring some food for the poor children next Sunday. [6]I felt very sorry for the poor children.

[7]Also, little envelopes were distributed to all the classes. [8]Each little boy and girl was to bring money for the poor, next Sunday. [9]The pretty Sunday school teacher explained that we were to write our names, or have our parents write them, up in the left-hand corner of the little envelopes. . . . [10]I told my mother all about it when I came home. [11]And my mother gave me, the next Sunday, a small bag of potatoes to carry to Sunday school. [12]I supposed the poor children's mothers would make potato soup out of them. . . . [13]Potato soup was good. [14]My father, who was quite a joker, would always say, as if he were surprised, "Ah! I see we have some nourishing potato soup today!" [15]It was so good that we had it every day. [16]My father was at home all day long and every day, now; and I liked that, even if he was grumpy. . . .

[17]Taking my small bag of potatoes to Sunday school, I looked around for the poor children; I was disappointed not to see them. [18]I had heard about poor children in stories. [19]But I was told just to put my contribution with the others on the big table in the side room.

[20]I had brought with me the little yellow envelope with some money in it for the poor children. [21]My mother had put the money in it and sealed it up. [22]She wouldn't tell me how much money she had put in it, but it felt like several dimes. [23]Only she wouldn't let me write my name on the envelope. [24]I had learned to write my name, and I was proud of being able to do it. [25]But my mother said firmly, no, I must not write my name on the envelope; she didn't tell me why. [26]On the way to Sunday school I had pressed the envelope against the coins until I could tell what they were; they weren't dimes but pennies.

_____ 1. At the time, the author did not realize he was a poor child himself.

_____ 2. The family had potato soup every day because it was so good.

_____ 3. The family had potato soup every day because it was so inexpensive.

_____ 4. The father's comment on potato soup showed his interest in nutrition.

_____ 5. The author feels that it is a bad idea to try to help the poor.

_____ 6. The author's mother didn't want his name on the envelope because she was ashamed of their small donation.

_____ 7. The author's father had probably lost his job.

_____ 8. The author soon stopped going to Sunday school.

INFERENCES: Mastery Test 6

A. (1–4.) Read the following textbook passage. Then check (✓) the **four** statements that are most logically supported by the information given.

^{1}Sitting alone in a dining room where bank officers had lunch, a researcher listened to what they were talking about at nearby tables. ^{2}When no woman was present, the men talked mostly about business. ^{3}They rarely spoke about people. ^{4}The next most popular topics were food, sports, and recreation. ^{5}When women talked alone, their most frequent topic was people, especially friends, children, and partners in personal relationships. ^{6}Business was next, and then health, including weight control. ^{7}Together, women and men tended to avoid the topic that each group liked best. ^{8}Instead, they settled on topics of interest to both, but they followed the style of the men-only conversations. ^{9}They talked about food the way men did, focusing on the food and restaurant rather than diet and health. ^{10}They talked about recreation the way men did, concentrating on sports figures and athletic events rather than on exercising for weight control. ^{11}And they talked about housing the way men did, dealing mostly with location, property values, and commuting time. ^{12}They did not talk about whether a house is suitable for the family, how safe the neighborhood is for the children, or what kinds of people live next door.

_____ 1. Men and women prefer different topics and styles of conversation.

_____ 2. Women never change their style of conversation.

_____ 3. Women have fewer personal relationships than men do.

_____ 4. Men tend not to talk about their personal relationships.

_____ 5. Women care more about food than men do.

_____ 6. Women speak differently when speaking to each other than they do when speaking with men.

_____ 7. Women are more interested in dieting than men are.

_____ 8. There's really very little difference between men's and women's conversations.

(Continues on next page)

B. (5–8.) Read the following textbook passage. Then check (✓) the **four** statements that are most logically supported by the information given.

> ¹The cause of cholera was not discovered until 1883. ²That's when Robert Koch, the famous scientist, led a group to Egypt that found the guilty germ. ³The deadly bacteria settle in the intestines of their victims. ⁴Dirty hands or raw fruits and vegetables often transmit the disease. ⁵But most cholera epidemics are spread by drinking water that has been polluted with raw sewage.
>
> ⁶Unfortunately, America's cities in 1832 had more than enough filth to encourage an epidemic. ⁷New York City was especially dirty. ⁸Residents were required by law to pile their garbage in the gutter in front of their homes for removal by the city. ⁹However, it seldom got collected. ¹⁰The only effective "sanitary engineers" in New York were the thousands of pigs that roamed the streets, eating the refuse.
>
> ¹¹Thanks to this filth, there was a great plague of death when cholera reached New York. ¹²Thousands died in the epidemic. ¹³There were so many bodies that the undertakers could not keep up with the volume. ¹⁴They had to stack corpses in warehouses and public buildings to await burial.
>
> ¹⁵In the midst of their suffering, New Yorkers could not help wondering why some people got the disease while others escaped it. ¹⁶Some of America's doctors thought they had an answer. ¹⁷People who kept God's laws, they explained, had nothing to fear.

____ 1. New York was the only American city to suffer from cholera.

____ 2. Cholera is more likely to spread in the countryside than in the city.

____ 3. In the early 1800s, the dangers of polluting water with garbage were not clear to New Yorkers.

____ 4. At the time of the plague in New York, doctors did not really know what caused cholera.

____ 5. Some doctors turned to religion to explain what they did not understand.

____ 6. Many victims of the New York cholera epidemic never got buried.

____ 7. In the 1800s, cholera was, in fact, easily cured.

____ 8. A cholera epidemic is unlikely to occur in the United States today.

9 Implied Main Ideas

This Chapter in a Nutshell

- Main ideas may be clearly suggested, or **implied**, rather than stated directly.
- In such cases, look closely at the supporting details. Then decide what general idea includes or summarizes those details.
- A general idea must "fit" the details; it must not be either too narrow or too broad for those details.

What Are Implied Main Ideas?

Main ideas are not always stated directly. Sometimes you must infer them from the evidence presented. For instance, what is the main idea of the poster below?

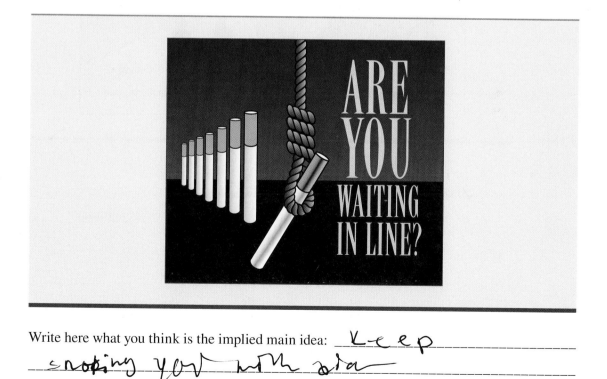

Write here what you think is the implied main idea: _Keep_
smoking you with ata

Explanation

Let's consider the details: There's a hangman's noose around one cigarette, and the other cigarettes are waiting in line for the noose. These details vividly express the idea that smoking kills, so anyone who smokes is waiting in line to die.

✓ Check Your Understanding

Look at the following cartoon. Put a check (✓) by the implied main idea.

Copyright © by Randy Glasbergen.
www.glasbergen.com

"This place is too cold, there's too much snow, and everybody looks the same."

— GLASBERGEN

____ 1. The speaker will not be happy anywhere.

✓ 2. The speaker wants to live somewhere else.

____ 3. The speaker does not get along with the other two penguins.

Explanation

The penguin is complaining about the place where he lives. And all of the things the speaker is unhappy about are things that cannot be changed—the temperature, the snow, and what others look like. These details all imply that the penguin wants to live somewhere else.

Finding Implied Main Ideas in Reading

In reading as well as in visual materials, the main idea is often not directly stated, but clearly implied. Such is the case with the paragraph below. See if you can infer its main idea. Check (✓) the letter of the statement that best summarizes all the supporting details.

> ¹I was in an alley dressed in light summer clothing. ²Coming out of the darkness at the end of the alley were hundreds of large gray rats. ³Their razor-sharp teeth glistened with saliva, and their eyes glowed red with a cold fury. ⁴I turned to run away, but attacking in the other direction were a dozen angry dogs—pit bulls! ⁵And these particular pit bulls were foaming at the mouth; they all had rabies. ⁶"Just my luck," I muttered and did my best to wake up as quickly as possible.

____ A. The writer is losing his mind.

____ B. Gray rats and pit bulls are scary animals.

____ C. Everyone has nightmares.

✓ D. The writer had a really bad dream.

Explanation

A. You may at first have thought the writer was indeed going mad. But the last sentence makes clear that the disturbing details of the paragraph were in a nightmare.

B. The statement that the rats and pit bulls are scary doesn't account for the last line of the paragraph, in which the writer reveals that all the details up to that point were in a nightmare.

C. The scary details of the paragraph are in one person's dream, but there's no support for the statement that everyone has nightmares.

D. The words "I . . . did my best to wake up as quickly as possible" plus all the scary details make clear that item D is the implied main idea.

As the above paragraph shows, a paragraph may lack a main idea *sentence*, but that doesn't mean it lacks a main idea. In this chapter, you will practice finding implied main ideas.

Following is a four-step process that will develop your skill at finding implied main ideas.

Step 1: Recognizing Implied General Ideas

Learning how to find unstated general ideas or subjects is a helpful step in finding unstated main ideas. Read the following list of specific items, and then write the letter of the general idea that best covers them. The answer will be the group to which all of the specific ideas belong.

____ *Specific ideas:* baseball cap, football helmet, Easter bonnet

The general idea is
A. sports hats.
B. clothing.
C. hats.

Since an Easter bonnet is not a sports hat, answer A is wrong—it is too narrow to cover all the specific ideas. It is true that all the specific ideas are items of clothing, but they have more in common than that—they are only items of clothing worn on the head. Thus answer B is much broader than necessary, and answer C is the correct choice.

When you are looking for the general idea, remember these points:

1 The general idea must cover all of the specific ideas. (*Hats* covers *baseball cap, football helmet*, and *Easter bonnet.*)

2 The general idea must not be so narrow that it excludes any of the specific ideas. (*Sports hats* is too narrow—it does not cover *Easter bonnet.*)

3 A general idea that covers many kinds of specific ideas in addition to the ones in the list is too broad. (*Clothing* is too broad—it covers specific ideas in addition to *hats*, such as *shoes* and *pajamas.*)

Check Your Understanding

Read the following list of specific items, and then write the letter of the general idea.

____ *Specific ideas:*
"I couldn't take the final because my grandmother died."
"I couldn't come in to work because I had a migraine headache."
"I couldn't study because I forgot to bring my book home."

The general idea is
A. common remarks.
B. common excuses.
C. common student excuses.

Explanation

The specific ideas are common remarks. Yet *common remarks* covers various types of remarks—common compliments, common greetings, common excuses, and so on. But all of the specific ideas on the previous page are one type of common remark—common excuses. Thus answer A is too broad, and answer B is the correct answer. Answer C is too narrow because only two of the three specific ideas are student excuses; one is a worker excuse.

> *Hint:* When you are trying to discover a general idea, ask yourself these questions:
>
> 1) Does a general idea cover **all** of the specific ideas listed? If not, it is **too narrow.**
>
> 2) Does a general idea cover **more** ideas than the specific ideas listed? If so, it is **too broad.**

PRACTICE 1

Read each group of specific ideas. Then, in the space provided, write the letter of the general idea that tells what the specific ideas have in common. Keep in mind that the correct general idea will not be too narrow or too broad.

B 1. *Specific ideas:* blueberries, strawberries, cranberries, cherries, peaches
   The general idea is
   A. foods.
   B. fruits.
   C. berries.

A 2. *Specific ideas:* worn brakes, body rust, weak battery, cracked windshield
   The general idea is
   A. car problems.
   B. external car problems.
   C. transportation problems.

A 3. *Specific ideas:* penny, nickel, dime, dollar bill
   The general idea is
   A. money.
   B. coins.
   C. folding money.

_B_ 4. *Specific ideas:* church, synagogue, temple, mosque

The general idea is
A. institutions.
B. religious institutions.
C. Christian institutions.

_A_ 5. *Specific ideas:* combs, brushes, razors

The general idea is
A. items for grooming.
B. women's items for grooming.
C. men's items for grooming.

_C_ 6. *Specific ideas:* eyeglasses, telescope, microscope, magnifying glass

The general idea is
A. inventions.
B. very recent inventions.
C. inventions for seeing.

_A_ 7. *Specific ideas:* letter, e-mail, telephone, smoke signal

The general idea is
A. forms of communication.
B. forms of electronic communication.
C. forms of written communication.

_C_ 8. *Specific ideas:* nose, pupil of an eye, bull's-eye, doughnut hole

The general idea is
A. objects.
B. body parts.
C. things in the middle.

_C_ 9. *Specific ideas:* "Mayor Reelected by Wide Margin." "Stocks Fall." "Stocks Rise." "Body Found in Trunk." "Storm Paralyzes City."

The general idea is
A. titles.
B. titles of books.
C. headlines in news articles.

_C_ 10. *Specific ideas:* syllable divisions, pronunciation, plural forms, meanings

The general idea is
A. information.
B. useful information.
C. information found in a dictionary entry.

Step 2: Putting Implied General Ideas into Your Own Words

Now that you have practiced recognizing general ideas, you are ready to practice stating such ideas on your own. Below is an example. Consider the four specific ideas, and then decide on a general idea that is neither too broad nor too narrow.

General idea: _Liquids_

Specific ideas: orange juice
water
milk
blood

At first glance it might seem that the general idea of these specific ideas is *beverages*. But blood does not fall into that category (except for Dracula). So you must use a broader general idea to include *blood*. Thus the general idea here is *liquids*.

PRACTICE 2

In the following lists, the specific ideas are given, but the general ideas are unstated. Fill in the blanks with the unstated general ideas. Parts of some answers are provided for you.

1. *General idea:* _Directions_
   Specific ideas: up
   down
   northwest
   south

2. *General idea:* _Seafood_
   Specific ideas: salmon
   lobster
   shrimp
   flounder

3. *General idea:* _Test_
   Specific ideas: multiple choice
   essay
   true-false
   fill in the blank

4. *General idea:* _____ Noises _____

   Specific ideas: squeak
   whistle
   shout
   buzz

5. *General idea:*   Parts of a _____ Book _____

   Specific ideas: cover
   table of contents
   chapters
   index

6. *General idea:*   Jobs in a _____ Restaurant _____

   Specific ideas: chef
   waitress
   cashier
   bus boy

7. *General idea:*   Things that are _____ White _____

   Specific ideas: snow
   wedding dress
   milk
   the President's house

8. *General idea:* _____ Baby _____ animals

   Specific ideas: kitten
   puppy
   chick
   lamb

9. *General idea:* _____ Signs _____

   Specific ideas: DO NOT ENTER
   REST ROOMS
   FIRE EXIT
   RIGHT TURN ONLY

10. *General idea:* _____ Opposites _____

   Specific ideas: *sick* and *well*
   good and *evil*
   cheap and *expensive*
   left and *right*

Step 3: Recognizing Implied Main Ideas I

Just as with the unstated general ideas above, your choice of an unstated main idea must not be too broad or too narrow. You must select a general statement that includes all or most of the specific ideas in a paragraph. The following practice will help you find unstated main ideas.

✓ ### *Check Your Understanding*

Begin by reading the supporting statements below. Then put a check (✓) by the idea that you think is the unstated point.

Support

- Men accuse women of not trusting them.
- Men complain that women have little interest in sports.
- Men say that women change the subject when they're losing an argument.

Point: The unstated main idea is:

_____ A. Men think women don't trust them.

_____ B. Men accuse women of talking too much.

__✓__ C. Men have various complaints about women.

_____ D. Men have strong positive and negative views about women.

Explanation

1. Item A is too narrow to be the unstated main idea. It applies to only one of the statements, the first one.

2. Item B is too narrow to be the main idea. It is a specific complaint, like each of the three supporting details above.

3. Item C is the main idea—it covers all three of the supporting statements (each of which is a specific complaint about women).

4. Item D is incorrect because it is too broad. It refers to positive views about women as well as negative ones.

PRACTICE 3

Read each group of three supporting details. Then, in the space provided, write the letter of the answer that best states the implied main idea of those details.

Group 1

Support

- The average part-timer earns three dollars an hour less than the average full-time worker.
- Part-time workers are easily laid off.
- Most part-time workers get no fringe benefits.

_A_ 1. The **implied main idea** is:
   A. Part-time workers have second-class status.
   B. Part-timers get paid lower salaries.
   C. Workers have numerous problems.
   D. Part-timers make up a significant part of our working population.

Group 2

Support

- Parents identified honesty, judgment, and obedience as the top three traits they value in their children.
- The second most desirable trait for children was "good sense and sound judgment."
- Obedience to parents came in third.

_A_ 2. The **implied main idea** is:
   A. For a survey, parents chose the traits they felt were most important for children.
   B. Parents feel it is more important for children to be honest than obedient.
   C. The trait most parents agree children should have is honesty.
   D. A survey shows that most people feel honesty is the most important human trait.

Group 3

Support

- An octopus can escape its enemies by shooting out a jet of water that gives it a burst of speed.
- The octopus can avoid being discovered by changing its body color so that it blends into the environment.

● The octopus can also avoid attack by releasing its ink, which dulls an attacker's sense of smell, making it harder to find the octopus.

_B_ 3. The **implied main idea** is:
   A. An octopus must protect itself from enemies.
   B. An octopus has several means of defense.
   C. An octopus has an interesting lifestyle.
   D. An octopus can change its coloring and blend into the environment.

Step 4: Recognizing Implied Main Ideas II

You have practiced finding implied main ideas for a group of supporting statements. The final step is to work at finding implied main ideas in paragraphs.

✔ **Check Your Understanding**

Read the following paragraph and see if you can choose the statement that best expresses its main idea.

> [1]If people stop to think about the plots in children's stories, they may be surprised. [2]Hansel and Gretel, for example, were abandoned by their father and stepmother and left to wander in a dark forest. [3]In another well-known story, Cinderella was treated like a slave by her stepmother and stepsisters. [4]Then there is the case of Little Red Riding Hood, who was eaten by a wild animal. [5]Finally, consider the example of the three blind mice. [6]As if being blind were not bad enough, they also had to deal with the horror of having their tails cut off by the farmer's wife.

___ The unstated main idea is:
   A. Children's stories are about stepfamilies.
   B. Cinderella was treated like a slave.
   C. Animals and children are important characters in children's stories.
   D. Children's stories often deal with evil and violence.

Explanation

An important clue to the main idea of this paragraph is the first sentence: "If people stop to think about the plots in children's stories, they may be surprised." From this we see that, in addition to having to cover most or all of the details, the main idea must be about something surprising in children's stories.

With these ideas in mind, let's examine the four answer options:

A. **Children's stories are about stepfamilies.**
Only two of the details of the paragraph are about stepfamilies, so answer A is too narrow to be the main idea. Also, it is not surprising.

B. **Cinderella was treated like a slave.**
Only one of the details in the paragraph is about Cinderella, so answer B is much too narrow to be the main idea.

C. **Animals and children are important characters in children's stories.**
The detail about Cinderella has nothing to do with animals and children. Also, this answer is not surprising—most people would expect animals and children to be common characters in children's stories.

D. **Children's stories often deal with evil and violence.**
The fact that children's stories deal with very mean and violent behavior could surprise people, since many think such themes are not suited to children. And all of the examples in the paragraph are about children's stories that include evil and violence. Thus statement D expresses the implied main idea of the paragraph.

PRACTICE 4

The following paragraphs have implied main ideas, and each is followed by four sentences. In the space provided, write the letter of the sentence that best expresses the implied main idea.

Paragraph 1

¹Personality plays a big role in who is chosen to be a TV game-show contestant. ²Producers of *The Price Is Right*, for instance, like contestants who almost jump onto the stage. ³Of course, another major factor is that contestants must be good game players. ⁴Appeal and energy are not enough if a person does not have skill at the game. ⁵Game-show producers find out just how good candidates are through tryouts. ⁶A third important factor, then, is that would-be contestants should live in the Los Angeles area. ⁷Except for a few shows that sponsor auditions around the country, most tryouts take place in Los Angeles.

_____ 1. The implied main idea is:
A. Producers of *The Price Is Right* like very energetic contestants.
B. Game-show contestants must have the right type of personality.
C. There are several factors involved in selecting TV game-show contestants.
D. Producing television shows is a very complicated process.

Paragraph 2

¹Jasmin was having trouble in her American Government class. ²Although she read her textbook carefully, she never got better than a C on an exam. ³She went to the study skills center to get help and discovered from her tutor that she was not taking good lecture notes in class. ⁴Because she listened rather than took notes, she did not get down a written record of what ideas her teacher considered most important for her to learn. ⁵The tutor made Jasmin realize that there was no way she could possibly remember everything the teacher said in class. ⁶As a result, it was very important for her to start taking plenty of notes in class and to rely heavily on those notes when preparing for a test. ⁷When Jasmin followed her tutor's advice, she soon began getting better grades.

__C__ 2. The implied main idea is:
   A. Textbook notes are more important than class notes in doing well in a course.
   B. Jasmin worked hard in her American Government class, but she was not successful.
   C. Thanks to a tutor, Jasmin learned to take detailed notes and improved her grades.
   D. All too often, students neglect to benefit from the helpful services at their school's study skills center.

Paragraph 3

¹The former talk show host Dick Cavett tells a story about his interview with a TV host named Raymond. ²Raymond wore a loud green jacket and matching tie. ³He also wore a cheap wig that said "bargain basement." ⁴Cavett had to work to keep his eyes off it. ⁵As the interview got underway, Raymond began to ask rude personal questions. ⁶For example, he asked Cavett, who is 5'6" tall, "Why does it bother you so much that you're so short?" ⁷And since Cavett had gone to Yale, Raymond asked, "Why do you think going to Yale has made you smarter than other people?" ⁸Cavett put up with these questions for a while but finally had had enough. ⁹"Raymond," he said, "'Why' seems to be your favorite word. ¹⁰May I ask you a 'Why' question?" ¹¹When Raymond nodded, Cavett asked, "Why do you wear a rug that looks like a wedge of blueberry pie sitting on top of your head?"

__D__ 3. The implied main idea is:
   A. Raymond was not a college graduate.
   B. Cavett was criticized by the TV network for his insulting remark.
   C. People who ask rude questions should not be given rude answers.
   D. Sometimes rude behavior calls for a rude response.

CHAPTER REVIEW

In this chapter, you learned the following:

- At times authors imply, or suggest, a main idea without stating it directly in one sentence.
- You can figure out an implied main idea by looking closely at the supporting details.
- To find the main idea, look for a general idea that exactly covers the details in question, rather than one that is too broad or too narrow.

The final chapter in Part One—Chapter 10—will deepen your ability to think in a clear and logical way.

On the Web: If you are using this book in class, you can visit our website for additional practice in recognizing implied main ideas. Go to **www.townsendpress.com** and click on "Learning Center."

REVIEW TEST 1

To review what you've learned in this chapter, answer each of the following questions.

1. A selection may have an _____imprred_____ main idea rather than a directly stated one.

2. When a main idea is not directly stated, you can often figure it out by considering carefully the _____supporting Details_____.

3. A general idea that is too (*narrow, broad*) _____narrow_____ is one that fails to cover some of the specific details in the passage.

4. A general idea that is too (*narrow, broad*) _____broad_____ is one that covers more kinds of specific ideas than the ones in the passage.

5. If a person talks about a movie and says that the acting is poor, the plot makes no sense, and the characters are boring, the implied main idea is that the movie _____is bad_____.

REVIEW TEST 2

A. (1.) Look at the following photograph, which appeared in an ad with the caption "Was last night really worth it?"

Write here what you think is the implied main idea: ___She's drunk___

B. Read each group of specific ideas. Then write the letter of the general idea that tells what the specific ideas have in common. Keep in mind that the correct general idea will not be too narrow or too broad.

___A___ 2. *Specific ideas:* Persian cats, cocker spaniels, elephants, canaries

   The general idea is
   A. animals.
   B. household pets.
   C. jungle animals.

___B___ 3. *Specific ideas:* a smile, a wave, a frown, a push

   The general idea is
   A. communication.
   B. nonspoken communication.
   C. friendly communication.

C. In the following lists, the specific ideas are given but the general ideas are unstated. Fill in the blanks with the unstated general ideas.

 4. *General idea:* _____Movied Titles_____

      Specific ideas: Dracula
                       The Call of the Wild
                       The Adventures of Tom Sawyer
                       A Tale of Two Cities

 5. *General idea:* _____Definitions_____

      Specific ideas: *Exploit* means "take advantage of."
                       Patron means "a regular customer."
                       Obstinate means "stubborn."
                       Recipient means "one that receives."

REVIEW TEST 3

A. Read each group of three sentences. Then, in the space provided, write the letter of the sentence that best states the implied main idea.

Group 1

Support

- In 1800, there was no "election day"; voting stretched from March to December.

- Less than 10 percent of the population had the right to vote.

- No paper ballots were provided; the voter had to bring his own ballot or vote by voice.

_P____ 1. The **implied main idea** of these sentences is:
    A. The election process was unfair in 1800.
    B. It was easier to win an election in 1800 than it is today.
    C. Elections are less honest today than they were in 1800.
    D. Voting in the election of 1800 was very different from voting today.

Group 2

Support

- In order to be able to go to work, single parents need daycare.

- The rise in divorce has increased the number of single-parent households.

- Families with two working parents also need daycare.

2. The **implied main idea** of these sentences is:
  A. The divorce rate has grown.
  B. The number of single-parent households continues to increase.
  C. There is a great need for daycare.
  D. Most mothers work outside the home.

Group 3

Support

- Children sometimes imitate the violent acts they see in TV cartoons.
- Television viewers may become less sensitive to violence.
- Potential lawbreakers sometimes get ideas for crimes from television shows.

___ 3. The **implied main idea** of these sentences is:
  A. Cartoons can be bad for children.
  B. Television may be contributing to aggression and violence in society.
  C. Television can make viewers less concerned about violence in real life.
  D. It is not unusual for television to show violent acts such as murder and rape.

B. Write the letter of the answer that best states the implied main idea in each paragraph.

___ 4. ¹Many of the "witches" executed in Salem, Massachusetts, in the 1690s were actually mentally ill. ²Their odd behavior made people believe they were in league with the devil. ³In other times and places, mentally ill people have been punished. ⁴Often they were beaten or chained up. ⁵It was thought that their illness was the result of an evil nature or lack of willpower. ⁶Only recently have people accepted the idea that mental illness can be a medical problem.

  A. Mentally ill people were once thought to be witches and were thus executed for being in league with the devil.
  B. Mental illness has become more common since the 1690s.
  C. The mentally ill are still treated badly today.
  D. Throughout history, there have been different views about the nature of mental illness.

___ 5. ¹The novel *Lord of the Flies* begins with a group of schoolboys who are left alone on an island after a plane crash. ²At first the boys are cooperative, helping one another to find food and shelter. ³Then they divide into two camps. ⁴One is led by a peaceful boy named Ralph; the other, by a violent boy named Jack. ⁵Jack's group then grows bigger and more powerful until Ralph is the only "civilized" person left on the island. ⁶He is nearly killed by the other boys before a rescue ship finally arrives.

The unstated main idea is:
A. *Lord of the Flies* is a fictional view of how young people interact with each other in various circumstances.
B. *Lord of the Flies* is a fictional view of what can happen when young people are alone and removed from civilization.
C. The author of *Lord of the Flies* feels that boys are basically more uncivilized than girls.
D. *Lord of the Flies* is a story about a rescue ship.

REVIEW TEST 4

Here is a chance to apply your understanding of implied main ideas to an essay that was written on the topic "Taking Charge of My Life." The author tells how, alone with three children and far from her native home, she managed to get past her despair and create a meaningful life for herself.

The selection is followed by questions on implied main ideas as well as on the reading skills you have practiced in earlier chapters.

Words to Watch

Below are some words in the reading that do not have strong context support. Each word is followed by the number of the paragraph in which it appears and its meaning there. These words are indicated in the selection by a small circle (°).

regal (2): royal
haze (3): confused state of mind
intervened (7): came in to change a situation
bleak (8): gloomy
bleary-eyed (18): with blurred vision
preoccupation (18): extreme concern with something
Morpheus (20): the god of dreams in Greek mythology
preemies (29): babies born prematurely

LIGHTING A MATCH

Regina Ruiz

1   I feel funny. So very funny, telling you about my life, my feelings, my secrets. I do not know how to welcome you into my heart and soul. You see, nobody ever asked me what I thought or how I felt about life's challenges. Or, maybe, they never really cared about what I thought.

2   My journey to Burlington County College began many years ago in Caracas, Venezuela, where I was born and grew to a young lady full of energy and life. My parents called me Regina because there was something regal° about the sound. They had high hopes of my marrying a local boy from a good, wealthy family. You know the kind—slick, black hair; long sideburns; driving a sports car. The kind who brings you flowers on every date and swears his undying love for you three days a week, and the other days he is sleeping with Maria, the local social worker.

3   To get even, or because I was in a romantic haze°, I met and married a U.S. Marine from Des Moines, Iowa, who was stationed at our local Embassy, where I also worked.

4   Marriage, a home in America, and three beautiful children occupied twenty-five years of my life.

5   Where did my life go? It went somewhere. But there is no lost-and-found department for a life lost in the years.

6   The marriage was bad. It was so bad that I cried every night for all those years. I would tell myself, "You are in a strange country—maybe the customs are different. The children need you, and you cannot admit failure to your parents back in Venezuela."

7   As luck would have it, fate intervened°. My ex-Marine husband found someone new and left me and the children with no money, very hurt and depressed.

8   I quickly took an inventory—foreign-born, with not a great command of the English language, no money, no job training, and two kids in college. The future looked bleak°.

9   But it did not stop. My father died. I loved him so much, and he was always my source of strength in need. Mother became ill.

10   I felt very hurt, lonely, angry, and very sorry for myself.

11   However, I remembered a saying my Dad would quote to me when things were going wrong and the future looked black. He may have gotten this quote from the Spanish edition of *Reader's Digest*. He would say, "My dear, it is always the darkest when you are fresh out of matches."

12   "Dad, I am out of matches." Or so I thought.

13   I decided to make my life something worthwhile by helping people. I wanted to help and heal and maybe, at the same time, heal myself.

14   I appeared before the college doors with my knees shaking and full of doubt. I said that I wanted to be a nurse.

15   I enrolled in college. I was proud of myself for not falling into the garbage pit waiting so close by.

16   Then the fun began—subjects that were very hard for me.

17   In order to survive, I managed to get two jobs to keep up with house payments and food. The kids found college money by working and by appealing to their father. I met my challenges on a daily basis.

18   Now, my days are very active and long. Before the sun makes its appearance, I stumble bleary-eyed° to the shower and afterwards select the day's outfit. After a quick check in the mirror, I make my way downstairs to prepare a quick breakfast along with my lunch, feed the cat (who happens to be my alarm clock), and do what seem like a million other small chores. Then I drive for forty-five minutes to the Pemberton Campus, while studying my chemistry notes on index cards before a test. I would do this with tears in my eyes. You see, at the same time I am worrying about the situation with my water heater that slowly but surely is leaking and may not last until the new one can be installed. In addition, I am anxious to schedule my exterminator's visit to treat the termites discovered in my basement. My preoccupation° with such household woes is due to a canceled appointment to have my furnace cleaned, which resulted in a periodic spray of soot.

19   After a hectic morning of classes, I rush to my car for a hurried thirty-minute ride to the office, where a desk piled high with import documents is waiting for me, along with innumerable phone

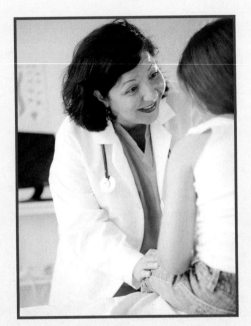

calls from the brokers, custom officials, and suppliers. Meanwhile, an impatient boss wants to know the precise location of one of the fifty containers traveling between eastern Europe and Burlington, New Jersey.

20   As the clock winds toward 5:00 p.m., I get ready to travel back to the Cinnaminson Campus for another round of classes. As I arrive on campus, I waste another thirty minutes searching for that nonexistent parking spot. My class continues until ten o'clock in the evening, and I praise the Lord it doesn't last longer. By that time, I am beginning to see double. I slowly make my way to the car and begin the long commute home, counting in my mind how many customers I will see as a result of my second job—hairdressing. On evenings when I have no classes scheduled, I take appointments to cut hair or give permanents. As I arrive home, I find a hungry son and starving

cat, both waiting to be fed. I usually cook something simple for us, then proceed to do the few dishes because I hate the thought of adding one more chore to my early morning schedule. By the time I finish getting ready for bed, it is midnight; I look up and see the stairway leading to the bedroom, which by then seems longer than the one outside the Philadelphia Museum of Art, and proceed to crawl in bed and into the arms of Morpheus°.

21 People question the wisdom of my studying to be a nurse. It may take four or five years.

22 "You will never last," they tell me.

23 "You will be too old to lift a bedpan," they mock.

24 But I am not discouraged. There are twenty more courses ahead of me before I get into the nursing area. While all these things challenge me, the greatest of all is to be able to hold my head high.

25 Somehow, just somehow, I think it might be all worth it—if I can hold the hand of someone dying all alone in a cold hospital ward and whisper in their ear, "You are not alone. I am here. I am here. I will never leave you."

26 Maybe, just maybe, I will find that life that was lost. It is out there somewhere.

27 But I know one thing—I am in charge, and I will never let go again. Never.

Update

28 Regina Ruiz successfully completed her registered nurse degree and is only a few credits away from earning her bachelor's degree at Jefferson University in Philadelphia. She is a nurse at Voorhees Pediatric Rehabilitation Hospital in New Jersey.

29 At the hospital, Regina's patients range in age from newborns to eighteen-year-olds. As she grows attached to particular patients, she requests that they be assigned to her daily shift, giving "extra love" to children battling illness, fear, and loneliness. "To see tiny preemies° and children who are so sick grow and get better and be released to their families—it is wonderful to be part of that. School was very difficult, and nursing is a demanding profession, but when I am at work, I am in heaven."

30 When she is not working, Regina takes pride in keeping her home beautiful. "After my divorce and through all those long, difficult years, I worried so much about not being able to keep up with things," she said. "The roof leaked so badly at one point I had trash cans sitting in the living room. So I had to learn to budget my money as well as my time. When I had three jobs, one was for tuition and food, and the others were for repairs—a roof, siding, new windows, everything. Now I can look at the house and feel so good. A little neighbor boy told me the other day, 'Mrs. Ruiz, you have the nicest house on the street.'"

31 Regina still does hair for a handful of longtime clients. "They were my friends for so many years," she said. "When I'd come home from a test crying because I was sure I'd failed, they'd be the ones to say, 'No, Regina! You're going to make it.' Now, maybe I don't have to cut hair anymore to earn a living," she says with a chuckle, "but how can I tell them to go jump in the lake?"

Reading Comprehension Questions

Vocabulary in Context

___D___ 1. In the sentence below, the word *appealing* (ə-pēl′ĭng) means
   A. paying.
   B. saying no.
   C. hiding their need.
   D. making a request.

   "The kids found college money by working and by appealing to their father." (Paragraph 17)

Central Point

___C___ 2. Which sentence best expresses the central idea of the selection?
   A. Ruiz got married to an American Marine and left her native land of Venezuela.
   B. Ruiz should not have married the Marine and moved so far from home.
   C. After a bad marriage, Ruiz learned to take charge of her life and build a worthwhile future.
   D. Ruiz is often exhausted by her schedule of school and two jobs.

Main Ideas

___A___ 3. A main idea may cover more than one paragraph. Which sentence best expresses the implied main idea of paragraphs 2–3?
   A. Born in Venezuela and betrayed by a boyfriend, Ruiz married an American Marine for mixed reasons.
   B. Ruiz wasn't particularly happy with the type of future her parents had in mind for her.
   C. Ruiz grew up in a wealthy family.
   D. Ruiz met the Marine she would marry at the Embassy in Caracas, where they both worked.

___B___ 4. Which sentence best expresses the implied main idea of paragraphs 10–13?
   A. Ruiz remembered a saying her father used to say.
   B. Ruiz at first saw no way out of a bad situation, but then thought of a worthwhile path.
   C. Ruiz's father may have gotten inspiration from the Spanish edition of *Reader's Digest*.
   D. Ruiz thought helping people was a worthwhile goal.

_A_ 5. Which sentence best expresses the main idea of paragraphs 18–20?

  A. "Now, my days are very active and long."

  B. "Before the sun makes its appearance. I stumble bleary-eyed to the shower and afterwards select the day's outfit."

  C. "I drive for forty-five minutes. . . . I would do this with tears in my eyes."

  D. "By the time I finish getting ready for bed, it is midnight. . . . "

_C_ 6. Which sentence best expresses the implied main idea of paragraphs 21–24?

  A. Others feel that Ruiz should not become a nurse.

  B. It may take Ruiz four or five years to become a nurse.

  C. Despite discouragement, Ruiz is determined to become a nurse.

  D. Ruiz still has twenty more courses ahead of her before she gets into nursing.

Supporting Details

_C_ 7. Ruiz's marriage ended when

  A. her father died.

  B. she enrolled in college and her husband divorced her.

  C. her husband left her for another woman.

  D. Ruiz's parents demanded that she come back to Venezuela.

Transitions

_C_ 8. The sentence below begins with a transition that shows

  A. addition.

  B. contrast.

  C. time.

  D. cause and effect.

  "After a hectic morning of classes, I rush to my car for a hurried thirty-minute ride to the office . . . " (Paragraph 19)

Patterns of Organization

_B_ 9. The main pattern of organization of the selection is

  A. list of items.

  B. time order.

  C. contrast.

  D. comparison.

Inferences

 10. We can infer that Ruiz
   A. wishes she had married "a local boy from a good, wealthy family."
   B. believes she married the U.S. Marine too quickly.
   C. regrets having three children.
   D. believes enrolling in the nursing program was not wise.

Discussion Questions

1. During the years of her unhappy marriage, Ruiz told herself, "The children need you, and you cannot admit failure to your parents back in Venezuela." Do these seem to you like understandable reasons for remaining in an unhappy relationship? Are they *good* reasons?

2. Ruiz writes that after she enrolled in college, she was proud of herself "for not falling into the garbage pit waiting so close by." What do you think she means by the words "the garbage pit waiting so close by"? Have you ever made a choice that you feel either saved you from or dropped you into a "garbage pit"?

3. Like Ruiz, adults who return to college often have a difficult time balancing the demands of their work, family, and classes. What challenges do you face as a student? What ways have you found to deal with them?

4. Ruiz briefly explains her decision to become a nurse. Why have you chosen your own course of study? What about it interests you? What do you hope it will offer to you after college?

Note: Writing assignments for this selection appear on page 609.

Check Your Performance

IMPLIED MAIN IDEAS

Activity		Number Right	Points			Score
Review Test 1	(5 items)	_____	× 2	=	_____	
Review Test 2	(5 items)	_____	× 6	=	_____	
Review Test 3	(5 items)	_____	× 6	=	_____	
Review Test 4	(10 items)	_____	× 3	=	_____	
			TOTAL SCORE	=	_____	%

Enter your total score into the **Reading Performance Chart: Review Tests** on the inside back cover.

IMPLIED MAIN IDEAS: Mastery Test 1

A. (1.) Look at the following cover for a book titled *Up from Slavery: An Autobiography* by Booker T. Washington. Put a check (✓) by the main idea that is implied by the information given on the cover.

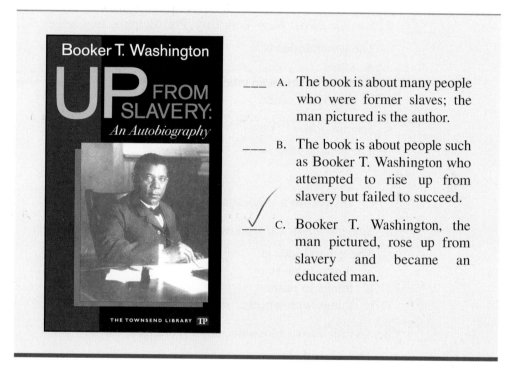

____ A. The book is about many people who were former slaves; the man pictured is the author.

____ B. The book is about people such as Booker T. Washington who attempted to rise up from slavery but failed to succeed.

✓ C. Booker T. Washington, the man pictured, rose up from slavery and became an educated man.

B. Read each group of specific ideas. Then, in the space provided, write the letter of the general idea that tells what the specific ideas have in common. Keep in mind that the correct general idea will not be too narrow or too broad.

__B__ 2. *Specific ideas:* toaster, microwave oven, dishwasher, coffeemaker

The general idea is

A. household appliances.

B. kitchen appliances.

C. cooking appliances.

__B__ 3. *Specific ideas:* sailboat, canoe, ship, raft

The general idea is

A. means of transportation.

B. means of water transportation.

C. military means of water transportation.

(Continues on next page)

_C_ 4. *Specific ideas:* rose, scarlet, pink, maroon

The general idea is
A. flowers.
B. colors.
C. shades of red.

_A_ 5. *Specific ideas:* New York City, Philadelphia, Los Angeles, London

The general idea is
A. cities.
B. eastern American cities.
C. American cities.

_B_ 6. *Specific ideas:* "Yes," "No," "Maybe," "Not now"

The general idea is
A. words.
B. answers.
C. answers to test questions.

_C_ 7. *Specific ideas:* cars, bikes, wheelchairs, supermarket carts

The general idea is
A. things to drive.
B. things to push.
C. things with wheels.

_C_ 8. *Specific ideas:* blossoms, apples, oranges, leaves

The general idea is
A. fruit.
B. things that grow.
C. things that grow on trees.

_B_ 9. *Specific ideas:* a cold, a baseball, a thief, a bus

The general idea is
A. things to avoid.
B. things to catch.
C. things to find.

_A_ 10. *Specific ideas:* Chapter 1, an appetizer, January, the letter A

The general idea is
A. beginnings.
B. parts of a book.
C. months.

IMPLIED MAIN IDEAS: Mastery Test 2

In the following items, the specific ideas are given, but the general ideas are unstated. Fill in the blanks with the unstated general ideas.

1. *General idea:* _____ TOOIS _____

   Specific ideas: saw
   hammer
   screwdriver
   drill

2. *General idea:* _____ Sports _____

   Specific ideas: football
   baseball
   basketball
   soccer

3. *General idea:* _____ cookies _____

   Specific ideas: chocolate chip
   oatmeal-raisin
   Oreo
   sugar

4. *General idea:* _____ Jobs _____

   Specific ideas: salesperson
   nurse
   auto mechanic
   computer programmer

5. *General idea:* _____ crimes _____

   Specific ideas: robbery
   murder
   rape
   illegal drug possession

6. *General idea:* _____ music _____

   Specific ideas: pop
   country
   classical
   rock

(Continues on next page)

7. *General idea:* _____Breakfast_____

   Specific ideas: oatmeal
   cereal
   bacon and eggs
   pancakes

8. *General idea:* _____Good Job_____

   Specific ideas: short travel time to work
   fair boss
   good pay
   friendly coworkers

9. *General idea:* _____wedding plan_____

   Specific ideas: Decide on whom to invite.
   Send out invitations.
   Order the bride's gown.
   Hire a photographer.

10. *General idea:* _____ways to fail class_____

    Specific ideas: Don't go to class much.
    Never take notes when you do go to class.
    Don't hand in assignments.
    Never study for quizzes or exams.

IMPLIED MAIN IDEAS: Mastery Test 3

Read each group of three supporting details. Then, in the space provided, write the letter of the answer that best states the implied main idea of those details.

Group 1

Support

- Young mothers tend to have fewer problems during pregnancy and childbirth.
- Young parents are likely to have more energy to cope with the demands of childcare.
- Young parents tend to be more in tune with their child when he or she reaches adolescence.

_C_ 1. The implied main idea of the above sentences is:
   A. Young parents never have problems with child rearing.
   B. Postponing parenthood is always a mistake.
   C. Having children early in life has certain advantages.
   D. Americans, on average, are having children earlier and earlier.

Group 2

Support

- In most fad diets, the dramatic initial weight loss is mostly just a loss of water from the body.
- Fad diets suggest unrealistic foods to eat and avoid, causing dieters to soon give up.
- Fad diets tend to ignore exercise, which is a crucial element of any good weight-loss program.

_B_ 2. The implied main idea of the above sentences is:
   A. Fad diets have become increasingly popular.
   B. Fad diets typically fail for several reasons.
   C. Dieters who lack willpower cannot succeed.
   D. Exercise is important not only for weight loss but also for preventing heart disease.

(Continues on next page)

Group 3

Support

- An unpopular child may be a child with a "chip on the shoulder," always looking for a fight.
- An unpopular child may be one who acts silly or seems babyish.
- An unpopular child may be a showoff or, at the other extreme, may be very shy and withdrawn.

_____ C 3. The implied main idea of the above sentences is:
   A. Unpopular children usually will "grow out of it."
   B. Unpopular children usually will not "grow out of it."
   C. Children become unpopular for several common reasons.
   D. Why some children are unpopular is a mystery to psychologists.

Group 4

Support

- The colon [:] is used to introduce a list.
- The colon is also used to introduce a long quotation.
- In addition, a colon can introduce an explanation.

_____ A 4. The implied main idea of the above sentences is:
   A. The colon is a punctuation mark with several specific uses.
   B. Some writers avoid using the colon.
   C. Student writers often make mistakes in using the colon.
   D. Correct punctuation is an important part of writing well.

IMPLIED MAIN IDEAS: Mastery Test 4

In the space provided, write the letter of the sentence that best expresses the implied main idea of each of the following paragraphs.

_____ 1. ¹Some workers skip breakfast and try to make up for it by eating a big lunch. ²Studies show that workers who do this lose as much efficiency at work as people who've missed a whole night's sleep. ³Workers who eat a high-protein breakfast and a light lunch, on the other hand, tend to be energetic and efficient throughout the day. ⁴Furthermore, a separate study proved that teens who eat breakfast do far better in school than their classmates who don't.

    A. Eating a good breakfast increases one's energy, efficiency, and performance all day.
    B. Skipping lunch probably does not make one less efficient.
    C. Teens who want to do well in school should eat a good breakfast.
    D. A glass of milk, whole wheat bread, and cheese make a good breakfast.

_____ 2. ¹One benefit of owning a pet is that an animal can make a person feel less lonely. ²According to the National Heart Association, owning a pet is also good for the heart. ³Studies show that stroking an animal can lower blood pressure and slow the heart rate. ⁴In addition, studies show that pet owners are more likely to survive during the first year after a heart attack than people who don't own pets. ⁵The elderly also benefit from pet ownership. ⁶Older people who own dogs are more likely to get daily exercise than those who don't. ⁷Moreover, feeding a pet encourages older people to pay better attention to their own diet.

    A. Pet ownership is more widespread than ever.
    B. People who have suffered a heart attack should consider getting a pet.
    C. Pets should be made available in elementary classrooms.
    D. Owning a pet has a number of advantages.

(Continues on next page)

_____ 3. ¹To make your clothes last longer, avoid using the dryer. ²Over time, the heat will fade colors and weaken fabrics. ³Instead, in cold weather, hang your clothing to dry inside the house. ⁴When the weather is warm, hang it outside—but away from direct sunlight, which can also fade colors. ⁵Also, don't use bleach more than is absolutely necessary. ⁶Bleach contains strong chemicals that can weaken fibers. ⁷In addition, never store knitted clothes on hangers—they can stretch out of shape. ⁸Instead, keep them folded in a drawer. ⁹Finally, get rid of stains promptly—if you let them set, they are much harder, if not impossible, to remove.

A. Most people don't know how to make their clothes last longer.
B. You can make your clothes last longer by following some simple guidelines.
C. Dryers and bleach are bad for your clothes.
D. There are several reasons to avoid using your dryer.

_____ 4. ¹Women who are poorly nourished before or during pregnancy are at risk for complications during pregnancy and delivery. ²They are more likely to bear low-birthweight babies or stillborn babies. ³Also, their babies are more likely to die soon after birth. ⁴The same is true for women who gain too much weight during pregnancy, or who were obese when they became pregnant. ⁵Their babies run a greater risk of medical problems than babies of mothers with normal weight.

A. The babies of poorly nourished women are more likely to die soon after birth.
B. A woman's diet and weight affect her and her baby's health during and after pregnancy.
C. Pregnant women tend to be poorly nourished or overweight before and during pregnancy.
D. Obesity is the cause of various medical problems for women and their children.

IMPLIED MAIN IDEAS: Mastery Test 5

In the space provided, write the letter of the sentence that best expresses the implied main idea of each of the following paragraphs.

_____ 1. ¹Most cases of baldness are caused by heredity. ²People with hereditary baldness gradually lose the bulbs from which new hair would grow. ³This type of hair loss is called male-pattern baldness, and it is the most common type of hair loss affecting men. ⁴This hair loss is permanent. ⁵Some types of hair loss, however, are not permanent. ⁶Their causes include high fevers and certain types of drugs, including drugs that are used to treat cancer. ⁷The hair may fall out as long as three or four months after the illness or treatment. ⁸Such hair loss is almost always temporary.

    A. Male-pattern baldness is permanent.
    B. Various factors may lead to temporary hair loss.
    C. Baldness may be either permanent or temporary.
    D. Hair loss, whether temporary or permanent, is much more common in men than in women.

_A_ 2. ¹One way that pigs show their intelligence is through curiosity. ²If you put something in their pens, such as a key chain, they'll sniff and poke at it to find out what it is. ³Also, hog farmers have noted that if a pig finds an escape hole in the pasture fence one summer and then is put in the barn for the winter, he'll head right over to the hole when he's back in the pasture next spring. ⁴One farmer said that he had a terrible time with one sow that learned how to use her snout to open the gate latch when it wasn't completely fastened. ⁵"She'd be checking it out every half hour to see if we'd slipped up, which we sometimes did," he said. ⁶More evidence that pigs are intelligent is the fact that they are more subject to psychological stress than other farm animals. ⁷They get bored and distressed when they're confined and there's nothing to do. ⁸In fact, like people, they can develop ulcers from an unfriendly environment.

    A. Pigs show their intelligence in many ways.
    B. Pigs have more curiosity than any other animal.
    C. Pigs react as strongly as people to stressful situations.
    D. Once pigs learn something, they are not likely to forget it.

(Continues on next page)

_____ 3. ¹A team of researchers surveyed patients who had suffered serious illnesses. ²Sixty of the patients had suffered a heart attack. ³Another thirty were breast cancer patients. ⁴All had completed therapy for their medical conditions at the time of the survey. ⁵Subjects were asked what positive changes had happened to them after their illness. ⁶About half reported healthy lifestyle changes. ⁷And over a quarter reported a greater appreciation of life and health as well as improved close relationships. ⁸Other common positive changes included feeling lucky to be given a second chance and an improved understanding of others.

A. A survey of patients was conducted to discover the changes that had happened to people with serious illnesses.
B. A survey of patients shows that serious illness can have positive effects.
C. Serious illness can result in better relationships with other people.
D. Recovering from serious illness can give a sense of gratitude and good fortune.

_____ 4. ¹If a child is having trouble seeing the difference between squares, circles, and triangles, that's one sign that he or she may have dyslexia, a common learning disorder. ²A second sign is seeing or writing scrambled or reversed messages. ³For instance, a dyslexic child may confuse "was" and "saw," "dog" and "bog," or even "hot" and "cold." ⁴The number 517 could be interpreted as 751. ⁵Also, a dyslexic child may have trouble distinguishing between right and left.

A. Reversing letters is a sure sign of dyslexia.
B. Dyslexia is one of the most common learning disorders.
C. There are several signs that a child has dyslexia.
D. A child who has trouble distinguishing between right and left is likely to be dyslexic.

IMPLIED MAIN IDEAS: Mastery Test 6

In the space provided, write the letter of the sentence that best expresses the implied main idea of each of the following textbook paragraphs.

_____ 1. ¹Newspapers are usually thrown out after a day. ²Magazines, however, may stay around the house or office for weeks or months. ³In addition, they may be passed from person to person. ⁴Therefore the ads in magazines have a better chance of being read and remembered. ⁵Magazines also allow for more colorful photography and artwork on quality paper. ⁶So they provide a way for advertisers to create a high-quality image with ads. ⁷Furthermore, many magazines now publish a range of editions aimed at specific areas and groups, instead of a single national edition. ⁸For example, *Time* magazine publishes 357 different editions worldwide. ⁹They include special editions for doctors, educators, and college students. ¹⁰Such editions make it possible for ads to be aimed at very specific audiences.

A. Magazines have some important advantages for advertisers.
B. Magazine ads are remembered longer than newspaper ads.
C. Television ads reach more people than magazine ads.
D. Magazines allow advertisers to reach specific market segments.

_____ 2. ¹Thomas H. Holmes, a psychiatrist, developed a scale to rate the amount of stress brought on by what he calls Life-Changing Units (LCUs). ²Some LCUs are obviously negative. ³They include the death of a spouse (rated at 100 points) or a jail term (63 points). ⁴Others may be positive: pregnancy (40 points) or an increase in responsibility at work (29 points). ⁵Holmes interviewed more than five thousand hospital patients as part of his study. ⁶He found that half the people who had scored between 150 and 300 LCUs in a year had become ill. ⁷About 70 percent of those scoring more than 300 LCUs in a year had gotten sick.

A. Life-changing events include jail or death.
B. A psychiatrist interviewed more than 5,000 hospital patients.
C. Even positive life-changing units can cause stress.
D. According to a psychiatrist's study, the stress of life-changing events makes people more likely to become sick.

(Continues on next page)

_____ 3. ¹It is widely believed that the institutions of marriage and the family are less stable today than ever before. ²It is true that divorce is very common these days. ³However, the divorce rate has been rising and falling for years. ⁴It was nearly as high during the 1920s as it is now. ⁵In addition, while divorce creates many single-parent households today, the same was true about death in earlier times. ⁶So many parents died early during the eighteenth and nineteenth centuries that most children spent at least part of their early lives growing up in single-parent households.

    A. The institutions of marriage and the family are unstable today.
    B. The institutions of marriage and family are no less stable today than at other times.
    C. Divorce is very common now; it was also common in the 1920s.
    D. Divorce and death have been responsible for creating many single-parent households.

_____ 4. ¹Mothers touch their little girls more than they touch their boys; they speak to their infant daughters more frequently and longer than they do to their sons. ²By age 2, girls generally prefer to play closer to their mothers than boys do. ³Little boys are more likely to be tossed, swung, and chased. ⁴In most cultures, they are also more likely than girls to be aggressive and to get into conflicts. ⁵The parents of boys are also more concerned with discipline and with pushing their child toward achievement than the parents of girls are. ⁶Fathers are more likely to reward their daughters for playing with other girls but punish their sons for playing with girls.

    A. Boys in most cultures are likely to be more aggressive than girls.
    B. By age 2, children are already beginning to show the effects of the way they are brought up.
    C. Some of the differences between boys and girls may be the result of being brought up differently.
    D. Fathers and mothers often disagree about how to raise children.

10 The Basics of Argument

This Chapter in a Nutshell

- A good thinker understands what it means to *make* a point.

- A good thinker understands what it means to *support* a point.

Look at the following cartoon and see if you can answer the questions that follow.

- What is Snoopy's argument here? In other words, what is his point?

    Your answer: His point is that _____

- What is his support for his point?

    Your answer: _____

Explanation

Snoopy's point is that dogs are superior to cats. But he offers no support whatsoever to back up his argument! There are two jokes here. First, he is a dog, and so naturally he believes that dogs are superior. The other joke is that his evidence ("they just are, and that's all there is to it!") is a lot of empty words. His somewhat guilty look in the last panel suggests that he knows he has not proved his point. To make a good argument and prove a point, you must offer real support.

Evaluating Arguments

A **critical thinker** is one who can look at an **argument**—a point and its support—and decide whether the support is solid or not. Look at the following point:

Point: You should not put your hand into that box.

Now, is there solid support for this point? In other words, is the person who made it thinking clearly and logically? Let's say the person goes on to provide these details:

Support

1. A flesh-eating spider the size of a large crab just crawled in there.
2. Inside the box are freshly cut leaves of poison ivy.
3. A loaded mousetrap is inside, ready to spring.

As you can see, the details do provide solid support for the point. They give us a basis for understanding and agreeing with the point. In light of the details, we probably won't be putting a hand anywhere near that box.

This is a small example of what critical thinking is about: recognizing a point and deciding whether there is support that effectively backs up the point. Let's look now at another example:

Point: Our meal in that new restaurant was unpleasant.

Is there support for this point? Is the person thinking clearly and logically? Let's say the person then goes on to provide the following details:

Support

1. Our meal took forty-five minutes to arrive.
2. The chicken we ordered was tough, and the rice and vegetables were cold.
3. The dessert choices were limited to stale cake and watery Jell-O.

Again, the details provide solid support for the point. They give us a basis for understanding and agreeing with the point. Having heard these details, we would not be eager to eat at that restaurant.

But what if the person had provided the reasons below for saying the meal at the restaurant was unpleasant?

Support

1. We had to wait fifteen minutes for the food to arrive.
2. The chicken we ordered was too juicy, and the vegetables were buttery.
3. The dozen dessert choices did not include my favorite, carrot cake.

We might question these reasons for not liking the restaurant. Waiting fifteen minutes is not so bad. Many people like juicy chicken and buttery vegetables, and many people would welcome a dozen dessert choices.

When evidence is provided, we can judge for ourselves whether or not there is enough logical support for a point. If the reasons above were the only ones given, we might decide to try the restaurant ourselves.

Argument in Everyday Life

In everyday life, people are constantly arguing all kinds of points and trying to provide convincing support. Here are some examples:

- A lawyer states, "So and so is guilty," and then tries to provide evidence to support his point. Another lawyer says, "So and so is not guilty," and attempts to back up her statement with different evidence.
- An advertiser tries to convince us that something is "a great product."
- A political candidate offers reasons why he or she is the person to vote for.
- Textbook authors or instructors advance and support all kinds of theories.
- Reviewers offer their thoughts about why a given book, movie, TV show, or restaurant is good or bad.
- Editorial writers, magazine columnists, and sportswriters argue their opinions on one issue or another.
- In everyday conversation, people make points, such as "Everyone likes the boss," "I hate my job," "She is a good friend," "You should help that person," "That child is troubled," and "She is the best teacher in the school." They then offer reasons to support their points.

In sum, all around us is a mix of points and support. If the points were always logically supported, the world would be in pretty fine shape. Unfortunately, many people are not skillful thinkers. The ideas they advance often lack reasonable support.

Chances are that you, like most people, will benefit greatly from sharpening your thinking skills. By learning to constantly ask, "What is the point?" "What is its support?" and "How logical is the support?" you can become an effective one-person jury. Such questions may seem simple, but learning to use them will not happen overnight. You must train your mind to become a critical thinker.

You have already learned a lot about critical thinking in this book as you have studied main ideas, supporting details, relationships, and inferences. In the pages that follow, you will have a chance to build on what you already know. The skill that you develop in thinking clearly and logically will prove of enormous value in all your college work.

Practice in Evaluating Arguments

1   Recognizing Point and Support

This first activity will review and sharpen your sense of the difference between a point and its support. As you learned earlier in the book, a **point** is a general idea; **support** is the specific information that backs up the point.

✔ ### *Check Your Understanding*

Look at the following group of items. It is made up of a point and three statements that logically support the point. See if you can put a **P** in front of the point and an **S** in front of the three supporting statements.

_____   A. The children argue and fight constantly.

_____   B. The mother looks as if she's scared to say anything.

_____   C. Our neighbors do not seem like a happy family.

_____   D. When I hear the father speak to the children, he's usually shouting.

Explanation

Statement A presents a specific fact about the neighbors. Statements B and D also contain specific facts about them. Statement C, on the other hand, is a general statement and expresses a point about the neighbors—that they are not happy. Therefore statement C is the point. The other statements support that point with specific examples.

PRACTICE 1

In each of the following groups, one statement is the point, and the other statements are support for the point. Identify each point with a **P** and each statement of support with an **S**.

Group 1

_____   A. People would look at me and ask, "Cat got your tongue?"

_____   B. I used to hide in my bedroom when visitors came.

_____   C. I cried on the first day of kingergarten.

_____   D. As a child, I was very quiet and shy.

Group 2

_____   A. Many jobs require you to apply online.

_____   B. Some teachers keep in touch with parents by e-mail.

_____   C. It's helpful to have regular Internet access nowadays.

_____   D. It's quick and easy to pay bills electronically.

Group 3

_____   A. It's not a good idea to buy bottled water.

_____   B. Bottled water costs about 5 cents an ounce, while tap water costs only about 1 cent per gallon.

_____   C. In most places, bottled water is no healthier than tap water.

_____   D. Bottled water produces up to 1.5 million tons of plastic waste every year.

Group 4

_____   A. Uniforms cost less than store-bought clothes.

_____   B. Studies show that students work better when they are dressed in uniforms.

_____   C. Requiring kids to wear uniforms to school is a good idea.

_____   D. Uniforms stop kids from teasing each other about the clothes they wear.

2   Identifying Logical Support I

Once you identify a point and its support, you need to decide if the support really applies to the point. The critical thinker will ask, "Is this support logical and relevant? Or is it beside the point?" In their enthusiasm to advance a point, people often bring up support that does not apply.

For example, say that a student claims her English instructor is a poor teacher. To support that point, the student may say, "He speaks so softly I can hardly hear him. In addition, he wears ridiculous clothes." A critical thinker will realize that although a soft voice may in fact interfere with an instructor's effectiveness, what the instructor wears has nothing to do with how well he teaches. The first reason for disliking the English teacher is relevant support, but the second reason is beside the point.

The following activity will sharpen your ability to decide whether evidence truly supports a point.

✓

Check Your Understanding

Read the following point and the three items of "support" that follow. Then check (✔) the letter of the **one** item that provides logical support for the point.

Point: That woman on the news was courageous.

Support

_____ A. [1]She collected bags of canned and boxed food for months and then brought it to the Golden Door Soup Kitchen to be used for Thanksgiving. [2]Thanks to her efforts, the soup kitchen was able to feed five hundred more people this year than last year. [3]That number includes over a hundred children.

_____ B. [1]She had at hand all the facts and figures to back up her statements, citing three different studies by experts in the field. [2]She handled the reporter's questions with ease and confidence.

_____ C. [1]When she saw the child being attacked, she went to his aid without a moment's hesitation. [2]She ran up, shouting "Let him go!" and then kicked the ferocious pit bull as hard as she could. [3]When the dog released the child, she grabbed the boy and pushed him to safety, even as the dog turned on her.

Explanation

A. The information here tells us that the woman on the news was kind and generous with her time. However, nothing she did required her to face danger, so no courage was required. You should not have chosen this item. It is about generosity, not courage.

B. The woman described here showed mastery of her subject and skill in being interviewed, but neither demands great courage. You should not have chosen this item either.

C. The woman referred to here put herself in danger to help a child. Clearly, to do so, she had to be courageous. If you checked the letter of this item, you were correct.

PRACTICE 2

Each item on the next page contains a point followed by three items of information. Put a check (✔) next to the **one** item that logically supports the point.

1. **Point: That child is very curious.**

    _____   A.   ¹He was reciting the alphabet when he was only three years old. ²By age seven, he was doing math at a fourth-grade level. ³He skipped third and fifth grades.

    _____   B.   ¹His favorite word is "NO!" ²He doesn't start picking up his toys until the fifth or sixth time he is told. ³Mealtime is a battle to get him to eat properly.

    _____   C.   ¹He has taken apart all the clocks in the house to see how they work. ²He borrowed his father's hammer to break rocks because he "wanted to see what they looked like inside." ³He is forever asking questions that start with "How" and "Why."

2. **Point: Aunt Isabel is my least favorite relative.**

    _____   A.   ¹When we meet, she always has something critical to say, such as "What have you done with your hair?" or "You look terrible in that color." ²She calls my sister "the smart sister" and me "the dumb one." ³On my birthday, she said, "I didn't think you wanted a present."

    _____   B.   ¹She works as a billing clerk at a hospital. ²She dropped out of high school, but earned her GED and then attended community college. ³She's held the job for more than 15 years and has been the hospital's "Employee of the Month" a number of times.

    _____   C.   ¹Isabel is about five foot seven and is a little on the heavy side. ²She wears her hair very short and always has on long dangly earrings. ³She's almost 50 but looks younger. ⁴She wears very little makeup— just some mascara and sometimes lip gloss.

3. **Point: The teenage boys at the dance were much more shy than the girls.**

    _____   A.   ¹They yelled and laughed out loud, drawing attention to themselves. ²One of them complained, "This sounds like music my grandmother would dance to!" ³Many leaned against the wall or sat at tables and made fun of the way girls were dancing. ⁴Then, many left with their friends to go to a nearby party.

    _____   B.   ¹They all gathered at one end of the room, away from the girls. ²They looked nervously at the girls who were dancing. ³When a group of girls approached them, they got quiet and pretended not to notice. ⁴Several girls had to drag them out in order for them to dance.

    _____   C.   ¹They walked right up to a group of girls and introduced themselves. ²They smiled broadly and asked the girls to dance. ³Before they left at the end of the night, they asked the girls for their phone numbers.

4. **Point: Our biology teacher is lazy.**

_____ A. ¹He has his top students present the lessons to the class so he doesn't have to do anything. ²If someone is having trouble in class, he tells him or her to get help from one of the other students. ³So he doesn't have to grade papers, he allows us to grade each other's homework and test papers, even midterm and final exams.

_____ B. ¹His favorite saying is, "There is no such thing as partial credit. ²Either the answer is right or it isn't." ³We can expect at least two hours of biology homework every night, and more on weekends and holidays. ⁴Even the best students in class have trouble finishing his tests before the end of the period, and the average grade for his class is a C.

_____ C. ¹He always arrives exactly on time for class; you could set your watch by him. ²He predictably begins with two or three questions, then lectures for most of the period, and with five minutes to go, writes on the board exactly what he wants us to read before the next class.

3 Identifying Logical Support II

✓

Check Your Understanding

Below is a point followed by five statements. Three of the statements logically support the point; two of the statements do not. In the spaces provided, write the letters of the **three** logical statements of support.

Point: English 102 was an extremely hard course.

A. The course included a research paper, five essays, three oral reports, and two major exams.
B. The course was required for my major.
C. The teacher called on students without warning and deducted points when they didn't know an answer.
D. The teacher has been at the school for over twenty years.
E. I had to do at least three hours of homework for every hour in class.

Items that logically support the point: _____   _____   _____

Explanation

The fact that a course is required doesn't make it more difficult, so item B does not support the point. Item D does not support the point either—how long a teacher has been at a school has nothing to do with how hard the course is. So you should have chosen items A, C, and E. Each one tells about a different difficulty experienced in taking the course.

PRACTICE 3

Each point is followed by three statements that provide logical support and two that do not. In the spaces, write the letters of the **three** logical statements of support.

1. **Point: I'm a perfect example of someone who has "math anxiety."**
    A. Fear of math is almost as widespread as fear of public speaking.
    B. I feel dread every time I sit down to take our Friday math quiz.
    C. During the math midterm, I "froze" and didn't even try to answer most of the questions.
    D. I also have a great deal of anxiety when I sit down to write a paper.
    E. I turned down a job as a salesclerk because I would have had to figure out how much change customers should get back.

    Items that logically support the point: _____   _____   _____

2. **Point: My kids are getting into the spirit of Halloween.**
    A. Today I found a plastic spider in my soup.
    B. Last night there was a bloody rubber hand on my pillow.
    C. Today a cardboard tombstone with my name on it appeared in the backyard.
    D. My kids also like to decorate the house on Thanksgiving.
    E. The other day, my oldest daughter said she was too old to go trick-or-treating.

    Items that logically support the point: _____   _____   _____

3. **Point:** Packing your lunch to take to work saves time and money.

   A. In many large cities, there are fast-food restaurants on nearly every block.
   B. Those who bring their lunch to work don't have to spend time getting their food.
   C. Packing a lunch allows you to keep reusing your containers and utensils.
   D. Those who consume a lot of calories at lunch tend to eat even more calories at dinner.
   E. People who pack a lunch often bring leftovers, allowing them to stretch their food budget.

   Items that logically support the point: _____   _____   _____

4. **Point:** People should be careful when buying used cars.

   A. Many used cars do not come with a guarantee, so you will have to pay if something breaks.
   B. Used cars are much cheaper than brand-new ones.
   C. A used car may have serious mechanical problems and still look fine on the outside.
   D. Some used cars come with a guarantee and are nearly as reliable as new cars.
   E. Used cars whose past owners did not take care of them are more likely to develop problems.

   Items that logically support the point: _____   _____   _____

5. **Point:** Schools should eliminate the summer vacation.

   A. It costs too much money for school buildings to remain empty in the summer months.
   B. Children have more energy than adults.
   C. Year-round school can better prepare students for year-round work in the adult world.
   D. During summer classes, schools should be air-conditioned.
   E. Recent studies show that children remember more and forget less if they attend school during the summer.

   Items that logically support the point: _____   _____   _____

4   Determining a Logical Point

This activity will develop your ability to come to a logical conclusion. You will look closely at supporting evidence and then decide what point is well supported by that evidence. The skill of making a reasonable judgment based upon the information presented is a significant part of critical thinking.

✓ *Check Your Understanding*

Look at the following three items of support:

Support

- ● Before underground plumbing, city people dumped raw sewage out of their windows and into the streets.

- ● In the days when city vehicles were horse-drawn, manure was piled high in the roadways.

- ● Before trash collection was available, pigs were set loose in city streets to eat the garbage thrown there.

Now check (✓) the **point** that is logically supported by the above evidence. Then read the explanation that follows.

_____   A. Cities of the past were probably pleasant places to live.

_____   B. Cities of the past were not all that different from today's cities.

_____   C. Cities of the past were troubled with crime.

_____   D. Cities of the past were very dirty.

Explanation

A. Obviously, none of the details suggest that cities of the past were pleasant places to live. So you should not have chosen this point.

B. The support clearly states that cities of the past were dramatically different places to live, with pigs in the streets, among other details. You should not have chosen this point.

C. The supporting statements make no mention of crime, so you shouldn't have chosen this point.

D. If the city streets were filled with raw sewage, manure, and garbage, they would certainly have been very dirty. This point is adequately supported. It is the one you should have chosen as the point.

PRACTICE 4

For each group, read the three items of supporting evidence. Then check (✓) the point that is most logically supported by that evidence.

Group 1

Support

- Dozens of angry bees attacked people sitting at the picnic table.
- A rain shower made all the food soggy and wet.
- Nearby kids threw a football onto the table, spilling all the drinks.

Point: Which of the following conclusions is best supported by all the evidence above?

_____ A. Picnics can be a fun way to spend an afternoon.

_____ B. The picnic was a disaster.

_____ C. Kids should be careful when they play outdoors.

_____ D. Everyone loves picnics.

Group 2

Support

- During the supposedly sad scenes in the movie, many people in the audience giggled.
- At least a third of the audience members left before the movie was over.
- As he left, one audience member said to people standing in line to buy tickets, "Don't waste your money!"

Point: Which of the following conclusions is best supported by all the evidence above?

_____ A. The movie was terrible.

_____ B. Today's movie audiences are difficult to please.

_____ C. Movie tickets cost too much.

_____ D. The movie was a comedy.

Group 3

Support

- A shrub brought into this country to stop soil from washing away eventually became a harmful weed that choked and killed countless other plants.
- Rabbits released in Australia for hunting quickly multiplied and destroyed much of the country's farmland.
- Caterpillars brought to the United States to start a silk industry broke free and destroyed large tracts of forest land.

Point: Which of the following conclusions is best supported by all the evidence above?

_____ A. Plants are difficult to grow properly.

_____ B. Great damage has been caused by bringing foreign plants and animals to new lands.

_____ C. Farmers should never use chemicals on their farms.

_____ D. There is no good way to stop soil from washing away.

Group 4

Support

- A study showed that regular churchgoers had lower blood pressure than non-churchgoers.
- Researchers have found lower rates of depression among religious people.
- A study found that patients who have strong faith have a much greater chance of surviving heart surgery than those who do not.

Point: Which of the following conclusions is best supported by all the evidence above?

_____ A. Scientists have some evidence that religious faith is good for one's health.

_____ B. Studies show that religious people are more intelligent than others.

_____ C. Medical science rejects the idea that religion can help people.

_____ D. Today, many hospitals encourage people to express their religious feelings openly.

CHAPTER REVIEW

In this chapter, you learned the following:

- A good argument is made up of a point, or a conclusion, and evidence to back it up.

- To think through an argument, you need to decide if each bit of evidence is relevant and logical.

- Critical thinking also includes looking at evidence and deciding what logical point, or conclusion, can be drawn from that evidence.

On the Web: If you are using this book in class, you can visit our website for additional practice in the basics of argument. Go to **www.townsendpress.com** and click on "Learning Center."

REVIEW TEST 1

To review what you learned in this chapter, fill in the blanks.

1. A point is the (*general idea, evidence, logic*) _____ that a speaker or writer advances.

2. A critical thinker is one who can look at an argument—a point and its support—and decide whether the _____ is solid or not.

3–5. To become an effective one-person jury, learn to constantly ask three questions:

   a. What is the _____?

   b. What is its _____?

   c. How logical is the _____?

REVIEW TEST 2

A. Here is another cartoon about Snoopy as a writer. Look at the cartoon, and then answer the question that follows.

_____ 1. This time Snoopy *does* support his point. What is his well-supported point?
   A. From the beginning, the hero pursued wealth, love, and fame.
   B. The hero wanted answers but found only questions.
   C. The "last car [that] drove away" must have been at the hero's funeral.
   D. The hero's life had been a disaster.

B. (2–9.) In each of the following groups, one statement is the point, and the other statements are support for the point. Identify the point with a **P** and each statement of support with an **S**.

Group 1

_____ A. It is good for people to limit the amount of time they watch TV.

_____ B. When people spend less time watching TV, they pursue healthier activities, including exercise.

_____ C. Studies show that when the TV is turned off, families talk and share more with each other.

_____ D. Watching less TV means that kids will be exposed to less violence.

Group 2

_____ A. Each year, Americans spend billions of dollars buying cold medications.

_____ B. Colds cause American businesses to lose millions of hours of work every year.

_____ C. The common cold is a major nuisance in America.

_____ D. The average child misses a week of school each year due to colds.

C. (10.) Read the three items of supporting evidence below. Then, in the space provided, write the letter of the point that is most logically supported by that evidence.

Support

● The worst disease in history—the Black Death—was spread by fleas living in the fur of rats.

● Malaria, a disease affecting millions each year, is often carried by a mosquito.

● Roaches are a major cause of the increase in asthma cases.

_____ **Point: Which of the following conclusions is best supported by all the evidence above?**

A. Insects play a major role in the spread of certain diseases.
B. Rats were an important link in the spread of the Black Death.
C. Rats are the biggest threat to human health today.
D. Asthma rates will continue to rise if the number of roaches increases.

REVIEW TEST 3

A. (1–4.) In the following group, one statement is the point, and the other statements are support for the point. Identify the point with a **P** and each statement of support with an **S**.

_____ A. Cell phones make it possible for people to talk to or text their friends and family almost anywhere at any time.

_____ B. Through e-mail, people can quickly exchange letters, no matter how far apart they are.

_____ C. Modern technology has helped connect people and strengthen relationships.

_____ D. Today's phones allow people to instantly take and share special photos with each other.

B. Each point is followed by three statements that provide logical support and two that do not. In the spaces, write the letters of the **three** logical statements of support.

5–7. **Point: The bus service on this route is unreliable.**

A. Several times each week, the bus on this route arrives more than a half hour late.
B. The buses on this route are at least twenty years old.
C. The transit authority is building a rail line to replace the bus route.
D. The bus schedule often gets changed without an announcement.
E. At least once per month, a bus on this route breaks down, causing long delays.

Items that logically support the point: _____   _____   _____

8–10. **Point: People should get rid of their credit cards.**

A. Many credit-card companies charge high yearly fees—even if the card is never used.
B. Having only one credit card keeps people from charging too much.
C. Having credit cards encourages people to spend more money than they have, resulting in high debts.
D. Not everyone is approved to get a credit card.
E. The interest rate on many credit cards is so high that people end up paying a lot more than the purchase price for what they buy.

Items that logically support the point: _____   _____   _____

REVIEW TEST 4

Here is a chance to apply all your reading skills to a full-length selection. In his book *Think Big*, Dr. Ben Carson tells us about the time he was in fifth grade and believed he was "the dumbest kid in the class." Read the excerpt to see how Carson turned his life around from a path that was leading to failure. Then go on to answer the questions covering all of the reading skills you've worked on since beginning this book.

Words to Watch

Below are some words in the reading that do not have strong context support. Each word is followed by the number of the paragraph in which it appears and its meaning there. These words are indicated in the selection by a small circle (°).

inasmuch as (13): because
potential (18): capacity for development and progress

solely (20): alone
rebellious (46): resisting authority
indifferent (58): uninterested
acknowledged (67): recognized
startled (75): surprised
astonished (81): surprised

DO IT BETTER!

Ben Carson, M.D., with Cecil Murphey

1   "Benjamin, is this your report card?" my mother asked as she picked up the folded white card from the table.

2   "Uh, yeah," I said, trying to sound casual. Too ashamed to hand it to her, I had dropped it on the table, hoping that she wouldn't notice until after I went to bed.

3   It was the first report card I had received from Higgins Elementary School since we had moved back from Boston to Detroit, only a few months earlier.

4   I had been in the fifth grade not even two weeks before everyone considered me the dumbest kid in the class and frequently made jokes about me. Before long I too began to feel as though I really was the most stupid kid in fifth grade. Despite Mother's frequently saying, "You're smart, Bennie. You can do anything you want to do," I did not believe her.

5   No one else in school thought I was smart, either.

6   Now, as Mother examined my report card, she asked, "What's this grade in reading?" (Her tone of voice told me that I was in trouble.) Although I was embarrassed, I did not think too much about it. Mother knew that I wasn't doing well in math, but she did not know I was doing so poorly in every subject.

7   While she slowly read my report card, reading everything one word at a time, I hurried into my room and started to get ready for bed. A few minutes later, Mother came into my bedroom.

8   "Benjamin," she said, "are these your grades?" She held the card in front of me as if I hadn't seen it before.

9   "Oh, yeah, but you know, it doesn't mean much."

10   "No, that's not true, Bennie. It means a lot."

11   "Just a report card."

12   "But it's more than that."

13   Knowing I was in for it now, I prepared to listen, yet I was not all that interested. I did not like school very much and there was no reason why I should. Inasmuch as° I was the dumbest kid in the class, what did I have to look forward to? The others laughed at me and made jokes about me every day.

14   "Education is the only way you're ever going to escape poverty," she said. "It's the only way you're ever going to get ahead in life and be successful. Do you understand that?"

15   "Yes, Mother," I mumbled.

16   "If you keep on getting these kinds of grades, you're going to spend the rest of your life on skid row, or at best sweeping floors in a factory. That's not the kind of life that I want for you. That's not the kind of life that God wants for you."

17   I hung my head, genuinely ashamed. My mother had been raising me and my older brother, Curtis, by herself. Having only a third-grade education herself, she knew the value of what she did not have. Daily she drummed into Curtis and me that we had to do our best in school.

18   "You're just not living up to your potential°," she said. "I've got two mighty smart boys and I know they can do better."

19   I had done my best—at least I had when I first started at Higgins Elementary School. How could I do much when I did not understand anything going on in our class?

20   In Boston we had attended a parochial school, but I hadn't learned much because of a teacher who seemed more interested in talking to another female teacher than in teaching us. Possibly, this teacher was not solely° to blame—perhaps I wasn't emotionally able to learn much. My parents had separated just before we went to Boston, when I was eight years old. I loved both my mother and father and went through considerable trauma over their separating. For months afterward, I kept thinking that my parents would get back together, that my daddy would come home again the way he used to, and that we could be the same old family again—but he never came back. Consequently, we moved to Boston and lived with Aunt Jean and Uncle William

Dr. Ben Carson today

Avery in a tenement building for two years until Mother had saved enough money to bring us back to Detroit.

21   Mother kept shaking the report card at me as she sat on the side of my bed. "You have to work harder. You have to use that good brain that God gave you, Bennie. Do you understand that?"

22   "Yes, Mother." Each time she paused, I would dutifully say those words.

23   "I work among rich people, people who are educated," she said. "I watch how they act, and I know they can do anything they want to do. And so can you." She put her arm on my shoulder. "Bennie, you can do anything they can do—only you can do it better!"

24   Mother had said those words before. Often. At the time, they did not mean much to me. Why should they? I really believed that I was the dumbest kid in fifth grade, but of course, I never told her that.

25   "I just don't know what to do about you boys," she said. "I'm going to talk to God about you and Curtis." She paused, stared into space, then said (more to herself than to me), "I need the Lord's guidance on what to do. You just can't bring in any more report cards like this."

26   As far as I was concerned, the report card matter was over.

27   The next day was like the previous ones—just another bad day in school, another day of being laughed at because I did not get a single problem right in arithmetic and couldn't get any words right on the spelling test. As soon as I came home from school, I changed into play clothes and ran outside. Most of the boys my age played softball, or the game I liked best, "Tip the Top."

28   We played Tip the Top by placing a bottle cap on one of the sidewalk cracks. Then taking a ball—any kind that bounced—we'd stand on a line and take turns throwing the ball at the bottle top, trying to flip it over. Whoever succeeded got two points. If anyone actually moved the cap more than a few inches, he won five points. Ten points came if he flipped it into the air and it landed on the other side.

29   When it grew dark or we got tired, Curtis and I would finally go inside and watch TV. The set stayed on until we went to bed. Because Mother worked long hours, she was never home until just before we went to bed. Sometimes I would awaken when I heard her unlocking the door.

30   Two evenings after the incident with the report card, Mother came home about an hour before our bedtime. Curtis and I were sprawled out, watching TV. She walked across the room, snapped off the set, and faced both of us. "Boys," she said, "you're wasting too much of your time in front of that television. You don't get an education from staring at television all the time."

31   Before either of us could make a protest, she told us that she had been praying for wisdom. "The Lord's told me what to do," she said. "So from now on, you will not watch television, except for two preselected programs each week."

32   "Just *two* programs?" I could hardly believe she would say such a terrible thing. "That's not—"

33   "And *only* after you've done your homework. Furthermore, you don't play outside after school, either, until you've done all your homework."

34   "Everybody else plays outside right after school," I said, unable to think of anything except how bad it would be if I couldn't play with my friends. "I won't have any friends if I stay in the house all the time—"

35   "That may be," Mother said, "but everybody else is not going to be as successful as you are—"

36   "But, Mother—"

37   "This is what we're going to do. I asked God for wisdom, and this is the answer I got."

38   I tried to offer several other arguments, but Mother was firm. I glanced at Curtis, expecting him to speak up, but he did not say anything. He lay on the floor, staring at his feet.

39   "Don't worry about everybody else. The whole world is full of 'everybody else,' you know that? But only a few

make a significant achievement."

40   The loss of TV and playtime was bad enough. I got up off the floor, feeling as if everything was against me. Mother wasn't going to let me play with my friends, and there would be no more television—almost none, anyway. She was stopping me from having any fun in life.

41   "And that isn't all," she said. "Come back, Bennie."

42   I turned around, wondering what else there could be.

43   "In addition," she said, "to doing your homework, you have to read two books from the library each week. Every single week."

44   "Two books? Two?" Even though I was in fifth grade, I had never read a whole book in my life.

45   "Yes, two. When you finish reading them, you must write me a book report just like you do at school. You're not living up to your potential, so I'm going to see that you do."

46   Usually Curtis, who was two years older, was the more rebellious°. But this time he seemed to grasp the wisdom of what Mother said. He did not say one word.

47   She stared at Curtis. "You understand?"

48   He nodded.

49   "Bennie, is it clear?"

50   "Yes, Mother." I agreed to do what Mother told me—it wouldn't have occurred to me not to obey—but I did not like it. Mother was being unfair and demanding more of us than other parents did.

51   The following day was Thursday.

After school, Curtis and I walked to the local branch of the library. I did not like it much, but then I had not spent that much time in any library.

52   We both wandered around a little in the children's section, not having any idea about how to select books or which books we wanted to check out.

53   The librarian came over to us and asked if she could help. We explained that both of us wanted to check out two books.

54   "What kind of books would you like to read?" the librarian asked.

55   "Animals," I said after thinking about it. "Something about animals."

56   "I'm sure we have several that you'd like." She led me over to a section of books. She left me and guided Curtis to another section of the room. I flipped through the row of books until I found two that looked easy enough for me to read. One of them, *Chip, the Dam Builder*—about a beaver—was the first one I had ever checked out. As soon as I got home, I started to read it. It was the first book I ever read all the way through even though it took me two nights. Reluctantly I admitted afterward to Mother that I really had liked reading about Chip.

57   Within a month I could find my way around the children's section like someone who had gone there all his life. By then the library staff knew Curtis and me and the kind of books we chose. They often made suggestions. "Here's a delightful book about a squirrel," I remember one of them telling me.

58   As she told me part of the story, I tried to appear indifferent°, but as soon

as she handed it to me, I opened the book and started to read.

59   Best of all, we became favorites of the librarians. When new books came in that they thought either of us would enjoy, they held them for us. Soon I became fascinated as I realized that the library had so many books—and about so many different subjects.

60   After the book about the beaver, I chose others about animals—all types of animals. I read every animal story I could get my hands on. I read books about wolves, wild dogs, several about squirrels, and a variety of animals that lived in other countries. Once I had gone through the animal books, I started reading about plants, then minerals, and finally rocks.

61   My reading books about rocks was the first time the information ever became practical to me. We lived near the railroad tracks, and when Curtis and I took the route to school that crossed by the tracks, I began paying attention to the crushed rock that I noticed between the ties.

62   As I continued to read more about rocks, I would walk along the tracks, searching for different kinds of stones, and then see if I could identify them.

63   Often I would take a book with me to make sure that I had labeled each stone correctly.

64   "Agate," I said as I threw the stone. Curtis got tired of my picking up stones and identifying them, but I did not care because I kept finding new stones all the time. Soon it became my favorite game to walk along the tracks and identify the varieties of stones. Although I did not

realize it, within a very short period of time, I was actually becoming an expert on rocks.

65   Two things happened in the second half of fifth grade that convinced me of the importance of reading books.

66   First, our teacher, Mrs. Williamson, had a spelling bee every Friday afternoon. We'd go through all the words we'd had so far that year. Sometimes she also called out words that we were supposed to have learned in fourth grade. Without fail, I always went down on the first word.

67   One Friday, though, Bobby Farmer, whom everyone acknowledged° as the smartest kid in our class, had to spell "agriculture" as his final word. As soon as the teacher pronounced his word, I thought, *I can spell that word.* Just the day before, I had learned it from reading one of my library books. I spelled it under my breath, and it was just the way Bobby spelled it.

68   *If I can spell "agriculture," I'll bet I can learn to spell any other word in the world. I'll bet I can learn to spell better than Bobby Farmer.*

69   Just that single word, "agriculture," was enough to give me hope.

70   The following week, a second thing happened that forever changed my life. When Mr. Jaeck, the science teacher, was teaching us about volcanoes, he held up an object that looked like a piece of black, glass-like rock. "Does anybody know what this is? What does it have to do with volcanoes?"

71   Immediately, because of my reading, I recognized the stone. I waited, but none of my classmates raised their

hands. I thought, *This is strange. Not even the smart kids are raising their hands.* I raised my hand.

72   "Yes, Benjamin," he said.

73   I heard snickers around me. The other kids probably thought it was a joke, or that I was going to say something stupid.

74   "Obsidian," I said.

75   "That's right!" He tried not to look startled°, but it was obvious he hadn't expected me to give the correct answer.

76   "That's obsidian," I said, "and it's formed by the supercooling of lava when it hits the water." Once I had their attention and realized I knew information no other student had learned, I began to tell them everything I knew about the subject of obsidian, lava, lava flow, supercooling, and compacting of the elements.

77   When I finally paused, a voice behind me whispered, "Is that Bennie Carson?"

78   "You're absolutely correct," Mr. Jaeck said, and he smiled at me. If he had announced that I'd won a million-dollar lottery, I couldn't have been more pleased and excited.

79   "Benjamin, that's absolutely, absolutely right," he repeated with enthusiasm in his voice. He turned to the others and said, "That is wonderful! Class, this is a tremendous piece of information Benjamin has just given us. I'm very proud to hear him say this."

80   For a few moments, I tasted the thrill of achievement. I recall thinking, *Wow, look at them. They're all looking at me with admiration. Me, the dummy! The one everybody thinks is stupid. They're looking at me to see if this is really me speaking.*

81   Maybe, though, it was I who was the most astonished° one in the class. Although I had been reading two books a week because Mother told me to, I had not realized how much knowledge I was accumulating. True, I had learned to enjoy reading, but until then I hadn't realized how it connected with my schoolwork. That day—for the first time—I realized that Mother had been right. Reading is the way out of ignorance, and the road to achievement. I did not have to be the class dummy anymore.

82   For the next few days, I felt like a hero at school. The jokes about me stopped. The kids started to listen to me. *I'm starting to have fun with this stuff.*

83   As my grades improved in every subject, I asked myself, "Ben, is there any reason you can't be the smartest kid in the class? If you can learn about obsidian, you can learn about social studies and geography and math and science and everything."

84   That single moment of triumph pushed me to want to read more. From then on, it was as though I could not read enough books. Whenever anyone looked for me after school, they could usually find me in my bedroom—curled up, reading a library book—for a long time, the only thing I wanted to do. I had stopped caring about the TV programs I was missing; I no longer cared about playing Tip the Top or baseball anymore. I just wanted to read.

85   In a year and a half—by the middle of sixth grade—I had moved to the top of the class.

Reading Comprehension Questions

Vocabulary in Context

_____   1. In the excerpt below, the word *trauma* (trou′mə) means
     A. love.
     B. knowledge.
     C. distance.
     D. suffering.

> "I loved both my mother and father and went through considerable trauma over their separating. For months afterward, I kept thinking that my parents would get back together, . . . but he never came back."
> (Paragraph 20)

Central Point and Main Ideas

_____   2. Which sentence best expresses the central point of the selection?
     A. Children who grow up in single-parent homes may spend large amounts of time home alone.
     B. Because of parental guidance that led to a love of reading, the author was able to go from academic failure to success.
     C. Most children do not take school very seriously, and they suffer as a result.
     D. Today's young people watch too much television.

_____   3. Which sentence best expresses the main idea of paragraph 56?
     A. Bennie's first experience with a library book was positive.
     B. The first book that Bennie ever checked out at a library was about a beaver.
     C. The librarian was very helpful to Bennie and Curtis.
     D. At first, Bennie could not read most of the animal books at the library.

Supporting Details

_____   4. To get her sons to do better in school, Mrs. Carson insisted that they
     A. watch less TV.
     B. finish their homework before playing.
     C. read two books every week.
     D. all of the above.

_____ 5. The major details in paragraphs 65–82 are
   A. books that Bennie Carson read.
   B. new skills Bennie Carson had gained.
   C. various people in Bennie Carson's elementary school class.
   D. two events that convinced Bennie Carson of the importance of reading books.

Transitions

_____ 6. The sentence below contains a transition that shows
   A. addition.
   B. contrast.
   C. an example.
   D. cause and effect.

   ". . . I hadn't learned much because of a teacher who seemed more interested in talking to another female teacher than in teaching us." (Paragraph 20)

_____ 7. The major details in paragraphs 65–82 are signaled by the addition words
   A. *Two, other.*
   B. *Two, One.*
   C. *One, other, finally, next.*
   D. *First, second.*

Patterns of Organization

_____ 8. The main pattern of organization of the selection is
   A. list of items.
   B. time order.
   C. contrast.
   D. definition and example.

Inferences

_____ 9. We can conclude that the author's mother believed
   A. education leads to success.
   B. her sons needed to be forced to live up to their potential.
   C. socializing was less important for her sons than a good education.
   D. all of the above.

Argument

_____ 10. Write the letter of the statement that is the point of paragraphs 70–80.
   A. Bennie knew that the name of the rock held by the teacher was obsidian.
   B. Bennie knew how to spell *agriculture*.
   C. Reading was the reason that Bennie became a better student.
   D. Bobby Farmer was the smartest kid in the class.

Discussion Questions

1. Why did Bennie consider himself "the dumbest kid in the class"? How did his image of himself affect his schoolwork?

2. The author recalls his failure in the classroom as an eight-year-old child by writing, "Perhaps I wasn't emotionally able to learn much." Why does he make this statement? What things in a child's home or social life might interfere with his or her education?

3. Part of Carson's mother's plan for helping her sons to improve their schoolwork was limiting their television watching to two programs a week. How much of a role do you think this limit played in the success of her plan? Do you agree with her that unrestricted television watching can be harmful to children?

4. Reading on a regular basis helped turn Carson's life around. Think about your daily schedule. If you were to do regular reading, where in your day could you find time to relax for half an hour and just read? What do you think would be the benefits of becoming a regular reader?

Note: Writing assignments for this selection appear on page 610.

Check Your Performance   **THE BASICS OF ARGUMENT**

Activity	Number Right	Points	Score
Review Test 1 (5 items)	_____	× 2 =	_____
Review Test 2 (10 items)	_____	× 3 =	_____
Review Test 3 (10 items)	_____	× 3 =	_____
Review Test 4 (10 items)	_____	× 3 =	_____
		TOTAL SCORE =	_____ %

Enter your total score into the **Reading Performance Chart: Review Tests** on the inside back cover.

THE BASICS OF ARGUMENT: Mastery Test 1

A. (1–8.) In each of the following groups, one statement is the point, and the other statements are support for the point. Identify each point with a **P** and each statement of support with an **S**.

Group 1

_____ A. My husband is a vegetarian.

_____ B. My mother, who lives with us, can't digest certain vegetables.

_____ C. One of my children is allergic to milk, wheat, and eggs.

_____ D. My family is difficult to cook for.

Group 2

_____ A. Hungry fans can buy anything from hot dogs to barbecued sandwiches to vegetarian food.

_____ B. The restrooms are large, plentiful, and well maintained.

_____ C. No matter where you sit, you always have a good view of the action.

_____ D. The new stadium is a great place to enjoy a game.

B. (9.) Below is a point followed by three items of information. Put a check (✓) next to the **one** item that logically supports the point.

Point: Margo is a very rude worker.

_____ A. [1]She can barely stay awake while at work. [2]Almost every day, she arrives at the store a few minutes late, having slept till the last minute. [3]She works in slow motion, and it takes her so long to do any one thing that people never ask for her help. [4]If she didn't spend the day pumping herself full of caffeine, she probably would not be able to move at all.

_____ B. [1]She keeps customers waiting while she talks with a coworker. [2]When someone asks her about a sale item, she snaps, "If it isn't on the shelf, we don't have it!" [3]When her boss isn't watching her, she answers the telephone by saying, "Yeah, what do you want?"

_____ C. [1]She can answer the phone, ring up a customer's purchases, and count large amounts of money all at the same time. [2]She often volunteers to help customers bring their bags to their cars. [3]She does not mind taking time to answer a customer's question or help someone stock a shelf.

(Continues on next page)

C. (10.) Read the three items of supporting evidence below. Then, in the space provided, write the letter of the point that is most logically supported by that evidence.

> *Support*
>
> ● Cats are relatively quiet, while dogs bark all the time.
>
> ● Unlike dogs, cats can be left on their own for a few days if their owner is traveling.
>
> ● Cats will use a litter box, rather than requiring several trips outside a day, as dogs do.

_____ **Point:** **Which of the following conclusions is best supported by all the evidence above?**

    A. Cats make better pets than dogs.

    B. Cats are quieter than dogs.

    C. Everyone should own a cat.

    D. Cats and dogs do not get along very well with each other.

THE BASICS OF ARGUMENT: Mastery Test 2

A. Each point is followed by three statements that provide logical support and two that do not. In the spaces, write the letters of the **three** logical statements of support.

1–3. **Point: Mel's new restaurant has a good chance of succeeding.**

    A. Another restaurant at the same location did not do well.

    B. The menu offers delicious dishes at reasonable prices.

    C. The restaurant itself is bright, clean, and attractive.

    D. Mel is a good host who makes customers feel welcome and special.

    E. The weekly specials at the restaurant change every Thursday.

Items that logically support the point: _____   _____   _____

4–6. **Point: I do not trust my sister's new boyfriend.**

    A. He likes one of my favorite bands very much and has seen it in concert three times.

    B. He gets calls on his cell phone at odd hours and then leaves without an explanation.

    C. He borrows money from my sister but has not paid any of it back.

    D. My sister met him at the pizza shop where she works.

    E. When I saw him in a restaurant with another girl, he acted very embarrassed and left before I could say hello.

Items that logically support the point: _____   _____   _____

7–9. **Point: Planting a garden in that vacant lot might benefit the neighborhood.**

    A. Farming was one of the earliest activities of civilization.

    B. Flowers would make the neighborhood look better and attract customers for local businesses.

    C. A garden could improve residents' diet by providing fresh produce to the neighborhood.

    D. Planting a garden might bring young and old people together, making the community stronger.

    E. There are many types of plants that could be planted in this climate.

Items that logically support the point: _____   _____   _____

(Continues on next page)

B. (10.) Below is a point followed by three items of information. Put a check (✓) next to the **one** item that logically supports the point.

Point: Greg is irresponsible.

_____ A. ¹He gives up his bus seat to elderly commuters. ²When he sees people carrying heavy packages or struggling with squirming children, he rushes to open doors to help them out.

_____ B. ¹No matter how much trouble I'm having with my English assignment, he refuses to do any of it for me. ²He says that between his own homework and his job, he doesn't have time. ³But he always gets B's, and I have trouble getting C's. ⁴Furthermore, when I need someone to cover for me at work so that I can see my girlfriend, he's always too busy with something else to help me out.

_____ C. ¹He never pays his bills on time. ²When he borrows things, he returns them damaged, or not at all. ³He is usually late for appointments, if he even remembers them at all.

THE BASICS OF ARGUMENT: Mastery Test 3

A. (1–8.) In each of the following groups, one statement is the point, and the other statements are support for the point. Identify each point with a **P** and each statement of support with an **S**.

Group 1

_____ A. The fans loudly boo the visiting team as soon as it appears.

_____ B. Recently, a man wearing a jacket from the opposing team was beaten up in the stands.

_____ C. Fans of our city's football team do not display good sportsmanship.

_____ D. Paper cups, beer cans, and even rocks are thrown onto the playing field during the game.

Group 2

_____ A. Play is an important part of a child's development.

_____ B. During physical play, kids strengthen muscles and improve coordination.

_____ C. When children "pretend," they develop imagination and creativity.

_____ D. By acting out stories, they learn to understand emotions and feelings.

B. (9.) Below is a point followed by three items of information. Put a check (✓) next to the **one** item that logically supports the point.

Point: That roller coaster is dangerous.

_____ A. [1]It is slower than any other roller coaster in the state. [2]The curves of its track are so wide and the hills are so shallow that a ride on this roller coaster seems like a drive in the country. [3]People don't scream when they ride it. [4]Instead, they enjoy the view from above the park.

_____ B. [1]It is known as one of the best roller coasters in the country. [2]People will wait in lines for hours just to try it. [3]At certain points it reaches the same speeds as cars do on highways. [4]The track is so tall and long that you can see it miles away.

_____ C. [1]Last year, it broke down several times, leaving people stranded in their cars sixty feet off the ground. [2]In most cars, the seatbelts are torn and don't always buckle properly. [3]One area of the track shakes and makes a strange grinding sound whenever a car passes over it.

(Continues on next page)

C. (10.) Read the three items of supporting evidence below. Then, in the space provided, write the letter of the point that is most logically supported by that evidence.

> *Support*
>
> ● In ancient times, "doctors" sometimes bored holes in the skulls of mentally ill people.
>
> ● In many parts of the world, mentally ill people were tortured to drive out their "evil spirits."
>
> ● Some societies in the past forced mentally ill people to live in colonies on deserted islands.

_____ **Point: Which of the following conclusions is best supported by all the evidence above?**

A. Mentally ill people should be treated with kindness, not cruelty.
B. In the past, mental illness was often treated harshly.
C. Not all ancient societies treated mentally ill people with cruelty.
D. Mentally ill people should never be held responsible for their actions.

THE BASICS OF ARGUMENT: Mastery Test 4

A. Each point is followed by three statements that provide logical support and two that do not. In the spaces, write the letters of the **three** logical statements of support.

1–3. **Point:** Raising the speed limit on America's highways is a bad idea.

   A. Raising the speed limit will make traffic accidents more severe, since cars will be hitting each other at higher speeds.
   B. Cars traveling at higher speeds produce more pollution.
   C. By traveling faster, people can get where they are going in less time.
   D. Cars get poorer gas mileage at higher speeds than at lower speeds.
   E. The higher speed limit will apply only to open highways, not to roads that are heavily crowded.

   Items that logically support the point: _____   _____   _____

4–6. **Point:** There are some simple ways to save money at the supermarket.

   A. Avoid products that charge extra for packaging, such as cheese wrapped individually by slice.
   B. Buy store brands of basic items instead of expensive name-brand products.
   C. Some people organize a shopping list alphabetically; others group items by categories.
   D. Shop when you are not hungry, so that you won't be tempted to buy pricey treats.
   E. Go to the store at odd hours or on weekdays to reduce the time you spend in lines.

   Items that logically support the point: _____   _____   _____

7–9. **Point:** Mayor Stump is the most dishonest politician I've ever seen.

   A. He used taxpayer money to buy expensive gifts for his family and friends.
   B. Before becoming mayor, Stump was a successful trial lawyer.
   C. Stump gave his daughter-in-law a "no-show" job that pays a salary of $80,000 a year.
   D. Our local newspaper says that Stump accepted bribes in exchange for government contracts.
   E. Stump is proud of the fact that several new businesses have opened in our town.

   Items that logically support the point: _____   _____   _____

(Continues on next page)

B. (10.) Below is a point followed by three items of information. Put a check (✓) next to the **one** item that logically supports the point.

Point: The meal I cooked for my girlfriend was horrible.

_____ A. ¹The chicken took an hour to prepare and two hours to cook. ²I had to travel for twenty miles to find a produce store that sold the vegetables I wanted. ³In order to make all this food, I had to buy a whole new set of pots and pans. ⁴Afterward, it took me hours to clean the kitchen and wash the dishes.

_____ B. ¹My girlfriend's car would not start when she wanted to come over. ²By the time she arrived, she was two hours late and very angry. ³As we sat down to eat, all she could talk about was how much it would cost to have her car fixed. ⁴When I tried to change the subject, she said I never listen to her, so I apologized. ⁵Then she accused me of apologizing too much. ⁶We both got so mad that we hardly touched dinner.

_____ C. ¹The chicken came out so tough and dry that I could barely cut it with a steak knife. ²I overcooked the fresh vegetables so much that they changed from a bright green color to the color of an army jeep. ³The cake I tried to bake collapsed into itself, turning into a shapeless chewy mass that resembled a giant cookie.

THE BASICS OF ARGUMENT: Mastery Test 5

A. (1–4.) In the following group, one statement is the point, and the other statements are support for the point. Identify the point with a **P** and each statement of support with an **S**.

_____ A. Hearing can be damaged by a number of common sounds.

_____ B. Loud music at a concert or in headphones can cause significant hearing loss.

_____ C. Machinery such as lawn mowers and leaf blowers can contribute to deafness.

_____ D. The noise level of many buses and trucks is high enough to damage hearing permanently.

B. The point below is followed by three statements that provide logical support and two that do not. In the spaces, write the letters of the **three** logical statements of support.

5–7. **Point: High-school proms should be banned.**

A. Proms pressure students to spend a ridiculous amount of money on gowns, tuxes, flowers, and even limos.

B. The social pressure to get a date for the prom makes many people miserable.

C. Prom preparations distract students for many weeks from the real business of school, which is education.

D. Proms usually feature a theme, and the room the prom is held in is decorated according to that theme.

E. At most schools, proms are chaperoned by teachers and administrators.

Items that logically support the point: _____   _____   _____

C. Each point below is followed by three items of information. Put a check (✓) next to the **one** item that logically supports each point.

8. **Point: Susan is a generous person.**

_____ A. ¹She bows her head and gives thanks before every meal, even when eating out. ²She spends most of every Sunday in church. ³She votes for political candidates who she feels have a strong connection to God.

(Continues on next page)

_____ B. ¹If I admire an outfit she's wearing, she'll offer to lend it to me. ²She often treats when we all go out for pizza. ³She can't pass a homeless person without giving away her loose change. ⁴And she donates two evenings a week to Big Sisters and an adult literacy program.

_____ C. ¹When her cousin failed to repay a loan, she said, "He told me he just can't get his life together," but this same cousin takes expensive vacations. ²She believed a salesman's story that the used car she bought had been owned by a little old lady who drove it only to church on Sundays.

9. **Point: Neil is a hypocrite—he usually does the opposite of what he says.**

_____ A. ¹He spent a half hour talking and laughing with someone yesterday, then later confided to me, "I can't stand that man!" ²He lectures his daughters about the dangers of drug addiction, but he is a heavy drinker and smoker.

_____ B. ¹He waits until December to put in winter storm windows, and his Christmas tree is often still up in March. ²He usually pays his bills a few days after they are due, and he never gets around to dental or medical checkups until real problems develop.

_____ C. ¹After thirty-seven years of marriage, he still writes love letters to his wife. ²He took early retirement so he could stay home and care for her when an illness left her bedridden. ³He never leaves the house without bringing her back something special.

10. **Point: My boss is considerate.**

_____ A. ¹She greets employees and customers alike with a warm smile and a hearty, "Hi! How are you today?" ²She is forever telling us, "A stranger is just a friend you haven't met yet."

_____ B. ¹Instead of giving us orders, she asks us to do things. ²She always thanks an employee for completing a task. ³She often helps out when she sees that things are getting stressful.

_____ C. ¹Getting a raise out of her is impossible—even for long-term employees. ²Her secretary is still using an old typewriter because the boss won't buy anything new. ³We had to have the retirement party for the office manager during our lunch hour, and the boss was waiting by the time clock when we got back—to make sure we weren't a minute late.

THE BASICS OF ARGUMENT: Mastery Test 6

A. (1–4.) In the following group, one statement is the point, and the other statements are support for the point. Identify the point with a **P** and each statement of support with an **S**.

_____ A. The authors do not define the new terms they use in each chapter.

_____ B. That sociology textbook is not very helpful.

_____ C. The sentences are long and hard to understand, and the material does not seem well organized.

_____ D. The book has few illustrations and no index.

B. The point below is followed by three statements that provide logical support and two that do not. In the spaces, write the letters of the **three** logical statements of support.

5–7. **Point: Early automobiles were uncomfortable and difficult to operate.**

A. The start of the factory assembly line made the price of the Model T drop from $440 in 1915 to $290 in 1925.

B. Hard, high-pressure tires on early cars made for very bumpy rides.

C. Early cars were open on top, and drivers choked on dust and dirt.

D. During World War II, many cars and trucks were made for military use.

E. A driver had to start the car's engine by cranking it by hand, and the crank sometimes sprang back and broke the driver's thumb.

Items that logically support the point: _____ _____ _____

C. (8–10.) For each group on the next page, read the three items of supporting evidence. Then, in the space provided, write the letter of the point that is most logically supported by that evidence.

(Continues on next page)

Group 1

Support

- It feels good to help people who are in need.
- You can meet a lot of interesting, friendly people while volunteering.
- You can learn new skills—some of which may help you land a paying job.

_____ **Point: Which of the following conclusions is best supported by all the evidence above?**

    A. Doing volunteer work is the best way to find a paying job.
    B. Doing volunteer work can be a rewarding experience.
    C. If you're looking for reliable friends, doing volunteer work is better than going online.
    D. These days, too many people lack food, clothing, and a decent place to live.

Group 2

Support

- Pigeons enjoy living in populated areas, especially big cities.
- Coyotes are increasing their numbers in populated suburban areas.
- Cities and suburbs are packed with an increasing number of squirrels.

_____ **Point: Which of the following conclusions is best supported by all the evidence above?**

    A. Coyotes may soon be a health problem for many suburban communities.
    B. Some wild animals are able to live near human beings.
    C. Big cities are dangerous places for all forms of wildlife.
    D. Many urban residents enjoy feeding and caring for pigeons.

Group 3

Support

- Buses and trains reduce air pollution.
- Traffic problems lessen where people take buses or trains to work.
- When more people take public transportation, fuel is saved.

_____ **Point: Which of the following conclusions is best supported by all the evidence above?**

    A. One answer to pollution is the use of public transportation.
    B. City streets would be safer if fewer people drove their cars to work.
    C. People should use public transportation more often.
    D. Highways should be built wider to reduce traffic accidents.

Part Two

Ten Reading Selections

1 Winners, Losers, or Just Kids?
Dan Wightman

Preview

Did a high-school teacher ever suggest that you'd never amount to anything? And when you were in high school, did you sometimes feel that happiness and success were going to happen to other people, but not to you? If so, like the author of this selection, you should realize that "A" students sometimes earn D's in life, and high-school losers sometimes turn out to be winners.

Words to Watch

coyly (1): with pretended shyness
flaunted (1): showed off
blotto (2): very drunk
swank (3): ritzy
metamorphoses (4): great changes
morose (7): gloomy
fare (8): do
endeared (9): made dear
sheepish (11): shamefaced
presumptuous (11): taking too much for granted
regressed (13): gone backward
quick (15): the sensitive flesh under the fingernails
stride (17): pace

1   If I envied anyone in high school, it was the winners. You know who I mean. The ones who earned straight A's and scored high on their Scholastic Aptitude Tests. The attractive ones who smiled coyly°, drove their own sport cars, and flaunted° those hard, smooth bodies that they kept tan the year round.

2   By contrast, my high-school friends were mostly losers. We spent a lot of time tuning cars and drinking beer. Our girlfriends were pale and frumpy, and we had more D's than B's on our report cards. After graduation, many of us went into the Army instead of to a university; two of us came back from the war in coffins, three more on stretchers. On weekends, when we drank Colt 45 together in my father's battered Ford, we'd laughingly refer to ourselves as the "out crowd." But, unless we were thoroughly blotto°, we never laughed hard when we said it. And I, for one, rarely got blotto when I was 16.

431

3   The reason I mention this is that last month 183 winners and losers from my Northern California high-school graduating class got together at a swank° country club for a revealing fifteen-year reunion.

4   Predictably, only happy and successful people attended. The strange thing, though, was that the people I once pegged as losers outnumbered the winners at this reunion by a visible margin. And, during a long session at the bar with my informative friend Paula, I got an earful about the messy lives of people I'd once envied, and the remarkable metamorphoses° of people I'd once pitied.

5   Paula reported that Len, a former class officer, was now a lost soul in Colorado, hopelessly estranged from his charming wife. Tim, one of the sorriest students I'd ever known, was a successful sportswriter, at ease with himself.

6   Estelle, who was modestly attractive in her teens, was now a part-time stripper in the Midwest, working to support her young son. Connie, a former car-club "kitten," had become a sophisticated international flight attendant.

7   Paula told me that Gary, a college scholarship winner, was overweight, underemployed, and morose°. Ron, who had shown little flair for music, had become a symphony violinist.

8   Sipping a piña colada, I thought to myself how terribly mistaken my senior counselor had been when she told me that high-school performance indicates how one will fare° later.

9   I looked at Paula, a high-school troublemaker with a naughty smile,

whose outgoing personality and rebellious spirit had endeared° her to me so long ago. Together, we once stole a teacher's grade book, changed some of our low marks, then dropped the book in the lost-and-found box. The savvy teacher never said a word about the incident, but at the end of the year, when report cards were issued, gave us the D's we deserved.

10   Now Paula was a housewife, a volunteer worker, and the mother of two sons. She wore a marriage-encounter pin on her modest dress, and sat at the bar tippling Perrier on ice.

11   She shook her head when I reminded her of the grade-book escapade, and the sheepish° look on her face reminded me how presumptuous° it is to predict the lives of others.

12   It also got me thinking about my own life since high school—how I'd gradually shaken my loser's image, gotten through college, found a decent job, married wisely, and finally realized a speck of my potential.

13   I thought about numerous situations where I could have despaired, regressed°, given up—and how I hadn't,

though others had—and I wondered why I was different, and had more luck, less guilt.

14   "The past is fiction," wrote William Burroughs. And, although I don't subscribe to that philosophy entirely, the people I admire most today are those who overcome their mistakes, seize second chances, and fight to pull themselves together, day after day.

15   Often they're the sort of people who leave high school with blotchy complexions, crummy work habits, fingernails bitten down to the quick°.

And of course they're bitterly unsure of themselves, and slow to make friends.

16   But they're also the ones who show up transformed at fifteen-year reunions, and the inference I draw is that the distinction between winners and losers is often slight and seldom crucial—and frequently overrated.

17   In high school especially, many people are slow getting started. But, finding their stride°, they quickly catch up, and in their prime often return to surprise and delight us—their lives so much richer than we'd ever imagined.

Vocabulary Questions

Use context clues to help you decide on the best definition for each italicized word. Then, in the space provided, write the letter of your choice.

___B___ 1. In the excerpt below, the word *pegged* (pĕgd) means
    A. feared.
    B. labeled.
    C. admired.
    D. envied.

    ". . . the people I once pegged as losers outnumbered the winners." (Paragraph 4)

___C___ 2. In the excerpt below, the word *estranged* (ĭ-strānjd′) means
    A. enriched.
    B. free.
    C. separated.
    D. rich.

    "...a lost soul ... hopelessly estranged from his charming wife." (Paragraph 5)

_____ 3. In the sentence below, the word *flair* (flâr) means
   A. dislike.
   B. inability.
   C. talent.
   D. money.

> "Ron, who had shown little flair for music, had become a symphony violinist." (Paragraph 7)

_____ 4. In the excerpt below, the word *savvy* (săv′ē) means
   A. foolish.
   B. cruel.
   C. misled.
   D. knowing.

> "The savvy teacher . . . gave us the D's we deserved." (Paragraph 9)

_____ 5. In the excerpt below, the words *subscribe to* (səb-skrīb′ tōō) mean
   A. agree with.
   B. disagree with.
   C. understand.
   D. pay for.

> "'The past is fiction,' wrote William Burroughs. And although I don't subscribe to that philosophy entirely, the people I admire . . . are those who overcome their mistakes . . . ." (Paragraph 14)

Reading Comprehension Questions

Central Point and Main Ideas

_____ 1. Which sentence best expresses the central point of the selection?
   A. High-school winners get good grades and are attractive.
   B. High-school losers drink beer and fix cars.
   C. The author attended his fifteen-year reunion.
   D. High-school performance doesn't show how well a student will do later in life.

_A_ 2. The main idea of paragraph 2 is best expressed in the
      A. first sentence.
      B. second sentence.
      C. third sentence.
      D. last sentence.

Supporting Details

_B_ 3. The author's old friend Paula, a troublemaker in high school,
      A. became a part-time stripper.
      B. became a housewife, mother, and volunteer worker.
      C. remained a troublemaker.
      D. told the author nothing about their classmates' lives.

_C_ 4. According to the author, high-school losers
      A. are less interesting than other people.
      B. have little potential for success.
      C. have a lot of potential for success.
      D. should try to become friends with winners.

Transitions

_____ 5. The relationship of paragraph 2 to paragraph 1 is one of
      A. comparison.
      B. contrast.
      C. an example.
      D. time.

_____ 6. In paragraph 17, the relationship of the second sentence to the first sentence is one of
      A. addition.
      B. illustration.
      C. comparison.
      D. contrast.

Patterns of Organization

_____ 7. The details in paragraphs 5–7 are organized in a pattern of
        A. time order.
        B. a list of items.
        C. cause and effect.
        D. definition and example.

Inferences

_____ 8. From the article, we can conclude that in high school, the author
        A. thought the winners would not always be winners.
        B. thought the winners did not deserve their grades.
        C. felt the winners did not know they were winners.
        D. might have wanted to trade places with the winners.

_____ 9. The author implies that
        A. people often think that high-school losers will remain losers.
        B. the difference between winners and losers in high school is usually very important to their futures.
        C. fifteen-year reunions change losers to winners.
        D. everyone knows that high-school losers often become winners.

_____ 10. The author implies that
        A. being a winner in high school is a poor start in life.
        B. being a high-school winner is more important to one's future than determination.
        C. determination and hope change people's lives.
        D. people's abilities are fully developed by high school.

Summarizing

Note: A **summary** is the reduction of a large amount of information to its most important points. The length and kind of summary will depend upon one's purpose as well as the material in question. Often, a summary will consist of a central point and its major supporting details. As a general guideline, a paragraph might be reduced to a sentence or two, an article (such as the one you have just read) might be reduced to a paragraph, and a textbook chapter might be reduced to about three or so pages of notes.

_____ 1. Write the letter of the statement that best summarizes the central point of "Winners, Losers, or Just Kids?" as expressed in the first four paragraphs.
   A. In high school, the author was a loser who envied the winners.
   B. High-school reunions can teach us important lessons about life in general.
   C. The reunion showed that many high-school winners and losers had not turned out as the author had expected.

_____ 2. Write the letter of the statement that best summarizes the first set of supporting details for the central point (paragraphs 5–12).
   A. At his reunion, the author found out what had happened to his classmates.
   B. The author's friend Paula had turned her life around and was now happily married and a contributor to society.
   C. The author realized that some losers in his high-school class, including himself, had done more with their lives than some of the winners he had once envied.

_____ 3. Write the letter of the statement that best summarizes the second set of supporting details for the central point (paragraphs 13–17).
   A. The winners in life include those who overcome early mistakes and problems and persist in building good lives for themselves.
   B. The winners in life are the ones who leave high school as attractive people with impressive records.
   C. The author began life as a loser but ended up as a winner.

Discussion Questions

1. What does Wightman really mean by "winners" and "losers"? Why does the title also say, "or Just Kids"?

2. Were you surprised that Wightman's classmates turned out as they did? Why or why not?

3. What is the meaning of the sentence "The past is fiction"? To what extent do you think it's true, if at all? In what ways *isn't* it true?

4. Wightman writes that he "wondered why he was different, and had more luck, less guilt" than others. What factors do you suppose are involved in determining whether or not people shake their "loser's image"? What factors does Wightman name?

Note: Writing assignments for this selection appear on page 610.

Check Your Performance   **WINNERS, LOSERS, OR JUST KIDS?**

Activity	Number Right	Points	Total
Vocabulary Questions (5 items)	_____	× 20 =	_____
		SCORE =	_____%
Reading Comprehension Questions			
Central Point and Main Ideas (2 items)	_____	× 8.5 =	_____
Supporting Details (2 items)	_____	× 8.5 =	_____
Transitions (2 items)	_____	× 8.5 =	_____
Patterns of Organization (1 item)	_____	× 8.5 =	_____
Inferences (3 items)	_____	× 8.5 =	_____
Summarizing (3 items)	_____	× 5 =	_____
		SCORE =	_____%

TOTAL SCORES: Vocabulary _____% Comprehension _____%

Enter your total scores into the **Reading Performance Chart: Ten Reading Selections** on the inside back cover.

2 The Right Words at the Right Time
Jeff Bezos

Preview

Sometimes we learn our most memorable lessons through the mistakes we make. In the following selection, the author (the founder and CEO of Amazon.com) recalls how the punishment he expected for a mistake he had made was replaced by words that would stay with him the rest of his life.

Words to Watch

vaccinate (1): to protect health with an injection of medicine
caravanning (2): traveling with others, usually in a long line
calculating (4): using math to solve problems
solemnity (5): seriousness
rebuke (8): scolding; punishment
essential (9): necessary

1   As a kid, I spent my summers with my grandparents on their ranch in Cotulla, Texas. I helped fix windmills, vaccinate° cattle, and did other ranch chores. It was hard work but a welcome change from my Houston life of school and playing *Star Trek* with my friends. I loved it.

2   One of the best, and strangest, parts of spending summers with my grandparents was caravanning° with the Wally Byam Caravan Club, a group of Airstream trailer owners who took road trips together around the United States and Canada. My grandparents were members and owned a thirty-one-foot Airstream that they towed behind their 1973 Oldsmobile. Every few summers, we would join the caravan—a line of some three hundred Airstream trailers, and it was during one of these trips that my grandfather said to me the right words at the right time.

3   I wasn't very old, maybe ten or eleven, but I was forming my opinions about the world, and, of course, I thought I knew much more about things than I actually did.

4   I was then, as I am now, a big reader and a fiend for numbers. Anyone who has been on a long road trip knows

that no matter how many books you bring, no matter how sparkling the conversation or beautiful the scenery, you still have too much time to think. So I spent a good deal of my extra time calculating°. I calculated gas mileage. I figured out the average per-item price of groceries bought over the course of the trip. And at some point, I saw an antismoking ad on TV. The announcer declared that every time a smoker took a puff of a cigarette, he was shortening his life span by two minutes. My grandmother was a smoker. I hated it, and not just because I knew that it was bad for her. My guess is that any kid who rides for thousands of miles sitting in the smoke-filled backseat of a 1973 Oldsmobile grows to hate smoking. So on one particularly long driving day, I decided to do the math.

Jeff Bezos today

5   I don't remember exactly what the number was—two minutes per puff, twenty puffs per cigarette, twenty cigarettes per pack, one pack a day for thirty years. About sixteen years? When I was satisfied that I had come up with a reasonably accurate number, I poked my head between the two front seats and tapped my grandmother on the shoulder. "You've taken sixteen years off of your life from smoking," I said, explaining the math, and with none of the solemnity° the disclosure deserved. She burst into tears.

6   It was not the "You're very clever— that's good math" reaction that I was expecting. But there's nothing like unintentionally stepping on a landmine to make you keenly aware of your effect on those around you. I felt terrible. I sat quietly in the backseat, unsure of what to do.

7   My grandmother cried, and my grandfather, who had been driving in silence, carefully pulled to the side of the road. He got out of the car and asked me to follow. Was I in trouble? How much trouble was I in? My grandfather had never said a harsh word to me, but this incident was unprecedented. I had no way to gauge how severe the consequences would be.

8   We walked a few paces back and stood between the trunk of the car and the front of the silver trailer. I watched the parade of Airstream trailers drive by and waited for the rebuke° I knew was coming. After a minute, my grandfather looked at

me, put his hand on my shoulder, and said: "You'll learn one day that it's much harder to be kind than clever."

9   With both his words and the gentle way in which he delivered them, my grandfather taught me an essential° lesson. I had always admired him for his intelligence, but that day I began to understand that his intelligence was only a gift that he had been given. It was the kindness with which he chose to apply it that he could be proud of. It's something I've been working on ever since.

Vocabulary Questions

Use context clues to help you decide on the best definition for each italicized word. Then, in the space provided, write the letter of your choice.

_____ 1. In the excerpt below, the word *fiend* (fēnd) means someone who is
   A. particularly good at something.
   B. afraid of something.
   C. very evil.
   D. very lazy.

   "I was then, as I am now, a big reader and a fiend for numbers. . . . So I spent a good deal of my extra time calculating. I calculated gas mileage. I figured out the average per-item price of groceries bought over the course of the trip." (Paragraph 4)

_____ 2. In the excerpt below, the word *disclosure* (dĭ-sklō′zhər) means
   A. obvious lie.
   B. funny story.
   C. interesting announcement.
   D. wild guess.

   "'You've taken sixteen years off of your life from smoking,' I said, explaining the math, and with none of the solemnity the disclosure warranted. She burst into tears." (Paragraph 5)

_____ 3. In the excerpt below, the word *keenly* (kēn′lē) means
  A. extremely.
  B. partly.
  C. pleasantly.
  D. sleepily.

  "But there's nothing like unintentionally stepping on a landmine to make you keenly aware of your effect on those around you. I felt terrible. I sat quietly in the backseat, unsure of what to do." (Paragraph 6)

_____ 4. In the excerpt below, the word *unprecedented* (ŭn-prĕs′ĭ-dĕn′tĭd) means
  A. surprising.
  B. angry.
  C. ordinary.
  D. happening for the first time.

  ". . . my grandfather, who had been driving in silence, carefully pulled to the side of the road. He got out of the car and asked me to follow. Was I in trouble? How much trouble was I in? My grandfather had never said a harsh word to me, but this incident was unprecedented." (Paragraph 7)

_____ 5. In the excerpt below, the word *gauge* (gāj) means
  A. judge.
  B. reject.
  C. welcome.
  D. share.

  "How much trouble was I in? My grandfather had never said a harsh word to me, but this incident was unprecedented. I had no way to gauge how severe the consequences would be." (Paragraph 7)

Reading Comprehension Questions

Central Point and Main Ideas

_____ 1. Which sentence best expresses the central point of the selection?
  A. It is often difficult for children to understand how to express their opinions politely.
  B. When we are young, we always believe that we know far more about the world than we do.
  C. One may be born smart, but being kind is something that takes work and focus.
  D. Grandparents often give the best advice to their grandchildren.

_____ 2. Which sentence best expresses the main idea of paragraph 4?
   A. The author entertained himself with numbers, leading to his figuring out how many years smoking had taken off his grandmother's life.
   B. Anyone who has ridden in a smoke-filled car for a long period of time has grown to hate smoking.
   C. The author was particularly good at math and was able to make a number of impressive calculations in his head very quickly.
   D. After the author grew tired of reading during the long trip, he switched to doing calculations about things he heard on the radio.

_____ 3. Which sentence best expresses the main idea of paragraph 7?
   A. The author's harsh words had upset his grandmother.
   B. The author's grandfather is going to punish him for what the author said about his grandmother.
   C. Since his grandfather had never punished him, the author is unsure about what is going to happen.
   D. The author's grandfather had never spoken a harsh word to him, so he would probably not punish him now.

Supporting Details

_____ 4. The author's grandparents lived
   A. in an Airstream trailer.
   B. on a ranch.
   C. in Houston.
   D. with the author's parents.

_____ 5. The author did math problems during the road trip because
   A. they were homework assignments.
   B. they helped him ignore his grandmother's smoking.
   C. his grandparents needed to know how much the trip was costing.
   D. they helped him pass the time.

Transitions

_____ 6. The two sentences below express a relationship of
   A. cause and effect.
   B. comparison.
   C. addition.
   D. illustration.

   "Anyone who has been on a long road trip knows that no matter how many books you bring, no matter how sparkling the conversation or beautiful the scenery, you still have too much time to think. So I spent a good deal of my extra time calculating." (Paragraph 4)

_____ 7. The relationship of the second sentence below to the first one is one of
   A. contrast.
   B. addition.
   C. time order.
   D. comparison.

   "I watched the parade of Airstream trailers drive by and waited for the rebuke I knew was coming. After a minute, my grandfather looked at me, put his hand on my shoulder, and said: 'You'll learn one day that it's much harder to be kind than clever.'" (Paragraph 8)

Patterns of Organization

_____ 8. Paragraph 4
   A. compares the author's love of reading to his love of numbers.
   B. presents a series of steps for passing time on a long trip.
   C. contrasts the author's love for his grandmother with his hatred of her smoking.
   D. lists several ways the author passed the time with numbers and calculations.

_____ 9. Overall, the main pattern of organization of this essay is
   A. time order.
   B. definition and example.
   C. comparison.
   D. list of items.

Inferences

_____ 10. In paragraph 9, the author suggests that
        A. he has never really learned to be as kind as his grandfather.
        B. his grandfather believes that intelligence is more important than kindness.
        C. kindness is more admirable than intelligence.
        D. his grandfather was proud of having the gift of intelligence.

Mapping

Following is a map of "The Right Words at the Right Time." Complete the map by filling in the letters of the missing major supporting details, which are listed below in random order. (One of the items has already been filled in for you.)

Central point: As a child, Jeff Bezos visited his grandparents one summer and learned an important lesson about kindness from his grandfather.

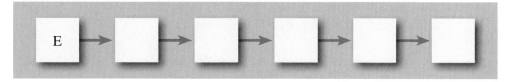

Major Supporting Details Missing from the Map
        A. Grandfather speaks to Bezos about kindness.
        B. Bezos tells his grandmother she has taken sixteen years off her life by smoking.
        C. Bezos begins doing number calculations.
        D. Grandmother begins to cry.
        E. Bezos becomes bored while on a long trip with his grandparents.
        F. Grandfather stops the car.

Discussion Questions

1. Bezos comments that he "helped fix windmills, vaccinate cattle, and did other ranch chores" and that he loved doing them. Why do you think these activities were fun for him? Would you "love" doing these kinds of things? Why or why not?

2. Why do you think the author did not consider that his "calculations" would hurt his grandmother's feelings? Do you think he was wrong to announce that his grandmother's life would be shortened by sixteen years due to smoking? Why or why not?

3. The author writes: "There's nothing like unintentionally stepping on a landmine to make you keenly aware of your effect on those around you." What does he mean by "a landmine"? While interacting with others, what kind of "landmines" have you—or people you know—unintentionally stepped on? What happened as a result?

4. Why is it "much harder to be kind than clever"? Why do think kindness is so difficult for some people?

Note: Writing assignments for this selection appear on page 611.

Check Your Performance   THE RIGHT WORDS AT THE RIGHT TIME

Activity	Number Right	Points		Total
Vocabulary Questions (5 items)	_____	×	20 =	_____
		SCORE	=	_____ %
Reading Comprehension Questions				
Central Point and Main Ideas (3 items)	_____	×	8 =	_____
Supporting Details (2 items)	_____	×	8 =	_____
Transitions (2 items)	_____	×	8 =	_____
Patterns of Organization (2 items)	_____	×	8 =	_____
Inferences (1 item)	_____	×	8 =	_____
Mapping (5 items)	_____	×	4 =	_____
		SCORE	=	_____ %

TOTAL SCORES: Vocabulary _____% Comprehension _____%

Enter your total scores into the **Reading Performance Chart: Ten Reading Selections** on the inside back cover.

3 Eye Contact
Ron Clark

Preview

In his book *The Essential 55*, Ron Clark, winner of the 2001 Disney Teacher of the Year Award, presents 55 rules that he thinks are essential for every classroom. Some of those rules are ones you'd probably expect, such as "Do your homework every day." But others are surprising, like the "rule" you are about to read.

Words to Watch

proposal (1): offer
emphasis (2): importance
torture (5): suffering
various (6): many different
custodians (6): people responsible for cleaning and general upkeep of a building
appreciated (6): valued
obvious (6): clear

1   Keeping eye contact is something that many people find hard to do, but it is important when you are trying to get your point across to people and show them you are serious about what you are saying. For example, if you go in to talk to your boss and ask for a raise, he is going to be far more likely to take you seriously if you are looking him in the eyes rather than glancing downward. If you are making a business proposal°, people will be more likely to trust you and believe in your ideas if they see that you are confident, sure of yourself, and making eye contact with them.

2   I spend a lot of time encouraging my students to make eye contact. In order to give them practice, I put the kids in groups of two. I then tell them that making eye contact when you make a statement gives what you are saying more emphasis° and emotion. When you look away or down at the floor, it shows you aren't sure of what you are saying and that you possibly aren't telling the truth. I also tell them that I have heard that repeated glances to the upper left-hand side mean you are being dishonest. Once they are in their groups, I have them practice talking to each other, taking note of how effective they are at maintaining eye contact with their partners.

3   Making eye contact is not only a way to show confidence, but it is also an important way to show respect. In class,

when a student is expressing an opinion, I make sure all of the other students turn and are focused on that individual. I don't allow them to raise their hands to make additional comments until that person is finished, because, if they do, it looks as if they are more concerned with what they want to say than with the opinions of the speaker. I tell them to imagine what it would be like if they were trying to express a thought and everyone around them kept waving their hands. It would make them feel like their opinions had no value, and so therefore, we don't do it.

4   I can remember when I was in school that it was awfully hard to daydream while staring at the teacher. If I could focus on the head in front of me or on my pencil, I was good to go, but watching the teacher just took something out of it. Therefore, I make sure to have all eyes on me at all times. That way, as I'm teaching, I can see the looks on the students' faces and can tell if they are confused and lost or entertained and attentive. Also, since I am a very visual learner and teacher, I am constantly making motions with my hands and on the board, and I want the kids to follow along with me and know exactly where I'm coming from.

5   I have worked many a day in fast food. I've spent countless hours making the doughnuts at Dunkin' Donuts and waiting tables at various restaurants. Serving the public can be a thrill, but it can also be torture° when you have to deal with difficult customers. I can remember how I always liked it when people would look me in the eyes to

give their order. It is far more respectful to look a person in the face. As they were leaving, I always expected them to say thank you; but many didn't, and it baffled me. What were they thinking? Many who did say thank you just said it as they turned away and drove off. Why not take one second to look the person in the eyes and say thank you as if you mean it?

6   I try to get my students to practice doing this with various° adults in the school who aren't teachers. Often the custodians°, cafeteria workers, secretaries, and teacher's aides aren't considered worthy of the respect teachers get, and I work hard to change that image in the minds of my students. I explain to the students the role of each person at the school and how his or her job makes it possible for kids to get a great education. I then tell them that people work harder and with more

effort if they feel appreciated° and that they are making a difference. I make sure to model the type of behavior I expect, as I interact with all members of the staff in a friendly and respectful manner. It doesn't take much effort before the students are following my lead, and the results are always obvious°. When we go to the lunchroom, the students aren't allowed to talk in the line, and when they get their food, they must look the cafeteria workers in the eyes and say "May I" when asking for anything. In turn, they always thank the lunchroom workers and tell them to have a good day. The workers always comment on how wonderful the class is and how much they appreciate the respect.

No matter how we are interacting   7 with others around us and regardless of what we are saying, we will be taken more seriously and our actions will be much more appreciated if they come with eye contact.

Vocabulary Questions

Use context clues to help you decide on the best definition for each italicized word. Then, in the space provided, write the letter of your choice.

_____ 1. In the sentence below, the word *maintaining* (mān-tān′ĭng) means
    A. continuing.
    B. asking for.
    C. stopping.
    D. risking.

"Once they are in their groups, I have them practice talking to each other, taking note of how effective they are at maintaining eye contact with their partners." (Paragraph 2)

_____ 2. In the sentence below, the words *focused on* (fō′kəst ŏn) mean
    A. taking a picture of.
    B. looking directly at.
    C. frightened by.
    D. wondering about.

"In class, when a student is expressing an opinion, I make sure all of the other students turn and are focused on that individual." (Paragraph 3)

_____ 3. In the sentence below, the word *visual* (vĭzh'oo-əl) means
   A. relating to the sense of hearing.
   B. relating to the sense of sight.
   C. boring.
   D. slow-moving.

   "Also, since I am a very visual learner and teacher, I am constantly making motions with my hands and on the board, and I want the kids to follow along with me and know exactly where I'm coming from." (Paragraph 4)

_____ 4. In the excerpt below, the word *baffled* (băf'əld) means
   A. angered.
   B. shocked.
   C. amused.
   D. puzzled.

   "As they were leaving, I always expected them to say thank you, but many didn't, and it baffled me. What were they thinking?" (Paragraph 5)

_____ 5. In the excerpt below, the word *model* (mŏd'l) means
   A. correct.
   B. see.
   C. be an example of.
   D. wear.

   "I then tell them that people work harder and with more effort if they feel appreciated and that they are making a difference. I make sure to model the type of behavior I expect, as I interact with all members of the staff in a friendly and respectful manner." (Paragraph 6)

Reading Comprehension Questions

Central Point and Main Ideas

_____ 1. Which sentence best expresses the central point of the selection?
   A. Clark treats all school staff members in a friendly and respectful way.
   B. Clark encourages his students to make eye contact because he knows that doing so will help them seem confident and earn respect.
   C. Although he is now a teacher, Clark spent a good deal of time working in fast food and waiting on tables in restaurants.
   D. Clark has students practice making eye contact with the adults in the school who are not teachers.

_____ 2. Which sentence best expresses the main idea of paragraph 4?
   A. When he was a student, Clark avoided daydreaming by focusing on the head in front of him or on his pencil.
   B. While teaching, Clark looks at his students' faces to make sure they aren't confused.
   C. Clark is a visual learner and teacher who always uses hand movements and writes on the board.
   D. Since he wants the students' full attention, Clark makes sure that his students keep their eyes on him.

Supporting Details

_____ 3. Clark tells his students that repeated glances to the upper left side mean that a person
   A. is left-handed.
   B. lacks confidence.
   C. is dishonest.
   D. is nervous.

_____ 4. Clark describes himself as
   A. an excellent teacher.
   B. a strict teacher.
   C. a visual learner and teacher.
   D. all of the above.

Transitions

_____ 5. The relationship between the two sentences below is one of
   A. addition.
   B. illustration.
   C. contrast.
   D. cause and effect.

   "If I could focus on the head in front of me or on my pencil, I was good to go, but watching the teacher just took something out of it. Therefore, I make sure to have all eyes on me at all times." (Paragraph 4)

_____ 6. The relationship of the second part of the sentence below (after the semicolon) to the first part is one of
   A. illustration.
   B. contrast.
   C. addition.
   D. cause and effect.

   "As they were leaving, I always expected them to say thank you; but many didn't, and it baffled me." (Paragraph 5)

Patterns of Organization

_____ 7. The selection mainly
   A. narrates important events in the author's life.
   B. contrasts those who make eye contact with those who don't.
   C. illustrates the importance of making eye contact.
   D. compares working in fast food with being a teacher.

Inferences

_____ 8. Which of the following statements would Clark probably agree with?
   A. "Because teachers are better educated than custodians and cafeteria workers, they should receive more respect."
   B. "If you look your boss in the eye when asking for a raise, he or she will probably become angry with you."
   C. "Working in fast food is something students should avoid."
   D. "Employees tend to work harder for bosses who treat them with respect than for those who don't."

_____ 9. We can infer from the selection that Clark
   A. is an easygoing teacher.
   B. has only been teaching a few years.
   C. believes that teachers should practice what they preach.
   D. has been a teacher for over twenty-five years.

_____ 10. The selection suggests that Clark
   A. is appreciated by the adults in his school who are not teachers.
   B. is too easygoing to be an effective teacher.
   C. once worked in a school cafeteria.
   D. looks down on people who work in the fast-food industry.

Summarizing

Complete the following summary of "Eye Contact" by filling in the blanks.

Because Ron Clark believes that making eye contact shows confidence and respect, he spends a lot of time encouraging his students to do so. One thing he has them do is practice talking to each other, while he _____ _____. In class, when a student is expressing an opinion, he makes sure all of the other students are focused on that individual. He doesn't allow them to _____ _____.

When he's teaching, he makes sure to have all eyes on him at all times. The many hours he spent working in fast food taught him that it is a sign of respect to look a person in the face. As a result, he _____ _____.

When his students go to the lunchroom, they aren't allowed to talk in the line, and when they get their food, they must _____ _____. In turn, they always thank the lunchroom workers and tell them to have a good day. The workers say _____ _____.

Clark concludes that we will be taken more seriously, and our actions will be much more appreciated, if we also make eye contact with the people we speak to.

Discussion Questions

1. Clark writes that he worked in fast food for "many a day." How do you think that working in the fast-food industry and in restaurants has affected his teaching?

2. Think of a person you know who is good at making eye contact. How does that person make you feel when she or he looks you in the eye? On the other hand, do you know anyone who is bad at making eye contact? What effect does his or her inability to make eye contact have on you?

3. Do you think you're good at making eye contact? In what situations might it be difficult for you to make eye contact? If you had the chance, would you sign up for Clark's class? Why or why not?

4. Eye contact is one form of nonverbal communication—in other words, communicating to others without using words. What are some other kinds of nonverbal communication? Under what circumstances might these alternate forms of communication be even more effective than spoken words? (For one response to this question, read "Body Language," page 203.)

Note: Writing assignments for this selection appear on page 611.

Check Your Performance   EYE CONTACT

Activity	Number Right	Points	Total
Vocabulary Questions (5 items)	_____	× 20 =	_____
		SCORE =	_____%
Reading Comprehension Questions			
Central Point and Main Ideas (2 items)	_____	× 8 =	_____
Supporting Details (2 items)	_____	× 8 =	_____
Transitions (2 items)	_____	× 8 =	_____
Patterns of Organization (1 item)	_____	× 8 =	_____
Inferences (3 items)	_____	× 8 =	_____
Summarizing (5 items)	_____	× 4 =	_____
		SCORE =	_____%

TOTAL SCORES: Vocabulary _____% Comprehension _____%

Enter your total scores into the **Reading Performance Chart: Ten Reading Selections** on the inside back cover.

4 Judge Judy Speaks

Judge Judy Sheindlin

Preview

As the saying goes, relationships are messy. And sometimes they are so messy that the two people involved end up in a courtroom. This next selection shows how a no-nonsense judge wastes little time in attempting to clean up the messes these couples have made.

Words to Watch

verbal (3): spoken
reap (5): gather, collect
obligation (5): duty
dictating (10): ordering

Payback Time

1 When people are in love and have stars in their eyes, they don't like to deal with the messy business of contracts. What really gets messy is when the relationship folds and one of the partners realizes too late that she doesn't have a leg to stand on. That's what happened to Amy.

2 **AMY:** When Paul and I met, I was an accountant, and he was driving a cab and going to school at night. Since we were planning a life together, we decided that he would go to school full-time and get his degree as a physical therapist. I would pay his tuition and the living expenses, and he'd help out with a part-time job. After he graduated, we'd get married and start a family, and then I would be the one to work part-time. Well, all went as planned, except he split when he graduated. I feel cheated, and I want to sue him for the money I laid out for his tuition. Isn't that fair?

3 **PAUL:** We both went into this relationship believing it was going to work out. I loved Amy. I believe she loved me. We made an arrangement that I would graduate from school early so we could get started on a family. Let me stress here that Amy was the one who really pushed for this arrangement. I was perfectly happy going to school part-time and paying for it myself. She insisted that it was better for us if I graduated sooner. The relationship didn't work out, and I regret that, but we never had an agreement that this was a loan. Never had a contract, verbal° or written, that said if things didn't work out, I would owe a cent.

4   **Judge Judy says:**

5   Amy, unfortunately, you should save the cost of filing a lawsuit. In order for you to be successful, you would have to establish that a contract existed between the two of you for Paul to reimburse his tuition and expenses, and there is no contract to that effect. This arrangement was an act of faith in your future, not a contract. Legally, Paul is absolutely right. Consider it money well spent on a good lesson for the future. Next time, make a contract, and memorialize your contribution as a loan. That's my legal answer. Don't sue; you'll lose. There are other issues here, too, having to do with common sense and judgment. Amy, since you were chomping at the bit to get started on your life plan together, which included marriage, why didn't you just go ahead and get married? Was something magical going to happen when Paul graduated? You left yourself without any protection whatsoever, because you didn't think things through. Paul, there is no legal claim against you, but that doesn't mean you're off the hook. She put you through school. You'll reap° the benefits of her hard work for the rest of your life, and you feel no moral obligation° to reimburse her? If that's the case, she's well rid of you.

JUDGE
JUDY SHEINDLIN

Just a Piece of Paper

6   It's the favorite refrain of gun-shy single people: "A wedding certificate is just a piece of paper!" Does anyone really believe that? Come on! Andrea certainly didn't believe it when Joe, her live-in of five years, tried it on her.

7   **ANDREA:** Joe and I have lived together for five years. We had both been divorced for many years when we met, and now we're in our mid-fifties. Even though he says he loves me and wants to be with me forever, Joe has a "thing" about marriage. He says since we're not planning to have children and we're both mature, it doesn't matter. But it matters to me.

8   **JOE:** We're more committed to each other than most of our married friends. We even wear rings. I just don't see the point. We aren't having children, and we've both been through the marriage thing before. We're perfectly happy just the way we are. Why change it?

9   **Judge Judy says:**

10   Do I hear the strains of "It's just a piece of paper?" You may be perfectly

happy, Joe, but Andrea isn't. If you love her and want to make her happy, you have to respect how important this is to her. Don't tell me that marriage is meaningless. You wouldn't be protesting so much if it were meaningless. I know something about this. After Jerry and I had been dating for about a year, I decided it was time to get married. He, on the other hand, suggested that marriage was merely a piece of paper, the state dictating° what the parameters of our lives should be. He, of course, noted that I had already been married, as had he. No one was even suggesting that I was a virgin, so living together would not have created the stir that it might have twenty years earlier. I listened to Jerry's arguments, and I didn't really know how to respond to him. I wasn't looking for a fight. Finally, I suggested that if he was committed to this concept and if he got my father's approval, I'd certainly be willing to go along with it. I knew full well that Jerry was scared to death of my father and would never even pose the question. We were married four months later. Joe, your excuses are weak. The fact that you're both mature and you're not planning to have children has nothing to do with saying "I do." Let me add that with old age creeping up on you, you should be eager to get married. Reliable health care providers are hard to come by.

It's the Money, Honey

11   Whenever someone says, "It's not about the money," I guarantee you, that's exactly what it's about—the money.

KEVIN: Martha and I started dating   12 about a year ago. We stopped seeing each other after about six months. While we were dating, Martha asked me to loan her some money. She had fallen behind in her car payments for two months. I trusted her, and I gave her almost $700. A couple of months later, we broke up. She never paid me back, and when I asked her about it, she said she shouldn't have to, because I used the car on the weekends, and it would have cost me more than $700 to rent one. That's beside the point. The money was a loan. She owes me.

MARTHA: This isn't about the   13 money, and Kevin knows it. He's bitter because I broke up with him. He wasn't talking loan when we were together, but now that we've split up, his tune has changed. Besides, he used my car, too. He should just leave me alone and get on with his life. I'm over him; I think he should try to get over me.

Judge Judy says: 14

Martha, stop acting like a princess.   15 You borrowed the money. Pay it back. Listen up out there in single-world land. WHEN IT'S A LOAN, GET IT IN WRITING. As a matter of fact, that's good advice for everyone: family loans, loans between friends. If you feel embarrassed asking for the written document, just say that Judge Judy insists. Blame me.

Vocabulary Questions

Use context clues to help you decide on the best definition for each italicized word. Then, in the space provided, write the letter of your choice.

 1. In the excerpt below, the word *memorialize* (mə-môr′ē-əl-īz′) means
   A. record.
   B. forget.
   C. celebrate.
   D. get rid of.

   "This arrangement was an act of faith in your future, not a contract. Legally, Paul is absolutely right. Consider it money well spent on a good lesson for the future. Next time, make a contract and memorialize your contribution as a loan." (Paragraph 5)

2. In the excerpt below, the word *reimburse* (rē′ĭm-bûrs′) means
   A. promote.
   B. repay.
   C. call.
   D. praise.

   "She put you through school. You'll reap the benefits of her hard work for the rest of your life, and you feel no moral obligation to reimburse her? If that's the case, she's well rid of you." (Paragraph 5)

3. In the sentence below, the word *refrain* (rĭ-frān′) means
   A. repeated phrase.
   B. moral lesson.
   C. food.
   D. type of event.

   "It's the favorite refrain of gun-shy single people: 'A wedding certificate is just a piece of paper!'" (Paragraph 6)

4. In the sentence below, the word *mature* (mə-tyŏŏr′) means
   A. disagreeing.
   B. older.
   C. confused.
   D. independent.

   "We had both been divorced for many years when we met, and now we're in our mid-fifties. Even though he says he loves me and wants to be with me forever, Joe has a "thing" about marriage. He says since we're not planning to have children and we're both mature, it doesn't matter." (Paragraph 7)

_C_ 5. In the excerpt below, the word *parameters* (pə-răm′ĭ-tərs) means
   A. joys.
   B. struggles.
   C. rules.
   D. events.

   > "After Jerry and I had been dating for about a year, I decided it was time to get married. He, on the other hand, suggested that marriage was merely a piece of paper, the state dictating what the parameters of our lives should be." (Paragraph 10)

Reading Comprehension Questions

Central Point and Main Ideas

_D_ 1. Which sentence best expresses the central point of this selection?
   A. Most people will try to get away without paying back loans when there is a breakup in the relationship.
   B. Judges typically understand relationships far better than most of us.
   C. Because many people in relationships are unable to solve their problems on their own, they go to court.
   D. Because relationships are complicated, partners should strive for clear communication and mutual respect.

_A_ 2. Which sentence best expresses the main idea of paragraph 5?
   A. Because Amy did not have a contract, she cannot sue Paul for the money she lent him.
   B. Amy's money was well spent, because it has taught her a lesson.
   C. Amy lent Paul the money because she thought they would have a future together.
   D. Paul knew more about the law than Amy when she paid for his tuition.

_D_ 3. Which sentence best expresses the main idea of paragraph 10?
   A. Men often have a fear of commitment and marriage.
   B. Jerry was more afraid of Judge Judy's father than of Judge Judy.
   C. Judge Judy believes that older people should be eager, not reluctant, to get married.
   D. Judge Judy, speaking from personal experience, points out that Joe's excuses for not marrying Andrea are weak.

Supporting Details

____F____ 4. TRUE OR FALSE? According to Judge Judy, friends should have a contract when borrowing money from each other, but contracts are not necessary with family members.

_____ 5. In his argument for why he and Andrea are just like married couples, Joe points out that they even
   A. own a home together.
   B. wear rings.
   C. have children.
   D. want to be together forever.

Transitions

_____ 6. The sentence below contains a(n)
   A. contrast signal.
   B. comparison signal.
   C. illustration signal.
   D. cause-effect signal.

   "You left yourself without any protection whatsoever, because you didn't think things through." (Paragraph 5)

Patterns of Organization

_____ 7. On the whole, paragraph 2
   A. lists the things Amy did for Paul during their relationship.
   B. compares and contrasts Paul's and Amy's ideas of what a "loan" is.
   C. defines *plans* and gives examples of them.
   D. uses time order to describe plans and what eventually happened.

_____ 8. Paragraph 8 is organized as a
   A. series of events that often lead to marriage.
   B. list of reasons why Joe doesn't think he and Andrea need to marry.
   C. contrast between married and unmarried couples.
   D. definition of marriage followed by examples.

Inferences

_____ 9. When Judge Judy says, "Do I hear the strains of 'It's just a piece of paper?'" we can infer that she
  A. thinks Joe and Andrea's problem is funny.
  B. has heard this same argument many times.
  C. is bitter about the fact that her husband once said the same thing.
  D. isn't sure what Joe is trying to say.

_____ 10. We can conclude from the reading that Judge Judy
  A. is not a real judge but only plays one on TV.
  B. often grows bored with hearing the same old legal problems.
  C. is a no-nonsense judge who sees through excuses and lies.
  D. once lent money to a friend without writing up a contract.

Summarizing

_____ Write the letter of the paragraph that best summarizes "Judge Judy Speaks."

  A. It is always best to form some sort of contract with a loved one when money is being lent so that there is no confusion later on about whether the money was a gift or a loan. Also, the idea that "it's only a piece of paper" is a weak excuse for not getting married. Judge Judy sees cases like the three presented in this selection frequently.

  B. Judge Judy offers advice on three common cases in this selection. Although her tone is often rather sharp and direct, television audiences enjoy watching her because she always sees through weak excuses and lies. It is clear that the judge has had a great deal of life experience and knows what she's talking about.

  C. In this selection, Judge Judy offers advice on three cases: two having to do with money being lent without a contract and one dealing with a couple that cannot agree on whether or not to get married. In her direct style, the judge indicates that the nature of relationships often makes couples reluctant to draw up contracts, but that is a mistake. Further, Judge Judy claims that saying "it's just a piece of paper" to avoid marriage is a weak excuse.

  D. It is not unusual for couples who were once in love to find themselves in a courtroom suing each other. Because relationships are complicated, most judges and lawyers recommend making up some sort of contract whenever money is lent, whether or not it makes the parties involved feel embarrassed or uncomfortable. Disagreeing about money is the number one reason for divorce, breakups, and lawsuits in the United States.

Discussion Questions

1. In the *Payback Time* story, Amy states, "Well, all went as planned, except he split when he graduated. I feel cheated." Do you think Amy should feel cheated? Or do you feel that "all is fair in love" and that Paul was not obligated to stay with Amy just because she was paying for (or lending money for) his education?

2. Even though there were no contracts written up when Paul and Martha received money from their respective girlfriend and boyfriend, Judge Judy indicates that paying the money back would still be the *right* thing to do. Do you agree with her? Or do you think the money was truly a gift and not a loan at the time it was given?

3. Joe's view that marriage is "just a piece of paper" is one that is shared by many people, male and female alike. Some feel that marriage is in the heart, not in a ceremony or a legally binding document. What do you think? Why is—or isn't—this "piece of paper" important?

4. Why are people reluctant to ask for a contract when they lend money to a friend or loved one? How would you feel if your boyfriend/girlfriend asked you to sign a contract before he or she gave you money? Alternatively, how would you feel about asking a boyfriend/girlfriend or family member to sign a contract before you made a loan? And if the person didn't pay you back, would you sue? Why or why not?

Note: Writing assignments for this selection appear on page 612.

Check Your Performance   JUDGE JUDY SPEAKS

Activity	Number Right	Points	Total
Vocabulary Questions (5 items)	_____	× 20 =	_____
		SCORE =	_____%
Reading Comprehension Questions			
Central Point and Main Ideas (3 items)	_____	× 8 =	_____
Supporting Details (2 items)	_____	× 8 =	_____
Transitions (1 item)	_____	× 8 =	_____
Patterns of Organization (2 items)	_____	× 8 =	_____
Inferences (2 items)	_____	× 8 =	_____
Summarizing (1 item)	_____	× 20 =	_____
		SCORE =	_____%

TOTAL SCORES: Vocabulary _____% Comprehension _____%

Enter your total scores into the **Reading Performance Chart: Ten Reading Selections** on the inside back cover.

5 Read All About It

Fran DeBlasio

Preview

When are people too old to turn their lives around? Ten? Twenty? Twenty-five? Here is the story of someone who made her life very different—and better— beginning at the age of thirty-five.

Words to Watch

decipher (1): read or make sense of something
unique (2): unusual
pass the buck (4): pass the responsibility on to someone else
chaos (5): disorder
landmarks (8): objects or structures that help people find their way
stunned (10): shocked

1   *For most of her life, Fran DeBlasio, 36, tried to conceal her shame. Unable to read the street signs or subway maps in her native Manhattan, let alone decipher° warning labels on medicine bottles, she lived, like many illiterates, in constant fear of the unknown. An even greater terror was that friends would discover her secret. "I was embarrassed," DeBlasio says. "I thought there must be something wrong with me."*

2   *DeBlasio's case is not unique°. Studies suggest that perhaps one in ten adult Americans is unable to read well enough to complete this article. The costs to society— in terms of welfare and unemployment payments and underproductivity—are enormous. With a growing awareness of the literacy crisis, a lucky few are getting help. DeBlasio enrolled last year in a program sponsored by Literacy Volunteers of New York City, a nonprofit organization, and can now read and write at a junior-high-school level. She described her personal triumph to reporter Jane Sugden.*

3   By the time I reached junior high school, I could read a little, but not very much. Whenever I was asked to read aloud in class, I felt terrible. I was afraid and nervous. I tried to tell myself, "Fran, you're smart. You have something up there." But I was confused and didn't know where to turn. My parents had separated when I was young, and my mother supported me and my two brothers by working as a cleaning lady. She was a traditional Italian woman who always told us how important it was to

get a good education. But even after she went to my school to try to find out why I was having problems, nothing changed.

4   I was going to public school in a working-class neighborhood in Manhattan. When I had to take written tests, I scribbled down some answers. I almost always flunked, but they still passed me on to the next grade anyway. When I told my teachers I was scared I wouldn't be able to keep up, they all gave me the same story: "Go home this summer and study hard on your vacation. If you work hard, you'll do better next year." But the impression I really had was they thought I was just too stupid to learn and would drop out sooner or later anyway. It's as if everyone just wanted to pass the buck° and get rid of me as quickly as possible. No one ever tried to give me any special help with my reading, and there weren't any experts at the school who knew how to teach people who didn't catch on right away. They just made me feel it was all my fault—that I didn't try hard enough. Meanwhile, I felt rejected and alone. Very alone. I get so angry when I think about that now.

5   Even though I had never been a discipline problem, in the seventh grade they put me in a class for kids who were troublemakers or wise guys. It was total chaos°. All day, the teacher yelled at the students, and they yelled back. It was no good for learning.

6   High school was worse. I went to an all-girls school where a lot of the kids were tough. Fights broke out

almost every day. I was too frightened to use the john because girls had been attacked there, sometimes sexually attacked by other girls. When I turned 17, I couldn't take it any more and quit. I figured, "What's the difference? I'm not learning anything anyway."

7   After quitting school, I didn't know what to do. Baby-sitting was one of the few jobs I could handle. I also worked at an amusement park in New Jersey, taking tickets for kiddie rides. Once I went to apply for a city job. I didn't understand most of the application, so I asked to take it home. But she said I had to fill it out there. I said, "Never mind. I don't want this job anyway," and ran out. I didn't want to be a bum, but I was very afraid of being rejected.

8   Trying to get a driver's license was impossible because I knew I couldn't pass the written test. Even simple street directions were a problem because I was not able to read signs. At the same time, I was ashamed to tell my friends I couldn't read, so I bluffed a lot. I memorized landmarks° in order to get around. Since I couldn't understand the menus at restaurants, I learned to be a

good actress. I asked my friends, "What are you having? What looks good?" Sometimes at parties, people wanted to play games like Scrabble, and I had to fake a headache. When people talked about the books they were reading— maybe a best-seller—I'd say, "I read sports books," because sports was one of the few subjects I could talk about.

9   By the time I was 25, my reading had improved slightly from studying the sports pages of the newspaper. Then a friend helped me fill out an application to work in the mail distribution department of a bank and—I couldn't believe it—I got the job. I had a tough time at first, learning to tell the difference between hundreds of different names. But my boss was very helpful. I learned to do the job well and began to feel much better about myself.

10   In June 1985, after ten years on the job, I was offered a promotion to assistant supervisor, but I was terrified because the new position involved a lot of paperwork. Luckily, a friend told me about Literacy Volunteers and arranged for me to meet with Barbara Greenfield, one of the coordinators of the program. When I told Barbara about my fear of taking on the new position, she volunteered to tutor me during her own free time. I was stunned° that someone would go out of her way to help me like that. When I walked out of her office, I felt born again.

11   Within a few months, I joined a small reading group which meets for two-hour sessions three times a week. When I first began, I would read a passage twenty-five times and not know what it meant. Or I would get hung up on one word for a half hour without getting a sense of the whole sentence. But during one session a few weeks later, one of my tutors asked me questions about something I read, and I suddenly realized I was giving her the answers. She said, "Fran, you understand!" I said, "Holy Christ! This is me. I can read."

12   The tutors also encouraged me to write. At first I had trouble putting down a single sentence, but before long I was writing stories and even poetry. I particularly like to write about my family. At a special meeting of my reading group one night, I recited a story I had written on my birthday about my mother, who died three years ago. When I finished, the whole group had tears in their eyes. I've written other pieces about my grandfather, who is ninety years old and lives with me. When he was in the hospital for a stroke three months ago, I sat with him every day and wrote about my feelings.

13   Things that once seemed impossible are now fun. I've read books about George Washington and Babe Ruth. I'm studying for my high-school equivalency exam and my driver's license test. I recently went to see an opera and was able to read an English translation of the story that they projected above the stage. Wow, that made me feel good! Even watching TV is different. Now I can read the ads. I understand street signs, menus, all those things. It's as if a great burden has been lifted off my back.

14   Recently, I've confessed to my friends about the problem I always had reading. One very close friend I used to play softball with moved to Florida several years ago and kept writing to me. She didn't know I couldn't write back, so she called me one time to ask why she hadn't received any letters from me. I said, "Oh, I'm just not very good about writing." I was ashamed to tell her the whole truth, so I had a friend write a letter for me. A few months ago, I wrote her a letter in my own handwriting and explained my problem. I told her how much I was learning and how exciting it was to finally be able to read. She wrote back and said, "I'm very proud of you. Very proud. I'm glad you told me." She understood.

Vocabulary Questions

Use context clues to help you decide on the best definition for each italicized word. Then, in the space provided, write the letter of your choice.

_____   1. In the excerpt below, the word *rejected* (rĭ-jĕkt′ĭd) means
   A. refused.
   B. hired.
   C. honored.
   D. forgotten.

   "I said, 'Never mind. I don't want this job anyway,' and ran out. I didn't want to be a bum, but I was very afraid of being rejected." (Paragraph 7)

_____   2. In the excerpt below, the word *bluffed* (blŭft) means
   A. coughed.
   B. talked.
   C. questioned.
   D. pretended.

   ". . . I was ashamed to tell my friends I couldn't read, so I bluffed a lot. I memorized landmarks. . . . I learned to be a good actress." (Paragraph 8)

_____ 3. In the excerpt below, the word *recited* (rĭ-sīt′ĭd) means
    A. thought about.
    B. sang.
    C. read aloud.
    D. examined.

> "At a special meeting of my reading group one night, I recited a story I had written. . . . When I finished, the whole group had tears in their eyes." (Paragraph 12)

_____ 4. In the excerpt below, the word *projected* (prə-jĕkt′ĭd) means
    A. read out loud.
    B. made appear.
    C. erased.
    D. forgot.

> "I . . . was able to read an English translation of the story that they projected above the stage." (Paragraph 13)

_____ 5. In the excerpt below, the word *burden* (bûr′dn) means
    A. shirt.
    B. load.
    C. bump.
    D. pleasure.

> "I understand street signs, menus, all those things. It's as if a great burden has been lifted off my back." (Paragraph 13)

Reading Comprehension Questions

Central Point and Main Ideas

_____ 1. Which sentence best expresses the central point of the selection?
    A. DeBlasio could not read.
    B. Learning to read has changed DeBlasio's life.
    C. DeBlasio felt ashamed that she couldn't read.
    D. DeBlasio didn't learn to read in school.

_____ 2. Which sentence best expresses the main idea of paragraph 7?
    A. DeBlasio could handle baby-sitting.
    B. DeBlasio once worked at an amusement park taking tickets for children's rides.
    C. DeBlasio couldn't fill out the application form for a city job.
    D. DeBlasio's inability to read limited her job opportunities and made applying for jobs difficult.

_____ 3. Which sentence best expresses the main idea of paragraph 13?
  A. DeBlasio is enjoying activities she thought she would never be able to do.
  B. DeBlasio can now read books.
  C. DeBlasio is studying for a high-school equivalency exam and a driver's license test.
  D. DeBlasio can even read the English translation of an opera.

Supporting Details

_____ 4. Before she was tutored by a Literacy Volunteers coordinator, DeBlasio
  A. could not read at all.
  B. never even wished she could read.
  C. could read a little.
  D. could read enough to feel very capable at work.

Transitions

_____ 5. Paragraph 7 begins with a transition that shows
  A. addition.
  B. time.
  C. an example.
  D. cause and effect.

_____ 6. The relationship expressed in the sentence below is one of
  A. contrast.
  B. cause and effect.
  C. time.
  D. addition.

  Trying to get a driver's license was impossible because I knew I couldn't pass the written test. (Paragraph 8)

Patterns of Organization

_____ 7. The pattern of organization of paragraph 13 is
  A. time order.
  B. list of items.
  C. definition and example.
  D. contrast.

Inferences

_____ 8. DeBlasio implies that
- A. she was too stupid to learn to read in public school.
- B. her teachers did the best they could for her.
- C. the schools she went to were not good places for her to learn in.
- D. in school she managed to keep her self-image strong despite the fact that she couldn't read.

_____ 9. TRUE OR FALSE? DeBlasio implies that she should not have been put in a class for students who were discipline problems.

_____ 10. From this article we can conclude that
- A. people can get along very well without reading.
- B. those who can't read may find ways of hiding that fact.
- C. when people don't learn to read in school, it is all their own fault.
- D. once people reach their thirties, it is almost impossible for them to learn new skills.

Summarizing

Complete the following summary of "Read All About It" by filling in the blanks.

DeBlasio didn't learn to read in her schools, which did a poor job of teaching her. After she quit high school, there were few jobs she could tackle, and her everyday activities were restricted because she couldn't read. Ashamed of her inability to read, DeBlasio hid it from her friends. By the time she was 25, however, her reading had improved a little, and she got a job _____.
After working at the bank for ten years, _____

_____. She wasn't sure, however, that she could handle the paperwork of the new job. Luckily, a friend told her about Literacy Volunteers, and she began to learn to read with the help of a tutor. Later she also joined _____ and began to write. DeBlasio is now able to enjoy many activities she once thought impossible for her. She feels much happier with herself and has even told _____

_____.

Discussion Questions

1.   Do you know anybody who has trouble reading? How does that trouble affect his or her life?

2.   Just how difficult is it to live in our society without being able to read? To get an idea of the answer to this question, think about your activities at home, at work or school, when shopping, in restaurants, and while driving. How much of what you do involves reading?

3.   DeBlasio gives a bleak picture of the schools she attended. In what ways were your own schools like, or unlike, hers? Why do you think her teachers behaved as they did?

4.   We tend to think that people don't learn important new skills as they get older, but DeBlasio's story contradicts that idea. Describe a person or persons you know who have been able to learn new skills as they get older. What skills have these people mastered, and what character traits might be responsible for their continued progress?

Note: Writing assignments for this selection appear on page 612.

Check Your Performance   READ ALL ABOUT IT

Activity	Number Right	Points	Total
Vocabulary Questions (5 items)	_____	× 20 =	_____
		SCORE =	_____ %
Reading Comprehension Questions			
Central Point and Main Ideas (3 items)	_____	× 8 =	_____
Supporting Details (1 item)	_____	× 8 =	_____
Transitions (2 items)	_____	× 8 =	_____
Patterns of Organization (1 item)	_____	× 8 =	_____
Inferences (3 items)	_____	× 8 =	_____
Summarizing (4 items)	_____	× 5 =	_____
		SCORE =	_____ %

TOTAL SCORES: Vocabulary _____ % Comprehension _____ %

Enter your total scores into the **Reading Performance Chart: Ten Reading Selections** on the inside back cover.

6 Erika Hilario
Beth Johnson

Preview

Many people, when faced with tremendous hardship, give up easily and accept the raw deal life has given them. Others, however, fight day after day and year after year for a better life and a fair deal. In the following selection, you will meet a remarkable woman who, having won that fight for herself, continues it for the sake of her children.

Words to Watch

recyclable (4): reusable
siblings (7): brothers and sisters
smuggle (18): to bring something in illegally to another country
desolate (20): empty and lonely
bilingual (36): able to speak in two languages (here, in English and Spanish)

1   *"Ándale! Apúrate!* Come on, *niños!* We're gonna be late!"

2   Luisa and Erick Hilario rush out of their room, carrying schoolbooks, a soccer ball, cleats, and water bottles. Their mom, Erika, hurries them out the door and down the narrow steps of their apartment building. She carries a cooler filled with cut-up fruit. They hit the sidewalk almost running.

3   The Hilarios are in a hurry. That is true on this particular day, when they're starting the two-plus-hour trip by train, bus, and foot from their neighborhood in Los Angeles to Pasadena. There, Luisa, 11, plays with one of the best soccer clubs in California. It is true on every other day as well. On weekends

and weekdays, from early mornings to late evenings, in Spanish and in English, the family hurries. On the soccer field, Luisa scores goals. Off the field, the family focuses on goals of another sort—goals that go far beyond the soccer field.

4   "Through soccer, Luisa sees another world," Erika says. In their own neighborhood, Boyle Heights, most residents have not finished high school. More Spanish is heard than English. Luisa's and Erick's father is a long-distance trucker who is rarely home. To earn money, Luisa decorates notebooks with colorful duct tape and sells them to her classmates, and Erick, 8, picks up recyclable° bottles

and cans. But in Pasadena, where the "CZ Elite" soccer club practices, Luisa plays alongside the children of doctors, lawyers, and professors. Those kids will go on to highly ranked universities. They will have professional careers, live in fancy houses, and be financially independent. These are all things that Erika desperately wants for her own children. Especially for Luisa. In Luisa, Erika sees the little girl she once was, and the chances that she never had.

5   "Life is very heavy for a woman," says Erika. "Women have to be the models if things *are* going to change." And Erika is determined things are going to change. Her brown-skinned children are going to enjoy the same opportunities as the wealthier Anglos around them, even if it takes her last ounce of strength to make it so. Although Erika's own life has indeed been heavy, she has taken her own pain and turned it into something amazingly strong and positive.

6   From the outside, Erika doesn't seem unusual. She didn't finish high school. She is a pretty woman, but she doesn't fuss over her appearance. Her usual uniform is sweat pants and T-shirts. Her beautiful red-brown hair is pulled back into a messy ponytail. She struggles with English, substituting the occasional Spanish word when she forgets. For work, she picks up a little money counting tortillas on a factory assembly line. But as she tells her own story, it becomes clear that she is extraordinary. Thinking back over the years, she can't keep tears from spilling down her cheeks. But she dries those tears and reminds herself, "Like I tell my kids—look forward, always forward. Never back."

7   Erika was born in Mexico City 32 years ago, to poor parents who could not read or write. Her father worked as a driver; her mother cleaned houses for rich families. Erika was the middle child of five siblings°. As she grew up, she realized that her father had another wife and children elsewhere in town. Nobody seemed to think that was unusual. And no one thought it was unusual that he beat Erika's mother and the children.

8   "My father was very *machista*," Erika says, using the Spanish word that means sexist, overbearing, and often abusive to women. "He controlled our home entirely. If my mother went to the market to buy a chicken, he might decide she was with another man. So he'd beat her when she came home. He would hit us for anything, even spilling a drop of water. We lived in a crowded city, but we had no friends. We weren't supposed to even say hello to people. We kids went to school and came home."

9   Worse yet, when Erika was 9, her father began to sexually abuse her. Erika tried to tell her mother, but it did no good. "In my house, to speak of sex was a sin," she says, tears running down her cheeks. "She never did anything to help me. But I do not blame her. I love my mother. She was ignorant, she was afraid. I can't judge her."

10   Instead of blaming her mother, Erika tried to help her. "My father would threaten to leave us, and she'd cry and say, 'No, no.' I'd tell her, 'Let him go! We'll be better off!' When he'd hit her, I'd try to pull him off."

11   Erika's strong spirit made her father angry. When she finished elementary school, he told her he would no longer pay her school fees. "I loved school," she says. "I threw myself at his feet, begging him to let me study. But he said that educating a girl was throwing money away."

12   And so, at the age of 11—the age Luisa is today—Erika went to work. She attended school in the morning, took the bus home, showered, and put on a work uniform. By 3 o'clock she was at a local market, where she and other children bagged groceries and stocked shelves for tips. By working until midnight, she was able to keep paying her school fees for three more years.

13   When Erika was 14, she began seeing a boy who was four years older. As her boyfriend, he was "sweet, nice. Never jealous." He taught her some valuable skills—how to drive a car, how to change a tire. She ran away from home to live with him, to get away from her abusive father.

14   But once Erika moved in with the boyfriend, everything changed. Now he began to act like her father—*machista*. He hit her if she so much as said "good morning" to another man. In addition, he used drugs, which he introduced Erika to.

15   Finally a crisis came. Erika was asleep when her boyfriend, crazy on drugs, attacked her with his fists, beating her savagely. "I truly thought I was going to die," she remembers. In great pain, blood streaming down her face, she ran from one neighbor's apartment to another, begging for help. (She learned later she had a fractured skull.) One after another, women turned her away. "They said they didn't want a problem," Erica says bitterly. They were too afraid of their husbands to help a beaten woman.

16   Afraid to stay in the same town with her ex-boyfriend, Erika fled to another part of Mexico to live with an uncle's family. There she thought about her options. Ahead of her, she could see two ways of life. "I could live like my mother. Or I could be with bad people, the drugs and all that. I said no, those are not for me."

17   Erika spoke to another uncle, one who was living in Los Angeles. He offered to help her come to the United States.

18   "He would pay a *coyote* (a person hired to smuggle° people) to take me across the border," she says. "I decided to go. I would live in L.A., pay him back, and start a new life."

19   Erika's first attempt to cross the border almost ended any hopes she had of a better life—or perhaps of life at all.

20   She was one of a group of 50 people, 49 of whom were men. They were guided by three *coyotes*. The group walked for two full days, through desolate° desert territory. One *coyote* attached himself to Erika, never leaving her side. As the group became more scattered, he separated her from the others.

21   "I didn't know where I was," Erika says. "We lost sight of the group, and I was alone with him. He began saying dirty things." She was terrified, but there was nowhere to go to get away. Finally they stopped to rest, sheltering under a rock. The *coyote* became aggressive. He tried to force Erika to touch him in sexual ways. She fought him off, moving as far from him as she could. Finally he fell asleep.

22   Alone in the desert night, Erika wept with rage and fear. She thought of her father's abuse, of her boyfriend's beatings. "I thought, 'WHY? Why me, again? Why do men treat women like this, like *basura*, like garbage? We are not objects just to be used!'"

23   Looking at the sleeping man, Erika thought of what he would do when he woke. She came to a decision. "I will not let this happen," she told herself. "If I have to kill him, I will do it." She searched for a heavy rock. She held it, thinking how she would smash his head.

24   And then the Border Patrol showed up.

25   "Thank God they came," Erika says, shaking her head at the horror of the memory. "I would have assassinated him."

26   Erika and the rest of the group were taken back into Mexico, where they were detained briefly in jail and then released. After a week, Erika was ready to try again. Again, she traveled with a group of 50 people, but this time the *coyote* "was a good person. He told us, 'If you have food, share it.' When it snowed, he covered me with his *chamarra*, his jacket."

27   Soon, Erika reached Los Angeles. In time, she gained legal residency in the United States. She met her husband, Luis, a gentle man 11 years older than she. As Luisa and then Erick came along, Erika discovered a passion for parenting. She threw herself into learning English. "In Mexico, we have a saying, '*A la tierra que fueres, haz lo que vieres.*' When you go to a new place, you do as those people do. And to help my children here, I have to speak English."

28   As the children started school, Erika became determined that though they were not rich, and were the children of immigrants, and didn't live in a fancy part of town, they were still going to get opportunities that more affluent American kids get. When classmates at Luisa's kindergarten teased her about her crooked teeth, making her self-conscious about smiling, Erika pulled Luisa out. She went to a local private school and begged until they gave her a discount on tuition. She enrolled Luisa (and later Erick), cut her household budget to the bone, and somehow found the money every month to pay the fees.

29   Erika watched her children's school progress like a hawk, demanding that they do their best. She posted learning tools, like multiplication tables and spelling lists, all over the house. She refused to install cable TV. "We can use that money for shoes and for lessons," she said. She went to library sales to buy inexpensive books to fill the bookcase that stands in Erick and Luisa's bedroom.

30   Today, all of Erika's efforts are paying off. The children are excellent students. Luisa is preparing to take the admission test to one of the highest-ranked middle schools in Los Angeles. "We will have to work very, very hard," says Erika. When Erika speaks of her children's futures, she always says, "We." Recently, the family was written about in a story in the *Los Angeles Times*. To everyone's delight, a reader offered to pay for Luisa to get her teeth straightened. She now proudly flashes a mouth full of braces. Friendly and giggly, she mentions that she dreams of being a professional soccer player.

31   Erika reminds her, "Maybe, but not many people can play professional soccer. You need Plan B."

32   Luisa agrees. "I'd also like to be a veterinarian," she says. Erika nods in approval. That is a more realistic goal.

33   Thanks to her mother, Luisa knows that her dreams can become a reality.

She can go to college. She can become a veterinarian, or a professional athlete. She lives in a world where women are not treated like *basura*.

34   "Luisa sees her teammates, and their families," her mom says. "I tell her, she can study and work, and she can live like them. She can be independent, not having to rely on anyone else. Or, she can stay in this house and be one of those." Erika points to the alley beside the house, where young people hang out to smoke marijuana.

35   "I don't judge them," she says of the pot smokers. "I was one of them. But my children—they deserve more."

36   Erika sends her children off to complete their homework. She'll check it when they are done. Later in the evening, she'll bring a whiteboard into the living room, where Luisa's soccer ribbons and trophies line a shelf, so they can have a Spanish lesson. Erika insists that the children be fully bilingual°, using perfect grammar in both languages.

37   As the children study, and Erika cleans up the kitchen from dinner, her words hang in the air: "Women have to be the models if things are going to change." Once beaten, abused, and denied an education, the amazing Erika Hilario has found the strength to become that model.

Vocabulary Questions

Use context clues to help you decide on the best definition for each italicized word. Then, in the space provided, write the letter of your choice.

_____ 1. In the sentence below, the word *overbearing* (ō′vər-bâr′ĭng) means
  A. drunk.
  B. bossy.
  C. weak.
  D. false.

  "'My father was very *machista*,' she says, using the Spanish word that means sexist, overbearing, and often abusive to women." (Paragraph 8)

_____ 2. In the excerpt below, the word *crisis* (krī′sĭs) means
  A. religious experience.
  B. happy ending.
  C. stressful event.
  D. puzzling mystery.

  "Finally a crisis came. Erika was asleep when her boyfriend, crazy on drugs, attacked her with his fists, beating her savagely. 'I truly thought I was going to die,' she remembers." (Paragraph 15)

_____ 3. In the excerpt below, the word *assassinated* (ə-săs′ə-nā′tĭd) means
  A. left.
  B. argued with.
  C. stayed with.
  D. killed.

  "'If I have to kill him, I will do it.' She searched for a heavy rock. She held it, thinking how she would smash his head.
  "And then the Border Patrol showed up.
  "'Thank God they came,' Erika says, shaking her head at the horror of the memory. 'I would have assassinated him.'" (Paragraphs 23–25)

_____ 4. In the sentence below, the word *detained* (dĭ-tānd′) means
  A. held in custody.
  B. entertained.
  C. judged.
  D. allowed to sleep.

  "Erika and the rest of the group were taken back into Mexico, where they were detained briefly in jail and then released." (Paragraph 26)

_____ 5. In the excerpt below, the word *affluent* (ăf′lōō-ənt) means
     A. athletic.
     B. wealthy.
     C. rude.
     D. eager.

> "As the children started school, Erika became determined that though they were not rich, and were the children of immigrants, and didn't live in a fancy part of town, they were still going to get opportunities that more affluent American kids get." (Paragraph 28)

Reading Comprehension Questions

Central Point and Main Ideas

_____ 1. Which sentence best expresses the central point of the selection?
     A. Erika Hilario had a very difficult childhood that affected her entire life.
     B. When you are living in a situation that will never get better, your best choice is to leave.
     C. Most mothers' dearest hope is that their children's lives will be better than theirs.
     D. By working hard, staying positive, and always looking forward, Erika overcame hardships and now teaches her children to do the same.

_____ 2. Which sentence best expresses the main idea of paragraphs 27–29?
     A. Erika has worked hard and done a number of things to improve her life and her children's lives.
     B. Because Luisa's classmates made fun of her teeth, Erika did everything she could to transfer Luisa to a better school.
     C. Hard work occasionally pays off.
     D. Erika's husband earns the money, and Erika is in charge of the household and the children's education and upbringing.

Supporting Details

_____ 3. The major supporting details of this reading are a series of
     A. questions about how Erika was able to overcome so many hardships.
     B. steps in the process of Erika's coming to the United States.
     C. techniques Erika used to improve her children's education.
     D. events in the lives of Erika and her family.

_____ 4. TRUE OR FALSE? Erika Hilario believes that those who move to the United States from Mexico should learn English.

Transitions

_____ 5. The sentence below begins with a transition that shows
    A. time.
    B. addition.
    C. cause and effect.
    D. contrast.

      "Instead of blaming her mother, Erika tried to help her." (Paragraph 11)

_____ 6. The signal words at the beginning of the sentence below show
    A. definition and example.
    B. contrast.
    C. time.
    D. addition.

      "Later in the evening, she'll bring a whiteboard into the living room, where Luisa's soccer ribbons and trophies line a shelf, so they can have a Spanish lesson." (Paragraph 36)

Patterns of Organization

_____ 7. On a whole, the main pattern of organization of this essay is
    A. list of items.
    B. time order.
    C. cause and effect.
    D. contrast.

_____ 8. The main pattern of organization of paragraph 8 is
    A. cause and effect.
    B. time order.
    C. contrast.
    D. definition and example.

Inferences

_____ 9. The sentence "Erika's first attempt to cross the border almost ended any hopes she had of a better life—or perhaps of life at all" implies that
    A. Erika's life was in real danger during her first attempt to cross the border.
    B. Erika was suicidal during that first attempt at crossing the border.
    C. There was no hope that Erika would ever make it to the United States.
    D. Erika made many mistakes when she first tried to come to the United States.

_____ 10. By the end of the selection, we can conclude that Erika's children
     A. will have a difficult time getting good enough grades to get into college.
     B. are more interested in sports than in school.
     C. will have far more opportunities than their mother ever had.
     D. are not particularly close to their father.

Summarizing

Complete the following summary of "Erika Hilario" by filling in the blanks.

Erika Hilario grew up poor in Mexico in a large family. When Erika was still a child, she discovered that her father was also married to a second woman across town. Worse than this, Erika's father beat her mother and the children and was extremely controlling. Worst of all, however, was the fact that _____

_____. Although Erika told her mother about it, her mother did nothing. Eventually, Erika left home and moved in with a boyfriend who also turned out to be abusive. At her wits' end, Erika decided to come to the United States with "coyotes" who led a group to the border. Although her first attempt to come into the United States was a disaster, her second attempt was successful. Soon, Erika arrived in Los Angeles, and in time she _____

_____. Erika gave birth to two children, Luisa and Erick, and was determined that their lives would be better than hers. Although they did not have a lot of money, Erika made certain that her children got many of the same opportunities given to privileged American kids. When classmates teased Luisa about her crooked teeth, _____

_____. Erika insists that her children study hard, and she spends money on books and lessons instead of luxuries like cable TV. Today, Erika's determination is paying off. Both children are excellent students, and even though Luisa says she'd like to be a professional soccer player, she _____

_____.

"Women have to be the models if things are going to change," Erika explains. Even though Erika was poor, beaten, abused and denied an education as a young girl, today _____.

Discussion Questions

1. Most fathers would be proud of a daughter who was emotionally strong. Why do you think "Erika's strong spirit made her father angry"?

2. Erika says that her mother never did anything to help her when she told her mother that her father was abusing her sexually. Today, Erika says that she doesn't blame or judge her mother. Should she blame her mother? Why or why not? What would you have done if you had been in her mother's position?

3. When Erika is attacked by the "coyote," she becomes angry and wonders, "WHY? Why me, again? Why do men treat women like this, like *basura*, like garbage?" In your opinion, why *do* some men treat women this way? How should a woman respond to this kind of treatment? Do you think Erika's responses were appropriate? Why or why not?

4. Why does Erika want her daughter to play soccer in a better neighborhood with more privileged kids? In general, would you say exposing a child to a different lifestyle is a good idea—or not? Explain.

Note: Writing assignments for this selection appear on page 613.

Check Your Performance   ERIKA HILARIO

Activity	Number Right	Points	Total
Vocabulary Questions (5 items)	_____	× 20 =	_____
		SCORE =	_____%
Reading Comprehension Questions			
Central Point and Main Ideas (2 items)	_____	× 8 =	_____
Supporting Details (2 items)	_____	× 8 =	_____
Transitions (2 items)	_____	× 8 =	_____
Patterns of Organization (2 items)	_____	× 8 =	_____
Inferences (2 items)	_____	× 8 =	_____
Summarizing (5 items)	_____	× 4 =	_____
		SCORE =	_____%

TOTAL SCORES: Vocabulary _____% Comprehension _____%

Enter your total scores into the **Reading Performance Chart: Ten Reading Selections** on the inside back cover.

7 How to Make It in College, Now That You're Here

Brian O'Keeney

Preview

Give yourself some credit—you're now a college student! But getting into college is only the first step. It's time to plan not only how to deal with the academic demands of college, but also how to cope with the additional demands of family, friends, and work. Based on interviews with college students, this article offers you practical, realistic steps to college success.

Words to Watch

hurdle (1): difficulty
coping with (2): dealing with
queasy (3): upset
distracted (4): sidetracked
relatively (4): compared with something else
plod (7): walk slowly and heavily
maintain (13): keep
hermit (13): one who lives alone, apart from others
simmer down (21): calm down

1 Today is your first day on campus. You were a high-school senior three months ago. Or maybe you've been at home with your children for the last ten years. Or maybe you work full-time, and you're coming to school to start the process that leads to a better job. Whatever your background is, you're probably not too concerned today with staying in college. After all, you just got over the hurdle° (and the paperwork) of applying to this place and organizing your life so that you could attend. And today, you're confused and tired. Everything is a hassle, from finding the classrooms to standing in line at the bookstore. But read my advice anyway. And if you don't read it today, save this article. You might want to look at it a little further down the road.

2 By the way, if this isn't your first day, don't skip this article. Maybe you

haven't been doing as well in your studies as you'd hoped. Or perhaps you've had problems juggling your work schedule, your class schedule, and your social life. If so, read on. You're about to get the inside story on making it in college. On the basis of my own experience as a final-year student, and on dozens of interviews with successful students, I've worked out a no-fail system for coping with° college. These are the inside tips every student needs to do well in school. I've put myself in your place, and I'm going to answer the questions that will cross (or have already crossed) your mind during your stay here.

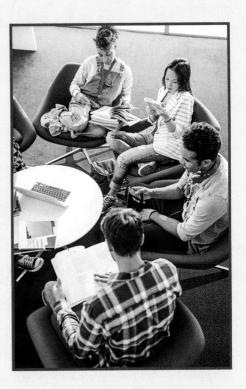

What's the Secret to Getting Good Grades?

3   It all comes down to getting those grades, doesn't it? After all, you came here for some reason, and you're going to need passing grades to get the credits or degree you want. Many of us never did much studying in high school; most of the learning we did took place in the classroom. College, however, is a lot different. You're really on your own when it comes to passing courses. In fact, sometimes you'll feel as if nobody cares if you make it or not. Therefore, you've got to figure out a study system that gets results. Sooner or later, you'll be alone with those books. After that, you'll be sitting in a classroom with an exam sheet on your desk. Whether you stare at that exam with a queasy° stomach, or whip

through it fairly confidently, depends on your study techniques. Most of the successful students I talked to agreed that the following eight study tips deliver solid results:

4   **1. Set up a study place.** Those students you see "studying" in the cafeteria or game room aren't learning much. You just can't learn when you're distracted° by people and noise. Even the library can be a bad place to study if you constantly find yourself watching the clouds outside or the students walking through the stacks. It takes guts to sit, alone, in a quiet place in order to study. But you have to do it. Find a room at home or a spot in the library that's

relatively° quiet—and boring. When you sit there, you won't have much to do except study.

5   **2. Get into a study frame of mind.** When you sit down, do it with the attitude that you're really going to get this studying done. You're not going to doodle on your notebook or make a list for the supermarket. Decide that you're going to study and learn now, so that you can move on to more interesting things as soon as possible.

6   **3. Give yourself rewards.** If you sweat out a block of study time, and do a good job on it, treat yourself. You deserve it. You can "psych" yourself up for studying by promising to reward yourself afterward. A present for yourself can be anything from a favorite TV show to a relaxing bath to a dish of double-chocolate ice cream.

7   **4. Skim the textbook first.** Lots of students sit down with an assignment like "read chapter 5, pages 125–150" and do just that. They turn to page 125 and start to read. After a while, they find that they have no idea what they just read. For the last ten minutes, they've been thinking about their five-year-old or what they're going to eat for dinner. Eventually, they plod° through all the pages but don't remember much afterward.

8   In order to prevent this problem, skim the textbook chapter first. This means the following: look at the title, the subtitles, the headings, the pictures, and the first and last paragraphs. Try to find out what the person who wrote the book had in mind when he or she organized the chapter. What was important enough to set off as a title or in bold type? After skimming, you should be able to explain to yourself what the main topics of the chapter are and even some of the main points. Unless you're the kind of person who would step into an empty elevator shaft without looking first, you'll soon discover the value of skimming.

9   **5. Take notes on what you're studying.** This sounds like a hassle, but it works. Go back over the material after you've read it, and jot down key words and phrases in the margins. When you review the chapter for a test, you'll have handy little things like "definition of rationalization" or "example of regression" in the margins. If the material is especially tough, organize a separate sheet of notes. Write down definitions, examples, lists, and main ideas. The idea is to have a single sheet or two that boil the entire chapter down to a digestible lump.

10   **6. Review after you've read and taken notes.** Some people swear that talking to yourself works. Tell yourself about the most important points in the chapter. Once you've said them out loud, they seem to stick better in your mind. If you can't talk to yourself about the material after reading it, that's a sure sign you don't really know it.

11   **7. Take a break when you're tired.** It's all right to let up for a bit when you've

had enough. You should try to make it through at least an hour, though. Ten minutes here and there are useless. When your head starts to pound and your eyes develop spidery red lines, quit. Rest for a bit with a short nap, and go back later.

12   **8. Take the college skills course if you need it.** Don't hesitate or feel embarrassed about enrolling in a study skills course. Many students say they wouldn't have made it without one.

How Can I Keep Up with All My Responsibilities without Going Crazy?

13   You've got a class schedule. You're supposed to study. You've got a family. You've got a husband, wife, boyfriend, child. You've got a job. How are you possibly going to cover all the bases in your life and maintain° your sanity? This is one of the toughest problems students face. Even if they start the semester with the best of intentions, they eventually find themselves tearing their hair out trying to do everything they're supposed to do. Believe it or not, though, it is possible to meet all your responsibilities. And you don't have to turn into a hermit° or give up your loved ones to do it.

14   The secret here is to organize your time. But don't just sit around half the semester planning to get everything together soon. Before you know it, you'll be confronted with midterms, papers,

family, and work all at once. Don't let yourself reach that breaking point. Instead, try these three tactics:

15   **1. Prepare a monthly calendar.** Get one of those calendars with big blocks around the dates. Give yourself an overview of the whole term by marking down the due dates for papers and projects. Circle test and exam days. This way those days don't sneak up on you unexpectedly.

16   **2. Make up a study schedule.** Sit down during the first few days of this semester and make up a sheet listing the days and hours of the week. Fill in your work and class hours first. Then try to block out some study hours. It's better to study a little every day than to create a huge once-or-twice-a-week marathon session. Schedule study hours for your hardest classes for the times when you feel most energetic. For example, I battled my tax law textbook in the mornings; when I looked at it after 7:00 p.m., I might as well have been reading Chinese. The usual proportion, by the way, is one hour of study time for every class hour.

17   In case you're one of those people who get carried away, remember to leave blocks of free time, too. You won't be any good to yourself or anyone else if you don't relax and pack in the studying once in a while.

18   **3. Use "to-do" lists.** This is the secret that singlehandedly got me through college. Once a week (or every day if

you want to), make a list of what you have to do. Write down everything from "write English paper" to "buy cold cuts for lunch." The best thing about a "to-do" list is that it seems to tame all those stray "I have to" thoughts that nag at your mind. After you finish something on the list, cross it off. Don't be compulsive about finishing everything; you're not Superman or Wonder Woman. Get the important things done first. The secondary things you don't finish can simply be moved to your next "to-do" list.

What Can I Do If Personal Problems Get in the Way of My Studies?

19   One student, Roger, told me this story:

> Everything was going okay for me until the middle of the spring semester. I went through a terrible time when I broke up with my girlfriend and started seeing her best friend. I was trying to deal with my ex-girlfriend's hurt and anger, my new girlfriend's guilt, and my own worries and anxieties at the same time. In addition to this, my mother was sick and on a medication that made her really irritable. I hated to go home because the atmosphere was so uncomfortable. Soon, I started missing classes because I couldn't deal with the academic pressures as well as my own personal problems. It seemed easier to hang around

my girlfriend's apartment than to face all my problems at home and at school.

20   And here's what another student, Marian, told me:

> I'd been married for eight years, and the relationship wasn't going too well. I saw the handwriting on the wall, and I decided to prepare for the future. I enrolled in college because I knew I'd need a decent job to support myself. Well, my husband had a fit because I was going to school. We were arguing a lot anyway, and he made it almost impossible for me to study at home. I think he was angry and almost jealous because I was drawing away from him. It got so bad that I thought about quitting college for a while. I wasn't getting any support at home, and it was just too hard to go on.

21   Personal troubles like these are overwhelming when you're going through them. School seems like the least important thing in your life. The two students above are perfect examples of this situation. But if you think about it, quitting or failing school would be the worst thing for these two students. Roger's problems, at least with his girlfriends, would simmer down° eventually, and then he'd regret having left school. Marian had to finish college if she wanted to be able to live independently. Sometimes, you've just got to hang tough.

22   But what do you do while you're trying to live through a lousy time? First of all, do something difficult. Ask yourself, honestly, if you're exaggerating small problems as an excuse to avoid classes and studying. It takes strength to admit this, but there's no sense in kidding yourself. You need to know if your problems are really bad in themselves or if you are perhaps making them worse than they are.

23   Second, if your problems are serious, and real, try to make some human contacts at school. Lots of students hide inside a miserable shell made of their own troubles and feel isolated and lonely. Believe me, there are plenty of students with problems. Not everyone is getting A's and having a fabulous social and home life at the same time. As you go through the term, you'll pick up some vibrations about the students in your classes. Perhaps someone strikes you as a compatible person. Why not speak to that person after class? Share a cup of coffee in the cafeteria, or walk to the parking lot together. You're not looking for a best friend or the love of your life. You just want to build a little network of support for yourself. Sharing your difficulties, questions, and complaints with a friendly person on campus can make a world of difference in how you feel.

24   Finally, if your problems are overwhelming, get some professional help. Why do you think colleges spend countless dollars on counseling departments and campus psychiatric services? More than ever, students all over the country are taking advantage of the help offered by support groups and therapy sessions. There's no shame attached to asking for help, either. In fact, almost 40 percent of college students (according to one survey) will use counseling services during their time in school. Just walk into a student center or counseling office and ask for an appointment. You wouldn't think twice about asking a dentist to help you get rid of your toothache. Counselors are paid—and want—to help you with your problems.

Why Do Some People Make It and Some People Drop Out?

25   Anyone who spends at least one semester in college notices that some students give up on their classes. The person who sits behind you in accounting, for example, begins to miss a lot of class meetings and eventually vanishes. Or another student comes to class without the assignment, doodles in his notebook during the lecture, and leaves during the break. What's the difference between students like this and the ones who succeed in school? My survey may be unscientific, but everyone I asked said the same thing: attitude. A positive attitude is the key to everything else—good study habits, smart time scheduling, and coping with personal difficulties.

26   What does "a positive attitude" mean? Well, for one thing, it means not

acting like a zombie. It means not only showing up for your classes, but also doing something while you're there. Really listen. Take notes. Ask a question if you want to. Don't just walk into a class, put your mind in neutral, and drift away to never-never land.

27   Having a positive attitude goes deeper than this, though. It means being mature about college as an institution. Too many students approach college classes like six-year-olds who expect first grade to be as much fun as *Sesame Street*. First grade, as we all know, isn't as much fun as *Sesame Street*. And college classes can sometimes be downright dull and boring. If you let a boring class discourage you so much that you want to leave school, you'll lose in the long run. Look at your priorities. You want a degree, or a certificate, or a career. If you have to, you can make it through a less-than-interesting class in order to achieve what you want. Get whatever you can out of every class. But if you simply can't stand a certain class, be determined to fulfill its requirements and be done with it once and for all.

28   After the initial high of starting school, you have to settle in for the long haul. If you follow the advice here, you'll be prepared to face the academic crunch. You'll also live through the semester without giving up your family, your job, or *Monday Night Football*. Finally, going to college can be an exciting time. As you learn things, the world truly becomes a more interesting place.

Vocabulary Questions

Use context clues to help you decide on the best definition for each italicized word. Then, in the space provided, write the letter of your choice.

_____ 1. In the excerpt below, the word *confronted* (kən-frŭnt′ĭd) means
   A. delighted.
   B. faced.
   C. finished.
   D. forgotten.

"But don't just sit around half the semester planning to get everything together soon. Before you know it, you'll be confronted with midterms, papers, family, and work all at once." (Paragraph 14)

_____ 2. In the excerpt below, the word *tactics* (tăk'tĭks) means
   A. methods.
   B. reasons.
   C. requirements.
   D. scenes.

   "The secret here is to organize your time. . . . try these three tactics: 1. Prepare a monthly calendar. . . . 2. Make up a study schedule. . . . 3. Use 'to-do' lists. . . ." (Paragraphs 14–18)

_____ 3. In the sentence below, the word *compulsive* (kəm-pŭl'sĭv) means
   A. overly concerned.
   B. careless.
   C. interested.
   D. honest.

   "Don't be compulsive about finishing everything; you're not Superman or Wonder Woman." (Paragraph 18)

_____ 4. In the excerpt below, the word *overwhelming* (ō'vər-hwĕl'mĭng) means
   A. silly.
   B. boring.
   C. overpowering.
   D. enjoyable.

   "Personal troubles like these are overwhelming when you're going through them. School seems like the least important thing in life." (Paragraph 21)

_____ 5. In the excerpt below, the word *compatible* (kəm-păt'ə-bəl) means
   A. unfriendly.
   B. easy to get along with.
   C. highly intelligent.
   D. concerned only about himself or herself.

   "Perhaps someone strikes you as a compatible person. Why not speak to that person after class? Share a cup of coffee in the cafeteria or walk to the parking lot together." (Paragraph 23)

Reading Comprehension Questions

Central Point and Main Ideas

_____ 1. Which sentence best expresses the central point of the selection?
   A. Going to college is exciting.
   B. There are ways to succeed in college and stay in control of your life.
   C. Most students are not concerned about staying in college.
   D. College can be confusing and tiring.

_____ 2. Which sentence best expresses the main idea of paragraph 27?
   A. First grade is less fun than kindergarten.
   B. College classes are sometimes quite boring.
   C. Students should be mature enough to tackle a class even when it's boring.
   D. A boring class encourages some students to leave school.

Supporting Details

_____ 3. The method of time control that was most helpful for the author was
   A. a monthly calendar.
   B. a study schedule.
   C. "to-do" lists.

Transitions

_____ 4. The sentence below expresses a relationship of
   A. illustration.
   B. comparison.
   C. contrast.
   D. cause and effect.

   "Don't let yourself reach that breaking point. Instead, try these three tactics." (Paragraph 14)

_____ 5. The sentence below expresses a relationship of
       A. illustration.
       B. comparison.
       C. contrast.
       D. cause and effect.

       "Soon, I started missing classes because I couldn't deal with the academic pressures as well as my own personal problems." (Paragraph 19)

Patterns of Organization

_____ 6. Just as paragraphs are organized according to patterns, so are groups of paragraphs. What is the main pattern of organization of paragraphs 3–12?
       A. List of items
       B. Time order
       C. Definition and example
       D. Comparison-contrast

_____ 7. Paragraph 19 combines the patterns of
       A. list of items and contrast.
       B. time order and cause-effect.
       C. definition/example and time order.
       D. definition/example and comparison.

_____ 8. TRUE OR FALSE? Paragraphs 26–27 contrast a positive attitude with a poor one.

Inferences

_____ 9. You can conclude that this article was written for
       A. incoming college students who have just completed high school.
       B. older students returning to college years after high-school graduation.
       C. high-school students considering college.
       D. students of any age who are beginning college.

_____ 10. The author suggests that many students who drop out of college
       A. have only themselves to blame.
       B. tried their best to do the work, but failed.
       C. were good students in high school.
       D. spent too much time making friends with classmates.

Outlining

Complete the following outline of the selection by filling in the five missing details.

> **Central point:** There are practical steps you can take to make yourself successful in college.

  A. Eight study tips will help:

     1. Set up a quiet place to study.

     2. _____

     3. Reward yourself for good studying.

     4. Learn to skim a textbook.

     5. Take notes on what you're reading.

     6. _____

     7. Take a break when you're tired.

     8. Take a study skills course if necessary.

  B. Three tactics will help organize time:

     1. Prepare a monthly calendar.

     2. _____

     3. _____

  C. Three approaches to personal problems can help:

     1. Ask yourself if you're exaggerating your problems.

     2. Make friends with other classmates so you feel less alone.

     3. _____

  D. A positive attitude can help.

Discussion Questions

1. What would you say is the single biggest obstacle between you and better grades? Do you need to get organized? Do you exaggerate your personal problems? How might O'Keeney's article help you overcome this obstacle?

2. Do you make "to-do" lists? If not, do you think you should? What are three items that you would put on your "to-do" list for today?

3. "Sometimes, you've just got to hang tough," O'Keeney tells us (paragraph 21). What does he mean? What are some techniques for hanging tough, instead of giving in, that have worked for you or for people you know?

4. O'Keeney writes in paragraph 27, "Look at your priorities. You want a degree, or a certificate, or a career." What are *your* priorities? Explain the kind of life you hope to have and how college fits into these plans.

    Note: Writing assignments for this selection appear on page 613.

Check Your Performance   HOW TO MAKE IT IN COLLEGE

Activity	Number Right	Points	Total
Vocabulary Questions (5 items)	_____	× 20 =	_____
		SCORE =	_____%
Reading Comprehension Questions			
Central Point and Main Ideas (2 items)	_____	× 8 =	_____
Supporting Details (1 item)	_____	× 8 =	_____
Transitions (2 items)	_____	× 8 =	_____
Patterns of Organization (3 items)	_____	× 8 =	_____
Inferences (2 items)	_____	× 8 =	_____
Outlining (5 items)	_____	× 4 =	_____
		SCORE =	_____%

TOTAL SCORES: Vocabulary _____%   Comprehension _____%

Enter your total scores into the **Reading Performance Chart: Ten Reading Selections** on the inside back cover.

8 Cooling Down Our Brains

Jason Peters

Preview

How good are your self-control and willpower? Can you resist that last donut? Will you stay home and study instead of going to the party? If your answers are No and No, you're not alone. Many people feel helpless when it comes to temptation. But as you will discover in the following selection, you can conquer that helplessness—it's just a matter of cooling down your brain.

Words to Watch

scenario (2): story line
exerted (6): put into use
competent (6): able, skilled
irrational (9): not logical, foolish
predestined (10): fated
harnessing (11): controlling
dominate (14): overpower

1 Suppose someone offered you fifty dollars. Obviously, you would be happy to take the money. However, suppose this person then told you that he or she would give you $100 in seven days if you could wait until then. If you didn't want to wait, you could have the $50 right now. What would you do—take the $50 now or the $100 later? And why would you make this choice?

2 This scenario° is the basis of an experiment, nicknamed "The Marshmallow Test," that took place over fifty years ago. Conducted by professor and researcher Walter Mischel, this experiment tested the willpower and self-control of young children. Children around the age of five were told they could have either one marshmallow now or two marshmallows fifteen minutes later. To an adult, fifteen minutes may not seem like a long time to wait for something, but to a small child, it is an eternity.

3 This eternity was made even longer by the fact that the children were left alone in a room with a single marshmallow sitting on a plate right in front of them. As Mischel and his assistants secretly watched from behind one-way glass, many of the children, as expected, could not resist the temptation and ate the marshmallow within a few minutes. However, at least

a third of the children made it through the fifteen minutes.

4   How did the children who waited do it? One girl found ways to distract herself through singing, fidgeting, or talking. If the marshmallow began to tempt her, then she would look away and begin to sing again. Others pushed the marshmallow as far away as possible and refused to look at it, pretending it wasn't there. One boy actually smelled and touched the marshmallow and then scolded himself angrily, reminding himself out loud that if he ate that one, it would be "too bad." "If I wait," he sighed happily, "then I will get two. Two marshmallows!" After this fierce reminder, the child put his head down on the table mumbling reminders to himself and waiting out the long minutes.

5   Mischel and his assistants were mostly interested in observing self-control techniques that children either used or ignored. When the "Marshmallow Test" was over, that seemed to be the end of it—but it wasn't.

6   Years later, in a follow-up study, Mischel made a surprising discovery. Generally, children who had resisted eating the marshmallow and had exerted° self-control were more competent° in school than children who had eaten the marshmallow right away. Several years later, another follow-up showed that the children (now young adults) who had "passed" the marshmallow test tended to have scored higher on the SAT than the children who had not. Additionally, the

children who had not given in to the allure of marshmallows twenty years earlier were shown to be more likely to reach long-term goals, avoid drug and alcohol abuse, and even maintain a healthy body weight. Children who had eaten the marshmallow were not nearly as successful.

What did all this mean? On the 7 surface, it appeared that children who had self-control would tend to be more successful in life than those who did not possess this skill. In addition, people assumed that willpower and self-control are innate abilities that one is born with. Much like intelligence or artistic talent, self-control was a quality that could not be learned. After the publication of Mischel's follow-up studies, many parents were alarmed and discouraged when they noticed that their own children seemed to lack self-control and the ability to work toward a delayed reward. They worried that their children would be low achievers in life. Wasn't there anything they could do to change what seemed to be a mindset established at birth?

8   Mischel wondered the same thing. He began researching the human brain and what happens to it when we either practice self-control or give in to temptation. And what he discovered may change forever the way we think about ourselves and what we can and cannot control.

9   Looking at brain scans of children and adults who were trying to control their desires or emotions, Mischel noticed that the front part of the brain, called the prefrontal cortex, lit up. This is the part of the brain that calms our desires, pain, fear, and obsessions— in other words, that cools us down. However, when subjects gave in to their desires and cravings, a different part of the brain near the back, called the amygdala, lit up. This "hot" part of the brain triggers immediate responses without thinking about consequences or dangers. It may keep us from quitting smoking, staying away from unhealthy foods, calming an irrational° fear, or even healing a broken heart. It is the devil on the shoulder that whispers, "Go ahead! You deserve it!"

10   Certainly, we are all predestined° to behave in certain ways to some extent when it comes to things like personality and self-control. But, Mischel wondered, is it possible to *train* our minds to make ourselves gain better control? Can we mentally make our brain's "cool" system override its "hot" system?

11   It turns out that we can. Our brains are, in fact, far more flexible and changeable than researchers and scientists had originally thought. It is

possible, in a real sense, to change our minds. In his book, *The Marshmallow Test*, Dr. Mischel discusses different methods for mentally training and harnessing° our brain's "cool" system of self-control.

12   How can we do it? To begin with, consider the behavior of the children who resisted the marshmallows. Some of their natural responses to avoiding temptation are exactly what Mischel suggests for training the brain to say No when the body and emotions are saying Yes. Among the various techniques Mischel describes are the following:

13   **Make up "If . . . then" rules.** Remember the child who, every time she was tempted by the marshmallow, began singing or chattering to herself? In her mind, she was thinking, *If I begin to want the marshmallow, then I will start to sing to keep me from eating it.* All of us tend to sabotage our best intentions (to diet, quit smoking, drink less) with established habits that come as naturally to us as brushing our teeth or turning on a light when we walk into a dark room. If we see candy we like, then we pick it up and eat it.

14   Mischel suggests changing the "then" with a new and unrelated habit. IF I see a bowl of candy in the office, THEN I will walk down the hall and get some water. IF I see a bar, THEN I will cross the street and walk on the opposite side. In time, the cues (candy, alcohol) will create a different response altogether if the "then" response is repeated over and over. Eventually, the desired behavior is

triggered automatically without effort. The cool part of the brain will dominate° the hot.

15   **Visualize the consequences; visualize the reward.** The child who was tempted by the marshmallow and then angrily reminded himself that if he ate it, it would be "too bad," was visualizing the consequences of not having self-control. When he dreamily reminded himself that if he could just wait, there would be two marshmallows, he was visualizing the reward. For adults, this cooling of the hot part of the brain and heating of the cool part of the brain is a particularly helpful technique.

16   Vividly imagining the negative consequences of lacking self-control can be powerful. A smoker might picture a black cancerous lung, perhaps even looking up real images online and viewing them several times a day. Overeaters might visualize themselves as obese and ill. In turn, keeping a mind's eye on the prize and visualizing positive outcomes heats up the cool, rational part of the brain and keeps us excited about our goals (Health! Marshmallows!). In time, constant visualizing will begin to change the way we respond to temptation; it won't be so tempting after all. In fact, it may even become annoying and disgusting.

17   **Distance yourself from the situation.** Finally, some of the children *literally* distanced themselves from temptation so that they could maintain control. They physically moved as far away from the marshmallow as possible and refused to look at it. As adults, we can distance ourselves both physically and mentally from things that are disrupting our lives.

18   How important are self-control and willpower? So important that they affect nearly everything we do. From getting up on time in the morning to our careers to relationships and far beyond, a good handle on self-control may make the difference between a happy, successful life or a disappointing and frustrating existence.

19   The bad news is that not everyone is born with a great deal of self-control. But the very good news is that there is not, as once thought, a limit to your willpower; you *can* develop it. You can exercise that cool part of your brain and master what you choose, where you go, and how you live.

20   So, knowing what you now know, would you take that $50 today—or wait for that $100 next week?

Vocabulary Questions

Use context clues to help you decide on the best definition for each italicized word. Then, in the space provided, write the letter of your choice.

_____ 1. In the sentence below, the word *eternity* (ĭ-tûr′nĭ-tē) means
   A. waiting period.
   B. endless amount of time.
   C. very boring experience.
   D. test.

   "To an adult, fifteen minutes may not seem like a long time to wait for something, but to a small child it is an eternity.'" (Paragraph 2)

_____ 2. In the sentence below, the word *allure* (ə-lŏor′) means
   A. threat.
   B. question.
   C. temptation.
   D. mystery.

   "Additionally, the children who had not given in to the allure of marshmallows 20 years earlier were shown to be more likely to reach long-term goals, resist drug and alcohol abuse, and even maintain a healthy body weight." (Paragraph 6)

_____ 3. In the excerpt below, the word *innate* (ĭ-nāt′) means
   A. strange.
   B. natural.
   C. helpful.
   D. lucky.

   "In addition, people assumed that willpower and self-control are innate abilities that one is born with. Much like intelligence or artistic talent, self-control was a quality that could not be learned." (Paragraph 7)

_____ 4. In the excerpt below, the word *sabotage* (săb′ə-täzh′) means
   A. reform.
   B. remember.
   C. repair.
   D. destroy.

   "All of us tend to sabotage our best intentions (to diet, quit smoking, drink less) with established habits that come as naturally to us as brushing our teeth or turning on a light when we walk into a dark room. If we see candy we like, then we pick it up and eat it." (Paragraph 13)

_____ 5. In the sentence below, the word *visualizing* (vĭz′hoo͞-ə-līz′ĭng) means

A. accepting.

B. forgetting.

C. imagining.

D. enjoying.

> "The child who was tempted by the marshmallow and then angrily reminded himself that if he ate it, it would be 'too bad,' was visualizing the consequences of not having self-control." (Paragraph 15)

Reading Comprehension Questions

Central Point and Main Ideas

_____ 1. Which sentence best expresses the central point of the selection?

A. Children who are able to practice self-control at a young age will have more successful lives.

B. Once a bad habit is formed, it is often very difficult to break it.

C. Research indicates that self-control can be improved through various mental exercises.

D. Young children are often more talented at coming up with unusual self-control techniques than are adults.

_____ 2. Which sentence best expresses the main idea of paragraph 4?

A. The children in the experiment found various ways to practice self-control.

B. It was not easy for the children to resist eating the marshmallows.

C. Children who physically pushed the marshmallow away were more easily able to resist it.

D. Children who could resist eating one marshmallow would be rewarded with two marshmallows later.

_____ 3. Which sentence best expresses the main idea of paragraphs 13 and 14?

A. Many of us sabotage our best intentions by falling back on old bad habits and routines.

B. When trying to break bad habits, creating a new "if-then" routine can help change a bad habit to a good habit.

C. Typically, the hardest habits for most adults to break have to do with diet, alcohol, and smoking.

D. One of the children who participated in the marshmallow test used a very good self-control technique.

Supporting Details

_____ 4. TRUE OR FALSE? Walter Mischel did two follow-up studies on the children who participated in the marshmallow test: one when they were still in school and one when they were adults.

_____ 5. According to the reading, the "hot" part of the brain
   A. is responsible for our immediate, unthinking responses.
   B. ignores the consequences or dangers of our actions.
   C. can prevent us from performing healthy activities.
   D. all of the above.

Transitions

_____ 6. The signal words at the beginning of the sentence below show
   A. addition.
   B. comparison.
   C. cause and effect.
   D. time.

   "Several years later, another follow-up showed that the children (now young adults) who had 'passed' the marshmallow test tended to have scored higher on the SAT than the children who had not." (Paragraph 6)

_____ 7. The relationship of the second sentence below to the first is one of
   A. time.
   B. contrast.
   C. cause and effect.
   D. addition.

   "The bad news is that not everyone is born with a great deal of self-control. But the very good news is that there is not, as once thought, a limit to your willpower; you *can* build it." (Paragraph 19)

Patterns of Organization

_____ 8. For the most part, paragraphs 2 and 3
   A. compare and contrast the different ways children dealt with temptation.
   B. use time order to describe the steps of the marshmallow test.
   C. list the reasons why children have a difficult time waiting.
   D. define willpower and self-control and give examples of them.

Inferences

_____ 9. In general, the essay implies that
     A. most of us have enough self-control and do not need to work on it using the techniques presented.
     B. most of us find it hard to resist temptation at times and will find the techniques presented helpful.
     C. learning better self-control is nearly impossible if one is not born with a fair amount of it.
     D. experiments using children as subjects are generally a bad idea.

_____ 10. When, at the very end of the essay, the author asks, "So, knowing what you now know, would you take that $50 today or wait for that $100 next week?" we can infer that he
     A. thinks we would still take the $50 today.
     B. really has no idea what we might choose.
     C. thinks we would wait for the $100.
     D. assumes that the average reader has poor self-control.

Outlining

The following outline of "Cooling Down Our Brains" is missing two major supporting details and three minor supporting details. Complete the outline by filling in the missing details, which are listed after the outline.

Central point: Research involving children's behavior has indicated that self-control can be improved through certain mental exercises.

1. The original experiment was nicknamed "The Marshmallow Test."
   A. _____

     _____

   B. One-third of the children were able to wait the 15 minutes.
   C. The children who waited were able to distract themselves, pretend the marshmallow wasn't there, or talk themselves out of eating the marshmallow.

2. _____

     _____

   A. They did better in school.

   B. _____

   C. They were more likely to reach long-term goals and avoid abusing drugs, drinking too much, and becoming overweight.

3. Additional research indicated that the brain has "hot" and "cool" areas, and that we can train the "cool" part of our brains to take control of our impulses.

    A. Make up "if . . . then" rules.

    B. _____

    C. _____

Major Details Missing from the Outline

    A. Follow-ups showed that the children who had self-control were more successful than those who gave in.
    B. Visualize the consequences and the reward.
    C. Distance yourself from the situation.
    D. They had higher SAT scores.
    E. Five-year-olds were told they could have one marshmallow now or two marshmallows in 15 minutes.

Discussion Questions

1. Before reading the rest of the essay, would you have taken the $50 right away? Did reading the essay change your mind? Explain.

2. The original "marshmallow test" was performed in the 1960s on preschool-age children while "Mischel and his assistants secretly watched from behind one-way glass." Today, some people think this kind of experimenting with children is a bad idea, because it might frighten or confuse a child. Do you agree? Why or why not?

3. When discussing the "hot" part of the brain, the author mentions "the devil on the shoulder that whispers, 'Go ahead! You deserve it!'" Have you ever encountered this annoying little devil? What were you tempted to do that, in your heart, you knew you should not do? Did you go ahead and do it anyway, or did you resist? Explain.

4. The author points out that self-control and willpower are needed for just about everything in life. Aside from the obvious (not overeating, controlling drinking, quitting smoking), what are some less obvious and even unusual activities that require willpower? Which of the three self-control techniques described near the end of the essay might be the most effective way to resist each of these activities?

Note: Writing assignments for this selection appear on page 614.

Check Your Performance   COOLING DOWN OUR BRAINS

Activity	Number Right	Points			Total
Vocabulary Questions (5 items)	_____	×	20	=	_____
		SCORE		=	_____ %

Reading Comprehension Questions

	Number Right	Points			Total
Central Point and Main Ideas (3 items)	_____	×	8	=	_____
Supporting Details (2 items)	_____	×	8	=	_____
Transitions (2 items)	_____	×	8	=	_____
Patterns of Organization (1 item)	_____	×	8	=	_____
Inferences (2 items)	_____	×	8	=	_____
Outlining (5 items)	_____	×	4	=	_____
		SCORE		=	_____ %

TOTAL SCORES: Vocabulary _____ % Comprehension _____ %

Enter your total scores into the **Reading Performance Chart: Ten Reading Selections** on the inside back cover.

9 Dealing with Feelings
Rudolph F. Verderber

Preview

Is it sometimes useful to conceal your feelings when you're hurt? Or when you're angry, is it usually best to simply yell out and let your anger loose? Finally, is it risky to tell others how you really feel? Think of your answers to these questions. Then read the following excerpt from the college textbook *Communicate!*, Sixth Edition, to see what the author says.

Words to Watch

self-disclosure (1): revealing information about oneself
decipher (2): figure out
seethe (2): become violently emotional
perceived (3): seen
undemonstrative (3): tending not to express feelings
inconsequential (4): unimportant
interpersonally (7): involving relations between people
potential (12): possible
net (14): final
triggered (16): set off
elated (17): very happy

1   An extremely important aspect of self-disclosure° is the sharing of feelings. We all experience feelings such as happiness at receiving an unexpected gift, sadness about the breakup of a relationship, or anger when we believe we have been taken advantage of. The question is whether to disclose such feelings, and if so, how. Self-disclosure of feelings usually will be most successful not when feelings are withheld or displayed but when they are described. Let's consider each of these forms of dealing with feelings.

Withholding Feelings

2   Withholding feelings—that is, keeping them inside and not giving any verbal or nonverbal cues to their existence— is generally an inappropriate means of dealing with feelings. Withholding feelings is best exemplified by the good poker player who develops a "poker face," a neutral look that is impossible to decipher°. The look is the same whether the player's cards are good or bad. Unfortunately, many people use poker faces in their interpersonal

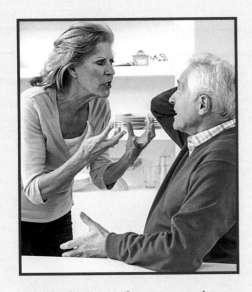

relationships, so that no one knows whether they hurt inside, are extremely excited, and so on. For instance, Doris feels very nervous when Candy stands over her while Doris is working on her report. And when Candy says, "That first paragraph isn't very well written," Doris begins to seethe°, yet she says nothing—she withholds her feelings.

3   Psychologists believe that when people withhold feelings, they can develop physical problems such as ulcers, high blood pressure, and heart disease, as well as psychological problems such as stress-related neuroses and psychoses. Moreover, people who withhold feelings are often perceived° as cold, undemonstrative°, and not much fun to be around.

4   Is withholding ever appropriate? When a situation is inconsequential°, you may well choose to withhold your feelings. For instance, a stranger's inconsiderate behavior at a party may bother you, but because you can move to another part of the room, withholding may not be detrimental. In the example of Doris seething at Candy's behavior, however, withholding could be costly to Doris.

Displaying Feelings

Displaying feelings means expressing 5
those feelings through a facial reaction, body response, and/or spoken reaction. Cheering over a great play at a sporting event, booing the umpire at a perceived bad call, patting a person on the back when the person does something well, or saying, "What are you doing?" in a nasty tone of voice are all displays of feelings.

Displays are especially appropriate 6
when the feelings you are experiencing are positive. For instance, when Gloria does something nice for you, and you experience a feeling of joy, giving her a big hug is appropriate; when Don gives you something you've wanted, and you experience a feeling of appreciation, a big smile or an "Oh, thank you, Don" is appropriate. In fact, many people need to be even more demonstrative of good feelings. You've probably seen the bumper sticker "Have you hugged your kid today?" It reinforces the point that you need to display love and affection constantly to show another person that you really care.

Displays become detrimental to 7
communication when the feelings you are experiencing are negative— especially when the display of a negative feeling appears to be an overreaction. For instance, when Candy stands over Doris while she is working on her report

and says, "That first paragraph isn't very well written," Doris may well experience resentment. If Doris lashes out at Candy by screaming, "Who the hell asked you for your opinion?" Doris's display no doubt will hurt Candy's feelings and short-circuit their communication. Although displays of negative feelings may be good for you psychologically, they are likely to be bad for you interpersonally°.

Describing Feelings

8   Describing feelings—putting your feelings into words in a calm, non-judgmental way—tends to be the best method of disclosing feelings. Describing feelings not only increases chances for positive communication and decreases chances for short-circuiting lines of communication; it also teaches people how to treat you. When you describe your feelings, people are made aware of the effect of their behavior. This knowledge gives them the information needed to determine whether they should continue or repeat that behavior. If you tell Paul that you really feel flattered when he visits you, such a statement should encourage Paul to visit you again; likewise, when you tell Cliff that you feel very angry when he borrows your jacket without asking, he is more likely to ask the next time he borrows a jacket. Describing your feelings allows you to exercise a measure of control over others' behavior toward you.

9   Describing and displaying feelings are not the same. Many times people think they are describing when in fact they are displaying feelings or evaluating.

10   If describing feelings is so important to communicating effectively, why don't more people do it regularly? There seem to be at least four reasons why many people don't describe feelings.

1. *Many people have a poor vocabulary of words for describing the various feelings they are experiencing.* People can sense that they are angry; however, they may not know whether what they are feeling might best be described as annoyed, betrayed, cheated, crushed, disturbed, furious, outraged, or shocked. Each of these words describes a slightly different aspect of what many people lump together as anger.   11

2. *Many people believe that describing their true feelings reveals too much about themselves.* If you tell people when their behavior hurts you, you risk their using the information against you when they want to hurt you on purpose. Even so, the potential° benefits of describing your feelings far outweigh the risks. For instance, if Pete has a nickname for you that you don't like, and you tell Pete that calling you by that nickname really makes you nervous and tense, Pete may use the nickname when he wants to hurt you, but he is more likely to stop calling you by that name. If, on the other hand, you don't describe your feelings to Pete, he is probably going to call you by that name all the time because he doesn't know any better. When you say nothing, you reinforce his behavior. The level of risk varies   12

with each situation, but you will more often improve a relationship than be hurt by describing feelings.

13   3. *Many people believe that if they describe feelings, others will make them feel guilty about having such feelings.* At a very tender age, we all learned about "tactful" behavior. Under the premise that "the truth sometimes hurts," we learned to avoid the truth by not saying anything or by telling "little" lies. Perhaps, when you were young, your mother said, "Don't forget to give Grandma a great big kiss." At that time you may have blurted out, "Ugh—it makes me feel yucky to kiss Grandma. She's got a mustache." If your mother responded, "That's terrible—your grandma loves you. Now you give her a kiss, and never let me hear you talk like that again!" then you probably felt guilty for having this "wrong" feeling. But the point is that the thought of kissing your grandma made you feel "yucky" whether it should have or not. In this case, what was at issue was the way you talked about the feelings—not your having the feelings.

14   4. *Many people believe that describing feelings causes harm to others or to a relationship.* If it really bothers Max when his girlfriend, Dora, bites her fingernails, Max may believe that describing his feelings to Dora will hurt her so much that the knowledge will drive a wedge into their relationship. So it's better for Max to say nothing, right? Wrong! If Max says nothing, he's

still going to be bothered by Dora's behavior. In fact, as time goes on, Max will probably lash out at Dora for other things because he can't bring himself to talk about the behavior that really bothers him. The net° result is that not only will Dora be hurt by Max's behavior, but she won't understand the true source of his feelings. By not describing his feelings, Max may well drive a wedge into their relationship anyway.

5. If Max does describe his feelings to   15
Dora, she might quit or at least try to quit biting her nails; they might get into a discussion in which he finds out that she doesn't want to bite them but just can't seem to stop, and he can help her in her efforts to stop; or they might discuss the problem and Max may see that it is really a small thing and not let it bother him as much. The point is that in describing feelings, the chances of a successful outcome are greater than they are in not describing them.

To describe your feelings, first   16
put the emotion you are feeling into words. Be specific. Second, state what triggered° the feeling. Finally, make sure you indicate that the feeling is yours. For example, suppose your roommate borrows your jacket without asking. When he returns, you describe your feelings by saying, "Cliff, I [indication that the feeling is yours] get really angry [the feeling] when you borrow my jacket without asking [trigger]." Or suppose that Carl has just reminded you of the very first time he brought

you a rose. You describe your feelings by saying, "Carl, I [indication that the feeling is yours] get really tickled [the feeling] when you remind me about that first time you brought me a rose [trigger]."

17   You may find it easiest to begin by describing positive feelings: "I really feel elated° knowing that you were the one who nominated me for the position" or "I'm delighted that you offered to help me with the housework." As you gain success with positive descriptions, you can try negative feelings attributable to environmental factors: "It's so cloudy; I feel gloomy" or "When the wind howls through the cracks, I really get jumpy." Finally, you can move to negative descriptions resulting from what people have said or done: "Your stepping in front of me like that really annoys me" or "The tone of your voice confuses me."

Vocabulary Questions

Use context clues to help you decide on the best definition for each italicized word. Then, in the space provided, write the letter of your choice.

_____ 1. In the excerpt below, the word *exemplified* (ĭg-zĕm′plə-fīd′) means
  A. challenged.
  B. illustrated.
  C. surprised.
  D. stolen.

  "Withholding feelings is best exemplified by the good poker player who develops a 'poker face,' a neutral look . . ." (Paragraph 2)

_____ 2. In the sentence below, the word *detrimental* (dĕt′rə-mĕn′tl) means
  A. useful.
  B. private.
  C. helpless.
  D. harmful.

  "For instance, a stranger's inconsiderate behavior at a party may bother you, but because you can move to another part of the room, withholding may not be detrimental." (Paragraph 4)

_____ 3. In the sentence below, the word *premise* (prĕm′ĭs) means
  A. question.
  B. choice.
  C. belief.
  D. disagreement.

  "Under the premise that 'the truth sometimes hurts,' we learned to avoid the truth by not saying anything or by telling 'little' lies." (Paragraph 13)

_____ 4. In the sentence below, the word *wedge* (wĕj) means
  A. something that divides.
  B. loyalty.
  C. friendship.
  D. many years.

  "Max may believe that describing his feelings to Dora will hurt her so much that the knowledge will drive a wedge into their relationship." (Paragraph 14)

_____ 5. In the excerpt below, the words *attributable to* (ə-trĭb′yōō-tə-bəl tōō) mean
  A. that cannot be explained by.
  B. that can be explained by.
  C. unrelated to.
  D. confused by.

  "As you gain success with positive descriptions [of feelings], you can try negative feelings attributable to environmental factors: 'It's so cloudy; I feel gloomy. . . .'" (Paragraph 17)

Reading Comprehension Questions

Central Point and Main Ideas

_____ 1. Which sentence best expresses the central point of the selection?
  A. Everyone has feelings.
  B. There are three ways to deal with feelings; describing them is most useful for educating others about how you want to be treated.
  C. Withholding feelings means not giving verbal or nonverbal clues that might reveal those feelings to others.
  D. Expressing feelings often leads to problems with others.

_____ 2. Which sentence best expresses the main idea of paragraph 3?
  A. Withholding negative feelings may lead to physical problems.
  B. Withholding negative feelings may lead to psychological problems.
  C. Withholding positive feelings can make one seem cold.
  D. Withholding feelings has several disadvantages.

_____ 3. Which sentence best expresses the main idea of paragraph 8?
  A. Describing your feelings can influence others' behavior toward you.
  B. It is possible to encourage friends to visit you again.
  C. It is possible to encourage friends to ask before they borrow things from you.
  D. It is possible to encourage friends.

Supporting Details

_____ 4. According to the author, you are more likely to create physical problems for yourself by
  A. withholding your feelings.
  B. displaying your positive feelings.
  C. describing your positive feelings.
  D. describing your negative feelings.

_____ 5. Describing your feelings means
  A. keeping your feelings inside.
  B. giving a nonverbal response to feelings.
  C. putting your feelings into words.
  D. telling "little" lies.

Transitions

_____ 6. The two parts of the sentence below express a relationship of
  A. time.   C. contrast.
  B. addition.   D. comparison.

  "Although displays of negative feelings may be good for you psychologically, they are more likely to be bad for you interpersonally." (Paragraph 7)

7. The two illustration words in paragraph 4 are _____

  and _____.

Patterns of Organization

_____ 8. The author develops paragraph 5 with
  A. a contrast.   C. a definition and examples.
  B. a comparison.   D. time order.

Inferences

_____ 9. From the reading, we can conclude that describing feelings
  A. is usually easy for people.
  B. is often a good way to solve problems.
  C. should be done only for positive feelings.
  D. should make you feel guilty.

_____ 10. Which sentence can we conclude is an example of displaying a feeling?
    A. Sonia refused to tell Tom that she hated his haircut.
    B. Betty told her son, "I enjoy reading your letters so much."
    C. The father clapped joyfully when the baby said, "Dada."
    D. Hakim avoided Jackie because he had forgotten her birthday.

Mapping

Below is a map of "Dealing with Feelings." Complete the map by filling in the central point (which Verderber presents in the first paragraph of the passage) and the three major supporting details.

Central point:

_____
_____
means

_____
_____
means

_____
_____
means

Discussion Questions

1. What is the difference between describing feelings and displaying them? How might Doris describe her feelings to Candy after Candy says, "That first paragraph isn't very well written" (paragraph 2)?

2. What do you think would be Verderber's advice on "little lies"? (See paragraph 13.)

3. Why do you think Verderber emphasizes describing feelings over the other two methods of dealing with feelings?

4. What are some examples from your own experience of withholding, expressing or displaying, and describing feelings? How useful was each method?

Note: Writing assignments for this selection appear on page 614.

Check Your Performance   DEALING WITH FEELINGS

Activity	Number Right	Points	Total
Vocabulary Questions (5 items)	_____	× 20 =	_____
		SCORE =	_____ %
Reading Comprehension Questions			
Central Point and Main Ideas (3 items)	_____	× 8 =	_____
Supporting Details (2 items)	_____	× 8 =	_____
Transitions (2 items)	_____	× 8 =	_____
Patterns of Organization (1 item)	_____	× 8 =	_____
Inferences (2 items)	_____	× 8 =	_____
Mapping (4 items)	_____	× 5 =	_____
		SCORE =	_____ %

TOTAL SCORES: Vocabulary _____ % Comprehension _____ %

Enter your total scores into the **Reading Performance Chart: Ten Reading Selections** on the inside back cover.

10 Not So Sweet
Alessa Staley

Preview

Only a generation ago, it was fairly unusual to see a very overweight child. Today, however, far more children (and adults) are overweight—even dangerously obese. Why? The answer can be complicated, but one of the main causes of weight problems is sugar. Most of us eat three and four times the sugar we should eat, and that's bad news. But here's even worse news: sugar is craftily—and intentionally—hidden in hundreds of foods where we would least expect it. Why would the food industry want to harm us? Read on to discover the very bitter truth about sugar.

Words to Watch

processed foods (4): packaged foods, usually treated with chemicals or other added materials to make them look and taste better
pediatrics (5): the branch of medicine that deals with infants and children
metabolism (6): the chemical processes in our bodies that keep us alive
nutrients (6): sources of nourishment
cirrhosis (6): a disease of the liver
insulin (6): a hormone that regulates the amount of sugar in our blood
justified (13): proved correct
litany (17): long list
rhetoric (17): empty words
lobbyists (18): people paid to influence politicians about various issues

1   *It's the sugar, stupid!*

2   *Fed Up*, a recent documentary film narrated by TV journalist Katie Couric, says it. A number of excellent books say it. Food writers, including Dr. Mark Hyman and the *New York Times*'s Mark Bittman, say it. **Sugar is killing us.** Most disturbingly, **it is killing our kids**.

3   What is it going to take to convince us? Forty years ago, a fat child was a rarity. Today, one in seven white children (ages 2–19) is obese. One in five black children is obese. One in four Latino children is obese. That's *obese*, which the dictionary defines as "grossly fat or overweight." We're not talking "plump" or "husky" or "big-boned." We're talking overweight to a degree that has life-threatening consequences. We're at the point that today's kids—for the first time in 200 years—have shorter life expectancies than their

parents. They will die, young, from heart disease, kidney failure, cancer, and Type 2 diabetes, a disease that until recently was so rare among children it was called "adult-onset diabetes." Now Type 2 diabetes is common among adolescents and teens.

4   So what has changed in the last 40 years that has made such a drastic difference in kids' health? Two things have happened. First, with both parents working outside the home in the majority of families, many Americans have turned away from cooking meals from scratch, preferring convenient "processed foods°." Second, as the competition for shoppers' dollars heated up, processed-food manufacturers made an earth-shaking discovery: *The more sugar they put into their products, the more sugar consumers wanted.* As the website for *Fed Up* says, "Sugar is added to food for one reason only. To make it taste better and make you eat more of it. It is addictive, and when you consume too much, you want more, which makes you buy more of the food industry's products. Better for them. Bad for you."

5   Whether it is called glucose solids, agave nectar, high-fructose corn syrup, maple syrup, sucrose, molasses, or any other of the 50-plus alternate names for sugar found on food labels, it's all the same stuff, and it's all equally deadly. "Sugar is poison," says Dr. Robert Lustig, professor of clinical pediatrics° at the University of California in San Francisco, and the author of *Fat Chance: Beating the Odds Against Sugar, Processed Food, Obesity, and Disease.*

How does sugar poison us? It's 6 not hard to understand, but it does require a very basic understanding of how our metabolism° works. When we eat, our digestive system breaks food down into its various nutrients°— proteins, vitamins, minerals, etc. Those nutrients are then used by different parts of the body—the brain, the muscles, etc. But sugar goes straight to our livers. That's not a problem when humans consume small amounts of sugar, as they did for thousands of years, mostly in the form of fruit. Our livers were designed to cope with that. But people following the Standard American Diet (so fittingly abbreviated as SAD) don't consume small amounts of sugar. They eat enormous quantities of it, because it's included in literally almost everything they eat. And when we eat large quantities of sugar, day after day, the liver can't keep up.

Overwhelmed, it turns the sugar into fat—not only the fat that makes you *look* fat, but *internal* fat, liver fat. And a fatty liver is a sick liver. It is at risk for developing cirrhosis°, liver scarring, and even liver cancer. It releases fats into the bloodstream, raising our "bad cholesterol" and increasing our risk of heart disease. It causes us to become insulin° resistant, a condition that can result in Type 2 diabetes.

7   That, in a nutshell, is what sugar does to us.

8   So clearly, we all need to eat less sugar, right? Right! But good luck with that, Jack. Because you and I might as well be living in a giant sugar bowl. Virtually every processed food we purchase is packed with the stuff.

9   Many of the worst offenders, the real sugar bombs, are obvious. For instance:

• A 20-ounce bottle of Coke contains about 17 teaspoons of sugar.

• A "venti"-sized Starbucks Caramel Frappuccino contains 16 teaspoons.

• One original size 3 Musketeers candy bar contains 7.3 teaspoons.

(To put those amounts in perspective: the American Heart Association recommends that teens eat no more than 5 teaspoons of sugar a day; adult males 9 teaspoons, and adult females 6 teaspoons.)

10   But you've always known that stuff like soda and candy is bad for you. If you're washing down your daily Krispy Kreme with a giant Mountain Dew, you probably aren't surprised to learn that you're taking in a whole lot of sugar.

What *is* surprising—make that 11 horrifying—is the huge amount of sugar hidden in innocent-sounding processed foods. The challenge is finding products that do *not* contain added sugar. Check out the labels on your next shopping expedition. And remember—sugar has more than 50 names. Whether it sounds "natural" and "healthy" (Honey! Agave nectar!) doesn't matter—to your body, it's all exactly the same toxic stuff. Here are just a few of sugar's aliases to aid you: Anything ending with *ose*—*glucose, maltose, fructose, sucrose,* etc. Then there's *barley malt. Beet sugar. Blackstrap molasses. Cane juice crystals. Caramel. Corn syrup. Dextran. Diastatic malt. Fruit juice. Maple syrup. Refiner's syrup. Rice syrup. Sorbitol. Sorghum. Turbinado sugar.*

So start reading ingredient lists. 12 You'll be astonished where you'll find significant added sugar. It's in almost everything, including foods that we don't think of as tasting sweet. You'll find it in ketchup. Baby food. Bagels. Spaghetti sauce. Pickles. Boxed macaroni and cheese. Bread. Instant oatmeal. Frozen pizza. Canned soups. Frozen waffles. Salad dressings. Boxed skillet meals. Deli meats. Even dog food! (And yes, our pets are getting fat and sick as well.)

Even more maddeningly, another 13 category of sugar-stuffed foods includes ones that we've been led to believe are "healthy." You know all those "low-fat" versions of food that you've been feeling righteous about buying? Sorry, Charlie. You've been had. The sad truth is that fat makes food taste good. And when you reduce the fat content of many processed foods, you end up with a product with all the taste appeal of cardboard. So what do manufacturers do in order to make the low-fat version tasty? You guessed it—they add sugar to it! Lots of sugar. Low-fat versions of cookies, crackers, peanut butter, muffins, frozen meals, salad dressings, candies, etc. contain an average of *20 percent more sugar* than their full-fat counterparts. Twenty percent! And you *know* that when you eat a "low-fat" snack, you feel justified° in having a second or a third helping, because hey! It's low-fat! That means healthier, right?

14   By this point, certain questions may be forming in your mind. You may be wondering, "If the food industry knows how bad sugar is for us, why do they put so much of it in foods? Don't they care that kids are getting fatter and sicker? And what's the government doing about all this? Aren't they supposed to protect us from things that hurt people, especially kids?"

15   Well, those would be very good questions. And the answers will make you angry. At least they should.

16   Because, yes. The processed-food industry knows exactly how bad much of their food is for us. They have the best food chemists in the world working for them. Those chemists have worked tirelessly for years to discover the exact combinations of sugary, salty, and fatty tastes that make the pleasure center in the human brain light up like a pinball

machine, much in the same way that cocaine does. And just as cocaine addicts require more and more coke to get the same pleasure rush, sugar addicts need larger and larger doses of sugar to feel satisfied. This is particularly disturbing news when we consider the fate of children who begin eating a sugar-heavy diet at a very young age. As they grow up, those children are doomed to crave ever greater amounts of sugar, leading to ever more devastating health consequences.

17   The other result of sugar's addictive qualities, of course, is that food manufacturers are making enormous profits. And when challenged to take more responsibility for the obesity epidemic and its related health problems, industry executives hide behind a litany° of weasel words and patriotic-sounding rhetoric°: *We're just giving people what they want. Americans are capable of making their own choices. No one wants a "nanny state" in which food choices are made by the government.*

18   And to a shameful extent, our government lets them get away with it. The processed-food industry has some of the highest paid and most influential lobbyists° in Washington, and they and the politicians they wine and dine and help get re-elected have fought food reform efforts every step of the way. When First Lady Michelle Obama decided to use her influence to battle childhood obesity, she came out of the gate strongly. She laid it on the line in an address to the Grocery Manufacturers Association:

19   *We need you not just to tweak around the edges, but to entirely rethink the products that you're offering, the information that you provide about these products, and how you market those products to our children. . . . While decreasing fat is certainly a good thing, replacing it with sugar and salt isn't. And it doesn't mean compensating for high amounts of problematic ingredients with small amounts of beneficial ones—for example, adding a little bit of Vitamin C to a product with lots of sugar, or a gram of fiber to a product with tons of fat, doesn't suddenly make those products good for our kids. . . . This isn't about finding creative ways to market products as healthy. As you know, it's about producing products that actually are healthy— products that can help shape the health habits of an entire generation.*

20   That was in 2010. Since then, food manufacturers have put out sugar-coated—oops, make that pleasant-sounding—statements about how very concerned they, too, are about children's health. And in the meantime, they're putting the same poison on the grocery shelves and making empty gestures like applauding Mrs. Obama's "Let's Move!" campaign, which encourages children to become more physically active.

21   But as made heartbreakingly clear in the documentary *Fed Up*, children cannot exercise their way out of obesity. As producer Laurie David says, "Exercise is essential for good health. But . . . just look at one small stat from the movie, which is a child who drinks one soda a day would have to be on a bicycle for an hour and 15 minutes to get rid of that soda. There really aren't enough hours in the day to exercise this food off." Food manufacturers also wage endless battles against food reform in schools. In December 2014, they succeeded in watering down standards for school lunches aimed at lowering their salt content and requiring that pasta and tortillas be made with whole grains. Meanwhile, the FDA (Food and Drug Administration, the branch of the government that oversees food safety) is so cowed by the might of the food industry that it hasn't even set a recommended daily allowance for sugar in our diet—a simple move that would make food labels much more meaningful to the average American consumer.

22   All of which leaves us, American consumers who care about our own health and those of our children, pretty much to our own devices. Our best option for saving ourselves from the sugar epidemic is to divorce ourselves from the Standard American Diet. Cook meals from scratch, concentrating on the non-processed or lightly processed foods that are found in the outermost aisles of the supermarket: meat, fish, vegetables, fruit, whole grains. But doing that requires an investment of time and know-how that many Americans are unwilling or unable to invest. The other option is to become far more savvy about the processed foods we *do* choose to buy. Learn to read

ingredient lists and to recognize added sugar where it hides. Don't be fooled by misleading labels that suggest food is "healthy" because its ingredients have been tweaked in some meaningless way. Begin tracking how much sugar you actually consume in a day. If you're eating too much sugar, consider taking the "Fed Up Challenge," which supports participants in eliminating sugar from their diet for ten days. The details are here: **http://fedupmovie.com/#/page/fedupchallenge**

Eliminating excess sugar from our 23 diets, as individuals and as a nation, isn't going to be easy. But it's absolutely necessary. Our future—our kids—depend upon it.

Vocabulary Questions

_____ 1. In the excerpt below, the word *drastic* (drăs′tĭk) means
   A. messy.
   B. pleasant.
   C. secret.
   D. extreme.

   "Today's kids—for the first time in 200 years—have shorter life expectancies than their parents. They will die, young, from heart disease, kidney failure, cancer, and Type 2 diabetes . . . So what has changed in the last 40 years that has made such a drastic difference in kids' health?" (Paragraphs 3–4)

_____ 2. In the sentence below, the word *counterparts* (koun′tər-pärts′) means
   A. treats.
   B. matching items.
   C. bad mistakes.
   D. small pieces.

   "Low-fat versions of cookies, crackers, peanut butter, muffins, frozen meals, salad dressings, candies, etc. contain an average of *20 percent more sugar* than their full-fat counterparts." (Paragraph 13)

_____ 3. In the excerpt below, the word *compensating* (kŏm′pən-sāt′ĭng) means
    A. making excuses.
    B. creating reasons.
    C. hoping.
    D. making up.

> "'While decreasing fat is certainly a good thing, replacing it with sugar and salt isn't. And it doesn't mean compensating for high amounts of problematic ingredients with small amounts of beneficial ones—for example, adding a little bit of Vitamin C to a product with lots of sugar, or a gram of fiber to a product with tons of fat, doesn't suddenly make those products good for our kids.'" (Paragraph 19)

_____ 4. In the excerpt below, the word *cowed* (kŏud) means
    A. strengthened.
    B. frightened.
    C. pleased.
    D. angered.

> "Food manufacturers also wage endless battles against food reform in schools. In December 2014 they succeeded in watering down standards for school lunches . . . Meanwhile, the FDA (Food and Drug Administration, the branch of the government that oversees food safety) is so cowed by the might of the food industry that it hasn't even set a recommended daily allowance for sugar in our diet—a simple move that would make food labels much more meaningful to the average American consumer." (Paragraph 21)

_____ 5. In the excerpt below, the word *savvy* (săv′ē)) means
    A. informed.
    B. careless.
    C. angry.
    D. amused.

> "The other option is to become far more savvy about the processed foods we *do* choose to buy. Learn to read ingredient lists and to recognize added sugar where it hides." (Paragraph 22)

Reading Comprehension Questions

Central Point and Main Ideas

_____ 1. Which sentence best expresses the central point of the selection?
   A. There is a serious problem in our country with sugar consumption, and nothing is being done about it.
   B. Eating too much sugar has created an obesity epidemic, so we need to become more aware of exactly what is in our food.
   C. Many of the food manufacturers in our country do not care about the health of Americans.
   D. There was a time when very few children were overweight, but today nearly one third of all children are either overweight or obese.

_____ 2. The main idea of paragraph 13 is
   A. stated in its first sentence.
   B. stated in its fifth sentence.
   C. stated in its sixth sentence.
   D. unstated.

_____ 3. The main idea of paragraph 16 is that
   A. sugar is like cocaine.
   B. children who become addicted to sugar will have health problems.
   C. most Americans do not realize how much sugar they are consuming.
   D. the food industry is intentionally trying to make us addicted to sugar.

Supporting Details

_____ 4. *Fill in the blanks:* Teens should have no more than _____ teaspoons of sugar a day, but just one 20-ounce bottle of Coke contains _____ teaspoons of sugar.
   A. 15, 15
   B. 5, 17
   C. 5, 4
   D. 10, 8

_____ 5. In what part of a supermarket can the healthiest foods be found?
   A. Around the edges and outermost aisles
   B. In the center of the store
   C. Near the checkout lanes
   D. In the frozen foods section

Transitions

_____ 6. The relationship between the sentences below is one of
   A. comparison.
   B. illustration.
   C. addition.
   D. time.

> "First, with both parents working outside the home in the majority of families, many Americans have turned away from cooking meals from scratch, preferring convenient "processed foods." Second, as the competition for shoppers' dollars heated up, processed-food manufacturers made an earth-shaking discovery: *The more sugar they put into their products, the more sugar consumers wanted.*" (Paragraph 4)

_____ 7. The relationship between the sentences below is one of
   A. time.
   B. addition.
   C. cause and effect.
   D. comparison.

> "Those chemists have worked tirelessly for years to discover the exact combinations of sugary, salty, and fatty tastes that make the pleasure center in the human brain light up like a pinball machine, much in the same way that cocaine does. And just as cocaine addicts require more and more coke to get the same pleasure rush, sugar addicts need larger and larger doses of sugar to feel satisfied." (Paragraph 16)

Patterns of Organization

_____ 8. The main pattern of organization of "Not So Sweet" is
   A. list of items.
   B. time order.
   C. cause and effect.
   D. definition and example.

Inferences

_____ 9. We can infer that the author
   A. was probably very overweight as a child.
   B. has experienced sugar addiction herself.
   C. has written a book about healthy eating.
   D. is very angry at the food industry for poisoning Americans with sugar.

_____ 10. We might conclude from paragraphs 20 and 21 that the food industry
   A. is making an effort to make food healthier for children.
   B. cares far more about profit than about the health of American children.
   C. fully supports Michelle Obama's "Let's Move!" campaign.
   D. is aware that exercise cannot burn enough calories to make up for all the sugar kids are eating.

Summarizing

Complete the following summary of "Not So Sweet" by filling in the blanks.

Too much sugar is creating a generation of sick kids. Because sugar (and too much of it) is in so many foods, children are suffering from obesity, leading to diabetes, cancer, and kidney failure. Amazingly, for the first time in 200 years, this generation of children _____

_____. And the food industry is well aware of just how terribly full of sugar many foods have become. The industry has loaded foods with sugar on purpose in order to make the food _____. They know that once children are hooked on sugar, they will continue buying the processed foods that contain sugar. All this sugar makes us sick because it interferes with the way our metabolism works. Our bodies can handle small amounts of sugar, but when too much is taken in, the _____ becomes overwhelmed and turns sugar into fat instead of breaking it down. Also, sugar is hidden in many foods we wouldn't expect to find it in. Making matters worse, even the word "sugar" is disguised on labels. But worst of all, our government lets the food industry get away with poisoning us. Highly paid food-industry lobbyists influence politicians, and the FDA is afraid to stand up to this powerful industry. Although Michelle Obama has worked hard to get kids active through her "_____

_____, exercise alone cannot combat the evils of sugar. Our best bet for saving our health and our children's health is to do two things: make meals from scratch and _____.

Discussion Questions

1. What information in this selection surprised you the most? Why?

2. After reading this selection, do you think you may be eating more sugar than you should? What are you eating that you should probably *not* be eating?

3. The "Let's Move!" campaign recommends one hour a day of "moderate to vigorous" activity for children. Do you think this amount is reasonable? Why or why not? Why do you think most children do not get an hour of exercise every day?

4. The food industry argues that they are simply "giving people what they want," and that Americans are capable of making their own choices without the government interfering by insisting on healthier food and clearer packaging. Do you agree or disagree with the food industry's position? Why or why not?

Note: Writing assignments for this selection appear on page 615.

Check Your Performance			NOT SO SWEET
Activity	*Number Right*	*Points*	*Total*
Vocabulary Questions (5 items)	_____	× 20 =	_____
		SCORE =	_____%
Reading Comprehension Questions			
Central Point and Main Ideas (3 items)	_____	× 8 =	_____
Supporting Details (2 items)	_____	× 8 =	_____
Transitions (2 items)	_____	× 8 =	_____
Patterns of Organization (1 item)	_____	× 8 =	_____
Inferences (2 items)	_____	× 8 =	_____
Summarizing (5 items)	_____	× 4 =	_____
		SCORE =	_____%
TOTAL SCORES: Vocabulary _____%		Comprehension _____%	

Enter your total scores into the **Reading Performance Chart: Ten Reading Selections** on the inside back cover.

Part Three

Active Reading, Relationships, and Combined Skills

1 An Introduction to Active Reading

Two Kinds of Readers

Many people are passive rather than active readers. Read the following description of passive and active readers and check (✓) the kind of reader that more fairly describes you. (It's OK to be honest.)

____ **Passive readers** read word after word without thinking much. Their attention may wander because they don't become interested in what they're reading. And since they aren't thinking about the material, they are likely to miss the main ideas and important details.

____ **Active readers** interest themselves by becoming involved in what they're reading. They think about what they read and ask themselves questions. Such active reading helps them to concentrate on what the author has to say. As a result, they are more likely than passive readers to understand and remember what they have read.

If you checked the first description, don't worry. You have already taken steps to break the habit of passive reading. With most chapters in this book, you have practiced an active reading skill:

- Guessing at the meaning of unfamiliar words
- Finding main ideas
- Recognizing key supporting details
- Understanding transitional words
- Identifying patterns of organization
- Making inferences
- Recognizing point and support

The goal of Part Three is to make you an active reader who is able to apply all of the skills, as needed. While you will practice here on short passages like those in standardized tests, the skills apply to material of any length.

Becoming an Active Reader

The following tips will help you read actively:

 TIP 1   When you read a passage for the first time, try to read it straight through. Frequent stops along the way will interfere with your getting the big picture. Don't feel you have to understand everything the first time through. Instead, focus on steady, active reading. After you have a good overall sense of the material, you can then go back to reread parts that were not clear at first.

 TIP 2   As you read, think about the main idea. Look for the main idea in the opening sentence or two. Ask yourself, "Is the main idea in one of these sentences? If not, where is it?" Just by asking this question, you'll get a head start on finding the main idea.

 TIP 3   As you read, think about the supporting details. As you continue reading the passage, actively ask yourself, "What is the main idea, and what is the support for that idea?" Again, asking questions helps you look for the answers. And if the main idea is unstated, the supporting details will help you figure out what the main idea is.

 TIP 4   As you read, look for relationships. Are there transitions that tell you, for example, that a list is being presented, or that two things are being contrasted, or that causes are being explained? Finding relationships is an important aid in understanding what you read.

 TIP 5   Along the way, make reasonable guesses. See if you can guess the meaning of any unknown words by looking at their context. And try to "read between the lines," guessing at some of the author's unstated meanings, when that seems to makes sense.

TIP 6   Reread as needed. Almost no one reads something just once and comes away with full comprehension. Instead, a careful first reading is often the first stage of understanding. Plan to go back and reread parts of the material as needed to gradually deepen your comprehension.

Most of all, the active reader is always trying to get to the heart of a passage: its main idea and the major details that support that idea. The two parts always go together; you cannot fully understand one without the other.

By now you may be saying to yourself, "Good grief. Active reading is asking a lot. I'm supposed to read a passage quickly but carefully, trying to understand it as best I can. I'm also supposed to be thinking about the main idea and its support as well as about relationships and implied ideas. Isn't this too much to do all at once?" The answer is definitely "No!" If you have the desire and if you practice, you will become a more effective reader.

A Model Passage

Read the passage below as quickly as you can with understanding. Look for the main idea in the opening sentence or two, and look for supporting details for the main idea. Then answer the questions and read the explanations that follow.

¹Elephants attracted to the odor of brewing beer have brought terror to some Indian villages. ²The beer is made from rice and is brewed after the rice harvest. ³The smell of the brew in one remote village attracted thirteen elephants, who drank the town's beer. ⁴Then they marched drunkenly through town, searching for more. ⁵In the process, they killed five people and injured twelve. ⁶Two thousand residents were forced to flee. ⁷Recently, similar disturbances by elephants have taken place in many villages, devastating more than fifteen thousand acres of rice paddies in one month.

_____ 1. In sentence 7, the word *devastating* means
    A. destroying.
    B. avoiding.
    C. planting.
    D. burning.

_____ 2. Which sentence expresses the main idea of the passage?
    A. "Elephants attracted to the odor of brewing beer have brought terror to some Indian villages."
    B. "The smell of the brew in one remote village attracted thirteen elephants, who drank the town's beer."
    C. "Two thousand residents were forced to flee."
    D. "Recently, similar disturbances by elephants have taken place in many villages, devastating more than fifteen thousand acres of rice paddies in one month."

_____ 3. TRUE OR FALSE? The elephants got drunk from rice beer.

_____ 4. The answer to question 3 can be found in sentence
      A. 1.
      B. 3.
      C. 4.
      D. 7.

_____ 5. The idea below is
      A. true according to the paragraph.
      B. false according to the paragraph.
      C. not mentioned in the paragraph.

        Elephants have been causing destruction in Indian villages for years.

_____ 6. Rice beer is brewed
      A. after the rice harvest.
      B. before the rice harvest.
      C. all year.
      D. every other year.

_____ 7. The relationship between sentences 3 and 4 is one of
      A. definition and example.
      B. time.
      C. contrast.
      D. comparison.

_____ 8. The passage implies that
      A. rice beer is no longer being made in India.
      B. the beer was brewed for the elephants.
      C. rice is an important crop in India.
      D. in India, rice is grown to feed the elephants.

Explanation

1. To find out the meaning of *devastating*, you could have asked, "What would drunken elephants do to acres of rice paddies that would be considered 'disturbances'?" Then you would have guessed the correct meaning of *devastating*: "destroying." So the answer to this question is A.

2. If you read the first sentence actively, you would have thought, "Is this sentence supported by the rest of the paragraph? Will I get details about terror in Indian villages?" In fact, you do, and the first sentence is the main idea. So the answer to this question is A.

3. Careful reading reveals that the answer to question 3 is *true*.

   > *Hint:* When questioned on a detail that you're not sure about, pick out key words in the question and look for those words in the passage. The key words in the question are *drunk* and *rice beer*. As you look for these key words in the passage, you quickly see that the elephants drank the beer and "marched drunkenly" through the town.

4. The answer is C—the answer to the third question can be found in sentence 4 in the words *they marched drunkenly*. Those words make it clear that elephants do, in fact, get drunk from the beer.

5. The answer is C, for the paragraph does not mention how long elephants have been causing the destruction. If you weren't sure of the answer to this question, a quick rereading would have given you the answer.

6. The answer to this question is A because sentence 2 tells us that the beer "is brewed after the rice harvest."

7. The answer is B. The transition *then* at the beginning of sentence 4 signals a time relationship: First, the elephants drank the town's beer; and after that, they marched through town, searching for more.

8. The correct answer is C. Sentence 7 tells us that many villages grow thousands of acres of rice. Nothing in the passage hints at answers A, B, or D.

✔

Check Your Understanding

Again, read the paragraph below as quickly as you can with understanding. Look for the main idea in the opening sentences, and look for supporting details for this idea. Then answer the questions and read the explanations that follow.

¹Officials often try to move homeless people to city shelters, where they can get a hot meal and a bed for the night. ²But for a variety of reasons, the homeless resist being helped. ³One reason is simple pride. ⁴If they remain on the street, they are their own bosses and do not feel humiliated by having to accept charity. ⁵In addition, many of the homeless are former mental patients who have difficulty getting along in society. ⁶For them, it is next to impossible to follow shelter rules and become part of a group of other homeless people. ⁷Finally, conditions in the shelters are not always pleasant. ⁸There may be noise and smells and disturbing sights, and drug use and petty theft are common.

_____ 1. In sentence 4, the word *humiliated* means
  A. hungry.
  B. shamed.
  C. the joy of being helped.
  D. a great deal richer.

_____ 2. Which would be the best title for this paragraph?
  A. Shelters for the Homeless
  B. Why the Homeless Avoid City Shelters
  C. Former Mental Patients
  D. Unpleasant Conditions in City Shelters

_____ 3. Which sentence expresses the main idea of the passage?
  A. Many homeless people are mental patients.
  B. City services often do not reach the people they are meant to help.
  C. Shelters can be unpleasant in various ways.
  D. Homeless people resist going to shelters for several reasons.

_____ 4. According to the passage, mental patients find it difficult to
  A. remain on the street.
  B. leave homeless shelters.
  C. follow shelter rules.
  D. all of the above.

_____ 5. The answer to question 4 can be found in sentence(s)
  A. 2.
  B. 3–4.
  C. 5–6.
  D. 7–8.

_____ 6. The relationship between sentences 1 and 2 is one of
   A. time.
   B. addition.
   C. contrast.
   D. comparison.

_____ 7. The paragraph is organized as
   A. a list of reasons.
   B. a series of events.
   C. a contrast between two things.
   D. a definition and examples.

_____ 8. From the passage we can infer that
   A. shelters actually have no rules to follow.
   B. city officials don't care about the pride of the homeless.
   C. the former mental patients eventually get better.
   D. homeless people face difficulties both on the street and in shelters.

Explanation

1. You could have guessed the correct meaning of _humiliated_ from sentences 3 and 4: "One reason is simple pride. If they remain on the street, they are their own bosses and do not feel humiliated by having to accept charity." These sentences suggest that a person who feels humiliated experiences the opposite of pride—in other words, shame. So the correct answer is B, "shamed."

2. A selection titled "Shelters for the Homeless" would tell us more about shelters—perhaps how they are run, what they do throughout a day, and so on. This paragraph tells us only one thing about the shelters—reasons the homeless resist going to them. So answer A is incorrect, and answer B is correct. Answer C could not be correct—it is too narrow. It mentions only former mental patients, but the paragraph is about all homeless people. Answer D is also too narrow—it refers to only one of the reasons the homeless avoid shelters.

3. Answers A and C are both too narrow—each is about only one part of the paragraph. Answer B is too broad—it refers to city services in general, but the paragraph is about only one specific service, city shelters. Answer D expresses the main idea of the passage, which is about the reasons the homeless resist going to shelters. (_A variety of reasons_ is an example of list words, as explained on page 128.)

4–5.   To find the answer to question 4, you had to remember (or go back and see) that only sentences 5–6 deal with mental patients. Those sentences say that "it is next to impossible" for mental patients "to follow shelter rules and become part of a group." So the correct answer for question 4 is C ("follow shelter rules"), and the correct answer for question 5 is also C ("sentences 5–6").

6.   The first word of sentence 2, *but*, signals a contrast, so the answer to this question is C. The author is contrasting the effort of city officials with the opposing response of the homeless.

7.   The supporting details are three reasons that explain why "the homeless resist being helped": 1) pride; 2) for mental patients, it is difficult to follow shelter rules and be part of a group of homeless people; and 3) shelters have unpleasant conditions. So the answer to this question is A, "a list of reasons." (The words *One, In addition,* and *Finally* are examples of addition words, as explained on page 129.)

8.   The passage suggests that people living out on the street have trouble getting a hot meal and a bed for the night. The paragraph also suggests that being in a shelter can be unpleasant. Thus answer D is correct. Answer A isn't correct. Sentence 6 says that shelters *do* have rules. Answer B is also incorrect. There is no evidence in the paragraph to tell us whether or not city officials care about the pride of the homeless. Nor is there evidence to support answer C— that former mental patients eventually get better. The paragraph states only that they have problems in shelters.

The relationships tests and combined-skills tests in the chapters that follow will help you develop your active reading skills.

2 Practice in Active Reading I: Relationships Tests

To think clearly and logically and have good comprehension, you need to understand relationships between ideas. The eight tests that follow will help you strengthen your understanding of the common types of relationships that have been explained in Chapters 6 and 7 of this book.

RELATIONSHIPS: Test 1

Here are some words that express relationships between ideas:

But (which means "however")
I liked Lola very much. *But* I did not love her.
Or: I liked Lola very much. *However*, I did not love her.

Because (which means "due to" or "the reason that")
Because I worked for ten hours straight, I was very tired.
Or: Due to working for ten hours straight, I was very tired.
Or: I was very tired. *The reason* was *that* I had worked for ten hours straight.

Therefore (which means "so" or "as a result")
My car would not start. *Therefore*, I decided to take a bus.
Or: My car would not start, *so* I decided to take a bus.
Or: My car would not start. *As a result*, I decided to take a bus.

Also (which means "and" or "in addition" or "moreover")
I wrote a paper for one of my classes. *Also*, I studied for an exam.
Or: I wrote a paper for one of my classes, *and* I studied for an exam.
Or: I wrote a paper for one of my classes. *In addition*, I studied for an exam.
Or: I wrote a paper for one of my classes. *Moreover*, I studied for an exam.

Then (which means "next" or "after")
In the morning, I drank some orange juice. *Then* I ate some oatmeal.
Or: In the morning, I drank some orange juice. *Next*, I ate some oatmeal.
Or: In the morning, I drank some orange juice. *After* that, I ate some oatmeal.

For each item below, write in the logical connecting word that describes the relationship between the two ideas.

1. **and, but, so**   It's easy to begin smoking, ____but____ it's much harder to quit.

2. **and, but, so**   I missed the bus, ____so____ I did not get to class on time.

3. **and, but, so**   My phone is missing, ____and____ my television stopped working.

4. **and, but, so**   My mother is mild-mannered, ____so____ my father can get very angry.

5. **Also, Then, Because**   I studied for three hours straight. ____Then____ I took a break.

6. **Also, Then, Because**   That color isn't right for you. ____Also / Because____, the style is wrong as well.

7. **Also, Then, Because**   ____Because____ the bill was not paid, our electricity was turned off.

8. **Therefore, However, In addition**   Some people are morning people. ____However____, I'm not one of them.

9. **Therefore, However, In addition**   I was out of jelly and butter. ____Therefore____, I spread yogurt on my toast.

10. **Therefore, However, In addition**   The dog walks on three legs. ____In addition____, its ear is chewed up.

RELATIONSHIPS: Test 2

For each item below, write in the logical connecting word that describes the relationship between the two ideas.

1. ***and, but, so***   I didn't hear my alarm this morning, __but__ I made it to class on time anyway.

2. ***and, but, so***   All the ice cream melted, __so__ we had cookies instead.

3. ***and, but, so***   The Christmas tree was too tall for the room, __and__ it also blocked the door.

4. ***and, but, so***   Our cat is very shy around strangers, __but__ she is friendly to us.

5. ***Also, Then, Because***   This cheese tastes weird. __also__, it smells really bad.

6. ***also, then, because***   Liz decided not to go to the party __because__ her ex-boyfriend was going to be there.

7. ***Also, Then, Because***   Everyone stood up and quieted down. __Then__ the national anthem began to play.

8. ***Therefore, However, In addition***   My brother wants to be on the basketball team. __However__, he's lazy about practicing.

9. ***Therefore,***
   However,
   In addition

People mostly download music today. _Therefore_, CD sales have declined.

10. ***Therefore,***
    However,
    In addition

You have a great singing voice. _In Addition_, you seem relaxed on stage.

RELATIONSHIPS: Test 3

For each item below, write in the logical connecting word that describes the relationship between the two ideas.

1. *and, but, so*   I'm very allergic to peanuts, ____SO____ I have
   to be careful about what I eat.

2. *and, but, so*   The parrot knew about fifty words, ___and___
   it could sing ten songs.

3. *and, but, so*   We thought it would be sunny in Florida, ___but___
   it rained the entire time we were there.

4. *and, but, so*   You may think that joke is funny, ___but___
   no one else does.

5. *also, then,*   People are buying smaller cars ___because___
   because   small cars get better gas mileage.

6. *Also, Then,*   I squinted at everything for a year. ___Then___
   Because   I realized I needed glasses.

7. *Also, Then,*   The ambulance is flashing its lights. _~~Because~~ Also_,
   Because   the siren is wailing.

8. *Therefore,*   My sister loves numbers. ___Therefore___, she plans
   However,   to study math in college.
   In addition

9. ***Therefore,***
    However,
    In addition

    Our dog is very friendly. _In addition_, she is very well-behaved.

10. ***Therefore,***
    However,
    In addition

    Mice are not particularly smart. _However_, rats are actually pretty intelligent.

RELATIONSHIPS: Test 4

For each item below, write in the logical connecting word that describes the relationship between the two ideas.

1. ***and, but, so***   I spent the entire day cleaning the house, ~~but~~ *so*
    I'm too tired to go out tonight.

2. ***and, but, so***   You never call me anymore, *and* you
    don't seem to want to see me.

3. ***and, but, so***   The moon was shining on the ocean, *and*
    the stars glittered in the sky.

4. ***and, but, so***   I like my coffee black, ~~and~~ *but* I put a lot of
    milk in my tea.

5. ***also, then,***   Jay says he likes playing the tuba *because*
    because   it's such an unusual instrument.

6. ***Also, Then,***   The tickets to the concert are much too expensive.
    Because   ~~because~~ *Also*, the only seats available are bad ones.

7. ***Also, Then,***   The jet climbed higher and higher. *Because*
    Because   it leveled out at cruising altitude.

8. ***Therefore,***   Bryant broke his leg when he was 10. *Therefore*,
    However,   he has a slight limp when he walks.
    In addition

9. ***Therefore,***
   However,
   In addition

I like pineapple on pizza. _In addition_ ~~However~~, I like thin crust better than thick.

10. ***Therefore,***
    However,
    In addition

The painters thought they had done a good job. _However_, they had used the wrong paint.

RELATIONSHIPS: Test 5

For each group below, choose the item in which the word or words in italics are used logically.

_____A_____ 1. You are smoking two packs of cigarettes a day. You are reducing your life expectancy.
   A. *Due to* smoking two packs of cigarettes a day, you are reducing your life expectancy.
   B. You are smoking two packs of cigarettes a day. *Also*, you are reducing your life expectancy.
   C. You are reducing your life expectancy. *Therefore*, you are smoking two packs of cigarettes a day.

 2. The posted starting time for the movie was 7:30 p.m. Twenty minutes of ads and previews preceded the movie.
   A. The posted starting time for the movie was 7:30 p.m., *but* 20 minutes of ads and previews preceded the movie.
   B. The posted starting time for the movie was 7:30 p.m., *and* 20 minutes of ads and previews preceded the movie.
   C. The posted starting time for the movie was 7:30 p.m. *Therefore*, 20 minutes of ads and previews preceded the movie.

 3. The killer was shocked by the jury's verdict. He thought he had fooled everyone.
   A. The killer was shocked by the jury's verdict. *Therefore*, he thought he had fooled everyone.
   B. The killer was shocked by the jury's verdict *because* he thought he had fooled everyone.
   C. The killer thought he had fooled everyone, *but* he was shocked by the jury's verdict.

_____A_____ 4. The earth is getting warmer. We will still have periods of cold weather.
   A. The earth is getting warmer. *However*, we will still have periods of cold weather.
   B. The earth is getting warmer. *Therefore*, we will still have periods of cold weather.
   C. The earth is getting warmer, *and* we will still have periods of cold weather.

_____C_____ 5. The movie was sold out. We went out for pizza instead.
   A. The movie was sold out, *but* we went out for pizza instead.
   B. *After* the movie was sold out, we went out for pizza instead.
   C. The movie was sold out, *so* we went out for pizza instead.

B 6. I worked two jobs and a lot of overtime last summer. I wanted to save money for college.
   A. I worked two jobs and a lot of overtime last summer, *so* I wanted to save money for college.
   B. *The reason* I worked two jobs and a lot of overtime last summer *was that* I wanted to save money for college.
   C. I wanted to save money for college, *but* I worked two jobs and a lot of overtime last summer.

B 7. Dolphins sleep with one eye open. Most birds sleep with one leg pulled up.
   A. Dolphins sleep with one eye open *due to* most birds sleeping with one leg pulled up.
   B. Dolphins sleep with one eye open, *and* most birds sleep with one leg pulled up.
   C. *Because* dolphins sleep with one eye open, most birds sleep with one leg pulled up.

C 8. Every time Maribel has to take a test, she feels sick. She finds it hard to breathe.
   A. Every time Maribel has to take a test, she feels sick, *but* she finds it hard to breathe.
   B. Every time Maribel has to take a test, she feels sick. *However,* she finds it hard to breathe.
   C. Every time Maribel has to take a test, she feels sick. *In addition,* she finds it hard to breathe.

A 9. My grandmother's family was poor when she was a girl. She is very careful with her money.
   A. My grandmother's family was poor when she was a girl. *Therefore,* she is very careful with her money.
   B. My grandmother's family was poor when she was a girl. *However,* she is very careful with her money.
   C. My grandmother's family was poor when she was a girl, *because* she is very careful with her money.

A 10. The English language has one word for snow. Eskimos have 15 words for snow.
   A. The English language has one word for snow, *but* Eskimos have 15 words for snow.
   B. *Because* the English language has one word for snow, Eskimos have 15 words for snow.
   C. The English language has one word for snow. *In addition,* Eskimos have 15 words for snow.

RELATIONSHIPS: Test 6

For each group below, choose the item in which the word or words in italics are used logically.

_____ 1. The *Titanic* was nicknamed "The Unsinkable." It struck an iceberg and sank on its very first voyage.
   A. The *Titanic* was nicknamed "The Unsinkable," *and* it struck an iceberg and sank on its very first voyage.
   B. *Because* the *Titanic* was nicknamed "The Unsinkable," it struck an iceberg and sank on its very first voyage.
   C. The *Titanic* was nicknamed "The Unsinkable," *but* it struck an iceberg and sank on its very first voyage.

_____ 2. People fear sharks. More people are killed by pigs each year than by sharks.
   A. People fear sharks. *However*, more people are killed by pigs each year than by sharks.
   B. *Due to* people's fear of sharks, more people are killed by pigs each year than by sharks.
   C. People fear sharks. *Therefore*, more people are killed by pigs each year than by sharks.

_____ 3. First, the firefighters rushed in and rescued the cat. They put out the spreading flames.
   A. First, the firefighters rushed in and rescued the cat. *However*, they put out the spreading flames.
   B. First, the firefighters rushed in and rescued the cat. *Moreover*, they put out the spreading flames.
   C. First, the firefighters rushed in and rescued the cat. *Next*, they put out the spreading flames.

_____ 4. Our oceans are 95 percent unexplored. Two-thirds of all ocean life is undiscovered.
   A. *After* our oceans are 95 percent unexplored, two-thirds of all ocean life is undiscovered.
   B. Our oceans are 95 percent unexplored. *Moreover*, two-thirds of all ocean life is undiscovered.
   C. Our oceans are 95 percent unexplored *because* two-thirds of all ocean life is undiscovered.

_____ 5. Gas prices are skyrocketing. We're not going on vacation this summer.
   A. Gas prices are skyrocketing, *because* we're not going on vacation this summer.
   B. *Due to* skyrocketing gas prices, we're not going on vacation this summer.
   C. We're not going on vacation this summer, *and* gas prices are skyrocketing.

_A_ 6. Houdini wanted to capture the attention of his audiences. He took death-defying risks.

   A. Houdini wanted to capture the attention of his audiences, *so* he took death-defying risks.

   B. Houdini took death-defying risks, *but* he wanted to capture the attention of his audiences.

   C. Houdini wanted to capture the attention of his audiences. *Moreover,* he took death-defying risks.

_A_ 7. The levees in New Orleans were not strong enough. Much of the city was flooded.

   A. The levees in New Orleans were not strong enough. *Therefore,* much of the city was flooded.

   B. The levees in New Orleans were not strong enough. *Then,* much of the city was flooded.

   C. The levees in New Orleans were not strong enough *because* much of the city was flooded.

_B_ 8. A baby robin eats about every 20 minutes. It eats about 14 feet of earthworms a day.

   A. A baby robin eats about every 20 minutes. *Next,* it eats about 14 feet of earthworms a day.

   B. A baby robin eats about every 20 minutes. *Also,* it eats about 14 feet of earthworms a day.

   C. A baby robin eats about 14 feet of earthworms a day. *However,* it eats about every 20 minutes.

_C_ 9. Using crutches can be frustrating. Crutches can cause backaches.

   A. Using crutches can be frustrating. *Next,* crutches can cause backaches.

   B. Using crutches can be frustrating. *As a result,* crutches can cause backaches.

   C. Using crutches can be frustrating. *Moreover,* crutches can cause backaches.

_B_ 10. There is a thunderstorm warning. Little League practice has been canceled.

   A. Little League practice has been canceled. *As a result,* there is a thunderstorm warning.

   B. *Due to* a thunderstorm warning, Little League practice has been canceled.

   C. There is a thunderstorm warning, *but* Little League practice has been canceled.

RELATIONSHIPS: Test 7

For each group below, choose the item in which the word or words in italics are used logically.

_____ 1. America is a wealthy country. Thirty million Americans regularly experience hunger.
   A. America is a wealthy country, *so* 30 million Americans regularly experience hunger.
   B. America is a wealthy country. *However*, 30 million Americans regularly experience hunger.
   C. America is a wealthy country. *Moreover*, 30 million Americans regularly experience hunger.

_____ 2. As a child, Einstein had a learning disability. He made only average grades in high school.
   A. As a child, Einstein had a learning disability. *In addition*, he made only average grades in high school.
   B. As a child, Einstein had a learning disability, *but* he made only average grades in high school.
   C. As a child, Einstein had a learning disability *because* he made only average grades in high school.

_____ 3. Adults laugh about 12 times a day. Most children laugh nearly 400 times a day.
   A. Adults laugh about 12 times a day, *but* most children laugh nearly 400 times a day.
   B. Adults laugh about 12 times a day. *Therefore*, most children laugh nearly 400 times a day.
   C. Most children laugh nearly 400 times a day, *because* adults laugh about 12 times a day.

_____ 4. In some parts of Africa, people have to walk far to get water. Water is very scarce.
   A. In some parts of Africa, people have to walk far to get water. *As a result*, water is very scarce.
   B. In some parts of Africa, people have to walk far to get water. *Therefore*, water is very scarce.
   C. In some parts of Africa, people have to walk far to get water *because* water is very scarce.

_____ 5. King George VI was afraid to speak in public. He had a terrible stutter.
   A. King George VI was afraid to speak in public *due to* his terrible stutter.
   B. King George VI was afraid to speak in public. *As a result*, he had a terrible stutter.
   C. King George VI had a terrible stutter, *but* he was afraid to speak in public.

_____ 6. Carter makes up excuses for not riding the roller coaster. He has a fear of heights.
   A. Carter makes up excuses for not riding the roller coaster. *Therefore*, he has a fear of heights.
   B. *After* Carter makes up excuses for not riding the roller coaster, he has a fear of heights.
   C. *The reason* Carter makes up excuses for not riding the roller coaster *is that* he has a fear of heights.

_____ 7. The coach threw his headset at a referee. The coach was ejected from the game.
   A. The coach was ejected from the game. *However*, the coach threw his headset at a referee.
   B. The coach threw his headset at a referee. *As a result*, the coach was ejected from the game.
   C. The coach threw his headset at a referee. *Moreover*, the coach was ejected from the game.

_____ 8. Sheryl wants to go skiing. Yesterday she sprained her ankle skating.
   A. Sheryl wants to go skiing. *Then* yesterday she sprained her ankle skating.
   B. Sheryl wants to go skiing. *Moreover*, yesterday, she sprained her ankle skating.
   C. Sheryl wants to go skiing. *However*, yesterday she sprained her ankle skating.

_____ 9. Our cat loves the taste of pine needles. We now have a fake Christmas tree every year.
   A. Our cat loves the taste of pine needles, *but* we now have a fake Christmas tree every year.
   B. Our cat loves the taste of pine needles, *because* we now have a fake Christmas tree every year.
   C. Our cat loves the taste of pine needles. *Therefore*, we now have a fake Christmas tree every year.

_____ 10. His mother told him to be home by midnight. She told him not to drink at the party.
   A. His mother told him to be home by midnight. *As a result*, she told him not to drink at the party.
   B. His mother told him to be home by midnight, *but* she told him not to drink at the party.
   C. His mother told him to be home by midnight. *Moreover*, she told him not to drink at the party.

RELATIONSHIPS: Test 8

For each group below, choose the item in which the word or words in italics are used logically.

_____ 1. Kyra saw live cells through a microscope. She became interested in biology.
   A. Kyra saw live cells through a microscope. *In addition*, she became interested in biology.
   B. *After* Kyra saw live cells through a microscope, she became interested in biology.
   C. Kyra saw live cells through a microscope. *However*, she became interested in biology.

_____ 2. People are not afraid of champagne corks. Flying corks can cause blindness and even death if they hit people in the eye or forehead.
   A. People are not afraid of champagne corks, *but* flying corks can cause blindness and even death if they hit people in the eye or forehead.
   B. People are not afraid of champagne corks. *As a result*, flying corks can cause blindness and even death if they hit people in the eye or forehead.
   C. People are not afraid of champagne corks *because* flying corks can cause blindness and even death if they hit people in the eye or forehead.

_____ 3. Seasons in Australia are the opposite of ours. Australians celebrate Christmas during their summer.
   A. Australians celebrate Christmas during their summer, *and* seasons in Australia are the opposite of ours.
   B. Seasons in Australia are the opposite of ours. *Therefore*, Australians celebrate Christmas during their summer.
   C. *After* seasons in Australia are the opposite of ours, Australians celebrate Christmas during their summer.

_____ 4. Water covers 70 percent of the earth. Only 3 percent of that water is drinkable.
   A. Water covers 70 percent of the earth. *Moreover*, only 3 percent of the water is drinkable.
   B. Water covers 70 percent of the earth. *Therefore*, only 3 percent of that water is drinkable.
   C. Water covers 70 percent of the earth. *However*, only 3 percent of that water is drinkable.

_____ 5. Many dogs love the taste of chocolate. Chocolate can damage a dog's heart.
   A. Many dogs love the taste of chocolate, *but* chocolate can damage a dog's heart.
   B. Many dogs love the taste of chocolate. *Then*, chocolate can damage a dog's heart.
   C. Many dogs love the taste of chocolate *because* chocolate can damage a dog's heart.

_____ 6. On January 1st, I began eating a lot of fruits and vegetables. I want to get healthier.
  A. I want to get healthier, *but* on January 1st, I began eating a lot of fruits and vegetables.
  B. On January 1st, I began eating a lot of fruits and vegetables. *Next,* I want to get healthier.
  C. On January 1st, I began eating a lot of fruits and vegetables *because* I want to get healthier.

_____ 7. New runners often get injured within the first month. They try to do too much too soon.
  A. *Because* they try to do too much too soon, new runners often get injured within the first month.
  B. New runners often get injured within the first month. *Then,* they try to do too much too soon.
  C. New runners often get injured within the first month. *Therefore,* they try to do too much too soon.

_____ 8. Some insects are packed with nutrients. Most people think eating insects is disgusting.
  A. Some insects are packed with nutrients *because* most people think eating insects is disgusting.
  B. Some insects are packed with nutrients, *but* most people think eating insects is disgusting.
  C. Some insects are packed with nutrients. *Also,* most people think eating insects is disgusting.

_____ 9. Learning to play the violin requires patience. It requires a lot of practice.
  A. Learning to play the violin requires patience. *Next,* it requires a lot of practice.
  B. Learning to play the violin requires patience. *As a result,* it requires a lot of practice.
  C. Learning to play the violin requires patience. *In addition,* it requires a lot of practice.

_____10. Cats' eyes glow in the dark. Some people believe cats are possessed by evil spirits.
  A. Cats' eyes glow in the dark. *As a result,* some people believe cats are possessed by evil spirits.
  B. Cats' eyes glow in the dark, *but* some people believe cats are possessed by evil spirits.
  C. Cats' eyes glow in the dark *because* some people believe cats are possessed by evil spirits.

3 Practice in Active Reading II: Combined-Skills Tests

ollowing are 20 tests that cover the skills taught in Part One and reinforced in Part Two of this book. Each test consists of a short reading passage followed by questions on any of the following: vocabulary in context, main ideas, supporting details, transitions, patterns of organization, and inferences.

COMBINED SKILLS: Test 1

Read the passage below. Then write the letter of the best answer to each question that follows.

¹A girl who had been late every day so far came up after class to inform me that she was probably going to be late a lot, and didn't want me marking her late. ²(Being late counts for one-third an absence.)

³"Why are you going to be late?" I asked. ⁴She explained that the traffic is heavy between her house and the school, and the drive takes longer than it should. ⁵"Doesn't that mean you need to leave your house earlier?" I asked. ⁶She looked exasperated and said, "No! I LEAVE at 7. ⁷I only live 30 miles away. ⁸It shouldn't take more than an hour to get here."

⁹There was a brief silence as I waited for her to say something that made sense. ¹⁰Nothing was forthcoming. ¹¹I finally said, "But apparently it does take more than an hour, so . . . I think the only solution is for you to leave earlier." ¹²She wailed, "But that would mean leaving home at SIX-THIRTY. ¹³Can't I do some extra credit work or something?"

¹⁴Again, we just looked at each other as I shook my head. ¹⁵Did she expect me to say to her, "Oh, of course, YOU don't have to be on time. ¹⁶Just the other students."

_____ 1. In sentence 6, the word *exasperated* means
    A. tired.
    B. frightened.
    C. frustrated.
    D. pleased.

_____ 2. In sentence 11, the word *apparently* means
    A. evidently.
    B. unfairly.
    C. not very often.
    D. strangely.

_____ 3. Which sentence best states the main idea of the selection?
    A. A student must get up at 6:30 a.m. to arrive on time for her class.
    B. A student asks her teacher for extra credit work because she knows she will often be late for class.
    C. A teacher gives a student some good advice about getting to class on time.
    D. A teacher is amazed that a student wants the rules about lateness bent just for her.

_____ 4. According to the passage, the student
A. lives an hour away from her school.
B. does not want to leave home before 7 a.m.
C. drives to school at a time when there is little traffic.
D. is a very cautious driver.

_____ 5. The main pattern of organization used in this passage is
A. list of items.
B. comparison.
C. definition and example.
D. time order.

_____ 6. We can infer from the passage that the writer
A. has had many students ask for favors.
B. knows the student has a good reason for being late.
C. is a teacher.
D. is a parent whose children are college students.

_____ 7. We can infer from the passage that the teacher
A. will no longer mark the student late for class.
B. will continue to mark the student late for class.
C. will probably give the student extra credit work.
D. will tell the student that she is acting like a spoiled brat.

_____ 8. The passage suggests that
A. teachers need to be more flexible about classroom rules.
B. it is not a good idea to schedule classes in the morning.
C. some students are unwilling to do what it takes to succeed in school.
D. the student will probably drop out of school.

COMBINED SKILLS: Test 2

Read the passage below. Then write the letter of the best answer to each question that follows.

[1]If you saw students sitting quietly in a lecture hall, you might think they were all involved in the lecture. [2]However, if you rang a bell at sporadic points during a lecture and asked the students to reveal their thoughts at each of those moments, you would find that very few of them were actively listening to the lecturer. [3]During a typical lecture, about 20 percent of the students are thinking sexual thoughts. [4]Another 20 percent are reminiscing about past events in their lives. [5]Only 20 percent are actually paying attention to the lecture. [6]And only 12 percent are actively listening. [7]The others are worrying, daydreaming, or thinking about lunch or—surprise!—religion.

_____ 1. In sentence 2, the word *sporadic* means
  A. zero.
  B. expected.
  C. high.
  D. occasional.

_____ 2. In sentence 4, the words *reminiscing about* mean
  A. forgetting about.
  B. talking about.
  C. looking back on.
  D. not thinking of.

_____ 3. The sentence that best expresses the main idea of the passage is sentence
  A. 2.
  B. 3.
  C. 4.
  D. 7.

_____ 4. The relationship of sentence 4 to the sentence before it is one of
  A. time.
  B. addition.
  C. an example.
  D. cause.

_____ 5. The main pattern of organization of this paragraph is
  A. time order.
  B. definition and example.
  C. cause and effect.
  D. list of items.

_____ 6. We can infer that a researcher must have
        A. guessed about what students were thinking at various points during school lectures.
        B. asked students what they were thinking at various points during school lectures.
        C. asked lecturers what they thought students were thinking at various points during school lectures.
        D. been in the lecture hall every day.

_____ 7. We can conclude that a lecturer might improve student attention by
        A. changing the beginning of a lecture.
        B. having students participate in class.
        C. ringing a bell at various times during the lecture.
        D. lecturing for a longer period of time.

_____ 8. The passage suggests that
        A. there is a difference between paying attention to something and actively listening to it.
        B. only very few people have the ability to listen actively.
        C. active listening is easy.
        D. most lectures are not very important.

COMBINED SKILLS: Test 3

Read the passage below. Then write the letter of the best answer to each question that follows.

¹One day, a man walked into a bank as if he was ready for war. ²He was carrying an ax, a stun gun, a smoke grenade, and a can of Mace. ³He demanded a lot of money in small bills right away. ⁴The tellers quickly loaded up a big bag with small bills. ⁵The problem was the robber was holding so many weapons he didn't have any hands left to carry the bag. ⁶Holding the bag as best he could, he took off out the door but then tripped. ⁷Another man passing by on the street jumped on him and held him down until the police arrived.

⁸Another incredible but true story is about the man in the Elvis mask who held up a store. ⁹He got the money and turned so fast to run that the mask didn't turn with him. ¹⁰It was now on backwards. ¹¹He sprinted toward the door anyway but then hit the doorframe so hard that he knocked himself out. ¹²He learned—the hard way—that a robber's mask might look good on TV, but it can be a problem in real life.

¹³And there was another would-be thief who tried the old paper-bag trick. ¹⁴Cutting two holes in the bag for his eyes, he tried to rob a convenience store. ¹⁵But he didn't cut out a hole for his mouth. ¹⁶As a result, the clerk couldn't understand what he was saying. ¹⁷"What?" the clerk kept asking. ¹⁸The robber flew into a rage. ¹⁹He tried to tear a hole for his mouth, but ended up tearing the bag right off his head. ²⁰The clerk looked at him and said, "Jerry?" ²¹Sure enough, the robber was another clerk who worked at the store.

_____ 1. In sentence 11, the word *sprinted* means
  A. walked.
  B. ran.
  C. looked.
  D. yelled.

_____ 2. Which sentence best states the main idea of the selection?
  A. It's not a good idea to wear a mask while robbing a bank or store.
  B. Some robberies are more successful than others.
  C. Robbing banks or stores is not really a serious crime.
  D. Some would-be criminals are really stupid.

_____ 3. The bank robber failed because
  A. he hit the door frame so hard that he knocked himself out.
  B. he was thrown off balance by all the stuff he was carrying.
  C. the can of Mace he was carrying went off in his face.
  D. he couldn't breathe through his mask.

_D_ 4. One robber became angry when
   A. his Elvis mask got turned around.
   B. the clerk in the store he was robbing recognized him as a coworker.
   C. he couldn't breathe through the mask he was wearing.
   D. a clerk couldn't understand what he was saying.

_A_ 5. The relationship of sentence 8 to the sentences that come before it is one of
   A. addition.
   B. time.
   C. contrast.
   D. cause and effect.

_C_ 6. The relationship of sentence 16 to sentence 15 is one of
   A. time.
   B. addition.
   C. cause and effect.
   D. an example.

_B_ 7. The first paragraph suggests that the bank robber
   A. was prepared to kill someone.
   B. felt he needed to carry as many weapons as possible.
   C. had robbed other banks.
   D. was angry at the way the bank had treated him in the past.

_D_ 8. We can infer from the passage that
   A. each of the would-be robbers had robbed other places.
   B. all of the criminals were caught.
   C. each of the robberies had been carefully planned.
   D. most robberies are unsuccessful.

COMBINED SKILLS: Test 4

Read the passage below. Then write the letter of the best answer to each question that follows.

¹Constant everyday fatigue and lack of energy can be due to various causes. ²One common cause, not surprisingly, is insufficient sleep. ³Many people simply do not allow themselves enough hours to sleep; and others have sleep disturbances, such as insomnia, that prevent them from getting the sleep they need. ⁴Another cause of fatigue is anemia—a low level of hemoglobin in the blood—which usually requires a better diet or nutritional supplements. ⁵Lack of exercise can also be a cause of fatigue. ⁶You might think that exercise will make you tired, but on the contrary, it tends to prevent fatigue. ⁷Low thyroid function can cause fatigue, too, unless remedied with hormone supplementation. ⁸Clinical depression, a serious but very treatable condition, is still another possible cause of fatigue. ⁹So, if you "feel tired all the time," could it be for one of these reasons?

_____ 1. In sentence 7, the word *remedied* means
    A. corrected.
    B. caused.
    C. damaged.
    D. invented.

_____ 2. The main idea of this passage is found in sentence
    A. 1.
    B. 2.
    C. 3.
    D. 4.

_____ 3. How many possible reasons for fatigue does the passage provide in support of the main idea?
    A. 3
    B. 4
    C. 5
    D. 6

_____ 4. A possible treatment for anemia is
    A. more exercise.
    B. a better diet.
    C. hormone supplements.
    D. more sleep.

_____ 5. One possible cause of fatigue is
    A. an overactive thyroid.
    B. extreme exercise.
    C. too much hemoglobin in the blood.
    D. an underactive thyroid.

_____ 6. The main pattern of organization used in this passage is
    A. cause and effect.
    B. time order.
    C. contrast.
    D. definition and examples.

_____ 7. The passage implies that
    A. most causes of everyday fatigue can be successfully treated.
    B. constant everyday fatigue is an increasingly common problem.
    C. lack of exercise is the most common reason for fatigue.
    D. people should be able to just "snap out" of being depressed.

_____ 8. We might conclude from the passage that
    A. it is natural to feel more fatigued as one grows older.
    B. most cases of constant fatigue are caused by serious medical problems.
    C. fatigue is usually a mental problem, not a physical one.
    D. if getting more sleep and exercise doesn't relieve fatigue, it's time to see a doctor.

COMBINED SKILLS: Test 5

Read the passage below. Then write the letter of the best answer to each question that follows.

[1]Touching is vital to human development. [2]During the nineteenth and early twentieth centuries, a large percentage of children died from a disease then called *marasmus*. [3]In Greek, this word means "wasting away." [4]In some orphanages, the mortality rate was nearly 100 percent. [5]However, even children in the most "advanced" homes and institutions died regularly from the disease. [6]Researchers finally found that the infants suffered from lack of physical contact with parents or nurses. [7]The children hadn't been touched enough, and as a result, they died. [8]From this knowledge came the practice in institutions of picking a baby up, carrying it around, and handling it several times each day. [9]At one hospital that began this practice, the death rate for infants fell from between 30 and 35 percent to below 10 percent.

_____ 1. In sentence 1, the word *vital* means
      A. necessary.
      B. beside the point.
      C. superior.
      D. an added bonus.

_____ 2. In sentence 4, the word *mortality* means
      A. health.
      B. death.
      C. Greek.
      D. touching.

_____ 3. The main idea of the paragraph is stated in sentence
      A. 1.
      B. 2.
      C. 8.
      D. 9.

_____ 4. *Marasmus* is
      A. an illness that struck people of all ages.
      B. mainly a Greek illness.
      C. an illness that killed children in orphanages and elsewhere.
      D. all of the above.

_____ 5. The relationship between the first and second parts of sentence 7 is one of
   A. comparison.
   B. contrast.
   C. cause and effect.
   D. time.

_____ 6. Within the context of the passage, touch is
   A. a cause.
   B. an effect.
   C. something compared.
   D. an example.

_____ 7. From this passage, we can assume that in the nineteenth and early twentieth centuries, children tended to get less attention
   A. at home, from their parents.
   B. in orphanages.
   C. in Greece.
   D. at hospitals where *marasmus* was understood.

_____ 8. From the passage, we can infer that touching is one advantage of
   A. giving birth to a child.
   B. breast-feeding a child.
   C. putting a child in a hospital.
   D. giving a child vitamins.

COMBINED SKILLS: Test 6

Read the passage below. Then write the letter of the best answer to each question that follows.

¹Feelings come and go within minutes. ²A mood, on the other hand, is a more sustained emotional state that colors our view of the world for hours or days. ³One researcher found that bad moods descend upon us an average of three out of every ten days.

⁴There are gender differences in dealing with moods. ⁵Men typically try to distract themselves (a partially successful strategy) or use alcohol or drugs (an ineffective tactic). ⁶Women are more likely to talk to someone (which can help) or to spend a long time thinking about why they feel bad (which doesn't help).

⁷The most effective way to banish a sad or bad mood is by changing what caused it in the first place. ⁸Keep in mind that most bad moods are caused by loss or failure—in school, in work, or in intimate relationships. ⁹If you can do anything to fix the loss or failure, take action and solve it. ¹⁰For example, ask to take a makeup exam. ¹¹Or tell your friend you feel bad about the argument you had with her.

¹²If there's nothing you can do, accept what happened and focus on doing things differently next time. ¹³Studies show that resolving to try harder actually can be as effective in improving a mood as taking action in the present.

¹⁴Another good option is to get moving. ¹⁵Studies have shown that exercise ranks as the single most effective way to banish bad feelings. ¹⁶Exercise can boost spirits, improve sleep and appetite, and reduce anxiety and anger.

_____ 1. In sentence 2, the word *sustained* means
      A. organized.
      B. negative.
      C. long-lasting.
      D. confusing.

_____ 2. In sentences 7 and 15, the word *banish* means
      A. understand.
      B. encourage.
      C. remember.
      D. drive away.

_____ 3. Which sentence best states the main idea of the selection?
      A. Moods last much longer than feelings.
      B. Men and women differ in the way they deal with bad moods.
      C. The most effective way to banish a sad or bad mood is by changing what caused it in the first place.
      D. There are several effective ways to banish a sad or bad mood.

_____ 4.   According to research,

      A. bad moods occur more often than good moods.

      B. one way to banish a bad mood is to spend a lot of time thinking about it.

      C. most bad moods are a response to loss or failure in some aspect of a person's life.

      D. feelings can sometimes last for hours or days.

_____ 5.   TRUE OR FALSE? One good way to get rid of a bad mood is to lie down and take a nap.

_____ 6.   The relationship of sentence 10 to sentence 9 is one of

      A. addition.

      B. illustration.

      C. comparison.

      D. cause and effect.

_____ 7.   This passage mainly

      A. lists ways to banish sad or bad moods.

      B. contrasts male and female behavior with regard to moods.

      C. explains why some people experience more bad moods than others.

      D. defines the terms *feelings* and *moods*.

_____ 8.   The passage suggests that

      A. women are more used to talking about their feelings than men are.

      B. some people never have bad moods.

      C. men try harder than women to banish bad moods.

      D. women experience bad moods more often than men.

COMBINED SKILLS: Test 7

Read the passage below. Then write the letter of the best answer to each question that follows.

¹Turn on your TV on a weekday afternoon or a Saturday, and you'll probably see cute cartoon characters urging kids to try the latest candy-coated cereal or rush out the door for some tasty fast food. ²For years, people have debated whether ads like these, which target young children, should be allowed on the air. ³The idea of banning children's ads is supported by many parents, teachers, and doctors. ⁴These people quote studies showing that young children often can't tell the difference between a TV program and a TV commercial. ⁵Because they don't understand the real purpose of ads, they think everything an ad says is true. ⁶But cereal companies, television networks, and major advertising agencies strongly disagree—and with good reason. ⁷They earn a lot of money producing these ads, broadcasting these ads, or selling products with these ads.

⁸The average American child now spends about 35 hours a week in front of a TV. ⁹This means that in one year, that child watches more than 25,000 TV commercials. ¹⁰Two-thirds of those ads are for junk food: soda, candy, sugary cereals, and burgers and fries. ¹¹As a result, children now see almost two hours of junk-food ads every week. ¹²Sadly, American kids aren't learning the truth about food, either in the classroom or on the Internet. ¹³Instead, they're being told what to eat by junk-food ads that they see over and over.

_____ 1. In sentence 3, the word *banning* means
   A. correcting.
   B. inventing.
   C. recognizing.
   D. doing away with.

_____ 2. Which sentence best states the main idea of the selection?
   A. The eating habits of American kids are shaped by watching TV commercials for junk food.
   B. American kids watch too much TV.
   C. American kids eat too much junk food.
   D. Banning ads targeted at children is opposed by some groups and supported by others.

_____ 3. The average American child
   A. watches 10,000 TV commercials a year.
   B. sees about 5 hours of junk-food ads a week.
   C. spends about 35 hours a week watching TV.
   D. sees about one hour of junk-food ads every day.

_____ 4. According to the passage, young children
   A. watch more TV than older children do.
   B. like to watch ads for junk food more than other types of ads.
   C. often learn about healthy eating before they start school.
   D. believe that what ads say is true.

_____ 5. The relationship of sentence 6 to the sentences before it is one of
   A. addition.
   B. cause and effect.
   C. illustration.
   D. contrast.

_____ 6. We can conclude from the passage that
   A. many breakfast cereals are not good for children's health.
   B. schools are doing a fine job of educating kids about healthy eating.
   C. cereal companies, television networks, and ad agencies put the health of American children above making money.
   D. all of the above.

_____ 7. The passage suggests that
   A. if parents, teachers, and doctors join together, they can ban TV advertising aimed at kids.
   B. cereal companies, television networks, and major ad agencies are more powerful than parents, teachers, and doctors.
   C. the people who work for cereal companies, television networks, and ad agencies do not have children.
   D. ads targeting kids will soon begin to show up on the Internet.

_____ 8. The author clearly implies that
   A. people have only recently begun to debate ads targeting kids.
   B. parents should not permit their children to watch more than a couple of hours of TV a week.
   C. in the next few years, TV stations will not be permitted to broadcast commercials aimed at kids.
   D. it would be a good idea to ban TV advertising aimed at kids.

COMBINED SKILLS: Test 8

Read the passage below. Then write the letter of the best answer to each question that follows.

[1]One beautiful sunny day, I was playing a Little League baseball game with other seven-year-olds. [2]Near the end of the game, as I stepped into the batter's box, my coach called me back to the dugout. [3]He asked if it would be all right if my brother hit for me. [4]My brother wasn't on the team. [5]He had never even played baseball due to his disability. [6]He couldn't stand, and he certainly couldn't hit. [7]But I responded very maturely for a kid my age. [8]"Of course he can hit for me," I said. [9]I was still puzzled as to how, though. [10]Thoughts ran through my mind: Would the kids make fun of him? [11]Would he hit the ball? [12]As my dad carried him to the plate, I realized that without his wheelchair, he would have to be held up. [13]The joy on his face couldn't be traded for anything in the world. [14]Just being on the field gave him all the happiness he needed. [15]What will the other kids think? I wondered. [16]I heard someone call out, "C'mon, hit it outta here." [17]Then came another, "You can do it!" [18]These words of acceptance showed me how great the moment really was. [19]On the first swing, which was pretty much my dad holding Sam's hands around the bat and my dad swinging, he—or they—hit the ball. [20]The kids on the other team did something amazing then, something seven-year-olds should never know how or why to do. [21]But in the spur of the moment, these seven-year-olds did. [22]They purposely overthrew the ball. [23]Three times. [24]Sam had hit his first and only home run. [25]And as my dad carried him around the bases, I knew this memory would stick with me and everyone else there forever.

_____ 1. In sentence 7, the word *maturely* means
    A. sadly.
    B. wisely.
    C. rudely.
    D. sincerely.

_____ 2. Which sentence best expresses the main idea of the paragraph?
    A. Sometimes young children do things that are surprising.
    B. The speaker had no idea that his brother could hit a home run.
    C. The opposing team overthrew the baseball on purpose.
    D. When everyone works together to help someone, it's a great moment.

_____ 3. When the speaker's dad held Sam at the plate, the speaker wondered
    A. who would cheer for Sam.
    B. if his team would win the game.
    C. how Sam would hit the ball.
    D. what the other kids would think.

_____ 4. The main pattern of organization for this paragraph is
     A. list of items.
     B. definition and example.
     C. comparison.
     D. time order.

_____ 5. The relationship of sentence 21 to sentence 20 is one of
     A. addition.
     B. illustration.
     C. contrast.
     D. cause and effect.

_____ 6. We can infer that the coach
     A. was not happy about having Sam bat.
     B. had spoken with Sam's dad about Sam batting.
     C. also has a disabled son.
     D. did not realize that Sam was disabled.

_____ 7. On the basis of the paragraph, we can conclude that the author was
     A. very athletic and competitive when he was young.
     B. often angry and frustrated with his brother.
     C. generous and loving toward his brother.
     D. shy and anxious around other seven-year-olds.

_____ 8. Sentences 20–23 suggest that the opposing team
     A. had rehearsed overthrowing the ball.
     B. had followed their coach's instructions to overthrow the ball.
     C. acted generously and on their own to overthrow the ball.
     D. overthrew the ball completely by accident.

COMBINED SKILLS: Test 9

Read the passage below. Then write the letter of the best answer to each question that follows.

¹On a Saturday morning in February, 1851, Shadrach Minkins was working as a waiter at a Boston coffeehouse. ²Suddenly, two men pretending to be customers grabbed him and announced that he was under arrest. ³Minkins, an escaped slave from Virginia, had thought he was safe in the "free state" of Massachusetts. ⁴But the Fugitive Slave Law of 1850 had changed that. ⁵Under this law, residents of free states had to cooperate with authorities capturing runaway slaves. ⁶If they didn't, they could be jailed and fined. ⁷Many residents of Boston were opposed to slavery, and the news of Minkins's capture made them furious. ⁸A crowd of black and white citizens quickly gathered at the courthouse where Minkins was being held. ⁹They forced their way past armed guards and carried Minkins away. ¹⁰After hiding him briefly in an attic, they smuggled him to safety in Canada. ¹¹Nine of the people who rescued Minkins were arrested, although charges against them were eventually dropped. ¹²The citizens of Boston had made their point: they would not cooperate with the Fugitive Slave Law.

_____ 1. In sentence 4, the word *fugitive* means
    A. dangerous.
    B. escaped.
    C. legal.
    D. pardoned.

_____ 2. In sentence 10, the word *smuggled* means
    A. kept from.
    B. accepted.
    C. chased.
    D. secretly took.

_____ 3. The main idea of the passage—a summary of the events described—is found in sentence
    A. 1.
    B. 2.
    C. 3.
    D. 12.

_____ 4. Under the Fugitive Slave Law of 1850,
    A. slavery was made illegal.
    B. it became illegal to hire a former slave.
    C. people in free states had to help authorities catch runaway slaves.
    D. Shadrach Minkins won his freedom.

_____ 5. Some of the people who helped Shadrach Minkins escape
   A. were arrested, but charges were later dropped.
   B. were fined and imprisoned.
   C. had to escape to Canada.
   D. chose to live in Canada.

_____ 6. The main pattern of organization used in this passage is
   A. comparison and/or contrast.
   B. list of items.
   C. definition and example.
   D. time order.

_____ 7. The relationship of sentence 4 to sentence 3 is one of
   A. contrast.
   B. illustration.
   C. comparison.
   D. time.

_____ 8. The passage implies that
   A. in 1851, slavery was still legal in Virginia.
   B. Shadrach Minkins was a well-known activist.
   C. only African-American people were concerned about slavery.
   D. Minkins was the first person arrested in Massachusetts under the Fugitive Slave Law.

COMBINED SKILLS: Test 10

Read the passage below. Then write the letter of the best answer to each question that follows.

[1]Driving has always been dangerous, but a new epidemic stretching across America's highways is making it even more risky. [2]Researchers call this problem "road rage"—an intense anger that makes drivers become violent. [3]Road rage is usually triggered by a minor traffic incident, such as someone honking a horn at another driver, or one person cutting in front of another. [4]But once it strikes, this rage instantly turns ordinary people into possible killers. [5]For example, recently one motorist on his way to work got angry when a car zipped in front of him, forcing him to slow down. [6]The driver was so enraged that he pulled out a gun, drove up to the side of the other car, and tried to shoot the driver. [7]Instead, he hit and killed the passenger—the driver's pregnant wife. [8]Sadly, stories like this have been reported all over the country, particularly in crowded urban areas.

[9]Psychologists think that road rage is caused by a buildup of stress that acts like a time bomb waiting to explode. [10]Once an event triggers the release of the tension, road rage strikes. [11]Since anyone on the road can be one of these "time bombs," police suggest that you drive carefully. [12]They also say to call them if someone looks particularly angry and is driving in an inconsistent way.

_____ 1. In sentence 3, the word *triggered* means
    A. imitated.
    B. shot.
    C. started.
    D. ended.

_____ 2. Which sentence best expresses the main idea of the first paragraph?
    A. Road rage is an intense anger felt by drivers.
    B. A motorist became so angry when another car cut in front of him that he tried to shoot the other driver, but shot the driver's passenger instead.
    C. Driving is more dangerous than ever because many drivers are becoming violently angry.
    D. People are more likely to become angry and violent in crowded urban areas than in other areas.

_____ 3. According to the passage, drivers with road rage often
   A. are angered by dangerous driving.
   B. become violent over minor events.
   C. are poor drivers.
   D. are excellent drivers.

_____ 4. Road rage is more likely to occur
   A. in crowded urban areas.
   B. on country roads.
   C. in parking lots.
   D. on suburban roads.

_____ 5. The idea below is
   A. true according to the passage.
   B. false according to the passage.
   C. not mentioned in the passage.

      People who drink are more likely to have road rage.

_____ 6. Sentences 9 and 10 explain
   A. a time relationship.
   B. a cause-effect relationship.
   C. contrasting situations.
   D. a comparison.

_____ 7. The author suggests that people with road rage often
   A. are young.
   B. are unemployed.
   C. drive very carefully.
   D. experience a lot of stress.

_____ 8. We might infer from the passage that
   A. we are very unlikely to bump into a person with road rage.
   B. drivers are less likely to become angry at female drivers.
   C. most drivers experience road rage.
   D. it is best to keep one's distance from aggressive drivers.

COMBINED SKILLS: Test 11

Read the passage below. Then write the letter of the best answer to each question that follows.

¹Research shows that we make assumptions about people on the basis of what they are wearing. ²In one study, a man and a woman were stationed in a hallway so that anyone who wished to go by had to respond to them in some way. ³They could either politely excuse themselves or rudely ignore them. ⁴Sometimes the conversationalists wore "formal daytime dress." ⁵At other times, they wore "casual attire." ⁶Passers-by behaved differently toward the couple, depending on the style of clothing being worn. ⁷They responded positively to the well-dressed couple and negatively when the same people were casually dressed. ⁸Similar results in other situations show the influence of clothing. ⁹Pedestrians were more likely to return lost coins to well-dressed people than to those dressed in low-status clothing. ¹⁰We are also more likely to follow the lead of high-status dressers, even when it comes to violating social rules. ¹¹For example, 83 percent of the pedestrians in one study followed a well-dressed jaywalker who crossed when a traffic light flashed "wait." ¹²But only 48 percent followed a jaywalker dressed in lower-status clothing.

_____ 1. In sentence 2, the word *stationed* means
  A. imagined.
  B. avoided.
  C. forced.
  D. placed.

_____ 2. In sentence 10, the word *violating* means
  A. breaking.
  B. understanding.
  C. following.
  D. learning.

_____ 3. Which sentence best states the main idea of the selection?
  A. In one experiment, people who passed a casually dressed couple responded negatively to them.
  B. The way people dress affects the way we view them and the level of influence they have over us.
  C. To get ahead in a career, dress in a high-status manner.
  D. Pedestrians were more likely to return coins to well-dressed people than to those dressed in low-status clothing.

_____ 4. According to the experiment, we are more likely to return lost coins to
   A. men.
   B. women.
   C. people in high-status clothing.
   D. people in low-status clothing.

_____ 5. People tend to react more positively toward
   A. men who are casually dressed.
   B. women.
   C. people who are dressed formally or in a high-status manner.
   D. couples who are dressed alike.

_____ 6. The relationship of sentence 8 to sentence 7 is one of
   A. time.
   B. illustration.
   C. comparison.
   D. contrast.

_____ 7. The relationship of sentences 11 and 12 to sentence 10 is one of
   A. time.
   B. illustration.
   C. contrast.
   D. comparison.

_____ 8. We can infer from this passage that our reactions are sometimes
   A. not thought out.
   B. based on appearances.
   C. illogical.
   D. all of the above.

COMBINED SKILLS: Test 12

Read the passage below. Then write the letter of the best answer to each question that follows.

¹People have a number of reasons for taking up smoking. ²It may be their response to stress or depression. ³It may be because their friends smoke or their parents do. ⁴It may be because cigarette companies spend billions of dollars each year on ads that falsely connect smoking to health, happiness, fitness, and sexual appeal.

⁵But whatever the reasons for lighting up that first cigarette, a very different factor keeps cigarettes burning pack after pack, year after year. ⁶In national polls, 7 out of 10 smokers say that they want to quit but can't. ⁷It's not simply because of a lack of willpower. ⁸Nicotine—the addictive ingredient in tobacco—is the reason.

⁹Nicotine has a much more powerful hold on smokers than alcohol does on drinkers. ¹⁰About 10 percent of alcohol users lose control of their intake of alcohol and become alcoholics. ¹¹On the other hand, as many as 80 percent of all heavy smokers have tried to cut down or quit smoking but cannot overcome their dependence.

¹²Nicotine causes dependence by at least three means. ¹³First, it acts on brain chemicals to provide a strong sensation of pleasure. ¹⁴In addition, it leads to fairly severe discomfort during withdrawal. ¹⁵Last, it creates cravings long after obvious withdrawal symptoms have passed. ¹⁶Few drugs act as quickly on the brain as nicotine does. ¹⁷It travels through the bloodstream to the brain in seven seconds—half the time it takes for heroin injected into a blood vessel to reach the brain. ¹⁸And a pack-a-day smoker gets 200 hits of nicotine a day—73,000 a year.

_____ 1. Which sentence best states the main idea of the passage?
   A. People start smoking for a number of reasons.
   B. Nicotine has a much more powerful hold on smokers than alcohol does on drinkers.
   C. Cigarette companies spend billions of dollars each year on ads that connect smoking to health, happiness, fitness, and sexual appeal.
   D. Whatever a person's reason for taking up smoking, the nicotine in cigarettes makes it extremely difficult to stop.

_____ 2. After it has been inhaled through smoking, how long does it take for nicotine to reach the brain?
   A. 7 seconds
   B. 10 seconds
   C. 14 seconds
   D. one minute

_____ 3. The percentage of people who drink and become alcoholics is
   A. 70%.
   B. 20%.
   C. 10%.
   D. 1%.

_____ 4. The relationship of sentence 11 to sentence 10 is one of
   A. comparison.
   B. cause and effect.
   C. illustration.
   D. contrast.

_____ 5. The main patterns of organization of paragraph 4 are list of items and
   A. time order.
   B. cause and effect.
   C. comparison.
   D. contrast.

_____ 6. By comparing the amount of time it takes nicotine and heroin to pass through the bloodstream to the brain, the author is suggesting that
   A. nicotine is a far less harmful drug than heroin.
   B. nicotine, like heroin, is a dangerous drug.
   C. people who inject heroin would be better off injecting nicotine instead.
   D. it is better to inhale heroin than to inject it.

_____ 7. We can conclude that
   A. most heavy smokers are aware that smoking is bad for their health.
   B. many heavy smokers are also alcoholics.
   C. most people start smoking to relieve depression.
   D. all of the above.

_____ 8. The passage suggests that
   A. cigarette companies do not realize that nicotine is addictive.
   B. cigarette companies hope that people will become addicted to the nicotine in cigarettes.
   C. people would still find smoking pleasurable if cigarettes did not contain nicotine.
   D. being an alcoholic or heroin addict is less dangerous than being a heavy smoker.

COMBINED SKILLS: Test 13

Read the passage below. Then write the letter of the best answer to each question that follows.

[1]Money appears to be very much on the minds of college freshmen, according to a recent survey of nearly 220,000 full-time freshmen at 300 colleges. [2]Colleges were advised to prepare for students who are "increasingly anxious" about the economy.

[3]The report states that students today are more likely to need loans than they were in the past. [4]More students than before are saying that an offer of financial aid is "very important" in choosing a college. [5]Moreover, a record 78 percent identified "being well-off financially" as a top objective. [6]That's higher than "raising a family" (74 percent) or "helping others in difficulty" (69 percent). [7]Forty years ago, the primary goal of most students was "to develop a meaningful philosophy of life." [8]Today, however, the main goal is to have financial security.

[9]There are other signs that financial concerns are intensifying. [10]Over 40 percent of students surveyed said that cost was a large factor in their choice of a school. [11]More students than in past surveys have an unemployed father and/or mother. [12]And more students than ever said a very important factor in selecting a college was whether its "graduates get good jobs."

_____ 1. In sentence 9, the word *intensifying* means
   A. becoming less serious.
   B. increasing.
   C. leveling off.
   D. becoming more difficult to notice.

_____ 2. The main idea of the passage is stated in sentence
   A. 1.
   B. 2.
   C. 3.
   D. 12.

_____ 3. TRUE OR FALSE? Most college freshmen choose what college to attend based on cost.

_____ 4. The report advises colleges to
   A. prepare to admit students who are not ready to do college-level work.
   B. provide more financial aid to incoming freshmen.
   C. offer students courses that will enable them to find good jobs.
   D. prepare for students who are anxious about the economy.

___D___ 5. The relationship of sentence 5 to sentences 3 and 4 is one of
  A. time order.
  B. contrast.
  C. definition and example.
  D. addition.

___C___ 6. The selection mainly
  A. compares male and female college freshmen.
  B. explains why so many of today's college students are applying for scholarships.
  C. provides facts and statistics that support the idea that today's college students are very concerned about money.
  D. provides examples of typical freshman behavior.

___A___ 7. The passage suggests that a college freshman today would be less likely to
  A. take courses simply because he or she enjoys them.
  B. seek financial aid.
  C. work at a part-time job while going to school.
  D. come from families who are struggling to pay their bills.

___B___ 8. The passage suggests that
  A. there are fewer college freshmen today than there were forty years ago.
  B. today's college freshmen fear that they may not be able to find jobs after they graduate.
  C. most college freshmen enroll in the least expensive college they can find.
  D. college students no longer major in impractical subjects such as art and music.

COMBINED SKILLS: Test 14

Read the passage below. Then write the letter of the best answer to each question that follows.

¹The next time you're in a busy public restroom, try a little experiment. ²Hang around for ten minutes or so. ³Pretend to be combing your hair or tying your shoe or fixing your makeup. ⁴While you're doing that, observe what percentage of people wash their hands after using the toilet. ⁵I mean *really* wash them, with soap, for at least 15 seconds. ⁶Chances are that your results will be "Not very many." ⁷Studies show that 15 percent of men and 7 percent of women don't wash their hands at all. ⁸Only 50 percent of male hand-washers use soap, while 78 percent of women do. ⁹And even among those who use soap, only 5 percent wash for long enough. ¹⁰Now, why should you care if other people don't wash their hands adequately? ¹¹Because after exiting that restroom, those people are all around you. ¹²They are touching doorknobs, ATM buttons, pens, phones, countertops, and armrests that you will later touch. ¹³They are shaking hands with you. ¹⁴They are handing you advertising flyers. ¹⁵They are preparing your food. ¹⁶And their unwashed hands are swarming with germs. ¹⁷This is a gross thought, but worth knowing: a tiny smudge of human feces—that's the fancy word for "poop"—can contain over one trillion germs. ¹⁸And those germs can cause everything from diarrhea to typhoid fever. ¹⁹There's not much you can do to make other people, especially strangers, wash their hands regularly. ²⁰However, your best defense against their germ-laden hands is to wash yours frequently, with plenty of soap, and for at least 15 seconds.

_____ 1. In sentence 16, the word *swarming* means
   A. fighting.
   B. becoming sick.
   C. overflowing.
   D. dangerous.

_____ 2. Which sentence best expresses the main idea of this passage?
   A. Men are less likely than women to wash their hands after using the restroom.
   B. Germs on unwashed hands can make you sick with anything from diarrhea to typhoid.
   C. Washing hands thoroughly after using the restroom is important for stopping the spread of germs and disease.
   D. Germs can spread from unwashed hands through food preparation, shaking hands, telephones, and even doorknobs.

_____ 3. According to the passage, hands should be washed for at least
   A. 5 seconds.
   B. 15 seconds.
   C. 45 seconds.
   D. 2 minutes.

_____ 4. We should care if other people don't wash their hands adequately
        because
        A. they are everywhere we are, and they are spreading their germs to us.
        B. many of them are sick with various illnesses.
        C. they are shaking our hands and preparing our food.
        D. they need to learn how to wash their hands properly.

_____ 5. The main pattern of organization of this passage is
        A. time order.
        B. comparison and contrast.
        C. a list.
        D. cause and effect.

_____ 6. The relationship of sentence 20 to sentence 19 is one of
        A. time order.
        B. illustration.
        C. comparison.
        D. contrast.

_____ 7. We can infer from this passage that the author
        A. often reminds people to wash their hands.
        B. is a woman.
        C. washes her or his hands thoroughly after using the restroom.
        D. is probably reluctant to shake hands or eat in restaurants.

_____ 8. Sentences 19 and 20 imply that
        A. you can avoid getting sick from others' germs by washing your
           hands well.
        B. people are basically inconsiderate and self-centered.
        C. it is a hassle to spend that long washing your hands, but you should
           do it.
        D. even if you tell people to wash their hands, they won't.

COMBINED SKILLS: Test 15

Read the passage below. Then write the letter of the best answer to each question that follows.

[1]Recently, a certain congressman suggested that poor children who receive free school lunches be made to work for those meals. [2]Why don't the poor kids sweep the cafeteria floors? he asked. [3]That, he suggested, would be an appropriate way to earn their food and to teach them the value of labor. [4]Well, I'd like to teach that congressman the value of a few things, starting with compassion and a sense of humanity. [5]You see, not long ago I was one of those poor kids receiving a federally subsidized school lunch. [6]And I'd like to assure that well-fed congressman sitting in the comfort of his office that I was absolutely aware of the cost of my "free lunch." [7]In my own childish way, I paid for every bite of that food. [8]I paid every time I endured the taunts of my better-off classmates or the pitying looks or sneers of the lunch ladies. [9]I paid every time I witnessed the shame and anger of my parents, who worked themselves to the bone but still could not pull themselves out of the pit of poverty. [10]I paid with every field trip I could not go on, every school picture I could not buy, every after-school club I could not afford to join. [11]And you, Mr. Congressman, would like to heap further humiliation on poor children by having them clean up the messes left by their wealthier classmates? [12]How dare you.

_____ 1. In sentence 8, the word *taunts* means
  A. interest.
  B. silence.
  C. smiles.
  D. insults.

_____ 2. The main idea of the paragraph is stated in sentence
  A. 1.
  B. 2.
  C. 3.
  D. 4.

_____ 3. The congressman suggests that poor children who get free school lunches sweep the cafeteria floors because the children will then
  A. be able to go on field trips.
  B. earn money to pay for things.
  C. learn the value of labor.
  D. buy a school picture.

_____ 4. The author of the selection "paid" for the free school lunch by
   A. seeing how ashamed and angry his or her parents were.
   B. joining after-school clubs.
   C. smiling at the lunch ladies.
   D. going on school field trips.

_____ 5. The pattern of organization in sentences 7–10 is
   A. cause and effect.
   B. comparison.
   C. list of items.
   D. time order.

_____ 6. The relationship of sentence 9 to sentence 8 is one of
   A. comparison.
   B. addition.
   C. contrast.
   D. time.

_____ 7. The selection implies that the congressman
   A. knows how hard the author's parents worked.
   B. understands the hardships that poor children face.
   C. has never experienced poverty himself.
   D. will not be reelected.

_____ 8. The author implies that
   A. the congressman lacks understanding and sympathy.
   B. the poor children would learn lessons by cleaning up after their classmates.
   C. the wealthier children should be cleaning up after the poor classmates.
   D. the congressman is caring and understanding.

COMBINED SKILLS: Test 16

Read the passage below. Then write the letter of the best answer to each question that follows.

[1]As one sociologist points out, adolescents and old people, as groups in our culture, are strikingly similar in certain ways. [2]First, they are both often segregated from the rest of society. [3]Young people are in schools, and old people are in retirement communities, assisted-living facilities, and nursing homes. [4]Second, they both tend to be poorer than young adults or middle-aged people. [5]Adolescents have less money because they do not yet have the education or experience to command high salaries, and old people have lower incomes because they are retired and living on their savings and social security. [6]Third, independence is important for both groups—they are conscious of wanting it, while young adults and middle-aged people take it for granted. [7]Adolescents want to become independent of their parents; old people want to keep their independence and not have to rely on their children or on institutions. [8]Fourth, they both tend to have a relatively large amount of leisure time or, at least, time that they can choose or not choose to fill with study, work, or hobbies. [9]However, young and middle-aged adults typically spend most of their time at their jobs or taking care of home duties such as child-rearing.

_____ 1. In sentence 5, the word *command* means
   A. pay.
   B. desire.
   C. deserve.
   D. avoid.

_____ 2. In sentence 6, the word *conscious* means
   A. bored.
   B. pleased.
   C. aware.
   D. tired.

_____ 3. The main idea of this passage is stated in sentence
   A. 1.
   B. 2.
   C. 5.
   D. 9.

_____ 4. One thing old people and adolescents tend to have a lot of is
   A. money.
   B. leisure time.
   C. independence.
   D. education.

_____ 5. This selection is mainly organized as
A. events in the lives of adolescents and the elderly, in a time order.
B. a list of comparisons between adolescents and old people.
C. definitions of adolescence and old age, with examples of each.
D. causes of problems in adolescence and old age.

_____ 6. The paragraph contrasts adolescents and old people with
A. unemployed people.
B. children and teenagers.
C. poor people.
D. middle-aged people and young adults.

_____ 7. The relationship between sentences 8 and 9 is one of
A. contrast.
B. comparison.
C. addition.
D. time.

_____ 8. The paragraph implies that people of all ages value
A. employment.
B. social security.
C. independence.
D. intellectual challenge.

COMBINED SKILLS: Test 17

Read the passage below. Then write the letter of the best answer to each question that follows.

[1]Men and women can get along better if they try to understand each other's communication style. [2]As sociologist Deborah Tannen says in her book *You Just Don't Understand*, for many men the purpose of talk is "information," while for many women it is "interaction." [3]These different purposes can lead to confusion, misunderstanding, and even anger between partners. [4]For example, if a woman asks her husband what he wants to do on Saturday night, he might answer simply, "I don't care." [5]And that is probably exactly what he means. [6]Going to a movie, going out to dinner, or going bowling all sound the same to him. [7]His wife, on the other hand, feels let down by his answer. [8]When she asked, "What do you want to do?" she was hoping to engage him in a real conversation about their plans. [9]She wanted to talk about the possibilities and share in the decision of what to do. [10]Such a conversation would make her feel closer and more in touch with her husband. [11]To her, his brief "I don't care" makes him seem indifferent to her and the time they spend together. [12]Because of their different communication styles, the husband and wife come away from the same conversation with completely different impressions of what happened. [13]The man believes that he answered her question honestly and that everything is OK. [14]The woman feels ignored by her husband and disappointed by his lack of response.

_____ 1. In sentence 2, the word *interaction* means
    A. argument.
    B. sharing.
    C. planning.
    D. confusion.

_____ 2. In sentence 8, the word *engage* means
    A. force.
    B. find.
    C. involve.
    D. trick.

_____ 3. The main idea of this passage is found in sentence
    A. 1.
    B. 3.
    C. 12.
    D. 14.

_____ 4. According to sociologist Deborah Tannen, the purpose of talk for many
            men is
            A. interaction.
            B. making plans.
            C. entertainment.
            D. information.

_____ 5. The main pattern of organization in this passage is
            A. time order.
            B. list of items.
            C. contrast.
            D. definition and example.

_____ 6. The relationship between the two parts of sentence 12 is one of
            A. addition.
            B. comparison.
            C. illustration.
            D. cause and effect.

_____ 7. We can infer from this passage that
            A. men in general often have a difficult time showing interest in plans.
            B. the woman in the passage was more interested in sharing than in
               actual plans.
            C. men and women will probably never be able to communicate well.
            D. the man in the passage is probably tired of trying to talk to his wife.

_____ 8. Sentences 4–6 imply that
            A. men are typically unconcerned about the specific details of a plan.
            B. bowling, going to a movie, or going to dinner are very similar
               activities.
            C. men are being honest, not indifferent, when they say, "I don't care."
            D. women often ask too many questions.

COMBINED SKILLS: Test 18

Read the passage below. Then write the letter of the best answer to each question that follows.

[1]Back when I was a teenager, young folks went on this thing called a "date." [2]A boy might ask a girl to go out with him at a specific time to a specific event. [3]For instance, he might say, "Would you like to go to the movies with me Sunday afternoon?" [4]If she said yes, he would go to her house, probably meet her parents, and then escort her to the event. [5]At the end of the date, if they had enjoyed each other's company, they might share a kiss, and he might say, "Can I call you again?" [6]Nowadays, I understand, young people don't date. [7]They hang out. [8]Hanging out usually involves a group, so nobody really knows who is or might be a couple. [9]The group goes to each other's places to watch movies. [10]Instead of talking face to face, or even on the phone, they text each other. [11]Rather than getting to know each other a bit and then deciding to date, they use websites that allow them to glance at strangers' photos and instantly decide "Yes" or "No." [12]Even when the group hanging out together involves people who are attracted to each other, everyone spends most of their time staring at their phones, reading texts or status updates from people who aren't there. [13]When asked if they are seeing anyone special, most say something like, "No, we're just hooking up." [14]No one knows what "hooking up" means. [15]Depending on whom you ask, it can mean anything from hanging out to—well, something else. [16]But by my old-time definition, it is definitely not dating.

_____ 1. In sentence 2, the word *specific* means
   A. random.
   B. unusual.
   C. exact.
   D. special.

_____ 2. Which sentence best expresses the main idea of this passage?
   A. Young people are not as interested in one another as they used to be.
   B. The way teens interact socially today is quite different from the way they interacted when the author was young.
   C. Dating was romantic, but hanging out is probably a lot more fun.
   D. Young people today never really get to know the people they are hanging out with.

_____ 3. The author points out that in the past, before leaving for a date with a girl, a boy would most likely
   A. open the car door for her.
   B. give her flowers.
   C. talk to her for a while at her house.
   D. meet her parents.

_____ 4. The author claims that when today's young people are in a group, they mainly
  A. watch TV.
  B. stare at their phones.
  C. look at computers.
  D. talk face-to-face.

_____ 5. The main pattern of organization in this passage is
  A. contrast.
  B. list of items.
  C. cause and effect.
  D. time order.

_____ 6. The relationship of sentence 1 to the four sentences that follow it is one of
  A. list of items.
  B. comparison.
  C. definition and example.
  D. addition.

_____ 7. We can infer from this passage that the author probably
  A. dated quite a lot when he or she was younger.
  B. does not approve of the new way that teens meet and interact.
  C. is secretly jealous of how much things have changed for young people.
  D. is not a very happy person.

_____ 8. Sentence 15 implies that "hooking up" can mean anything from hanging out to
  A. going to a movie.
  B. seeing only one person.
  C. texting.
  D. sexual activity.

COMBINED SKILLS: Test 19

Read the passage below. Then write the letter of the best answer to each question that follows.

[1]If we knew better, we would cry far more often than we do. [2]Life is difficult. [3]Some people pretend that it is not, that we should be able to breeze through. [4]Yet hardly a week passes in which most of us don't have something worth crying about. [5]Men seem to have a particularly hard time with this. [6]We are taught not to cry. [7]We are expected to tough it out, to not let our feelings show, lest we be regarded as weak and soft. [8]Yet, at times of loss, an acknowledgment of weakness and softness suggests a full heart. [9]If there is a single person who can't find something worth crying about, I would not want to meet him. [10]Many of us men have a hard time crying because we are afraid of our feelings. [11]Every time we express ourselves emotionally, we lose some control. [12]For those of us who become skilled at maintaining control, the results can be disastrous. [13]We take our feelings and strangle them. [14]Then we are nothing but closed, tight, frightened little people, pretending that we have grown up and hoping that no one will notice how deeply we really do care. [15]At first it is an act, a hard act, but over time, as we get better at it, it may become less difficult. [16]If we fail to practice caring, hurting, and crying, over time we may forget how.

_____ 1. In sentence 8, the word *acknowledgment* means
   A. refusal.
   B. acceptance.
   C. fear.
   D. love.

_____ 2. The main idea of this paragraph is best expressed in sentence
   A. 1.
   B. 4.
   C. 5.
   D. 11.

_____ 3. What is the main point of sentences 1-4?
   A. For some people life is hard, but it is a breeze for others.
   B. Some of us pretend life is easy, but life can be hard.
   C. We should be able to breeze through life without crying.
   D. We should all cry at least once every week.

_____ 4. Many men have a hard time crying because
  A. they don't have much to cry about.
  B. it isn't natural for a man to cry.
  C. they are afraid to express their feelings.
  D. they are rarely in a private place where they feel comfortable crying.

_____ 5. The main pattern of organization for this paragraph is
  A. a list.
  B. definition and example.
  C. comparison and contrast.
  D. cause and effect.

_____ 6. The relationship of sentence 8 to sentence 7 is one of
  A. addition.
  B. comparison.
  C. contrast.
  D. cause and effect.

_____ 7. We can infer that the writer of this paragraph
  A. cries a lot.
  B. is a man.
  C. resents the fact that women, unlike men, find it easy to show their emotions.
  D. has forgotten how to care, hurt, and cry.

_____ 8. TRUE OR FALSE? In this paragraph, the author is suggesting that we should cry whenever anything upsets us, no matter how small or unimportant it might be.

COMBINED SKILLS: Test 20

Read the passage below. Then write the letter of the best answer to each question that follows.

¹There's a thirty-second video that I never tire of watching. ²A young man in a fancy car pulls up to a stop sign. ³Crossing the street in front of him is an old woman, carrying a heavy bag. ⁴She's moving slowly. ⁵*Very* slowly. ⁶Quickly growing impatient, the rude young guy revs his engine and lays on the horn. ⁷Without changing expression, the old lady raises her heavy bag and smashes it onto the hood of the car, making its airbag inflate. ⁸She then goes on her slow way while the young man is left sitting helplessly in his disabled car. ⁹And I am left laughing out loud, saying, "You GO, lady! ¹⁰How are you feeling NOW, punk?" ¹¹In other words, I am enjoying the sweet, sweet taste of revenge. ¹²And by "revenge," I don't mean something as tacky as yelling insults or punching someone. ¹³I mean a clever, unexpected way of paying back someone who has been a jerk. ¹⁴For instance, a guy was bothering a girl who wouldn't go out with him by sending her creepy texts and photos of himself. ¹⁵She got revenge by forwarding the texts—to his mom. ¹⁶Or do you know the revenge story of musician Dave Carroll? ¹⁷When United Airlines broke his $3,500 guitar and refused to pay the damages, he recorded a song about it on YouTube. ¹⁸Within days, the video had 4 million hits, and United's stock value dropped more than 10 percent. ¹⁹Ouch! ²⁰Why do we love great payback stories? ²¹It's not hard to understand. ²²Every one of us has at some time been treated badly by someone else. ²³Most of the time we just let it go. ²⁴So it is extremely satisfying to learn about someone who came up with a great, effective form of revenge.

_____ 1. In sentence 8, the word *disabled* means
  A. dented.
  B. unable to be driven.
  C. suddenly stopped.
  D. expensive.

_____ 2. In sentence 12, the word *tacky* means
  A. funny.
  B. intelligent.
  C. in obvious bad taste.
  D. surprising.

_____ 3. Which sentence best expresses the main idea of this passage?
  A. Rude people never expect someone they've hurt to take revenge on them.
  B. Everyone, at some point, has been treated badly by someone else.
  C. Revenge is sweet.
  D. An old woman and a musician took revenge on people who were mean to them.

_____ 4. In the video, when the old woman hits the car with her bag,
        A. the driver yells at her.
        B. the bag dents the hood of the car.
        C. the driver revs his engine and honks the horn.
        D. the car's airbag inflates.

_____ 5. The main pattern of organization in this passage is
        A. comparing and contrasting types of revenge.
        B. listing several stories involving revenge.
        C. defining _revenge_ and giving examples.
        D. using time order to tell one story of revenge from start to finish.

_____ 6. The relationship of sentence 17 to sentence 18 is one of
        A. cause and effect.
        B. comparison.
        C. illustration.
        D. addition.

_____ 7. We can infer that Dave Carroll's YouTube video about United Airlines
        A. was entertaining.
        B. pointed out how rudely United had treated him.
        C. both of the above.
        D. neither of the above.

_____ 8. We can assume that the author of this passage
        A. has paid someone back for treating him or her badly.
        B. has, at some point, been treated badly and just let it go.
        C. believes that everyone should practice revenge regularly.
        D. feels regret for having mistreated someone in the past.

Sample Answer Sheet

Use the form below as a model answer sheet for the twenty combined-skills tests on the preceding pages.

Name _____ Date _____

Section _____ SCORE: (Number correct) _____ x 12.5 = _____ %

COMBINED SKILLS: Test ____

1. _____

2. _____

3. _____

4. _____

5. _____

6. _____

7. _____

8. _____

Appendixes

Separating Fact from Opinion

Fact

A **fact** is information that can be proved true through objective evidence. This evidence may be physical proof or the spoken or written testimony of witnesses. For instance, there are some foods at McDonalds that cost only one dollar. One can visit a McDonalds and confirm this statement is true.

Following are some more facts—they can be checked for accuracy and thus proved true.

Fact: The Quad Tower is the tallest building in this city.

(A researcher could go out and, through inspection, confirm that the building is the tallest.)

Fact: Albert Einstein willed his violin to his grandson.

(This statement can be checked in historical publications or with Einstein's estate.)

Fact: On September 11, 2001, terrorists destroyed the New York World Trade Center, killing thousands.

(This event was witnessed in person or on television by millions, and it's in records worldwide.)

Opinion

An **opinion** is a belief, judgment, or conclusion that cannot be objectively proved true. As a result, it is open to question. For example, "McDonalds is a terrible place to eat" is an opinion. While some people might argue that fast food in general is harmful to one's health, other people enjoy the convenience and taste of fast food.

Or consider this example: After watching a movie, someone might state that the film was boring. The statement is an opinion because it cannot be objectively proved. Another person might see the same movie and find it exciting. Neither statement can be proved; both are opinions.

Here are some more opinions:

Opinion: **The Quad Tower is the ugliest building in the city.**

(There's no way to prove this statement because two people can look at the same building and come to different conclusions about its beauty. *Ugly* is a **value word**, a word we use to express a value judgment. Value, or judgment, words are signals that an opinion is being expressed. By their very nature, these words represent opinions, not facts.)

Opinion: **Einstein should have willed his violin to a museum.**

(Who says? Not his grandson. This is an opinion.)

Opinion: **The attack on the World Trade Center was the worst act of terrorism in the history of humankind.**

(Whether something is "worst" is always debatable. *Worst* is another value word.)

Points about Fact and Opinion

There are several points to keep in mind when considering fact and opinion.

1 **Value words** (ones that contain a judgment) often represent opinions. Here are examples of these words:

best	worse	lovely	bad
worst	great	disgusting	good
better	terrible	beautiful	wonderful

Value words often express judgments—they are generally subjective, not objective. While factual statements *report on* observed reality, subjective statements *interpret* reality. For example, the observation that it is raining outside is an objective one. The statement that the weather is bad, however, is subjective, an evaluation of reality. (Some people—for example, farmers whose crops need water—consider rain to be good weather.)

2 The words *should* and *ought to* often signal opinions. Those words introduce what people think should, or ought to, be done. Other people will disagree.

Couples should definitely not live together before marriage.

Couples ought to live together before getting married to be sure they are compatible.

3 Don't mistake widely held opinions for facts. Much information that sounds factual is really opinion. A real estate agent, for example, might say, "At the price listed, this rancher is a great buy." Buyers would be wise to wonder what the value word *great* means to the agent. Or an ad may claim that a particular automobile is "the most economical car on the road today," a statement that at first seems factual. But what is meant by *economical*? If the car offers the most miles per gallon but the worst record for expensive repairs, you might not agree that it's economical.

4 Finally, remember that much of what we read and hear is a mixture of fact and opinion. The reality is that most of what matters in life is very complex and cannot be separated into simple fact and opinion. Our challenge always is to arrive at the best possible informed opinion, and even then there will be people who disagree with us.

Fact and Opinion in Reading

In general, textbook authors try to be as factual as possible. Most textbook material is based on scientific observation and study, and textbook authors do their best to present us with all the facts and objective informed opinions. On the other hand, many essays, editorials, political speeches, and advertisements may contain facts, but those facts are often carefully selected to back up the authors' opinions.

 PRACTICE 1

To sharpen your understanding of fact and opinion, read the following statements and decide whether each is fact or opinion. Put an **F** (for "fact") or an **O** (for "opinion") beside each statement. Put **F+O** beside the **two** statements that are a mixture of fact *and* opinion.

> *Hint:* Remember that opinions are signaled by value words—words such as *great* or *hard* or *beautiful* or *terrible* that express a value judgment. Take care to note such words in your reading.

_____ 1. Last night, a tree outside our house was struck by lightning.

_____ 2. The waiters at that restaurant are rude, and the food costs twice as much as it's worth.

_____ 3. Ostriches do not hide their heads in the sand.

_____ 4. Brad Pitt and Jennifer Lopez are the most gorgeous movie stars in Hollywood today.

_____ 5. Low-flow showerheads save water, so all homeowners should be required to buy and install them in their showers.

_____ 6. *Watchers*, by Dean R. Koontz, is a terrifying story that is bound to keep you awake at night.

_____ 7. The Grimm brothers collected their fairy tales from other storytellers.

_____ 8. There is nothing like a bottle of Coca-Cola to satisfy thirst.

_____ 9. In the late 1890s, when Coke was first sold, it included a small amount of cocaine, which was then legal.

_____ 10. One of the most delicious of soft drinks, Coca-Cola was first intended to cure various ills, including headaches.

PRACTICE 2

Some of the statements below are facts, and some are opinions; in addition, **two** include fact and opinion. Label facts with an **F**, opinions with an **O**, and statements of fact *and* opinion with an **F+O**.

_____ 1. German shepherds are the scariest dogs alive.

_____ 2. The dog that bites people the most often, according to one twenty-seven-year study, is the German shepherd.

_____ 3. German shepherds, which always make poor pets, are used in police work and as guide dogs for the blind.

_____ 4. Smoking has been found to be one cause of lung cancer.

_____ 5. Executives of corporations that pollute the environment should be jailed.

_____ 6. According to scientists, all the water on Earth has been recycled for millions of years, and we drink the same water as the dinosaurs did.

_____ 7. Because many studies have concluded that smoking is a health hazard, cigarettes should be banned.

_____ 8. Scientists predict that one-third of people who begin smoking under the age of 18 will die prematurely because of their habit.

_____ 9. There's no illness harder to cope with than depression.

_____ 10. Depression is most common among persons between the ages of 25 and 44.

On the Web: If you are using this book in class, you can visit our website for additional practice in separating fact from opinion. Go to **www.townsendpress.com** and click on "Learning Center."

Identifying an Author's Purpose and Tone

Purpose

Authors write with a reason in mind, and you can better evaluate their ideas by determining what that reason is. The author's reason for writing is also called the **purpose** of a selection. Three common purposes are as follows:

- To **inform**—to give information about a subject. Authors with this purpose wish to provide facts that will explain or teach something to readers.

  For example, the author of an informative paragraph about sandwiches might begin, "Eating food between two slices of bread—a sandwich—is a practice that has its origins in eighteenth-century England."

- To **persuade**—to convince the reader to agree with the author's point of view on a subject. Authors with this purpose may give facts, but their main goal is to argue or prove a point to readers.

  The author of a persuasive paragraph about sandwiches might begin, "There are good reasons why every sandwich should be made with whole-grain bread."

- To **entertain**—to amuse and delight; to appeal to the reader's senses and imagination. Authors with this purpose entertain in various ways, through fiction and nonfiction.

  The author of an entertaining paragraph about sandwiches might begin, "What I wanted was a midnight snack, but what I got was better—the biggest, most magical sandwich in the entire world."

While the cover and title of anything you read—books, articles, and so on—don't necessarily suggest the author's main purpose, often they do. On the next page are the covers of three books. See if you can guess the primary purpose of each of these books.

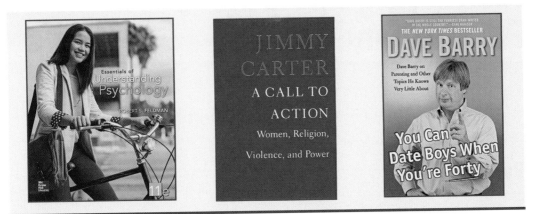

As you probably concluded, the main purpose of the textbook is to inform; the main purpose of Jimmy Carter's *A Call to Action* is to persuade; and the main purpose of Dave Barry's *You Can Date Boys When You're Forty*—whose humorous subtitle reads, "Dave Barry on Parenting and Other Topics He knows Very Little About"—is to entertain.

PRACTICE 1

Read each of the three paragraphs below and decide whether the author's purpose is to inform, to persuade, or to entertain.

1. Each Saturday morning, TV commercials advertise fast foods and high-calorie cereals directly to children. These ads teach children unhealthy eating habits and have been linked to childhood obesity. Parents must realize how harmful such commercials are and should pressure companies to stop marketing unhealthy products to children.

   Purpose: _____

2. About 113 billion people have lived and died in the history of our planet, according to scientific estimates. Of all these people, the names of about 7 billion, or approximately 6 percent, are recorded in some way—on monuments or in books, manuscripts, and public records. The other 106 billion people are gone without a trace.

   Purpose: _____

3. Because of the war between his medium-size shirts and pants and his extra-large-size body, my brother has made a commitment to eat only three meals a day. His definition of a meal, however, is as broad as his belly. If we spot a pretzel salesman or a hot-dog stand on our way to a restaurant, for example, he is not beyond suggesting that we stop. "It'll make a good appetizer," he says.

   Purpose: _____

PRACTICE 2

Label each item according to its main purpose: to inform (**I**), to persuade (**P**), or to entertain (**E**).

_____ 1. Professional athletes do not deserve their inflated salaries, nor does their behavior merit so much media attention.

_____ 2. The career of a professional athlete is usually quite short.

_____ 3. Nurses assigned to intensive-care units should be given shorter shifts and higher pay because the work is unusually demanding and stressful.

_____ 4. On average, women dream more than men, and children dream more than adults.

_____ 5. The best approach to take when you feel the urge to exercise is to lie down quickly in a darkened room until the feeling goes away.

_____ 6. It's easy to quit smoking; I've done it hundreds of times.

_____ 7. More women should get involved in local politics and support the growing number of female candidates for public office.

_____ 8. An artificial odor is added to natural gas so that people can tell whether or not gas is leaking.

_____ 9. Once football season begins, Matt starts jogging every night—to the refrigerator during commercial breaks.

_____10. The first person to die of radiation poisoning was a co-discoverer of radium, Marie Curie.

Tone

A writer's **tone** reveals the attitude that he or she has toward a subject. Tone is expressed through the words and details the writer selects. Just as a speaker's voice can project a range of feelings, a writer's voice can project one or more tones, or feelings: anger, sympathy, hopefulness, sadness, respect, dislike, and so on. Understanding tone is, then, an important part of understanding what an author has written.

To appreciate the differences in tone that writers can employ, look at the following versions of a murder confession. Then read them aloud—in the tone of voice appropriate in each case.

"I just shot my husband five times in the chest with this .357 Magnum." (*Tone:* matter-of-fact, objective.)

"How could I *ever* have killed him? I just can't *believe* I did that!" (*Tone:* shocked, disbelieving.)

"Oh, my God. I've murdered my husband. How can I *ever* be forgiven for this dreadful deed?" (*Tone:* guilty, regretful.)

"That dirty rat. He's had it coming for years. I'm glad I finally had the nerve to do it." (*Tone:* revengeful, self-satisfied.)

Words That Describe Tone

Here are some words often used to describe tone. Except for *matter-of-fact* and *objective*, the words reflect a feeling or judgment.

admiring	concerned	grateful	self-pitying
affectionate	critical	humorous	serious
amused	cruel	insulting	sorrowful
angry	curious	joyous	sympathetic
apologetic	defensive	loving	threatening
ashamed	doubtful	matter-of-fact	tragic
calming	encouraging	objective	warm
caring	excited	playful	worried
cheerful	forgiving	praising	
conceited	frightened	respectful	

PRACTICE 3

Below are five statements expressing different attitudes about a boss. Five different tones are used:

admiring	critical	objective	sympathetic	worried

For each statement, write the tone that you think is present. Use each tone once.

_____ 1. Tony is an excellent manager—the best one I've ever had.

_____ 2. I know Tony's daughter has been sick. Naturally it's hard for him to concentrate on work right now.

_____ 3. Tony's too ambitious for his own good. That ambition may destroy both him and the company.

_____ 4. Since Tony Roberts became manager, sales in the appliance division have increased 30 percent.

_____ 5. I'm afraid there's something wrong with Tony. For the last month or so, he's seemed distracted. Sometimes he repeats himself. And I've seen him taking pills several times a day.

PRACTICE 4

Following are five reactions to a fender-bender accident (a collision that results in minor damage to an automobile). Label each statement with the tone of voice that you think is present. Choose each tone from the following box, and use each tone only once.

A. angry	**B.** apologetic	**C.** calm
D. concerned	**E.** defensive	

_____ 1. "Are you hurt? Are you sure you're okay? Don't move too quickly. Take your time getting out of the car."

_____ 2. "I am really sorry. I was daydreaming a bit, which is no excuse. I should have been more careful."

_____ 3. "You idiot! If you hadn't stopped short, I would never have hit you. You should be tossed in jail. You could have gotten us both killed."

_____ 4. "It's no big deal. Neither of us was hurt, which is all that counts. The damage is slight. Don't worry about it."

_____ 5. "Hey, this wasn't my fault. Don't even think about blaming me. You're the one that stopped too quickly, not me. I did nothing wrong here."

On the Web: If you are using this book in class, you can visit our website for additional practice in identifying an author's purpose and tone. Go to **www.townsendpress.com** and click on "Learning Center."

Writing Assignments

A Brief Guide to Effective Writing

Here in a nutshell is what you need to do to write effectively.

Step 1: Explore Your Topic through Informal Writing

To begin with, explore the topic that you want to write about or that you have been assigned to write about. You can examine your topic through **informal writing**, which usually means one of three things.

First, you can **freewrite** about your topic for at least ten minutes. In other words, for ten minutes, write whatever comes into your head about your subject. Write without stopping and without worrying at all about spelling or grammar or the like. Simply get down on paper all the information about the topic that occurs to you.

A second thing you can do is to **make a list of ideas and details** that could go into your paper. Simply pile these items up, one after another, like a shopping list, without worrying about putting them in any special order. Try to accumulate as many details as you can think of.

A third way to explore your topic is to **write down a series of questions and answers** about it. Your questions can start with words like *what, why, how, when,* and *where*.

Getting your thoughts and ideas down on paper will help you think more about your topic. With some raw material to look at, you are now in a better position to decide on just how to proceed.

Step 2: Plan Your Paper with an Informal Outline

After exploring your topic, plan your paper, using an informal outline. Do two things:

- **Decide on and write out the point of your paper.** It is often a good idea to begin your paragraph with this point, which is known as the **topic sentence**. If you are writing an essay of several paragraphs, you will probably want to include your main point somewhere in your first paragraph. In a paper of several paragraphs, the main point is called the **central point**, or **thesis**.

- **List the supporting reasons, examples, or other details that back up your point.** In many cases, you should have at least two or three items of support.

Step 3: Use Transitions

Once your outline is worked out, you will have a clear "road map" for writing your paper. As you write the early drafts of your paper, use **transitions** to introduce each of the separate supporting items (reasons, examples, or other details) you present to back up your point. For instance, you might introduce your first supporting item with the transitional words *first of all*. You might begin your second supporting item with words such as *another reason* or *another example*. And you might indicate your final supporting detail with such words as *last of all* or *a final reason*.

Step 4: Edit and Proofread Your Paper

After you have a solid draft, edit and proofread the paper. Ask yourself several questions to evaluate your paper:

1 Is the paper **unified**? Does all the material in the paper truly support the opening point?

2 Is the paper **well supported**? Is there plenty of specific evidence to back up the opening point?

3 Is the paper **clearly organized**? Does the material proceed in a way that makes sense? Do transitions help connect ideas?

4 Is the paper **well written**? When the paper is read aloud, do the sentences flow smoothly and clearly? Has the paper been checked carefully for grammar, punctuation, and spelling mistakes?

Writing Assignments for the Twenty Readings

Note: Your instructor may also permit you to write a paper that is based upon one of the discussion questions that follow each reading.

Part One Readings

Responsibility

1. Peck writes about the great lengths people will go to "avoid assuming responsibility for personal problems." Think of times you have observed people blaming someone else or circumstances for their own problem. Then write a paper that begins with the following topic sentence:

   > Just like M. Scott Peck, I have seen someone refuse to take responsibility for his (*or* her) own problem.

   Then go on to develop your paper by explaining who the person is, what the person's problem was, how he or she helped to create it, and how he or she blamed others or circumstances rather than accepting responsibility.

2. Peck explains that the only way to solve a problem is to solve it—in other words, to take responsibility for the problem and find a solution. Write a paper about a time in your own life when you had to accept responsibility for a problem and figure out a solution for it. In choosing a topic for this assignment, it can be helpful to list areas in which you have experienced problems. Following, for example, is one such list:

   - Getting along with parents
   - Balancing a budget
   - Use of alcohol
   - Obeying the law
   - Holding a job

   When you have your list, ask yourself which of those problems you have accepted responsibility for and solved or improved. Once you have decided on a topic to write about, you might begin with a statement like this:

   > After years of scraping together just enough money to get from one week to the next, I've taken steps to deal with my money problems.

   Support your opening statement with the following: 1) one or more examples of the problem, 2) an explanation of how and when you began to understand the problem, and 3) a detailing of the steps you have taken to deal with the problem.

All the Good Things

1. In life, we often forget to let others know how much they have helped us. Sister Helen learned of the value of her work with her students only after one of them died. Write about someone to whom you are grateful, and explain what that person has done for you. Begin by introducing the person and the relationship he or she has to you. For example:

    > My brother Roy has been an important part of my life.
    >
    > My best friend Ginger helped me through a major crisis.
    >
    > Mrs. Morrison, my seventh-grade English teacher, taught me a lesson for which I will always be grateful.

    Then provide detailed examples that show what the person did for you and how important that person has been for you.

2. Early in her essay, Sister Helen describes how a "teacher's mistake" forced her to punish a student in front of the class. Write about a time when you were pressured to do something because others around you expected it. Explain what the situation was, just what happened, and how you felt afterward. Here are two sample opening sentences:

    > Even though I knew it was wrong, I went along with some friends who shoplifted at the mall.
    >
    > Just because my friends did, I made fun of a kid in my study hall who was a slow learner.

Group Pressure

1. Have you had the following experience? From conversation with a friend, you believe you know his or her opinion on some matter. But when the two of you are with a larger group, you hear the friend agree with the general group opinion, even though it is different from the one he or she held before. The opinion might be about something unimportant, such as the quality of a new movie or TV show. Or it may be on something more important, such as whether or not someone is likable. Write a description of that experience. An opening statement for this paper might be something like this one:

    > I believe that group pressure caused _____ to change his (or her) opinion about someone new at school.

2. The "lines on the card" experiment gives just a hint of the kind of pressure group opinion can bring to bear on an individual. What bigger, more important examples of group pressure can you think of? They might be ones occurring in your family, in your town, in your school, in your city, in the country, or in the world. Write a paper in which you describe one or more examples that you believe show group pressure on individual behavior. Here are a few topics to consider writing about:

- Making fun of a particular student
- Being part of a gang
- Racial problems in a school or city
- Being a fan of a sports team
- The use of drugs or alcohol within a group of friends

As you describe someone's behavior, be sure to include details that help show group pressure.

A Door Swings Open

1. When Roxanne found out she had lupus, she had to learn, very quickly, a great deal about the disease. Like Roxanne, people are often forced to learn new things rapidly when they are put into an unfamiliar situation. Write about a time that you had to become informed quickly about a new situation that affected you. You might consider writing about what you had to learn:

- when you moved to a new town
- when you entered a new school
- when a loved one developed an illness
- when you started a new job

As you write, be specific about *what* sort of things you had to learn and *how* you found the information you needed.

2. When little Michelle died, Roxanne learned a painful lesson: life is not fair. What experience in *your* life made you think, "Life isn't fair"? Write a description of that experience, explaining in what way you think its outcome was unfair. Here are some sample first lines from papers like the one you might write:

It wasn't fair that my grandmother had to suffer so much at the end of her life.

It wasn't fair that my hard-working parents lost their house.

It wasn't fair that my mean neighbor won the lottery.

Body Language

1. This essay describes body language in two settings: a job interview and a singles' bar. In what other setting have you observed body language at work? Write a paper that describes where and how you have seen people communicating without words. You can write about any setting, including any of the following:

    - A family dinner
    - An office or other workplace
    - A date
    - A classroom

    In the opening of your paper, explain the setting, the participants, and the general mood that was being communicated by the nonverbal behavior. For example, here are some opening sentences:

    > The body language in our math class shows students are bored and confused.

    > Anyone who watches my parents together can tell that they are still in love.

    Go on to describe in detail the body language you observe and what you believe it means and why.

2. Johnson states in her essay that some body language comes from our roots in the animal world. Think of behavior you've observed in an animal—a pet dog or cat, for example. What body language have you observed? Can the animal communicate its needs or desires through its actions? Describe all the ways you can think of that a pet communicates through body language. Here's a sample of a sentence that expresses the main point for this paper:

    > My dog, Red, has a large "vocabulary" of body language.

Behind Closed Doors: Violence in the Family

1. Have you ever been aware that someone was being abused in the home of a neighbor, friend, or relative? Write a paper about the situation. (You may use made-up names if you feel uncomfortable using the people's real identities.) Explain who you believe was being hurt and why you believe it. Then explain what, if any, action you took and what (if anything) happened to change the situation.

2. The essay makes this statement: "In effect, parenthood confers a 'license for hitting' in our society." Do you believe that parents are justified in sometimes hitting a child? Write a paper that supports one of the following statements:

    > I think there are times when a parent has the right to hit a child.

    > It is a bad idea, under any circumstances, for parents to hit their children.

Support your main point with reasons that back up your opinion. If you take the first point of view, describe specific times when you think hitting would be justified. If you take the second point of view, write about circumstances when hitting a child would be tempting, and explain why you think it would be the wrong thing to do. Suggest alternate ways of dealing with the situation.

Conversing in Real Life

1. Certainly, some conversations are disasters, leaving both parties feeling awkward and frustrated. However, all of us have experienced conversations that we may remember for the rest of our lives. Perhaps we learned something important from the conversation. Perhaps we fell in love during it. Perhaps it has simply remained a sweet and heartwarming memory of someone close to us.

   Write a paper about such a conversation. Start by describing the person with whom you had the conversation and explaining what he or she meant/means to you. Then describe the conversation, using dialog—the actual words spoken—to bring it to life. Finally, write about how this conversation affected you, what you learned from it, how it may have changed your life.

   Your opening sentence can be as simple and direct as "One of the most memorable conversations I've ever had was with _____."

2. The author suggests that electronic interaction has made real human conversation a bit of a lost art. Although the age of electronic communication is relatively new, it has already changed (or is changing) more than just conversation when it comes to human interaction. Write a paper that discusses a few ways that technology has changed the way we all communicate and interact. If you need some ideas, researching "How has technology changed us?" or "How technology has changed communication" should help you out.

A Path to Marriage

1. It is apparent that Jean and Rod Sutton have a good marriage. Among the couples you know, who do you think has the best relationship? Write about that couple, focusing on how they treat each other. Include details about their words and actions that reveal why you admire their relationship.

2. As she grew to know Rod, Jean noticed some very specific characteristics she admired in him—for instance, his work ethic, his ability to communicate, and his respectful attitude toward older people. What are two or three characteristics that *you* would like to see in a potential mate? Write about those characteristics and why they are important to you. As Jean does, give examples of how those characteristics can be expressed.

Lighting a Match

1. Ruiz and her parents had very different ideas about whom she should marry. How well have your plans for your life fit your parents' hopes for you? Write a paper about a decision in your life on which you and your parents have either clashed or agreed. Tell exactly what your parents had in mind and how they communicated their hopes to you. Also explain clearly your decision and the reasons for it. You may wish to conclude by telling how you feel now about your decision. Here are some sample openings for this assignment:

   > Although my parents urged me to become a teacher, I am studying to be a veterinary assistant.

   > My parents did not want me to marry my high-school girlfriend, and I surprised them—and myself—by doing what they wanted.

2. Ruiz writes about her typical morning, from stumbling out of bed to getting to and through school. She tells in detail about getting ready in the morning, studying for a test while driving to school, and thinking about her "household woes" at the same time. Write a paper describing your typical morning. To make sure you have plenty of interesting specific details, do some freewriting or list making, or both. Then think of a sentence that will cover all of the details you will write about. Here, for instance, is one possible statement of the main point:

   > Though a typical morning in my life starts slowly, it develops into some very productive—but hectic—hours.

   Before writing your final draft, double-check your opening point to see if it still covers the details in your paper or if it needs adjusting. (Perhaps you realized your morning doesn't start so slowly after all.) Also, use a few time transitions to make the sequence of events clear to your reader. You could write, for example, "*First* I hear my alarm go off at 6 a.m. *Then* I take a shower, ending with a few seconds of ice-cold water to wake up my body and my brain."

Do It Better!

1. "Do It Better!" suggests that television can interfere with children's academic progress. Write a paper on what you believe is another unfortunate effect that television has on children. To find a topic and then to gather colorful details, you may find it helpful to spend a few sessions in front of the TV with a notebook. Below are sample points you might choose to write about:

   ● TV advertising encourages children to want to buy too much.
   ● TV sitcoms promote poor family values.
   ● Television keeps children from more useful recreational activities.

   Support your paper's main point with specific details and examples.

2. Reading helped Bennie, and it can do a lot for adults too. Most of us, however, don't have someone around to insist that we do a certain amount of personal reading every week. In addition, many of us don't have the amount of free time that Bennie and Curtis had. How can adults find time to read more? Write a paper listing several ways adults can add more reading to their lives.

   A good prewriting strategy for this assignment is list making. Simply write out as many ways as you can think of. Don't worry about putting them in any special order. You will select and organize the methods you wish to include in your paper after accumulating as many ideas as you can.

Part Two Readings

Winners, Losers, or Just Kids?

1. No matter what we we're like in high school, we change in important ways as we get older. Write about some good changes in your life since high school and perhaps about changes you would like to make in the future. Your main point for this paper might be similar to this: "My life has changed in important ways since high school, and I'm hoping for even more and better changes in the future."

2. Write about someone you know who has changed a great deal since high school. The change could be for the good—or not so good. Describe what that person was like in high school, how he or she is today, and what you think might have caused the changes. You might, for instance, write about one of the following:

   ● A person who was once a successful student who is now having problems in life
   ● A person you thought would never achieve anything who is now doing well
   ● A person who once was mean or unfriendly but is now pleasant

The Right Words at the Right Time

1. In his essay, Jeff Bezos recalls that he "felt terrible" when he realized that what he had said had upset his grandmother so much. Clearly, he didn't realize he was doing the wrong thing until he'd already done it. Can you remember a time in your childhood when you accidentally said or did something that really upset someone? How did you feel? What happened? Write a paper describing your experience.

2. Bezos's grandfather points out that it is "harder to be kind than clever." At first, this may seem like an unusual comment, because we don't often think about kindness as being something that is "hard." However, more and more often in our culture, people complain that others are rude, inconsiderate, and even downright mean. There is, in fact, something of a "rudeness epidemic" these days, in which grown people regularly speak as carelessly and thoughtlessly as the young Bezos did.

   Why is this "epidemic" taking place? What can be done about it?

   Write a paper about rudeness in our society. Begin by presenting examples of rude behavior you've seen or know about. Next, suggest reasons *why* so many people seem to suffer from a lack of kindness. Finally, write about specific ways people could be more thoughtful and kind. If you have difficulty thinking of how others could be kinder, Google phrases such as "random acts of kindness" or "unusual kindnesses" to come up with ideas.

Eye Contact

1. "Making eye contact" is not something that is talked about in many classrooms, but Ron Clark makes it part of his students' education. Do you think that it's appropriate to talk in school about topics like making eye contact, showing respect to school employees, and the other kinds of behavior that Clark refers to? Or should teachers discuss only the particular subject they are teaching? Write a paragraph that supports one of these two topic sentences:

   I think Ron Clark is right to talk to his students about eye contact and showing respect.

   I don't think it's a teacher's job to talk to students about things like eye contact and showing respect.

   Explain why you chose the topic sentence you did and how you see a teacher's role in his or her students' lives.

2. In his classroom, Ron Clark insists on some rules such as "make eye contact," "do not interrupt a student who is speaking," and "keep your eyes on the teacher." If you were a teacher, what are some rules you would make for your students? Write about two or three rules you would put in place and why they are important to you.

Judge Judy Speaks

1. In her statement, Amy indicates that she feels "cheated," since as soon as Paul obtained his degree (with money she gave him), he broke up with her. Have you ever felt taken advantage of in a relationship or friendship? Or have you taken advantage of someone who trusted you? Write a paper about this experience.

2. When speaking to Andrea and Joe, Judge Judy presents some of the advantages of being married as opposed to remaining in a relationship without the "piece of paper." What are other advantages of marriage? Or, conversely, what are the advantages of remaining unmarried? Write a paragraph that argues either in favor of or against marriage. If you need some more ideas, a quick Internet search of "advantages of marriage" or "disadvantages of getting married" will help you get started.

Read All About It

1. Write about someone (even yourself) who, like DeBlasio, changed his or her life as an adult. Discuss what the person's life was before, what he or she did in order to change, and what that person's life is like now. Below are some of the many topics you might write about:
   - Someone who married or had a child late in life
   - Someone who changed careers
   - Someone who got divorced
   - An adult who learned to read (or drive, or type, or perform any other important skill)

   Begin with a sentence telling who and what you are writing about. For instance:

   > Chris has changed dramatically since he was in trouble with the law.
   >
   > I am no longer the shy person I used to be in high school.

   Then provide details that show what the person used to be like and what he or she is like today.

2. If you could improve any of the schools you attended, what would you do? Write about two or three changes you would make. Provide specific details to show precisely what you would change and why you would change it. In your opening sentence, state the things you would change so that readers will know exactly what your paper is about. For example:

   > If I were in charge of my college, I would change the cafeteria food and the cost of tuition.
   >
   > If I were in charge of my high school, there are three things I would change: the athletic facilities, the way tests are graded, and the books that are used.

   Then go on to explain exactly what the changes would be and why you would make these changes.

Erika Hilario

1. The author reveals that after an article appeared in the Los Angeles *Times* about the Hilario family, a reader paid for Luisa to get braces to fix her crooked teeth. Random acts of kindness like this happen all the time, though we often don't hear about them. Imagine that you had the money or resources to do someone, even a stranger, a remarkable favor. What would you do? Write a paper about it. Explain why you would choose the person you chose. Describe how you would help this individual and how your action might help him or her.

2. After Erika is beaten by her boyfriend and suffers a fractured skull, she runs out into the neighborhood, blood streaming down her face, begging for help. However, "one after another, women turned her away. 'They said they didn't want a problem,' Erika says bitterly."

    It's often been said that turning a blind eye to domestic abuse only encourages it. The idea that "domestic abuse is everyone's problem" has become a rallying cry. And it is no longer just a good idea to become involved if you suspect a friend is being abused—it's absolutely necessary. So what can you do if you discover that your friend/sister/relative is being abused? What steps can you take to help her?

    Do a little research. Typing "helping abused women" or "how to help a friend who is being abused" or "domestic violence help" into search engines should give you a lot of information. Then write a paper about this important topic. Include at least three different ways to help someone who is being abused. Your opening sentence could be as simple as "There are several important ways to help a victim of domestic violence."

How to Make It in College, Now That You're Here

1. What particular pressures do you deal with as you go to school? Write a paper that describes some of the biggest problems that stand in the way of your doing your best job as a student. Describe how each of them affects you, and briefly state how you try to overcome them. Here are some typical problems many students might mention:

    - Roommate problems
    - Personal difficulties
    - Money worries
    - Distractions (parties, etc.)

2. Drawing upon your own experience as a student, write about "making it" at your particular school. Come up with three or four "secrets of success" that you believe would benefit other students. They may be serious or lighthearted—anything from "avoid the first floor of the library—it's too noisy to study there" to "stay away from the cheese fries at the snack shop." You may use the following or something similar for your main point: "There are a few things new students at this school would benefit from knowing." Then discuss each of your three or four suggestions, choosing colorful details to explain your points.

Cooling Down Our Brains

1. At some point, we all experience a lack of willpower or self-control. When this happens, we typically end up doing something that we later regret. However, the experience may serve as a starting point for making a change in our lives. Write a paper describing a time when you could not resist temptation. What did you do? How did you feel about it? Did it make you change something about your life? Or are you still struggling with that particular area of low self-control?

2. Understandably, some of the parents of children who showed poor self-control during the marshmallow test were worried. Since follow-up studies revealed that children with better self-control skills were often more successful as teens and young adults, parents were anxious to know if there was *anything* they could do. Until that point, it was widely believed that self-control was something you were born with and that it could not be changed or improved.

   As this essay reveals, previously held beliefs were wrong. Scientific research proved that we can train our brains to have more willpower. Can you think of other recent or not-so-recent scientific discoveries that have changed the way we live or think of ourselves? Write a paper describing one such discovery and how it has changed our lives. Researching "recent scientific discoveries" can give you some starting points.

Dealing with Feelings

1. Can you think of times that you (or someone else) *withheld* or *displayed* feelings—when *describing* them would have been more useful? Write about one such time. You might begin with something like this statement of the main point:

   > An experience I had recently showed that describing is often the best strategy for dealing with feelings.

   Then narrate the event, showing how feelings were withheld or displayed and what the result was. Finally, contrast the outcome of the event with what might have happened if feelings had been described.

2. "Dealing With Feelings" lists and discusses several ways to deal with feelings. Write a paper in which you present three ways to do something else. Your tone may be serious or humorous. You might write about three ways to

   - cut expenses.
   - meet people.
   - criticize in a helpful manner.
   - ruin a meal.
   - embarrass your friends.
   - hurt a relationship.

   Here is a possible opening sentence for this assignment:

   > In order to ruin a meal, you must follow three simple steps.

Not So Sweet

1. How healthy is your daily food intake? Do you even know? Near the end of this selection, the author recommends that we learn to read labels, look at how much sugar is in what we eat, and keep track of how much sugar we eat each day. For this paper, you will need to spend at least a day or two looking at *everything* you eat. Write down what you discover. (Grams of sugar are usually listed on packaging nutrition charts. If you eat in a restaurant, most chain restaurants have nutritional information printed in the menu or posted online.) Refer to the information in the selection to discover if your sugar intake is normal or, like most Americans, too high. Remember that adult men should have no more than 9 teaspoons (or 36 grams); adult women should have no more than 6 teaspoons (24 grams).

    Take your findings and write a paper. First, discuss what you like to eat and what a typical day of eating might look like. Next, reveal how much sugar you have discovered is *really* in your diet (be honest!). Which foods surprised or shocked you? Which foods were the worst offenders? Describe how you felt about your discoveries. Finally, explain how you could go about changing your diet and getting healthier. How might you change what you buy at the grocery store or eat in restaurants? What could you do to further educate yourself about what you are putting into your body?

2. In an attempt to avoid making any changes to food or packaging, food industry executives argue that they do not want to create a "nanny state." By this, they mean that neither they nor the government should be treating American citizens as though they are children who can't make their own decisions about what foods to eat. The food industry feels, or at least claims to feel, that any kind of government interference when it comes to personal choices is wrong. Healthy food is available, so those who want it can buy it. Those who prefer to eat processed and unhealthy foods should have that personal choice too. It is not up to elected officials to tell us what we can and cannot eat.

    However, those who think the government *should* get involved point out, as does this selection, that it is no longer a simple issue of choice—it is an issue of poisonous food that is truly sickening a generation of children.

    What do you think? Should our government become more involved and overhaul the food industry, its products, labeling, and advertising? Or is food a matter of personal choice that should be left up to individuals? Write a paper arguing your position on this popularly debated question. Come up with three convincing reasons why our government should or should not get involved in changing the kinds of foods that are available and how they are labeled. Searching the Internet for phrases such as "Should government regulate sugar?" or "Should government have control over our diets?" will give you ideas for your essay.

Limited Answer Key

An important note: To strengthen your reading skills, you must do more than simply find out which of your answers are right and which are wrong. You also need to figure out (with the help of this book, the teacher, or other students) *why* you missed the questions you did. By using each of your wrong answers as a learning opportunity, you will strengthen your understanding of the skills. You will also prepare yourself for the review and mastery tests in Part One, the reading comprehension questions in Part Two, and the combined-skills tests in Part Three, for which answers are not given here.

Answers to the Practices in Part One

1 Dictionary Use

Practice 1
1. pelican, Peking, penalty kick
2. exact, evil, ewe
3. kindergarten, killing, kilowatt
4. during, duplicate, dunk
5. stumble, subcompact, style

Practice 2
1. occasion
2. duty
3. decided
4. accident
5. neighbor
6. autumn
7. remember
8. attention
9. experiment
10. photocopy

Practice 3
2. dis•close, 2
3. hur•ri•cane, 3
4. un•der•tak•er, 4
5. in•hu•man•i•ty, 5

Practice 4
1. A
2. A
3. B
4. A
5. A
6. B
7. B
8. B
9. B
10. B

Practice 5
A. 2. majority, 1
   3. isolate, 1
   4. artificial, 2
   5. natural, 2

B. 7. ăd′və-kāt′
   8. ŏp′tə-mĭst
   9. ăr′ə-gənt
   10. hī-pŏth′ĭ-sĭs

Practice 6
1. 4; second
2. 4; second
3. 3; first
4. 5; second
5. 3; second

Practice 7
1. noun, verb
2. noun, verb
3. noun, verb, adjective
4. preposition, adverb
5. noun, verb, adjective, adverb

Practice 8
1. verb
   wrote; written; writing
2. adjective
   craziest
3. noun
   qualities

Practice 9
1. Definition 1
2. Definition 2
3. Definition 2

2   Vocabulary in Context

Practice 1: Examples

1. Examples: *numerous paper cups, ticket stubs, sandwich wrappings, cigarette butts;* C
2. Examples: *white bread, rice, mashed potatoes;* C
3. Examples: *New York, Boston, Philadelphia;* B
4. Example: *extra calcium, large doses of vitamin C;* A
5. Examples: *backing his car into the side of his boss's Cadillac, trying to walk through a glass door;* B
6. Examples: *the death of a child, the death of a spouse;* B
7. Examples: *buying or selling a product;* C
8. Examples: *baptisms, church weddings, funeral services;* B
9. Examples: *play with humans, eat out of their hands, nuzzle them;* A
10. Examples: *car dealerships, department stores, frozen-yogurt stands, online drugstores;* B

Practice 2: Synonyms

1.	self-important	6.	discussion
2.	powerful	7.	force
3.	cloudy	8.	rich
4.	secret	9.	prove
5.	believable	10.	variety

Practice 3: Antonyms

1. Antonym: *in-depth;* A
2. Antonym: *temporary;* A
3. Antonym: *allowed;* C
4. Antonym: *old;* A
5. Antonym: *order;* B
6. Antonym: *planned;* B
7. Antonym: *expert;* C
8. Antonym: *making progress;* C
9. Antonym: *concerned;* C
10. Antonym: *carefully thought-out;* B

Practice 4: General Sense

1.	C	6.	B
2.	A	7.	C
3.	A	8.	B
4.	C	9.	A
5.	A	10.	C

3   Main Ideas

Practice 1

1.	S	6.	S
	S		S
	G		S
	S		G
2.	S	7.	S
	S		G
	S		S
	G		S
3.	S	8.	G
	G		S
	S		S
	S		S
4.	G	9.	S
	S		S
	S		G
	S		S
5.	S	10.	S
	S		S
	S		S
	G		G

Practice 2

Answers will vary. Here are some possibilities:

1. milk, coffee
2. football, basketball
3. father, nephew
4. tuna, egg salad
5. newspaper, magazine
6. shrimp, crabmeat
7. angry, pleading
8. selfishness, dishonesty
9. loyalty, honesty
10. "Hi there," "Good morning"

Practice 3

1.	S	3.	S
	S		S
	P		S
	S		P
2.	S	4.	P
	S		S
	S		S
	P		S

Practice 4

1.	S	3.	S
	S		P
	S		S
	P		S
2.	S	4.	P
	S		S
	P		S
	S		S

Practice 5

Group 2		Group 4	
A.	SD	A.	SD
B.	MI	B.	SD
C.	T	C.	T
D.	SD	D.	MI

Group 3

A. SD
B. SD
C. MI
D. T

Practice 6

Paragraph 1
1. *Topic:* B
2. *Main idea:* Sentence 1

Paragraph 2
1. *Topic:* A
2. *Main idea:* Sentence 1

Paragraph 3
1. *Topic:* C
2. *Main idea:* Sentence 1

Paragraph 4
1. *Topic:* A
2. *Main idea:* Sentence 2

Practice 7

1. a number of advantages
2. several ways
3. three major inventions
4. A series of mistakes
5. two important steps
6. some alarming facts
7. First of all
8. In addition
9. Also
10. Finally

4   Supporting Details

Practice 1 (*Wording of answers may vary.*)

Passage 1
1. Serious money problems
   a. Checks that bounce
   b. Minimal monthly payment on credit card cannot be made
2. Distinct mood pattern
   a. Tension before shopping
3. Shoplifting
4. Other addictive behaviors

Words that introduce a list: signs of addiction to shopping

Words that introduce:
   First major detail: One
   Second major detail: second
   Third major detail: Another
   Fourth major detail: Last of all

Passage 2
1. Cheaper
   b. Another $30 for drinks and snacks
2. More comfortable
   a. No bumper-to-bumper traffic
3. More informative
   a. Close-ups and instant replays
   b. Detailed explanations by commentators

Words that introduce a list: several advantages

Words that introduce:
   First major detail: One
   Second major detail: Morover
   Third major detail: Finally

Practice 2 (*Wording of answers may vary.*)

Passage 1

Be specific.   Stick to the present.
Don't use insults.   Complain privately.

Words that introduce a list:
   several sensible guidelines

Words that introduce:
   First major detail: First
   Second major detail: Second
   Third major detail: In addition
   Fourth major detail: last

Passage 2
Chest discomfort
Pain or discomfort in upper body
Shortness of breath
Lightheadedness, nausea, or cold sweat

> *Words that introduce a list:*
> various signs

> *Words that introduce:*
> *First major detail:* For one thing
> *Second major detail:* Next
> *Third major detail:* Also
> *Fourth major detail:* Finally

5   Locations of Main Ideas

Practice 1
1. *Main idea:* Sentence 1
2. *Main idea:* Sentence 2
3. *Main idea:* Sentence 9
4. *Main idea:* Sentence 5

Practice 2
1. *Main idea:* Sentence 8
2. *Main idea:* Sentence 1
3. *Main idea:* Sentence 2
4. *Main idea:* Sentence 3

Practice 3
1. *Main idea:* Sentence 2
2. *Main idea:* Sentence 1
3. *Main idea:* Sentence 7
4. *Main idea:* Sentence 2

6   Relationships I

Practice 1
1. B Another
2. A also
3. D In addition
4. C For one thing
5. E second

Practice 2 *(Answers may vary.)*
1. A After
2. E When
3. D Then
4. B Before
5. C during

Practice 3 *(Wording of answers may vary.)*
A. Main idea: Research has revealed three different types of kindness.
1. Natural
2. Rule-guided
3. Imitative

B. Main idea: Opossums cope with danger by using a few defense methods.

Play	Scare off
dead	enemies

Practice 4 *(Wording of answers may vary.)*
Main idea: All of us have certain fears at different points in our lives.
1. Young children worry about something bad happening to their parents.
2. Teenagers fear social rejection.
3. Parents fear that their children will be harmed.
4. Elderly people are afraid of poor health and death.

Practice 5 *(Wording of answers may vary.)*
Main idea: To study a textbook effectively, follow a few helpful steps.
> Read and mark the selection.
> Write study notes.
> Study the notes.

Practice 6
1. B
2. A
3. A
4. B
5. A
6. B
7. A
8. B
9. A
10. B

7 Relationships II

Practice 1 *(Answers may vary.)*

1. For example
2. Once
3. such as
4. For instance
5. example

Practice 2

A. Term being defined: *stimulant;*
   definition—3; *example 1*—4;
   example 2—5

B. Term being defined: *jargon;*
   definition—1; *example 1*—3;
   example 2—4

Practice 3 *(Answers may vary.)*

1. just as
2. Similarly
3. as
4. similar
5. just like

Practice 4 *(Answers may vary.)*

1. but
2. Although
3. on the other hand
4. Despite
5. however

Practice 5 *(Wording of answers may vary.)*

A. Comparison: Abraham Lincoln and John
   F. Kennedy
B. Contrast: high school and college

Practice 6 *(Answers may vary.)*

1. Because
2. Therefore
3. resulted in
4. As a result
5. reason

Practice 7 *(Wording of answers may vary.)*

A. **Main idea** *(the effect):* Two reasons
   explain weight gain among the Japanese.
   Cause 1: Less active lifestyles
   Cause 2: High-fat diet

B. **Main idea** *(the cause):* Increases in the
   numbers of elderly people will have a
   major impact in Europe, Canada, and the
   United States.
   Major supporting details (the effects):
   1. Fewer people available to fill jobs
   2. Bigger demand on pension systems
   3. Great strain on national medical
      services

Practice 8

1. B	6. A
2. A	7. C
3. C	8. B
4. B	9. A
5. C	10. C

8 Inferences

Practice 1

A. 1. C
   2. A
   3. B

B. 4. B
   5. C
   6. C

Practice 2

1, 4, 6, 7, 10

Practice 3

A. 2, 3
B. 2, 4

9   Implied Main Ideas

Practice 1

1. B	6. C
2. A	7. A
3. A	8. C
4. B	9. C
5. A	10. C

Practice 2 *(Wording of answers may vary.)*

1. Directions
2. Seafood
3. Tests (*or* Test questions)
4. Noises (*or* Sounds)
5. book
6. restaurant
7. white
8. Baby
9. Signs
10. Opposites (*or* Words with opposite meanings)

Practice 3

1. A
2. A
3. B

Practice 4

1. C
2. C
3. D

10   The Basics of Argument

Practice 1

Group 1	Group 3
A. S	A. P
B. S	B. S
C. S	C. S
D. P	D. S

Group 2	Group 4
A. S	A. S
B. S	B. S
C. P	C. P
D. S	D. S

Practice 2

1. C	3. B
2. A	4. A

Practice 3

1. B, C, E
2. A, B, C
3. B, C, E
4. A, C, E
5. A, C, E

Practice 4

Group 1: B
Group 2: A
Group 3: B
Group 4: A

Answers to the Practices in the Appendixes

Separating Fact from Opinion

Practice 1

1. F
2. O
3. F
4. O
5. F+O
6. O
7. F
8. O
9. F
10. F+O

Practice 2

1. O
2. F
3. F+O
4. F
5. O
6. F
7. F+O
8. F
9. O
10. F

Identifying an Author's Purpose and Tone

Practice 1

1. To persuade
2. To inform
3. To entertain

Practice 2

1. P
2. I
3. P
4. I
5. E
6. E
7. P
8. I
9. E
10. I

Practice 3

1. admiring
2. sympathetic
3. critical
4. objective
5. worried

Practice 4

1. D
2. B
3. A
4. C
5. E

Acknowledgments

Text Credits

Bassis, Michael S., Richard J. Gelles, and Ann Levine. "Behind Closed Doors: Violence in the Family." From *Sociology: An Introduction*, 3rd ed. Copyright © 1998 by McGraw-Hill, Inc. Reprinted by permission.

Bezos, Jeff. "The Right Words at the Right Time." From *The Right Words at the Right Time,* edited by Marlo Thomas, published 2002 by Atria Books. Reprinted by permission of Jeff Bezos.

Black, Roxanne. "A Door Swings Open." Originally published as "In the Beginning." From *Unexpected Blessings* by Roxanne Black, copyright © 2008 by Roxanne Black. Used by permission of Avery Publishing, an imprint of Penguin Group (USA) Inc.

Carson, Ben, M.D., with Cecil Murphey. "Do It Better!" Taken from *Think Big* by Dr. Benjamin Carson; Cecil Murphey. Copyright © 1992. Used by permission of Zondervan. All rights reserved.

Clark, Ron. "Eye Contact." From *The Essential 55: An Award-Winning Educator's Rules for Discovering the Successful Student in Every Child* by Ron Clark. Copyright © 2003 Ron Clark. Used by permission of Hachette Books. All rights reserved.

DeBlasio, Fran. "Read All About It." From *People Weekly*, © 1986 by *Time*, Inc.

Johnson, Beth. "Body Language" and "Erika Hilario." Reprinted by permission.

Langan, Paul. "One Reader's Story." Reprinted by permission.

Mrosla, Sister Helen P. "All the Good Things." Originally published in *Proteus*, Spring 1991. Reprinted by permission as edited and published by *Reader's Digest*.

O'Keeney, Brian. "How to Make It in College, Now That You're Here." Reprinted by permission.

Peck, M. Scott. "Responsibility." Reprinted with the permission of Simon & Schuster, from *The Road Less Traveled*, by M. Scott Peck, M.D. Copyright © 1978 M. Scott Peck.

Peters, Jason. "Cooling Down Our Brains." Reprinted by permission.

Rice, Sarah. "Conversing in Real Life." Reprinted by permission.

Ruiz, Regina. "Lighting a Match." Reprinted by permission.

Sheindlin, Judge Judy. "Judge Judy Speaks." From Judy Sheindlin, *You're Smarter Than You Look*. Originally published by Cliff Street Books as *Keep It Simple, Stupid; You're Smarter Than You Look*. Copyright © 2000 by Judge Judy Sheindlin. Reprinted by permission of HarperCollins Publishers, Inc.

Staley, Alessa. "Not So Sweet." Reprinted by permission.

Stark, Rodney. "Group Pressure." From *Sociology*, 3rd ed. Copyright © 1989 South-Western, a part of Cengage Learning, Inc. Reproduced by permission. **www.cengage.com/permissions**

Sutton, Jean. "A Path to Marriage." Originally published as "Jean Sutton Speaks" in *Sister to Sister: Black Women Speak to Young Black Women*, ed. by Beth Johnson. Copyright © 2010 by Townsend Press, Inc. Reprinted by permission of the author.

Verderber, Rudolph F. "Dealing with Feelings." From *Communicate!*, 6th ed. Copyright © 1990 Wadsworth, a part of Cengage Learning, Inc. Reproduced by permission. **www.cengage.com/permissions**

Wightman, Dan. "Winners, Losers, or Just Kids?" Originally published in *Los Angeles Times*, July 25, 1979. Reprinted with permission of the author.

Wilson, Craig. "In Fall, a Young Man's Fancy Turns to His Teacher." Copyright © September 23, 1997, *USA Today*. Reprinted by permission.

Photo Credits

Introduction

Chapter 1, p. 6 courtesy Beth Johnson; Chapter 2, pages 16, 20, 24 courtesy Ryan Klootwyk.

Part One

Chapter 1, p. 58 © UK Stock Images Ltd./Alamy; Chapter 2, p. 97 © age fotostock/Superstock; Chapter 3, p. 137 © Hal Taylor; Chapter 4, p. 174 © Hal Taylor; Chapter 5, p. 204 © Image Broker/Alamy; Chapter 6, p. 245 © Sinisha Karich/Shutterstock; Chapter 7, p. 289 © Leila Cutler/Alamy; Chapter 8, p. 336 courtesy Jean Sutton; Chapter 9, p. 369 © Steven Boniface, NZ; p. 374 © Blend Images/Alamy; Chapter 10, p. 409 courtesy The Carson Scholars Fund.

Part Two

Chapter 1, p. 432 courtesy Gina Carson; Chapter 2, p. 440 © Amazon.com; Chapter 3, p. 448 © Image Source/Alamy; Chapter 4, p. 456 © Sonja Flemming/CBS; Chapter 5, p. 464 © Terry Lorant; Chapter 6, p. 472 courtesy Beth Johnson; Chapter 7, p. 482 © Gregg Vignal/Alamy; Chapter 8, p. 494 © Keith Beaty/GetStock.com; Chapter 9, p. 504 © Monkey Business Images/Shutterstock; Chapter 10, p. 513 © Leila Cutler/Alamy.

Index